A Companion to Narrative Theory

Blackwell Companions to Literature and Culture

A COMPANION TO

NARRATIVE THEORY

EDITED BY **JAMES PHELAN AND PETER J. RABINOWITZ**

Blackwell
Publishing

BLACKWELL PUBLISHING
350 Main Street, Malden, MA 02148-5020, USA
9600 Garsington Road, Oxford OX4 2DQ, UK

First published 2005 by Blackwell Publishing Ltd
First published in paperback 2008 by Blackwell Publishing Ltd

1 2008

Library of Congress Cataloging-in-Publication Data

A companion to narrative theory / edited by James Phelan and Peter J. Rabinowitz.
p. cm.—(Blackwell companions to literature and culture; 33)
Includes bibliographical references and index.
ISBN 978-1-4051-1476-9 (hardcover)—ISBN 978-1-4051-8438-0 (pbk)
1. Narration (Rhetoric)   I. Phelan, James, 1951–   II. Rabinowitz, Peter J., 1944–   III. Series.

PN212.C64 2005
808—dc22
2004025184

A catalogue record for this title is available from the British Library.

Set in 11/13 pt Garamond 3
by SPi Publisher Services, Pondicherry, India

For further information on
Blackwell Publishing, visit our website at
www.blackwellpublishing.com

To our students

Contents

Notes on Contributors

H. Porter Abbott is Professor of English at the University of California, Santa Barbara. He works primarily in the areas of narrative, modernism, autobiography, literature and evolutionary theory, and the art of Samuel Beckett. His most recent book is *The Cambridge Introduction to Narrative* (2002). He is currently at work on a study of Darwin, modernism, and representations of the conversion experience.

Alison Booth, Professor of English, has taught at the University of Virginia since 1986. Among her publications are *Greatness Engendered: George Eliot and Virginia Woolf* (1992), the edited collection *Famous Last Words: Changes in Gender and Narrative Closure* (1993), and articles in *Narrative, Victorian Studies, American Literary History, Kenyon Review*, and other journals and essay collections. Her interest in prosopography sparks her current project on "homes and haunts" and the location of national canons in authors' houses.

The late **Wayne C. Booth** (1921–2005) was one of the most influential narrative theorists of the twentieth-century. The author of *The Rhetoric of Fiction* (1961), *A Rhetoric of Irony* (1974), and *The Company We Keep* (1988), among other important books and articles, he did groundbreaking work on the rhetorical and ethical dynamics of communications among authors, narrators, and readers. For the cloth edition of this volume, he wrote the following author's note: Wayne C. Booth sees himself now as having spent a lifetime trying to improve communication, both by teaching and by producing books and articles. That effort has often led him to the thesis of his chapter here. In most situations, and especially in reading literature, you cannot fully understand (and thus communicate well) unless you distinguish the author implied by the text from both the flesh-and-blood author and the diverse characters and narrators met in any text. Every author and speaker attempts to create an implied version superior to the everyday Self. And no one who tries to understand anyone can hope to succeed without listening closely enough to spot the differences among two – and sometimes three – contrasting personae."

Peter Brooks is author of a number of books, including *The Melodramatic Imagination* (1976), *Reading for the Plot* (1984), *Body Work* (1993), and *Troubling Confessions* (2000). *Realist Vision* will be published in 2005. For many years professor of comparative literature and French at Yale University, he is currently University Professor (English and Law) at the University of Virginia.

Royal S. Brown is a Professor at Queens College in the City University of New York – where he currently chairs the Department of European Languages and Literatures – and in the PhD Programs in Music, French, and Film Studies at the City University of New York Graduate Center. He is the author of *Focus on Godard* (1972) and *Overtones and Undertones: Reading Film Music* (1994) as well as numerous articles and critiques dealing mostly with film and film music.

Alison Case is a Professor of English at Williams College, Williamstown, MA. She is the author of *Plotting Women: Gender and Narration in the Eighteenth- and Nineteenth-Century British Novel* (1999) and of several articles on Victorian narratives and narrative techniques. She is currently collaborating with Harry Shaw on a guide to nineteenth-century British fiction.

Seymour Chatman is Professor Emeritus of Rhetoric and Film Studies at the University of California, Berkeley. He is the author of *Story and Discourse* (1978), *Coming to Terms* (1990), *Antonioni, or the Surface of the World* (1985), and *Antonioni: The Complete Films* (2004). His recent articles include discussions of narratology, film adaptation, parody, and the term "literary theory."

Melba Cuddy-Keane is Professor of English and a Northrop Frye Scholar at the University of Toronto, and a former President of the International Virginia Woolf Society. She has published widely on modernist narrative, media, and culture and is the author of *Virginia Woolf, the Intellectual, and the Public Sphere* (2003).

Monika Fludernik is Professor of English Literature at the University of Freiburg, Germany. She is the author of *The Fictions of Language and the Languages of Fiction* (1993), *Towards a "Natural" Narratology* (1996), winner of the 1998 Perkins Prize from the Society for the Study of Narrative Literature, and *Echoes and Mirrorings: Gabriel Josipovici's Creative Oeuvre* (2000). She has edited a special issue of *Style* on second-person fiction, a special issue of *EJES* on "Language and Literature, and (co-edited with Donald and Margaret Freeman) a special issue of *Poetics Today* on "Metaphor and Beyond: New Cognitive Developments." Work in progress includes a project on the development of narrative structure in English literature between 1250 and 1750.

Susan Stanford Friedman teaches at the University of Wisconsin-Madison. *Mappings: Feminism and the Cultural Geographies of Encounter* (1998) won the 2000 Perkins Prize from SSNL. She has also published *Psyche Reborn: The Emergence of H.D.* (1991),

Penelope's Web: Gender, Modernity, H.D.'s Fiction (1990), *Analyzing Freud: Letters of H.D., Bryher, and Their Circle* (2002), *Joyce: The Return of the Repressed* (1993), and numerous essays on narrative poetics.

David Herman teaches in the English Department at Ohio State University. The editor of the *Frontiers of Narrative* book series published by the University of Nebraska Press, he is the author, editor, or coeditor of a number of books on narrative and narrative theory, including *Universal Grammar and Narrative Form* (1995), *Narratologies* (1999), *Story Logic* (2002), *Narrative Theory and the Cognitive Sciences* (2003), the *Routledge Encyclopedia of Narrative Theory* (coedited with Manfred Jahn and Marie-Laure Ryan, 2005), and *The Cambridge Companion to Narrative* (2007). A new book, *Basic Elements of Narrative*, is forthcoming from Wiley-Blackwell.

Linda Hutcheon is Distinguished University Professor of English and Comparative Literature at the University of Toronto. **Michael Hutcheon** is Professor of Medicine at the University of Toronto. Together they have written *Opera: Desire, Disease, Death* (1996), *Bodily Charm: Living Opera* (2000) and *Opera: The Art of Dying* (2004).

Emma Kafalenos teaches comparative literature at Washington University in St Louis. She has published extensively on narrative theory, often in relation to the visual arts or music, in journals including *Poetics Today, Comparative Literature, 19th-Century Music, Visible Language, Studies in Twentieth Century Literature*, and *Narrative*. She is the guest editor of the May 2001 issue of *Narrative*, devoted to contemporary narratology.

Catherine Gunther Kodat is associate professor of English and American Studies at Hamilton College, Clinton, NY. She writes on dance, music, cinema, and literature; her essays have appeared in *American Quarterly, Representations*, and *Mosaic*. An essay on Faulkner and Godard is forthcoming in the *Blackwell Companion to William Faulkner*.

Susan S. Lanser is Professor of English and Comparative Literature and Chair of the Women's Studies Program at Brandeis University. She works in the fields of narrative theory, gender studies, and eighteenth-century European culture and literature. Her publications on narrative include *The Narrative Act* (1981) and *Fictions of Authority: Women Writers and Narrative Voice* (1992), as well as many articles and essays.

Fred Everett Maus is an Associate Professor of Music at the University of Virginia. He has written widely on such subjects as theory and analysis, gender and sexuality, popular music, aesthetics, dramatic and narrative aspects of instrumental music. Recent publications include the entries "Criticism: General Introduction" and "Narratology, Narrativity" in the *New Grove Dictionary of Music and Musicians*.

Brian McHale is Distinguished Humanities Professor in English at The Ohio State University. He has been associated for many years with the journal *Poetics Today*, most recently as coeditor. He is the author of *Postmodernist Fiction* (1987), *Constructing Postmodernism* (1992), and *The Obligation Toward the Difficult Whole: Postmodernist Long Poems* (2004), as well as many articles on modernist and postmodernist poetics, narratology, and science fiction.

J. Hillis Miller taught for many years at the Johns Hopkins University and then at Yale University, before going to the University of California at Irvine in 1986, where he is now UCI Distinguished Research Professor. He is the author of many books and essays on nineteenth- and twentieth-century English, European, and American literature, and on literary theory. His most recent books are *Others* (2001), *Speech Acts in Literature* (2002), *On Literature* (2002), and *Zero Plus One* (2003). He is at work on a book on speech acts in the novels and stories of Henry James. A *J. Hillis Miller Reader* is forthcoming.

Alan Nadel, Professor of literature and film at Rensselaer Polytechnic Institute, Troy, NY, is the author of numerous books and essays on American literature, film, and culture. His books include *Invisible Criticism* (1988), *Containment Culture* (1995), *Flatlining on the Field of Dreams* (1997), and the forthcoming *White America in Black-and-White: Cold War Television and the Legacy of Racial Profiling*. His essays have won prizes from *Modern Fiction Studies* and *PMLA*, and his poetry has appeared in several journals including *Georgia Review*, *New England Review*, *Paris Review*, *Partisan Review*, and *Shenandoah*. The chapter in this volume is excerpted from his nearly complete work-in-progress: *The Historical Performative: Essays on the Cogency of Narrative Media*.

Ansgar Nünning has been Professor and Chair of English and American Literary and Cultural Studies at the Justus-Liebig-University of Giessen, Germany, since 1996, following a 10-year period at the University of Cologne. He is the founding director of the Giessen Graduate School for the Humanities (GGK), and the Project Coordinator of the International PhD study course "Literary and Cultural Studies." He is the author of monographs on the structure of narrative transmission and the functions of the narrator in George Eliot's novels, historiographic metafiction, the development of the historical novel in England since 1950, and the twentieth-century English novel. He has edited the *Metzler Encyclopedia of Literary and Cultural Theory* (1998), collections of articles on unreliable narration and multiperspectivism, the *Metzler Encyclopedia of English Authors* (2002, with Eberhard Kreutzer), *Konzepte der Kulturwissenschaften – Theoretische Grundlagen – Ansätze – Perspektiven* (2003) and *Kulturwissenschaftliche Literaturwissenschaft* (2004, with Roy Sommer).

James Phelan is Humanities Distinguished Professor of English at Ohio State University. He is the editor of the journal *Narrative* and the author of several books in narrative theory, the most recent of which are *Living to Tell About It: A Rhetoric and Ethics of Character Narration* (2005) and *Experiencing Fiction: Judgments, Progressions, and* *the Rhetorical Theory of Narrative* (2007). He coedits, with Peter J. Rabinowitz, the Ohio State University Press series on the Theory and Interpretation of Narrative.

Peggy Phelan is the Ann O'Day Maples Chair in the Arts and Professor of Drama, Stanford University. She is the author of the Survey essays for *Art and Feminism* (ed. Helena Reckitt, 2001) and *Pipilotti Rist* (2001). She is also the author of *Mourning Sex: Performing Public Memories* (1997) and *Unmarked: The Politics of Performance* (1993). She coedited *The Ends of Performance* (1997) with Jill Lane, and with the late Lynda Hart, she coedited *Acting Out: Feminist Performances* (1993). Currently she is writing a book entitled *Twentieth Century Performance*.

Gerald Prince is Professor of Romance Languages at the University of Pennsylvania. The author of several books, including *Narratology* (1982), *A Dictionary of Narratology* (1987), and *Narrative as Theme* (1992), he is editor of *French Forum* and he coedits the "Parallax" series for the Johns Hopkins University Press as well as the "Stages" series for the University of Nebraska Press.

Peter J. Rabinowitz is Professor and Chair of Comparative Literature at Hamilton College. His previous publications include *Before Reading* (1987) and *Authorizing Readers* (coauthored with Michael Smith, 1998). He is also a music critic and serves as a contributing editor of *Fanfare*. He coedits, with James Phelan, the Ohio State University Press series on the Theory and Interpretation of Narrative.

Brian Richardson teaches in the English Department of the University of Maryland. He is the author of *Unlikely Stories: Causality and the Nature of Modern Narrative* (1997) and the editor of *Narrative Dynamics: Essays on Time, Plot, Closure, and Frames* (2002). He has written articles on many aspects of narrative theory and reader response, and is currently completing a book on extreme narration and unusual narrators in contemporary fiction.

David H. Richter is Professor of English at Queens College and the Graduate Center, City University of New York. He is the author of *The Progress of Romance* (1996) and *Fable's End* (1974) and the editor of *The Critical Tradition* (1998) and *Falling into Theory* (2000). Richter is currently working on two research projects: on indeterminacy in biblical narrative and on a case of identity theft in the late eighteenth century.

Shlomith Rimmon-Kenan is Professor of English and Comparative Literature at the Hebrew University of Jerusalem, where she also holds the Renee Lang Chair for Humanistic Studies and currently heads the School of Literatures. Her current research concerns the concept of narrative in various disciplines (psychoanalysis, historiography, law), an offshoot of which is her work on illness narratives.

Marie-Laure Ryan, a native of Geneva, Switzerland, is an independent scholar based in Colorado. She is the author of *Possible Worlds, Artificial Intelligence and Narrative*

Theory (1991), and of *Narrative as Virtual Reality: Immersion and Interactivity in Literature and Electronic Media* (2001), which received the Jeanne and Aldo Scaglione Prize for Comparative Literature from the Modern Language Association. She is also the editor of *Cyberspace Textuality* (1999) and *Narrative Across Media* (2004), as well as a coeditor, with David Herman and Manfred Jahn, of the *Routledge Encyclopedia of Narrative* (2004).

Harry E. Shaw is Professor of English at Cornell University, where he has served as Chair of the Department of English and is now Senior Associate Dean of the College of Arts and Sciences. He is the author of *The Forms of Historical Fiction: Scott and his Successors* (1983) and *Narrating Reality: Austen, Scott, Eliot* (1999). Essays on Scott, J. L. Austin, and narrative theory have appeared in such journals as *JEGP*, *diacritics*, *Narrative*, and *European Romantic Review*. He is currently at work on a book on the nineteenth-century British realist novel for a general audience, in collaboration with Alison Case.

Dan Shen is Changjiang Professor of English and Director of the Center for European and American Literatures at Peking (Beijing) University. Apart from her numerous books and essays published in China, she has published more than 30 essays in North America and Europe on narrative theory, stylistics, literary theory, and translation studies.

Sidonie Smith is Martha Guernsey Colby Collegiate Professor of English and Women's Studies and Chair of the Department of English at the University of Michigan. As well as the works coauthored and coedited with Julia Watson, she is the author of five other books on autobiography, the most recent of which is *Human Rights and Narrated Lives: The Ethics of Recognition* (with Kay Schaffer, 2004).

Meir Sternberg is Artzt Professor of Poetics and Comparative Literature at Tel-Aviv University and Editor of *Poetics Today*. His publications include *Expositional Modes and Temporal Ordering in Fiction* (1978), *The Poetics of Biblical Narrative: Ideological Literature and the Drama of Reading* (1985), *Hebrews Between Cultures: Group Portraits and National Literature* (1998), and the two-part interdisciplinary review "Universals of Narrative and their Cognitivist Fortunes" for *Poetics Today*.

Richard Walsh is a lecturer in English and Related Literature at the University of York, UK. His publications include *Novel Arguments: Reading Innovative American Fiction* (1995), and articles on narrative in *Poetics Today*, *Style*, and *Narrative*.

Robyn R. Warhol, Professor of English at the University of Vermont, has published *Having a Good Cry: Effeminate Feelings and Popular Forms* (2003), *Feminisms* (1997), and *Gendered Interventions: Narrative Discourse in the Victorian Novel* (1989).

Julia Watson is Associate Professor of Comparative Studies at Ohio State University. With Sidonie Smith she has coauthored *Reading Autobiography: A Guide for Interpreting*

Life Narratives (2001) and coedited four collections of essays, most recently *Interfaces: Women, Autobiography, Image, Performance* (2002).

Tamar Yacobi teaches at Tel-Aviv University. Her primary interests include narration, (un)reliability, reading, ekphrasis, the dramatic monologue, and Isak Dinesen. Recent publications include "Ekphrasis and Perspectival Structure," in *Cultural Functions of Intermedial Exploration* (ed. Erik Hedling and Ulla-Britta Lagerroth, 2000) and articles in *Poetics Today* and *Narrative*.

Acknowledgments

The editors would like to thank, first, all of our contributors because they have made working on this volume a consistent source of intellectual pleasure and energy. We also would like to thank several people who have provided invaluable editorial advice: Jamie Abaied, Elizabeth Jensen, Jessica Kent, Nancy Rabinowitz, Greta Rosenberger, and James Weaver. Aaron McKain has earned our eternal gratitude through his patient and thorough work on the index. We are grateful as well to Andrew McNeillie, who recruited us to edit this Companion, and to Jennifer Hunt, who guided us in the first stages of its preparation. We owe a special thanks to Emma Bennett and Karen Wilson, who so ably guided the manuscript through production. Above all, we are indebted to Jenny Roberts, copy-editor extraordinaire.

The editors and publishers are also grateful to the following for their kind permission:

Introduction: Tradition and Innovation in Contemporary Narrative Theory

James Phelan and Peter J. Rabinowitz

Writing an introduction to a wide-ranging collection of essays is always a matter of navigating between Scylla and Charybdis – but in this book, the metaphor has more specificity than usual. Scylla, you'll recall, was a monster who inhabited a cave in a cliff on a spit of land jutting off from the coast; her many arms plucked sailors from the boats that came too near. Charybdis was a whirlpool that threatened any boats that tried to evade the cliff. Elements of those images impinge on this introduction – and on narrative theory itself – in several ways.

How, for instance, should the introduction be structured? On the one hand, we can aim for clarity, simply summarizing the contents. Such a *Cliffs Notes* approach may provide a certain stony intelligibility, but it runs the risk of plucking the spirit from both the essays and our readers. On the other hand, we're faced with the ever-expanding whirlpool of self-reflexivity. An introduction, after all, can itself easily become a narrative – and a narrative about the current study of narrative (which in turn includes a history of the study of narrative) risks spinning into an endless loop, especially when written by authors who are, by disciplinary training, acutely self-conscious.

The task is made more difficult still because Scylla and Charybdis are not simply potential dangers to be evaded. Like the Sirens (and it's appropriate that the volume includes three essays on music and one that deals tangentially with musical issues), they offer seductions as well. Indeed, one can argue that the discipline of narrative theory itself divides into two attractive and productive ways of doing things, ways parallel to the distinction between the cliff and the whirlpool. On the one hand, we have the search for a stable landing, a theoretical bedrock of the fundamental and unchanging principles on which narratives are built. This approach is often associated with what is called structuralist (or classical) narratology, and especially after the rise of post-structuralism, it is often viewed as old-fashioned, even quaint – and it is often believed to yank the life out of the works it considers. But as we hope this collection will make clear, it's still an enormously vital area of study, and it's still producing illuminating work, though nowadays its claims tend to be more modest – about "most narratives" or "narratives of a certain historical period" rather than about "all narratives."

On the other hand, we have a discipline experiencing a voracious spin. That whirlpool is generated in part by the self-conscious and self-critical nature of much narrative theory. What the two of us have in the past labeled "theorypractice," for instance, uses the interpretive consequences of particular theoretical hypotheses as a way of testing and re-examining those very hypotheses. But the vortex of narrative theory comes as well from what's often called the "narrative turn," the tendency of the term "narrative" to cover a wider and wider territory, taking in (some would say "sucking in") an ever-broadening range of subjects for inquiry. Narrative theory, over the years, has become increasingly concerned with historical, political, and ethical questions. At the same time, it has moved from its initial home in literary studies to take in examination of other media (including film, music, and painting) and other nonliterary fields (for instance, law and medicine).

It should therefore be no surprise that our volume represents both Scylla and Charybdis, both the search for enduring fundamentals of narrative theory and the engagement with the many turnings of contemporary theory. True, the introduction steers, on the whole, closer to the cliff, largely because so many of the essays themselves offer sufficient spin to satisfy anyone in search of the pleasures of the whirlpool. Nonetheless, we are sufficiently self-conscious to warn you that, if writing this introduction involved navigating a familiar but tricky path, so too does reading it. For reasons that will become increasingly clear, we urge you to recognize that our navigational choices were not inevitable. You very well might have charted a different route – though of course you can't choose that route until you've read much more than this introduction.

The book opens with a prologue that sets out narrative theory's modern history. In the first essay, "Histories of Narrative Theory (I): A Genealogy of Early Developments," David Herman surveys the origins of the field. But since Herman is strongly influenced by the notion of "genealogy" promoted by Nietzsche and Foucault, his essay refuses to move in a simple linear fashion. He is particularly concerned with the way early structuralist narratology – an attempt to study narrative by treating "particular stories as individual narrative messages supported by a shared semiotic system" – grew out of "a complex interplay of intellectual traditions, critico-theoretical movements, and analytic paradigms distributed across decades, continents, nations, schools of thought, and individual researchers." Herman uses Wellek and Warren's influential *Theory of Literature* as a nodal point, moving in and out from there to show the overlapping connections among a wide range of superficially competing critics who nonetheless represent, if not "a singular continuous tradition of research," then at least "a cluster of developments marked by family resemblances." One of

Herman's key points is that what can be assimilated from any theorist's work at any given time is fundamentally dependent on the paradigms in force at the time of reading. His history thus twists back on itself, as he demonstrates how "old" theoretical works in "new" contexts take on new resonances.

In "Histories of Narrative Theory (II): From Structuralism to the Present," Monika Fludernik likewise resists a linear chronology in which gradual developments contribute to an ever-more complete critical arsenal. Rather, Fludernik self-reflexively applies narrative theory to the history of narrative theory itself, setting out two competing "plots." She then follows the second of these to show how narrative theory has spread out in widening branches. Specifically, she moves from formalist study to pragmatics (including issues of gender and politics) on to the study of media and of the narrative turn in a variety of social sciences, coming finally to issues of linguistics and cognition. Her essay dexterously ends with both a return to its opening and a possible glimpse of the future.

The prologue ends with Brian McHale's "Ghosts and Monsters: On the (Im)Possibility of Narrating the History of Narrative Theory." Here McHale questions the work of Herman and Fludernik by using the insights of narrative theory to question the task we assigned to them. Specifically, McHale defines two different kinds of history — what he calls "history of ideas" and "institutional history" — and argues that the friction between them makes a true history of narrative theory an impossibility. In even more provocative terms, McHale suggests that there is an irreconcilable opposition between narrative theory that privileges "structure" (the Scylla of classical narratology) and narrative theory that privileges "history" (the Charybdis of narrative turnings). Though the necessity of sequence dictates that McHale's essay be last in the prologue, that does not mean that you should take his word as final. Our own position is that the prologue is a provocation that opens up more questions than it settles.

Part I, "New Light on Stubborn Problems," looks at some of the disputes that have continued as an undertow in the flow of narrative theory for the past 40 or 50 years — disputes that therefore remain central to its continued movement. In the first essay, "Resurrection of the Implied Author: Why Bother?," Wayne C. Booth — already introduced in Herman's and Fludernik's histories — returns to a concept that he first introduced in *The Rhetoric of Fiction* in 1961: the implied author, the author's "second self" as reflected in a text. Many subsequent theorists (including several contributors to this volume) have argued that the concept is either useless or redundant; Booth, in contrast, believes that it's more important than ever. Starting from a reconsideration of the concerns that led him to develop the idea in the first place, Booth goes on to show how the concept improves our understanding, not only of fiction (for which it was developed), but also of poetry and of the way we present ourselves in our day-to-day interactions.

The next two essays deal, in different ways, with another key narratological term introduced by Booth in *The Rhetoric of Fiction*: the "unreliable narrator." The first is by

Ansgar Nünning, one of the critics dissatisfied with Booth's concept of the implied author. In "Reconceptualizing Unreliable Narration: Synthesizing Cognitive and Rhetorical Approaches," Nünning uses that dissatisfaction as an entry into a detailed account of the battles that have erupted over unreliable narration, with particular attention to the question of how readers in fact recognize unreliability when they come across it in the text. He argues that unreliability cannot be defined simply in terms of the text's "structural or semantic" aspects; it also involves the "conceptual frameworks" brought to the text by its readers. More generally, he contends that an adequate model of unreliability needs to combine the latest insights offered by the apparently divergent arguments of rhetorical and cognitive narrative theorists. He ends his essay, provocatively, with a series of six questions that remain to be answered.

If Nünning hopes to reduce the difficulties involved in accounting for unreliable narration by developing a new synthetic theory, Tamar Yacobi ("Authorial Rhetoric, Narratorial (Un)Reliability, Divergent Readings: Tolstoy's *Kreutzer Sonata*") offers a somewhat different perspective on the same terrain by moving up to the next level of generality. Yacobi argues that unreliability is best understood as a "reading-hypothesis" that allows readers to resolve apparent textual contradictions. She makes her case by looking at the wide disparities that separate different readings of Tolstoy's novella. After grouping these disparate readings into a few sets with common features, she goes on to show how all these groups are in turn generated by the operation of a small number of shared integrative mechanisms that readers use to deal with incongruities that arise when processing a text.

The essays by J. Hillis Miller and Dan Shen take up a different complex of problems that have long puzzled narrative theorists, problems that often show up in terms of the relation of form to content or style to meaning – or form to substance, as Miller puts it in his close reading of Henry James's *The Awkward Age* ("Henry James and 'Focalization,' or Why James Loves Gyp"). Although many narratologists have argued that the purpose of theory is not to produce new readings, Miller insists that narratological distinctions are only valuable if they serve interpretation – indeed, more radically in an age that often seems to resist judging interpretations, that they "are useful only if they lead to better readings or to better teachings of literary works." A good reading for Miller, though, is not necessarily a simple or a stable one: it can well end in a whirlpool of its own. His patient, theoretically sophisticated analysis demonstrates how, in this formally anomalous narrative (anomalous, at least, within the James canon), James succeeds in breaking down the distinction between substance and form and how the "right reading" of the text turns out to be one that reaches "undecidability" as its conclusion.

Shen, in "What Narratology and Stylistics Can Do for One Another," starts by looking at a familiar assumption: there is a rough equivalence between the story/discourse distinction central to narratological thinking (the distinction between "what" is told and "how" it is told) and the content/style distinction (what is expressed and how it is expressed) central to much stylistic thinking. Using a brief interchapter from Ernest Hemingway's *In Our Time* as her case in point, she goes on to show that the similarities are only superficial – and that a full understanding of style in narrative requires an interdisciplinary approach that synthesizes the insights of both narratology and stylistics.

The final essay in Part I, Richard Walsh's "The Pragmatics of Narrative Fiction," turns to one of the most enduring, and most vexing, problems of narrative theory – the nature of fiction. Walsh surveys the history of attempts to explain what fiction is and how it operates, pointing out that, for all their rich variety, "modern accounts of fictionality generally turn upon one or more of a small repertoire of theoretical gambits." In addition, as he demonstrates through patient exploration of central modern accounts, especially those based in speech act theory and possible worlds theory, all these maneuvers reduce to various kinds of displacement "by detaching the fictive act from the domain of truth." (Despite their differences, there are interesting methodological similarities between Walsh's and Yacobi's essays.) As an alternative, Walsh offers a pragmatic account of fictionality in which relevance, rather than truth, becomes the key term, and he demonstrates its explanatory power by analyzing the opening of Kafka's *The Trial*.

Part II, "Revisions and Innovations," groups together essays that offer significantly new views of some basic concepts in narrative theory. The authors arrive at their fresh takes on these concepts in different ways: some focus on narratives that cannot be adequately addressed with our existing understandings, others focus on the logic of theory itself or on the uncomfortable fit between theory and readerly experience, and some use a combination of these methods. All of these essays engage in "theorypractice"; in this respect, the section provides the self-conscious reader not only with some provocative new theorizing but also an implicit primer in how to revise existing theory.

Focusing primarily on James Joyce's *Ulysses* and bringing in other avant-garde narratives of the twentieth century, Brian Richardson deftly moves "Beyond the Poetics of Plot" to consider "Alternative Forms of Narrative Progression." Richardson begins by pointing out that the dominant models, developed by R. S. Crane, Paul Ricoeur, Peter Brooks, and others, conceive of plot as a sequence of logically connected events involving coherent characters that provides, in Brooks's words, "design and intention" for a narrative. But Richardson casts doubt on these models by pointing to a tradition of novel writing that rejects this conception, moving its reader from beginning to end through radically different logics. Richardson then delivers the big payoff: an insightful survey into the range of these alternatives, starting with the multiple principles of progression in *Ulysses* and ending with what he calls the aleatory progressions of the Dadaists and their descendants such as William Burroughs.

In "They Shoot Tigers, Don't They? Path and Counterpoint in *The Long Goodbye*," Peter J. Rabinowitz's primary concern is with time – and our tools for accessing its representation. Rabinowitz starts by puzzling over similarities and differences between treatments of time in music and narrative, and he ends by proposing that narrative theory needs a new concept, one that refers to the order in which a character experiences the events of a narrative. He calls this concept *path*, and he sees it as supplementing the well-established distinction between "story" or *"fabula"* (referring to the chronological order of events) and "discourse" or *"sjuzhet"* (referring to the order of presentation of those events). We need the concept, he argues, because characters may experience events neither in the story order nor in the discourse order, and that difference can matter for readers. Rabinowitz demonstrates the interpretive value of this concept through a revisionary reading of Raymond Chandler's *The Long Goodbye*, carefully tracing the story order, the discourse order, and the paths of Philip Marlowe and the other characters involved in the "tiger trap" episode. Recognizing the counterpoints among the different paths not only leads us to reinterpret the significance of that episode but also exposes Marlowe's failure to understand it, a revelation that overturns the standard readings of the novel.

In moving from Rabinowitz's essay to Susan Stanford Friedman's "Spatial Poetics and Arundhati Roy's *The God of Small Things*," we shift attention from time to space. Friedman observes that narrative theory has privileged time over space, and she wants to redress the balance – not by demoting time but by restoring space "to its full partnership with time as a generative force for narrative." Drawing on other theorists who have advocated more attention to space, such as Edward Soja, Mikhail Bakhtin, Franco Moretti, and Lawrence Grossberg, she proposes that we stop regarding space as a static background and begin recognizing it as an "active, mobile, and 'full'" component of narrative. More specifically, Friedman proposes that we pay more attention to the role of borders and border crossings in the generation, development, and resolution of narratives. Exploring the consequences of her spatial poetics through an energetic and insightful reading of Roy's novel, Friedman shows how the spaces in the novel contain "multiple borders of desirous and murderous connection and separation, borders that are continually erected and transgressed in movement that constitutes the kinetic drive of the plot."

Susan S. Lanser's essay, "The 'I' of the Beholder: Equivocal Attachments and the Limits of Structuralist Narratology," makes an interesting companion piece to Walsh's as it takes a fresh look at the well-known assumption that the "I" of fiction is different from the author, while the "I" of nonfiction is identical to the author. Arguing that this assumption oversimplifies the situation, she proposes a more complex scheme with three primary categories. Attached texts such as letters to the editor and scholarly essays are those in which the primary "I" and the author are identical. Detached texts are those in which the primary "I" and the author are not identical (e.g., the Pledge of Allegiance; any fiction with an unreliable narrator) or in which the relation between the two is not consequential for textual meaning (e.g., a joke, a national anthem). Equivocal texts are those in which the primary "I" is both associated with and distinct from the author, moving between being attached and detached. Novels and poems are typically equivocal texts. Lanser builds on this taxonomy by arguing that genres such as lyric and narrative have default conditions – lyrics are attached, while novels are detached – but that under many conditions these default lines are transgressed. Readers intuitively know how to navigate these fault lines, but theorists have rarely paid attention to how they manage to do so. Lanser's essay, with its suggestive analyses of how we read such different works as Sharon Olds's poem "Son," Ann Beattie's short story "Find and Replace," and Philip Roth's novel *The Human Stain*, provides a theoretical scheme that accounts for these interpretive practices.

In "Neonarrative; or, How to Render the Unnarratable in Realist Fiction and Contemporary Film," Robyn Warhol offers a different kind of taxonomy, one based on the conventions governing what can and cannot be represented in narrative. Warhol examines the phenomena of the "disnarrated" and "the unnarrated" as instances of the larger category of the "unnarratable" in order to identify genre conventions and changes in those conventions. The disnarrated, first identified by Gerald Prince, is the narration of something that might have happened or was imagined to have happened but did not actually happen. The unnarrated is the lack of narration about something that did happen; it can be found in those passages in a narrative "that explicitly do not tell what is supposed to have happened, foregrounding the narrator's refusal to narrate." Both the disnarrated and the unnarrated are, for Warhol, strategies for representing the unnarratable, which she divides into four types: the subnarratable (that which is taken for granted and so not worthy of narration); the supranarratable (that which is ineffable); the antinarratable (that which social convention labels as unacceptable for narration); and the paranarratable (that which formal conventions render unnarratable). Building on these categories, Warhol shows how, over time, Hollywood films have created what she calls "neonarratives" by transgressing the formal or social conventions governing the unnarratable.

In "Self-consciousness as a Narrative Feature and Force: Tellers vs. Informants in Generic Design," Meir Sternberg turns to a neglected feature of narrative representation, self-consciousness – not just of narrators but also of characters. Sternberg makes three crucial claims: (1) self-consciousness should be mapped along a continuum from total to totally absent, from what he calls tellers who are fully aware of audiences other than themselves to informants whose only audience is themselves; (2) self-consciousness is always mediated – the narrator's mediated by the author, the characters' by the narrator and the mimetic situation; and (3) the significance of self-consciousness for narrative's form and functioning has not yet been appreciated. Sternberg offers a careful elaboration and exemplification of these points, including an analysis of why the phenomenon has not yet been given its due. The result is a persuasive case that the phenomenon of self-consciousness – in particular, the unself-conscious end of the continuum – deserves much more attention.

In "Effects of Sequence, Embedding, and Ekphrasis in Poe's 'The Oval Portrait,'" Emma Kafalenos offers another approach to understanding the structure of narrative, as she employs function analysis to explore the interrelation of the three terms of her title in Poe's story. Revising models proposed in the work of Vladimir Propp and Tzvetan Todorov, Kafalenos's function analysis focuses on how events in narrative proceed through a series of five stages: equilibrium, disruption, efforts by characters (or actants) at alleviating the disruption, the success or failure of those efforts, and finally the establishment of a new equilibrium. In examining the Poe story, which involves both ekphrasis (the representation of a visual composition in a literary work) and an embedded narrative, Kafalenos makes good on her contention that "function analysis demonstrates the magnitude of the effect that the way events are told can have on interpretations of the causes and effects of those events." More specifically, Kafalenos shows how the final paragraph in Poe's story, which narrates the death of a young girl, has one effect in a function analysis of the embedded narrative and another, different, effect in a function analysis of the story as a whole. Furthermore, she identifies the factors that contribute to this difference, paying special attention to the role of ekphrasis. This insightful reading of "The Oval Portrait" thus serves as a model for the way we understand (1) the link between the events of an embedded narrative and those in its frame, and (2) the role of ekphrasis in narrative.

Kafalenos focuses on one kind of "intratextuality," as she examines the interaction of several texts represented or embedded within a single story. Seymour Chatman's essay, "*Mrs. Dalloway's* Progeny: *The Hours* as Second-degree Narrative," shifts attention to intertextuality. His exploration builds on Gérard Genette's work in *Palimpsests* on second-degree texts (texts that are explicitly intertextual with a prior, source text). After sorting out the different kinds of relations a second-degree narrative can have to its source, Chatman turns to Michael Cunningham's *The Hours*, his homage to Virginia Woolf's *Mrs. Dalloway*. Chatman illuminates Cunningham's novel by considering it as what Genette calls a "transposition," a work that invents new characters but uses the source text as a basis for either revisions or patterns. More specifically, Chatman treats *The Hours* as a "complement" to *Mrs. Dalloway*, a narrative that does not seek to displace the source even as it transforms it. Within this framework, Chatman focuses on the "how" of the transposition, tracing many relations between elements of the two novels. Because Chatman attends both to similarities and to differences, he is able to show Cunningham's indebtedness to Woolf as well as Cunningham's creative use of his source. More generally, Chatman's analysis works to illuminate the specific craft of each novel – and the value of his approach to second-degree narratives.

Part III brings together essays that consider "Narrative Form and Its Relationship to History, Politics, and Ethics." This section moves from biblical narrative to contemporary medical narrative, that last essay providing a bridge to Part IV's move "Beyond Literary Narrative."

David Richter's "Genre, Repetition, Temporal Order: Some Aspects of Biblical Narratology" begins with an acknowledgment of the challenges biblical narrative presents to narratological models: it is not written by clearly identifiable authors, its coherence cannot be assumed, and, indeed, its generic identity is often unclear. What, then, can narratology offer to biblical studies? Richter answers that a flexible, historically informed application of the concepts of genre, repetition, and temporal order can yield significant interpretive dividends. He starts by showing that different readings of the book of Jonah stem from different assumptions about its genre. Richter defends the view that it is satirical fable, but he emphasizes that such a generic classification is likely to meet resistance because it entails accepting the idea that some parts of the Bible are fiction. With his second example, the multiple uses of repetition in the first book of Samuel, Richter works through their many possible interpretations to arrive at the significant role of the redactor. He then proposes that the repetitions end up making Samuel 1 a precursor of *Rashomon* or Faulkner's *Absalom, Absalom*, in which the motives of the tellers take on greater interest than the story they tell. Richter's third example is the temporal order of the second book of Samuel; here late revelations lead to a radical reconfiguration of our understanding of David's character. These narratologically grounded interpretations help explain, Richter argues, why religions have preferred to focus on "pericopes" (short segments detached from context) rather than the Bible as a continuous narrative whole.

Questions about the historical stability of narratological categories continue in Harry E. Shaw's "Why Won't Our Terms Stay Put?: The Narrative Communication Diagram Scrutinized and Historicized." Shaw argues for the necessary relation among our understanding of basic tools of narrative theory, our larger conceptions of narrative, and the history of narrative. Focusing on the famous diagram that charts the movement of narrative communication from real author through implied author, narrator, text, narratee, implied reader, and, finally to real reader, Shaw begins by showing how our different interests give different meanings to elements of the diagram. Those committed to a rhetorical view of narrative find the concept of the implied author a necessary element, while those committed to a view of narrative as information find the concept unnecessary. (In this part of his argument, Shaw is offering his own intervention in the debate about implied authors raised at the beginning of the volume in the essays by Booth and Nünning.) Developing the distinction between rhetoric and information further, Shaw notes that Genette's Law – the dictum that as we move across the diagram from tellers to audiences, the entities become less substantive – is especially relevant for the rhetorician: while information-oriented theorists can give solidity to the narratee by restricting it to its observable presence in the text, rhetoricians are better served by folding their insights about the narratee back into their understanding of the narrator. After demonstrating the consequences of this view for his reading of Thackeray's narrator in *Vanity Fair*, Shaw makes a self-conscious turn, showing the historical inflection of his *own* argument. He notes that his theoretical predilections are part and parcel of his interest in accounting for a specific period in the history of narrative, the nineteenth-century British novel.

Alison Case's "Gender and History in Narrative Theory: The Problem of Retrospective Distance in *David Copperfield* and *Bleak House*" continues Shaw's focus on the necessary connection between form and history in the nineteenth-century British novel, though her view of the terrain is different because she looks through the lens of feminist narratology. Her essay, in effect, adds a missing historical dimension to James Phelan's account of "paradoxical paralipsis" in *Narrative as Rhetoric*. Phelan explains that the technique is in play when the narration of a naïve character narrator is not informed by the changes that his or her narrative eventually reveals. Phelan also contends that the technique, though it violates strict mimesis, is often effective because it allows the author to render the character's change with the most emotional force. Case argues that Phelan's account works for twentieth-century cases but that in the nineteenth century the technique is often part of "a gendered literary code." Specifically, paradoxical paralipsis marks a narrator as "feminine" – which does not necessarily mean "female" – by revealing a lack of authoritative control over the narrative. Case develops her argument by contrasting Dickens's different approaches to the same problem in *Bleak House* and in *David Copperfield*: how to use a retrospect-ive character narrator to represent sympathetically that figure's prior naïve conscious-ness. In Esther Summerson's narration, Dickens uses paradoxical paralipsis and other devices that signal Esther's lack of narrative mastery, whereas in David's narration, he uses commentary from the narrator's perspective that calls attention to David's mastery. Furthermore, Case argues, in establishing these links among gender, tech-nique, and narrative mastery, Dickens is typical of his age.

James Phelan's "Narrative Judgments and the Rhetorical Theory of Narrative: Ian McEwan's *Atonement*" shifts from a focus on form and history to a focus on form and ethics. Phelan's major theoretical claim is that the concept of narrative judgment is central to a rhetorical understanding of narrative form, narrative ethics, and narrative aesthetics, because judgment functions as the hinge that allows each domain to open into the other two. Phelan develops the claim through his identification of three kinds of judgments (interpretive, ethical, and aesthetic), his articulation of six theses about their interrelation, and his analysis of *Atonement*, a complex novel that intertwines the problems of ethical judgments by its characters with the problems of readers' ethical judgments of its storytelling. *Atonement* is overtly concerned with the relation be-tween transgression and atonement as it shows, first, 13-year-old Briony Tallis's well-meaning misidentification of her sister's lover as a sexual assailant and, second, Briony's realization of her mistake and her efforts to make amends. But after showing Briony on the verge of atonement, McEwan reveals that he has encouraged a mis-identification on his audience's part: this novel we have been reading is not only his but Briony's. Furthermore, within the world of both their novels, Briony's error has been real but her atonement is pure fiction: her sister and her lover were never reunited and, in fact, died before such a reunion could even be possible. Thus we need to come to terms both with the ethics of Briony's decision to fictionalize her past and with the ethics of McEwan's misidentification of the narrative we have been reading. Phelan contends that McEwan guides us to see Briony's justification as ethically and aesthetically deficient even as he succeeds in making his own misiden-tification increase the aesthetic and ethical power of the novel.

The next two essays deal with lifewriting. Alison Booth's "The Changing Faces of Mount Rushmore: Collective Portraiture and Participatory National Heritage" inves-tigates the connection between portraits and biographies and between collective biography and politics. Her method is to focus on decisions about whose portrait/

biography gets included in galleries of literary figures and at sites designed to memorialize significant parts of American history such as Mount Rushmore and the Hall of Fame of Great Americans. In each case, Booth traces a complex interaction among the choice of an individual portrait (and its implied biography), the development of a collective portrait (for which she uses the term "prosopography"), and the significance of that collective portrait for the larger national community. Prosopography inevitably raises the political question of representativeness, of who gets included or excluded and why. Consequently, as Booth notes in her summary, prosopography involves its "presenters as well as the audience in collective memorial representation, claiming a certain kinship in cultural heritage, forming a conjunction of biography and history, and leaving a palpable afterimage of what is missing."

Sidonie Smith and Julia Watson continue the focus on lifewriting in "The Trouble with Autobiography: Cautionary Notes for Narrative Theorists" – but they do so by raising significantly different kinds of questions. They explore four particular trouble spots in autobiographical practice that deserve more attention from narrative theory. First, Smith and Watson analyze different motives for and effects of hoaxes (and claims about hoaxes), though they conclude this section by underlining how, whatever the motives, an autobiographical hoax induces a feeling of betrayal in its reader. Their discussion of the second trouble spot, the postcolonial play with the borders of fiction and nonfiction, includes both claims for autobiography in telling the story of another and claims for fiction in telling the story of oneself. Such experimentation, Smith and Watson contend, interrogates "the complicity of the autobiography canon and its critics with dominant modes of self-representation and truth-telling." Next they turn to autobiographical narratives that bear witness to human rights abuses, which often place the autobiographical subject in the position of speaking for the collective and of appealing to the audience for recognition. These appeals, in turn, place a particular ethical burden on the audience since recognizing the writer's experience also entails doing something with that recognition. Finally, in a discussion of materiality, Smith and Watson note that contemporary mixed media autobiography raises questions about the links among the body, the medium of representation, and the autobiographical subject. Like so many essays in the collection, this one ends in a kind of self-conscious spin: all four trouble spots, Smith and Watson contend, simultaneously receive illumination from and offer challenges to contemporary narrative theory.

Gerald Prince picks up one thread of Smith and Watson's discussion of postcolonial lifewriting and weaves it into a larger essay "On a Postcolonial Narratology." Prince explains that his version of this hybrid "would...adopt and rely on the results of (post)classical narratology but would inflect it and perhaps enrich it by wearing a set of postcolonial lenses to look at narrative." Prince elaborates on this conception by moving, with impressive swiftness and clarity, through a remarkable number of narratological categories and suggesting how they would look from this new perspective. To take just a few examples, with voice, one would focus on its "linguistic power or communal representativeness"; with narrator, one would look at postcolonial status and diegetic situation. Most notably from the perspective of this volume, one would do with space what Susan Friedman does in her essay – pay attention to border crossings and heterotopia. Prince concludes the essay by placing his sketch of a postcolonial narratology within a larger vision of three important projects for contemporary and future narrative theory: (1) the continued re-examination and revision of existing categories through the consideration of new examples of narrative – as in this essay; (2) studying the role of various elements of narrative as part of an effort to establish an empirical basis for narratology; and (3) reviving the effort to develop a model of narrative competence. In this portion of his essay, Prince looks back to the kinds of concerns motivating the essays in Parts I and II, while also looking ahead to those raised in the Epilogue.

This look to the future continues in Melba Cuddy-Keane's "Modernist Soundscapes and the Intelligent Ear: An Approach to Narrative Through Auditory Perception." This essay could serve as another model for the first of Prince's projects for the future, since it seeks to develop a vocabulary and methodology for dealing with representations of sound in narrative. At the same time, the essay resonates with the work of Shaw and Case when it makes a historical claim that "modernity occasioned new experiences for the 'human sensorium,' stimulating both a new perceptual knowledge and a new apprehension of perception," especially auditory perception. Cuddy-Keane brings these two main concerns of the essay together in her analysis of Virginia Woolf's representations of sound perception in her fiction. Drawing on such terms as *auscultation, auscultize,* and *auscultizer* (patterned on focalization, focalize, and focalizer, narratology's terms for describing vision) as well as *soundmark* and *soundscape* (patterned on landmark and landscape), Cuddy-Keane demonstrates the range, innovation, and importance of Woolf's use of soundscapes from "Kew Gardens" to *The Years*. Cuddy-Keane's supple analyses show that "by reading for sonics rather than semantics, . . . we discover new forms of making narrative sense."

Shlomith Rimmon-Kenan's essay, "In Two Voices, or: Whose Life/Death/Story Is It, Anyway?," is a meditation on the ethics of the double illness narrative by Ilana Hammerman and her husband Jürgen Nieraad, *Under the Sign of Cancer: A Journey of No Return*. The first half of the book is Nieraad's account of his terminal illness, acute myeloid leukemia; the second half is Hammerman's account of that same illness told from her perspective after Nieraad's death. Rimmon-Kenan structures her treatment as "a series of concentric circles: the relations between the dying husband and his wife, the twofold act of narration, the appropriation of both husband and wife by the medical 'system,' published responses to the narrative by doctors and other readers, and my own appropriation as evidenced in this essay." The result is an analysis that, like Phelan's, links matters of narrative form and ethics, though Rimmon-Kenan's focus on this nonfictional illness narrative and published responses to it – as well as her own reflections on her personal investment in the issues raised by the narrative – leads her to a rather different set of ethical questions. Is Hammerman's narrative inevitably an appropriation of Nieraad's experience? Is it a just indictment of the medical system? Is Rimmon-Kenan's own analysis yet another appropriation? By taking on these questions with intelligence and rigor and refusing to answer definitively the question of her title, she offers a compelling example of the intellectual whirlpools that can result from a serious ethical engagement with narrative.

As we've said, narrative theory has an expansionist quality; and in Part IV, "Beyond Literary Narrative," we gather up seven essays that exemplify its ability to contribute to fields well beyond the traditionally literary. Contribute to – or swallow up? Even among narrative theorists, there are doubts about the impact of this expansionist (one might even say imperialist) potential, as revealed by the questions raised in several of these essays.

The section moves, generally, from verbal to nonverbal fields. We begin with two essays discussing the power of unacknowledged narrative mechanisms in contemporary culture. First, in "Narrative in and of the Law," Peter Brooks reflects on the "role of storytelling" in the legal realm. Stories are absolutely central to legal practice, but, according to Brooks, the law rarely admits their centrality openly. Instead, it recognizes the importance of stories only implicitly and only negatively, through "its efforts at policing narrative," a policing that manages "the conditions of telling" so that "narratives reach those charged with judging them in controlled, rule-governed forms." Narrative content, in other words, is repressed – and kept "under erasure." Brooks ends his essay by calling for a "legal narratology," especially one that deals with the reception and construction of stories by the listeners: judges and juries.

Alan Nadel, in "Second Nature, Cinematic Narrative, the Historical Subject, and *Russian Ark*," studies the impact of unacknowledged conventions in narrative cinema. Although most viewers have come to accept their position while watching narrative films as "natural," in fact such films "naturalize a counterintuitive experience by creating the illusion that the viewer has acquired a privileged window on reality." This naturalization requires viewers to engage in a kind of learning as forgetting which has significant social and psychological consequences. Nadel focuses on the conventions of the "Classical Hollywood Style" – exemplified here in particular by the use of the close-up – and concludes with an analysis of Alexander Sukurov's 2002 film *Russian Ark* that shows how it "calls into question that style and the history of cinematic narrative in which it participates."

The next three essays deal with music, an area that would seem, at first, even further removed from narrative concerns than law and film. In "Narrativizing the End: Death and Opera," Linda and Michael Hutcheon argue that, in order to account for opera's synthesis of music and story, standard narratological models need to be significantly altered. They demonstrate the power of such an alteration by turning to a question about operas that center on suffering and death: how do such works of art produce pleasure? Expanding the work of traditional narrative theorists (especially that of Frank Kermode), they propose that the shared public experience of opera, much like the Early Modern practice of *contemplatio mortis*, allows its audience to "rehearse death" and to confront its "mortal anxieties."

In "Music and/as Cine-Narrative; Or, *Ceci n'est pas un leitmotif*," Royal S. Brown looks at a different kind of music attached to an independent story: film music. Traditional accounts of film music have privileged the narrative aspects of this independent story, reducing the music to little more than a catalog of themes and motifs that double the narrative that we see on the screen. Brown looks instead at the "quasi-narrative properties" found in the music itself in the form of the codes on which Western music depends. He zeroes in on the ways in which film music interacts with our notions of time in the title sequences composed by Hugo Friedhofer for *The Best Years of Our Lives* and by Bernard Herrmann for *North by Northwest*. His analysis demonstrates how film music, "through violations of strictly musical codes" familiar from the concert hall, "often rises above" the literal-minded duplication of the screen action, providing a commentary that, at its best, provides "a kind of meta-text whose 'story' is the very substance of narrative."

In the last of the musical essays, "Classical Instrumental Music and Narrative," Fred Everett Maus deals with music that seems, on the surface, even further removed from narrative concerns: nonprogrammatic instrumental music. Maus charts out the major arguments in the debates that have arisen since musicologists first started to take narrative theory seriously in the 1970s, with particular attention to the work of Marion A. Guck, Susan McClary, and Anthony Newcomb. He then offers his own intervention, arguing that the relationship between music and narrative is a loose analogy and that we should think more carefully about the "poetics" of texts *about* music (rather than considering them simply as literal representations of the music they discuss). From this base, he launches his most important argument: we should think not about musical works as ideal objects that are stable and consistent but rather about the "diversity of the dramatic successions that different performers may create, even when starting from the same score." Maus demonstrates this point with a careful analysis of several different performances of a passage from Beethoven's Fifth Symphony.

Most of the essays in this collection ground their arguments in the details of a particular text. In "'I'm Spartacus!'" Catherine Gunther Kodat does something substantially different – she studies a particular figure, Spartacus, who shows up in many different narratives, posing the question of why we continue to be fascinated by a figure (a term she picks with care) so inextricably tied to defeat. To answer the question, Kodat chooses to treat the repetition of Spartacus figures as an instance of what she calls, after J. M. Bernstein, eidetic variation. At first glance, Kodat argues, Spartacus appears to reveal "the strength of a single figure to hold together a crumbling narrative (the fragmentary, incomplete, and contradictory early histories of a slave rebellion in which Spartacus is the common thread)"; but her exploration of the various versions of "Spartacus" in different media (especially Howard Fast's novel, Stanley Kubrick's film, and Aram Khachaturian's ballet) reveals, rather, an underlying tension between narrative (as ground) and Spartacus as a figure that narrative cannot, in fact, contain. In the end, Spartacus emerges as a queer figure whose story is inevitably "our" story.

The most radical essay in this section is arguably the one by Peggy Phelan, "Shards of a History of Performance Art: Pollock and Namuth Through a Glass, Darkly."

Focusing on the history of performance art, Phelan self-consciously explores both the need for and (like Kodat) the limitations of narrative. Taking as her primary example the action painting of Jackson Pollock, she confronts a glaring paradox. On the one hand, narrative is necessary for anyone who wants to produce a history of performance art. On the other hand, as she shows in her account of the way Pollock's work has been treated by critics (in particular critics who discuss it through the mediation of Namuth's photographs of Pollock's work), narrative itself serves to counteract the very spirit of performance art, whose purpose is "to unsettle the distinction between subject and object, between doing and telling." The essay ends with one of her experiments in "performative writing," as she reflects on Pollock's action painting via prose "that remains alive to action, whose telling force resides in each breath of the renewing present tense."

The Epilogue contains two essays that, like the end of Gerald Prince's, consider recent developments in narrative and implicitly or explicitly point the way toward the future of both narrative and narrative theory. Marie-Laure Ryan's "Narrative and Digitality: Learning to Think With the Medium" explores the development of digital narrative over the last 25 years by focusing on the relation between the potential of software systems and the realization of that potential in actual narratives. Ryan offers a skillful survey of what she calls the "affordances" of three major kinds of digital narrative: interactive fiction based on Infocom software; hypertext narrative based on Storyspace software; and mixed-media narrative based on Flash software. She then builds on the survey to develop her larger theoretical point about "thinking with the medium," her phrase for taking advantage of the potentiality of software. Thinking with the medium "is not the overzealous exploitation of all the features offered by the author-ing system, but an art of compromise between the affordances of the system and the demands of [narrative] meaning." From this perspective, one should not judge digital narrative by the criteria of print narrative because the technologies underlying each kind of narrative provide very different affordances. In other words, digital narrative should not be found wanting because it is not as good as Shakespeare or Proust but rather should be judged by how well it takes advantage of its potential to offer "freely explorable narrative archives; dynamic interplay between words and image; and active participation in fantasy worlds," such as we find in multiplayer online computer games.

The final essay, H. Porter Abbott's "The Future of All Narrative Futures," is a meditation on the power of narrative form and its consequences for the future of narrative, based on Abbott's analysis of current "technologically assisted" narrative entertainments. Although he begins by noting that such narratives (MOOs and MUDs as well as the kinds Ryan analyzes) have expanded the domain of narrative and focused more attention on interactivity, Abbott ultimately sees more similarity than difference between the fundamental structures of these narratives and print narrative than Ryan does. But Abbott takes the investigation further by asking whether the shifts in emphasis of our digital age signal a developing shift in our behavior and cognition, one moving us away from coherent master-narratives toward more fragmentary, open-ended, local narratives. Turning to a reading of the contemporary political scene, including a consideration of the conflicting master-narratives of the September 11, 2001 terrorists and of George W. Bush and his followers, Abbott again suggests that the old structures remain in place. This answer, however, suggests the next question: what is the relation between current developments in narrative e-entertainments and the old structures? Abbott finds in these developments a resistance to "the givenness of narrative," and a correspondingly greater interest in the "prenarratable," that is, experience that is not yet shaped into narrative. More generally, Abbott suggests that this oscillation between the prenarratable and narrative corresponds with a similar oscillation between living and narrating our lives, an oscillation that he sees as necessary for our mental health. Consequently, "the often wonderful developments in the technology of entertainment will continue largely to take place within constraints, narrative or otherwise, that give us the illusion that time itself has a shape and that somehow we are equipped to read it."

As we look back on this introduction's navigation – and that of our contributors – between the stony clarity of apparently well-grounded knowledge and the whirling waters of theoretical and interpretive innovation, we see several larger conclusions. (1) Contemporary narrative theory is a flourishing enterprise precisely because it remains strongly aware of its history and tradition even as it pursues its commitment to innovation. If one navigational mistake is to steer too close to either Scylla or Charybdis, an equally grave mistake is to sail on oblivious to both. (2) There is no one best way to navigate between tradition and innovation, and the field is flourishing because its scholars have developed multiple paths even as they continue to invent new ones. (3) The ongoing work of our contributors will play a substantial role in the further flourishing of the field.

Prologue

1

Histories of Narrative Theory (I): A Genealogy of Early Developments

David Herman

[A fact becomes] historical posthumously, as it were, through events that may be separated from it by thousands of years.

(Benjamin 1969: 265)

Introduction

When Tzvetan Todorov coined the French term *narratologie* ("narratology") in his 1969 book *Grammaire du "Décaméron,"* he used the word in parallel with *biology, sociology,* and so forth to denote "the science of narrative," describing his work as a fledgling effort within a field not yet fully born. Participating in a broader structuralist revolution that sought to use Saussurean linguistics as a "pilot-science" for studying cultural phenomena of all sorts (Dosse 1997: 59–66), Todorov built on precedents set by theorists such as the early Roland Barthes ([1957] 1972), who had characterized diverse forms of cultural expression (advertisements, photographs, museum exhibits, wrestling matches, etc.) as rule-governed signifying practices or "languages" in their own right (Culler 1975). Founding narratology as a subdomain of structuralist inquiry, researchers like Barthes, Claude Bremond, Gérard Genette, A. J. Greimas, and Todorov followed Saussure's distinction between *la langue* (= language viewed as system) and *la parole* (= individual utterances produced and interpreted on that basis); they construed particular stories as individual narrative messages supported by a shared semiotic system. And just as Saussurean linguistics privileged *la langue* over *la parole*, focusing on the structural constituents and combinatory principles of the semiotic framework of language, the narratologists privileged narrative in general over individual narratives. Their chief concern was with transtextual semiotic principles according to which basic structural units (characters, states, events, etc.) are combined, permuted, and transformed to yield specific narrative texts.

I revisit the methods, aims, and legacies of structuralist narratology in the section on "The Structuralist Synecdoche" below (see also Prince 1995). But it is worth emphasizing at the outset that, despite the narratologists' own claims for novelty, and notwithstanding the profound impact their work has had on the study of narrative since the 1960s, structuralist theories were not in fact as revolutionary as the heady language in some of their more programmatic statements might suggest (see, e.g., Barthes [1966] 1977). Rather, French structuralist narratology emerged from a complex interplay of intellectual traditions, criticotheoretical movements, and analytic paradigms distributed across decades, continents, nations, schools of thought, and individual researchers. Marked by regions of nonsynchronous evolution (Bloch 1988) and criss-crossing vectors of change, this complex of related research initiatives makes it difficult to fix the exact geotemporal coordinates of any particular innovation in the field. Accordingly, as I will argue in this chapter, a quite complicated story needs to be told about the rise – or diffusion – of methods for studying stories.

Adopting a case-study approach, the next section examines René Wellek and Austin Warren's chapter on narrative fiction in their 1949 book *Theory of Literature*. I focus on this influential text, published in mid twentieth-century North America but bearing the traces of earlier German, Czech, and Russian scholarship, to underscore how modern-day research on narrative was shaped by the discontinuities and dislocations associated with World War II, among other disruptive events. Caught up in these events, Wellek and Warren's chapter in *Theory of Literature* provides a point of entry into the network of historical tendencies that conspired to make narrative theory what it was and is. Subsequent sections of my chapter then zoom out to reveal the broader contexts in which approaches to narrative theory emerged, interacted, and re-emerged in different form.[1] As my account suggests, early Anglo-American initiatives in the field, though they have contributed importantly to recent research on narrative (see section "Morphology II" below), must also be situated within a complex of discourses and traditions that were rooted in Europe, and that later manifested themselves in the structuralist narratology developed in France beginning in the 1960s. The final section of the chapter returns to Wellek and Warren's account, reassessing their discussion in light of the larger historical developments of which I here attempt to give an overview.

A preliminary note about my title: I use the term *genealogy* in the sense pioneered by Friedrich Nietzsche ([1887] 1968) and reinvigorated by Michel Foucault ([1971] 1984); in this usage, genealogy is a mode of investigation that seeks to uncover forgotten interconnections; reestablish obscured or unacknowledged lines of descent; expose relationships between institutions, belief-systems, discourses, or modes of analysis that might otherwise be taken to be wholly distinct and unrelated. Genealogy in this way seeks to denaturalize "the contingent [social, institutional, discursive, or other] structures we mistakenly consider given, solid, and extending without change into the future as well as into the past" (Nehamas 1986: 110). Hence, in referring to the chapter as a genealogy, I mean to clarify its aims: to situate recent theories of narrative in a complex lineage, a network of historical and conceptual affiliations, and thereby underscore how those theories constitute less a singular continuous tradition of research than a cluster of developments marked by family resemblances. Such resemblances are readily recognized yet notoriously difficult to define (Wittgenstein [1953] 1958; see the final section below).

Theory of Literature and Narrative Theory: A Case Study

Published during the heyday of the New Criticism, Wellek and Warren's *Theory of Literature* helped shape Anglo-American formalist literary theory in general, as well as research on narrative fiction in particular. The chapter on fiction reflects the authors' overarching aim of developing an "intrinsic" as opposed to an "extrinsic" approach to literary study; they eschewed "positivist" methods that subordinated literature to the objects studied in other disciplines (e.g., history, social groups, or philosophical arguments), advocating instead a theory of literature based on the nature of literary objects in particular. In turn, in specifying the nature of narrative fiction as a particular object of study, the chapter sets out many of the research foci that have persisted as central concerns for later theorists of narrative:

- the notion that narrative fiction, including novels and short stories, constitutes only a particular subtype of narratively organized discourse, not the canonical form of narrative as such (Wellek and Warren 1949: 225);
- the jointly causal and temporal logic of stories, or narrative's fusion of sequence and consequence (p. 222);
- the distinction between the basic situations and events that form the story-stuff or *fabula* of a narrative and the composition of those basic elements into the plot or *sjuzet* (pp. 224–6); that is, the distinction between "story" and "discourse" (Chatman 1978) that was exploited so productively by Francophone structuralists such as Todorov (1966) and Genette ([1972] 1980);
- mechanisms of characterization, including the social and anthropological bases for character-types in fiction (pp. 226–8);
- point of view (pp. 230–3);
- framed tales, and the modes of narrative embedding that result from stories-within-stories (p. 230) (cf. Genette [1972] 1980);
- the noncoincidence of author and narrator in fictional discourse (p. 230) (cf. Booth 1961);
- strategies for the representation of characters' consciousness as well as speech (pp. 233–4); and
- the notion that the "truth" of narrative fiction arises from the way its components hang together to form a *Kosmos* sufficient unto itself, whereas the truth of a

historical account depends on the extent to which it matches, in some sense, the way the world is (pp. 219–22).

But is it the case that by targeting these issues the authors in fact anticipated or prefigured subsequent approaches to narrative theory – for example, approaches enabled by the birth of narratology in France? The story, as I have suggested, is not that simple.

Thanks in part to Wellek's own background as a specialist in English language and comparative literature who was once affiliated with the Prague Linguistic Circle, and who thus helped transmit ideas deriving from earlier European and Slavic scholarship (including Saussurean linguistics), *Theory of Literature* constitutes a node within a network of discourses and intersecting historical trends.[2] Besides interacting synergistically with the guiding principles of the Anglo-American New Critics, whose insistence on the autonomy of verbal art mirrored the Russian Formalists' emphasis on "literariness,"[3] the same Formalist ideas that helped shape Wellek and Warren's approach also affected the development of structuralist narratology. Influenced in their own right by German scholars working on questions of narrative in the early years of the twentieth century (see my next section), Viktor Shklovskii, Boris Tomashevskii, Vladimir Propp, and other Formalists helped establish not only the universe of discourse on which Wellek and Warren drew in their 1949 text, but also the basis for some of the most recognizable topoi of narratology: for example, the decomposition of the story level or content level into obligatory and optional components, and the rethinking of characters as actants (see the next section and the section on "The Structuralist Synecdoche" below for further discussion).

By the same token, rather than unfolding along a single timeline, the history of narrative theory has acquired its structure from the distribution of research concerns across parallel developmental trajectories; genealogy allows these trajectories to be grouped together into a larger historical constellation. The student of narrative theory would thus do well to look for family resemblances, but not necessarily causally determinative relations, between Wellek and Warren's characterization of narrative as a transgeneric phenomenon and the later analogous account outlined by Barthes ([1966] 1977). The same goes for *Theory of Literature*'s use of the story–discourse distinction and Genette's use of it in *Narrative Discourse*, as well as for Wellek and Warren's probe into the anthropological bases of character types and Greimas's anthropologically inflected theory of actants, or general behavioral roles encoded in narrative plots.

But what accounts, exactly, for the special synergy of the discourses and traditions from which Wellek and Warren's chapter on narrative fiction took rise, and to which their study in turn contributed? In other words, when it comes to early developments in narrative theory, what is the nature (and scope) of the historical constellation in which Czech, Russian, French, and Anglo-American ideas and approaches can be situated? The remainder of my chapter explores these questions.

Early Twentieth-Century Narrative Poetics: "Morphological" Models in Germany and Russia

In his own history of occidental poetics during the period stretching from Aristotle (1971) to the Prague School semioticians, Lubomír Doležel (1990) has identified a constellation in terms of which a number of ideas about narrative can be grasped as related developments. Doležel suggests that in the aftermath of Romanticism, ostensibly diverse approaches to (narrative) poetics were united by their common descent from a broadly "morphological" research tradition. Tracing the morphological paradigm back to Goethe, and building on previous work by Victor Erlich (1965) and Peter Steiner (1984: 68–98; cf. Steiner and Davydov 1977), Doležel characterizes the emergence of morphological poetics in the Romantic era as a manifestation of a broader epistemological shift.[4] At issue is the replacement of a mechanistic by an organic model for understanding the structure of the world (Doležel 1990: 55). As Doležel puts it, "Anatomy and morphology share the assumption that an organism is a set of parts. . . . [But whereas] anatomy is satisfied with separating and identifying the parts, morphology informs us that the diverse parts make up a higher-order, structured whole. Morphology is a theory of the formation of complex structures from individual parts" (p. 56).

In the domain of narrative poetics, the morphological method was pioneered in Germany in the early years of the twentieth century (Doležel 1990: 126–41; see also Doležel 1989). It was then further developed by Russian Formalist theorists and subsequently by Prague structuralists who built on the Formalists' work.[5] Foundational works of narrative morphology include a programmatic 1912 manifesto by the German philologist Otmar Schissel von Fleschenberg, who analyzed higher-order narrative structures into "rhetorical artistic devices," and the Germanist Berard Seuffert's studies of what he identified as schematic building blocks of literary narratives.[6]

As Doležel notes, German scholars such as Schissel, Seuffert, and also Wilhelm Dibelius distinguished between the *disposition* (logical arrangement) and *composition* (artistic arrangement) of the structural elements contained within narratives. They focused on two aspects of compositional patterning in particular: patterns of action and acting personae. Thus, in his 1910 study of the English novel, Dibelius anticipated Propp's morphological study of Russian folktales by defining the notion of "role" as a "character in a certain function of the whole" (quoted by Doležel 1990: 133–4). Like Dibelius, Propp subordinated character to plot, focusing not on particularized actors but on recurrent, plot-based "functions" instantiated by various individuals across specific tales (see below). In turn, anticipating the idea of actants that Greimas developed on the basis of Propp's work, Seuffert studied the system of characters as an ingredient of narrative composition. Schissel, for his part, focused on the composition of action rather than characters per se, parsing narrative structures into the patterned distribution of scenes and episodes, and identifying the ring (*Kranz*) and frame (*Rahmen*) as basic compositional principles.

Grounded in a broadly morphological approach, this early focus on narrative composition shaped later German narrative theory. Relevant studies include André Jolles's *Einfache Formen*, a Goethe-inspired morphology of "simple forms" (anecdotes, sayings, legends, etc.) (Doležel 1990: 205 n.31), and two works on which Gérard Genette drew in presenting the influential narratological model outlined in *Narrative Discourse* ([1972] 1980): Günther Müller's *"Erzählzeit und erzählte Zeit"* (Narrative Time and Narrated Time), originally published in 1948 and reprinted in Müller's 1968 book *Morphologische Poetik* (*Morphological Poetics*), and Eberhard Lämmert's (1955) *Bauformen des Erzählens* (*Structural Components of Narrative*). These later German studies, extended by Genette, exploited the semantic potential of the idea of composition itself; they investigated how incidents may acquire idiosyncratic time-scales and event structures when composed into narratives, that is, integrated into a complex of other events to form a narrative whole. In parallel with this line of research, the Russian Formalists had mapped the idea of "composition" onto that of "plot" (= *sjuzet*); for Shklovsky ([1929] 1990) plot encompassed not only the arrangement of incidents "but also all the 'devices' used to interrupt and delay the narrative" (Erlich 1965: 242; cf. Wellek and Warren 1949: 226).

Meanwhile, German work on narrative composition was well-known in Russia by the 1920s (Doležel 1990: 134–6). There, too, the morphological model flourished (Erlich 1965: 171–2, 239, 249, Steiner 1984: 68–98), producing studies that would mold later research on narrative theory, particularly the structuralist narratology developed in France some four decades later. The Russian Formalists were committed to developing stylistic models for the widest possible range of prose forms, including the full gamut of narrative genres (Erlich 1965: 230–50, Shklovsky 1990 [1929]). They studied, for example, narrative techniques such as the *skaz*, whereby a personified narrator figure in a written narrative prominently mediates between the author and the audience to produce the illusion of spontaneous vernacular storytelling (Erlich 1965: 238, Prince 1987: 87–8). Concerned with such higher levels of narrative structure, the Formalists studied prose narratives of all sorts, from Tolstoy's historically panoramic novels to tightly plotted detective novels to (Russian) fairy tales. This widened investigative focus would prove to be a decisive development in the history of modern-day narrative theory. The new focus helped uncouple theories of *narrative* from theories of the *novel*, shifting scholarly attention from a particular genre of literary writing to all discourse or, in an even broader interpretation, all semiotic activities that can be construed as narratively organized. The Formalists thus set a precedent for the transgeneric and indeed transmedial aspirations of later French structuralist theorists such as Bremond (1964) and Barthes ([1966] 1977) (Herman 2004). Further, the Formalists' attempt to create a stylistics suitable for prose texts constituted a starting-point for Bakhtin's ([1929] 1984) (anti-Formalist) research on the polyphonic or multivoiced profile of Dostoevsky's fictions. A half-century later, Bakhtin's research helped shape the contextualist approaches to narrative that took issue with structuralist narratology, which in turn traced its roots back to the Russian Formalists (see section on "The Structuralist Synecdoche" below).

Adopting the German theorists' morphological approach to narrative composition, and extending their framework of inquiry to include narratives of all types, the Russian Formalists authored a number of pathbreaking studies. For example, in distinguishing between "bound" (or plot-relevant) and "free" (or nonplot-relevant) motifs, Boris Tomashevsky ([1925] 1965) provided the basis for Barthes's distinction between "nuclei" and "catalyzers" in his "Introduction to the Structural Analysis of Narratives" (Barthes [1966] 1977). Renamed *kernels* and *satellites* by Seymour Chatman (1978), these terms refer to core and peripheral elements of story-content, respectively. Delete or add to the kernel events of a story and you no longer have the same story; delete or add to the satellites and you have the same story told in a different way. Related to Tomashevsky's work on free versus bound motifs, Viktor Shklovsky's ([1929] 1990) early work on plot as a structuring device provided what I have already alluded to as one of the grounding assumptions of narratology: namely, the *fabula–sjuzet* or story–discourse distinction, that is, the distinction between the what and the how, or what is being told about versus the manner in which it is told.

What is arguably the most important Formalist precedent for modern narrative theory, however, was furnished by Vladimir Propp's *Morphology of the Folktale* ([1928] 1968), whose first English translation appeared in 1958. Explicitly associating his approach with Goethean morphology (Doležel 1990: 141), Propp distinguished between variable and invariant components of higher-order narrative structures – more specifically, between changing dramatis personae and the unvarying plot functions performed by them (e.g., act of villainy, punishment of the villain, etc.). In all, Propp abstracted 31 functions, or character actions defined in terms of their significance for the plot, from the corpus of Russian folktales that he used as his data-set; he also specified rules for their distribution in a given tale. Lévi-Strauss ([1955] 1986), in a protonarratological study that influenced French structuralists such as Bremond (1973) and Barthes ([1966] 1977), would later build on Propp's concept of functions to formulate a deep-structural analysis of the "mythemes," or "gross constituent units," structuring the Oedipus myth. Further, Propp's approach constituted the basis for structuralist theories of characters as "actants." Extrapolating from what Propp had termed "spheres of action," Greimas ([1966] 1983) sought to create a typology of general roles to which the (indefinitely many) particularized actors in narratives could be reduced.

But before detailing the ways in which structuralist narratologists of the 1960s and early 1970s built on the work of previous researchers, I need to explore another branch within the genealogy of modern-day narrative theory. At issue is the Anglo-American tradition of narrative poetics in which Wellek and Warren's *Theory of Literature* intervened in the mid twentieth century, but which extends back at least to the tradition of novel theory that originated with Henry James (see Miller 1972) and was codified by Percy Lubbock ([1921] 1957). This tradition began with an organicist emphasis that can be traced back to Aristotle's concern with the way well-made plots (*mythoi*) comprise elements contributing to a larger whole. Jamesian organicism was congruent, on the one hand, with the emerging New Critical conception of literary artifacts as "organic wholes" and, on the other hand, with the German, Czech, and Russian theories of narrative morphology that surface in Wellek and Warren's chapter on fiction. But what is more, beginning as long as two decades before the Francophone structuralists exposed the limits of earlier, linguistically oriented European and Slavic models, Chicago School neo-Aristotelians such as R. S. Crane (1953) and his student Wayne Booth (1961) leveled powerful critiques at analogous trends in Anglo-American theories of fiction. Anglo-American and French structuralist approaches to narrative thus underwent a kind of staggered development, following parallel evolutionary trajectories at nonsynchronous rates of change.

Morphology II: Organic Form, Anglo-American Formalism, and Beyond

Henry James's influential 1884 essay on "The Art of Fiction" (Miller 1972: 27–44) provided important foundations for Anglo-American novel theory. Three interconnected aspects of the model outlined by James can be singled out for discussion here: its characterization of fictions as organic wholes, its adoption of a descriptive rather than prescriptive approach to narrative analysis, and its skeptical attitude toward exact recipes or protocols for the *production* of fictional texts. The subsequent course of early to mid twentieth-century Anglo-American narrative theory can be mapped out as a series of (more or less dialectically related) responses to these aspects of James's approach.

In parallel with Aristotelian poetics as well as the later morphological models discussed in my previous section, James characterizes narrative fictions as higher-order verbal structures greater than the sum of their parts. For James, too, the components of fiction derive their functional properties from their relation to the gestalt in which they participate. But James's metaphorical equation of literary works with living organisms is even more explicit than that adopted by the Russian Formalists. Questioning such standard oppositions as incident vs. description and description vs. dialogue, James remarks: "A novel is a living thing, all one and continuous, like any other organism, and in proportion as it lives will it be found, I think, that in each of the parts there is something of each of the other parts" (Miller 1972: 36). It is in this same context that James poses his famous two-part rhetorical question, suggesting that characters and events cannot be understood in isolation from the plot by which they are linked together and from which they acquire their significance in the first place: "What is character but the determination of incident? What is incident but the illustration of character?" (p. 37). Similarly, refusing to distinguish between the form and content of fiction, James writes: "This sense of the story being the idea, the starting-point of the novel, is the only one that I see in which it can be spoken of as something different from its organic whole" (p. 40). Precisely because for James the content of fiction must be allowed to determine its form, and vice versa, his account remains resolutely antiprescriptivist. He argues that it is impossible to dictate, *a priori*, what makes for successful narrative fiction. Rather, "the good health of an art which undertakes so immediately to reproduce life must demand that it be perfectly free. It lives upon exercise, and the very meaning of exercise is freedom" (p. 33).

Percy Lubbock ([1921] 1957) took his inspiration from James's novelistic practice as well as his theory of fiction. Working in tandem with his New Critical contemporaries, who characterized verbal artifacts as organic wholes such that removing or altering one part would destroy the entire work (Brooks [1947] 1992), Lubbock espoused the doctrine of organic unity in fiction; he thus privileged James's own well-wrought fictions over the more sprawling creations produced by writers such as Tolstoy. However, Lubbock made the issue of "point of view" the cornerstone of his account – to an extent not necessarily warranted by James's own approach (Miller 1972: 1, Booth 1961: 24–5). In doing so, Lubbock appropriated James's ideas to produce a markedly prescriptive framework. His chief concern was to draw an invidious distinction between showing ("dramatizing" events) and telling ("describing" or "picturing" events), suggesting that description is inferior to dramatization, picturing to scene-making: "other things being equal, the more dramatic way is better than the less. It is indirect, as a method; but it places the thing itself in view, instead of recalling and reflecting and picturing it" (Lubbock 1957: 149–50). But if in systematizing James's ideas Lubbock transformed them from more or less tentative descriptions into prescriptions, by the same token he construed fictional techniques as part of a craft rather than mysterious emanations of artistic genius. More specifically, in advocating for and not just describing the techniques whereby events are dramatized by being filtered through a reflector figure or fictional center of consciousness, Lubbock suggested that specific methods or procedures are at the heart of the craft of fiction.

In response, maintaining a focus on issues of narrative technique, but seeking to restore the qualifications and complexities evident in James's original statement of his theory (as well as in his novelistic practice), Wayne C. Booth (1961) inverted the terms of Lubbock's argument. Instead of privileging showing over telling, Booth accorded telling pride of place – making it the general narratorial condition of which "showing" is a localized effect, or rather an epiphenomenon. Thus, unlike Lubbock, Booth resisted making point of view the paramount concern of the theory of fiction. Indeed, Booth's brilliant account revealed difficulties with the very premise of the telling-versus-showing debate. He characterized showing as an effect promoted by certain deliberately structured kinds of tellings, organized in such a way that narratorial mediation (though inescapably present) remains more or less covert. Booth also suggested that an emphasis on showing over telling has costs as well as benefits, cataloging important rhetorical effects that explicit narratorial commentary can be used to accomplish – for example, relating particulars to norms established elsewhere in the text, heightening the significance of events, or manipulating mood.

More generally, Booth's rigorous exposé of the incoherence of calls for artistic purity – his demonstration that it is in fact impossible to "purify" narrative fiction of rhetoric, as if separating the wheat from the chaff – aligns his account with neo-Aristotelian approaches to literary theory. Given Booth's affiliation with the Chicago School (see Crane 1953, Richter forthcoming, Vince 1993), it is not surprising that he would take issue with the formalist orientation of critics such as Allen Tate (cf. Booth 1961: 28–9), who echoed other New Critics in insisting on the autonomy and self-sufficiency of the work of art, defined as a particular use of (or orientation toward) language. Booth's model can be situated instead in the context of the critical framework developed by neo-Aristotelians such as Crane, Elder Olson, and Richard McKeon, who used Aristotle's taxonomy of causes as an approach to analyzing literary texts – in effect using Aristotle's own ideas to recontextualize the organicism that the New Critics had derived from the *Poetics*. In this framework, causes of verbal art include the *efficient* cause (= the author), the *final* cause (= effect on readers), the *material* cause (= the language), and the *formal* cause (= the mimetic content) (Vince 1993: 117).[7] Accordingly, from a neo-Aristotelian perspective, New Critical theories of literary art in general and narrative fiction in particular were guilty of reducing all the causal forces operating on and manifested in verbal art to the material cause alone. Rather than consigning to the intentional fallacy a concern with efficient causes, or to the affective fallacy a concern with final causes, the neo-Aristotelian approach suggested that all of these concerns are legitimate research foci. Analogously, factoring in efficient and final as well as material causes, Booth studied how particular kinds of fictional designs prompt specific kinds of rhetorical transactions between authors and audiences.

Furthermore, Booth's wide-ranging discussion of narrative types ranging from Boccaccio's *Decameron* to ancient Greek epics to novels and short fictions by authors as diverse as Cervantes, Hemingway, and Céline encouraged subsequent theorists in the Anglo-American tradition to explore various kinds of narratives, rather than focusing solely on the novel. This uncoupling of narrative theory from novel theory – a process that had been initiated independently by the Russian Formalists some 40 years earlier – culminated in such wide-scope works as Robert Scholes and Robert Kellogg's study of *The Nature of Narrative* (1966). Significantly, Scholes and Kellogg's study was published the same year as *Communications* 8, which effectively launched structuralist narratology with a similarly transgeneric focus.

The Structuralist Synecdoche: Narratology after Russian Formalism

In rejecting the New Critics' exclusive emphasis on the material cause of verbal art, the neo-Aristotelian Chicago School had, by the time of the so-called "structuralist revolution," already taken issue with the narrative = language equation that is at the heart of structuralist narratology. Nonetheless, when Barthes, Bremond, Genette,

Greimas, and Todorov initiated the project of narratology, their efforts hearkened back to a major "theoretical synecdoche" (Steiner 1984) used by the Russian Formalists. Citing a 1928 statement by the Formalist Viktor Zirmunsky – "Insofar as the material of poetry is the word ... the classification of verbal phenomena provided by linguistics should be the basis for a systematically constructed poetics" – Steiner points out that "the model described by Zirmunsky is a synecdoche, a *pars pro toto* relationship. It substitutes language – the material of verbal art – for art itself, and linguistics – the science of language – for literary studies" (p. 138). The narratologists repeated this trope, but drew on Saussure's work to lend the synecdoche hermeneutic authority as well as quasi-scientific status. Ironically, however, in reinstating the Formalists' synecdoche on what they viewed as rigorously structuralist-linguistic grounds, narratologists exposed the limits of the very linguistic models that they used to make their case, that is, to reassert the argument that narrative is (preeminently) a kind of language.[8]

In any event, the use of (Saussurean) linguistics as a pilot-science or "theoretical synecdoche" shaped the object, methods, and overall aims of structuralist narratology as an investigative framework (see Herman 2002: 2–4). Narratology's grounding assumption is that a common, more or less implicit, model of narrative explains people's ability to recognize and interpret many diverse productions and types of artifacts as stories. In turn, the *raison d'être* of narratological analysis is to develop an explicit characterization of the model underlying people's intuitive knowledge about stories, in effect providing an account of what constitutes humans' narrative competence. Hence, having conferred on linguistics the status of a "founding model" (Barthes [1966] 1977: 82), Barthes identifies for the narratologist the same object of inquiry that (*mutatis mutandis*) Ferdinand de Saussure ([1916] 1959) had specified for the linguist: the system (*la langue*) from which the infinity of narrative messages (*la parole*) derives and on the basis of which they can be understood as stories in the first place.

Further, narratologists like the early Barthes used structuralist linguistics not just to identify their object of analysis, but also to elaborate their method of inquiry. This adaptation of linguistic methods was to prove both enabling and constraining.[9] On the positive side, the example of linguistics did provide narratology with a productive vantage-point on stories, affording terms and categories that generated significant new research questions. For example, the linguistic paradigm furnished Barthes with what he characterized as the "decisive" concept of the "level of description" (Barthes 1977: 85–8). Imported from grammatical theory, this idea suggests that a narrative is not merely a "simple sum of propositions" but rather a complex structure that can be analyzed into hierarchical levels – in the same way that a natural-language utterance can be analyzed at the level of its syntactic, its morphological, or its phonological representation. Building on Todorov's (1966) Russian Formalist-inspired proposal to divide narrative into the levels of story and discourse, Barthes himself distinguishes three levels of description: at the lowest or most granular level are *functions* (in Propp's and Bremond's sense of the term); then *actions* (in the sense used by Greimas in his work on actants); and finally *narration* (which is "roughly the level of 'discourse' in Todorov" [1977: 88]) (cf. Genette [1972] 1980).

Yet narratology was also limited by the linguistic models it treated as paradigmatic. Ironically, the narratologists embraced structuralist linguistics as their pilot-science just when its deficiencies were becoming apparent in the domain of linguistic theory itself (cf. Herman 2001). The limitations of the Saussurean paradigm were thrown into relief, on the one hand, by emergent formal (e.g., generative-grammatical) models for analyzing language structure. On the other hand, powerful tools were being developed in the wake of Ludwig Wittgenstein, J. L. Austin, H. P. Grice, John Searle, and other post-Saussurean language theorists interested in how contexts of language use bear on the production and interpretation of socially situated utterances. These theorists began to question what they viewed as counterproductive modes of abstraction and idealization in both structuralist linguistics and the Chomskyan paradigm that displaced it. Research along these lines led to the realization that certain features of the linguistic system – implicatures, discourse anaphora, protocols for turn-taking in conversation, and so forth – emerge only at the level beyond the sentence.

Accordingly, Barthes unintentionally reveals the limits of structuralist narratology when he remarks that "a narrative is a long sentence, just as every constative sentence is in a way the rough outline of a short narrative," suggesting that one finds in narrative, "expanded and transformed proportionately, the principal verbal categories: tenses, aspects, moods, persons" (Barthes 1977: 84). Other early narratologists shared with Barthes the assumption that all the categories pertaining to sentence-level grammar could be unproblematically scaled up to the discourse level, without compromising the descriptive or explanatory power of the grammatical machinery involved. Todorov's study of Boccaccio's *Decameron* borrowed categories from traditional grammars to compare narrated entities and agents with nouns, actions and events with verbs, and properties with adjectives (Todorov 1969). Genette ([1972] 1980) drew on the same grammatical paradigm in using tense, mood, and voice to characterize the relations between the narrated world, the narrative in terms of which it is presented, and the narrating that enables the presentation.

Indeed, the narratologists' appropriation of ideas from structuralist linguistics not only determined their object and method of inquiry, but also shaped the overall purpose of the narratological enterprise itself. In Jonathan Culler's phrase, "linguistics is not hermeneutic" (Culler 1975: 31); that is, linguistic analysis seeks to provide not interpretations of particular utterances, but rather a general account of the conditions of possibility for the production and processing of grammatically acceptable forms and sequences. Similarly, narratologists argued that the structural analysis of narrative should not be viewed as a handmaiden to interpretation. The aims of narratology were, rather, fundamentally taxonomic and descriptive. Structural analysis of stories concerned itself not with *what* narratively organized sign systems mean but rather with *how* they mean, and more specifically with how they mean *as* narratives. The narratologists therefore adhered to Jakobson's (1960) distinction between poetics and criticism; in privileging the code of narrative over particular stories supported by that code, they pursued narrative poetics, not narrative criticism. The critic engages in serial readings of individual stories; the narratologist studies what allows an assemblage of verbal or other signs to be construed as a narrative in the first place.

Thus the structuralist narratologists made into an explicit methodology the theoretical synecdoche that was a more or less implicit background assumption for the Russian Formalists. In essence, the narratologists looked to language theory for model-building purposes. In the process, they confirmed the fruitfulness of transferring into the domain of narrative theory ideas incubated in other disciplines (Herman 2002). But there is another lesson to be learned from the history of narratology as well: namely, that when it comes to research on narrative, cross-disciplinary transfers need to be managed with care, on pain of overextending ideas and methods whose limits of applicability have already made themselves manifest in other contexts.

Wellek and Warren Revisited: A Genealogical Perspective

Overall, the account offered in this chapter suggests that the history of early developments in narrative theory should be viewed, not as a series of events linked by a single causal chain and lending themselves to neat periodizations (Russian Formalism, New Criticism, narratology, etc.), but rather as fields of forces sometimes unfolding in parallel, sometimes temporally staggered, but emerging at different rates of progression and impinging on one another through more or less diffuse causal networks. In sketching the beginnings of modern-day research on narrative, I have thus subscribed to the genealogical method, as characterized by R. Kevin Hill (1998):

> History, according to genealogists, is not teleological (as it is for Hegel). They cannot identify a goal of a historical process, and then go on to show how it gradually emerged from its embryonic beginnings. Rather, they chart the processes that, by contingent confluence, produce a contemporary result. Hence the metaphor: no individual is the goal of a family history. Rather, a family is a vast fabric of relationships, and any one individual represents only one among many confluences of past lines of descent.
>
> (Hill 1998: 1)

Likewise, no individual approach or school is the "goal" of the history (better, histories) of narrative theory. The field constitutes, instead, a cluster or family of related developments with intersecting lines of descent; in this context, earlier developments have a shaping but not determinative influence on later ones, and whereas some modes of analysis branch out from and feed back into a shared historical tradition, others represent theoretical innovations that have not had a larger continuing impact on this research domain.

Viewed from a genealogical perspective, Wellek and Warren's chapter on narrative fiction did not "anticipate" structuralist narratology. Rather, it was itself shaped by

German, Czech, and Russian lines of development that also led, through multiple routes of historical, biographical, and conceptual influence, to the formation of the narratologists' models and methods. Drawing on a common stock of ideas, both the authors of *Theory of Literature* and the narratologists parsed narrative structure into story and discourse, shifted their interest from specific characters to character types (or actants), highlighted the interconnectedness of causality and chronology in narrative representations, and pointed (more or less explicitly) to the benefits of a transgeneric focus on narratives of all kinds.[10]

But then there are elements of Wellek and Warren's account that were simply unassimilable by structuralist narratology as originally constituted. Because of their own Saussurean heritage, the structuralists were ill-equipped to handle the problem of fictional reference, that is, the question of what (fictional and other) narratives refer to. Thus, in broaching the idea of the fictional *Kosmos* – the storyworld underlying and evoked by fictional representations – Wellek and Warren's account highlighted problems of narrative semantics that would remain undeveloped for some three or four decades, until another complex of discourses began to reshape narrative theory and alter its genealogical profile.[11]

NOTES

1   Even so, given the limited scope of my account, I will not be able to deal with all of the contexts in which modern-day research on narrative has developed – in some cases yielding approaches very different in focus and method from those discussed in this chapter. For example, since theories of narrative were entangled until quite recently with theories of the novel, Georg Lukács's ([1920] 1971, [1938] 1990) Hegel- and Marx-inflected studies of the novel constitute relevant sources for a broader survey of early developments in the field. Similarly, during the mid twentieth century, Frankfurt School Marxists such as Walter Benjamin (1969: 28–109) and Ernst Bloch (Bloch 1988: 245–77) explored ideas that are important for narrative theory. Of course, recent non-Western approaches to narrative theory would also need to be included in a more comprehensive survey.

2   Born in Austria in 1903, Wellek was an inaugural member of the Prague Linguistic Circle, which was established in 1926 (Doležel 1995: 34, Erlich 1965: 156). Wellek was familiar with key ideas advanced by the Russian Formalists, whose work preceded the founding of the Czech group and (through Roman Jakobson) helped set its agenda (Steiner 1984: 27–33). After Hitler invaded Czechoslovakia, Wellek emigrated to the United States and served as the Chair of the Comparative Literature Program at Yale from 1946–72 (see Lawall 1993).

3   See, however, Thompson's (1971) account of underlying differences between the Russian and Anglo-American varieties of formalism.

4   In a controversial essay, Darby (2001) also traces back to Goethe's (and Schiller's) work tendencies in modern-day research on narrative. But whereas my chapter builds on the constellation sketched by scholars like Doležel (1990), Erlich (1965), and Steiner (1984), and uses the cross-disciplinary idea of morphology to explore affiliations among German, Slavic, Anglo-American, and Francophone theories of narrative, Darby instead proposes a bifurcated genealogy. For him, there is a radical split between the German *Erzähltheorie* that gained momentum in the 1950s, on the one hand, and a "French-American" tradition originating with structuralist narratology, on the other hand.

5 In this chapter, I focus mainly on Russian Formalist extensions of the morphological model and their bearing, in turn, on later French structuralist narratological theories. However, in their own analyses of narrative semiotics Prague structuralists such as Felix Vodička, who wrote an important 1948 study of Czech fictional prose, also worked in what can be construed as a broadly morphological tradition (see Doležel 1989, 1995: 44–5).

6 A fuller genealogy of German narrative theory would also need to include discussion of an important work mentioned by Darby (2001) but not treated here, namely, Spielhagen's (1883) book on the theory and technique of the novel.

7 David Richter (in an email message dated 4 November 2003) notes that members of the Chicago School found in Aristotle's work grounds for dividing both the efficient and the final cause into "external" and "internal" subtypes. Whereas the author or maker is the external efficient cause, the manner in which something is done can be construed as an internal efficient cause. Likewise, whereas the effect produced on an audience constitutes the external final cause of a work, the work's internal final cause might be thought of as "a purpose inherent in the thing made, a kind of entelechy of the artifact."

8 Todorov's (1965) translation of key Formalist texts served as a connecting link between Russian and French versions of the theoretical synecdoche in question. Meanwhile, as Doležel (1995: 39–40) points out, though they were developing their ideas several decades before the French, Prague School structuralists refrained from making this sort of *pars pro toto* argument (cf. Doležel 1990: 147–75).

9 See Pavel (1989) for a wide-ranging critique of structuralist appropriations of ideas from linguistics.

10 On the connection between causality and temporality in stories, see Barthes's ([1966] 1977: 94) famous characterization of narrative as a systematic application of the logical fallacy *post hoc propter hoc* ("after this, therefore because of this").

11 I am grateful to Brian McHale, Monika Fludernik, Manfred Jahn, James Phelan, Peter Rabinowitz, and David Richter for their insightful feedback on earlier drafts of this chapter, and to Lubomír Doležel, Uri Margolin, and Peter Steiner for invaluable bibliographic assistance.

References and Further Reading

Aristotle (1971). *Poetics*. In H. Adams (ed.), *Critical Theory Since Plato* (pp. 48–66). San Diego: Harcourt Brace Jovanovich.

Bakhtin, M. M. ([1929] 1984). *Problems of Dostoevsky's Poetics*, ed. and trans. C. Emerson. Minneapolis: University of Minnesota Press.

Barthes, R. ([1957] 1972). *Mythologies*, trans. A. Lavers. New York: Hill and Wang.

Barthes, R. ([1966] 1977). "Introduction to the Structural Analysis of Narratives." In S. Heath (trans.), *Image Music Text* (pp. 79–124). New York: Hill and Wang.

Benjamin, W. (1969). *Illuminations*, ed. H. Arendt, trans. H. Zohn. New York: Schocken.

Bloch, E. (1988). *The Utopian Function of Art and Literature: Selected Essays*, ed. J. Zipes, trans. J. Zipes and F. Mecklenburg. Cambridge, MA: MIT Press.

Booth, W. C. (1961). *The Rhetoric of Fiction*. Chicago: University of Chicago Press.

Bremond, C. (1964). "Le message narratif." *Communications* 4, 4–32.

Bremond, C. (1973). *Logique du récit*. Paris: Seuil.

Brooks, C. ([1947] 1992). "The Heresy of Paraphrase." In H. Adams (ed.), *Critical Theory Since Plato*, revised edn. (pp. 961–68). Fort Worth: Harcourt Brace Jovanovich.

Chatman, S. (1978). *Story and Discourse: Narrative Structure in Fiction and Film*. Ithaca, NY: Cornell University Press.

Crane, R. S. (1953). *The Languages of Criticism and the Structure of Poetry*. Toronto: University of Toronto Press.

Culler, J. (1975). *Structuralist Poetics: Structuralism, Linguistics, and the Study of Literature*. Ithaca, NY: Cornell University Press.

Darby, D. (2001). "Form and Context: An Essay in the History of Narratology." *Poetics Today* 22(4), 829–52.

Doležel, L. (1989). "Two Narratologies: Propp and Vodička." In K. Eimermacher, P. Grzybek, and G. Witte (eds.), *Issues in Slavic Literary and Cultural Theory* (pp. 13–27). Bochum: Universitätsverlag Dr. Norbert Brockmeyer.

Doležel, L. (1990). *Occidental Poetics: Tradition and Progress*. Lincoln: University of Nebraska Press.

Doležel, L. (1995). "Structuralism of the Prague School." In R. Selden (ed.), *The Cambridge History of Literary Criticism*, vol. 8 (pp. 33–57). Cambridge, UK: Cambridge University Press.

Dosse, F. (1997). *History of Structuralism*, vol. 1, trans. D. Glassman. Minneapolis: The University of Minnesota Press.

Erlich, V. (1965). *Russian Formalism: History – Doctrine*, 2nd edn. The Hague: Mouton.

Foucault, M. ([1971] 1984). "Nietzsche, Genealogy, History," trans. D. F. Bouchard and S. Simon. In P. Rabinow (ed.), *The Foucault Reader* (pp. 76–100). New York: Pantheon Books.

Genette, G. ([1972] 1980). *Narrative Discourse: An Essay in Method*, trans. J. E. Lewin. Ithaca, NY: Cornell University Press.

Greimas, A. J. (1983). *Structural Semantics: An Attempt at a Method*, trans. D. McDowell, R. Schleifer, and A. Velie. Lincoln: University of Nebraska Press.

Herman, D. (2001). "Sciences of the Text." *Postmodern Culture*, 11, 3. <www.iath.virginia.edu/pmc/text-only/issue.501/11.3herman.txt>.

Herman, D. (2002). *Story Logic: Problems and Possibilities of Narrative*. Lincoln: University of Nebraska Press.

Herman, D. (2004). "Toward a Transmedial Narratology." In M.-L. Ryan (ed.), *Narrative Across Media: The Languages of Storytelling* (pp. 47–75). Lincoln: University of Nebraska Press.

Hill, R. K. (1998). "Genealogy." In E. Craig (ed.), *The Routledge Encyclopedia of Philosophy*, vol. 4 (pp. 1–5). London: Routledge.

Jakobson, R. (1960). "Closing Statement: Linguistics and Poetics." In T. A. Sebeok (ed.), *Style in Language* (pp. 350–77). Cambridge, MA: MIT Press.

Lawall, S. (1993). "Wellek, René." In I. Makaryk (ed.), *Encyclopedia of Contemporary Literary Theory*

(pp. 484–5). Toronto: University of Toronto Press.

Lévi-Strauss, C. ([1955] 1986). "The Structural Study of Myth," trans. C. Jacobson and B. G. Schoepf. In H. Adams and L. Searle (eds.), *Critical Theory Since 1965* (pp. 809–22). Tallahassee: University Presses of Florida.

Lubbock, P. ([1921] 1957). *The Craft of Fiction*. London: Jonathan Cape.

Lukács, G. ([1920] 1971). *The Theory of the Novel*, trans. A. Bostock. London: Merlin Press.

Lukács, G. ([1938] 1990). *The Historical Novel*, trans. H. and S. Mitchell. Lincoln: University of Nebraska Press.

Miller, J. E., Jr. (ed.). (1972). *Theory of Fiction: Henry James*. Lincoln: University of Nebraska Press.

Nehamas, A. (1986). *Nietzsche: Life as Literature*. Cambridge, MA: Harvard University Press.

Nietzsche, F. ([1887] 1968). *On the Genealogy of Morals*. In W. Kaufman (ed.), *Basic Writings of Nietzsche*, trans. W. Kaufman (pp. 437–599). New York: The Modern Library.

Pavel, T. G. (1989). *The Feud of Language: A History of Structuralist Thought*, trans. L. Jordan and T. G. Pavel. Oxford: Blackwell.

Prince, G. (1987). *A Dictionary of Narratology*. Lincoln: University of Nebraska Press.

Prince, G. (1995). "Narratology." In R. Selden (ed.), *The Cambridge History of Literary Criticism*, vol. 8 (pp. 110–30). Cambridge, UK: Cambridge University Press.

Propp, V. ([1928] 1968). *Morphology of the Folktale*, trans. L. Scott, revised by L. A. Wagner. Austin: University of Texas Press.

Richter, D. H. (forthcoming). "Chicago School, The." In D. Herman, M. Jahn, and M.-L. Ryan (eds.), *The Routledge Encyclopedia of Narrative Theory*. London: Routledge.

Saussure, F. de ([1916] 1959). *Course in General Linguistics*, ed. C. Bally and A. Sechehaye, in collaboration with A. Riedlinger, trans. W. Baskin. New York: The Philosophical Library.

Scholes, R. and R. Kellogg (1966). *The Nature of Narrative*. Oxford: Oxford University Press.

Shklovsky, V. ([1929] 1990). *Theory of Prose*, trans. B. Sher. Elmwood Park, IL: Dalkey Archive Press.

Spielhagen, F. (1883). *Beiträge zur Theorie and Technik des Romans*. Leipzig: Staakmann.

Steiner, P. (1984). *Russian Formalism: A Metapoetics*. Ithaca, NY: Cornell University Press.

Steiner, P. and Davydov, S. (1977). "The Biological Metaphor in Russian Formalism: The Concept of Morphology." *SubStance* 16, 149–58.

Thompson, E. M. (1971). *Russian Formalism and Anglo-American New Criticism: A Comparative Study*. The Hague: Mouton.

Todorov, T. (1965). *Théorie de la littérature: Textes des formalistes russes*. Paris: Seuil.

Todorov, T. (1966) "Les catégories du récit littéraire." *Communications* 8, 125–51.

Todorov, T. (1969). *Grammaire du "Décaméron."* The Hague: Mouton.

Tomashevsky, B. ([1925] 1965). "Thematics." In L. T. Lemon and M. J. Reis (eds.), *Russian Formalist Criticism* (pp. 61–95). Lincoln: University of Nebraska Press.

Vince, R. W. (1993). "Neo-Aristotelian School." In I. Makaryk (ed.), *Encyclopedia of Contemporary Literary Theory* (pp. 116–19). Toronto: University of Toronto Press.

Wellek, René and Warren, Austin (1949). "The Nature and Modes of Narrative Fiction." In *Theory of Literature* (pp. 219–34). New York: Harcourt Brace.

Wittgenstein, L. ([1953] 1958). *Philosophical Investigations*, eds. G. E. M. Anscombe and R. Rhees, trans. G. E. M. Anscombe, 3rd edn. Oxford: Blackwell.

2

Histories of Narrative Theory (II): From Structuralism to the Present

Monika Fludernik

The history of narratology has recently been cast in two different plots. The first plot, entitled "The rise and fall of narratology," consists in a story that starts with early beginnings in Todorov, Barthes, and Greimas; finds its climax in Gérard Genette (with a few adjacent peaks taken up by F. K. Stanzel, Mieke Bal, Seymour Chatman, Gerald Prince and Susan Lanser); and thereafter plunges to a decline, thus suitably bracketing the discipline between the "death of the author" and the "death of narratology." This account is now widely considered to be outmoded (Herman 1999: 1), even by Carlo Romano (2002) in his recent piece in the *Chronicle of Higher Education*. In her introduction to *Neverending Stories*, Ingeborg Hoesterey (1992) provides a bridge to an alternative plot of narratological development by distinguishing between an "'archaic' phase of narratological scholarship" (roughly equivalent to the period discussed by David Herman in the previous chapter of this volume), a second phase of "classical" narratology based on the structuralist paradigm (from which Herman took his term "postclassical narratologies"), and a third phase of so-called "critical" narratology which Hoesterey describes as a "new Hellenism" (Hoesterey 1992: 3). The model is designed, positively, to reassure us that narratology keeps flourishing, but bears some traces of the first plot. Although meant to be descriptive on the pattern of styles of Greek architecture and sculpture, the term "Hellenism" – despite the associated label "critical" – hints not only at the current proliferation of scholarship but also at a dilution of aesthetic standards usually associated with the Hellenistic period, implying a discipline past its prime that is experiencing a final flourish before sinking into well-deserved oblivion.

The second, alternative plot, now dominant, sees classical narratology as a stage in the much more encompassing development of narrative theory. It bears the title "The rise and rise of narrative" (cf. Cobley's "The Rise and Rise of the Novel").[1] In this competing plot, the adolescence of narratology was followed by a reorientation and diversification of narrative theories, producing a series of subdisciplines that arose in reaction to post-structuralism and the paradigm shift to cultural studies. (See, for instance, the telltale plural in the title of David Herman's 1999 collection *Narratologies* and the surveys provided by Richardson 2000, Fludernik 2000a, and Nünning 2000.) Among these subdisciplines the most frequently mentioned are the psychoanalytic narrative approach (e.g., work by Ross Chambers 1984 and Peter Brooks 1985); feminist narratology (see especially Lanser 1992, 1999, Warhol 1989, 2003); cultural studies-oriented narrative theory (e.g., Steven Cohan and Linda Shires 1988 or Nancy Armstrong and Leonard Tennenhouse 1993); as well as more recent work concentrating on postcolonial (readings of) narrative. This extension, if not proliferation, of paradigms also has terminological consequences. Some critics still identify themselves as narratologists (especially Herman, Ryan, Lanser, Fludernik, Nünning), whereas others restrict the use of the term *narratology* to what I here call "classical narratology" (Barthes, Todorov, Genette, Prince, Chatman, early Lanser, Cohn, possibly Stanzel). In the spirit of this volume, I will therefore be using *narrative theory* and *narratology* interchangeably (but compare Nünning 2003 for a complex terminological proposal). Plot number two, perhaps to be entitled alternatively "De pluribus progressio," moreover ends as a success story. Out of the diversity of approaches and their exogamous unions with critical theory have now emerged several budding narratologies which betoken that the discipline is in the process of a major revival. Among recent achievements one can count developments from possible worlds theory to information-based and media technology-based approaches (linked especially to the work of Marie-Laure Ryan 1991, 1999, 2001); the combination of philosophy, linguistics, and conversation analysis[2] in David Herman's oeuvre (1995, 2002); the cognitivist and cultural studies-oriented work of Ansgar Nünning (especially 1997, 2000); the marriage of the empirical sciences with narratology in Duchan, Bruder, and Hewitt (1995) and Bortolussi and Dixon (2003); the organicist and historical approach represented by Fludernik (especially 1996, 2003a); the extension of rhetorics and ethics into discrete narratological paradigms in the wake of Wayne C. Booth's *Rhetoric of Fiction* and *The Company We Keep* (Booth [1961] 1983, 1988, Phelan 1989a, 1996, Phelan and Rabinowitz 1994, Rabinowitz and Smith 1998); as well as the expansion of narrative theory to cover other media and genres in Wolf (2002, 2003).

In the following I will outline what I see as major aspects of narrative theory in its various phases since Roland Barthes. It will obviously be impossible to name all important narrative theorists or to do justice to the diversity and originality of narratological work written in the past 40 to 50 years. My presentation will moreover be biased in favor of individual schools, widely influential contributions, and theoretical monograph publications – an emphasis that tends to disadvantage a number of important scholars.[3]

Structuralist Narratology: The Rage for Binary Opposition, Categorization, and Typology

Structuralism, based on Ferdinand de Saussure's linguistic insights into the structure of language as a system (*langue*) irrespective of speakers' faulty performances in their *parole*, set the parameters for early literary structuralism of which narratology was one important offshoot. In imitation of de Saussure and phonology, the most fundamental building stone of the narratological edifice became the structure of binary opposition. Thus, in Bremond's plot analysis (1973), decisions taken between two alternative courses have to be taken at each juncture of the hero's quest. Even more prominently, Gérard Genette's typology of narrative forms (1980) sports a panoply of binary oppositions: homodiegetic vs. heterodiegetic narrative (the narrator is or is not a character in the tale); extradiegetic vs. intradiegetic (the narrator's act of narration is situated inside or outside the story); *focalization interne* vs. *externe*, and so forth. The last example is instructive in the way Genette takes three categories and turns them into a hierarchy of binaries. Although Genette actually has three types of focalization, *focalization zéro* is defined as unlimited in contrast to limitation of perspective (subdivided as external vs. internal). Where binary opposition does not do the job, three or four categories must be offered. This tradition endures beyond Genette in F. K. Stanzel's structuralist reworking of his 1955 (trans. 1971) typology in *A Theory of Narrative* ([1979] 1984) where he introduced three axes constituted by binary oppositions, which in turn constitute his three narrative situations (see below). A passion for typology and classification also characterizes much of the early narratological work of Mieke Bal, Gerald Prince, and Susan Lanser, and is prominent today in the work of Ansgar Nünning.

The emphasis on binarism and typology highlights two prevalent features of narratology – its aspirations to scientificity (via a "quasi"-linguistic formalism and empiricity) and its ultimately descriptive aims. Narratology's "geometric imaginary" (Gibson 1996) projects the illusion that narrative is knowable and describable, and therefore that its workings can be explained comprehensively. Narratology promised to provide guidelines to interpretation uncontaminated by the subjectivism of traditional literary criticism. This attitude presupposes that texts are stable entities and that readers react to them in foreseeable ways. More recent pragmatically oriented and post-structuralist proponents of narrative theory, by contrast, have queried the stability of the text, arguing that textual analysis becomes affected by the reader's interaction with it,[4] and some of them critique the very categories of linguistic binarism and narratology's obsession with typology (Gibson 1996).

The major problem of narratology in its early structuralist and typological phase, however, lay in the difficult relation between theory and practice. On the one hand, narratology claims to deliver a set of instruments for analyzing texts (this "toolbox" rationale of narratology is most prominently displayed in Nünning's work); on the other hand, narratology focuses on the why and the wherefore, the semiotics and grammar of narrative. In other words, narratology is both an applied science and a theory of narrative texts in its own right. As applied narratology it faces the critical challenge "So what? – What's the use of all the subcategories for the understanding of texts?" As a theory, narratology – like deconstruction or Lacanian psychoanalysis – encounters the criticism that its theoretical proposals do not help to produce significant readings. Unlike postcolonial or feminist interpretations of literature, narratological analyses do not in themselves tend to produce entirely new readings of a text; they frequently highlight *how* the text manages to have certain effects and explain *why* these occur, thus providing arguments for existing interpretations of the text. This is why narratology has performed so well with postmodernist narrative where its instruments are eminently suited to demonstrating how mimetic traditions are being contravened and playfully refunctionalized. Excellent studies in this area are McHale ([1987] 1996, 1992) and Wolf (1993). Research on postmodernist texts has also significantly extended narratological theorizing, for instance in relation to the category of person (Fludernik 1994, Margolin 2000) and tense (Margolin 1999a). From this perspective, narratology, therefore, is really a subdiscipline of aesthetic and literary semiotics in so far as these specifically relate to narrative.

Narratology in its classical phase can be grouped into schools, although the adequacy of a classification relying on mere nationality may be queried. Most prominent is, obviously, the paradigm instituted by Gérard Genette in *Narrative Discourse* (1980), whose international influence was cemented by its early translation into English and by its adoption on the part of prominent American (Prince 1982, 1987), European (Bal [1985] 1997, 1999) and Israeli (Rimmon-Kenan [1983] 2002) scholars. Genette's narratological oeuvre is noteworthy above all for its careful attention to the temporality of narrative, prominently displayed in Genette's distinction between order, duration (tempo), and frequency. Thus, Genette's term for a flashback, *analepsis*, has become a household word in literary criticism, and – especially in work dealing with postmodernist fiction – the term *metalepsis*, which refers to a transgression of narrative levels, occurs again and again (e.g., McHale 1992, [1987] 1996).[5] Genette's temporal model of order, tempo, and frequency decisively extends Günther Müller's 1948 distinction between *Erzählzeit* (narrating or discourse time) and *erzählte Zeit* (narrated or story time). The category of tempo (including pause, [stretch],[6] scene, summary, and ellipsis) summarizes and systematizes Müller; but Genette adds the important aspects of order (i.e., the narrative reordering of story elements)[7] and frequency, noting that events can be told more than once or that recurring story elements may be condensed into one typical representation. Genette, moreover, was the first to recognize that retrospective narration is not the only possible temporal relationship between narration and story, drawing attention to the existence of simultaneous and intercalated storytelling.

If Genette's insights into narrative temporality proved attractive, even more so did his distinction between homodiegesis and heterodiegesis, since this once and for all eschewed the problem of having to explain why narrators such as in Fielding's *Tom Jones* are "third person" narrators even though they refer to themselves as "I." Genette's term heterodiegesis clarifies simply and elegantly that the narrator is not part of the story world. However, Genette's use of the root term *diegetic* in many technical terms (homo-/heterodiegetic, extra-/intradiegetic, metadiegetic, etc.), though usefully allowing distinctions of person and level, at the same time introduced the problem that *diegesis*, in the Greek original, actually referred to the narratorial discourse, that is, to the act of telling, rather than to the story (the *muthos* or – in later narratological parlance – the *histoire*). It is one of the reasons why German-speaking academics have largely resisted the Genettean terminology.

Genette's model, besides the named major insights, moreover was responsible for establishing the concept of focalization in narrative studies, which has largely replaced the traditional terms *perspective* and *point of view*. Genette's famous distinction between "who speaks" (the narrator) and "who sees" (what Bal calls the focalizor [1997: 146–9]) helped to promote a narratology that maximizes discreteness and precision in classification. Genette thus set himself apart from the much earlier model of F. K. Stanzel ([1955] 1971) which was based on a holistic conception of prototypical narrative situations in line with organicist and "morphological" frames current in earlier (Friedemann [1910] 1865, Müller [1948] 1968) and contemporary (Lämmert 1955, Hamburger [1957] 1993) German work on narrative. Stanzel additionally integrated American new critical insights by Percy Lubbock and Norman Friedman, themselves inspired by Henry James.

Stanzel's *magnum opus*, A Theory of Narrative, first published as *Theorie des Erzählens* in 1979 and translated from the German revised 1982 edition in 1984, was, and to some extent still is, the canonical narratological model in German-speaking countries and in parts of Eastern Europe. In this book Stanzel revised his original model of three narrative situations arranged around a "typological circle" along structuralist lines by introducing three axes based on binary oppositions, with one pole of each axis constituting the prototype of a narrative situation. Stanzel's model differs from Genette's in its organicist and holistic frame, its emphasis on prototypicality, its historical outlook, and its attention to textual dynamics.[8] In lieu of Genette's pervasive binaries, Stanzel proposes a tripartite theoretical setup in three *narrative situations* (NRSs) which correspond to prototypical versions of historically influential novel types. The *authorial NRS*, figured in Fielding's *Tom Jones*, combines an omni-communicative (Sternberg [1978] 1993) narratorial presence up and above the world of fiction (extradiegetic and heterodiegetic with zero focalization) with a panoramic view of the fictional world and easy access to characters' thoughts and emotions. The narrator is typically intrusive and indulges in much metanarrative comment. By contrast, in the prototypical *figural NRS* (e.g., Joyce's *A Portrait of the Artist as a Young Man*) the narrative conveys the illusion of unmediated access to the main protagonist's mind and there is no foregrounded narrator persona. Finally, there is the *first-person NRS* (e.g., Dickens's *David Copperfield*) in which the narrator looks back on his previous experience, evaluating it in his function as a narrating self, but often immersing himself and the reader in his past experiencing self. Since the three NRSs are merely *prototypes*, individual texts may combine characteristics of these NRSs. In particular, nineteenth-century fiction displays what Stanzel calls the authorial-figural continuum, the frequent move of the narrative between external and internal perspectives in a given section of the narrative.

In his revision of the original typology in 1979, Stanzel grounded the three NRSs on three axes. The category person (homo-/heterodiegesis) is founded on the identity vs. nonidentity of narratorial and fictional worlds with the first-person NRS prototypically situated at the pole of identity, the category perspective (external vs. internal) defines the authorial NRS as prototypically dominated by external perspective, and the category mode (teller vs. reflector mode) defines the figural NRS as constituted by the reflector pole. Stanzel placed these NRSs on a *typological circle* not only for the sake of categorization but in order to illustrate the continua between narrative forms and the principal openness of categorization. Despite these confessed aims, the model provoked heated debates (Stanzel 1978, 1981, Cohn 1981, Genette 1988, Chatman 1990).

In addition to these typological arrangements, Stanzel was particularly concerned with the history of the novel and the primacy of authorial narrative before first-person texts and later the figural novel. Stanzel also analyzed the way in which novel openings tend to foreground narratorial discourse and how later in the book, the profile of the narrator weakens. He thus implicitly incorporated the reader into his account and anticipated the pragmatic and historical emphasis of later narratological studies.

Among the most influential scholars coming after Stanzel and Genette in narratology's classical phase, three will be discussed specifically at this point.[9] Gerald Prince not only provided readers with the first dictionary of narratological terms (now complemented by the Schellinger 1998 *Encyclopedia of the Novel* and the Herman, Jahn, and Ryan forthcoming *Routledge Encyclopedia of Narrative Theory*); he was also responsible for two important refinements of the Genettean model – the introduction of the narratee (*narrataire*), the text-internal figure whom the narrator addresses, and, secondly, the extensive definition of narrativehood[10] (what makes a narrative narrative) and of degrees of narrativity (the well-formedness of narratives). The first innovation has given rise to a spate of communication-oriented models (e.g., Coste 1989, Sell 2000). Prince's attempt to define the basic requirements for a text to be considered a narrative inspired major reformulations of the term and concept of "narrativity" in White (1980), Chatman (1990), Ryan (1992), Sturgess (1992), Fludernik (1996), Prince (1995, 1999), McHale (2001), Sternberg (2001), and Herman (2002).

The second critic I wish to discuss here is the Dutch scholar Mieke Bal, who proposed an originally controversial and now quite current extension of Genette's focalization theory. According to Bal, focalization properly defined requires both a focalizor and an object of focalization. She therefore distinguishes between who does the focalizing (an extradiegetic narrator, a character) and what is being focused on (the external behavior of a character or the character's mind – this corresponds to Genette's external vs. internal focalization).[11] Bal therefore rewrites Genette's model which was based on the limitation of perspective – zero focalization (no limitation) vs. limited external or internal focalization – into a neat binarism of focalizors and focalized. This then results in the introduction of a narrator-focalizor, a narrator who "sees." Bal's second important innovation was her extension of narratology to cover film (already discussed in Chatman 1978: 96), ballet, and drama (Bal 1997: 5). Bal – despite her keen interest in the ideological functions of narrative – opposed the current anthropomorphization of the narrator figure, marking the merely functional quality of the narrational instance with the impersonal pronoun "it." In her later postnarratological research, Bal went on to focus on painting as narrative and as ideology, particularly in relation to biblical subjects and from a feminist perspective. In this she anticipated later developments in New Historicism and cultural studies.

The third of the triumvirate to be specifically noted in this section is Seymour Chatman, who wrote the standard textbook of narratological study in the United States, *Story and Discourse* (1978).[12] Chatman's shrewd presentation of the two fundamental levels of narrative – story (what the narrative is about) and discourse (the text) – served to reformulate the question of what constitutes a narrative by extending the definition to cover a variety of narrative media, especially film. Narrative discourse in Chatman's model can therefore come in different shapes – narratorial discourse, filmic sequences, and so on. Chatman's definition of narrativity in *Story and Discourse* reposes on the dynamic interrelation of the two levels of story (plot) and discourse (medial representation). Chatman's important second theoretical volume, *Coming to Terms* (1990), significantly expanded his concept of narrativity by integrating narrative with other text types (like argument, description, etc.), thus opening the way for a cross-generic and linguistic discussion of the specifics of narrative.[13] Besides introducing the useful distinction between covert and overt narrators, Chatman has additionally enriched our terminology by his distinction between narratorial *slant* and character-related *filter* to denote limitations on perspective; this attempt to separate ideological from perception-based types of point of view has been extremely influential in studies of focalization and unreliability.[14] Moreover, Chatman was one of the first critics to analyze film as a narrative genre. He thus initiated a line of enquiry into film as narrative that complements key studies by Metz (1971), Branigan (1984, 1992), Bordwell (1985), and others. More controversially, Chatman also introduced the concept of the "cinematic narrator" (1990: 126–34) to film studies, thus attempting to supply filmic discourse with an equivalent of verbal narratives' narrator function.

Classical narratology, as we have seen, developed a terminology to describe textual diversity and it instituted a number of key categories for a narrative grammar and poetics. Among these, the story–discourse distinction is perhaps the most fundamental. Secondly, the conception of narrative as communication resulted in a more extended list of narrative instances besides the author and the narrator (invented as a separate figure by K. Friedemann and Wolfgang Kayser): the narratee, the implied author (Booth [1961] 1983), and the implied reader (Iser [1972] 1990). At the same time, the pronominal, temporal, and expressive features of narrative came into view and engendered a plethora of new categories as mentioned above (Stanzel's narrative situations; Genette's homo-/heterodiegesis, order, tempo, frequency; Chatman's slant and filter; Bal's focalizor; Lanser's communicational and perspective categories, etc.). The issue of tense in narrative especially gave rise to numerous incisive studies (Weinrich [1964] 1985, Ricoeur 1984–88, Fleischman 1990). Alongside focalization, the issue of narrative level and especially the status of characters' discourse also attracted extensive attention. A major preoccupation of narratologists has been the presentation of consciousness in narrative, especially in the shape of free indirect discourse (Cohn 1978, McHale 1978, 1983, Banfield 1982, Sternberg 1982, Fludernik 1993).

Although classical models started out with a structuralist fixation on plot and narrative grammars[15] in Todorov, Barthes, Bremond, and Greimas, narratology in the 1970s and 1980s was mostly concerned with discourse and narration rather than plot. Plot only moved back into focus in Peter Brooks's psychoanalytic study *Reading for the Plot* (1985) and, more recently, in the work of Marie-Laure Ryan (1991, 1992) and David Herman (2002). Curiously, another area of narratology that has remained somewhat underresearched is that of setting and character, even though there are at least some superb essays on the latter topic by Philippe Hamon (1972), Uri Margolin (1990, 1995, 1996) and Ralf Schneider (2001).[16] Finally, narrative mimesis and the issue of fictionality became major focusing points, particularly in the context of postmodernist literature which seemed to contradict the narratological models of Genette and Stanzel since these were based on the eighteenth-century to early twentieth-century realist novel. Whereas classic narratology started out by analyzing postmodernist texts as deviating from realistic and verisimilar parameters (no plot, contradictory character, illogical concatenation of action sequences, etc.), studies such as Wolf (1993) have helped to go beyond the description of defamiliarizing devices to the analysis of metafictional strategies in the framework of fictionality and the constitution of aesthetic illusion. Important studies contrasting fiction and historical narrative were Ricoeur's *Time and Narrative* (1984–8) and essays by Gérard Genette and Dorrit Cohn (republished in Genette 1991 and Cohn 1999). The extension of narratological analysis to historiography and generally to nonfictional narrative occurred in the wake of the "narrative turn" in historical studies which is centrally linked to the name of Hayden White. White, in his analyses of nineteenth-century historiography, demonstrated the presence of literary generic frames in the narrative writing of history (especially 1973, 1987). More importantly, he argued that plot construction (i.e., narrativization) affects historiographic discourse as much as it does literary narrative. The narratological analysis of twentieth-century historical texts (Carrard 1992) and research on faction (the nonfiction novel)[17] moreover increasingly emphasized the continuity between literary and nonliterary narrative and advanced the issue of narrative strategies employed in different ways or combinations in either realm.

Let us now turn to the first major paradigm shift in narrative studies which set in in the early 1980s and was closely related to contemporary trends in critical theory in the United States.

Beyond Form: Pragmatics, Gender, and Ideology

Contextual narratology emerged from two main sources. The first source can be identified as the native American tradition in the wake of Henry James's *The Art of the Novel* (1907–17; James [1934] 1953), followed by work on narrative perspective (Percy Lubbock 1921 and Norman Friedman 1955), which reached its apogee in Wayne C. Booth's studies of irony in *The Rhetoric of Fiction* ([1961] 1983) and *A Rhetoric of Irony* (1974).[18] A second major source was the pragmatic revolution in linguistics which displaced linguistic structuralism and generative grammar and reintroduced semantics, context-orientation, and textual issues to the study of language. Whereas earlier, the linguistic model had inspired the development of text grammars (e.g., van Dijk 1972, Petöfi and Rieser 1973, Petöfi 1979) and semiotics (Lotman 1977), these were now displaced by the models of text linguistics, speech act theory, sociolinguistics, and conversation analysis which were offering methodologies and concepts eminently suitable for literary application. In particular, linguistic pragmatics emphasized the notion of function in ways that allowed for multiple relations between form and function. Thus, Meir Sternberg's and other members' work at the Porter Institute for Poetics and Semiotics in Tel Aviv established that one form could correspond to several functions, and one function be marked with several surface structure elements. This research decisively promoted functional analysis and frame-theoretical concerns, thus laying the foundation for more cognitivist studies in the 1990s.[19]

Conversational narrative, analyzed by William Labov in the 1970s and by Deborah Tannen, Wallace Chafe, and others in the 1990s, had become a key area of narratological research in Germany in the late 1970s (Harweg 1975, Ehlich 1980, Quasthoff 1980, 1999, Stempel 1986) and centrally influenced postclassical narratological work by David Herman (1997, 2002) and Monika Fludernik (1991, 1993, 1996). At the same time, the aesthetic and quasi-fictional aspects of everyday storytelling were increasingly being discussed in linguistics (Tannen 1982, 1984, Norrick 2000, Ochs and Capps 2001). This research has resulted in an extension of the narratological corpus, now including oral language narrative as well as the novel and short story.

A second major area of narratological research came to fruition in the context of feminist literary criticism. In 1988, a heated debate arose between Susan Lanser (1986, 1988) and Nilli Diengott (1988) about the blindness of narratology regarding issues of gender. Lanser, who is still the major proponent of gender-oriented narratology (Lanser 1992, 1995, 1999), mainly concentrates on the genderization of narrator figures (cf. also Fludernik 1999). Thus, the question of a narrator's properties (overt/covert, homo-/heterodiegetic, etc.) is extended into the field of sex and gender;

the explicit naming, description, or actions of narrator figures need to be compared with implied genderization by means of dress codes, behavioral patterns, and cultural presuppositions. Such analyses are pragmatic in the original linguistic sense of the term since they involve the readers' interpretative strategies, speculations, and guess-work. Instead of seeking to rewrite the major narratological categories, Robyn Warhol has proposed the concept of the "engaging narrator" in an attempt to discuss different types of narratorial discourse in male- and female-authored texts (Warhol 1989, 2003). Here, too, narratees and actual readers are signally involved. Besides the issue of narratorial sex or gender, "female" vs. "male" plot structures (Mezei 1996, Page 2003) and revisions of the history of narrative from a female perspective (e.g., Aphra Behn as first novelist – Fludernik 1996) have been additional foci of research. At the same time, Roof (1996) and Lanser (1995, 1999) have extended feminist research into queer studies.[20]

A third vast area of narratological research that developed in the 1980s and 1990s is ultimately ideological in orientation. The emphasis in this work derives from newer theoretical disciplines such as postcolonial criticism, New Historicism, or cultural studies. To take postcolonial criticism as an example, in this kind of narratological analysis, the main point concerns the question of how the text is imbued with (neo)colonial discourse that colludes with the oppression of the native population and how the discourse at the same time ends up undermining this ideology. Post-colonial and feminist theory or gender studies frequently join forces in the analysis of orientalist, exoticist, and colonial discourses since patriarchal and (neo)colonial patterns can be observed to operate in tandem in literary texts, travelogues, or historical writing. Postcolonial narratological criticism attempts to describe how the choice of specific narrative techniques helps to transmit underlying orientalist or patriarchal structures and how the narrative, by its choice of focalization, plot structure, or use of free indirect discourse sometimes resists these structures, undermines or deconstructs them. Finally, postcolonial narratology is concerned with experimental narrative techniques that correlate with the celebration of cultural hybridity or the symbolic liberation of the subaltern. (For criticism in this vein, see Pratt 1992, Spurr 1993, Fludernik 2000b, Richardson 2001a.)

Lack of space prevents me from illustrating similar research for earlier Marxist or cultural materialist analyses of narrative or to discuss the new-historicist uses of narrative theory. (For good surveys see Eagleton 1996 and Cobley 2001.) Marxist readings of the novel and the uses of the concept of ideology by Marx and Engels as well as Althusser were already crucially concerned with narrative and the novel (as witness the work of Georg Lukács). What I want to emphasize here, however, is the increasing turn within feminist, gender-oriented, postcolonial, and ideological criticism in general toward a *symptomatic reading* of texts. Like earlier psychoanalytic work, critical discussion of texts and genres attempts to locate textual strategies that signal unconscious or repressed psychological or ideological "drives" which the critic uncovers, reading "against the grain" of the text. This disclosure of the text's secret motivations, of which the author may be entirely unaware, tends to change the

pattern of interpretation of narrative techniques as well. There are narrative and
rhetorical techniques used by the author to convey his or her meanings, but these
techniques become split between their ostensible signifying functions and their secret
and insidious conveyings of ideological purport. The scenario is even further complicated by the fact that postcolonial, feminist, and Marxist critics frequently detect
signs in which the text surreptitiously seems to undermine or put in doubt its
ostensible ideological drift – as when, by seemingly praising patriarchal structures,
a criticism of them can be gleaned from the text. Thus, in many of Kipling's short
stories, the narrative voice ostensibly participates in a colonialist and orientalist
discourse, but the plots of the tales undermine the lessons of British superiority and
contempt for the natives, and the narrator seems to be uttering his commonplaces
tongue in cheek ("Beyond the Pale" is a good example of such a constellation). What
has not been systematically analyzed in narratology are the structural patterns to
which such readings resort (but see Chambers 1991, Sinfield 1992): how is it possible
for narrative techniques to mean both one thing and its opposite at the same time?
What types of narrative techniques are at issue in such cases? Most frequently, no
specific formal elements signal ideological symptoms or their subversion; rather, the
frame within which the texts are read opens up avenues of interpretation that within a
different (patriarchal, colonial, capitalist, etc.) frame were not initially salient in the
reading process.

   This kind of broadening of the complexity of narrative issues takes me to the next
section in which recent extensions of the term narrative are discussed. Whereas, in the
1960s, everything became a text (including Paris viewed from the Eiffel Tower), we
are now experiencing a "narrative turn."

The "Narrative Turn" and the Media

In this section I want to discuss developments in media studies and the generalization
of the term "narrative" (see Bal 1999) within a wide spectrum of the social sciences,
resulting in the application of narratological paradigms to legal, medical, psychological, or economic discourses. Such extensions are always charged with tension since
the appropriation of narratological frameworks by nonliterary disciplines often results
in the dilution of the narratological basis, in a loss of precision, and the metaphoric
use of narratological terminology. On the other hand, as Rimmon-Kenan has argued
(2001), narrative theory needs to come to terms with the deployment of its concepts
in nonnarratological contexts. In psychoanalytic practice, the example she gives,
patients are encouraged to construct life stories for themselves that allow them to
project a positive identity (cf. Eakins 1999). As Cohn (1999: 38–57) demonstrates,
Freud's clinical narratives were significantly different from fictional and real-world
storytelling. What is particularly interesting in this context is that odd uses of the
concept "narrative" frequently occur in conjunction with acts of storytelling. Thus,
many social sciences use narratives from interviews as their source material to then

construct what they call a "narrative" of, say, homelessness or a "narrative" of criminality. These narratives are rationalizations of the behavior and experience observed in their subjects but not narratives in any traditional narratological sense. Even in policy training, narrative strategies are prominent these days (Roe 1994). Instead of merely rejecting the application of narratological terminology to different subjects, narrative theory must try to theorize the extension of the concept and propose theoretical frameworks that counteract the attendant loss of precision (Nünning and Nünning 2002: 3–5).

I would like to start with psychoanalysis, whose narratological heyday goes back to the 1980s when Ross Chambers (1984) and Peter Brooks (1985) published important studies using psychoanalytic frameworks. In narrative, three main applications of psychoanalytic concepts are possible: analyzing the author, analyzing the character(s), and subjecting the reader's relation to the text to psychoanalytic interpretation. Depending on the various paradigms, such analysis can be based on Freudian, Lacanian, Kleinian, or other theoretical frameworks. Major psychoanalytic literary studies also focus on specific concepts such as repression, transference, or hysteria, and many literary critics have been particularly concerned with the treatment of women in the text, reading the often phallocentric psychoanalytic frameworks against their grain.[21] By contrast, recent work in psychoanalysis not only relies on patients' storytelling but methodologically utilizes dialogue and narrative for clinical purposes (Schafer 1992). Such uses of narrative in therapy and in the theoretization of the therapeutic process deploy narrative concepts in an interdisciplinary manner – not that literary texts are studied by recourse to the framework of classical psychoanalysis, but therapist–client interaction is analyzed within a narrative framework and methodology.

In legal discourse, too, narrative has for a long time played a crucial role. Witnesses and defendants tell stories; police, prosecutors, defense lawyers, and judges produce narratives of legitimation that juries need to find convincing. Moreover, narratives of guilt or innocence are frequently based on the interpretation of evidence similar to psychoanalytic reconstructions from patients' symptoms. In the past 20 years, a new area of research called "Law and Literature" has developed which is concerned with literary thematizations of legal concerns (Weisberg 1984, 1992, Dimock 1996, Brooks 2000, Thomas 1987, 2001) and with the influence of legal (especially metaphorical) language on legal practice (Hyde 1997).[22] Much of this research involves narrative concerns.

Although narrative has become an important term in many other disciplines, the two discussed above should suffice to make the point that narratology is increasingly appealed to as a master discipline. Narratology thus finds itself confronted with nonliterary and even nonlinguistic uses of the concept of narrative among which the literary and poetic framework of traditional narratology seems to lose in significance.

Besides these extensions of the term narrative, new departures in narrative study also include possible worlds theory and its recent transfer of narratological analysis into hypertext and communication studies. Possible worlds theory has a long philosophical tradition starting with Saul A. Kripke. It originally emerged from the attempt to solve the problem of fictional reference. The concept of possible worlds (in which reference is no longer a problem) was first utilized in narratological research by Thomas G. Pavel and Lubomír Doležel (Pavel 1986, Doležel 1998a, 1998b)[23] and is now associated with the work of Marie-Laure Ryan (1991, 1999, 2001). Its recent proposals have been especially important to the elucidation of plot structure, the reader's manipulation of alternative plot developments, or the characters' planned or fantasized alternative action series. One of the major innovations of this approach is the concept of transworld identity which characterizes protagonists like Napoleon or Charlemagne in fictional texts. Ryan has used insights from possible worlds theory to reformulate the concept of narrativity (Ryan 1992) and to analyze hyperfictions from a narratological perspective (Ryan 2001). Parallel work touches on the grammar of virtuality (Margolin 1999b), which is closely linked to possible world scenarios.

Other transgeneric and intermedial extensions of narratology are presented in a recent survey volume by Nünning and Nünning (2002). Especially noteworthy is the increasing attention paid in narrative study to drama (Richardson 1987, 1988, 2001b, Jahn 2001) – a genre formerly excluded from narratology by nearly everyone except Mieke Bal (1997) and Manfred Pfister, whose influential theory of drama utilizes many categories from narratology (Pfister [1977] 1991). Nünning's subsumption of drama under the umbrella of transgeneric narratology is indeed partly based on his adoption of Pfister's theory of open versus closed perspective structure which was developed for the analysis of plays but which Nünning and Nünning (2000, 2002) have now centrally reintegrated into narratology (cf. Fludernik 2003b). Nünning and Nünning (2002) additionally include an analysis of cartoons, painting, poetry, and music as narrative (see especially Wolf 1999, 2002). Pictorial narrative and music also figure prominently in Marie-Laure Ryan's *Narrative Across Media* (2004) and are discussed in separate essays in this volume.

The Present: The Cognitivist Turn and the Resurrection of the Linguistic Model

Concurrently with the "narrative turn" in the social sciences and narrative theory's move into media studies, another major shift was taking place which one could dub the "cognitivist turn" (Jahn 1997). Increasingly, narrative theory began to reorient itself toward the cognitive roots already present in the structuralist and morphological traditions (Herman 2002), additionally absorbing insights from cognitive linguistics and empirical cognitive studies. One way to map the history of narratology is therefore to see it as adopting linguistic paradigms one by one as they arose in the twentieth century – structuralism (classical narratology); generativist linguistics (text grammars); semantics and pragmatics (speech act theory, politeness issues, etc.); text linguistics (conversation analysis and critical discourse analysis); and now cognitive linguistics (cognitivist narratology). Cognitive linguistics analyzes the way in which language structure is predetermined by human cognition. Cognitive linguistic approaches cover a wide range of subjects. These include the lexicalization of color terms and spatial reference, the analysis of constitutive body schemata as they affect metaphoric and conceptual thinking, and the crucial importance of schemata and prototypes in human cognition and hence in language structure.

The cognitivist turn in narrative study concerns two basic levels. On the one hand, it focuses on humans' perceptions of actions and events from a cognitive viewpoint; on the other hand, it analyzes narrative structures (as transmitted in texts) and how these obey fundamental cognitive parameters or frames (see van Dijk and Kintsch 1983).[24] Whereas David Herman's monumental *Story Logic* (2002) concentrates on the first approach, Fludernik's model of the narrative episode and its textual surface structures tends to focus on the second level. At the same time, the cognitivist paradigm shift has produced two major lines of methodology, one focusing on conversation analysis and narrative in the oral language as a prototype for literary and written narrative; the other focusing on constructivist presuppositions about the reader–text relationship. In practice, the various studies share aspects of all of these orientations. It is, however, useful to provide a rough pattern of developments since this enables one to place individual projects as offshoots of one rather than the other axis of analysis. Many of these approaches are represented in Herman (2003).

Basically, David Herman's *Story Logic* is focused on conversational narrative, which he sees as a paradigm for narrative in general. Herman's major cognitivist thrust concerns the introduction of preference rules that are generically based and could be expanded historically. Following Herman's timely collection of essays, *Narratologies* (1999) – a survey of current narratological criticism at the turn of the millennium – his magisterial *Story Logic* delves into philosophy, linguistics, conversation analysis, and cognitive theory to propose a system of microdesigns and macrodesigns governing the logic of story(telling). In this important book traditional narratological categories like plot, perspective, person, or narratees (among others) are integrated into a larger framework inspired by a wide range of theoretical approaches based in (philosophical) linguistics. Whereas Herman's emphasis is on the *logic* of narrative and his focus is on story rather than discourse, Marisa Bortolussi's and Peter Dixon's timely *Psychonarratology* (2003) privileges the empirical analysis of readers' engagements with texts and demonstrates how ever more sophisticated experiments can help determine which textual features are responsible for certain "literary" reactions on the part of readers, or whether narratological categories like focalization are useful in actual empirical work.

Fludernik (1996, 2003a), by contrast, combines a strong emphasis on the prototypicality of conversational narrative with an emphasis on textual surface structure and a diachronic perspective. The approach relies on cognitivist paradigms to the extent that it analyzes narrative patterns whose shape is determined not merely by linguistic markers on the surface structure but in addition by the active narrativization of the text on the part of readers. Fludernik's work moreover displays a strong interest in historical or diachronic issues. Previously, Stanzel had been the only early

theoretician with an important historical orientation. The history of narrative forms
also played a role in feminist studies and in a number of German habilitations
(e.g., Korte 1997). Fludernik (1996, 2003a) put the diachronic analysis of narrative
back on the agenda, particularly with its focus on the development of narrative from
the Middle English period to the early novel. The analysis of medieval and early
modern texts promises to have important theoretical repercussions since current
narratological categories are still by and large based on the novel between (maximally)
1700 and the 1990s.

Another major proponent of the cognitivist turn is Ansgar Nünning, who explicitly declares his narratological oeuvre an effort in constructivism.[25] Nünning started
out with analyses of the narratorial functions in the nineteenth-century novel (1989)
and quickly came to focus on a critique of the implied author (see Nünning's chapter
in this volume) and the revision of the concept of unreliable narration (Nünning
1999a, 1999b).[26] Nünning's work tries to steer a middle course between the textual
analysis of signals helping the reader to recognize unreliability and the reader's active
construction of an unreliable narrator by way of interpretative strategy. Nünning and
Nünning's more recent work on multiperspectivism (2000) expands this line of
argument to its logical conclusion by tackling the general process of assigning overall
meaning to narratives, replacing the implied author concept by a theory of constructivist attributions of overall textual meaning. This work – despite its criticism of
Booth – actually closely relates to the ethics of narrative which is one of Booth's major
legacies.

This brings us back to Wayne C. Booth and to the closing of a circle that originated
with classical narratology and its typological preferences and has meanwhile encompassed a decisive broadening of the subject and the methodologies of narrative theory.
Having started out with a focus on the novel, narratology is now held responsible for
explaining narrative in general – and this includes conversational storytelling, narrative representations in medical or legal contexts, historiography, news stories, films,
ballets, plays, video clips, and much more. At the same time, narratology has
absorbed insights from critical theory, molded itself into feminist, psychoanalytic,
and postcolonial shapes, and has adopted text linguistic, cognitivist, constructivist,
and empirical models for its various frameworks. Perhaps this flexibility has earned
the discipline its present vitality and productivity – disciplines chained to one specific
methodology like deconstruction have had a harder time surviving in the competitive
climate of the 1990s. Like David Herman, I too see the developments between the
1970s and the present as a conflux of different outlooks and emphases that combine in
interesting ways in the work of individual narratologists. Nevertheless, the cognitivist turn in narratology also allows one to postulate an entirely different story – namely
that of a resuscitation of linguistic models in recent narratological research. On this
view, classical narratology was unable to prove the empirical relevance of its linguistic
categories in interdisciplinary research; with the move of linguistics into cognitive
studies the research produced by narratologists seems to have acquired a new lease on
life. Thanks to the narrative turn in the humanities even linguists are taking

narratology more seriously. The cognitivist paradigm shift could thus pave the way for a much closer companionship of narratology with the empirical sciences and, perhaps, come a long way towards fulfilling narratology's original aspirations toward a scientific image.[27]

Notes

1   This is the title of Chapter 3 in Cobley's *Narrative* (2001).

2   Although the term discourse analysis is current, I have avoided it in this presentation because of its connotations of Foucauldian discourse analysis and linguistic analogues in critical discourse analysis (e.g., Fairclough 1995).

3   For introductions to narrative theory and narratological terms for beginners see Chatman (1978, 1993), Jahn and Nünning (1994), Bal (1997), Rimmon-Kenan (2002), and Jahn's homepage (Jahn 2003) which includes a study course for German MA students.

4   See especially Sternberg (1982, 1983, 1987, [1978] 1993), Yacobi (1981, 1987, 2000), Fludernik (1993, 1996), and Herman (2002).

5   In November 2002 there was even a symposium on metalepsis in Paris, at which Gérard Genette participated (see Pier and Schaeffer forthcoming).

6   Some narratologists have added a "slow motion" category (Chatman 1978: 72–3, Martinez and Scheffel 1999: 43–4).

7   This topic has meanwhile received an even more extensive treatment by Ireland (2001). Genette's analepses and prolepses reformulate Eberhard Lämmert's analyses (1955: 100–89).

8   For a good summary of Stanzel's model see Stanzel (1978, 1981) and Cohn (1981).

9   Although Lanser (1981) is a major landmark in narrative theory, I have shifted a discussion of her work to the feminist section since her later feminist contributions are the ones that were most influential.

10   Subsequently renamed "narrativeness" (Prince 1999).

11   See also the incisive reformulations in French criticism (Vitoux 1982, Cordesse 1988) as well as Lanser (1981), Nelles (1990), Edmiston (1991), Jahn (1996, 1999), Niederhoff (2001), Shen (2001), and Nieragden (2002).

12   Chatman also authored a very handy introduction to narrative theory (Chatman 1993), which unfortunately is no longer in print.

13   Compare also Fludernik (1996: 352–8, 2000c) as well as Wolf (1998) on narrative vs. lyric poetry and narrative in painting and music (Wolf 2002).

14   See the essays by Prince and Phelan in van Peer and Chatman (2001).

15   On text grammars in the 1970s see Petöfi (1979) as representative of a group of text linguists as well as Pavel (1973).

16   See also Phelan (1989b).

17   See Hollowell (1977) and Foley (1986).

18   Booth's work is part of what is sometimes called the Chicago School of literary criticism which displayed a strong emphasis on rhetorical models (see also Phelan 1996) and on narrative ethics, a subject to which Booth contributed significantly in his later books. On ethics in literature see also Gibson (1999).

19   See especially Sternberg (1983).

20   For a good survey of a gender-focused narratology see also Nünning and Nünning (2004) and Prince (1996).

21   Relevant studies are too numerous to mention. Note the early work by Shoshana Felman (1982, 1985) and several studies by Elisabeth Bronfen (1992, 1998).

22   For a good survey see Kayman (2002).

23   For a good summary see Doležel (1998b).

24   Another related strand of cognitive poetics is closely aligned with cognitive metaphor theory (Stockwell 2002, Semino and Culpepper 2002).

25 Nünning and Nünning (2002) emphasizes the cognitive basis of narrativity.

26 The original volume of essays in German came out in 1998; the two papers from 1999 modify the earlier model.

27 A first draft of this paper has received extremely generous feedback from J. Alber, D. Herman, M. Jahn, U. Margolin, and

G. Olson, to whom I wish to express my grateful acknowledgment for constructive criticisms of the piece. Revisions were also made in response to comments from Brian Richardson. Given the many partly conflicting suggestions I received, I take full responsibility for this final version of the paper.

References and Further Reading

Armstrong, N. and Tennenhouse, L. (1993). "History, Poststructuralism, and the Question of Narrative." *Narrative* 1(1), 45–8.

Bal, M. ([1985] 1997). *Narratology: Introduction to the Theory of Narrative*, 2nd edn. Toronto: University of Toronto Press.

Bal, M. (1999). "Close Reading Today: From Narratology to Cultural Analysis." In W. Grünzweig and A. Solbach (eds.), *Grenzüberschreitungen: Narratologie im Kontext/Transcending Boundaries: Narratology in Context* (pp. 19–40). Tübingen: Narr.

Banfield, A. (1982). *Unspeakable Sentences: Narration and Representation in the Language of Fiction*. Boston: Routledge & Kegan Paul.

Booth, W. C. (1974). *A Rhetoric of Irony*. Chicago: University of Chicago Press.

Booth, W. C. ([1961] 1983). *The Rhetoric of Fiction*, 2nd edn. Chicago and London: University of Chicago Press.

Booth, W. C. (1988). *The Company We Keep: An Ethics of Fiction*. Berkeley: University of California Press.

Bordwell, D. (1985). *Narration in the Fiction Film*. Madison: University of Wisconsin Press.

Bortolussi, M. and Dixon, P. (2003). *Psychonarratology: Foundations for the Empirical Study of Literary Response*. Cambridge, UK: Cambridge University Press.

Branigan, E. (1984). *Point of View in the Cinema: A Theory of Narration and Subjectivity in Classical Film*. Berlin: Mouton.

Branigan, E. (1992). *Narrative Comprehension and Film*. London: Routledge.

Bremond, C. (1973). *Logique du récit*. Paris: Seuil.

Bronfen, E. (1992). *Over Her Dead Body: Death, Femininity and the Aesthetic*. Manchester, UK: Manchester University Press.

Bronfen, E. (1998). *The Knotted Subject: Hysteria and its Discontents*. Princeton, NJ: Princeton University Press.

Brooks, P. (1985). *Reading for the Plot: Design and Intention in Narrative*. New York: Vintage.

Brooks P. (2000). *Troubling Confessions: Speaking Guilt in Law and Literature*. Chicago: Chicago University Press.

Carrard, P. (1992). *Poetics of the New History: French Historical Discourse from Braudel to Chartier*. Baltimore: Johns Hopkins University Press.

Chafe, W. L. (1994). *Discourse, Consciousness, and Time: The Flow and Displacement of Conscious Experience in Speaking and Writing*. Chicago: University of Chicago Press.

Chambers, R. (1984). *Story and Situation: Narrative Seduction and the Power of Fiction*. Theory and History of Literature, 12. Minneapolis: University of Minnesota Press.

Chambers, R. (1991). *Room for Maneuver: Reading Oppositional Narrative*. Chicago: University of Chicago Press.

Chatman, S. (1978). *Story and Discourse: Narrative Structure in Fiction and Film*. Ithaca, NY: Cornell University Press.

Chatman, S. (1990). *Coming To Terms: The Rhetoric of Narrative in Fiction and Film*. Ithaca, NY: Cornell University Press.

Chatman, S. (1993). *Reading Narrative Fiction*. New York: Macmillan.

Cobley, P. (2001). *Narrative: The New Critical Idiom*. London: Routledge.

Cohan, S. and Shires, L. M. (1988). *Telling Stories: A Theoretical Analysis of Narrative Fiction*. New York: Routledge.

Cohn, D. (1978). *Transparent Minds: Narrative Modes for Presenting Consciousness in Fiction*. Princeton, NJ: Princeton University Press.

Cohn, D. (1981). "The Encirclement of Narrative: On Franz Stanzel's *Theorie des Erzählens.*" *Poetics Today* 2(2), 157–82.

Cohn, D. (1999). *The Distinction of Fiction.* Baltimore: Johns Hopkins University Press.

Cordesse, G. (1988). "Narration et focalisation." *Poétique,* 19(76), 487–98.

Coste, D. (1989). *Narrative as Communication.* Theory and History of Literature, 64. Minneapolis: University of Minnesota Press.

Couturier, M. (1995). *La Figure de l'auteur.* Paris: Seuil.

Diengott, N. (1988). "Narratology and Feminism." *Style,* 22(1), 42–51.

Dijk, T. van (1972). *Some Aspects of Text Grammars: A Study in Theoretical Linguistics and Poetics.* The Hague: Mouton.

Dijk, T.A. van and Kintsch, W. (1983). *Strategies of Discourse Comprehension.* New York: Academic Press.

Dimock, W.-C. (1996). *Residues of Justice: Literature, Law, Philosophy.* Berkeley, CA: University of California Press.

Doležel, L. (1998a). *Heterocosmica: Fiction and Possible Worlds.* Baltimore, MD: Johns Hopkins University Press.

Doležel, L. (1998b). "Possible Worlds of Fiction and History." *New Literary History* 29, 785–810.

Duchan, J. F., Bruder, G. A., and Hewitt, L. E. (eds.) (1995). *Deixis in Narrative: A Cognitive Science Perspective.* Hillsdale, NJ: Erlbaum.

Edmiston, W. F. (1991). *Hindsight and Insight: Focalization in Four Eighteenth-Century French Novels.* University Park, PA: Pennsylvania State University Press.

Eagleton, T. (ed.) (1996). *Marxist Literary Theory: A Reader.* Oxford: Blackwell.

Eakins, P. J. (1999). *How Our Lives Become Stories: Making Selves.* Ithaca, NY: Cornell University Press.

Ehlich, K. (ed.) (1980). *Erzählen im Alltag.* Frankfurt/Main: Suhrkamp.

Fairclough, N. (1995). *Critical Discourse Analysis: The Critical Study of Language.* London: Longman.

Felman, S. (1982). *Literature and Psychoanalysis.* Baltimore, MD: Johns Hopkins University Press.

Felman, S. (1985). *Writing and Madness: Literature/Philosophy/Psychoanalysis.* Ithaca, NY: Cornell University Press.

Fleischman, S. (1990). *Tense and Narrativity: From Medieval Performance to Modern Fiction.* Texas Linguistics Series. Austin: University of Texas Press.

Fludernik, M. (1991). "The Historical Present Tense Yet Again: Tense Switching and Narrative Dynamics in Oral and Quasi-Oral Storytelling." *Text* 11(3), 365–98.

Fludernik, M. (1993). *The Fictions of Language and the Languages of Fiction: The Linguistic Representation of Speech and Consciousness.* London: Routledge.

Fludernik, M. (ed.) (1994). *Second-Person Narrative.* Special issue, *Style* 28.3.

Fludernik, M. (1996). *Towards a "Natural" Narratology.* London/New York: Routledge.

Fludernik, M. (1999). "The Genderization of Narrative." In J. Pier (ed.), *GRAAT* 21: *Recent Trends in Narratological Research: Papers from the Narratology Round Table,* ESSE 4, Debrecen, September 1997 (pp. 153–75). Tours: Publications des Groupes de Recherches Anglo-Américaines de l'Université François Rabelais de Tours.

Fludernik, M. (2000a). "Beyond Structuralism in Narratology: Recent Developments and New Horizons in Narrative Theory." *Anglistik* 11(1), 83–96.

Fludernik, M. (2000b). "The Hybridity of Discourses about Hybridity: Kipling's 'Naboth' as an Allegory of Postcolonial Discourse." In T. Steffen (ed.), *Crossover: Cultural Hybridity in Ethnicity, Gender, Ethics* (pp. 151–68). Tübingen: Stauffenberg.

Fludernik, M. (2000c). "Genres, Text Types, or Discourse Modes – Narrative Modalities and Generic Categorization." *Style* 34(2), 274–92.

Fludernik, M. (2003a). "The Diachronization of Narratology." *Narrative* 11(3), 331–48.

Fludernik, M. (2003b). Review of A. Nünning & V. Nünning (eds.) (2000) *Multiperspektivisches Erzählen: Zur Theorie und Geschichte der Perspektivenstruktur im englischen Roman des 18. bis 20. Jahrhunderts. GRM* 53, 262–7.

Foley, B. (1986). *Telling the Truth: The Theory and Practice of Documentary Fiction.* Ithaca, NY: Cornell University Press.

Friedemann, K. ([1910] 1965). *Die Rolle des Erzählers in der Epik.* Darmstadt: Wissenschaftliche Buchgesellschaft.

Friedman, N. (1955). "Point of View in Fiction. The Development of a Critical Concept." *PMLA* 70, 1160–84.

Füger, W. (1978). "Das Nichtwissen des Erzählers in Fieldings *Joseph Andrews*: Baustein zu einer Theorie negierten Wissens in der Fiktion." *Poetica* 10, 188–216.

Genette, G. (1980). *Narrative Discourse: An Essay in Method.* Ithaca, NY: Cornell University Press.

Genette, G. (1988). *Narrative Discourse Revisited.* Ithaca, NY: Cornell University Press.

Genette, G. (1991). *Fiction et diction.* Paris: Seuil.

Gibson, A. (1996). *Towards a Postmodern Theory of Narrative.* Edinburgh: Edinburgh University Press.

Gibson, A. (1999). *Postmodernity, Ethics, and the Novel.* London: Routledge.

Hamburger, K. ([1957] 1993). *The Logic of Literature*, 2nd revised edn, trans. M. J. Rose. Bloomington, IN: Indiana University Press.

Hamon, P. (1972). "Pour un statut sémiologique du personnage." *Littérature* 6, 86–110.

Harweg, R. (1975). "Perfekt und Präteritum im gesprochenen Neuhochdeutsch. Zugleich ein Beitrag zur Theorie des nichtliterarischen Erzählens." *Orbis* 24(1), 130–83.

Herman, D. (1995). *Universal Grammar and Narrative Form.* Durham, NC: Duke University Press.

Herman, D. (1997). "Scripts, Sequences, and Stories: Elements of a Postclassical Narratology." *PMLA* 112(5), 1046–59.

Herman, D. (ed.) (1999). *Narratologies: New Perspectives on Narrative Analysis.* Theory and Interpretation of Narrative Series. Columbus: Ohio State University Press.

Herman, D. (2002). *Story Logic: Problems and Possibilities of Narrative.* Lincoln, NE: University of Nebraska Press.

Herman, D. (ed.) (2003). *Narrative Theory and the Cognitive Sciences.* Stanford, CA: Publications of the Center for the Study of Language and Information.

Herman, D., Jahn, M. and Ryan, M.-L. (forthcoming). *The Routledge Encyclopedia of Narrative Theory.* London and New York: Routledge.

Hoesterey, Ingeborg (1992). "Introduction." In A. Fehn, I. Hoesterey, and M. Tatar (eds.), *Neverending Stories: Towards a Critical Narratology* (pp. 3–14). Princeton, NJ: Princeton University Press.

Hollowell, J. (1977). *Fact & Fiction: The New Journalism and the Nonfiction Novel.* Chapel Hill, NC: University of North Carolina Press.

Hrushovski, B. (1984). "Fictionality and Fields of Reference: Remarks on a Theoretical Framework." *Poetics Today* 5(2), 227–51.

Hyde, A. (1997). *Bodies of Law.* Princeton, NJ: Princeton University Press.

Ireland, K. (2001). *The Sequential Dynamics of Narrative: Energies at the Margins of Fiction.* Madison, WI: Fairleigh Dickinson University Press/London: Associated University Presses.

Iser, W. ([1972] 1990). *The Implied Reader: Patterns of Communication in Prose Fiction from Bunyan to Beckett.* Baltimore, MD: Johns Hopkins University Press.

Jahn, M. (1996). "Windows of Focalization: Deconstructing and Reconstructing a Narratological Concept." *Style* 30(2), 241–67.

Jahn, M. (1999). "More Aspects of Focalization: Refinements and Applications." In J. Pier (ed.), *GRAAT* 21: *Recent Trends in Narratological Research: Papers from the Narratology Round Table*, ESSE 4, Debrecen, September 1997 (pp. 85–110). Tours: Publications des Groupes de Recherches Anglo-Américaines de l'Université François Rabelais de Tours.

Jahn, M. (1997). "Frames, Preferences, and the Reading of Third-Person Narratives: Towards a Cognitive Narratology." *Poetics Today* 18(4), 441–68.

Jahn, M. (2001). "Narrative Voice and Agency in Drama: Aspects of a Narratology of Drama." *New Literary History* 32(3), 659–79.

Jahn, M. (2003). "Narratology: A Guide to the Theory of Narrative" <www.uni-koeln.de/~ame02/pppn.htm>.

Jahn, M. and Nünning, A. (1994). "Forum: A Survey of Narratological Models." *Literatur in Wissenschaft und Unterricht* 27(4), 283–303.

James, H. (1907–17). *The Novels and Tales of Henry James, Vol. I – Vol. 26.* New York: Scribner.

James, H. ([1934] 1953) *The Art of the Novel,* introduction R. P. Blackmur. New York: Scribner.

Kayman, M. A. (2002). "Law-and-Literature: Questions of Jurisdiction." *REAL: The Yearbook of Research in English & American Literature* 18, 1–20.

Kayser, W. (1957). "Wer erzählt den Roman?" *Neue Rundschau* 68, 444–59.

Korte, B. (1997). *Body Language in Literature*. Toronto and Buffalo, NY: University of Toronto Press.

Labov, W. (1972). *Language in the Inner City: Studies in the Black English Vernacular*. Philadelphia: University of Pennsylvania Press.

Lämmert, E. (1955). *Bauformen des Erzählens*. Stuttgart: Metzler.

Lanser, S. S. (1981). *The Narrative Act: Point of View in Prose Fiction*. Princeton, NJ: Princeton University Press.

Lanser, S. S. (1986). "Toward a Feminist Narratology." *Style* 20(3), 341–363.

Lanser, S. S. (1988). "Shifting the Paradigm: Feminism and Narratology." *Style* 22(1), 52–60.

Lanser, S. S. (1992). *Fictions of Authority: Women Writers and Narrative Voice*. Ithaca, NY: Cornell University Press.

Lanser, S. S. (1995). "Sexing the Narrative: Propriety, Desire, and the Engendering of Narratology." *Narrative* 3(1), 85–94.

Lanser, S .S. (1999). "Sexing Narratology: Toward a Gendered Poetics of Narrative Voice." In W. Grünzweig and A. Solbach (eds.), *Grenzüberschreitungen: Narratologie im Kontext/Transcending Boundaries: Narratology in Context* (pp. 167–84). Tübingen: Narr.

Lotman, J. M. (1977). *The Structure of the Artistic Text*. Michigan Slavic Contributions. Ann Arbor: University of Michigan Slavic Department.

Lubbock, P. (1921). *The Craft of Fiction*. London: Jonathan Cape.

McHale, B. (1978). "Free Indirect Discourse: A Survey of Recent Accounts." *Poetics and Theory of Literature* 3, 249–87.

McHale, B. (1983). "Unspeakable Sentences, Unnatural Acts: Linguistics and Poetics Revisited." *Poetics Today* 4(1), 17–45.

McHale, B. (1992). *Constructing Postmodernism*. London: Routledge.

McHale, B. ([1987] 1996). *Postmodernist Fiction*. London: Routledge.

McHale, B. (2001). "Weak Narrativity: The Case of Avant-Garde Narrative Poetry." *Narrative* 9(2), 161–8.

Margolin, U. (1990). "The What, the When, and the How of Being a Character in Literary Narrative." *Style* 24(3), 105–20.

Margolin, U. (1995). "Characters in Literary Narrative: Representation and Signification." *Semiotica* 106(3–4), 373–92.

Margolin, U. (1996). "Characters and Their Versions." In C.-A. Mihailescu and W. Hamarneh (eds.), *Fiction Updated: Theories of Fictionality, Narratology, and Poetics* (pp. 113–32). Toronto: University of Toronto Press.

Margolin, U. (1999a). "Of What is Past, is Passing, or to Come: Temporality, Aspectuality, Modality, and the Nature of Literary Narrative." In D. Herman (ed.), *Narratologies: New Perspectives on Narrative Analysis* (pp. 142–66). Theory and Interpretation of Narrative Series. Columbus: Ohio State University Press.

Margolin, U. (1999b). "Story Modalised, or the Grammar of Virtuality." In J. Pier (ed.) *GRAAT 21: Recent Trends in Narratological Research: Papers from the Narratology Round Table*, ESSE 4, Debrecen, September 1997 (pp. 49–62). Tours: Publications des Groupes de Recherches Anglo-Américaines de l'Université François Rabelais de Tours.

Margolin, U. (2000). "Telling in the Plural: From Grammar to Ideology." *Poetics Today* 21(3), 591–618.

Martinez, M. and Scheffel, M. (1999). *Einführung in die Erzähltheorie*. Munich: C. H. Beck.

Metz, C. (1971). *Langage et cinéma*. Paris: Larousse.

Mezei, K. (ed.) (1996). *Ambiguous Discourse. Feminist Narratology and British Women Writers*. Chapel Hill, NC: University of North Carolina Press.

Müller, G. ([1948] 1968). "Erzählzeit und erzählte Zeit." In *Morphologische Poetik*. Darmstadt: Wissenschaftliche Buchgesellschaft.

Nelles, W. (1990). "Getting Focalization into Focus." *Poetics Today* 11(2), 365–82.

Niederhoff, B. (2001). "Fokalisation und Perspektive: Ein Plädoyer für friedliche Koexistenz." *Poetica* 33, 1–22.

Nieragden, G. (2002). "Focalization and Narration: Theoretical and Terminological Refinements." *Poetics Today* 23(4), 685–97.

Norrick, N. (2000). *Conversational Narrative. Storytelling in Everyday Talk*. Amsterdam: John Benjamins.

Nünning, A. (1989). *Grundzüge eines kommunikationstheoretischen Modells der erzählerischen Vermittlung: Die Funktionen der Erzählinstanz in den*

Romanen George Eliots. Horizonte, 2. Trier: Wissenschaftlicher Verlag.

Nünning, A. (1997). " 'But Why *Will* You Say That I Am Mad?': On the Theory, History, and Signals of Unreliable Narration in British Fiction." *Arbeiten aus Anglistik und Amerikanistik* 22(1), 83–105.

Nünning, A. (1999a). "Reconceptualizing the Theory and Generic Scope of Unreliable Narration." In J. Pier (ed.), *GRAAT* 21: *Recent Trends in Narratological Research: Papers from the Narratology Round Table*, ESSE 4, Debrecen, September 1997 (pp. 63–84). Tours: Publications des Groupes de Recherches Anglo-Américaines de l'Université François Rabelais de Tours.

Nünning, A. (1999b). "Unreliable, Compared to What?: Towards a Cognitive Theory of *Unreliable Narration*: Prolegomena and Hypotheses." In W. Grünzweig and A. Solbach (eds.), *Grenzüberschreitungen: Narratologie im Kontext/Transcending Boundaries: Narratology in Context* (pp. 53–74). Tübingen: Narr.

Nünning, A. (2000). "Towards a Cultural and Historical Narratology: A Survey of Diachronic Approaches, Concepts, and Research Projects." *Anglistentag 1999 Mainz: Proceedings*, ed. Bernhard Reitz and Sigrid Rieuwerts (pp. 345–73). Trier: WVT.

Nünning, A. (2003). "Narratology or Narratologies?: Taking Stock of Recent Developments, Critique and Modest Proposals for Future Usages of the Term." In T. Kindt and H.-H. Müller (eds.), *What is Narratology? Questions and Answers Regarding the Status of a Theory* (pp. 239–75). Berlin: de Gruyter.

Nünning, A. and Nünning, V. (eds.) (2000). *Multiperspektivisches Erzählen: Zur Theorie und Geschichte der Perspektivenstruktur im englischen Roman des 18. bis 20. Jahrhunderts.* Trier: WVT.

Nünning, A. and Nünning, V. (eds.) (2002). *Erzähltheorie transgenerisch, intermedial, interdisziplinär.* WVT Handbücher zum literaturwissenschaftlichen Studium, 5. Trier: WVT.

Nünning, A. and Nünning, V. (eds.) (2004). *Erzähltextanalyse und Gender Studies.* Stuttgart: Metzler.

Ochs, E. and Capps, L. (2001). *Living Narrative: Creating Lives in Everyday Storytelling.* Cambridge, MA: Harvard University Press.

Page, R. (2003). "Feminist Narratology? Literary and Linguistic Perspectives on Gender and Narrativity." *Language and Literature* 12, 43–56.

Pavel, T. G. (1973). "Some Remarks on Narrative Grammars." *Poetics* 8, 5–30.

Pavel, T. G. (1986). *Fictional Worlds.* Cambridge, MA: Harvard University Press.

Peer, W. van and Chatman, S. (eds.) (2001). *New Perspectives on Narrative Perspective.* Albany, NY: State University of New York Press.

Petöfi, J. (ed.) (1979). *Text vs Sentence: Basic Questions of Text Linguistics: First Part.* Papiere zur Textlinguistik, 20.1. Hamburg: Buske.

Petöfi, J. and Rieser, H. (1973). *Studies in Text Grammar.* Dordrecht: Reidel.

Pfister, M. ([1977] 1991). *The Theory and Analysis of Drama*, trans. J. Halliday. Cambridge, UK: Cambridge University Press.

Phelan, J. (ed.) (1989a). *Reading Narrative: Form, Ethics, Ideology.* Columbus: Ohio State University Press.

Phelan, J. (1989b). *Reading People, Reading Plots: Character, Progression, and the Interpretation of Narrative.* Chicago: University of Chicago Press.

Phelan, J. (1996). *Narrative as Rhetoric: Technique, Audiences, Ethics, Ideology.* Columbus: Ohio State University Press.

Phelan, J. (2001). "Why Narrators Can Be Focalizers – And Why It Matters." In W. van Peer and S. Chatman (eds.), *New Perspectives on Narrative Perspective* (pp. 51–64). Albany, NY: State University of New York Press.

Phelan, J. and Rabinowitz, P. J. (eds.) (1994). *Understanding Narrative.* Columbus: Ohio State University Press.

Pier, J. and Schaeffer, J.-M. (eds.) (forthcoming). *Actes du colloque "La Métalepse, Aujourd'hui."* Paris: Editions du CNRS.

Pratt, M. L. (1977). *Toward a Speech Act Theory of Literary Discourse.* Bloomfield, IN: Indiana University Press.

Pratt, M. L. (1992). *Imperial Eyes: Travel Writing and Transculturation.* London: Routledge.

Prince, G. (1982). *Narratology: The Form and Functioning of Narrative.* Berlin: Mouton.

Prince, G. (1987). *A Dictionary of Narratology.* Lincoln and London: University of Nebraska Press.

Prince, G. (1995). "On Narratology: Criteria, Corpus, Context." *Narrative* 3(1), 73–84.

Prince, G. (1996). "Narratology, Narratological Criticism, and Gender." In C.-A. Mihailescu and W. Hamarneh (eds.), *Fiction Updated: Theories of Fictionality, Narratology, and Poetics* (pp. 159–64). Toronto: University of Toronto Press.

Prince, G. (1999). "Revisiting Narrativity." In W. Grünzweig and A. Solbach (eds.), *Grenzüberschreitungen: Narratologie im Kontext/Transcending Boundaries: Narratology in Context* (pp. 43–51). Tübingen: Narr.

Prince, G. (2001). "A Point of View on Point of View or Refocusing Focalization." In W. van Peer and S. Chatman (eds.), *New Perspectives on Narrative Perspective* (pp. 43–50). Albany, NY: State University of New York Press.

Quasthoff, U. M. (1980). *Erzählen in Gesprächen: Linguistische Untersuchungen zu Strukturen und Funktionen am Beispiel einer Kommunikationsform des Alltags.* Tübingen: Narr.

Quasthoff, U. M. (1999). "Mündliches Erzählen und sozialer Kontext: Narrative Interaktionsmuster in Institutionen." In W. Grünzweig and A. Solbach (eds.), *Grenzüberschreitungen: Narratologie im Kontext/Transcending Boundaries: Narratology in Context* (pp. 127–46). Tübingen: Narr.

Rabinowitz, P. J. and Smith, M. W. (1998). *Authorizing Readers: Resistance and Respect in the Teaching of Literature.* New York: Teachers College Press.

Richardson, B. (1987). " 'Time is Out of Joint.': Narrative Models and the Temporality of the Drama." *Poetics Today* 8(2), 299–310.

Richardson, B. (1988). "Point of View in Drama: Diegetic Monologue, Unreliable Narrators, and the Author's Voice on Stage." *Comparative Drama* 22(3), 193–214.

Richardson, B. (2000). "Recent Concepts of Narrative and the Narratives of Narrative Theory." *Style* 34(2), 168–75.

Richardson, B. (2001a). "Construing Conrad's *The Secret Sharer*: Suppressed Narratives, Subaltern Reception, and the Act of Interpretation." *Studies in the Novel* 33(3), 306–21.

Richardson, B. (2001b). "Voice and Narration in Postmodern Drama." *New Literary History* 32(3), 681–694.

Ricoeur, P. (1984–88). *Time and Narrative, Vol. I-III,* trans. K. McLaughlin and D. Pellauer. Chicago: University of Chicago Press.

Rimmon-Kenan, S. (2001). "Narrative as Paradigm in the Interface between Literature and Psychoanalysis." Lecture given at the IAUPE conference in Bamberg, July 2001.

Rimmon-Kenan, S. ([1983] 2002). *Narrative Fiction: Contemporary Poetics.* London: Routledge.

Roe, E. (1994). *Narrative Policy Analysis: Theory and Practice.* Durham, NC: Duke University Press.

Romano, C. (2002). "Is the Rise of 'Narratology' the Same Old Story?" *The Chronicle of Higher Education* June 28, B12.

Roof, J. (1996). *Come As You Are: Sexuality and Narrative.* New York: Columbia University Press.

Ryan, M.-L. (1991). *Possible Worlds, Artificial Intelligence, and Narrative Theory.* Bloomington: Indiana University Press.

Ryan, M.-L. (1992). "The Modes of Narrativity and Their Visual Metaphors." *Style* 26(3), 368–87.

Ryan, M.-L. (ed.) (1999). *Cyberspace Textuality. Computer Technology and Literary Theory.* Indianapolis: Indiana University Press.

Ryan, M.-L. (2001). *Narrative as Virtual Reality: Immersion and Interactivity in Literature and the Electronic Media.* Baltimore: Johns Hopkins University Press.

Ryan, M.-L. (ed.) (2004). *Narrative Across Media: The Languages of Storytelling.* Lincoln: University of Nebraska Press.

Schafer, R. (1992). *Retelling a Life: Narration and Dialogue in Psychoanalysis.* New York: Basic Books.

Schellinger, P. (ed.) (1998). *Encyclopedia of the Novel,* 2 vols. Chicago: Fitzroy Dearborn.

Schneider, R. (2001). "Toward a Cognitive Theory of Literary Character: The Dynamics of Mental-Model Construction." *Style* 35(4), 607–40.

Sell, R. (2000). *Literature as Communication: The Foundations of Mediating Criticism.* Amsterdam and Philadelphia: John Benjamins.

Semino, E. and Culpepper, J. (eds.) (2002). *Cognitive Stylistics: Language and Cognition in Text Analysis.* Amsterdam and Philadelphia: John Benjamins.

Shen, D. (2001). "Breaking Conventional Barriers: Transgressions of Modes of Focalization." In W. van Peer and S. Chatman (eds.), *New Perspectives on Narrative Perspective* (pp. 159–72). Albany: State University of New York Press.

Sinfield, A. (1992). *Faultlines: Cultural Material-ism and the Politics of Dissident Reading*. Oxford: Clarendon Press.

Spurr, D. (1993). *The Rhetoric of Empire: Colonial Discourse in Journalism, Travel Writing and Imper-ial Administration*. Durham, NC: Duke University Press.

Stanzel, F. K. ([1955] 1971). *Narrative Situations in the Novel*: Tom Jones, Moby Dick, The Ambassadors, Ulysses. Trans. J. P. Pusack. Bloomington: Indiana University Press.

Stanzel, F. K. (1978) "Towards a 'Grammar of Fiction.' " *Novel* 11, 247–64.

Stanzel, F. K. (1981). "Teller-Characters and Re-flector Characters in Narrative Theory." *Poetics Today* 2(2), 5–15.

Stanzel, F. K. ([1979] 1984). *A Theory of Narrative*, trans. C. Goedsche. Cambridge, UK: Cambridge University Press.

Stempel, W.-D. (1986). "Everyday Narrative as 'Prototype.' " *Poetics* 15, 203–16.

Sternberg, M. (1982). "Proteus in Quotation-Land: Mimesis and the Forms of Reported Discourse." *Poetics Today* 3(2), 107–56.

Sternberg, M. (1983). "Mimesis and Motivation: The Two Faces of Fictional Coherence." In J. Strelka (ed.), *Literary Criticism and Philosophy. Yearbook of Comparative Criticism, 10* (pp. 144–88). University Park, PA: Pennsylvania State University Press.

Sternberg, M. (1987). *The Poetics of Biblical Narrative: Ideological Literature and the Drama of Reading*. Bloomington: Indiana University Press.

Sternberg, M. ([1978] 1993). *Expositional Modes and Temporal Ordering in Fiction*. Bloomington: Indiana University Press.

Sternberg, M. (2001). "How Narrativity Makes a Difference." *Narrative* 9, 115–22.

Stockwell, P. (2002). *Cognitive Poetics: An Introduc-tion*. London: Routledge.

Sturgess, P. J. M. (1992). *Narrativity: Theory and Practice*. Oxford: Clarendon Press.

Tannen, D. (ed.) (1982). *Analyzing Discourse: Text and Talk*. Georgetown University Round Table on Languages and Linguistics 1981. Washing-ton, DC: Georgetown University Press.

Tannen, D. (1984). *Conversational Style: Analyzing Talk Among Friends*. Norwood, NJ: Ablex.

Thomas, B. (1987). *Cross-Examinations of Law and Literature: Cooper, Hawthorne, Stowe and Melville*. Cambridge, UK: Cambridge University Press.

Thomas, B. (ed.) (2001). *Law and Literature*. Tübingen: Narr.

Vitoux, P. (1982). "Le jeu de la focalisation." *Poé-tique* 51, 358–68.

Warhol, R. (1989). *Gendered Interventions: Narrative Discourse in the Victorian Novel*. New Brunswick, NJ: Rutgers University Press.

Warhol, R. (2003). *Having a Good Cry: Effeminate Feelings and Pop-Culture Forms*. Columbus: Ohio State University Press.

Weinrich, H. ([1964] 1985). *Tempus: Besprochene und erzählte Welt*. Sprache und Literatur, 16. Stuttgart: Kohlhammer, 4th edn. based on 2nd revised edition 1971.

Weisberg, R. H. (1984). *The Failure of the Word: The Protagonist as Lawyer in Modern Fiction*. New Haven, CT: Yale University Press.

Weisberg, R. H. (1992). *Poethics, and Other Strat-egies of Law and Literature*. New York: Columbia University Press.

White, H. (1973). *Metahistory: The Historical Imagination in Nineteenth-Century Europe*. Balti-more, MD: Johns Hopkins University Press.

White, H. (1980). "The Value of Narrativity in the Representation of Reality." *Critical Inquiry* 7, 5–27.

White, H. (1987). *The Content of the Form: Narrative Discourse and Historical Representation*. Baltimore: Johns Hopkins University Press.

Wolf, W. (1993). *Ästhetische Illusion und Illusions-durchbrechung in der Erzählkunst. Theorie und Geschichte mit Schwerpunkt auf englischem illusions-störenden Erzählen*. Tübingen: Niemeyer.

Wolf, W. (1998). "Aesthetic Illusion in Lyric Poetry?" *Poetica* 30, 251–89.

Wolf, W. (1999). *The Musicalization of Fiction: A Study in the Theory and History of Intermedial-ity*. IFAVL, 35. Amsterdam: Rodopi.

Wolf, W. (2002). "Das Problem der Narrativität in Literatur, bildender Kunst und Musik: Ein Beitrag zu einer intermedialen Erzähltheorie." In A. Nünning and V. Nünning (eds.), *Erzähltheorie transgenerisch, intermedial, interdiszi-plinär* (pp. 23–104). Trier: WVT.

Wolf, W. (2003). "Narrative and Narrativity: A Narratological Reconceptualization and its

Applicability to the Visual Arts." *Word & Image* 19(3), 180–97.

Wolf, W. (2004) "Aesthetic Illusion as an Effect of Fiction." In M. Fludernik and U. Margolin (eds.), *German Narratology,* Special issue. *Style* 38 (3–4).

Yacobi, T. (1981). "Fictional Reliability as a Communicative Problem." *Poetics Today* 2(2), 113–36.

Yacobi, T. (1987). "Narrative and Normative Pattern: On Interpreting Fiction." *Journal of Literary Studies* 3, 18–41.

Yacobi, T. (2000). "Interart Narrative: (Un)Reliability and Ekphrasis." *Poetics Today* 21(4), 711–49.

3

Ghosts and Monsters: On the (Im)Possibility of Narrating the History of Narrative Theory

Brian McHale

A Ghost in the Machine

A specter is haunting narrative theory – or at least, it haunts David Herman's and Monika Fludernik's histories of narrative theory. That specter is none other than Mikhail Bakhtin. The author of (among other things) two landmark works of narrative theory, and implicated somehow or other in the production of a third,[1] Bakhtin (1895–1975) is certainly the most ubiquitous narrative theorist of the last quarter of the twentieth century, and arguably one of the most influential. He is the one narrative theorist about whom every graduate literature student is certain to know something, even if he or she knows nothing else about narrative theory. Nevertheless, Bakhtin is conspicuous by his near-absence from both Herman's and Fludernik's histories of narrative theory – complete absence in the case of Fludernik, scant mention in the case of Herman. How did everyone's favorite narrative theorist all but vanish from history – or at least, from these histories?

Perhaps the division of labor is to blame. Herman covers early developments in narrative theory through structuralism, and Fludernik developments since structuralism, but Bakhtin, due to his long mid-career silence and his belated reception in the West (about which I'll say more in a moment), straddles that divide. A contemporary of the Russian Formalists as well as, through the vagaries of his reception, of 1980s and 1990s contextual narratology, Bakhtin belongs in *both* histories. Perhaps Herman and Fludernik each thought the other would take responsibility for him. But if so, this would be a trivial oversight, and easily remedied. What are editors for, if not to catch such slips?

I don't believe Bakhtin's absence is a trivial oversight. Rather, it is symptomatic of an important tension within the history of narrative theory, and ultimately within narrative theory itself. Bakhtin, it seems to me, has slipped through the cracks between two approaches to narrating the history of narrative theory.[2] Herman and

Fludernik vacillate between these two approaches, in either of which Bakhtin might figure, but in each of which he would figure differently. His strange disappearance is largely attributable to this vacillation, and its consequence is to throw the entire enterprise of history and theory, of historicizing theory, into sharp relief.

What kind of history might a history of narrative theory be? As I see it, one might approach such a history from one of two angles. One might begin from the *system of ideas* that has come to comprise narrative theory, identifying the sources of its basic concepts and terms, tracing their refinements and complications at the hands of later theorists, and juxtaposing different states of the system. This approach is akin to the "history of ideas" in the classic mode of A. O. Lovejoy, the historiographer of "romantic," "primitive," "the Great Chain of Being," and other "unit-ideas" (his own term; see Lovejoy [1936] 1957 and [1938] 1948). Herman practices this kind of history when he specifies the "research foci" that Wellek and Warren share both with the Russian Formalist tradition and with subsequent narrative theory (this volume, pp. 21), while Fludernik practices the same sort of idea-oriented history when, for instance, she traces the refinements introduced by Bal into Genette's original notion of focalization (this volume, pp. 40–1).

Alternatively, one might approach the history of narrative theory from the perspective of the latter's *institutional existence*. I understand "institutional" here in an extended but, I hope, still recognizable sense, including not only academic institutions, research collaborations, disciplinary circuits, conditions of publication and dissemination, and professional career trajectories, but also informal networks and even personal relationships of intellectual affinity, mentorship, role modeling, and so forth – in short, the whole *social* life of ideas. Institutional history, in this extended sense, preoccupies itself not just with unit-ideas and their pedigrees, but with who knew whom, who taught whom, who published what and when (and who was prevented from publishing), who read what, when, and under what circumstances, who brought the word from Moscow to Prague and what happened to it when it got there, and so on. This is the kind of history that Herman characterizes as "seek[ing] to uncover forgotten interconnections; reestablish obscured or unacknowledged lines of descent: expose relationships between institutions, belief-systems, discourses, or modes of analysis that might otherwise be taken to be wholly distinct and unrelated" (this volume, p. 20). Following Nietzsche and Foucault, he calls this mode "genealogy."[3]

From the perspective of the history of ideas, Bakhtin's place seems to be relatively secure. We might take as representative the forthcoming *Routledge Encyclopedia of Narrative Theory*, which aspires to serve as a sort of roadmap of the system of concepts in narrative theory. Here Bakhtin's name appears in connection with a number of the key concepts that he contributed, including "dialogism," "dual-voice hypothesis," "heteroglossia," and no doubt several others. In the perspective of institutional history, however, the picture looks quite different. Here Bakhtin – or rather the writings for which the name "Bakhtin" has come metonymically to stand – including, problematically, those of the other members of the so-called "Bakhtin Circle," V. N. Vološinov and P. N. Medvedev, is profoundly *dis*placed.

Initially associated with the intellectual ferment surrounding the Russian Formalists, against whom he polemicized (through his spokesmen or personae, Vološinov and
Medvedev), Bakhtin was consigned to silence and provincial obscurity during the
Stalinist era, the victim, apparently, of guilt by association (his brother Nikolai, a
veteran of the counterrevolutionary White Army, was living in exile in Britain). He
ought to have been a precursor of Wellek's and Warren's narrative poetics, derived in
part from the Slavic context, but in fact there is scant evidence that Wellek himself or
his Prague School teachers before him knew much, if anything, about the Bakhtin
Circle. Bakhtin re-emerged in the 1960s, both in his native Russia and among
Western Slavists, who by the early 1970s had made his work widely available in
translation. His integration into Western poetics, however, really only began in the
late 1960s, when he was taken up by the Paris structuralists through the mediation of
Julia Kristeva.[4] By the 1980s, Bakhtin was enjoying an extraordinary posthumous
career, especially in the United States, but eventually in Russia as well. The story of
his reception over the past two decades involves serial appropriations and misappro-
priations, decontextualizations and recontextualizations, as he has migrated from one
institutional context to another, passing ghost-like through the walls separating
paradigms and disciplines, uncannily splitting and multiplying until now we have
a whole host of spectral Bakhtins. There is an American liberal-humanist Bakhtin
(sponsored by Wayne Booth, who wrote the introduction to the 1984 retranslation of
Problems of Dostoevsky's Poetics), a post-structuralist Bakhtin, a materialist Bakhtin, a
feminist Bakhtin, an African-Americanist Bakhtin (where "double-voiced" becomes
conflated with "double consciousness"), a postcolonial Bakhtin, a post-Soviet religious
Bakhtin, and no doubt many others.[5]

The conspicuous absence (or near-absence) of Bakhtin from both Herman's and
Fludernik's histories is mainly attributable to their vacillation between the history-of-
ideas mode and the genealogical mode, between accounting for the system of narrative
theory and narrating its institutional fortunes. They apparently felt obliged to try to
do both, perhaps in a spirit of nonpartisanship, conscious that, if they opted for one
mode to the exclusion of the other, they would be taking sides in an internecine
division that runs right through narrative theory (as we shall see in the next section).
They also apparently felt that they could reconcile the two modes, which (as we'll also
see in the next section) is harder to do than one might imagine – perhaps impossible.
Instead of reconciling them, they only mixed them up, producing histories that are
neither all one thing nor all the other, nor even some synthesis of the two, but a little
of this and a little of that, a little history of ideas mixed in with a little genealogy.

Bakhtin, in particular, is placed at a disadvantage by this mixed approach. As we
have seen, his place seems secure as far as the history of ideas is concerned, but
anything but secure in an institutional perspective. Institutionally, Bakhtin is a
nomad, a sort of wandering Jew or hungry ghost, doomed restlessly to crisscross the
intellectual world without ever settling in any particular niche. A contemporary and
antagonist of the Russian Formalists, he ought to figure in histories of Formalism, but
rarely does. Instead, he appears as a fellow-traveler of a range of contemporary

contextual narratologies – materialist, African-American, feminist, postcolonial, and so on – with whom his institutional affiliation is not only entirely posthumous, but largely dependent on various forms of misprision and intellectual press-ganging. One readily sees how a historian of narrative theory, confronted with the vagaries and incoherence of Bakhtin's institutional career, might prefer to treat him instead as a figure in the history of ideas, where his position seems so much more stable: Bakhtin, father of "dialogism."

Unfortunately, the same nomadism that makes it hard to integrate him into the institutional history of narrative theory also tends to undermine his place in the history of ideas. The very facility with which "dialogue," "dialogism," "heteroglossia," and so on have been taken up across such a wide range of practices, both inside the disciplinary sphere of narrative theory and well beyond it, is apt to arouse one's suspicions. Perhaps these "traveling concepts" don't really belong to narrative theory after all; perhaps, after all, Bakhtin is not really a narrative theorist, and ought not to be covered in a history of the discipline. And so, institutionally unplaceable, disciplinarily suspect, neither here or there, Bakhtin slips through the cracks.

Surely there is something uncanny, or maybe something karmic, in Bakhtin's historical displacement. Bakhtin charged the Formalists with having excluded the contingencies of social experience and social context from their account of how language operates in verbal art – with having, in effect, excluded the historical existence of language, with having dehistoricized it.[6] Is it some kind of poetic justice, then, or maybe karmic justice, that Bakhtin should himself undergo dehistoricization, historical decontextualization? Bakhtin, contemporary of the Formalists, has become *everybody's* contemporary, unmoored in time and space, available for assimilation (or so it sometimes seems) to *anyone's* system of ideas. Of course, it is precisely his insistence on *historicizing* language, on restoring it to its place in a historically contingent social realm, that has made Bakhtin so congenial to so many varieties of historicist and contextualist theory in our own time. It is this, more than anything else, that has made him such an attractive candidate for serial reappropriation and recontextualization. Cut loose to drift through history precisely because he sided *with* historicism *against* dehistoricized form, Bakhtin falls prey to so many complex historical ironies that one cannot help but regard his situation as uncanny. Remember, too, that Bakhtin's attacks on the Formalists were conducted under the cover of others' names, Vološinov's and Medvedev's; that is to say, they were (or so some authorities maintain) *ghost-written*.

Structure Versus History

The Bakhtin case serves here, as I intimated earlier, as a kind of parable of the tension in these histories of narrative theory between, precisely, *history* and *narrative theory* – between the obligation incumbent upon these historians to reconstruct the successive states of the system of narratological concepts, and their obligation to place that system and those concepts in the context of institutional history, to historicize them. This tension runs right through these histories, indeed (as I shall argue below) right through our discipline, where it is replicated at every level, under various terms. It is reflected in the current tension within the field between, on the one hand, its "classically" structuralist *narratological* tendencies and its *contextualist* tendencies (see Chatman 1990), broadly construed to include feminist narratology and other historicist varieties. Of all the terms that one might use to capture this tension, the most canonical of all are the ones with which I have titled the present section: *structure* versus *history*.[7]

It would be nice to be able to say that the two orientations, historicist and structuralist, were *complementary*, that narratology in the structuralist lineage complemented contextualist narrative theory and vice versa; unfortunately, the relationship between them is not as happy or untroubled as that would imply. Quite the reverse, in fact: under the big tent of narrative theory, structuralism and historicism jockey for position, each seeking to outflank or overcome the other, to *contain* the other, and if that doesn't work, then to forget or *repress* the other – a risky strategy since, as we know, the repressed is apt to return. The accusation, on the part of historicist narrative theory, that narratology represses history is a familiar one, of course; this was already the substance of the Bakhtin Circle's attack on the Formalists, and later of Jameson's critique of Formalism and structuralism alike. But the reverse is also arguably true: that historicist narrative theory represses its narratological Other.

To illustrate how historicism seeks to outflank and contain narratology, one need look no further than several of the chapters in the present *Companion*. In essays by, for instance, Alison Case ("Gender and History in Narrative Theory"), Alan Nadel ("Second Nature, Cinematic Narrative, the Historical Subject, and *Russian Ark*") and Harry Shaw ("Why Won't Our Terms Stay Put?"), narratological categories are revisited from a historical perspective, and rethought as historically contingent and variable, rather than as permanent features of a system that *applies* differently at different epochs. As part of his period-based narratology, for instance, Shaw proposes to treat the communications model not as a universal "given" of narratives everywhere, but as malleable and adjustable, varying from period to period. On the other side, structuralist maneuvers to outflank historicism are readily illustrated from the writings of the Russian Formalists themselves, who from the very outset were subject to the pressure of a competing Marxist-historicist mode of explanation, and who responded by seeking to contain or pre-empt the historical in various ways. One such maneuver can be seen in Jakobson's and Tynjanov's thesis on "Problems in the Study of Language and Literature" ([1928] 1971), dating from very near the end of the Formalists' brief flowering, after Jakobson had already decamped for Prague, in which the model of the literary text as a systematic relation of parts is scaled up to the level of literary history itself. Reconceived in systemic terms, history now falls within the Formalists' purview, instead of being left "outside," the province of hostile historicists.[8]

Even more powerfully pre-emptive, however, is the concept of *motivation*, which was already in place in some of the earliest versions of Formalist narrative poetics (Tomashevsky [1925] 1965, Shklovsky [1929] 1990). If, as the Formalists posited, a work of verbal art comprises a series of devices – devices of estrangement, of retardation, and impeded form, and so on – then the artist must choose either to lay his or her devices bare (as Sterne notoriously does in *Tristram Shandy*) or to produce alibis for them, masking their arbitrariness behind a scrim of naturalness and inevitability – to *motivate* the devices. Thus, to adapt one of Shklovsky's simpler examples (Shklovksy 1990: 110), if Sherlock Holmes requires an opposite number, a chronically misguided detective whose incompetence can be played off against Holmes's own infallibility, then it doesn't much matter in strictly formal terms whether the nincompoop is another private detective or a civil servant. Given Conan Doyle's historical moment, however, the obvious choice, the one that most satisfactorily *motivates* the device, is the civil servant – Inspector Lestrade, of course – allowing the author to profile the superiority of the bourgeois individual against a background of state bungling. Shklovsky suggests that, in a proletarian regime, the role assignments might be reversed – the successful detective might be the civil servant, while the bungler might be the private eye – but the device, and the necessity for *some* motivation of it, would be identical. The concept of motivation thus allows historical contingency to be drawn into the very fabric of formal structure; the historical is placed at the service of the device. This opening of structure to historical contingency through the concept of motivation has a long legacy in subsequent narrative theory. It reappears, with some variations, in Paris structuralist theory under the names of *vraisemblance* (Genette [1968] 2001) and naturalization (Culler [1975] 2002: 153–87), and persists as a central concept of Tel Aviv school narratology down to the present (e.g., Sternberg 1983).

Seeking to contain its narratological Other, historicism represses narratology, just as, vice versa, narratology represses history – or so I have claimed. Let me see whether I can justify my claim, and in particular my use of the term "repress," which will have struck some readers, I'm sure, as rhetorical overkill. I can make my case most efficiently by way of example, so let me briefly revisit a pair of undisputed classics in our field: Henry Louis Gates's account of free indirect discourse in Zora Neale Hurston's *Their Eyes Were Watching God*, from his book *The Signifying Monkey* (1988) and elsewhere, and Gérard Genette's poetics of Proustian narrative in *Narrative Discourse* ([1972] 1980).

Gates's work is a landmark in the historicizing of narratological description. He introduces narratological categories, for the first time ever in any systematic way, into the discussion of the history of novelistic representations of African-American speech. Nevertheless, in order to interpret and contextualize Hurston's handling of free indirect discourse (FID) Gates must, in a sense, "forget" narratology. He insists on the uniqueness and novelty of FID in *Their Eyes Were Watching God* – on the way, for instance, that narration and FID converge stylistically, almost to the point of identity, and the way FID is used to represent not only individual characters' speech and thought, but the collective speech and thought of a whole community. There's no disputing the special semantic charge and the extra load of cultural meaning that these features bear in *Their Eyes*. Nevertheless, *as formal features* they are hardly as unique or unprecedented as Gates makes them out to be, but rather belong to the range of possibilities that FID encompasses as a quasi-universal category of narrative discourse. In making his historicist and contextualist case for Hurston's innovations, Gates downplays their basis in the system of narrative discourse, laying himself open to the counterargument that Hurston's practice isn't all that special or unprecedented after all, that her FID is more "standard," formally and functionally, than he is willing to admit.[9] Structure trumps history; repressed narratology returns.

Genette, conversely, undertakes to describe a particular novelist's narrative practice – Proust's – against the backdrop of a general system of narratological categories that aspires to universal and transhistorical applicability. Or rather, he tries to do two things at once: on the one hand, to capture the idiosyncrasies of Proust's poetics, which can only be grasped relative to some "norm" of narrative practice; on the other hand, to develop a system of general categories using Proust's *Recherche* as the primary example. Genette performs a tricky balancing act between polar opposites – anomaly and exemplarity, idiolect and system. In the end, however, it's clearly the system of norms that holds the upper hand in his approach.

But what if we upended Genette's approach, and gave anomaly the upper hand over norm? There are several perspective from which this might be undertaken. First, we might simply abandon the appeal to transhistorical norms altogether, and develop a poetics of Proustian narrative that was frankly one-of-a-kind, elevating Proust's anomalies into idiosyncratic norms. Alternatively, we might do what Culler proposes in his foreword to the English translation of *Narrative Discourse* (Genette 1980: 12–13) and acknowledge the anomalous character of *all* literary narrative relative to norms that are based, after all, on models of reality. Between these two moves – custom-tailoring to the exact specifications of Proustian narrative, on the one hand, and wall-to-wall literary anomaly, on the other – there is a third possible move, the *historicist* one. This is the sort of move that Randall Stevenson (forthcoming) adumbrates when he notes the close correlation between the areas of Genette's most valuable contributions to narrative theory – focalization and relations of time – and the innovations of modernist fiction, not least of all Proust's fiction, with respect to perspective and temporality. In other words, suppose we viewed Proust's practice, not as anomalous relative to some transhistorical norm, but rather as typical of a particular historically determined *period style* – the period style of high modernism? From this perspective, the categories that Genette imagined to be universals actually appear to reflect a particular modernist historical practice, and his supposed transhistorical system comes to share an unexpected kinship with Shaw's period-based narratology. With this move, structure is trumped, and repressed history returns.

Frankenstein as Narratologist

Again, it would be nice to be able to say that these two orientations, structuralist and historicist, were, if not complementary, at least *reconcilable*. My sense, however, is that their relationship has always been, and is likely to remain, a conflicted one. It may be that structure and history are finally irreconcilable; or rather, they may be reconciled, but only on terms congenial to one of the rival orientations and not to the other. To practice narratology in the structuralist tradition, it would seem, is to strive to get the better of the historical, to outflank it or trump it or take it in charge, to become its horizon; and vice versa, to practice contextualist or historicist narratology is to strive to outflank or trump structure. To practice one is to repress the other, and, as we have seen, the repressed Other always seems to return.

At the end of her history of narrative theory since structuralism, as in her own recent narratological work (e.g., Fludernik 2003), Monika Fludernik promises a new reconciliation of structure and history, in the form of a *historicist cognitive narratology*. She advances strong claims for the potential of tools derived from cognitive science to rejuvenate historicist approaches to narrative. I am a good deal less sanguine than she is about the chances for any such reconciliation. As a case in point, I might cite a special issue of *Poetics Today* in Spring 2002 dedicated to "Literature and the Cognitive Revolution," one section of which bears the promising title, "Cognitive Historicism." The guest editors claim that the papers in this section "address the complex interaction of evolved neurocognitive structures and contingent cultural environments with an eye to specific examples of cultural change." These papers demonstrate, according to the editors, that "issues in literary history, far from being occluded by approaches that recognize the validity of human universals and species-specific cognitive mechanisms, can be productively reopened in ways that have eluded criticism that relies on purely constructivist notions of the subject" (Richardson and Steen 2002: 5). I remain unpersuaded. I don't see how "neurocognitive structures" and "species-specific cognitive mechanisms" that have evolved over tens of millennia, and that are presumably stable and permanent features of modern-day *homo sapiens*, are likely to give us much purchase on change occurring at the historical scale of decades and centuries; and if they don't capture change and difference at that time-scale, then I don't see how the approaches that evoke such structures and mechanisms can claim to be "historicist."[10]

In my view, these essays in "cognitive historicism" neither cognitivize historical difference nor historicize cognitive structures. They don't after all reconcile cognitivism and historicism, whatever they (or Fludernik) may promise. What they actually *do* do is alternate between cognitivist moments and historicist moments, between structure and history – first one thing, then the other. This is not the same thing as reconciliation; it's more like ships passing in the night.

Moreover, I would argue that what these essays do, we all do, whether we call ourselves cognitive historicists or something else – plain-vanilla historicists, or

cultural materialists, or contextualists, or diehard old-school narratologists, or feminist narratologists, or whatever. I venture to say that many, if not most, of the
contributors to the present *Companion* believe not only that structure and history
can be reconciled, but moreover that they themselves have done so in their own essays,
seamlessly integrating the tools and insights of narratology with the contingencies of
history. I suspect that, insofar as they hold this belief, they are probably mistaken.
Whatever we may think we're doing when we study narrative, we're probably not
reconciling history and structure. On the other hand, neither are we successfully
pursuing one to the exclusion of the other because, as I've tried to demonstrate, the
repressed always returns. What we're really doing, at best, is alternating between
narratological moments and historicist moments. There is no "pure" practice of
narratology to be found, and no "pure" historicist narrative theory either, but neither
is there any stable synthesis or seamless integration of the two – only a messy
patchwork, a little of this and a little of that, first one thing and then the other.

I recently had the opportunity to examine an unpublished doctoral dissertation by a
young Finnish scholar (Samuli Hägg) who has undertaken to do for Pynchon's
Gravity's Rainbow what Genette did for Proust's *Recherche* – in other words, to produce
a narratology of Pynchon that at the same time reflects critically on the system of
narratological categories, just as Genette produced a narratology of the *Recherche* that
also elaborated a general system of narrative discourse. He encountered many of the
same difficulties as Genette, in particular the problem of what to treat as anomalous
in Pynchon's practice, relative to a systematic narratology, and what in Pynchon's
practice to try to integrate into that system. This in turn entails confronting the
question of what kind of narratology one would have if anomalies such as those
encountered in *Gravity's Rainbow* were treated as integral rather than anomalous,
brought "inside" rather than left "outside." He concludes that the results could only
be, not some coherent "narratology of *Gravity's Rainbow*," but "a monstrous narratology crudely stitched together from incompatible organs and lumps of flesh."[11] He
goes on: "Disturbingly enough…this description seems to fit pretty well *any*
conception of narratology" – or of historicist or contextualist narrative theory, for
that matter.

If this is true, and *every* narrative theory is monstrous, then a history of narrative
theory, such Herman's or Fludernik's, could only be an account of how the monster
got stitched together from a little of this and a little of that, here a little structure and
there a little history – in other words, a retelling of *Frankenstein*. Either that, or it
would have to be a ghost story.[12]

NOTES

1   See Bakhtin's *Problems in Dostoevsky's Politics*
    ([1963] 1984), a revision of a work first pub-
    lished in 1929, and his *Dialogic Imagination*
    ([1975] 1981). Bakhtin's role in Vološinov
    ([1929] 1973) is controversial: was he its
    pseudonymous author? Vološinov's shadow

collaborator? His mentor and muse? Nobody knows for sure.

2   Nor is he the only the figure to slip through the cracks in this way. Alan Nadel suggests (personal communication) that Kenneth Burke presents a problem comparable to that of Bakhtin. This is true, but only up to a point; Bakhtin's belated currency and astonishing ubiquity has no parallel in the Burke case.

3   The distinction between the history-of-ideas approach to narrative theory and the institutional or genealogical approach roughly parallels the distinction between traditional history of science and the sociological or cultural studies approach to "science studies," as practiced by Bruno Latour, Evelyn Fox Keller, Timothy Lenoir, Bruce Clarke and others; see, e.g., Morrison's (2002) review-article.

4   In a parallel development, the Tel Aviv school of poetics also "discovered" Bakhtin at roughly the same time, through the mediation of Benjamin Hrushovski (Harshav). However, the distinctive Tel Aviv synthesis of narrative poetics would not become widely known outside Israel until almost a decade later, when the Tel Aviv theorists began publishing in English.

5   On Bakhtin in general, see Clark and Holquist (1984) and Morson and Emerson (1990). On his Russian reception in particular, see Emerson (1997); on his American reception, see Hale (1998: 113–27, 197–220). DeMan suggested that the only type of theorist who might *not* find any use for Bakhtin would be one like himself, one "concerned with tropological displacements of logic" (1983: 104) – in other words, a deconstructionist. But he might have been wrong about that; others have found it possible to reconcile Bakhtinian ideas with deconstruction.

6   Jameson would launch a similar (and immensely influential) critique against the Formalists in his *The Prison-House of Language* of 1972, but apparently in ignorance of his precursors in the Bakhtin Circle, whose main works had only just begun to appear in French and German, and would only appear in English over the course of the next several years.

7   Another terminological option, equally canonical, would be *synchrony* versus *diachrony*, but

this casts the opposition in terms "native" to the structuralist camp, one of the parties to the controversy. Better, surely, to stick with the somewhat more neutral, "nonaligned" terminology of *structure* versus *history*.

8   This move, involving a change of scale from text-as-system to literature-as-system, leaves a long legacy in subsequent literary theory, from the "historical structuralism" of the Prague school (Galan 1984) to the literary semiotics of Lotman and the Tartu school (Shukman 1977) to the polysystem theory of Even-Zohar and the Tel Aviv school (Even-Zohar 1990).

9   Moreover, as Fludernik has pointed out, Gates actually misidentifies the discourse mode in at least one passage from *Their Eyes Were Watching God*, remarking on the dual-voice potential of FID apropos of a passage in which no sentence of FID is to be found. Fludernik is referring not to *The Signifying Monkey*, but to an analysis in an essay on Hurston and Alice Walker (Gates 1989: 148–9). Gates's lapse, writes Fludernik, "shows how grossly narratological discussions of free indirect discourse can be misread in the interests of metaphor and thematic speculation" (1993: 82) – I would prefer to say, in the interests of *historicizing* narratological categories. On African-Americanist appropriations of narrative theory, compare Hale (1998: 197–220). See also my parallel critique (McHale 1994: 60–2) of D. A. Miller's abuse of the poetics of FID in his *The Novel and the Police*.

10 I may be wrong about this. Work on cognitive approaches presented at the 2004 Society for the Study of Narrative Literature Conference, especially Ellen Spolsky's and Lisa Zunshine's papers on "theory-of-mind theory," seem to me promising harbingers of what may prove to be a genuinely historicist cognitivism. Stay tuned.

11 Hägg presumably has in mind the account of "narrative and monstrosity" in Gibson (1996: 236–74), though he does not allude to it directly here.

12 I am grateful to the participants in "Contemporary Narrative Theory: The State of the Field," for their feedback, and especially to

Monika Fludernik and David Herman. I have also profited from the advice of Lubomír Doležel, Bob Griffin, Steve Kern, Randall Stevenson, and the editors of the present volume.

REFERENCES AND FURTHER READING

Bakhtin, M. ([1963] 1984). *Problems in Dostoevsky's Poetics*, ed. and trans. C. Emerson. Minneapolis: University of Minnesota Press.

Bakhtin, M. ([1975] 1981). *The Dialogic Imagination: Four Essays*, ed. and trans. C. Emerson and M. Holquist. Austin: University of Texas Press.

Chatman, S. (1990). "What Can We Learn from Contextualist Narratology?" *Poetics Today* 11(2), 309–28.

Clark, K. and Holquist, M. (1984). *Mikhail Bakhtin*. Cambridge, MA and London: Harvard University Press.

Culler, J. ([1975] 2002). *Structuralist Poetics: Structuralism, Linguistics and the Study of Literature*. London: Routledge.

DeMan, P. (1983). "Dialogue and Dialogism." *Poetics Today* 4(1), 99–107.

Emerson, C. (1997). *The First Hundred Years of Mikhail Bakhtin*. Princeton, NJ: Princeton University Press.

Even-Zohar, I. (1990). *Polysystem Studies*. Special Issue, *Poetics Today* 11(1).

Fludernik, M. (1993). *The Fictions of Language and the Languages of Fiction: The Linguistic Representation of Speech and Consciousness*. London and New York: Routledge.

Fludernik, M. (2003). "The Diachronization of Narratology." *Narrative* 11(3), 331–48.

Galan, F. W. (1984). *Historic Structures: The Prague School Project, 1928–1946*. Austin: University of Texas Press.

Gates, H. L. (1988). *The Signifying Monkey: A Theory of African-American Literary Criticism*. New York and Oxford: Oxford University Press.

Gates, H. L. (1989). "Color Me Zora: Alice Walker's (Re)writing of the Speakerly Text." In P. O'Donnell and R. C. Davis (eds.), *Intertextuality and Contemporary American Fiction* (pp. 144–67). Baltimore, MD: Johns Hopkins University Press.

Genette, G. ([1972] 1980). *Narrative Discourse*, trans. J. E. Lewin. Ithaca, NY: Cornell University Press.

Genette, G. ([1968] 2001). "*Vraisemblance* and Motivation," trans. D. Gorman. *Narrative* 9(3), 239–58.

Gibson, A. (1996). *Towards a Postmodern Theory of Narrative*. Edinburgh: Edinburgh University Press.

Hale, D. J. (1998). *Social Formalism: The Novel in Theory from Henry James to the Present*. Stanford CA: Stanford University Press.

Jakobson, R. and Tynjanov, J. (1971 [1928]). "Problems in the Study of Language and Literature." In L. Matejka and K. Pomorska (eds.), *Readings in Russian Poetics: Formalist and Structuralist Views* (pp. 79–81). Cambridge, MA: MIT Press.

Jameson, F. (1972). *The Prison-House of Language: A Critical Account of Structuralism and Russian Formalism*. Princeton, NJ: Princeton University Press.

Lovejoy, A. O. ([1938] 1948). "The Historiography of Ideas." In *Essays in the History of Ideas* (pp. 1–13). Baltimore, MD: Johns Hopkins University Press.

Lovejoy, A. O. ([1936] 1957). "Introduction: The Study of the History of Ideas." In *The Great Chain of Being: A Study of the History of an Idea* (pp. 3–23). Cambridge, MA: Harvard University Press.

McHale, B. (1994). "Whatever Happened to Descriptive Poetics?" In M. Bal and I. E. Boer (eds.), *The Point of Theory: Practices of Cultural Analysis* (pp. 56–65). Amsterdam: Amsterdam University Press.

Morrison, M. (2002). "Why Modernist Studies and Science Studies Need Each Other." *Modernism/Modernity* 9(4), 675–82.

Morson, G. S. and Emerson, C. (1990). *Mikhail Bakhtin: Creation of a Prosaics*. Stanford, CA: Stanford University Press.

Richardson, A. and Steen, F. (2002). "Literature and the Cognitive Revolution: Introduction." *Poetics Today* 23(1), 1–8.

Tomashevsky, B. ([1925] 1965). "Thematics." In L. T. Lemon and M. J. Reis (eds.), *Russian Formalist Criticism: Four Essays* (pp. 61–95). Lincoln: University of Nebraska Press.

Shklovsky, V. ([1929] 1990). *Theory of Prose*, trans. B. Sher. Normal, IL: Dalkey Archive Press.

Shukman, A. (1977). *Literature and Semiotics: A Study of the Writings of Yu. M. Lotman.* Amsterdam and New York: North-Holland Press.

Sternberg, M. (1983). "Mimesis and Motivation: The Two Faces of Fictional Coherence." In J. P. Strelka (ed.), *Literary Criticism and Philosophy* (pp. 145–88). University Park, PA: Pennsylvania State University Press.

Stevenson, R. (forthcoming). "Modernist Narrative." In D. Herman, M. Jahn, and M.-L. Ryan (eds.), *The Routledge Encyclopedia of Narrative Theory*. London and New York: Routledge.

Vološinov, V. N. ([1929] 1973). *Marxism and the Philosophy of Language*, trans. Ladislaw Matejka and I. R. Titunik. Cambridge, MA: Harvard University Press.

PART I
New Light on Stubborn Problems

4
Resurrection of the Implied Author: Why Bother?

Wayne C. Booth

It will surprise no reader here that the author of *The Rhetoric of Fiction* ([1961] 1983) is appalled by the number of critics who have embraced the "death of the author." (Actually it has always been only the *implied* author;[1] no one has claimed that the *flesh-and-blood* author never existed.) How could anyone ever believe that the author's intentions about a work are irrelevant to how we read it? The critics were of course justified in claiming that the author's expressed intentions, *outside* the text, could be in total contrast to the intentions finally realized in the finished text. But does not that difference dramatize the importance of the implied author/author distinction?

This whole essay could be devoted to refuting this or that absurd assassination attempt, followed by a report on the best efforts at resuscitation. Some of the latter, like Jim Phelan's and Peter Rabinowitz's, are so good that I'm tempted simply to copy them. Instead I shall offer one more sermon on why we should all work to keep the concept alive, regardless of how we define it.

When I first wrote about the implied author (IA), I was driven by at least three motives, all triggered by anxiety about the critical scene in the 1950s.

1 Distress about the widespread pursuit of so-called objectivity in fiction. Defensible novelists, many were saying, must engage in *showing*, not *telling*, thus leaving it to the reader to perform all judgments. Praiseworthy novelists must kill off all open signs of the author's opinions. Authorial commentary is not just frequently dull; it is *always* a violation of true "poetic" quality.

Long before Barthes and Foucault and others made that assassination attempt explicit, critics were proclaiming that genuinely admirable fiction purged itself of all signs of the writer's opinions about what was *artistically* shown. Praiseworthy fiction had to be presented *objectively*, with the author's opinions about characters and events not merely concealed but fully purged.[2]

This view often led to a downgrading of the narrative mastery practiced by geniuses like Joseph Fielding, Jane Austen, and George Eliot – not to mention many great European and Russian novelists; often it led to outright misreadings. Many of the "point-of-viewists" simply ignored the ways in which openly expressed authorial rhetoric can in itself be a major aesthetic creation. If space allowed I would quote a couple of lengthy authorial commentaries by "George Eliot," the male IA created by the woman genius, Marian Evans; her/his aggressive "intrusions" had not only aided me in reading her novels but led me to admire, and even love, the creator. Would I have fallen in love with Marian Evans if I'd known her? Depends on the circumstances in which I encountered the flesh-and-blood person (the FBP). But her IAs, employing manifold self-conscious intrusions, are fabulous.

2 Annoyance over students' misreadings. Though my college students were not at all bothered by the *telling* practices of the great self-conscious narrators (they had read none of the diatribes), they seemed too often ignorant about the differences between the narrators and the IAs, and between the IAs and the FBPs creating them. Too many of them had never learned to distinguish – especially as they read the so-called objective modern fictions – the *narrative* voice from that of an author deliberately creating a partially or totally *unreliable* voice.

My most troubling example of frequent misreadings, as I now remember it, was Salinger's *Catcher in the Rye*. Students consistently identified so fully with Holden Caulfield that they missed the ironic clues that Salinger provided about his hero's serious faults and weaknesses. Most of Holden's words were taken as if the author wanted everything he said to be read as straight. The critical neglect of such widespread misreading bothered me a lot.

3 A "moralistic" distress about how critics ignored the value of rhetorical ethical effects – the bonding between authors and readers. This one produced many attacks against my emphasis on ethics, as critics went on asserting that not only poems but novels should not "mean but be," and that novels, like poems, "make nothing happen." Though fewer critics made this "aestheticist" assertion about fiction, many did buy into assertions like Oscar Wilde's "There is no such thing as a moral or immoral book. Books are well written or badly written. That is all."[3] Though that rejection of ethical concerns is still widespread, more critics these days than in the 1950s are acknowledging that there is such a thing as an ethics of fiction. In the responses to J. M. Coetzee's Nobel Prize in 2003, for example, we encountered again and again open claims about how the justified winner's novels, laden as they are with depressing episodes, have improved our ways of responding to the floods of cruelty and suffering that we encounter in the shit-laden world. Unlike the "pure" "poetic" critics back then, most critics are admitting, some only tacitly, that great fiction educates us ethically – unless we misread it.[4] But in the 1950s and 1960s, increasing numbers embraced a movement soon to be called "reader response," claiming that interpretation is all a matter of the *reader's* responsibility: "My reading of what Henry James's characters are doing is much more important than James's intention, so what do I have to learn from him? Nothing."[5]

Those three motives are now reinforced by a fourth, as I've done more thinking about how authorial creation of IAs relates to the universality of our daily, hourly, dependence on constructive and destructive role playing. In every corner of our lives, whenever we speak or write, we imply a version of our character that we know is quite different from many other selves that are exhibited in our flesh-and-blood world. Sometimes the created versions of our selves are superior to the selves we live with day by day; sometimes they turn out to be lamentably inferior to the selves we present, or hope to present, on other occasions. A major challenge to all of us is thus to distinguish between beneficial and harmful masking. And that challenge is especially strong in literary criticism.

Some decades ago Saul Bellow dramatized wonderfully the importance of authorial masking, when I asked him, "What're you up to these days?" He said "Oh, I'm just spending four hours each day revising a novel, to be called *Herzog*." "What does that amount to, spending four hours every day revising a novel?" "Oh, I'm just wiping out those parts of my self that I don't like."

In almost all of our utterances we imitate Bellow, consciously or unconsciously–especially when we have time for revision. We simply wipe out those selves that we don't like, or that at least seem inappropriate for the moment. If everything we said were unrevised, simply a blurting out of "sincere" blasts of undoctored feelings and thoughts, wouldn't life become intolerable? Would you want to go to a restaurant where the boss instructs waiters never to smile unless they sincerely *feel* like smiling? Would you want to go on teaching if your administration required you never to perform a more cheerful, knowledgeable persona than you felt you were as you walked toward class? Would you want to read poems by Yeats if they were nothing but undoctored records of his deeply troubled life? Our lives would be disastrous, hour by hour, if everyone swore to be "sincere" at every moment.

Even more important is the fact that if we don't think about the differences between good and bad masking, we are much more likely to get sucked in destructively by the bad kinds – such as politicians' dishonest rhetrickery. And won't we also fail to appreciate our ethical dependence on the good kinds: the IAs created by our spouses, at their best, our bosses, at their best, our journalists, at their best, and . . . well, name your favorite beneficial posers. For me, as this essay will demonstrate, they are the authors who know how to wipe out the selves they do not like.

The plain ethical fact is that we all, at least to some degree, derive our models of how to live by taking in, absorbing, the better selves, the IAs, created by others – especially authors. It's of course true that, for most of us, the people we live with – our parents and siblings and friends – have even stronger effects on us as models – good and bad – than any literary IAs we meet. But even those friends and relatives have influenced us by managing, at least some of the time, to wipe out those selves they do not like. And for most of us, they are the ones who first managed to engage us in *literary* engagement – filling our lives from infancy on with IAs of amazing diversity.

What is good and what is questionable about the inescapable universality of such influence by projected – often totally faked – selves? They are always to some degree masks covering much more complex, and too often much less admirable, selves. Should we celebrate what some people would call mere hypocrisy, such wearing of false masks? Is it good for us, because it provides models for living better than would be provided by the authors' actual lives, or should we condemn all of it as if it were Schwarzenegger's kind of hypocritical performances?

Saving such threatening questions for a possible book about it, I for now retreat into the corner that seems to me the most important one: *literary* masking of the kind Bellow reports. I am certain that we should all feel deeply grateful to Bellow for the wiping out he did. Through my years of knowing him personally I encountered other versions that nobody would like – Bellow-versions that, if allowed to dominate his novels, would have totally destroyed them. What's more, those who have studied his manuscripts (as I have not) find confirmation for that claim: he chose, from thousands of pages, a few hundreds that presented IAs he really liked, and that I love.

Obviously every judgment of authorial character must be tentative. But only the cynic could ever claim that there are no real moral distinctions: "Since it's *all* chicanery, why bother?" When seriously engaged authors grant us their works, the FBP has created an IA who aspires, consciously or unconsciously, for our critical joining. And the IAs are usually far superior to the everyday lives, the FBPs.

Since most of my work about that point has concentrated on fiction, I'll shift here to poetry. The point will be not only that IAs are valuable to us as models but that our knowledge of the difference between cleansed IAs and contemptible FBPs can actually enhance our admiration of the literary works presenting the IAs. (So far as I know, this point has never before been dramatized.)

What differences from fictional IAs do we meet when we read poems? Most obviously, we less often meet ironic portraits of *deliberately* flawed, intentionally unreliable narrators. Only rarely does a poet create a consistently dubious voice like that of Huck Finn or Kazuo Ishiguro's butler in *The Remains of the Day*. What we more often meet are, more reliably speaking, thoroughly cleansed personae who imply a total identity with the IA whom the FBP hopes we will join: "I, the poet, speak to you directly in my true voice." But if we probe the biographies and autobiographies of any great poet from ancient times to the present, we discover that the poetic self has emerged dressed up elegantly, exhibiting a sensitivity to life's woes and blisses that careful readers find themselves longing to possess – *but* that the FBP has often violated in everyday behavior. To paraphrase Yeats's point about it: it is by struggling with our selves that we create poetry, in contrast with the rhetoric we produce when we struggle with others. (I would of course expand the word "rhetoric" to include the internal quarrels.)

It's true that some poets, like Browning, have created deliberately unreliable poetic voices.[6] And there are many others, in recent times, who, like Sylvia Plath, have beautifully revealed and recreated their self-destructive faults and miseries – as if practicing total undoctored honesty. But in doing so, they are still realizing, during the very act of creating the poems, selves far superior to those who cursed their spouses over breakfast.

Some readers are deeply troubled when biographies reveal just how awful was the life of the FBP. When a biographer of a highly admired poet uncovers "warts and all," many feel that the poetry has been sullied. How can we admire T. S. Eliot's poems as much as we did formerly, now that we know how hard he worked to clean out from them aspects of his emotional life that he thought would "overpersonalize" them? Poetry, Eliot claimed, is "not a turning loose of emotion, but an *escape from* emotion; it is not the expression of personality, but an *escape from* personality. But, of course, only those who have personality and emotions know what it means to want to escape from such things" (Eliot [1917] 1932: 10). In escaping emotion and personality of one kind, while creating emotions and personality of another kind, isn't Eliot's masking contemptible? Wouldn't he have been an even greater poet if he had decided to "let it all burst out"?

Not surprisingly, some would answer "yes," attacking Eliot and other poets for thus producing poetry less "honest" than poetry ought to be. There is by now almost a whole industry devoted to "outing" authors' various suppressions of their questionable selves, often suggesting that the poems would be better if the poets had been more honest. It should not surprise you that my answer is "No!" Most of the poetry we admire would be much worse if the authors had failed to put on a mask. Shouldn't we be grateful for their cleansing?[7] And should we not admire them for their ability in performing that laundry work?

As the first of only two examples here, consider Robert Frost, a poet who has been almost viciously "outed" by some biographers. Who is the Robert Frost we meet in his poem, "A Time to Talk"?

> When a friend calls to me from the road
> And slows his horse to a meaning walk,
> I don't stand still and look around
> On all the hills I haven't hoed,
> And shout from where I am, "What is it?"
> No, not as there is a time to talk,
> I thrust my hoe in the mellow ground,
> Blade-end up and five feet tall,
> And plod: I go up to the stone wall
> For a friendly visit.

(Frost [1916] 1939: 156)

First, what kind of person is the narrator, the speaker here?

He's a man whom I cannot resist admiring and do not *want* to resist: a dutiful, hard-working farmer who, though facing the pressing task of hoeing the hills, cares so much about friendship that he'll drop his important work and chat. He's a man who loves the mellow farmland, but leaves it for the sake of a friendly visit; good talk, in a rural scene with a friend, is for him a higher value.

But who, behind that narrator, is the IA creating him? Well, in one sense they are identical; the IA obviously intends no ironies against the speaker. But he is not only a friendly farmer; though sharing the virtues of the speaker, he is a much more complex man devoted to poetic form, working hard – probably for hours or days – to achieve effective rhymes that obey his rule that no reader should be able to claim that a rhyme was determined only by the rhyming: road, hoed; walk, talk; around, ground; tall, wall; and – separated by six lines – "What is it" and "friendly visit." He's also working hard with meter and line length, so that he can surprise us with the only short line, the final one: "For a friendly visit." To me that's a lot harder work than plowing a field (I've worked at both), and it's wonderful to meet a man who, though he rightly loves farming, considers friendly talk even more important, and yet considers most important of all the writing of a beautiful poem; for all we know he hasn't touched a hoe for years. The result: though the poem is by no means Frost's greatest, his IA is moving in the direction of greatness. He is a weirdly richer character than the reliable narrator, though not in shocking contrast: after all, a devoted farmer could also be a poet, and both a farmer and a poet could love to chat with a neighbor.

But where meanwhile is FBP Frost? You may want to join those who refuse to ask that question, because the answer may diminish the pleasure of the poem. The contrast between those first two Frosts with the Frosts portrayed in his biographies is shocking.[8] The first and most influential of the negative exposures called him "an appalling man, petty, vindictive, a dreadful husband and parent . . . a monster, a man of systematic cruelty . . . a man who pretended to be a rustic peasant type but who was always well-to-do and urbane" (Thompson 1966: 27).[9] The more recent biographers don't portray him as quite that bad, and some, without denying appalling faults, portray him much more favorably (see Parini 1999).[10] But none of them reveal a man I would like to have as a close neighbor or relative or lunch companion. The man I'd love to have as a next door neighbor or brother is the one who emerges from that poem, or from the even better ones, or the wonderful poser whose lecture I attended when a college student.

Does this contrast diminish my admiration for the poems, or, as I claim here, actually somehow raise it a bit?

An even more complex collection of contrasting selves is presented by Sylvia Plath. Of all the relatively small number of poets whose lives I've studied, she is top contender for prize as "FBP With Largest Collection of Contradictory IAs." As her husband, and her journals, and her many biographers, have revealed, she herself felt divided about just which of her poems really fit the person she wanted to appear to be. She simply did not trust any one of her many voices, even when she felt that the poems and stories they created were good. As she said when explaining why, after many other changes of title for her first collection of poems, she chose *The Devil of the Stairs*: "... this title encompasses my book and 'explains' the poems of despair, which is as deceitful as hope is" (Plath 1981: 13).

She had a terrible time deciding not just between the voice of despair and the voice of hope but the voices of anger, of physical violence, of revenge, of sexual bliss and disappointment. Ted Hughes explains that when she finally settled on the title *Ariel*, not long before she committed suicide, she "omitted some of the more personally aggressive poems from 1962, and might have omitted one or two more if she had not already published them herself in magazines" (Plath 1981: 15). Responding to Plath's mother's distress at how she is portrayed in the poems, Janet Malcolm rightly explains:

> It seems never to have occurred to Mrs. Plath that the persona of *Ariel* and *The Bell Jar* was the persona by which Plath wished to be represented and remembered – that she wrote this way for publication because this was the way she wished to be perceived, and that the face she showed her mother was not the face she wished to show the reading public.
>
> (Malcolm 1994: 15)

I would put it even more strongly, as "the self her mother knew was not the self she hoped really to *be*" (Malcolm 1994: 18).

When Hughes decided, after Plath's death, to publish a collection, he weeded out some of the contradictions, explaining in his Introduction to the book: "Several advisers had felt that the violent contradictory feelings expressed in those [late] pieces might prove hard for the reading public to take.... This apprehension showed some insight" (Plath 1981: 15). Her journal entries (only a fraction of which I've read) are full of stories, many perhaps true and some obviously jazzed up with the thought of turning them into publishable versions, her disliked selves now wiped out. But in most of them we can detect a genuine effort to find and project this or that superior "self," and particularly the self that will know how to deal with being not just a woman but – too often – a miserable woman.

Throughout her poetry, Plath does often reveal that she is trying hard to give an honest portrait of some kind of *real* damaged self. But we can obviously thank our good fortune that most of those selves were escaped when she sat down to write the poems about them. Should we feel any regret that she did not write a poem about the time when, furious with Ted Hughes for his philandering, she tore "into small pieces all his work in progress of the winter of 1961, as well as his copy of Shakespeare" (Malcolm 1994: 18)?

Even her latest poems about the approaching suicide imply an author who is still very creatively alive, while contemplating death. Here is the concluding moment, from what was probably her last poem, "Edge":

The woman is perfected.
Her dead

Body wears the smile of accomplishment,
The illusion of a Greek necessity

Flows in the scrolls of her toga,
Her bare

Feet seem to be saying:
We have come so far, it is over.

Each dead child coiled, a white serpent,
One at each little

Pitcher of milk, now empty.
She has folded

Them back into her body as petals
Of a rose close when the garden

Stiffens and odors bleed
From the sweet, deep throats of the night flower.

The moon has nothing to be sad about,
Staring from her hood of bone.

She is used to this sort of thing.
Her blacks crackle and drag.

(Plath 1981: 272–3)

After reading that poem aloud several times, I find myself not just admiring it but in effect loving the author implied by every stroke: a wonderfully different person from the one I have met in her diaries and in some of her more careless poems. She is of course thinking about suicide, contemplating it, even planning it. But for the time being, she is creating a beautiful poem about how contemplating suicide *feels*. She is *thinking* about the awful way in which to commit suicide will for her be a metaphorical killing of her children: her past life with them will disappear, the loveliness somehow disappearing into – no, not sadness: the moon (the world that transcends human emotion) has nothing to be sad about.

At the end she – the creator she chooses to project, no matter what Plath had actually felt five minutes before or yesterday – is attempting to place her coming death, with poetic force, into the general truth about the universality of death. And meanwhile, probing for that truth, she is also aspiring for poetic beauty, excellence of poetic structure. Thinking as a dying self, she is creating a self capable of writing a beautiful poem while feeling suicidal. At the risk of boring those of you who have by now read the poem aloud, note how she handles the rhymes: "in the scrolls of her t*o*ga," and on through r*o*se, cl*o*se, *o*dors, thr*o*ats, b*o*ne. It's as if she were sighing: Oh, oh, oh, death where is thy sting?

But the flowing "o"s change to nastier vowel rhymes and harsh, explosive alliteration and half alliteration:

> Each dead child coiled, a white serpent . . .

And finally a concentration of rhyme and alliteration:

> blacks crackle and drag.

Where do her blacks drag Plath and her readers?[11] Into a powerful confrontation with death!

We are told that Plath wrote "Edge," and others of her best poems, in those final hours, waking at 5 a.m. in a freezing unheated apartment, financially desperate, miserably angry against Ted for his affair, overwhelmed with the care of the two children, desperate for financial help from friends. She must have felt, for a few hours each morning as she labored with the poems, that she had finally found the true self that she wanted to express. And she did it. But as we've seen, that creative self was still a mask – a mask that was torn off each morning as soon as the children awoke. Throughout her life she had been troubled by self-consciousness about her masking – sometimes as a totally passive, dutiful domesticated woman, sometimes as almost a whore, sometimes as . . . who knows?

Meanwhile, who are the diverse selves you and I enact as readers of such a poem? The full value of a poet's masking can be understood only when we acknowledge the importance of what it does to our own diverse masks – what we gain from the encounter. (At the risk of overdramatizing, I'll label them as diverse "Booths," but you as reader may want to substitute your own name.)

Well, first there is Booth$_1$, the totally engaged reader who initially tried to follow the poem faithfully and accurately at every point, laboring to join the IA in every word, hoping to become the Implied Reader the IA hoped for.

Booth$_1$ attempts to exercise Coleridge's total suspension of disbelief, not allowing thoughts to intrude about the complex critical matters labored on in an essay like this. He attempts simply to enter the poem, to join the IA, even wishing that he could himself, when the time comes to face death, emulate Plath by writing something creative about it.

In that sympathetic reading, Booth$_1$ is consciously or unconsciously joining all lovers of poetry, and especially lovers of the special type who love to read thoughts about death. They are not those old-fashioned readers who abhor free verse, or those optimists who abhor poems that fail to be "nice" and cheerful, or those *hyper*-"objective" folks who detest obvious rhyming. The implied readers – Peter Rabino-witz's ([1987] 1998) "authorial audience" – must have read a good deal of other modern poetry or they'll fail in reading this one. Yet they are also lovers of prosodic richness as amazing as Alexander Pope's, with his commandment: "The sound must seem an echo to the sense": close attenders to details, appreciating the subtle free-verse lyrical effects I have only partially traced.

Meanwhile there is a version of Booth$_1$, call it Booth$_{1a}$, who happens to know throughout the time of reading – unlike some other possible poetry lovers reading carefully – that this poet committed suicide shortly after writing this poem; the implied "Plath" must have sensed that such a reader will be especially touched, as I am, by her managing this creative moment at such a desperate time of life. Just think of how differently we would read this poem if we did not know that she committed suicide.

While aspiring to join that authorial audience, thinking of myself as sincerely putting on those quite different masks, I must of course confess to the presence here of several additional Booths. There is, most embarrassingly, the intrusive critic, Booth$_2$, who is exploiting the poem in order to write this essay. Motivated by his book-effort grappling with good and bad masking, sometimes even labeling it "hypocrisy upward and downward," he has imposed his critical interests in a way that would no doubt feel offensive, or at least irrelevant, to any one version of Plath's selves. Booth$_2$ has partially crippled Booth$_1$, deflecting him somewhat from a full joining: Booth$_2$ stands cruelly above – or should I say "below"? – the IA, the creating, suffering, persona. He would of course like to claim that he is himself an example of constructive masking or posing: except for this sentence, his mind, his soul, his self is totally occupied with the honest critical pursuit of truth about posing and masking, and its relation to this poem.

Meanwhile, Booth$_3$, the FBP, takes a break, goes to the toilet, reads a page or two of the daily paper – and thinks a bit about how to revise the not-yet-good-enough section of this essay dealing with Plath's poem. He is troubled by an aching back as he sits too long at his computer: "what the hell, just abandon it and mail it in!" Actually he's writing under some pressure because in a few moments friends will come to play string quartets, and he really ought to be practicing the cello part for Beethoven's Op. 59 #3 that they'll play this morning; he's thus almost totally distracted from any full engagement with the poem or with thinking about it. He's especially troubled by having stumbled earlier today on a passionately negative review of one of his books.

Next day, back to the draft, feeling good about the Beethoven, Booth$_4$, the lifetime moralizer, finds himself thinking not about the poem but about suicide. Unlike many other readers in the audience that Plath must have expected, this Booth has never personally contemplated or attempted suicide. His feelings will be very different from those of any reader who happens to have failed in an attempt last year. He actually has an uncertain but real conviction that suicide is an immoral act that everyone should resist to the last possible moment. He thus has an irrelevant, aesthetically destructive, temptation to lecture the FBP-Plath for what her act did to the world, by ennobling suicide. Yet meanwhile he should be aware that the whole thesis of this essay – thought about IAs must not be abandoned, because IAs improve us – moves into Booth$_4$'s territory.

As the other Booths have read and reread the poem, as they have revised and rerevised these sentences about the reading, Booth$_2$, the critic, goes on masking here as a totally scholarly/critical persona: the objective pursuer of nothing but the truth about how poets enrich us with their maskings. Thus he dissociates himself uneasily from the various other implied or actual audiences: he becomes the critic anxious about getting his own essay into good shape, thinking of scores of trivial matters that not only would Plath consider irrelevant but that he knows are irrelevant – to the poem. He knows that he thus risks harming the poem, imposing on it the *over*standing that can diminish poetic *under*standing. Only Plath's poem can rescue him from that kind of unfair intrusion. And meanwhile, at this very moment, he is working hard to imply an author of total honesty.

No reader, of whatever moral or intellectual persuasion, can avoid objecting to at least some of Plath's maskings, once they are revealed. I (that is, Booth₃) cannot help thinking that if she somehow had resisted the "modernist individualism" that her culture – and family, her friends, her English teachers, the books she read – had imposed on her, if she could somehow have managed to diminish the anguished search for the one true self, she might have avoided that suicide. She had the gifts to become, as some critics have claimed (though Ted Hughes has denied it) a great novelist. All we can do, at the end of the story, is thank *our* fate that she finally found the mask that freed her to write those final poems. That mask, alas, did not save her from turning on the oven gas. Booth₃ is tempted to say (but he's probably wrong): we would all be a lot better off if, at the end, she could just have gone on grappling with life, saying, "In celebrating suicide, I was just masking as a true poet absorbed in making beautiful poetry about it."

It is important to stress, as we move toward conclusion, that none of this suggest that masking as a poetic self is a hoax. The created IA is not – as some biographers have suggested and others have often implied – someone whose very creation should lead us to condemn the creator as a deplorable phony. The IAs are not only as genuine versions of Frosts and Plaths as are the FBP sinners. They are in one sense *more* genuine, and of course far more admirable and influential: in wiping out the selves they do not like, the poets have created versions that elevate both their worlds and ours. Just think how impoverished our lives would be without such acting out of superior versions.

Meanwhile a chorus of past assassinators of the IA shout at us: why bother about all these irrelevant – or fake – distinctions? Why not just live with the text, interpreting it in whatever way seems right? Forget about FBPs, kill off the IAs, and *interpret the poem*! Another chorus, though believing in the notion of IAs, will accuse me of having besmirched Frost and Plath by dwelling on the warts. Why even mention the gruesome facts about the author's life? Just enjoy the poem.

I can only repeat the one simple answer that has been implicit throughout: I find my admiration for the works of Frost and Plath and other effective maskers actually *rising* a bit when I learn some contemptible details about their FBPs. How could creatures with such faults and miseries manage to produce such beautiful moving works? Well, obviously, they can do it because they have aspired not just to *appear* better but to *be* better than those parts of their FBPs that they deplored. They create a realer, truer, more genuine version of their selves than those selves who plagued the world with base behavior. As they sit polishing their works, they either wipe out the parts of their selves that they do not like, or, when the darker selves get dramatized, as happens so often in Plath, the superior IA conquers the other versions of FBP by polishing the poem or novel or play: "That's who I really am, the person able to exhibit those values and brilliant strokes."

Another chorus, much smaller, intrudes now to express annoyance at my having dodged the problem of the difference between the implied author and the actual text. How can I go on talking as if the actual person implied by the text is the same as the text itself? Well, that's because I still don't think there *is* a real difference, at any moment of reading of the kind Booth₁ has attempted. It is only when we start thinking (Booth₂) about different time frames and cultural contrasts that we create versions of the IA that the author would never have dreamt of as he or she created the text. Of course the IA I recreate by reading the text *now* is not identical with the IA I would have recreated 40 or 20 years ago. But my claim is that what I see as the actual text implies, in every stroke as I read now, the choices I believe were made by the author then, which in turn imply the chooser. It's true that the text is always in one sense "out there," divorced from the creator, subject to innumerable readings and misreadings. But *at the time of creation*, and at the time of my recreation, unless I am imposing *over*standing, the two have been identical. (I resist offering examples of the appalling flood of current distortions of texts by readers who "know" in advance what they are going to find in them – and therefore find it, regardless of what the IA wanted them to find.)

Others may be troubled by my obsession with ethical effect. To that objection I can only reply, a bit rudely: are you sure that you are not echoing those author-assassinators who were in fact *over*standing *mis*readers? As they pursued only theoretical or structural questions, they in fact failed to *experience* the work as intended. Having experienced no emotional bonding with the author through the characters, they could thus dismiss ethical effect. Only readers who have known the thrill of joining authors in their full engagement, their full achievement, their full cleansing or purification, leaving abstract critical questions to one side until the poem has been fully experienced – only such fully hooked readers ever discover how that joining changes one's life.

As we merge ourselves with the created self who has created the work, as we recreate the work as intended, we resemble more and more the IA who achieved the creation. And when we learn of the shoddy selves behind the creation, we not only can admire the creations even more than previously; we observe models of how we ourselves might do a bit of creating of better selves.

Though we may later decide that some of our joinings were harmful, even disastrous, the subject of that joining cries out for persistent study, as we encounter the daily flood of IAs – constructive and destructive – not only in literature but in politics, in journalism, in scholarly works, and in the classroom.

NOTES

1 See Booth 1988, especially index entries under "Author, implied."

2 For a selection from innumerable attacks on authorial intrusions, *before* the death of the author movement, see Lubbock (1921), Ford Madox Ford (1932), and Caroline Gordon and Allen Tate (1950).

3 From the Preface to *The Picture of Dorian Gray*. For a persuasive argument that Wilde was not an extreme aestheticist but was always actually in pursuit of moral or ethical effects – under idiosyncratic definitions – see Richard Ellmann's (1988) *Oscar Wilde*.

4 For a first-class demonstration of why ethical matters cannot be escaped in narrative, see Yehoshua (2000).

5 There were innumerable excesses in this shocking elevation of reader over author, often by brilliant critics like Stanley Fish (e.g., Fish 1980). I resist documenting their absurdities – partly because I am these days more willing to agree that *some* of their claims were sound. The best treatment of the proper balance between reader-response concerns and full respect for intention is to me

Louise Rosenblatt's (1995) *Literature as Exploration*.

6 See for example Browning's brilliantly ironic "My Last Duchess" and "Mr. Sludge, the Medium."

7 For example, in his work in progress *Modernism and the Ethics of Impersonality*, Tim Dean argues that *The Waste Land* would not be as great as it is if Eliot had spent his time laboring with his homosexual Self.

8 Well summarized by Denis Donoghue (1999).

9 No doubt because of the flurry such an indictment produced, Thompson's many later accounts were somewhat less severe. But they still revealed ways in which Frost's "arrogance" produced suffering in those around him.

10 A small number portray Frost, somewhat dishonestly in my view, as almost a saint: as pretty much the man who is implied by the wonderfully complex, honest poetry.

11 I can't figure out why she chooses the word "blacks," except for the rhyme – and of course the suggestion of gloom.

REFERENCES AND FURTHER READING

Beach, J. W. (1932). *The Twentieth Century Novel: Studies in Technique*. London: The Century Company.

Booth, W. C. ([1961] 1983). *The Rhetoric of Fiction*. Chicago: The University of Chicago Press, 2nd edn., with added final chapter.

Booth, W. C. (1968). "The Rhetoric of Fiction and the Poetics of Fictions." *Novel* 1 (Winter), 105–17.

Booth, W. C. (1988). *The Company We Keep: An Ethics of Fiction*. Berkeley, CA: The University of California Press.

Crane, R. S. ([1957] 1967). "Criticism as Inquiry; or, The Perils of the 'High Priori Road,'" In *The Idea of the Humanities*, vol. II (pp. 25–44). Chicago: The University of Chicago Press.

Donoghue, Denis (1999). "Lives of a Poet." *New York Review of Books* 46 (18), 55–7.

Eliot, T. S. ([1917]1932). "Tradition and Individual Talent." In *Selected Essays: 1917–1932* (pp. 3–11). New York: Harcourt Brace.

Ellmann, R. (1988). *Oscar Wilde*. New York: Alfred Knopf.

Fish, S. (1980). *Is There a Text in This Class? The Authority of Interpretive Communities*. Cambridge, MA: Harvard University Press.

Ford, F. M. (1932). *The Twentieth-Century Novel: Studies in Technique*. London: Duckworth.

Frost, R. ([1916] 1939). *Mountain Interval*. New York: Henry Holt.

Gordon, C. and Tate, A. (1950). *The House of Fiction*. New York: Scribner.

Lubbock, P. (1921). *The Craft of Fiction*. London: J. Cape.

Malcolm, J. (1994). *The Silent Woman: Sylvia Plath and Ted Hughes*. New York: Alfred Knopf.

Parini, J. (1999). *Robert Frost: A Life*. New York: Henry Holt.

Phelan, J. (1989). *Reading People, Reading Plots: Character, Progression, and the Interpretation of Narrative*. Chicago: The University of Chicago Press.

Phelan, J. and Rabinowitz, P. J. (eds.) (1994). *Understanding Narrative*. Columbus: Ohio State University Press.

Plath, S. (1981). *Sylvia Plath: The Collected Poems*, ed. with introduction T. Hughes. London: Faber and Faber.

Rabinowitz, P. J. ([1987] 1998). *Before Reading: Narrative Conventions and the Politics of Interpretation*. Columbus: Ohio State University Press.

Rosenblatt, L. ([1965] 1995). *Literature as Exploration*. New York: The Modern Language Association.

Thompson, L. (1966). *Robert Frost*. New York: Holt, Rinehart, and Winston.

Wimsatt, W. K., and Beardsley, M. C. (1954). "The Intentional Fallacy." In W. K. Wimsatt, *The Verbal Icon: Studies in the Meaning of Poetry* (pp. 3–18). Lexington: University Press of Kentucky.

Yehoshua, A. B. ([1998] 2000). *The Terrible Power of a Minor Guilt*, trans. Ora Cummings. Syracuse, NY: Syracuse University Press.

5

Reconceptualizing Unreliable Narration: Synthesizing Cognitive and Rhetorical Approaches

Ansgar F. Nünning

Introducing the Unreliable Narrator

Ever since Wayne C. Booth first proposed the unreliable narrator as a concept it has been considered to be among the basic and indispensable categories of textual analysis. Booth's well-known formulation, "I have called a narrator *reliable* when he speaks for or acts in accordance with the norms of the work (which is to say the implied author's norms), *unreliable* when he does not" (1961: 158–9), has become the canonized definition of the term and was only challenged quite recently. According to Booth, the distinction between reliable and unreliable narrators is based on "the degree and kind of distance" (p. 155) that separates a given narrator from the implied author of a work. A comparison of the definitions provided in standard narratological works, in scholarly articles, and in glossaries of literary terms shows that the great majority of narratologists have followed Booth, providing almost identical definitions of the unreliable narrator.

What most critics seem to have forgotten, however, is that Booth himself freely admitted that the terminology for "this kind of distance in narrators is almost hopelessly inadequate" (1961: 158). There is indeed a peculiar discrepancy between the importance generally attributed to the question of reliability in narrative and the unresolved issues surrounding the concept: "There can be little doubt about the importance of the problem of reliability in narrative and in literature as a whole.... [But] the problem is (predictably) as complex and (unfortunately) as ill-defined as it is important" (Yacobi 1981: 113). While critics and theorists working within the tradition of rhetorical approaches to narrative consider the implied author to be among the important and indispensable categories of textual analysis, structuralist and cognitive narratologists have argued for the abandonment of the implied author and for a radical reconceptualization of the unreliable narrator. In contrast to many other narratological categories (e.g., such well-defined and familiar terms as events and actions, homodiegetic and heterodiegetic narrators, order, duration, and frequency) both of these key concepts of narrative theory have become the subject of intense debates and even heated controversy.

As the debates surrounding unreliable narration have shown, the topic attracts a great deal of attention from most of the main current approaches to narrative, ranging all the way from rhetorical and ethical approaches, from which the concept originates, over narratological and feminist approaches to cognitive narratology. There are many reasons why unreliable narration has become such a central issue in contemporary narrative theory. First, the topic of narratorial unreliability is an extremely rich theme, involving a number of intriguing theoretical problems (e.g., the vexed question of whether or not we need the implied author and the equally intricate question of how readers negotiate textual inconsistencies and ambiguities). Second, since unreliable narration is situated at the interface of aesthetics and ethics as well as of description and interpretation, it combines important theoretical and interpretive enquiries, with any decision about a narrator's (un)reliability having far-reaching interpretive consequences. Third, the fact that unreliable narration is very widespread in both modern and postmodern fiction provides a great challenge both to every critic and to our usual definition of an unreliable narrator (cf. Wall 1994). Last but not least, unreliable narration as a phenomenon is, of course, not confined to narrative fiction, but can be found in a wide range of narratives across the genres, the media, and different disciplines.

As the title of this chapter suggests, it attempts to survey recent work on unreliable narration, showing that narrative theory has made considerable progress in dealing with this very slippery and complex topic. Narratologists have not only identified the main problems in traditional accounts, but have also provided a number of useful terminological and taxonomic distinctions as well as theoretical refinements. Attempts to reconceptualize unreliable narration mainly involve four areas: (1) the theory and definition of unreliable narration; (2) typological distinctions of different kinds of unreliability; (3) the textual clues and frames of reference involved in projections of unreliable narrators; (4) the respective roles of the reader, the text, and the (implied) author.

Realigning the relation between the cognitive and the rhetorical approaches, this chapter attempts to show that recent work in cognitive narratology and rhetorical theory provides the basis for reconceptualizing unreliable narration. The next section outlines the cognitive reconceptualization of unreliable narration, which can shed more light on the usually unacknowledged presuppositional framework on which theories of unreliable narration have hitherto been based. This is followed by a section that combines the insights of cognitive and rhetorical approaches and argues that the whole notion of unreliable narration only makes sense when we bear in mind that ascriptions of unreliability involve a tripartite structure that consist of an authorial agency, textual phenomena (including a personalized narrator and signals of unreliability), and reader response. The final section then provides a brief summary, suggesting that much more work needs to be done in this fascinating field of narrative theory.

A Critique of Conventional Theories of Unreliable Narration and a Cognitive Reconceptualization: The Role of the Reader and His/Her Frames of Reference

Unreliability is an effect that most readers intuitively recognize. Though Booth's attempt to explain that effect in the particular way outlined above provided a landmark contribution to narrative theory, that way creates as many problems as it sets out to solve. The definition of an unreliable narrator provided by Gerald Prince in his *Dictionary of Narratology* provides a good starting point for understanding why this is so: "A narrator whose norms and behavior are not in accordance with the implied author's norms; a narrator whose values (tastes, judgments, moral sense) diverge from those of the implied author; a narrator the reliability of whose account is undermined by various features of that account" (Prince 1987: 101). Despite the good job Prince does in summarizing the *communis opinio*, this definition is marred by vagueness, because the only yardstick it offers for gauging a narrator's unreliability is the implied author, whose status and norms are more difficult to ascertain than one might think. Nonetheless, most theorists and critics who have written on the unreliable narrator take the implied author both for granted and for the only standard according to which unreliability can be determined. In what are arguably some of the best critiques of classical theories of unreliable narration to date, Tamar Yacobi (1981, 1987) and Kathleen Wall (1994) hold on to the implied author as though he or she, or rather it, was the only possible way of accounting for unreliable narration. Critics who argue that a narrator's unreliability is to be gauged in comparison to the norms of the implied author just shift the burden of determination onto a critical passepartout that is itself notoriously ill-defined (cf. Nünning 1997b).

Some narratologists have pointed out that the concept of the implied author does not provide a reliable basis for determining a narrator's unreliability. Not only are "the values (or 'norms') of the implied author [. . .] notoriously difficult to arrive at," as Rimmon-Kenan ([1983] 2003: 101) observes, but the implied author is itself a very elusive and opaque notion. From a theoretical point of view, the concept of the implied author is quite problematic because it creates the illusion that it is a purely textual phenomenon. But it is obvious from many of the definitions that the implied author is a construct established by the reader on the basis of the whole structure of a text. If the implied author is conceived of as a structural phenomenon that is voiceless, one should look at it not as a speaker involved in the structure of narrative transmission, but as a component of the reception process, as the reader's idea of the author, or "as a construct inferred and assembled by the reader from all the components of the text" (Rimmon-Kenan [1983] 2003: 87). When Chatman (1990: 77) writes that "we might better speak of the 'inferred' than of the 'implied' author," he implicitly concedes that one is dealing with something that has to be worked out by the reader. From a Boothian perspective, however, the notion of an inferred author is quite different from an implied author: the latter is a creation by the author, which the reader may or may not gauge in practice, whereas an inferred author is a creation by the reader, which may or may not correspond to the implied author projected by the flesh-and-blood person who wrote the text (see Booth's contribution to the present volume). As Phelan (2005: 41–2) persuasively argues, this difference means that Chatman's (1990: chap. 5) "Defense of the Implied Author" is not really a defense of Booth's concept but a redefinition masquerading as a defense.

The controversy about the concept of the implied author matters because it carries far-reaching theoretical implications. First, the concept of the implied author reintroduces the notion of authorial intention, though through the back door, by providing a terminological link to the sphere of the actual author and authorial values. As Chatman (1990: 77) has pointed out, "the concept of implied authorship arose in the debate about the relevance of authorial intention to interpretation." For many critics, the implied author provides a terminologically acceptable way of talking about the author and his or her intention, under the guise of talking about textual phenomena. Second, allegedly representing the work's norms and values, the implied author is intended to serve both as a yardstick for an ethical kind of criticism and as a check on the potentially boundless relativism of interpretation. Third, the use of the definite article and the singular suggest that there is only one correct interpretation. In short, the concept of the implied author appears to provide the critic again with a basis for judging both the acceptability of an author's moral position and the correctness of an interpretation.

The main objections to the concept of the implied author involve its lack of clarity and theoretical incoherence. Structuralist narratologists have pointed out that it is a contradiction in terms to define the implied author as the structure of the text's norms and to thus conflate it with the text as a whole, while also casting it in the role of the addresser in the communication model of narrative. They have argued that an entity cannot be both a distinct agent in the sequence of narrative transmission and the text itself; furthermore, if the implied author is equivalent to the whole text, and if his or her counterpart the implied reader is also presumed to be a textual function, then the implied author is equivalent to or a subsumption of the implied reader (Nünning 1997b). About the only thing that is clear, then, is that such an incoherent concept cannot provide a basis for determining unreliability.

Conventional theories of unreliable narration are also methodologically unsatisfactory because they leave unclear how the narrator's unreliability is apprehended in the reading process. The metaphors that Chatman uses in order to explain how the reader detects a narrator's unreliability are a case in point. He resorts to what is arguably one of the two most popular metaphors in this context, that of "reading between the lines." Chatman (1978: 233) argues that readers "conclude, by 'reading out,' between the lines, that the events and existents could not have been 'like that,' and so we hold the narrator suspect." Such observations, though vivid, fail to shed much light on how a narrator's unreliability is actually determined by the reader. The second common metaphor is that something is going on "behind the narrator's back" (cf. Riggan 1981: 13, Yacobi 1981: 125). Chatman (1978: 233), for instance, suggests that the implied author establishes "a secret communication with the implied reader." Riggan (1981: 13) not only uses almost exactly the same phrase but he also states quite unequivocally that "the presence of the implied author's hand is always discernible behind the narrator's back" (p. 77). In contrast to Booth (1974), whose four steps for reading stable irony, outlined in part I of *A Rhetoric of Irony*, constitute a specific method for discerning much unreliable narration, Riggan does not, however, enlighten the uninitiated as to how the hand of the omnipresent implied author behind the narrator's back may in fact be discerned.

Despite what common sense would appear to tell us, definition apparently *is* a problem with the unreliable narrator because most theories leave unclear what unreliability actually is and fail to distinguish between moral and epistemological shortcomings. Most definitions in the wake of Booth have emphasized that unreliability consists of a moral distance between the norms of the implied or real author and those articulated by the narrator. But other theorists have pointed out that what is at stake is not a question of moral norms but of the veracity of the account a narrator gives. Thus Rimmon-Kenan's ([1983] 2003: 100) definition leaves open whether unreliability is to be gauged in comparison to the accuracy of the narrator's account of the story or to the soundness of his or her commentary and judgments: "An unreliable narrator [. . .] is one whose rendering of the story and/or commentary on it the reader has reasons to suspect." The "and/or" construction sounds very open and flexible but actually it is a bit too nonchalant. Most would agree that it *does* make a difference whether we have an ethically or morally deviant narrator who provides a sober and factually veracious account of the most egregious or horrible events, which, from his point of view, are hardly noteworthy, or a "normal" narrator who is just a bit slow on the uptake and whose flawed interpretations of what is going on reveal that he or she is a benighted fool. It is thus unclear whether unreliability is primarily a matter of misrepresenting the events or facts of the story or whether it results from the narrator's deficient understanding, dubious judgments, or flawed interpretations.

Aware of these problems, some narrative theorists have suggested terminological refinements and typological distinctions. Lanser (1981: 170–1) was among the first to suggest that one should distinguish between an unreliable narrator, that is, a narrator whose rendering of the story the reader has reasons to suspect, and an untrustworthy one, that is, a narrator whose commentary does not accord with conventional notions of sound judgment. Pursuing the same line of inquiry, Olson (2003) distinguishes between factual unreliability associated with a fallible narrator, that is, a narrator whose rendering of the story the reader has reasons to suspect, and normative unreliability displayed by an untrustworthy narrator whose commentary and interpretations do not accord with conventional notions of sound judgment, emphasizing that the two types elicit different responses in readers.

Moreover, there may be a number of different reasons for unreliability, including "the narrator's limited knowledge, his personal involvement, and his problematic value-scheme" (Rimmon-Kenan [1983] 2003: 100). Depending on the reason for unreliability, one can distinguish different types of unreliable narrators such as the madman, the naïve narrator, the hypocrite, the pervert, the morally debased narrator, the picaro, the liar, the trickster, or the clown (cf. Riggan 1981). Such a typology "corresponds to an already semanticized classification of unreliable narrators" (Fludernik 1999: 76) which is based on social and literary conventions.

In one of the most sophisticated recent articles on the subject, Phelan and Martin (1999) have developed the most systematic and useful classification of kinds of unreliability to date, while also addressing some of the most important theoretical issues regarding the problem of narrative unreliability. Their heuristic typology is based on the fact that narrators tend to perform three main functions: (1) they report on characters, facts, and events; (2) they evaluate or regard the characters, facts, and events; (3) they interpret or read the characters, facts, and events. Each of these functions or roles can be thought of as existing along one axis of communication, resulting in a different kind of unreliability: (1) unreliable reporting occurs along the axis of facts/events; (2) unreliable evaluating occurs along the axis of ethics/evaluation; (3) unreliable reading or interpreting occurs along the axis of knowledge/perception. Distinguishing these three axes of unreliability, Phelan and Martin have also pointed out that narrators can be unreliable in two different ways along each axis, either by falling short or by distorting. Consequently, they distinguish six main types of unreliability: underreporting and misreporting, underregarding and misregarding (or misevaluating), underreading and misreading.

In contrast to typologies like Riggan's, which are based on real-life parameters, the taxonomy proposed by Phelan and Martin is not only much more systematic, it also has the great merit of being based on a rhetorical model, focusing as it does on the relations among authorial agency, narrator, and authorial audience. Moreover, Phelan and Martin emphasize that, regardless of the axis, all deviations require the authorial audience to infer an understanding of the report, the evaluations, or the interpretations different from those offered by the narrator. Nevertheless, their rhetorical approach fails to provide a satisfactory answer to the question of *how* readers actually recognize an unreliable narrator (in his or her role as reporter, as evaluator, and/or as interpreter or reader) when they see one.

Narrative theorists working within a cognitive and constructivist approach to understanding unreliable narration have argued that the link that has been forged between the unreliable narrator and the implied author deprives narrative theory of the possibility of accounting for the pragmatic effects of unreliability. Focusing on the interactivity between textual modes of representation and readers' choices in constructing narrative worlds, some theorists (e.g., Yacobi 1981, 1987, 2001, Nünning 1998, 1999) have located unreliability in the interaction of text and reader. Indeed, they have argued that unreliability is not so much a character trait of a narrator as it is an interpretive strategy of the reader. This move has led them to propose a conceptualization of the relevant phenomena in the context of frame theory as a projection by the reader who tries to resolve ambiguities and textual inconsistencies by projecting an unreliable narrator as an integrative hermeneutic device. The reader or critic accounts for whatever incongruity he or she may have detected by reading the text as an instance of dramatic irony and by projecting an unreliable narrator. Culler (1975: 157) has clarified what is involved here: "At the moment when we propose that a text means something other than what it appears to say we introduce, as hermeneutic devices which are supposed to lead us to the truth of the text, models which are based on our expectations about the text and the world." Similarly, I regard unreliable narration as not only a structural or semantic aspect of the text but also a phenomenon that involves the conceptual frameworks readers bring to it.

Determining whether a narrator is unreliable is not just an innocent descriptive act but a subjectively tinged value judgment or projection governed by the normative presuppositions and moral convictions of the critic, which as a rule remain unacknowledged. Recent work on unreliable narration confirms Culler's hypothesis about the impact of realist and referential notions for the generation of literary effects. Culler (1975: 144) argues that "most literary effects, particularly in narrative prose, depend on the fact that readers will try to relate what the text tells them to a level of ordinary human concerns, to the actions and reactions of characters constructed in accordance with models of integrity and coherence." Riggan's book provides a case in point. Riggan distinguishes four types of such narrators, which he designates "picaros," "madmen," "naïfs," and "clowns." These typological distinctions can best be understood as a way of relating texts to accepted cultural models or to literary conventions. Riggan (and critics like him) integrate previously held world-knowledge with textual data or even impose pre-existing conceptual models on the text. The models used for accounting for unreliable narration provide a context which resolves textual inconsistencies and makes the respective novels intelligible in terms of culturally prevalent frames.

The information on which the projection of an unreliable narrator is based derives at least as much from these models and the conceptual schema in the mind of the beholder as from textual data. In other words: whether a narrator is regarded as unreliable not only depends on the distance between the norms and values of the narrator and those of the text as a whole (or of the implied author) but also on the distance that separates the narrator's view of the world from the reader's or critic's world-model and standards of normalcy, which are themselves, of course, subject to change. This process of course raises the question of what particular schema are deemed relevant.

An analysis of the presuppositional framework on which most theories of unreliable narration rest is overdue since research into unreliable narration has been based on a number of questionable conceptual presuppositions, which as a rule remain implicit and unacknowledged. These underlying presuppositions include certain

(1) epistemological and ontological premises; (2) assumptions that are rooted in a liberal humanist view of literature; and (3) psychological, moral, and linguistic norms, all of which are based on stylistic and other deviational models. An analysis of the presuppositional framework on which most theories of unreliable narration are based reveals that the orthodox concept of the unreliable narrator is a curious amalgam of a realist epistemology and a mimetic view of literature.

The epistemological and ontological premises consist of realist and by now doubtful notions of objectivity and truth. More specifically, the traditional notion of unreliability presupposes that an objective view of the world, of others, and of oneself can be attained. The concept of unreliable narration also implies that human beings are principally taken to be capable of providing veracious accounts of events, proceeding from the assumption that "an authoritative version of events" (Wall 1994: 37) can in principle be established or retrieved. Theories of narrational unreliability also tend to rely on realist and mimetic notions of literature. The concept of the unreliable narrator is based on what Yacobi (1981: 119) has aptly called "a quasi-human model of a narrator," and, one might add, an equally anthropomorphic model of the implied author.

In addition, theories of narrational unreliability are also heavily imbued with a wide range of unacknowledged notions that are based on stylistic deviation models or on more general notions of deviation from some norm or other. The notion of unreliability presupposes some default value that is taken to be unmarked "reliability." This is usually left undefined and merely taken for granted. Most critics agree, however, that reliability is indeed the default value. Lanser (1981: 171), for instance, argues that "the conventional degrees zero [are] rather close to the poles of authority." Wall is the first theorist of unreliable narration to shed some light on the presuppositions on which this "*reliable* counterpart" of the unreliable narrator rests when she argues that the reliable narrator "is the 'rational, self-present subject of humanism,' who occupies a world in which language is a transparent medium that is capable of reflecting a 'real' world" (1994: 21). Vague and ill-defined though this norm of reliability may be, it supplies the standard according to which narrational unreliability is gauged.

Probing further, we can distinguish some other presupposed norms underlying determinations of unreliability: (1) all those notions that are usually referred to as "common sense," (2) those standards that a given culture holds to be constitutive of normal psychological behavior, (3) some conception of linguistic norms, and (4) culturally agreed-upon moral and ethical standards. One problem with all of these tacit presuppositions is that the establishment of norms is much more difficult than critics acknowledge.

Furthermore, in both critical practice and in theoretical work on unreliable narration, these different sets of norms are usually not explicitly set out but merely introduced in passing, and they seldom if ever receive any theoretical examination. Let me give one typical example: in what is the only book-length study of the unreliable first-person narrator, Riggan (1981: 36) suggests that the narrator's unreliability may be revealed by the "unacceptability of his [moral] philosophy in terms of normal moral standards or of basic common sense and human decency." By saying this, he lets the cat out of the bag: it is not the norms and values of the implied author that provide the critic with the yardstick for determining how abnormal, indecent, immoral, or perverse a given narrator is, but "normal moral standards," "basic common sense," and "human decency." The trouble with seemingly self-explanatory yardsticks like "normal moral standards" and "basic common sense" is that no generally accepted standard of normality exists which can serve as the basis for impartial judgments. In a pluralist, postmodernist, and multicultural age like ours it has become more difficult than ever before to determine what may count as "normal moral standards" and "human decency." In other words: a narrator may be perfectly reliable compared to one critic's notions of moral normality but quite unreliable in comparison to those that other people hold. To put it quite bluntly, a pederast would not find Humbert Humbert, the fictitious child molester and narrator of Nabokov's *Lolita*, unreliable, though even pederasts may have moral codes that Humbert violates; a male chauvinist fetishist who gets his kicks out of making love to store mannequins is unlikely to detect any distance between his norms and those of the mad monologist in Ian McEwan's (1979) "Dead As They Come"; and someone used to watching his beloved mother disposing of unwelcome babies would not even find the stories collected in Ambrose Bierce's *The Parenticide Club* in any way objectionable.

In addition, there are a number of definable textual clues to unreliability, and what is needed is a more subtle and systematic account of these signals. Unreliable narrators tend to be marked by a number of textual inconsistencies, including paratextual elements as well as conflicts between story and discourse. Other textual elements that signal a narrator's unreliability may range from internal contradictions within the narrator's discourse over discrepancies between their utterances and actions (cf. Riggan 1981: 36, who calls this "a gaping discrepancy between his conduct and the moral views he propounds"), to those inconsistencies that result from multiperspectival accounts of the same event (cf. Rimmon-Kenan [1983] 2003: 101). The range of clues to unreliability that Wall (1994: 19) simply refers to as "verbal tics" or "verbal habits of the narrator" (p. 20) can and should be further differentiated, for example by specifying the linguistic expressions of subjectivity. Due to the close link between subjectivity on the one hand and the effect called unreliability on the other the virtually exhaustive account of categories of expressivity and subjectivity that Fludernik (1993: 227–79) has provided is useful for drawing up a list of grammatical signals of unreliability, which can be further differentiated in terms of the linguistic expressions of subjectivity. The establishment of a reading in terms of unreliable narration frequently depends on the linguistic and stylistic evocation of a narrator's subjectivity or cognitive limitations.

To develop a more viable theory of unreliability, we need a pragmatic and cognitive framework that takes into consideration the world-model, values and norms, and conceptual information previously existing in the mind of reader or critic, and the interplay between textual and extratextual information. To put it another way, we need an interactive model of the reading process and a reader-oriented pragmatic or cognitive framework. Fludernik's (1993: 353) explanation of irony illuminates how this might be conceptualized: "textual contradictions and inconsistencies alongside semantic infelicities, or discrepancies between utterances and action (in the case of hypocrisy), merely *signal* the interpretational incompatability [...] which then requires a recuperatory move on the reader's part – aligning the discrepancy with an intended higher-level significance: irony." An interactive model of the reading process alerts theorists of unreliable narration that the projection of an unreliable narrator depends upon both textual information and extratextual conceptual information located in the reader's mind. As Culler, Yacobi, Wall, and others have remarked, this view of unreliable narration sees it as one kind of naturalization, that is, a way of bringing the text "into relation with a type of discourse or model which is already, in some sense, natural or legible" (Culler (1975: 138).

Noticing and clarifying those unacknowledged frames of reference that allow us to naturalize unreliability also provides the clue to reconceptualizing the phenomenon. One might begin by distinguishing between frames of reference derived from every-day experience – what we can call referential frames – and those that result from knowledge of literary conventions. A first referential frame should be based on the readers' empirical experience and criteria of verisimilitude. This frame depends on the assumption that the text refers to or is at least compatible with the so-called real world and allows us to determine reliability according to the narrator's behavior in relation to the norms of that world. A second referential frame depends on the reader's knowledge of the social, moral, or linguistic norms relevant for the period in which a text was written and published (cf. Yacobi 1987) and a third on knowledge of relevant psychological theories of personality or implicit models of psychological coherence and normal human behavior.

A second set of models brought into play in order to gauge a narrator's possible unreliability involves a number of specifically literary frames of reference. These include, for example, general literary conventions; conventions and models of literary genres (cf. Yacobi 1981: 115f.); intertextual frames of reference, that is references to specific pretexts; stereotyped models of characters such as the picaro, the *miles gloriosus*, and the trickster; and last but not least the structure and norms established by the respective work itself. The generic framework determines in part which criteria are used when a narrator's potential unreliability is gauged (cf. Yacobi 1987: 20f.). A narrator who is considered to be unreliable in psychological or realistic terms may appear quite reliable if the text belongs to the genre of science fiction.

In addition to such a cognitive turn in the theory of unreliable narration, Zerweck (2001: 151) has called for a "second fundamental paradigm shift, one toward greater historicity and cultural awareness." Since the development of the narrative technique known as unreliable narration and such cultural frames of reference as norms and values are subject to historical change, the whole notion of (un)reliability needs to be historicized and be seen in the context of broader cultural developments. V. Nünning and Zerweck argue that, because the ascription of (un)reliability involves interpretive choices and strategies, it is culturally and historically variable. Using Oliver Goldsmith's novel *The Vicar of Wakefield* as a test case of a cultural-historical narratology, Vera Nünning ([1998] 2004) has demonstrated that only when the historical variability in the construction of meaning and the values of the period in which the work was written, read, and reviewed are taken into consideration will a narratological analysis of unreliable narration become valid and historically meaningful. Readers and critics who do not take cultural and historical differences into account are apt to misread a sentimental novel like *The Vicar of Wakefield*, including misreading the (un)reliability of a narrator like Dr Primrose.

Detecting Unreliable Narration in Practice: The Role of the Text and the Role of the Author

Proponents of rhetorical approaches to narrative have taken cognitive narratologists to task for throwing out the textual baby with the bathwater of the implied author. They have criticized the cognitive theory of unreliable narration for overstating the role of the reader at the expense of the author's agency and the textual signals of unreliability. Moreover, Phelan (2005: 48) has rightly pointed out that the radically constructivist and cognitive conceptualization of unreliable narration fails to identify the multiple constraints imposed not just by texts and conventions of reading but also by those who design those texts, namely (implied) authors. The interpretive move to read textual inconsistencies as a signal of unreliability after all does not make much hermeneutic sense if it does not proceed from the assumption that someone designed the inconsistency as a signal of unreliability (cf. Phelan 2005: 48).

In contrast to cognitive narratologists who seek to relocate unreliability only in the interaction of reader and text (e.g., Nünning 1998, 1999, Zerweck 2001), Phelan (2005: 38–49) has re-examined the concept and reconsidered the location of unreliability in light of the recent debates surrounding the implied author and unreliable narration. Reminding us of Booth's notion of continuity without identity between the real and the implied author, he retains the implied author, but moves him or her outside the text, thus re-establishing a closer link between the flesh and blood author and the implied author (see also Booth's essay in the present volume). Rejecting both the reader-response version of an "inferred author" and the conflation of the implied author with the text, Phelan (2005: 45) stresses the continuity that pertains between the real author and his or her implied counterpart by redefining the latter as a construction by and a partial representation of the real author, as "*a streamlined version of the real author, an actual or purported subset of the real author's capacities, traits, attitudes, beliefs, values, and other properties that play an active role in the construction of the particular text*" (italics in original). According to this account, the implied author is not a product or structure of the text but rather the agent responsible for bringing the text into existence. Phelan convincingly argues that the notion of unreliable narration presupposes both a rhetorical view of narrative communication and the assumption that authors fashion their texts in a particular way in order to communicate sharable meanings, beliefs, attitudes, and values and norms.

Phelan and Martin as well as Greta Olson have reminded us that the different models of unreliable narration all have "a tripartite structure that consists of (1) a reader who recognizes a dichotomy between (2) the personalized narrator's perceptions and expressions and (3) those of the implied author (or the textual signals)" (Olson 2003: 93). Phelan's rhetorical model in particular provides a timely reminder that meaning arises from the recursive relations among authorial agency, textual phenomena, and reader response, and that not only readers but also authors draw on conceptual and cultural schema: "But if readers need conceptual schema to construct interpretations, authors also need conceptual schema to construct structural wholes" (Phelan 2005: 49). While acknowledging that the same textual phenomena can and often will be construed in different ways by different readers, his rhetorical approach is much better suited to accounting for the many ways in which readers might indeed share understandings, values, and beliefs with authors and with each other, thus opening up a useful way of exploring the ethical dimensions of narratives.

In contrast to a radically constructivist and cognitive theory of unreliable narration, Phelan's rhetorical and ethical approach to unreliable narration focuses on the interplay between authorial agency, text-centered phenomena or signals, and reader-centered elements in the reading process. This approach leads him to argue that "while a text invites particular ethical responses through the signals it sends to its authorial audience, our individual ethical responses will depend on the interaction of those invitations with our own particular values and beliefs" (Phelan and Martin 1999: 88–9). The concept of unreliable narration presupposes the existence of a constructive agent who builds into the text explicit signals and tacit assumptions for the authorial or hypothetical ideal audience in order to draw readers' attention to an unreliable narrator's unwitting self-exposure or unintentional betrayal of personal shortcomings. From the point of view of a rhetorical approach to unreliable narration, Zerweck's (2001: 156) thesis that the "unintentional self-incrimination of the personalized narrator is a necessary condition for unreliability" thus needs to be supplemented by the insight that the narrator's unintentional self-incrimination in turn presupposes an intentional act by some sort of higher-level authorial agency, though it may be open to debate whether we should attribute the constructive and intentional acts to "the implied author" or "the real author."

A brief look at Ian McEwan's macabre and grotesque short story "Dead As They Come" (1978) may serve as a convenient example to show how the cognitive and rhetorical approaches can be synthesized to solve many of the problems outlined above and to shed more light on the questions faced by any critic doing interpretive analysis: What textual and contextual signals suggest to the reader that the narrator's reliability may be suspect? How does an implied author (as redefined by Phelan) manage to furnish the narrator's discourse and the text with clues that allow the critic to recognize an unreliable narrator when he or she sees one? In short: how does one detect a narrator's unreliability? McEwan's story is told by a 44-year-old, rich and egotistic mad monologist (and misogynist) who, after three failed marriages, falls madly in love with a "fashionable woman" who turns out to be a dummy (store mannequin), which he decides to buy and to call Helen. After a couple of months of what the narrator describes as emotional and sexual bliss and "perfect harmony" (p. 71) he suddenly begins to suspect that "Helen" is having an affair with his chauffeur Brian. What makes him more and more suspicious is that "Helen was not listening at all" (p. 72), that "she said nothing, absolutely nothing" (p. 73), and that what he believes to see when he looks into her eyes is "quiet, naked contempt" (p. 76). The story reaches its horrible climax, alluded to in the title, when in a frenzied fit of passionate madness the narrator conceives "two savage and related desires. To rape and destroy her. [. . .] I came as she died" (p. 76).

To begin with, while the narrator's factual reliability, that is, his rendering of the story, is only impaired by his highly idiosyncratic view of the world and his deranged and disintegrating mind, the reader has plenty of reasons to suspect both the nameless narrator's commentary on and evaluation of the details of the events, and the way in which the narrator reads and interprets, for example, what he deems to be Helen's feelings. The main reason for this is that the narrator violates both many of the standards that today's culture holds to be constitutive of normal psychological behavior and widely accepted norms and values. Right from the very beginning the implied author leaves the reader in no doubt that the narrator's view of the world is radically separated from any sane reader's world-knowledge, which will immediately tell the reader that the narrator is merely walking past a store window and that he is stopped in his tracks by a well-dressed dummy:

> I do not care for posturing women. But she *struck* me. I had to stop and look at her. The legs were well apart, the right foot boldly advanced, the left trailing with studied casualness. She held her right hand before her, almost touching the window [. . .] Head well back, a faint smile, eyes half-closed with boredom or pleasure. I could not tell. Very artificial the whole thing, but then I am not a simple man.
>
> (McEwan 1979: 61–2)

The narrator's explicit self-characterization includes a number of opaque statements like "I am a man in a hurry" (pp. 61, 62) and "I am not a simple man" (p. 62) but he also provides the reader with plenty of information about himself, unwittingly exposing many of his personal shortcomings:

> I must tell you something about myself. I am wealthy. Possibly there are ten men resident in London with more money than I. Probably there are only five or six. Who cares? I am rich and I made money on the telephone. I shall be forty-five on Christmas Day. I have

been married three times, each marriage lasting, in chronological order, eight, five and two years. The last three years I have not been married and yet I have not been idle. I have not paused. A man of forty-four has no time to pause. I am a man in a hurry.

(McEwan 1979: 62)

As in most other cases, the structure of unreliable narration underlying McEwan's story can be explained in terms of dramatic irony or discrepant awareness because it involves a contrast between the narrator's deranged view of the fictional world and the divergent state of affairs which the reader can grasp. In the case of McEwan's unreliable narrator, dramatic irony results from the discrepancy between the highly unusual intentions and questionable value system of the narrator and the general world-knowledge, values, and norms of the average reader. For the reader, both the internal lack of harmony between many of the statements and acts of the narrator and contradictions between the narrator's perspective and the reader's own concept of normality suggest that the narrator's reliability is indeed highly suspect. The reader interprets what the narrator says in two quite different contexts. On the one hand, the reader is exposed to what the narrator wants and means to say, that is, the narrator's version of his tragic and fatal love story with Helen. On the other hand, however, the statements of the narrator take on an additional meaning for the reader, a meaning the narrator is not conscious of and does not intend to convey. Without being aware of it, McEwan's unreliable narrator continually gives the reader indirect information about his idiosyncrasies and deranged state of mind.

In addition to the peculiar characteristics, strange beliefs, and perverse behavior explicitly attributed to the narrator in the text, the implied author has also endowed the story with a wide range of signs and signals that invite the reader to make inferences pertaining to the narrator beyond what is stated in the text. These "inference invitations" (Bortolussi and Dixon 2003: 80–1) include, for instance, the bookkeeping manner in which the narrator reviews his marriages "in chronological order," the breathless and self-centered quality of his narratorial effusions, the excess and incoherence of the information he provides, his disdain for others, and his predilection for "silent women" (p. 63). Readers are thus invited to draw inferences pertaining to the narrator and his questionable values, constructing him as a complete egotist, misogynist, and monologist who has no respect for others, and who, as the decreasing lengths of his marriages indicates, has apparently become increasingly intolerable, and who is only interested in satisfying his own needs, interests, and carnal pleasures.

It is thus not just the distance that separates the narrator's highly idiosyncratic view of the (fictional) world from the reader's or critic's world-knowledge, standards of normalcy, and norms and values that indicates to the reader that the narrator is highly unreliable, but also a wide range of textual features that serve as signals of unreliability. Like many other texts featuring unreliable narrators, the narrative of McEwan's monologist is marked by a number of definable textual inconsistencies which function as clues to unreliability. Two of the most prominent of these are internal contradictions within the narrator's discourse and discrepancies between his utterances and actions. McEwan's narrator provides an especially amusing example:

> My ideal conversation is one which allows both participants to develop their thoughts to their fullest extent, uninhibitedly, without endlessly defining and refining premises and defending conclusions. . . . With Helen I could converse ideally, I could *talk* to her. She sat quite still . . . Helen and I lived in perfect harmony which nothing could disturb. I made money, I made love, I talked, Helen listened.
>
> (McEwan 1979: 70–1)

The implied author has furnished the story with many other textual signals of the narrator's unreliability such as conflicts between story and discourse, between the narrator's representation of events and the explanations, evaluations, and interpretations of them that the narrator gives. In such cases as the description of the scene in which the narrator actually buys "Helen," his commentary "is at odds with the evidence presented in the scene he comments upon" (Wall 1994: 25). The reader or critic can establish such a difference by analyzing those utterances in which the narrator's subjective bias is particularly apparent and comparing the worldview these imply with the story itself. In "Dead As They Come," for example, the narrator's expressive statements such as subjective comments, evaluations, and general remarks are completely at odds with the view of the events and characters that is projected by such narrative modes as description, report and scenic presentation, as well as by numerous small dramatic details. In his factually accurate report of how he managed to get Helen, the narrator, for instance, mentions that the five female salesclerks "avoided my eye" (p. 65) and that "[t]hey smiled, they glanced at each other" (p. 65) after he has made his strange request to buy "the dummy (ah my Helen)" (p. 65), but he completely fails to interpret correctly why they are doing this.

In addition to such internal contradictions the implied author (once again as redefined by Phelan) has carefully equipped the narrator with idiosyncratic verbal habits which also serve as clues to unreliability. The narrator's stylistic peculiarities and his violation of linguistic norms and of Grice's conversational postulates play an important role in detecting the narrator's unreliability. There are, for instance, pragmatic indications of unreliability such as frequent occurrences of speaker-oriented and addressee-oriented expressions. One does not need to take a word-count or employ ponderous statistical methods to show that the unreliable narrator of McEwan's story as well as those of Martin Amis's *Money* or Julian Barnes's *Talking It Over* are compulsive monologists as well as egotists. The vast majority of their utterances are indeed speaker-oriented expressions beginning with their favorite word, "I." Similarly, it is virtually impossible not to notice the plethora of addressee-oriented expressions that these and many other unreliable narrators tend to use. There are also syntactic indications of unreliability such as incomplete sentences, exclamations, interjections, hesitations, and unmotivated repetition. McEwan's "Dead as They Come" is full of them, and so are Patrick McGrath's novels. One could also mention such lexical indications of unreliability like evaluative modifiers, expressive intensifiers, and adjectives that express the narrator's attitudes, all of which feature prominently in McEwan's short stories and McGrath's novels. All of these stylistic expressions of subjectivity indicate a high degree of emotional involvement and they provide clues for the reader to process the narrator as unreliable along the axis of facts/events, the axis of ethics/evaluation, and/or the axis of knowledge/perception (see Phelan and Martin 1999).

As these examples may serve to show, the projection of an unreliable narrator does not hinge upon the reader's frames of reference or on conventions of reading alone, as cognitive approaches suggest, because texts and those who design those texts, namely (implied) authors, impose multiple constraints on the ways in which narrators are processed. Rhetorical approaches to narrative remind us that the projection of an unreliable narrator, far from being hit or miss, presupposes the existence of a creative agent who furnishes the text and the narrator with a wide range of explicit signals and inference invitations in order to draw readers' attention to a narrator's unwitting self-exposure and unreliability.

Conclusion and Suggestions for Further Research

To sum up: by synthesizing concepts and ideas from both cognitive and rhetorical approaches, this essay has attempted to advance our understanding of unreliable narration and of how readers negotiate and process texts featuring an unreliable narrator, creating a somewhat more detailed (though by no means exhaustive) inventory of the presuppositions, frames of reference, and textual signals involved in the projection of unreliable narrators. If the rhetorical approach with its emphasis on the recursive relations among (implied) author, textual phenomena or signals, and reader response encompasses the cognitive narratologist's emphasis just on reader and text, then the cognitive approach can nevertheless provide more finely nuanced tools for recognizing an unreliable narrator. Though the suggested synthesis of the two approaches still leaves several questions unanswered (e.g., what is the respective degree of importance of the various items in the inventory outlined above?), it can arguably yield new insights into unreliable narration and open up productive avenues of inquiry for narrative theory, the more so because it is just as relevant for the ways in which, for example, literary characters, events, and plots are constructed (by implied authors) and processed (by readers) and for the role conceptual schema play on the production and reception side.

Though agreement has been reached that ascriptions of unreliability involve the recursive relationship among the author, whether implied or not, textual phenomena, and reader response, accounts of unreliable narration still differ significantly with regard to the respective degree of importance they attribute to each of these three factors. While cognitive narratologists single out reader response and the cultural frameworks that readers bring to texts as the most important basis for detecting unreliability, narrative theorists working in the tradition of rhetorical approaches to narrative have redressed the balance. Most theorists agree, however, that to determine a narrator's unreliability one need not rely merely on intuitive judgments, because a broad range of definable signals provides clues to gauging a narrator's unreliability. These include both textual data and the reader's pre-existing conceptual knowledge of the world and standards of normality. In the end it is both the structure and norms established by the respective work itself and designed by an authorial agency, and the reader's knowledge, psychological disposition, and system of norms and values that provide the ultimate guidelines for deciding whether a narrator is judged to be reliable or not.

The suggested synthesis of cognitive and rhetorical approaches is chiefly offered as a means to rethink, and to stimulate further debate on, the intricate problem of explaining how readers and critics intuitively consider narrators to be instances of unreliable narration. Much more work, however, needs to be done if we want to come to terms with the complex set of narrative strategies that ever since Booth's early work have been subsumed under the wide umbrella of the term "unreliable narration." There are at least six important areas that have yet to be adequately explored. One of them is the development of an exhaustive and full-fledged theory of unreliable narration integrating the insights recently provided by cognitive and rhetorical narrative theorists. Second, what is needed is a more subtle and systematic account of the clues to unreliable narration, including more sophisticated analyses of the interplay between textual data and interpretive choices. Third, the different uses of the unreliable narrator in the works of both contemporary novelists and authors from earlier periods, and the ways in which they reflect or respond to changing cultural discourses, are just waiting to be explored. Fourth, the history of the development of the narrative technique known as "unreliable narration" has yet to be written because no one has dared to provide an historical overview spanning the period from the eighteenth century to the twentieth (for brief sketches see Nünning 1997a, Zerweck 2001). Fifth, since the generic scope of unreliable narration has as yet neither been properly defined nor even gauged, unreliability across different genres, media, and disciplines provides a highly fertile area of research. Notwithstanding a small number of articles on the subject (see Bennett 1987, Richardson 1988), the use of the unreliable narrator in genres other than narrative fiction – for instance in dramatic genres like the memory play or in the dramatic monologue – as well as in other media and domains (including law and politics) deserves more attention than it has hitherto been given. Lastly, taking a new look at the development of narrative techniques like unreliable narration and of the history of the reception of individual unreliable narrators (see V. Nünning 2004) could be an important force in the current attempts to historicize narrative theory.

REFERENCES AND FURTHER READING

Bennett, J. R. (1987). "Inconscience: Henry James and the Unreliable Speaker of the Dramatic Monologue." *Forum* 28, 74–84.

Booth, W. C. (1961). *The Rhetoric of Fiction.* Chicago: University of Chicago Press.

Booth, W. C. (1974). *A Rhetoric of Irony.* Chicago: University of Chicago Press.

Bortolussi, M. and Dixon, P. (2003). *Psychonarratology: Foundations for the Empirical Study of Literary Response.* Cambridge, UK: Cambridge University Press.

Chatman, S. (1978). *Story and Discourse: Narrative in Fiction and Film.* Ithaca, NY and London: Cornell University Press.

Chatman, S. (1990). *Coming to Terms: The Rhetoric of Narrative in Fiction and Film.* Ithaca, NY and London: Cornell University Press.

Culler, J. (1975). *Structuralist Poetics: Structuralism, Linguistics and the Study of Literature.* London: Routledge & Kegan Paul.

Fludernik, M. (1993). *The Fictions of Language and the Languages of Fiction: The Linguistic Representation of Speech and Consciousness.* London: Routledge.

Fludernik, M. (1999). "Defining (In)Sanity: The Narrator of The Yellow Wallpaper and the Question of Unreliability." In W. Grünzweig and A. Solbach (eds.), *Grenzüberschreitungen: Narratologie im Kontext/Transcending Boundaries: Narratology in Context* (pp. 75–95). Tübingen: Narr.

Lanser, S. S. (1981). *The Narrative Act: Point of View in Prose Fiction.* Princeton, NJ: Princeton University Press.

McEwan, I. (1979 [1978]). "Dead As They Come." In *In Between the Sheets* (pp. 61–77). London: Pan Books.

Nünning, A. (1997a). "'But Why *Will* You Say That I Am Mad?' On the Theory, History, and Signals of Unreliable Narration in British Fiction." *Arbeiten aus Anglistik und Amerikanistik* 22, 83–105.

Nünning, A. (1997b). "Deconstructing and Reconceptualizing the 'Implied Author': The Resurrection of an Anthropomorphicized Passepartout or the Obituary of a Critical 'Phantom?'." *Anglistik. Mitteilungen des Verbandes Deutscher Anglisten* 8(2), 95–116.

Nünning, A. (ed.) (1998). *Unreliable Narration: Studien zur Theorie und Praxis unglaubwürdigen Erzählens in der englischsprachigen Erzählliteratur.* [*Unreliable Narration: Studies in the Theory and Practice of Unreliable Narration in English Narrative Fiction*]. Trier, Germany: Wissenschaftlicher Verlag Trier.

Nünning, A. (1999). "'Unreliable, Compared to What? Towards a Cognitive Theory of Unreliable Narration: Prolegomena and Hypotheses." In W. Grünzweig and A. Solbach (eds.), *Grenzüberschreitungen: Narratologie im Kontext/Transcending Boundaries: Narratology in Context* (pp. 53–73). Tübingen: Narr.

Nünning, V. ([1998] 2004). "Unreliable Narration and the Historical Variability of Values and Norms: *The Vicar of Wakefield* as Test-case for a Cultural-Historical Narratology." *Style* 38.

Olson, G. (2003). "Reconsidering Unreliability: Fallible and Untrustworthy Narrators." *Narrative* 11, 93–109.

Phelan, J. (1996). *Narrative as Rhetoric: Technique, Audiences, Ethics, Ideology.* Columbus: Ohio State University Press.

Phelan, J. (2005). *Living To Tell About It: A Rhetoric and Ethics of Character Narration.* Ithaca, NY and London: Cornell University Press.

Phelan, J. and Martin, M. P. (1999). "'The Lessons of Weymouth': Homodiegesis, Unreliability, Ethics and *The Remains of the Day.*" In D. Herman (ed.), *Narratologies: New Perspectives on Narrative Analysis* (pp. 88–109). Columbus: Ohio State University Press.

Prince, G. (1987). *A Dictionary of Narratology.* Lincoln: University of Nebraska Press.

Richardson, B. (1988). "Point of View in Drama: Diegetic Monologue, Unreliable Narrators, and the Author's Voice on Stage." *Comparative Drama* 22, 193–214.

Riggan, W. (1981). *Picaros, Madmen, Naifs, and Clowns: The Unreliable First-Person Narrator.* Norman: University of Oklahoma Press.

Rimmon-Kenan, S. ([1983] 2003). *Narrative Fiction: Contemporary Poetics.* London, New York: Methuen.

Wall, K. (1994). *"The Remains of the Day* and its Challenges to Theories of Unreliable Narration." *Journal of Narrative Technique* 24, 18–42.

Yacobi, T. (1981). "Fictional Reliability as a Communicative Problem." *Poetics Today* 2, 113–26.

Yacobi, T. (1987). "Narrative and Normative Patterns: On Interpreting Fiction." *Journal of Literary Studies* 3(2), 18–41.

Yacobi, T. (2001). "Package Deals in Fictional Narrative: The Case of the Narrator's (Un)reliability." *Narrative* 9, 223–9.

Zerweck, B. (2001). "Historicizing Unreliable Narration: Unreliability and Cultural Discourse in Narrative Fiction." *Style* 35, 151–78.

6

Authorial Rhetoric, Narratorial (Un)Reliability, Divergent Readings: Tolstoy's *Kreutzer Sonata*

Tamar Yacobi

My subject brings together a famous story, an ongoing debate on its interpretation, and a theoretical common denominator that, I would argue, underlies its divergent readings as alternative ways to resolution. The combination of theory, history, and reading, especially in the service of accounting for disagreements about the narrator's reliability, demonstrates the explanatory power of the Tel-Aviv school of narratology to which I subscribe. I'll begin with an overview of the critical controversy triggered by the *Kreutzer Sonata* and of the proposed theoretical framework. The greater part of the essay will show how the various readings of the tale, even where incompatible, are all embedded and explicable within the framework of this theory.

Tolstoy's *The Kreutzer Sonata* (first published 1891) is the story of Pozdnyshev, a Russian nobleman who has murdered his wife because he suspected her of adultery. After his trial and acquittal, he tells it all to a chance fellow traveler on a train. His account is anything but typical. Instead of claiming, say, temporary insanity, he admits premeditation and minutely details the murder scene. Moreover, unlike his murderous jealousy at the time, the teller now pities his dead wife and represents them both as equally helpless victims of the socioeconomic system. In self-defense, perhaps, he mounts a direct attack on it, with a radical and extraordinary reform as a solution: since sexual intercourse generates all social evils, it should be abolished, even between husband and wife. The consequent extinction of the human race does not deter him. Both tale and reform plan are set within the framing written report of Pozdnyshev's original addressee and traveling companion.

The controversy over *The Kreutzer Sonata* started with its first readers, who either applauded or denounced its radical message. The censor banned it but couldn't prevent handwritten copies from being circulated all over Russia. Peter Ulf Møller, in his meticulous survey of the early reception, also delineates the parties to the debate: conservative vs. liberal critics; religious as against secular thinkers; abused wives, who embraced, and feminists, who repudiated, the doctrine at issue; or those who agreed with Tolstoy about the problem of sexual life but not with his solution, as opposed to those who disputed his very premises (Møller 1988: 39–162). In many cases, the divergence among readers on the author's ideology came together with their views of the speaker's reliability: "a typical modern husband or a particularly debauched deviant," and "intended as a character whose misapprehensions were to be exposed or as the author's spokesman"? (Møller 1988: 134–5).

A hundred years later, the debate goes on, and with it, in effect, the quarrel over Pozdnyshev's mediation between author and reader. The sheer wonder at his incongruity, even counterproductiveness in this role, would appear inexhaustible. Among most critics, as one slavicist generalizes, Tolstoy's "views . . . on chastity are said to be presented so unsubtly as to be beyond explication, while the rhetorical strategy of placing them in the mouth of a preachy and unrepentant murderer is held to be unfathomable" (Herman 1997: 16, n.4). As we'll find below, commentators roughly divide into three basic positions: (1) those who take the narrator as Tolstoy's reliable spokesman; (2) others who assert his unreliability; and (3) still others who locate the problem not (or not only) in the narrator's but in the author's own unacceptable ideology and/or confused discourse. The first two views, which judge the narrator by his (dis)harmony with the author, are symmetrical and in principle mutually exclusive; the third complicates the division in preferring or proceeding to judge the author himself as thinker, artist, persuader, and always, it so happens, to negative effect at that. How this third position subdivides, relative to the first two, inter alia, will appear below.

It is not my intention, or the task of narratology, to resolve "once and for all" the crux of *The Kreutzer Sonata*. Instead, I want to show that the diverse interpretive positions are best mapped and correlated as alternative hypotheses under the umbrella of a proper theory of interpretation, wide-ranging yet specifically narrative-oriented. Most wanted here is a theory that can bridge the apparent gulf between readings that explain the story by pointing to the narrator's unreliability and those that cast the blame on the author. To anticipate my fundamental thesis: even contrasted readings of speaker and author, speaker vis-à-vis author, operate, knowingly or otherwise, by the same deeper principle, namely, explaining ostensible discordance by reference to an appropriate integration mechanism.

"Unreliability" famously comes from Wayne Booth, who defines it as the narrator's distance from the implied authorial norms of the text (1961: 158–9). Booth elaborates on the "variation" in both "distance" and "norms," suggesting the flexibility of our conception of a speaker's (un)reliability. But why, how, and where does a "distance" arise, or fail to arise, between a speaker and the implied author?

Hence my operational theory, influenced by Meir Sternberg's idea of fictional discourse as a complex act of communication (e.g., 1978: 254–305, 1983) to be motivated or otherwise integrated. I have accordingly long defined unreliability as a reading-hypothesis: one that is formed in order to resolve textual problems (from unaccountable detail to self-contradiction) at the expense of some mediating, perceiving, or communicating agent – particularly the global speaker – at odds with the author (e.g., Yacobi 1981, 1987, 2001). Let me briefly re-emphasize the hypothetical nature of such an interpretive move, which, like any conjecture, is open to adjustment, inversion, or even replacement by another hypothesis altogether. Fictional unreliability is not a character trait attaching to the (probabilistic) portrait of the narrator but a feature ascribed (or lifted) ad-hoc on a relational basis, depending on the (equally hypothetical) norms operative in context. What is deemed "reliable" in one context, including reading-context, as well as authorial and generic framework, may turn out to be unreliable in another, or even explained outside the sphere of a narrator's failings.

By ordinary standards, for instance, the teller of Bashevis-Singer's "Gimpel the Fool" may indeed look like the fool that his neighbors see and trick; yet his apparent folly is readable in context as genuine innocence, hence as the very merit that qualifies Gimpel to speak for his creator's deeper norms. A mirror image of this hard-won reliability would be the suspicion that Thackeray's showman of *Vanity Fair* lapses at times into inconsistencies that betray an untrustworthy judgment (on this comparison, see Yacobi 2001, with further references). Likewise with tensions in matters of fact, rather than ethics or ideology. A paradigm of suppressive omniscient narration, Fielding's *Tom Jones* thus goes to show how a narrator's deliberate concealment of the truth – false statements included – may yet be accordant with his reliability: explicable as an authorized tactic by appeal to the text's rules and goals (Stenberg 1978: 248, 265–8, 1983: 172ff., 2001: esp. 150ff.).

In short, there is no automatic linkage between textual incongruities and narratorial unreliability. The less so because the same perceived tensions, difficulties, incompatibilities – down to linguistic oddities – are always open to alternative principles or mechanisms of integration. Among them, my earlier work has singled out the existential, the functional, the generic, and the genetic mechanisms as rivals to the perspectival way, specifically to (un)reliability judgments. The fact that all five are relevant to *The Kreutzer Sonata* debate (though in varying degrees) qualifies the story for a test case of my theoretical framework. Let me briefly outline the set of mechanisms as they operate on this ground to diverse interpretive effect.

1 The *existential* mechanism refers incongruities to the level of the fictive world, notably to canons of probability that deviate from those of reality. The worlds of fairy tale, science fiction, or Kafka's "Metamorphosis" are extreme examples. In our novella, part of the debate concerns the applicability of Pozdnyshev's generalizations on issues as significant as love, education, sexual morality, and women's emancipation. Pozdnyshev asserts throughout that his marital crisis is typical, with implications for our judgment of him. To the extent that the claim holds true of the world, his tale reliably embodies a widespread problem in need of

solution; if, on the other hand, his crisis is unique, let alone morbid, his insistence on its prevalence betrays unreliability.

2 The *functional* mechanism imposes order on the deviant in terms of the ends requiring or justifying that deviance. Whatever looks odd – about the characters, the ideas, the structure – can be motivated by the work's purpose, local or overall, literary or otherwise. Here, Tolstoy's religious worldview and iconoclastic theory of art may explain not just the text's normative hierarchy but the problematic manner of its representation. Apropos the *Sonata*, Tolstoy emphasizes the low status of "artistry," to which he has " 'only given . . . just enough room for the terrible truth to become visible' " (quoted in Møller 1988: 10). Such a defiant admission might warn us against expecting a high norm of unity here. For Tolstoy, Pozdnyshev is a useful mouthpiece as long as he delivers "the terrible truth." Seemingly apart from (un)reliability, then, functionality, like existence (and, next, genre), interacts with it.

3 The *generic* principle appeals to a certain encoded model or simplification of reality, like the causal freedoms of comedy vis-à-vis the stricter tragic plot. Here, J. M. Coetzee analyzes our tale within the generic frame of secular *confession*, defined as "a mode of autobiographical writing" with "an underlying motive to tell an essential truth about the self" (Coetzee 1985: 194). Coetzee accordingly juxtaposes Pozdny-shev's claim to tell the truth with the telling's numerous incongruities, wondering in turn how reliable his confession is, how persuasive his conversion. The generic context and "motive" possibly explain away such internal tensions, or, failing to do so, raise the question of whose responsibility it is: the confessing agent's or his creator's?

4 The *perspectival* or unreliability principle enables *The Kreutzer Sonata* reader to explain a variety of incongruities – in matters of fact, action, logic, value, aesthetics – as symptoms of narrator/author discord: clues to Pozdnyshev's unknowing misrepresentation of Tolstoy, Tolstoy's organized exposure of Pozdnyshev. Such a reading, insofar as it appeals to the teller's unreliability, presupposes a further hypothesis about the implied norms that not only govern fact, action, and so forth, but also determine the choice of this kind of teller.

5 Finally, the *genetic* mechanism relegates fictive oddities and inconsistencies to the production of the text; above all, where unresolved otherwise, they are blamed on the (e.g., wavering, negligent, or ideologically fanatic) author. This explanation most differs from all others. When incongruities are shifted from any of the four discourse contexts to the context of the creator, they become more intelligible, but not necessarily more acceptable. Just consider "one inconsistency [that] seems like a slip on Tolstoy's part: in chap. 14, Pozdnysheva is said to have borne six children, while elsewhere it is five" (Isenberg 1993: 167, n.29). On the other hand, evidence of an author's writing process (diaries, letters), as well as related genetic circum-stances, may support other integration mechanisms to favor one interpretive hypothesis over its alternative(s). Here, too, the well-documented genesis of the story, including its nine versions and "Sequel," will be found to play a large role.

Again, like the perspectival mechanism, the genetic explains textual oddities at the expense of someone associated with the story as told. The difference in the identity of the responsible party, however, opposes the descriptive concept of unreliable narrator to the sheer evaluative implications of the inept or offensive or self-contradicting author. A genetic explanation thus often imputes some loss of control – whether over a minor detail like "how many children had Mrs Pozdnyshev," or over significant issues such as character, plot, and ideology. Yet, though arising from and judged as incongruity, the consequent irony – now directed against the author himself – is unintended on every level of the text. By contrast, to hypothesize a fallible narrator is to assume the ironic mastery of a deliberate communicator behind the scenes. On such a reading, the fictive message divides between the narrator's surface oddities and the underlying coherence of the implied communication that we hypothesize as both their source and point.

The perspectival and the genetic mechanisms are also the most relevant to the explanation of the *Kreutzer Sonata* debate. The others, particularly the existential and the functional, serve there to support or reject or complement the main readings. Generally, the first set of readings (Pozdnyshev is reliable) all imply that there are no significant inner tensions in the telling as such, and those that still remain should be integrated between the existential mechanism (his problems represent a common human condition) and the functional principle (apparent discordances are effective in context). For if the narrator is indeed the author's spokesman, then all his choices, selections, and combinations must somehow operate for reliability. On the other hand, readings that reject Pozdnyshev's viewpoint emphasize the incongruities, but disagree about the responsible agent: the teller (within a perspectival or unreliability mechanism) and/or his creator (a genetic solution). These two models of integration produce the second and third sets of the story's readings.

The Selling of a Madman: Rhetoric in the Service of Reliability

First, to judge Pozdnyshev reliable means that all significant inner tensions in his discourse have been contrived to promote the author's like-minded thematic and rhetorical goals. In turn, such promotion against, amid, and through tension, demands an authorial rhetoric in the promoter's favor. Every reliability hypothesis entails persuasion, but selling the end to sexual intercourse, from the mouth of a wife killer, too, escalates the need along with the difficulty. What, then, are the rhetorical countermeasures, and how do the various integration mechanisms work *or* substitute for this thrust?

In text order, the first rhetorical step is a multiform extension of the normative crux and thesis beyond the idée-fixe of one individual, who himself claims their extension. Even before Pozdnyshev's monologue, two devices work to this validating effect – the epigraph and the opening scene (compare Isenberg 1993: 80–2).

The epigraph, like the title, has been chosen by an independent party (the anonymous frame-narrator, and/or the author). Moreover, Tolstoy appeals here to a high authority, quoting two of Christ's sayings on sexual morality (Matthew 5: 28, 19: 10–12): the second explicitly recommends celibacy "for the sake of the kingdom of heaven." Christ's approval of the hero's thesis endows it in advance with ideological weight and prestige as well as temporal depth. Pozdnyshev himself duly (re)quotes and explicates one of these verses (Tolstoy 1963: 313) to suit his new ideology. And as Møller notes, "in the eighth draft version," he also "concludes...by repeating his interpretation of Matthew 5: 28" (Møller 1988: 28; Tolstoy 1960: 448–9, n.100). In further genetic support for the commonality, hence reliability of the thesis, the same Matthew quotes recur in Tolstoy's "Sequel to the Kreutzer Sonata" (1929: 163).

Next, the long opening dialogue scene brings out the topical relevance of the problem. Although the murderer's lecture dominates the story, it is set within a framing tale and presented as a response to an exchange of views by an apparently random group of passengers. Yet the group's "choice" and "discussion...are by no means fortuitous" (Møller 1988: 20; also Isenberg 1993: 86–9). There arise issues like the frequency of divorce, women's rights and education, the institution of marriage, the deterioration of family ethics. The crisis becomes manifest in the growing abandonment of the orthodox code of behavior for imported new ideas, and in the spread of marital conflict to remote villages. Moreover, the two chief debaters, a conservative old merchant and an emancipated lady, "represent...two fairly easily datable stages in the history of sexual morality in Russia...but both still very much present as poles in the range of contemporary attitudes" (Møller 1988: 23). Hence the advance support of Pozdnyshev's claim that his predicament is not exceptional but a symptom of what was known as "the woman question" (Mandelker 1993: 21–30). As the opening contestants all agree that marriage has become an insoluble problem for all classes, they enable the author to expand the scope even beyond the fictive to the real Russian world of his time. Who would disagree? Mirroring an actual state of affairs, the "existential mechanism" supports the speaker's claim for generality.[1]

While dramatizing the issue's scope, the dialogue also looks ahead to the extraordinary value-judgment to be made. First, via the negation of rival worldviews. Those attacked by Pozdnyshev (and his creator, on this reading) are already espoused by such speakers as defeat their own claims. On the side of modernity, education for women, and marriage for love, we find the lady whose "mannish" appearance bespeaks in contemporary context an object of ridicule, or mixed response, while her illogical interventions are supposed to misfire even outside the fictive debate. Her conservative antagonist is an old merchant whose practice (he has taken part in an orgy) contradicts his preaching traditional religion and a hard line with promiscuous females. Genetically, moreover, Tolstoy transformed him from a decent man in the earlier versions to a hypocrite (Møller 1988: 20–3).

Finally, the dispute is resolved dramatically. The merchant evades the anonymous narrator's clear allusion to his sexual practice; his adversary, the lady, under Pozdnyshev's provocative questions, likewise retires without an answer. The failure of the two "representative" voices infects their respective ideologies. "Unfair" rhetoric, perhaps, but integral – or at least available – to fiction. The resemblance to a real-life controversy is only illusive, the realistic facade of a fixed fight. In life, interlocutors are *directly* responsible for their attitudes and arguments, for their power relation and the resolution. Here, as a fictive character, Pozdnyshev confronts the rival ideologues and ideologies in what is, for him, the reality of his life. But it is the implied author who – for his thematic and rhetorical purposes – reduces these antagonists to "straw people," confused or hypocritical, and accordingly authorizes his own spokesman's line of fundamental reform (cf. Isenberg 1993: 83, 87, 88).

Those choices are doubtless functional. Tolstoy could have created an intelligent female antagonist, or an attractive and happily married one, like Natasha Rostov at the end of *War and Peace*. Similarly, the religious "delegate" could be modeled on Levin from *Anna Karenina*, and so would practice what he teaches (as indeed his earlier versions do). In short, by leading the group discussion to the marriage crisis and by first giving the floor to such inferior doctrinal exponents, Tolstoy would persuade us of the need for reform. Narratively, at least, he both raises our interest in a suitable new doctrine and motivates Pozdnyshev's response.

Not satisfied, however, with the rhetoric of negation, Tolstoy multiplies positive devices. On the plot level, Pozdnyshev's "marriage functions paradoxically as an example of a completely normal marriage" (Møller 1988: 12). Its normalcy (e.g., the trivial causes and the frequency of marital conflict) ensures its existential scope or generality; its tragic ending is supposed to act as a warning and an incentive for a radical change. In between, Tolstoy needed an exciting force strong enough to push the couple from the normal hell of marriage to an explosion beyond the pale. And among all forces, he picked Beethoven's Sonata, "the titillating, exciting" catalyst "of ethically unengaged art" (Møller 1988: 16–17), to trigger the husband's murderous fury.

On the level of the monologist's own discourse, rhetorical figures abound: appeal to statistics, rhetorical questions, anaphoric repetitions, analogies between sexual and other addictions. Pozdnyshev's shock tactics include the deautomatizings of family life: love assimilated to lust, or wives equated with whores as kept women. In marriage, "an innocent girl is sold to a dissolute man and the sale is attended by fitting rites" (Tolstoy 1963: 309). Or observe how the speaker's emotional upheaval goes with his reasoned argument and chronological tale (Møller 1988: 36). Tolstoy needs, and values, both extremes: the marks of Pozdnyshev's sincerity and the clear narrativized reasoning. How to join such persuasive forces? Their incongruity might undermine the reliability hypothesis: on its own, Pozdnyshev's monologue could look like a mixture of a religious tract and nervous tics (Møller 1988: 35–7).

Hence the crucial rhetorical function that is assigned to Pozdnyshev's inside addressee and future recorder. That he is impressed by Pozdnyshev's sincerity mediates it much better than would any self-declaration. Likewise, his quoting of the long monologue foregrounds (e.g., via the added chapter divisions) its (chrono)logical order, while his comments on the original way of speaking "document Pozdnyšev's agitation" (Møller 1988: 36–7). Further, as is widely agreed, the anonymous narrator serves as the reader's delegate within the fictive world: the global framing communicator (the implied author, "Tolstoy") persuades his addressee (the implied reader) by dramatizing the process along which the inset speaker (Pozdnyshev) affects *his* auditor. The latter thus serves as "a kind of Directions for Use attached to the work" (Møller 1988: 38). To enhance this symmetrical device, the dramatized addressee, unlike the opening disputants, is a reasonable person. Neither quick to change his mind nor deaf to new ideas, he qualifies as our deputy.

This rhetorical process accordingly falls into two parts. During the first, Pozdnyshev's addressee frequently interrupts his amazing monologue with questions, objections, and surprised exclamations.

> "What do you mean by the domination of women?" I said. "The law gives the advantage to man."
>
> (Tolstoy 1963: 306)

> "Vice, you say?" I put in. "But you are speaking of the most natural human function." . . .
> "But how," said I, "is the human race to be perpetuated?"
>
> (p. 310)

> I found his ideas new and shocking.
> "But what is to be done?" I said. "If what you say is true, then a man can make love to his wife only once in two years; but men —"
>
> (p. 318)

Such responses verbalize the reader's expected wonder and possible reservations about Pozdnyshev's value system and no-sex thesis. Consistently built up throughout the opening half (chaps. 3–15), the listener's dependability as persuasively modulates in the closing part (chaps. 16–28), when his responses undergo a change. He stops asking questions, yet continues to express his interest in the new ideas, even when addressing himself to the reader. At one point, when left alone in the carriage – thus the narrator about his experiencing self – "I" got "so lost" in "going over in my mind all he had said . . . that I did not notice him come back"; at parting, he is even moved "to tears" (Tolstoy 1963: 330–1, 369).

Moreover, unlike the satiric treatment of the inside speakers in the opening scene, the author takes care to moderate the addressee's rhetorical role. Hence, as in the above quote, we never know if he was actually converted by Pozdnyshev or has only become convinced that the severity of the marriage crisis and the uselessness of other solutions at least give the extraordinary proposal a claim to a wider public hearing.[2] So even a skeptical reader should find the lower limit hard to resist and even pushed up toward assent by the rest of the author's rhetoric, mediated as well as (like the epigraph) wholly implicit.

Thus, reconsider the story's communicative structure. As the official narrator who quotes and frames and publishes the murderer's tale, the former listener to it is responsible for the selection and combination of the given text. This position lends greater authority to, inter alia, his own quoted responses. Were Pozdnyshev the global teller, he might have mistaken them for conversion or even fabricated them for persuasion by example. But as it is, we take these pregnant responses at face value and as a guide to our own in authorial reading. Inversely with the turning of the *un*reliability mechanism on others to support the counterspeaker's reliability. It is not Pozdnyshev, the would-be reformer, but the narrator himself who chose to juxtapose the early contestants' failures (of appeal, logic, consistency, honesty, etc.) with the protagonist's viewpoint.

Finally, Tolstoy's own "Afterword" or "Sequel" leaves no doubt concerning his like-minded authorial intent. It begins with five points on sexual relations and their outcome, which condense Pozdnyshev's argument. Then, even more radically, it explicates Christ's teaching on sexual morality (notably the epigraph verses) counter to the rulings of the Church. As Ernest Simmons (1960: 128) sums up, the "Afterword" displays the basic agreement between creator and creature, except that Tolstoy's "idealistic but logically developed thought" varies from "the extravagant conviction of the deranged Pozdnyshev." In effect, Simmons qualifies the spokesman's reliability on the level of presentation alone.

The Sequel's genetic evidence is reinforced by further data about the underlying drive. The story's eight earlier versions and the work in progress on *What Is Art?*, as well as the writer's diary and correspondence, show how Tolstoy gradually shaped his unconventional ideology along with the communicative and rhetorical strategy (Møller 1988: 1–38, 181–99). Such evidence would appear to confirm what the finished novella implies: that the reliability hypothesis best explains an array of puzzling textual features. Why the New Testament epigraph? Why the debate prior to Pozdnyshev's monologue, including the given debaters, traits, ideologies, ironies, undignified withdrawal? What is the function of Beethoven's *Sonata*? Why the inside addressee, complete with his early wonder and changing attitude? Why assign the overall narration to this anonymous figure rather than to Pozdnyshev? And, of course, why did Tolstoy, contrary to his habit, append a "Sequel," and to this like-minded effect?

So the hypothesis that the author endows a deviant speaker with reliability looks the likeliest in context because it provides the fullest and most interconnected answers: even the oddest parts make joint sense within a rhetorical strategy devised to create a bridge between Tolstoy's ideological representative and the presumable beliefs of the common reader.[3]

Yet the controversy over *The Kreutzer Sonata* still goes on; and it will, I suspect, persist in face of the case made here for reliability by appeal to overall difficult coherence. J. M. Coetzee comments on the text's "lack of armament against other, unauthorized readings, other truths" (1985: 204). Reviewing "the critical tradition," Isenberg concludes that "from a narratological perspective, the most remarkable thing about 'The Kreutzer Sonata' is its power to evoke readings against its own grain" (1993: 107). Both scholars destabilize the reliability of the protagonist and the control of his author alike. But then, my interest in the conflicting interpretations is the theoretical basis that they share with the reliable-mediator alternative. Even diametrically opposed readings of speaker vis-à-vis author operate, knowingly or otherwise, by the same deeper principle, namely, accounting for ostensible discordance by reference to an appropriate integration mechanism.

Opposing the Reliable Mediator: The Perspectival Hypothesis Inverted

One line of counterreading deems Pozdnyshev an unreliable communicator. Its exponents (predictably, on my account of unreliability) detect tensions among the data that seem unproblematic or authorized to the first set of readers. For Keith Ellis, "the moralizing in the novel or the statement of purpose in the 'Afterword'... cannot fully account for the action"; and "interpretation... may be detrimentally restricted by stated authorial purpose" (1971: 892). Isenberg finds a "conflict between surface meaning and latent significance," namely, "between the theory of gender proposed by the text and the vision of gender performed by it" (1993: 93).

For comparison with the above argument for reliability, it is worth noting what kinds of tensions these inverters allege or emphasize and what kinds get downgraded or passed over altogether. Ellis thus ignores the epigraph, barely mentions the opening discussion as "setting," and regards the anonymous frame-narrator as an "attentive though unobtrusive audience," who "limits his comments to occasional requests for clarification" and is "properly uncritical" (1971: 893, 894).[4]

Instead, the argument for unreliability focuses on the problematic speaker and speech. As Coetzee rightly observes, his "agitation," "funny little sounds," odd ideas, and odious crime produce a bad impression from the very start, contributing to an *expectation* of an unreliable narrator, one whom "we are all too easily able to read... *against* himself" (Coetzee 1985: 196; emphasis in original). The monologist's character thus becomes both a cause and a signal of unreliability, ironically targeted by the implied communication. Accordingly, others highlight Pozdnyshev's jealousy ("once its distorting presence is noticed we cannot wholly trust the narrator's judgments" [Ellis 1971: 898]); still others dwell on his mental disorder ("a man who sees the phallus everywhere" [Coetzee 1985: 198]; others see him as a latent homosexual who is sexually drawn to his wife's lover [Isenberg 1993: 96–9]); and so forth.

As a reflex of his psychological problems, many have predictably found (or imagined) Pozdnyshev's theory to be distorted or marred by contradictions. Those found between "theory" and "vision" of gender, "moralizing" and "action," have specific equivalents. For instance, at one point he defines sex as an acquired, artificial habit; at another, as an unconscious bestiality (Isenberg 1993: 92–3). Or, as Ellis (1971) suggests, he "blames, first men for pursuing women, and then women for capturing husbands." Again, "[i]n attacking women's subjection to men's sexual pleasure he gives a strong and sensitive defense of women's rights, but criticizing elsewhere their cunning, he declares that 'the result of all this is the ascendancy of women, from which the whole world is suffering.'" He oscillates between the insistence that every marriage leads to divorce, suicide, and murder and the opposite claim that the horror of his deed marks his own experience as unique. Further, the perpetrator's "untidy generalizations . . . may well be interpreted as a desperate attempt at rationalizing the act" (Ellis 1971: 894–6). Symptoms of his unacknowledged guilt-complex are detected, for instance, in his misunderstanding of the lawyer's reference to "critical moments in married life" as an allusion to his own crime (Gustafson, in Isenberg 1993: 166, n.23). In Ellis's account, such incongruities are explicitly reconciled via a psychopathology beyond Pozdnyshev's rational control: "by regarding jealousy as the motivating force in *The Kreutzer Sonata* and antithesis as the dominant stylistic trait[,] an interpretation is offered that would seem to reveal the novel's unity and coherence" (Ellis 1971: 899). So the search for a principle of integration drives this reading type as well – but away from reliability. Accepting neither the protagonist's existential claim (the prevalence of the marriage crisis), nor his drastic solution, the unreliability hypothesis (over)-focuses and subjectivizes the monologue's infelicities. Their repatterning ensues from the inverted perspective: both the given account of past events and the scheme for a reform are diagnosed as symptoms of delusion. In turn, the workings of the wife-killer's mind become the central object of implied, ironic interest. The text's norms and designs are supposedly concerned not with moral ideology (as transmitted by an unusual spokesman) but with the speaker's ongoing psychopathology.

Opposing Authorial Intention or Composition: The Genetic Alternative

Yet the problematic ideology, not surprisingly, has given rise to a third, mainly genetic, set of readings. Thereby, tensions and failures are again diagnosed in the text, yet now found unresolvable within its own coordinates, and so blamed on the author himself. The shift of responsibility from the explicit to the implicit communicator intersects not just (as in the reliable vs. unreliable polarizing of the narrator) with an alternative model of interpretation, but with questions of evaluation and canonicity. Here are some variants.

1 Some readers refuse to become Tolstoy's implied audience because of their violent antagonism to his proposed ideology in the *Sonata* – whether his iconoclastic religion or his attitude to women. On either issue, the clash arises not inside the text but between the advocated thesis and a reader's imported counterthesis. The issue and the import favored often express group interests: they jointly oppose

the thesis from diverse, even mutually hostile, viewpoints. Thus the acrimonious responses of contemporary church dignitaries (in Møller 1988: 145–62) as against the "counter-literature" written as polemic parallel to the *Sonata* (Møller 1988: 163–80) or the historical and cultural anachronism of later feminist attacks on Tolstoy (reviewed by Mandelker 1993: 15–57).[5]

2 More frequently, readers acknowledge the text's ideological and didactic center of interest, and take the monologist's reliability as normative. Yet they find inconsistencies within the proposed ideology (say, women changing roles between victim and pursuer; the spirit/body split; the blindness to scientific facts). Since they find no distance between author and spokesman, they blame the author for the tensions. Some have indeed banished the *Sonata* from their Tolstoy canon, as "a grossly imperfect work" (Davie 1971: 326), which "shows the worst side of Tolstoy" (Spence 1961: 227).[6] Others have ingeniously differentiated the artist from the ideologist as two conflicting Tolstoyan personalities. One "strong tradition" would have Tolstoy "during the creative process ... split into" these "personalities, each attempting to dupe the other" and applauds "when the artist, as the more sympathetic of the two, comes out the winner" (Møller 1988: 17).

Elsewhere the split migrates to the text's readings, differentiated by appeal to its addressees. Thus, after enumerating Pozdnyshev's many failures of fact, interpretation, ideology, and self-scrutiny, Isenberg suggests that readers of the *Sonata* can follow Tolstoy's directive and echo the "three kinds of responses" voiced by his "primary listener": either absolving the protagonist, or taking his lesson to heart, or, at least, being "seduced" by his tale without analyzing "its disruptions of meaning." But this, for Isenberg, is the response of the "submissive" reader who "cave[s] in" on the model of the equally submissive frame narrator. Instead,

> the resisting reader who accepts the work's surface intentions as the only possible guide ... may well end up pronouncing it a tendentious failure – or the reader may recognize his or her stake in making it work as a story, not as received wisdom, even if this means rejecting its homiletic aims and making Tolstoy of the devil's party without his knowing it.
>
> (Isenberg 1993: 107)

In fact, then, Isenberg offers here three principled lines of reading, roughly corresponding to the three groups of actual readers, and divided among the relevant integration mechanisms. The reliable alternative (itself threefold) is possible, he maintains, but only for those who accept Tolstoy's homily and dictate, closing their eyes to the many confusions in the text. Those alive and resistant to the text's incongruities, vis-à-vis the author's extratextual intentions, end up with a genetic reading, and pronounce the *Sonata* "a tendentious failure." At best, they will save the text by "rejecting its homiletic aims" in favor of a storied, ironic reading, counter to the writer's and presumably the narrator's viewpoint.

As this example illustrates, quite a few of the tensions adduced by a genetic approach coincide with those discovered or imagined or magnified by advocates of the perspectival hypothesis – except that, on the genetic reading, they point to the failure of the author instead of his mediator. It's the ideology and generalizations (on women, marriage, physicians, etc.) that are most often attacked for their factual and logical deficiencies, up to self-contradiction. But sometimes the genetic drive corresponds to the unreliability hypothesis in uncovering a psychopathology: now again Tolstoy's own, or his own as well as the character's, and beyond the artist/ideologue split.

3   For such readers, Pozdnyshev's oddities reflect the psychological (even psychotic) disturbances of his creator. So Daniel Rancour-Laferriere, in *Tolstoy on the Couch* (1998), traces Pozdnyshev's mental disorders (above all, his misogyny) to Tolstoyan traumas, as far back as the loss of his mother at the age of two. This analyst even denies that Pozdnyshev's words on marriage are representative but judges them "self-oriented, that is, narcissistic" (p. 62). Nor is the epigraph, for him, quoted "to propagandize Christianity, but to express" Tolstoy's personal beliefs (p. 76). Such a reading, by the usual genetic logic, locates unity (but not coherence) somewhere outside the text, namely, in the unbalanced personality of the author.

4   Some genetic judgments are transformed into or linked with textually coherent (and hence authorized – reliable or unreliable) readings. Thus Emmanuel Velikovsky declares that "the jealous murderer Pozdnishef is presented as a homosexual who did not know his own nature; even the author, Tolstoy, failed to realize this" (1937: 18). Still, Tolstoy is congratulated throughout on his wonderful, if unconscious, "intuition" in dramatizing repressed homosexuality, and various of Pozdnyshev's lapses allegedly compare with the behavior of a psychotherapist's real patients. So, judged by Freudian insight or (self-)knowledge, the author ultimately comes out in a positive light, while the diagnosed hero is exposed in his unreliability. The publication of this essay in the *Psychoanalytic Review* underscores the external criteria for evaluating the text's success.[7]

From a literary viewpoint, Coetzee arrives at another balance between perspectival and genetic reading. To begin with, Coetzee juxtaposes the various oddities, culminating in the murder, that imply Pozdnyshev's unreliability with various signals of his reliability. The notable contribution to the latter hypothesis is the argument from genre: that Tolstoy did not dramatize Pozdnyshev's (debatable) conversion, because he was more interested in advocating the truth than in the psychic experience of its revelation. Given this downgrading of psychology, we need to follow the lead of the anonymous narrator who, as listener, supports the protagonist's version of the truth by his "silence" (sic) throughout the confession (Coetzee 1985: 204).

So far, Coetzee's analysis is another variant of the reliability hypothesis. But then he identifies a genetic oddity: why did the author of *Anna Karenina*, with his brilliant psychological insight, write "so naïve and simple-minded a book, in which the truth that the truth-teller tells emerges as a bald series of dicta" (1985: 231)? Coetzee's answer links the author's peculiar character and history with the peculiarities of our story. First, he reminds us, even the earlier Tolstoy ranked truth above the dramatic process of illumination. More importantly, though still able to make this text psychologically "richer" or "deeper," "by making it ambiguous," he has lost interest in this "machinery." Coetzee therefore ends with a speculation on the genetic process of *The Kreutzer Sonata*: "Tolstoy's impatience with the novelistic motions" could have led to his "(rash?) decision to *set down the truth*, finally, as though after a lifetime of exploring one had acquired the credentials, amassed the authority, to do so" (p. 232; emphasis in original). This genetic hypothesis supplies an answer to yet another problem, namely, that the *Sonata* is open not only to Tolstoy's intended (reliable-narrator) reading but to counterreadings, including the unreliability hypothesis. Tolstoy's "lack of armament against other, unauthorized readings" (p. 204) would thus signify his ideological rejection of the well-made tale along with the larger one of art as a goal.[8]

I will now leave aside further variants that reinforce the point. Owing to this diversity of interpretations, and of elements cited for and/or against, *The Kreutzer Sonata* offers an effective test case of my theoretical framework. Its exemplarity largely springs from the fact that no reading is strong enough, nor any worldview consensual enough, to decide the issue in accounting for all major problems. Less contested texts will be distributed along fewer, simpler, or more stable lines among the various integration mechanisms that it exemplifies. However, amid the shift from one perspectival reading (Pozdnyshev is reliable) to its opposite (he is unreliable) or even to a genetic failure, both the logic of integration as such and the principled power structure of the text (author above mediating narrator, Pozdnyshev the creature of Tolstoy) remain in force. Whatever the final diagnosis, the interpretation necessarily concerns (at least) two discourse-contexts: one explicit and freely problematic, the other implicit and determinative for better or worse. Unlike real-life communication, a fictive speaker's reliability is determined neither by some objective truth (of fact or idea) or poetic rule ("artistry"), nor on the basis of equality (of subjects, evidence, attitudes), but in relation, concordant or conflictual, to the hypothesized norms and goals of the author.

NOTES

1   Andrea Dworkin is so much in agreement with Tolstoy on the problem's universality, that she opens her feminist book on *Intercourse* with a discussion of this tale (1987: 3–20). Felman (1997) suggests the ongoing relevance of the Tolstoy/Pozdnyshev analysis of gender relations, opposing Pozdnyshev's laudable con-

fession of guilt with O. J. Simpson's plea of not guilty.

2   Contrast Isenberg's (1993: 107) threefold division of those inside responses: the confessor's absolving function; the sermon audience's taking the lesson to heart and disseminating it; the model reader seduced by the tale without

noticing its inner tensions. For more on this reading, see below.

3 Other critics who endorse the reliable reading differ mainly concerning the relevant normative scale. For example, Spence affirms that nowhere is "Pozdnyshev's theory...contradicted" by the later Tolstoy, being "the logical outcome of the despairing passages of the *Confession*" (Spence 1963: 161–2). For Herman, the mystery that torments both author and narrator is "the problem of art's likeness to adultery" (Herman 1997: 17); etc.

4 Likewise, Christian (1969: 231), Bayley (1966: 283–4), Herman (1997: 34) or Coetzee (1985: 204) either ignore or belittle the function of the inside addressee.

5 Of particular "counter-literary" interest is the story by Countess Tolstoy, which retells the murder plot from the wife's viewpoint, in a double sense. Among modern feminists, Dworkin is surprisingly ambivalent about this "androcentric" tale, "crazed with misogyny and insight." Her solution is in effect antigenetic, differentiating Tolstoy's art ("he articulates with almost prophetic brilliance the elements that combine to make and keep women inferior") from his own revolting behavior to his wife (Dworkin 1988: 4, 19). She thus accepts the implied author, concedes reliability to his homicidal speaker – no-sex program included – and repudiates the sexual beast who wrote the text.

6 Anton Chekhov first applauded the *Sonata* for its art, but particularly because "it is extremely thought-provoking," even when it fluctuates between "true" and "ridiculous" points (Chekhov 1971: 97). But he changed his mind after reading the "Sequel," pronouncing Tolstoy's philosophy stupid, arrogant, and ignorant (Chekhov 1971: 98); see Møller's fine chapter on his critical and literary response (Møller 1998: 208–58).

7 Whereas Velikovsky compliments Tolstoy's intuition, Isenberg, with his very similar diagnosis of the hero's psychopathology, emphasizes the tension between the writer's intended reliable mediator and the homily-resisting or unreliable alternative.

8 Recall Tolstoy, as quoted in Møller, on the fuss made about the tale's artistry, to which he has actually given "just enough room for the terrible truth to become visible" (Møller 1988: 10). See also Herman (1997: 32, 34–6).

References and Further Reading

Bayley, J. (1966). *Tolstoy and the Novel*. London: Chatto & Windus.

Booth, W. C. (1961). *The Rhetoric of Fiction*. Chicago: University of Chicago Press.

Chekhov, A. (1971). From *Selected Letters*. In Henry Gifford (ed.), *Leo Tolstoy: A Critical Anthology*, trans. S. Lederer (pp. 97–8). Harmondsworth, UK: Penguin.

Christian, R. F. (1969). *Tolstoy: A Critical Introduction*. Cambridge, UK: Cambridge University Press.

Coetzee, J. M. (1985). "Confession and Double Thoughts: Tolstoy, Rousseau, Dostoevsky," *Comparative Literature* 37, 193–232.

Davie, D. (1971). "The Kreutzer Sonata." In H. Gifford (ed.), *Leo Tolstoy: A Critical Anthology* (pp. 326–34). Harmondsworth, UK: Penguin.

Dworkin, A. (1987). *Intercourse*. New York: Free Press.

Ellis, K. (1971). "Ambiguity and Point of View in Some Novelistic Representations of Jealousy." *Modern Language Notes* 86(6), 891–909.

Felman, S. (1997). "Forms of Judicial Blindness, or the Evidence of What Cannot Be Seen." *Critical Inquiry* 23, 738–88.

Herman, D. (1997). "Stricken by Infection: Art and Adultery in *Anna Karenina* and Kreutzer Sonata." *Slavic Review* 56(1), 15–36.

Isenberg, C. (1993). *Telling Silence: Russian Frame Narratives of Renunciation*. Evanston, IL: Northwestern University Press.

Mandelker, A. (1993). *Framing Anna Karenina: Tolstoy, the Woman Question, and the Victorian Novel*. Columbus: Ohio State University Press.

Møller, P. U. (1988). *Postlude to the Kreutzer Sonata: Tolstoj and the Debate on Sexual Morality in Russian Literature in the 1890s*, trans. J. Kendal. Leiden, Netherlands: Brill.

Rancour-Laferriere, D. (1998). *Tolstoy on the Couch: Misogyny, Masochism and the Absent Mother*. New York: New York University Press.

Simmons, E. J. (1960). *Leo Tolstoy: The Years of Maturity 1880–1910*, vol. II. New York: Vintage Books.

Spence, G. W. (1961). "Tolstoy's Dualism." *Russian Review* 20(3), 217–31.

Spence, G. W. (1963). "Suicide and Sacrifice in Tolstoy's Ethics." *Russian Review* 22(2), 157–67.

Sternberg, M. (1978). *Expositional Modes and Temporal Ordering in Fiction*. Baltimore, MD: Johns Hopkins University Press.

Sternberg, M. (1983). "Mimesis and Motivation: The Two Faces of Fictional Coherence." In J. Strelka (ed.), *Literary Criticism and Philosophy* (pp. 145–88). University Park: Pennsylvania State University Press.

Sternberg, M. (2001). "Factives and Perspectives: Making Sense of Presupposition as Exemplary Inference." *Poetics Today* 22, 129–244.

Tolstoy, L. N. (1929). "Sequel to the Kreutzer Sonata," trans. A. Maude. In *Master and Man, The Kreutzer Sonata, Dramas* (pp. 155–70). New York: Charles Scribner's Sons.

Tolstoy, L. (1960). "Appendix to *The Kreutzer Sonata*." In *Great Short Works of Leo Tolstoy*, trans. L. and A. Maude (pp. 429–49). New York: Harper & Row.

Tolstoy, L. ([1891] 1963). "The Kreutzer Sonata," trans. M. Wettlin. In *Six Short Masterpieces by Tolstoy* (pp. 284–369). New York: Dell.

Velikovsky, I. (1937). "Tolstoy's Kreutzer Sonata and Unconscious Homosexuality." *Psychoanalytic Review* 24, 18–25.

Yacobi, T. (1981). "Fictional Reliability as a Communicative Problem." *Poetics Today* 2, 113–26.

Yacobi, T. (1987). "Narrative and Normative Pattern: On Interpreting Fiction." *Journal of Literary Studies* 3, 18–41.

Yacobi, T. (2001). "Package-Deals in Fictional Narrative: The Case of the Narrator's (Un)Reliability." *Narrative* 9, 223–9.

7

Henry James and "Focalization," or Why James Loves Gyp

J. Hillis Miller

Henry James's prefaces to the New York Edition of his novels and tales develop many wonderful narratological concepts, concepts inexhaustible for meditation. One of these is the proposition that limitation to a single "center of consciousness," in works of fiction, is a basic requisite of good form. It is the best way to avoid producing what James, in the preface to *The Tragic Muse*, disdainfully called "large loose baggy monsters" (James 1971–9, vol. 7: x). Examples James gives are *War and Peace*, *Les Trois Mousquetaires*, and *The Newcomes*. James opposed such monsters to "a deep-breathing economy and an organic form," in which he said he "delighted" (ibid.). James's inordinate imagination and his tendency to "sprawl" and to create misplaced middles (James, 1971–9, vol. 26: 299, vol. 7: xi-xii, xxi) made some principle of limitation especially necessary for him. The first half of James's *The Golden Bowl* is, for the most part, limited to the Prince's consciousness of things and people, while the second half makes Maggie the center of consciousness. *The Ambassadors* is limited, with magnificent consistency, to Strether's "point of view." It can be argued, of course, that the real "center of consciousness" in these novels is the encompassing "omniscient narrator" who presents through free indirect discourse the way things looked to Prince Amerigo, to Maggie, or to Strether. One of James's dominant linguistic strategies is not interior monologue but free indirect discourse, the presentation, in the narrator's past-tense language, of the present-tense language of the character, or, sometimes, of the character's unworded interiority. That narrator might be defined as a consciousness of the consciousness of others. The narrator is almost a collective or community consciousness, if indeed anything like a community is presupposed in James's fiction.

Other names for "center of consciousness" are the now old-fashioned term "point of view" and, in subtly elaborated recent narratological theory, "focalization." None of these terms is innocent. Each in one way or another begs the question it is meant to clarify. All three, for example, evade the fact that novels are made of words. They tend to imply either that a novel is a matter of "looking" or that it is made of "consciousnesses." The term "focalization" is drawn from optics. Its figurative base does not differ from "point of view," except that it defines "point of view" not as a matter of looking from a certain position, but rather as a matter of getting things in focus when looking through some device or other, such as a telescope, binoculars, a microscope, or a mind/body compound considered as a focalizing apparatus. Such terms elide the way the essential mode of existence of any literary fictional work is linguistic through and through. There ain't nothing there but words.

Another way to put this is to say that though such terms as "center of conscious-ness," "point of view," or "focalization" may be essential to present-day narrative theory, they are figures of speech. No consciousness as such exists in any novel, only the representation of consciousness in words. No looking or bringing into focus exists in any novel, only the virtual phantasm of these as expressed in words. This is not a trivial distinction. The term "free indirect discourse," on the contrary, is a genuinely linguistic term.

Most narratologists of course know all this. In spite of sometimes seeming to take more delight in subtle refinements of distinction among various forms of "focaliza-tion" than in demonstrating how these formal features are related to meaning, narratologists, for the most part, know that their distinctions are not useful in themselves. They are useful only if they lead to better readings or to better teachings of literary works. Narratological distinctions and refinements are not valuable in themselves, as "science." At least they are not valuable in quite the same way as decoding the human genome is valuable. The latter not only finds out new facts – those facts are also socially useful. They lead to new medicines and to new cures for diseases. Narratological distinctions, unlike scientific discoveries, are not facts about the external world. They are disciplinary artifacts concocted for heuristic purpose to allow talk about certain features of human language. Narratological distinctions are useful primarily as aids to better reading, which *is* socially useful. As Henry James understood, form is meaning. Sticking to the formal principles he has chosen for *The Awkward Age*, James says in the preface to that novel, "helps us ever so happily to see the grave distinction between substance and form in a really wrought work of art signally break down" (James 1971–9, vol. 9: xxi).[1] All good reading is therefore formalist reading.

In this essay I want to demonstrate this "breaking down" of the distinction between form and substance by reading, at least partially, a quite anomalous work by James, *The Awkward Age* (1899). This work is anomalous, that is, if we assume that for James the principle that there must be a "center of consciousness" in order to achieve economy of form was a universal law. The oddness, or lawlessness, of *The Awkward Age* is that it eschews both the omniscient narrator and, almost entirely, what he calls in the preface "going behind" (p. xvii) the objective presentation of the characters. This novel has neither an omniscient narrator in the usual sense nor, for the most part, any centers of consciousness or points of view or focalizations in the minds and feelings of the characters. The novel describes objectively what the characters said and did, how they looked, their clothes, faces, gestures, and other behavior, the things with which they have surrounded themselves. The reader must from this "superficial" or manifest evidence figure out what is going on behind the objective signs. Additional resources are cross-references, repetitions, allusions, echoes, and the like. These link one scene or utterance in the novel to others. Gérard Genette ([1972] 1980) identifies this technique as "external focalization," reading it as evidence that the narrator knows less than the characters know. Genette's example is Dashiell Hammett (p. 190). In James's case, however, the reader senses that the narrator knows all that is going on in the characters' minds and could reveal it if he would. The evidence is those few places where the narrator does enter the mind of a character, especially Vanderbank's mind in scenes early in the novel.

James, in the preface, is quite specific about his procedures. What he says comes in the context of defending his scrupulous obedience, in *The Awkward Age*, to the laws of a stage play. In such a work, he says, he can "escape poverty" and attain "beauty," "*even though* the references in one's action can only be, with intensity, to things exactly on the same plane of exhibition with themselves" (p. xx). In this novel, he goes on to say, there are no obnoxious "loose ends," that obtrude like "the dangle of a snippet of silk or wool on the right side of a tapestry. We are shut up wholly to cross-relations, relations all within the action itself, no part of which is related to anything but some other part – save of course by the relation of the total to life" (ibid.). James remains true here to the general principles, endorsed throughout all the prefaces, of a mimetic realism that values literature for its representational value, its imitation of real life. That relation, however, is not to be measured by bits and parts, but by "the relation of the total to life." The total in itself, however, draws its intrinsic meaning from cross-relations, not from the referential value of the parts. In Saussure's theory of language, in an analogous way, words or phonemes draw their meanings not from reference, but from their differential relation to one another. In *The Awkward Age* these elements are all "exactly on the same plane of exhibition." They all obey the law that only what a sharp onlooker would have seen and heard can be "exhibited," that is, brought into the open. The rest remains hidden, secret.

Why in the world does James in this case avoid just those narrative techniques that are usually his most powerful tools, for example in the three great masterpieces that followed just a few years after *The Awkward Age*, that is, *The Ambassadors, The Wings of the Dove*, and *The Golden Bowl*? If I can answer that question I may be able to exemplify what it means to say that form is meaning, or that the distinction between substance and form signally breaks down in a "really wrought work of art."

First I must identify the models James claims, in the preface, that he followed in *The Awkward Age*. One is the stage play. In the preface James tells the reader, somewhat ruefully and ironically, how he presented to the editors of *Harper's Weekly*, where the novel first appeared "during the Autumn of 1898 and the first weeks of winter" (p. xv), a diagram on a sheet of paper of his plan for the novel. The comedy is that he now suspects the editors did not have the slightest idea what he was talking about:

I remember that in sketching my project for the conductors of the periodical I have named I drew on a sheet of paper – and possibly with an effect of the cabalistic, it now comes over me, that even anxious amplification may have but vainly attenuated – the neat figure of a circle consisting of a number of small rounds disposed at an equal distance about a central object. The central object was my situation, my subject in itself, to which the thing would owe its title, and the small rounds represented so many distinct lamps, as I liked to call them, the function of each of which would be to light with due intensity one of its aspects. I had divided it, didn't they see? into aspects – uncanny as that little term might sound (though not for a moment did I suggest we should use it for the public), and by that sign we would conquer. [...]

Each of my "lamps" would be the light of a single "social occasion" in the history and intercourse of the characters concerned, and would bring out to the full the latent color of the scene in question and cause it to illustrate, to the last drop, its bearing on my theme. I reveled in this notion of the Occasion as a thing by itself, really and completely a scenic thing, and could scarce name it, while crouching amid the thick arcana of my plan, with a large enough O.

(pp. xvi-xvii)

The reader will note that the "lamps" here are not centers of consciousness, but objectively presented social scenes, the give and take of conversation in a drawing room.

It might appear at first that James is presenting the reader with another exclusively visual figure for the procedures of the novelist, another figure like "focalization" or "point of view." A careful reading, however, shows that matters are not quite so simple. James's figure is presented overtly, up front, as a figure, a trope, and an "arcane," "cabalistic," or "uncanny" one at that. What is cabalistic, arcane, or uncanny about it? These terms refer to a code for something secret and to the experience of something spooky that nevertheless seems somehow familiar, something in short, in Freud's term for uncanny, *"unheimlich."* The mystery lies in the impossibility of naming, in so many words, the "central object," his "situation." That central object is uncanny because it appears only in ghosts or revenants, doubles of itself, never in itself or as itself. James nowhere says what he put down, as a picture of this central object, on his mystic sheet of paper, over which he "crouched" like some medieval mage. Was it a point, or another circle, or the drawing of some object or other? He does not say. He does not say because he cannot say. He can only shine lamps on the object and reveal its "aspects" one by one through that method. The rhetorical label for this procedure, that is, for the tropological naming of something that does not have a literal name, is "catachresis." Each of James's "Occasions" are catachreses for an unnamed central object, the situation, which can be named in no other way.

To call each "Occasion" a "lamp" to "light with due intensity one of its aspects" differs fundamentally, moreover, from the figure of "focalization." The latter implies that the object of the narration is there to be seen. It is just a matter of getting it into focus. James's figure of "Occasions" that illuminate a central object, on the contrary, implies that the object is in the dark, to some degree permanently in the dark. It, or rather just one of its "aspects," can only be brought into the light by way of a given "Occasion." The latter functions performatively to expose it, or, rather, to expose one of its aspects. "Occasion": the word names something that happens or befalls, a fortuitous event. The word comes from Latin *occidere* (past participle *occasus*), to fall down. The difference between a lamp and a focalizer is analogous to Meyer Abrams's ([1953] 1971) famous distinction between the mirror and the lamp. Abrams set the mirror of classical theories of mimesis against the quasi-constitutive force of poetic language. The latter is figured in romantic theories as a lamp.

What justifies my implicit claim, when I speak of catachreses, that these Occasions are acts of language figured by the optical images James uses, not literally matters of seeing at all? The answer is that these Occasions are, according to James's strict formal or generic rule in this novel, made of conversational exchanges in some social scene. Each Occasion brings two or more of the chief characters together in talk, with a minimum of stage directions. A given "lamp" illuminating some aspect of the central situation is made up almost exclusively of what the characters say, plus their gestures and bodily behavior as reported by the narrator. The Occasion is made, that is, of what a hovering, invisible spectator might have seen or heard, especially heard.

A leitmotif of *The Awkward Age* occurs in sentences like the following: "As the reflection of her tone might have been caught by an observer in Vanderbank's face it was in all probability caught by his interlocutress [Nanda], who superficially, however, need have recognized there – what was all she showed – but the right manner of waiting for dinner" (p. 389; see also, among other examples, pp. 148, 238, 269, 400, 424, 449, 514, 535–6). David Herman, in terms that are perhaps a little unnecessarily barbarous or even misleading, calls this "direct hypothetical focalization" or the use of a "counterfactual focalizer" (Herman 1994: 237). He means by this that no real witness existed. This is true enough if we imagine the events as having really taken place, but of course the whole story is "counterfactual" in the sense that it precisely did not take place. It exists only in the words for it. The hypothetical witness is the narrator as surrogate for the reader. The latter is imagined to be in the situation of an audience-member carefully watching a stage play. Such a spectator is limited, in the evidence for his or her interpretation, to what the actors say and how they behave and look.

That this was James's deliberate strategy in this novel, and that he was aware that it differed markedly from his normal procedure, is confirmed by what follows the passage in the preface about the uncanny little circles arranged in a cabalistic circle around a mysterious central object. Here James says explicitly that his model was the stage play:

The beauty of the conception was in this approximation of the respective divisions of my form to the successive Acts of a Play – as to which it was more than ever a case for charmed capitals.[2] The divine distinction of the act of a play – and a greater than any other it easily succeeds in arriving at – was, I reasoned, its special, its guarded objectivity. This objectivity, in turn, when achieving its ideal, came from the imposed absence of that "going behind," to compass explanations and amplifications, to drag out odds and ends from the "mere" storyteller's great property-shop of aids to illusion: a resource under denial of which it was equally perplexing and delightful, for a change, to proceed. Everything, for that matter, becomes interesting from the moment it has closely to consider, for full effect positively to bestride, the law of its kind. "Kinds" are the very life of literature, and truth and strength come from the complete recognition of them, from abounding to the utmost in their respective senses and sinking deep into their consistency. I myself have scarcely to plead the cause of "going behind," which is right and beautiful and fruitful in its place and order; but as the confusion of kinds is the inelegance of letters and the stultification of values, so to renounce that line utterly and do something quite different instead may become in another connection the true course and the vehicle of effect.

(p. xvii)

This seems clear enough, but just why does James renounce "going behind"? Why does he give up his special line, give up what he is famous for doing? Why does he attempt to write a novel that is as much as possible like a stage play, or, one might say, is like the report of an imaginary play as if seen by a clever spectator? Why does this "form" seem to James especially appropriate for this particular "substance," this "central object," this "situation," this "subject in itself," this "theme"? The answer, though one hopes this is not the case, may be that no particular consonance between form and substance, in this instance, exists. James just wanted to try something different for a change. The novel could have been written as *The Portrait of a Lady* or *The Golden Bowl* or *The Ambassadors* is written. James just decided to experiment with dramatic or scenic form. Once he had decided to do that, an aesthetico-moral obligation not to confuse kinds required that he be strictly consistent. Moreover, one might argue, James was still feeling angry and humiliated by the failure in 1895 of his stage play, *Guy Domville*. The audience hissed the play and hissed James off the stage when he appeared there after the curtain. He was especially humiliated because, at the moment James's play failed, Oscar Wilde's *An Ideal Husband* was a resounding success in another nearby London theater. The paragraphs in the preface that follow the passage I have just quoted are, by way of a discussion of Dumas and Ibsen (Wilde of course is not mentioned), an angry and defensive attack on the British play-going public as having no more than "infantine intelligence" (p. xviii). I'll show the world, James may secretly have thought, that I can do something of the stage play "kind," though in my own métier, the novel. I'll go Wilde – who is a scandalous person in any case – one better after all.

The other model James claims to have followed suggests, however, that some other deeper reason may have dictated adoption of dramatic form in *The Awkward Age*. Though no one seems to have noticed, says James, he was copying the procedures of "the ingenious and inexhaustible, the charming philosophic 'Gyp'" (p. xii). Who in the world was Gyp? Many specialists in modern French literature have never heard of her, as I have found out by asking around. Nor have critics of *The Awkward Age* often followed up this precious clue. "Gyp" was the pseudonym of a nineteenth- and twentieth-century French writer with the almost unbelievable name, so resonant of the French Revolution, of Sibylle Gabrielle Marie Antoinette Riqueti de Mirabeau, Comtesse de Martel de Janville (1849–1932). I kid you not! Gyp was the author of many novels, plays, and other works. Friedrich Nietzsche, of all people, also greatly admired her. He mentions her in *Ecce Homo* as a model writer. What Nietzsche admired especially was the wonderful economy and presto tempo of Gyp's novels, along with the limpidity of her idiomatic French. I too admire these. A shared admiration for Gyp is about the only overt connection between James and Nietzsche that I know of.

That "happiest of forms," of which Gyp was mistress, was the use of dialogue in novels that dispensed almost altogether with narrative comment or "going behind." Gyp often indicates the speaker simply by giving the character's name, accompanied by "said," for example "Chiffon said."

This "Gyp taint" of *The Awkward Age*, as James calls it (p. xiv) may suggest that the dramatic form James chose for it is appropriate because the novel is somehow in substance as well as in form like Gyp's novels, for example *Le mariage de Chiffon* (1894). This novel has parallels with *The Awkward Age*, and James may possibly have read it in its 1895 edition.

Just what was that "substance," the "situation," the "subject" of *The Awkward Age*? James explains in the preface that the focus is on what happens when a young girl of marriageable age is, at that particular "awkward" moment in English social history, first brought downstairs to hear the talk of adults. The term "the awkward age" refers not only to a moment of adolescence, but also to the historical moment of transition that is the novel's setting. "The awkward age" is another name for "le fin de siècle."

What is awkward about the awkward age seems almost ludicrous to present-day readers. An act of the historical imagination is required to take it seriously. Girls were still at that time supposed (in what must always have been something of a fiction) to go to their marriage beds totally ignorant of the facts of sex. At the same time, "talk," as James calls it, in middle- and upper-class drawing rooms was becoming freer and freer. Young girls were more and more allowed to hear that talk. The talk among Mrs Brookenham's "set" is almost entirely focused on speculation about the sexual misdeeds of themselves or of people they know. Impasse! Aporia! Social behavior contradicted old-fashioned assumptions about necessary virginity of mind as well as of body in unmarried girls of marriageable age who can hope to get married.

James distinguishes carefully the English situation from the continental or American one. In the United States no such talk occurs, or indeed, in James's view, any talk whatsoever that is at all interesting. In France or Italy such talk occurs, but unmarried young women are carefully sequestered from it. Nanda Brookenham, the heroine of *The Awkward Age*, is brought down too soon and hears all the talk in her mother's drawing room and elsewhere. She spends time, for example, with a newly married friend, Tishy Grendon, who fears her husband is betraying her. Nanda learns all about sex, especially illicit sex. Therefore, though she is wonderfully attractive and intelligent, a little like Gyp's Chiffon, she becomes, in her particular community or "set," unmarriageable. Chiffon, by the way, also knows all about sex and about the sexual misdeeds of her elders, but this does not prevent a happy ending. Chiffon engages herself to her rich "Uncle Marc" at the end of the novel and will presumably live happily ever after.

The central event of *The Awkward Age* is Vanderbank's tacit refusal to marry Nanda Brookenham. This happens even though Mr Longdon, a rich older man from the country, who loved Nanda's grandmother and was refused by her, has promised a fortune to Vanderbank, by way of a dowry to Nanda, if he will marry her. Why does Vanderbank renounce this opportunity? How is his renunciation related to James's choice of what is, for him, such an anomalous form?

I suggest several answers to these questions, all of which may be supported by citations from the text. The text is, after all, all the evidence we have, plus the preface, an entry or two in the Notebooks, and comments in the letters. The latter three may or may not be misleading, deliberately or otherwise. In a letter to Mrs Humphry Ward, James tells her, "I 'go behind' left and right in 'The Princess Casamassima,' 'The Bostonians' . . . just as I do it consistently *never at all* (save for a false and limited *appearance*, here and there, of doing it a *little*, which I haven't time to explain) in 'The Awkward Age'" (James 1974–84, vol. 4: 110). Well, what does the evidence show?

One may begin by saying that if Vanderbank had married Nanda, as Chiffon is to marry Uncle Marc, in Gyp's *Le mariage de Chiffon*, it would have gone against the almost universal law of James's fiction. This law says that renunciation is the final act in almost all his fictions. His novels and stories almost all end with a giving up. This giving up most often, though not always, is of ordinary marriage or heterosexual relations. Strether refuses Maria Gostrey's offer of herself, in *The Ambassadors*. The unnamed narrator of "The Aspern Papers" refuses to marry Miss Tina, though that is the only way he can get the papers. Isabel, in *The Portrait of a Lady*, refuses Caspar Goodwood's offer to free her from her bad marriage to the perfidious Gilbert Osmond, if she will run away from him. Kate Croy refuses to marry Merton Densher, in *The Wings of the Dove*, though she has earlier sworn that she gives herself to him forever. Densher is so much "in love with her [Milly's] memory," as Kate says (James 1976–9, vol. 20: 404), that he will not take Milly's money and then marry Kate, which is the condition Kate sets. The adept reader of James's fiction expects that somehow or other Nanda's passion for Vanderbank will remain unsatisfied. The astute reader will have noted that "renounce" and "sacrifice" are the words James uses in the preface (p. xvii) to define his decision, in this case, not to "go behind." Novelistic form, for James, is always a matter of sacrifice, a matter of cutting out, a matter of renunciation or giving up, in order to avoid sprawl, but he is in *The Awkward Age* sacrificing a procedure especially dear to him and essential to most of his work. This sacrifice is necessary in order to conform to the law that form must match theme.

Why, in this particular case, does the main protagonist decide to renounce? One answer, hinted at by various details in the novel, is that Vanderbank, like James himself, is not the marrying sort. He may be, however covertly and circumspectly this is presented, gay. I note that many of the papers presented at a conference on James in Montreal in May 2004 were within the discipline of "queer theory." They explored the ramifications of James's supposed queerness and of its inscription, however covertly, in his writing. Mrs Brookenham says firmly at one point in *The Awkward Age* that she knows her daughter's love for Vanderbank is doomed to be disappointed: "Poor little darling dear!...he'll never come to the scratch. And to feel that as *I* do...can only be, don't you also see? to want to save her" (p. 91). When the Duchess asks Mrs Brookenham, "What's Mr. Vanderbank looking for?" meaning looking for as a wife, Mrs Brook answers, "Oh, *he*, I'm afraid, poor dear – for nothing at all!" (p. 62). In another place she tells Vanderbank she must protect Nanda from him because, "'...so far as they count on you, they count, my dear Van, on a blank.' Holding him a minute as with the soft, low voice of his fate, she sadly but firmly shook her head. 'You won't do it.'" (p. 295). It may be that Vanderbank is a "blank" because he is incapable of feeling heterosexual desire.

Vanderbank is said repeatedly to inspire a "sacred terror" (e.g., p. 308) in the other characters. This is perhaps because he is outside and above them, in sovereign independence. He has, it may be, no wish or ability to participate in the exchanges of heterosexual love that motivate most of the characters. The warmest and most natural friendships and conversational interchanges in the novel are, it must be said, those between men. They often involve Vanderbank, for example in the opening scene between Mr Longdon and Vanderbank, or in scenes between Vanderbank and Mitchy. A good bit of spontaneous mutual affection, of relaxed warmth, or of what is called "homosociality," appears in these scenes. Vanderbank, by contrast, is always uneasy and embarrassed with both Mrs Brookenham (who wants him for herself) and with Nanda (who also wants him). A more or less explicit reference to "the love that dares not speak its name" appears in one place. When Mr Longdon and Vanderbank are discussing the former's offer of a fortune to Nanda if Vanderbank marries her, Vanderbank at one point says, "Well then, we're worthy of each other. When Greek meets Greek –!" (p. 265). Well, when Greek meets Greek, then comes the Tug of War, as the old adage avers, but "Greek love" was also a code name in the fin de siècle for homosexual love.

This is an exceedingly satisfying answer. It is satisfying because it conforms to a currently fashionable tendency to explain everything in James by way of his covert homosexuality. It is satisfying because, since James had not by any means come out of the closet, he had every reason to keep this explanation for Vanderbank's refusal implicit, hinting at it in ways that "Greeks" would recognize. This would be a happy explanation of why James chose the "Gyp form" for this novel, that is, a form that prohibited him from "going behind" his characters' speech and overt behavior, or from revealing directly their secret desires and distastes. Choosing this form kept Vanderbank (and James himself) safely in the closet, while allowing him to write covertly or secretly about the effects of homosexuality in a set like Mrs Brookenham's. Going for this explanation also satisfies a somewhat prurient desire to "out" James. "See, here is another one!" the triumphant critic exclaims.

Only one problem impedes accepting this tempting proffered satisfaction: so much evidence can be cited from the novel and from outside the novel that goes against this conclusion. Just as strong a case, based on citations, can be made for arguing that Vanderbank is straightforwardly heterosexual, but that he is either too proud, too ethically upright, too unwilling to accept a lifelong indebtedness, to allow himself to be bribed by Mr Longdon, or that he accepts the social code of his day and finds Nanda unacceptable, nice though she is, because she knows too much about sex, knows more and more, until she is, as she says of herself, "a sort of a little drain-pipe with everything flowing through" (p. 358). James's initial notes for the novel, in the *Notebooks*, supports this reading:

> A young man who likes her – wants to take her out of it – feeling how she's exposed,
> etc. . . . The young man hesitates, because he thinks she already knows too much; but all
> the while he hesitates she knows, she learns, more and more. He finds out somehow how
> much she *does* know, and, terrified at it, drops her: all her ignorance, to his sense, is
> gone.
>
> (James 1987: 118)

The "sacred terror" in this note is on Vanderbank's side. He is "terrified" of a young unmarried woman who "knows," though Nanda, in a touching scene, tells Vanderbank that he inspires in her an indefinable fear. "I don't know. Fear is fear," she says when he asks her to specify what she is afraid of in him (p. 212).

Of course James may have changed his mind when he came to write the novel, or he may not have known what he was doing, that is, he may have written a queer novel without intending to do so. The "sacred terror" Vanderbank inspires is, however, when the phrase first appears in the novel, unmistakably defined as a sexual radiance that attracts women's desire. Mitchy turns to Vanderbank, when they are discussing Nanda's infatuation with Vanderbank and refusal of Mitchy, and tells him, "The great thing's the sacred terror. It's you who give *that* out" (p. 308). This, in its context, seems to be saying clearly enough that "sacred terror" refers to Vanderbank's heterosexual charm, not to his covert homosexuality. In the climactic scene between Nanda and Mr Longdon, in which she agrees to join him in his country house, she defends Vanderbank's refusal by making clear, at least in her understanding, what his reasons are, and to make absolutely sure that Mr Longdon understands that she is as Vanderbank thinks she is. Vanderbank's refusal, she argues, is justified: ". . . it's I who am the horrible impossible and who have covered everything else with my own impossibility" (p. 541). "I *am* like that," she says. And in answer to Mr Longdon's "Like what?" she says, "Like what he thinks" (p. 543). What that is, the novel has made clear, is an unmarried young woman who knows too much and therefore cannot utter traditional marriage vows. Her knowledge disables her performative power, except for those anomalous performative speech acts that are uttered within a now "unworked community." Such vows cannot depend on community sanctions for their efficacy. An example of such a speech act is Nanda's promise to live permanently with Mr Longdon.

I conclude that *The Awkward Age* is what is called "undecidable" in meaning. A set of incompatible and contradictory answers to the basic question the narrative raises, in this case the question of why Vanderbank refuses to marry Nanda, can be adduced. Each can be supported by citations, but no decisive evidence is given endorsing a choice among them. According to one reading, Vanderbank's refusal arises from his covert homosexuality. According to the other, it arises from his being too proud to be bribed and from his distaste for Nanda because she knows too much about sex. I claim that a right reading of *The Awkward Age* reaches this undecidability as its conclusion.

My phrase "unworked community" is an allusion to Jean-Luc Nancy's book of that name (Nancy 1991). An unworked (or inoperative) community is made up of a congregation of singularities who cannot ever fully understand one another. This collection cannot be gathered together in a traditional community of individuals who are like one another and who understand one another because they share most assumptions. One evidence for the breakdown of traditional community in *The Awkward Age*, the kind of community assumed in most Victorian novels, is the way speech acts, guaranteed in J. L. Austin's (1962) speech act theory by the existence of a community with firm institutions, all tend to misfire or to be "infelicitous" (Austin's word) in this novel. Many Victorian novels end with a community-sanctioned and "felicitous" "I do" uttered in a marriage ceremony. This happy marriage joins the hero and the heroine. It passes on an inheritance or a title to the next generation, that is, to the children who will be born of the marriage. Nothing of this sort happens in *The Awkward Age*. The novel is full of people who have betrayed their marriage vows or are about to do so. It could be described as a novel about the breakdown of marriage in fin de siècle English culture. Vanderbank will not sign, so to speak, the contract or compact Mr Longdon offers him. Nanda will die unmarried.

This breakdown of community in *The Awkward Age* corresponds to a breakdown of the usual form of Victorian fiction. A so-called omniscient narrator tells most of those stories. That narrator, as in George Eliot's novels or in Anthony Trollope's, is a spokesperson for the collective consciousness of the community. This narrator can interpret the characters for the reader. He (or she, or it) can utter wise commentary on the meaning of the story. This commentary guides the reader's understanding and evaluation. The narrator can penetrate the deepest recesses of consciousness in the characters and report to the reader, in free indirect discourse, just what the characters at a given moment were thinking and feeling. This happens by way of what Nicolas Royle correctly identifies as an uncanny species of telepathy (Royle 2003: 256–76).

All that has almost completely vanished in *The Awkward Age*. No going behind. No wise omniscient narrator who explains everything and speaks for a collective wisdom. Whatever may be the proprieties of Gyp's use of a stichomythic dialogue form with a minimum of intervention by a narrator, in its relation to the stories told in her novels, the form of *The Awkward Age*, as James adopted and altered Ibsen's form, or Gyp's, corresponds to its substance. That substance, or central object, or situation, can be defined in the broadest terms as the "unworking" of community in late nineteenth-century middle- and upper-class England.

What about the readers of *The Awkward Age*? Do they not form a secret and dispersed community of those who have had a shared experience? It is true that a fairly large number of recent essays about the novel exist. If they did not tend to disagree with one another quite sharply, they might be taken as evidence that the novel has generated a community. In James's own time, in any case, no such community existed. James ruefully reports, in a sad confession, as sad, almost, as Nanda's renunciation of any hopes of marriage, that the publisher of the book version of the novel, after James waited vainly for news of how his work was selling, reported to him when asked: "I'm sorry to say the book has done nothing to speak of; I've never in all my experience seen one treated with more general and complete disrespect" (p. xv).

NOTES

1 Citations from this novel will henceforth be indicated by page numbers only.

2 "Charmed" is another word in the vocabulary range of "uncanny," "arcane," and "cabalistic."

REFERENCES AND FURTHER READING

Abrams, M. ([1953] 1971). *The Mirror and the Lamp: Romantic Theory and the Critical Tradition.* New York: Oxford University Press.

Austin, J. L. (1962). *How To Do Things With Words.* Oxford: Oxford University Press.

Genette, G. ([1972] 1980). *Narrative Discourse: An Essay in Method*, trans. J. E. Lewin. Ithaca, NY: Cornell University Press.

Herman, D. (1994). "Hypothetical Focalization." *Narrative* 2(3), 230–53.

James, H. (1971–9). *The Novels and Tales*, 26 vols, reprint of the New York Edition. Fairfield, NJ: Augustus M. Kelley.

James, H. (1974–84). *Letters*, 4 vols, ed. Leon Edel. Cambridge, MA: Harvard University Press.

James, H. (1987). *The Complete Notebooks*, ed. Leon Edel and Lyall H. Powers. New York: Oxford University Press.

Nancy, J.-L. (1991). *The Inoperative Community*, ed. P. Connor, trans P. Connor, L. Garbus, M. Holland, and S. Sawhney. Minneapolis: University of Minnesota Press.

Royle, N. (2003). *The Uncanny.* Manchester, UK: Manchester University Press.

8

What Narratology and Stylistics Can Do for Each Other

Dan Shen

On the surface the narratological distinction between story and discourse seems to match stylistics' distinction between content and style. "Discourse" refers to "how the story is told" and "style" to "how the content is presented." But in this essay I will argue that (1) the surface similarity conceals an essential difference and (2) recognizing that difference reveals the necessity and the value of synthesizing narratological and stylistic approaches to "how narrative is presented." I will also demonstrate the payoff of this interdisciplinary approach by analyzing a short story by Ernest Hemingway and offer suggestions for future studies.

Differences Between "Discourse" and "Style"

The relation between narratology's "discourse" and stylistics' "style" is one of superficial similarity and essential difference because discourse is primarily concerned with modes of presentation that go beyond strictly linguistic matters, and style is in general concerned more narrowly with choices of language. The narratological distinction between story and discourse is one between "what" is told and "how" to transmit the story (Chatman 1978: 9, see also Shen 2001, 2002); similarly, the traditional stylistic distinction between content and style is one between "what one has to say" and "how one says it" (Leech and Short 1981: 38). In his *Linguistics and the Novel*, Roger Fowler writes:

> The French distinguish two levels of literary structure, which they call *histoire* [story] and *discours* [discourse], story and language. Story (or plot) and the other abstract elements of novel structure may be discussed in terms of categories given by the analogy of linguistic theory, but the *direct* concern of linguistics is surely with the study of *discours*.
>
> (Fowler [1977] 1983: xi, original italics)

But, in effect, the *"discours"* in French narratology is to a large extent different from what Fowler calls "the language proper of fiction" (ibid.), that is, from "style" in stylistics. There is an implicit boundary separating the two, with a limited amount of overlap.

In narratology, the most influential work on discourse is Gérard Genette's *Narrative Discourse* ([1972] 1980), which classifies "discourse" into three basic categories: tense (the relation between story time and discourse time), mood (forms and degrees of narrative representation), and voice (the way in which the narrating itself is implicated in the narrative). The first category "tense" comprises three aspects: order, duration, and frequency. In terms of "order" (the relation between the chronological sequence of story events and the rearranged textual sequence of the events), the analysis is conducted both on the microstructural and the macrostructural levels. At the micro level, the object of analysis is a short episode, which is classified into temporal sections according to the change of position in story time. Genette's main concern, however, is the macro level, at which Proust's *Recherche* is divided into a dozen temporal sections, some lasting for more than 200 pages. When analysis is conducted on such an abstract level, linguistic features simply become irrelevant.

In Genette's discussion of narrative order, he focuses on various kinds of "anachrony," that is, discordance between the two orderings of story and discourse, such as analepsis (flashback) and prolepsis (flash-forward). Such anachronies fall outside the concern of stylistics with only one exception, namely beginning *in medias res* (beginning the story from the middle), an anachrony that is often related to the use of definite expressions. A case in point is the first sentence of Hemingway's "The Short Happy Life of Francis Macomber": "It was now lunchtime and they were all sitting under the double green fly of the dining tent pretending that nothing had happened." The use of "they" without any antecedent, the use of the definite article "the" and the reference to something that had happened prior to this "now" all indicate that Hemingway begins *in medias res*.

In *Style in Fiction*, a seminal work in the stylistics of fiction, Geoffrey Leech and Michael Short devote quite some attention to sequencing on the microstructural level. They offer a distinction between three kinds of sequencing: presentational, chronological, and psychological (1981: 176–80, 233–9). An example of chronological sequencing is "The lone ranger saddled his horse, mounted, and rode off into the sunset" (versus "The lone ranger rode off into the sunset, mounted, and saddled his horse"), which is apparently a matter of syntactic ordering. As for psychological sequencing, a case in point goes as follows:

> Gabriel had not gone to the door with the others. . . . A woman was standing near the top of the first flight, in the shadow also. He could not see her face but he could see the terracotta and salmon-pink panels of her skirt which the shadow made appear black and white. It was his wife.
>
> (James Joyce, "The Dead," from Leech and Short 1981: 177)

Here the readers "seem to be with Gabriel, looking up the stairs towards a vague figure in the shadow, face hidden. . . . The effect [of the psychological sequencing] would have been nullified if Joyce had begun his third sentence: 'His wife was standing . . .'" (Leech and Short 1981: 177–8). This is essentially a matter of the author's choice of words in reflecting a particular point of view. It is worth noting that on the micro plane, the examples Leech and Short have chosen are usually in the mode of scenic presentation, with only one temporal position "now." These examples, that is to say, do not involve the reordering of the different temporal positions of past, present, and future, but involve rather different ways of using language to create different effects.

The second temporal aspect of "discourse" is "duration" (narrative speed), which is defined by the relationship between the actual duration of the events and textual length (Genette 1980: 87–8). In Proust's *Recherche*, the "range of variations" goes from "150 pages for three hours to three lines for twelve years, viz. (very roughly), from a page for one minute to a page for one century" (Genette 1980: 92), a kind of variation that surely goes beyond linguistic features. A narrative, in Genette's view, "can do without anachronies, but not without anisochronies [accelerations or slowdowns], or, if one prefers (as one probably does), effects of *rhythm*" (pp. 87–8, original emphasis). Such narrative "rhythm" (normal speed, acceleration, slowing-down, ellipsis, pause) as investigated by narratologists is essentially different from the verbal rhythm that stylisticians are concerned with, the latter being a matter of the features of words and their combination (e.g., the alternation between stressed and unstressed syllables, the use of punctuation, the length of words, phrases, sentences). Indeed, to a narratologist, no matter what words describe an event, the narrative speed will remain unchanged as long as those words take up the same textual space. A stylistician, on the other hand, will concentrate on what words are used to describe an event, while hardly paying attention to the narrative "rhythm" involved.

The last temporal aspect of narratologists' "discourse" is "narrative frequency." A narrative "may tell once what happened once, n times what happened n times, n times what happened once, once what happened n times" (Genette 1980: 114). Now, whether to tell an event once or more than once is not a choice of language itself, hence also beyond the concern of stylistics proper.

Of the above-mentioned tripartite distinction of discourse – tense, mood, and voice – the latter two categories have more to do with the linguistic medium, especially focalization (point of view)[1] and modes of speech presentation, and have hence attracted attention from both narratologists and stylisticians. But even here, some elements are nonlinguistic in essence. As for different types of narration, the narratological "analysis of narrators emphasizes the structural position of the narrator *vis à vis* the story he narrates rather than a linguistic characteristic like grammatical person" (Rimmon-Kenan 1989: 159), the latter being the concern of stylisticians. Indeed, two narrators with the same structural position may speak in radically different ways due to different language choices. But only stylistics takes into account the different language choices.

Narratology's discourse is sometimes also concerned with characterization, especially the different modes of characterization such as direct definition, indirect presentation, and reinforcement by analogy (Rimmon-Kenan 2002: 59–71). While narratology is concerned with what counts as direct definition and what structural function it serves, stylistics focuses on what specific words are used in describing a character and what effects those words convey as opposed to other potential choices. As for indirect presentation, Rimmon-Kenan makes a structural distinction between (different categories of) action, speech, external appearance, and environment. Stylistics usually takes for granted such narrated action, appearance, and environment, and proceeds to investigate what words the author has chosen to represent those "fictional facts" (for a purposeful exception, see Mills 1995: 159–63).

Like narratology, stylistics has developed with the times and become increasingly interested in reader and context, though its interests reflect developments more in linguistics than in critical theory. By now, we have numerous branches of stylistics, such as literary (practical) stylistics, functional stylistics, discourse stylistics, critical discourse analysis, feminist stylistics, literary pragmatics, and cognitive stylistics, among others (see Wales 2001). Whatever the linguistic model or critical frame adopted, whatever the definition of style, and whatever the relation to reader and context, stylistics is in general marked by a concentration on the functions and effects of language features.

Reasons for the Boundary

The boundary between "discourse" and "style" is in part a result of the different ways in which narratology and stylistics relate to poetic analysis. The stylistic analysis of prose fiction is not much different from the stylistic analysis of poetry. Both focus on the use of language, a use manifested in different forms. By contrast, narratological analysis of prose fiction has departed from the poetic analytical tradition, focusing attention on the relation between story events and their rearrangement. In investigating prose fiction, stylisticians have adopted the Prague school's concept of "foregrounding," a concept initially based on the investigation of poetry. Not surprisingly, the concept of "foregrounding," as a matter of psychological prominence due to "*deviations* from the expected or ordinary use of language" (Stockwell 2002: 14), has not entered the realm of narratology. What figures prominently in narratology is the concept of "anachrony" as mentioned above, which takes the form of various kinds of deviation from the causal chronological sequence of events.

Another fundamental reason for the boundary between "discourse" and "style" is that narratology and stylistics have established different relations to the discipline of linguistics. Stylistics uses the findings of linguistics in the analysis of verbal texts. It both gains analytical strength from linguistics and, at the same time, is subject to the confinement of linguistics – to verbal texts and to the use of language itself. By contrast, narratology uses the findings of linguistics metaphorically. As mentioned above, Genette has adopted the linguistic term "tense" to cover "order," "duration," and "frequency." In terms of "order," anachronies often do not have to do with tense (e.g., "When she first *went* to school . . ." or "Five years later, I *saw* him again"). It is important to note that verbal tense normally goes with the natural temporal facts (e.g., past tense is used to describe past happenings), but Genette's "anachrony" ("flashback" or "flash-forward") concerns how the discourse deviates from the natural sequence of story events. In this sense, the relation between Genette's "anachrony" and verbal tense change is essentially one of opposition rather than similarity. And absolutely no real similarity can be perceived between verbal tense and "duration" or "frequency" as such. The relation between the grammatical term "mood" and "mood" in narrative discourse (narrative distance and focalization) is no less metaphorical. Similarly, the area of "voice" – mainly in the form of levels and types of narration – is miles apart from the grammatical category of "voice" (active voice versus passive voice).

Across the Boundary

It is worth noting that the boundary between "style" and "discourse" has been crossed by some especially broad-minded scholars. Of the two camps of narratologists and stylisticians respectively, the interdisciplinary attempts have come mostly from the stylistic side. On the narratological side, Rimmon-Kenan in 1989 published a provocative and insightful paper "How the Model Neglects the Medium," which puts forward the "counterintuitive" claim that "the exclusion of language" constitutes a fundamental reason for the crisis of narratology. But Rimmon-Kenan treats language in a rather different way:

> But what exactly do I mean by "language"? I have in mind two senses of the term: 1) language as medium, or the fact that the story in question is conveyed by words (rather than by cinematic shots, mimed gestures, and the like); 2) language as act, or the fact that the story in question is told by someone to someone, and that such telling is not only constative but also performative.
>
> (Rimmon-Kenan 1989: 160)

A note is added to explain the first sense of language: "This paper takes a different direction from the one chosen by Phelan [in *Worlds from Words* (1981)], who says: 'Nevertheless, my questions about the medium of fiction shall not lead out toward questions about the similarities and differences among language and other representational media, but shall lead in toward questions of style' (6–7)" (1989: 164 n. 4). Due to the "different direction," attention is shifted from "style" to certain properties of language itself: its linearity, its digital nature, its differential character, its arbitrariness, its indeterminacy, its iterability, and its abstract nature. With the emphasis set on such "technical and semiotic properties of the media themselves,"

Rimmon-Kenan (p. 162) purposefully overlooks the problem of style. As for the second sense of language – language as act – what comes under focus is the general function and motivation of narration, rather than style. Not surprisingly, Rimmon-Kenan does not draw on stylistics.

The few interdisciplinary publications on the narratological side have typically come from literary linguists such as Monika Fludernik (1996, 2003) and David Herman (2002). The two established narratologists started their careers doing both stylistics and narratology, but gradually moved to the narratological side, bringing with them their remarkable expertise in stylistics or linguistics, an expertise that is still evident in their narratological books and essays. The fact that stylistics has not exerted much influence on other narratologists may be accounted for mainly by the following: (1) narratologists' conscious or unconscious "exclusion of language"; (2) the linguistic technicalities in stylistics; (3) the fact that although stylistics has flourished in Britain (also on the Continent and in Australia), its development has been limited in America, where, however, the majority of narratologists of the English-speaking world are based.

As for the stylistic camp, numerous interdisciplinary attempts have appeared, including Paul Simpson (1993), Sara Mills (1995), Jonathan Culpeper (2001), and Peter Stockwell (2002).[2] Those works are typically marked by multidisciplinarity, incorporating various approaches, but still retaining a distinctive stylistic identity because of the focus on language and the dependence on linguistics. Not surprisingly, since the case is one of stylistics drawing on narratology, narratological models or concepts are typically used as frameworks for investigating the functioning of language.

It is worth mentioning that recent interdisciplinary attempts tend to draw on cognitive linguistics or cognitive science. Cognitive stylistics (cognitive rhetoric, cognitive poetics), which did not come into being until the 1990s, is developing fast, parallel to the cognitive turn on the narratological side (see Herman 2002, Bortolussi and Dixon 2003). The complementary relation between stylistics and narratology may be inferred from the following observation made by Stockwell in his *Cognitive Poetics*:

> This view of schema theory in a literary context points to three different fields in which schemas operate: **world schemas, text schemas,** and **language schemas.** World schemas cover those schemas considered so far that are to do with content; text schemas represent our expectations of the way that world schemas appear to us in terms of their sequencing and structural organisation; language schemas contain our idea of the appropriate forms of linguistic patterning and style in which we expect a subject to appear. Taking the last two together, disruptions in our expectations of textual structure or stylistic structure constitute **discourse deviation,** which offers the possibility for schema refreshment.... However, the headers and slots within schemas and the tracks through schemas can also be discussed in terms of their *stylistic* and *narratological* features.
>
> (Stockwell 2002: 80–2, original italics and boldface)

Here we can see clearly the distinction between story (the content area) and discourse (the two presentational areas), although, of course, the schemas in the three areas will be working simultaneously and interacting with each other in the interpretive process. Significantly, the "discourse" consists of two areas: the textual/organizational (narratology's discourse)[3] and language/linguistic (stylistics' style). This is directly related to the point I'm driving at: since the level of presentation contains both organizational (narratological) and language (stylistic) choices, focusing only on one aspect will result in a partial picture of "how the story is presented." In order to gain a fuller picture of narrative presentation, it is both desirable and necessary to combine the concerns of narratology and stylistics.

To illustrate the point, I would like to offer an interdisciplinary analysis, within the limited scope of the essay, of a mininarrative by Ernest Hemingway:

> They shot the six cabinet ministers at half past six in the morning against the wall of a hospital. There were pools of water in the courtyard. There were wet dead leaves on the paving of the courtyard. It rained hard. All the shutters of the hospital were nailed shut. One of the ministers was sick with typhoid. Two soldiers carried him downstairs and out into the rain. They tried to hold him up against the wall but he sat down in a puddle of water. The other five stood very quietly against the wall. Finally the officer told the soldiers it was no good trying to make him stand up. When they fired the first volley he was sitting in the water with his head on his knees.
>
> (Hemingway [1925] 1986: 51)

This is one of the vignettes that constitute the Paris edition of *in our time* (1924), and that appear as interchapters in *In Our Time* (first published 1925). This vignette is based on an actual historical event: the atrocious executions of six Greek cabinet ministers, including the ex-Premier, in Athens in 1922 after Greece's unsuccessful campaign against Turkey (see Simpson 1996: 120–2).

Narratologically, a notable feature is what Genette calls "repeating" narration: narrating twice what happened only once. The narrative begins with a summary of the event, then, after a description of the setting, moves to a scenic re-presentation of the same event. The more condensed presentation interacts with the more detailed presentation so that they reinforce each other.

While reading the vignette, readers feel a strong tension between the terrifying nature of the executions and the naturalness as conveyed by the presentation. This tension results in part from a narratological feature: the detached and merely observing position of the external narrator, and in part from a stylistic feature: the neutral reporting style chosen by Hemingway. The initial summary "They shot the six cabinet ministers at half past six in the morning against the wall of a hospital" sounds matter-of-fact, as if the executions were an ordinary event, one that can be reported on without the need of evaluating or characterizing it. Compare Hemingway's vignette with a newspaper account of the same event Hemingway had read: "*ATROCITIES MARKED GREEK EXECUTIONS OF FORMER LEADERS,*" which contains phrases like "To begin the *horrors* of that morning...a *ghastly* line...an *appalling* instance..." (quoted from Simpson 1996: 121, my emphasis). When Hemingway wrote this short story, he had already experienced the atrocities of World War I, which, coupled with his experience as a reporter covering crime stories, led him to focus on war, bull-fighting, and murder in the vignettes. Indeed, Hemingway's world is a world of violence and death, where atrocities are treated as commonplace. As in this vignette, Hemingway often uses the discrepancy between the horror of what is represented and the matter-of-fact quality of how it is presented to call attention to that horror. The effect will be even more striking in relation to readers who are not accustomed to such inhuman atrocities and who are more easily shocked by such a "commonplace treatment" of the illegal executions of cabinet ministers.

While the narration is detached, the readers are immediately drawn into the story by a notable stylistic feature at the beginning: the definite expressions *"They"* and *"the* six cabinet ministers." Suspense is created leading to a series of questions: who were "they"? Who were "the six cabinet ministers"? In which part of the (fictitious) world did this happen? In which year (month, date) did this (fictitious) event take place? Although Hemingway wrote the story only three months after the historical event, readers could not get access to the published story until two or more years later, and most readers, especially later ones, may not associate this vignette with the historical event. Since the answers cannot be found in the text, the event takes on a sense of universality due to the lack of specification of time, place, and even nationality (the nationalities of the ministers and the soldiers remain unspecified). Hemingway, by suppressing such information, seems to suggest that such murders can take place anywhere and any time in the world.

Interestingly, in the first sentence, there appears an indefinite article "a," which conflicts with the preceding definite expressions. Compare the more natural:

> They shot the six cabinet ministers at half past six in the morning against the wall of the hospital.
> A group of soldiers shot six cabinet ministers ... against the wall of a hospital.

In these more natural contexts, "hospital" appears psychologically less prominent. In Hemingway's version, the indefinite article "a" in the "definite context" signals that "a hospital" is a piece of new information that is not to be taken for granted. The deviant choice of the indefinite article "a" seems to emphasize the point that the executions do not take place on an ordinary execution ground but in a hospital that is supposed to save lives. The clash of the nature of the event and that of the setting heightens the cruelty of the executions in an unobtrusive way. In fact, the historical executions were carried out at a place "about one and a half miles outside of the city" at about noon time (quoted from Simpson 1996: 121). The ex-Premier, who was sick, was taken there from a hospital, while the other five ministers were taken from a prison. In the Hemingway text, all six are shot dead "against the wall of a hospital" at dawn when life just begins to wake up, resulting in a strong ironic effect.

In the scenic re-presentation of the event, most of the textual space (five out of six sentences) is devoted to the minister sick with typhoid. In the historical event, one minister died on the way to the execution ground but his dead body was still "propped up" and executed together with the live ministers. Why does Hemingway omit this highly inhuman fact and only give the sick minister such structural prominence? The reasons seem to be both personal and artistic. Hemingway was severely wounded while fighting on the western front in Italy, and this traumatic experience may have rendered him particularly attentive to and compassionate towards the sick. In this light, we may appreciate better why Hemingway has chosen "a hospital" as the setting for the murdering. Artistically, Hemingway's structural highlighting of the sick minister conveys in a very effective way the inhuman nature of the executions. In the historical event, the sick minister was made to stand up in front of the firing party through injections of strychnine. In the Hemingway version, we have instead the climactic progression from "Two soldiers carried him . . ." (the sick man could not walk) to "They tried to hold him up against the wall . . ." (the sick man could not stand up) and, finally, to "he was sitting in the water with his head on his knees" (the sick man could not even hold his head while sitting). The last clause occupies the end-focus position of the text and is psychologically very prominent. It may arouse strong indignation and compassion on the part of readers: how can one bear to shoot a man who cannot even sit up? As for the only sentence devoted to the rest of the victims – "The other five stood very quietly against the wall" – it seems to convey, in a highly economic manner, Hemingway's heroic code of behavior: face death and destruction calmly and undauntedly. This, on the one hand, counterpoints the miserable sight of the sick man and, on the other hand, may produce a startled and admiring reaction through conflicting with the expectations of readers.

The most notable narratological feature of the vignette, however, is what Genette calls "descriptive pause": scenic description from the perspective of the external narrator, a description that takes up textual space but does not take up story time, hence the "pause" of story time. This descriptive pause, which is sandwiched between the summary and the detailed re-presentation of the event, takes up one fourth of the whole textual space:

> *There were* pools of water in *the courtyard. There were* wet dead leaves on the paving of *the courtyard.* It rained hard. All the shutters of the hospital were nailed shut. (my emphasis)

Of the other vignettes functioning as interchapters in *In Our Time*, action and dialogue predominate and pure scenic description is kept to the minimum. Indeed, of the other eight vignettes narrated in third person, six do not contain any pure scenic description and the remaining two contain much less in textual proportion. Stylistic analysis can help explain why Hemingway devotes so much textual space to a pure scenic description in this vignette. In this structurally prominent descriptive pause, three stylistic features are foregrounded: (1) the redundant repetition of "there were" and "the courtyard," (2) the abnormal syntactic boundary between the first and the second sentence, and (3) the reversal of the cause-and-effect relationship. Compare:

> It rained hard. There were pools of water on the ground and wet dead leaves on the paving of the courtyard.

This paraphrase is just a straightforward description of the setting, but Hemingway's original takes on additional symbolic meaning. As will soon become clear, the foregrounded repetition and redundancy function to draw attention to the symbolic association of "pools of water" with "pools of blood," and "dead leaves" with "dead bodies." In English, one may say "All my old buddies were gone. I was like the last leaf on the tree" or "as insignificant and slight as an autumn leaf." The six ministers were important figures in human history, but they are now treated as useless leaves to be got rid of. Their dead bodies are no more significant than dead leaves. This apparently has to do with Hemingway's nihilistic view of the world. Significantly, the clumsy verbal repetition and the syntactic boundary add to the semantic weight of the two symbolic objects, an effect reinforced by placing "It rained hard" *after* rather than before the two sentences involved. In the paraphrase offered above, the order is reversed, a change that increases the psychological prominence of "It rained hard" and reduces the symbolic weight of "pools of water" and "dead leaves." Moreover, in the Hemingway version, the repetition of "the courtyard" signals that what we have are not ordinary "pools of water" or "dead leaves" like those elsewhere, but "pools of blood" and "dead bodies" *in the courtyard where the bloody executions take place*. Furthermore, the deviant syntactic ordering placing the effect first and the cause next functions to loosen the natural cause and effect relationship (it is not just a matter of rain leading to . . .), signaling and highlighting in a very subtle manner the symbolic significance of "pools of water" and "dead leaves." In this light, "wet dead leaves" may be viewed as symbolizing dead bodies soaked in blood. And in this light, we may understand better the related repetition: "he sat down *in a puddle of water*" and "he was sitting *in the water* with his head on his knees" – a pathetic view of a sick man huddled up in blood. While the courtyard symbolizes a bloody killing ground, the hospital itself seems to symbolize a big tomb: "All the shutters of the hospital were nailed shut." These symbols of setting unobtrusively counterpoint the repeated presentation of the executions, greatly intensifying the effect.

All in all, in order to appreciate "how the story is presented" in Hemingway's vignette, we need to carry out both narratological and stylistic analyses. The former focuses on the structural techniques, such as the mutual reinforcement between the curt summary and the more detailed scenic re-presentation, which together interact with the structurally prominent descriptive pause sandwiched in between; the detached observing position of an external narrator; the structural highlighting and progressive description of what happens to the sick man, which counterpoints the brief description of the other victims. The stylistic analysis, on the other hand, focuses on the initial definite expressions, which form a contrast with the following indefinite article "a"; the lack of verbal specification of time, place, and nationality of the characters; the neutral style and matter-of-fact tone; the foregrounded verbal repetition, sentence boundary, and deviant syntactic sequencing in the descriptive pause. The narratological features and stylistic features interact and reinforce each other, and it is necessary to see their interaction in order to understand the "how" of Hemingway's art.

Current Practices and Future Studies

In view of the implicit boundary between narratology's "discourse" and stylistics' "style," and the fact that despite the appearance of numerous interdisciplinary attempts, the majority of existing publications and courses are purely stylistic or narratological, I would like to offer the following suggestions for future studies.

In terms of theoretical discussions, it is necessary to give more specific definitions of stylistics' "style" and narratology's "discourse." As regards narratives in the verbal medium, it needs to be pointed out in the first place that "narrative presentation" or "how the story is told" consists of two aspects: one organizational and the other verbal, with a certain amount of overlap in between. Thus, "style" may be defined as "the language aspect of how the story is presented." Accordingly, "stylistic features" will be understood as choices of *verbal* form or *verbal* techniques. On the narratological side, while "discourse" can still be defined as "how the story is presented" or "the signifier, statement, discourse or narrative text itself" (Genette 1980: 27), it is necessary to point out that in narratological investigations of "discourse," attention is focused on the structural organization of story events, leaving aside style or language choices. Accordingly, "narratological features" will be understood as narrative strategies or organizational techniques.

Moreover, in a stylistic book, it would be productive to refer to narratology's concern with narrative strategies. Since many stylisticians are not yet narratologically informed, it is necessary to promote the introduction of narratology to stylisticians. Interestingly, in Britain where stylistics has been thriving, the development of narratology has been much slower than in America, despite the fact that the British-based Poetics and Linguistics Association and its official journal *Language and Literature* have played an important role in promoting the interface of stylistics and narratology.

In a narratological book, it would be helpful to delineate the scope of inquiry for readers, and to point out that in order to gain a fuller view of "how the story is presented", more attention needs to be paid to the writer's "style," which is well defined by James Phelan in *Worlds from Words*: "'Style' is the specific term, used to refer to particular uses of [the language] system. 'Style' also has another sense, which I shall develop more fully later: *those elements of a sentence or passage that would be lost in a paraphrase*" (Phelan 1981: 6, my emphasis). Narratological investigations often do not bear on "those elements of a sentence or passage that would be lost in a paraphrase." But as shown by Phelan's illuminating analyses, those are also very important elements of "how the story is presented" in many literary narratives. Indeed, a comparison of Phelan's *Worlds from Words* (and works in stylistics) with his 1996 *Narrative as Rhetoric* (and other works in narratology) will surely lead to the double realization that paying close attention to the functioning of language can lead to fruitful results in narrative analysis, and that in order to gain a fuller picture, attention should be devoted not only to verbal techniques but also to organizational techniques. Many of the interdisciplinary attempts as referred to above, such as Monika Fludernik's 2003 paper "Chronology, Time, Tense and Experientiality in Narrative," well demonstrate the gains of treating narratological concerns (e.g., chronology) and stylistic concerns (e.g., tense) together.

Now, although the works by Fludernik and Herman exemplify how narratology can benefit from stylistic or linguistic analysis, narratologists and students majoring in literature may be put off by the linguistic technicalities in many stylistic publications. However, many other stylistic works are intended for readers and students of both language and literature with linguistic technicalities kept to the minimum, such as those in "The Interface Series: Language in Literary Studies" published by Routledge. Or as an alternative, attention may be directed to "close reading." As we all know, close reading was prevalent for a time but has been discredited for the past two decades or so because of its ideological limitations. It has to a great extent been replaced by stylistics in Britain, but in America, where stylistics itself has been very much excluded, "style" has been to a great extent overlooked since the "death" of close reading. Interestingly, on May 15, 2003, the America-based NARRATIVE listserv posted a call for proposals: "Henry James and new formalisms" which directs attention to close reading: "Long discredited as a conservative, parochial, and even 'oppressive' critical practice, 'close reading' is showing signs of return. Yet this return is marked by considerable anxiety... In what sense are New Formalisms new? In what ways might they return to the New Criticism yet discern its limitations?...."[4]

While doing close reading, we certainly should try to eliminate the earlier limitations. Now, no matter whether it is stylistics or close reading, a language-oriented approach may reveal many things about "how the story is presented" that go beyond the concerns of the structure-oriented narratology. In view of this fact, students should be encouraged to take courses and read books in both areas of study. It is hoped that, with a clear awareness of the complementarity between "style" and "discourse" (as investigated by narratology), more conscious efforts will be made to combine the concerns of narratology and stylistics/close reading in narrative criticism.

Moreover, as an extension of Rimmon-Kenan's earlier call, both narratological and stylistic investigations of narrative presentation can be enriched by looking out at the relation between the linguistic medium and other media, as can be seen in the increasing fruits of media studies especially on the narratological side. As regards the Hemingway vignette, we can look out at how the structural and verbal techniques can or cannot be conveyed either directly or indirectly on screen. Since film is scenic in nature, the initial summary can only be replaced by a scene showing, say, soldiers firing at the six ministers or the six dead bodies after the killing, where the contrast between the definite expressions and the indefinite "a" can hardly be conveyed, and where the concealment of nationalities may be difficult to achieve because of the appearance and clothes/uniform of the persons involved. With this initial scene, the following re-presentation will function as a flashback. But as distinct from the natural re-presentation in the Hemingway text, this re-presentation on screen will appear much less natural, since on screen we can only have a double scenic presentation rather than a summary substantiated by a scene. On screen, while there is no difficulty in conveying the structural highlighting of the sick minister in the re-presentation, it may be less easy to bring out the symbolic significance of the setting, as signaled by the joint function of unusual structural prominence, verbal repetition, deviant syntactic boundary and ordering in the Hemingway text. It is true that a close-up of "wet dead leaves" may succeed in conveying the symbolic meaning, but a close-up of "pools of water" may not help and the way out is perhaps to show pools of water mixed with blood or present analogous scenes of pools of water and pools of blood.

And finally, in terms of the investigation on "style," we can further look out, where applicable, for an interlingual comparison, which may shed interesting light on how the author's stylistic choices are related to the properties of the specific language involved.

NOTES

1 The choice of different modes of focalization is essentially a structural choice, but different modes of focalization have different linguistic indicators, hence attracting attention from stylisticians.
2 Katie Wales's *A Dictionary of Stylistics* also contains numerous narratological concepts, implicitly calling for an incorporation of narratological concerns.
3 And of course we also have other elements of textual organization, such as chapter titles, chapter division, paragraphing, etc.
4 The email was sent by Beartooth <karhunhammas@Lserv.com> on May 14, 2003, and resent from NARRATIVE-error@ctrvax.Vanderbilt.Edu on May 15, 2003.

REFERENCES AND FURTHER READING

Bortolussi, M. and Dixon, P. (2003). *Psychonarratology*. Cambridge, UK: Cambridge University Press.

Chatman, S. (1978). *Story and Discourse*. Ithaca, NY: Cornell University Press.

Culpeper, J. (2001). *Language and Characterization in Plays and Texts*. London: Longman.

Fludernik, M. (1996). *Towards a "Natural" Narratology*. London and New York: Routledge.

Fludernik, M. (2003). "Chronology, Time, Tense and Experientiality in Narrative." *Language and Literature* 12, 117–34.

Fowler, R. ([1977] 1983). *Linguistics and the Novel*. London: Methuen.

Hemingway, E. ([1925] 1986). *In Our Time*, Collier Books Edition. New York: Macmillan.

Herman, D. (2002). *Story Logic*: Lincoln and London: University of Nebraska Press.

Genette, G. ([1972] 1980). *Narrative Discourse*, trans. J. E. Lewin. Ithaca, NY: Cornell University Press.

Leech, G. N. and Short, M. H. (1981). *Style in Fiction*. London: Longman.

Mills, S. (1995). *Feminist Stylistics*. London and New York: Routledge.

Phelan, J. (1981). *Worlds from Words*. Chicago: The University of Chicago Press.

Phelan, J. (1996). *Narrative as Rhetoric*. Columbus: Ohio State University Press.

Rimmon-Kenan, S. (1989). "How the Model Neglects the Medium: Linguistics, Language, and the Crisis of Narratology." *The Journal of Narrative Technique* 19, 157–66.

Rimmon-Kenan, S. ([1983] 2002). *Narrative Fiction*, 2nd edn. London and New York: Routledge.

Semino, E. and J. Culpeper (eds.) (2002). *Cognitive Stylistics*. Amsterdam and Philadelphia: John Benjamins.

Shen, D. (2001). "Narrative, Reality and Narrator as Construct: Reflections on Genette's Narration." *Narrative* 9, 123–9.

Shen, D. (2002). "Defence and Challenge: Reflections on the Relation Between Story and Discourse." *Narrative* 10, 422–43.

Simpson, P. (1993). *Language, Ideology, and Point of View*. London and New York: Routledge.

Simpson, P. (1996). *Language Through Literature*. London and New York: Routledge.

Stockwell, P. (2002). *Cognitive Poetics*. London and New York: Routledge.

Wales, K. ([1990] 2001). *A Dictionary of Stylistics*, 2nd edn. Harlow, UK: Pearson Education.

9

The Pragmatics of Narrative Fictionality

Richard Walsh

> Thoughts about his case never left him now. Several times he had considered whether it would not be advisable to prepare a written document in his defence and lodge it with the court. His idea was to present a short account of his life and, in the case of each relatively important event, explain the reasons for his action, say whether he now thought that course of action should be condemned or approved, and give his reasons for this judgement.
>
> (Kafka [1925] 1994: 89)

Josef K., the protagonist of Kafka's *The Trial*, finds himself in a situation in which his efforts to establish his innocence, to explain himself, have no focus and no boundaries: he can only envisage a plea in the form of an exhaustive narrative of his life. Our own efforts to make sense of the extraordinary circumstances surrounding K.'s envisaged narrative act are crucially related to a distinctive fact about Kafka's: while K. contemplates autobiography, Kafka engages in fiction. Fiction is usually understood to have a second-order relation to the real world, via the mimetic logic of fictional representation: it represents events, or imitates discourses, that we assimilate through nonfictional modes of narrative understanding. So even where (as here) the fiction is in some respects unrealistic, it is comprehensible in terms of its relation to familiar types of narrative: not only the accused person's effort of self-justification, and the discourse of moral autobiography, but also psychological narratives of guilt, and the several kinds of legal narrative that inform the global frame of reference of *The Trial*.

On the other hand, the place of narrative in nonfictional contexts such as legal studies has itself attracted a lot of attention in recent years. H. Porter Abbott's *Cambridge Introduction to Narrative* devotes a whole chapter to "narrative contestation," for which his paradigm case is the competing narrative efforts of the prosecution and defense in the notorious 1893 trial of Lizzie Borden, accused (and acquitted) of murdering her father and stepmother (Abbott 2002: 138–55). Abbott emphasizes the way in which the prosecution and defense, in this as in all trials, strive to establish narrative credibility by aligning their representation of events with rhetorically advantageous "masterplots," by which he means familiar skeletal narratives with an established cultural authority. So Lizzie Borden's apparent "lack of affect" in the face of the murders is narrativized by one side as the shock of a virtuous daughter, by the other as the cold-blooded viciousness of a Lady Macbeth (pp. 147–9). In a legal context, the issue of narrative truth is especially pointed (Lizzie Borden, after all, stood in jeopardy of the death penalty): yet the explanatory power of narrative here depends less upon its relation to fact than its relation to other narratives, and it is in these terms that both sides make their case. Indeed they can do no other, even in those self-reflexive moments when they accuse each other of doing so.

The general point here is that all narrative, fictional and nonfictional, is artifice: narratives are constructs, and their meanings are internal to the system of narrative. For some theorists this general quality of narrativity subsumes the concept of fictionality entirely: if all narratives derive their meaning from their relation to other narratives, rather than any direct purchase upon reality, then it no longer makes sense to use this second-order kind of relation specifically to characterize fiction. Yet the awkward fact remains that the narratives elaborated by prosecution and defense in the Lizzie Borden trial made truth claims that Kafka's novel does not make, and accordingly these two cultural modes of narrative invoke quite different interpretative assumptions. In this respect the rise of the general concept of narrativity, far from superseding the issue of fictionality, has actually exposed it as a theoretical problem. If the logic of narrative representation does not provide for a defensible distinction between fiction and nonfiction, then the focus of theoretical attention is necessarily displaced from the substance of fictional narrative to the act of fictive narration; from the product to the production of fiction. How are we to understand fictive narration as a referential act, or as an act of communication? It is in this context that I want to advocate a pragmatic approach to the issue of fictionality: one that draws upon philosophical and linguistic fields of inquiry into the communicative use of language, and in particular invokes the conceptual framework of relevance theory.

Modern accounts of fictionality generally turn upon one or more of a small repertoire of theoretical gambits, which can be collectively understood as gestures of disavowal, achieved through several kinds of displacement. That is to say, these accounts variously respond to the problem of fictionality as a problem of truthfulness, and resolve it by detaching the fictive act from the domain of truth, that is, from any codified system of representation or language. The kinds of theoretical move I have in mind are: the institution of a narrator as the source of the fictive discourse, the redescription of fictional artefacts as props in a game of make-believe, the notion of pretended speech acts, and the recuperation of fictional reference as actual reference to fictional worlds. The first two moves place the language of fiction itself within the fictional frame; the third move disqualifies it, as nonserious language, from communicative accountability; the fourth move allows the language of fiction to be literal and serious but not exactly fictive (that is, to the extent that fictive language does not make referential commitments), since fictionality has been redefined as a matter of ontological modality. The nub of fictionality always turns out to be elsewhere: it is as if fictionality were not a problem *except* in relation to language. This is odd, given that language, I take it, is what makes fiction possible – and again by a language here I mean broadly any codified system of representation, such that fictions in any medium are equally dependent upon a language, a representational code, and not merely upon cognitive illusion.

Fictionality, I want to suggest, functions within a communicative framework: it resides in a way of using a language, and its distinctiveness consists in the recognizably distinct rhetorical set invoked by that use. I assume that narrative fictionality is worth distinguishing from narrativity in general: that is to say, I want to grant full force to the claim that all narrative is artifice, and in that very restricted sense fictive, but maintain nonetheless that fictional narrative has a coherently distinct cultural role, and that a distinct concept of fictionality is required to account for this role. It is best explained in functional and rhetorical terms, rather than in formal terms: true, there are formal qualities strongly associated with fiction, but they do not supply necessary or sufficient conditions of fictionality. To say instead that fictionality is a functional attribute is to say that it is a use of language; to say that it is rhetorical is to say that this use is distinguished by the kind of appeal it makes to the reader's or audience's interpretative attention. No model that treats fictive discourse as framed by formal, intentional, or ontological disavowal can meet these criteria for a concept of fictionality. If fictionality consists in a distinct way of using language, it is not explained by attaching its distinctiveness to some quarantine mechanism conceived precisely to maintain its conformity with nonfictional usage, at the cost of detaching it, in one way or another, from its actual communicative context. The rhetorical distinctiveness of fiction, then, is consistent with a communicative continuity between fictional and nonfictional uses of language. Fictionality is a rhetorical resource integral to the direct and serious use of language within a real-world communicative framework.

I want to reformulate the age-old problem of fiction's claim upon our attention, the challenge that has prompted various defenses of poesy, or expulsions from republics, down through the centuries, as the problem of reconciling fictionality with relevance. The concept of relevance appears, in several quite specific senses, within two distinct well-demarcated theoretical domains that have been important to recent discussions of fictionality: one is fictional worlds theory, which focuses upon the referential act; the other is speech act theory, especially those accounts that engage with Gricean "conversational implicature" (Grice 1989), where the focus is upon the communicative act. Relevance theory itself is a related approach to communication from the perspective of pragmatics and cognitive linguistics, and although this field of research has not included any detailed consideration of fictionality, it does suggest that a pragmatic theory of fiction has much to gain from pursuing the relation between fictionality and relevance.

The issue of relevance arises in fictional worlds theories in two respects: the first and narrowest is internal to a given fictional world, and relates to the problem of incompleteness; the second is external, and concerns the global pertinence of fictional worlds to the reader. Incompleteness is a problem for fictional worlds theory because the text of a fiction cannot be expected to fully specify a world, nor even provide a sufficient basis for a comprehensive inferential process. There are always going to be gaps and indeterminacies in the interpretative construction of fictional worlds, which is a significant divergence from the philosophical model of possible worlds upon which fictional worlds theory is based, since it is axiomatic that possible worlds are logically complete. The theoretical response has been to invoke two complementary recuperative strategies. The first, proposed by Marie-Laure Ryan, is to bring fictional worlds into line with the logical framework of possible worlds theory by assuming a "principle of minimal departure": the principle of minimal departure dictates that the world of the text is to be understood as complete, and identical to the actual world except for the respects in which it deviates from that model, either explicitly or implicitly, both in its own right and by virtue of any genre conventions it invokes (Ryan 1991: 51). In this case, then, the fictional world itself is complete after all, even if the reader's actualization of it in interpretation of the text is not. But if the problem really is logical incompleteness, the principle of minimal departure cannot help: there are indeterminacies in relation to the narrative particulars of any fiction for which the model of the actual world offers no decisive guidance (exactly how many times did K. consider the idea of preparing a short account of his life?). On the other hand, if the principle of minimal departure is assumed just to have a supplementary role in providing for a "reasonably comprehensive" world (Ryan 1991: 52), it raises a question: how far does the reader pursue the gap-filling process it licenses? What criterion limits that interpretative pursuit? However we may choose to define the goals of interpretation, the criterion required is one of relevance to those goals.

Ryan's answer to the problem of incompleteness in fictional worlds is cited by Thomas Pavel, whose alternative solution is to conceive them as worlds of various sizes, determined by the texts from which they are constructed and open to extra-textual information provided for by the principle of minimal departure, without being "maximal" (Pavel 1986: 107–8). So we might just conceivably infer that K. has an appendix, in the absence of any textual information to the contrary, but neglect to infer that his maternal great-grandfather had an appendix – although the latter inference would be better founded, on the basis of minimal departure, since an appendectomy would not then have been available. Pavel's explanation introduces the crucial notion of relevance: "Some form of gradual opacity to inference, some increasing resistance to maximal structures, must be at work in most fictional worlds, keeping them from expanding indefinitely along irrelevant lines" (Pavel 1986: 95). Once the idea of relevance is admitted, however, it entirely supersedes that of completeness. It makes no practical difference whether the "facts" of a fictional world are understood maximally, independent of textual interpretation, or contingently, on the basis of what it is possible to infer from the text; because in either case the scope of inference is, in principle, nonfinite. The horizon of the reader's encounter with a fiction is determined, not by what it is possible to infer, but by what is worth inferring: the reader will not pursue inferential reasoning beyond the point at which it ceases to seem relevant to the particulars of the narrative, in a specific context of interpretation. This is a pragmatic limit, but only such a limit can provide for the fact that fictional representations do not merely exist (in whatever qualified sense), but are communicated.

Such considerations invoke the other sense in which the notion of relevance arises in fictional worlds theory. Pavel declares a "principle of relevance" as one of only two fundamental principles of fictional reference (1986: 145); but the kind of relevance he has in mind here is quite distinct from the internal relevance presupposed by the discussion so far. Instead, it articulates an external global relation between worlds, and is therefore contingent upon the reader's realization of the fictional world. Yet as we have already seen, that realization itself must be contingent upon relevance criteria of a quite different order, if it is not to be an endless project. This relation between worlds, then, is a strangely cumbersome reprise of the reader's supposed original effort of world construction, which (under the rubric of "minimal departure") was to be pursued precisely in terms of difference. Are these two kinds of relevance, internal and external, ultimately distinct? Or do they, under closer scrutiny, collapse into each other, in the process extinguishing the concept that intervenes between them, which is the concept of fictional worlds itself? In fictional worlds theory, the concept of relevance is bounded by two assumptions that I want to resist: one is that the "facts" of fiction are meaningfully independent of considerations of relevance; the other is the idea that relevance can be internal to the fictional world; that it can ever mean something independently of the communicative act. My counterclaim is that the reader's interpretative agenda cannot be understood within the bounds of a fictional world, or indeed in relation to its fictional existence rather than its actual communication; and that relevance, even when it is described internally as relevance to story, is always, reciprocally, relevance to the reader.

The issue of communication, of course, is central to the relation between fictionality and speech act theory. The standard speech act account of literary discourse, as first elaborated by Richard Ohmann (1971) and John Searle (1975), is the imitation speech act model, in which the authorial speech act is not seriously made, but pretended, which effectively suspends the appropriateness conditions (or felicity conditions) normally attaching to the performance of that speech act. But the imitative model is undermined by the fact that third-person novels routinely deviate from the norms of any nonfictional, real-world speech act, for instance in such ordinary narrative strategies as omniscient narration. The pretended speech act frame does not account for fictionality because the rhetoric of fictionality often inhabits the narration itself: the first sentence of my quote from *The Trial*, for example, resists recuperation as a pretended nonfictional speech act in both content (access to the thoughts of another) and form (the dual temporal perspective of internal focalization, manifested in the otherwise anomalous "now").

A more promising alternative, advanced by Mary Louise Pratt (1977), looks instead to H. P. Grice's model of conversational implicature: Grice argued that the appropriateness conditions applicable to speech acts were best understood, not as attaching to the semantics of specific sentences, but in relation to a few general maxims. These maxims together constitute a Cooperative Principle, which is the foundation of successful communication: the crucial ones for my purposes are the Maxim of Relation, "be relevant," and the first Maxim of Quality, "do not say what you believe to be false" (Grice 1989: 27). Grice's approach allows a great deal of flexibility in the interpretation of speech acts, because what is actually said may be supplemented by inferences, or implicatures, in order to maintain the shared assumption that the Cooperative Principle is in place. Pratt proposes that one way in which speech acts may be relevant is by being "tellable," by which she means of intrinsic interest, or worthy of display: a tellable speech act constitutes an invitation to contemplate, to interpret, to evaluate. This allows her to propose a distinct category of speech act called "narrative display text," which embraces both fictional narratives and the nonfictional "natural narratives" she cites from the sociolinguistic studies of William Labov (Pratt 1977: 132–6). These texts adhere to Grice's Maxim of Relation, and fulfill the appropriateness conditions of relevance, not by being informative, but by being exhibitive – by being tellable.

Pratt, however, stops short of addressing the issue of fictionality itself and does not inquire into the hierarchical relation between Grice's maxims of Quality and Relation, truthfulness and relevance. To accommodate fiction, Pratt ultimately falls back upon the standard speech-act account she had originally rejected, and concedes that fictive discourse is, on the author's part, an imitation display text, attributed to a narrator within the frame of fiction (1977: 173, 207–8). Pratt might have offered an account of fictive discourse independent of the pretence model: she has a plausible basis for the relevance of the authorial speech act in the notion of tellability, and comes very close to seeing tellability as sufficient for a felicitous authorial speech act irrespective of truth criteria. In short, she makes progress with the aspects of the Gricean model that emphasize relevance, but is blocked by her assumption that the issue of relevance is ultimately secondary to that of truthfulness, which precludes any direct authorial model of fictive discourse.

Pratt's case leads me on to relevance theory, which I want to introduce in relation to Grice. Grice's model of "conversational implicature" was developed in recognition of the fact that the code model of language was often not sufficient to account for communication, and needed to be supplemented by an inferential model. The innovation of relevance theory, as expounded by Dan Sperber and Deirdre Wilson, is to argue that inference is not a supplementary component of communication, but its core. For Grice, an utterance is either literally relevant in a given context, or literally irrelevant, prompting an inferential search for implicatures that might redeem the Cooperative Principle. Sperber and Wilson argue that the order of events in this process of comprehension should be reversed: "It is not that first the context is determined, and then relevance is assessed. On the contrary, people hope that the assumption being processed is relevant (or else they would not bother to process it at all), and they try to select a context which will justify that hope: a context which will maximise relevance" (Sperber and Wilson 1995: 142). To clarify some of this slightly technical terminology, a *context*, here, is a set of assumptions adopted by an individual, a subset of the individual's cognitive environment (1995: 15). A *cognitive environment* is the total set of facts or assumptions manifest to an individual at a given time (p. 39). Something is *manifest* if it is available to perception or inference (p. 39). An *assumption* is a thought (a conceptual representation) treated by the individual as true of the actual world (p. 2). The relevance of a new assumption to an individual is *maximized* when its processing achieves an optimal balance between the effort involved and the contextual effects (or more strictly, the positive cognitive effects) derived (pp. 144, 265). A *contextual effect* is a modification of the context arising from the interaction between old assumptions and new assumptions; it is a *positive cognitive effect* if it benefits an individual's cognitive functions or goals (pp. 109, 265). To illustrate, albeit simplistically, consider a situation in which Dan tells Deirdre that the kettle is on. Deirdre's cognitive environment at the time includes all the perceptible physical phenomena of the office in which she is writing an article, the knowledge of relevance theory that she is bringing to bear upon the article, the understanding she has gleaned from past experience about the uses of kettles, her evaluation of Dan's friendly disposition and his knowledge of her beverage preferences, and so forth, as well as the new assumptions made manifest by the words he has just spoken (that he is talking to her, that he is informing her that he has put the kettle on, etc.). She draws upon a subset of her old assumptions (kettles are used to make tea; Dan knows she likes tea, milk but no sugar, etc.) as a context within which to process the implications of these new assumptions (Dan is making tea for her, he expects her to join him in the kitchen, etc.). In order to maximize the relevance of these new assumptions she strikes a balance between the effort required to draw those implications (and retrieve old assumptions) and the cognitive benefits of doing so. She may not bother to draw some inferences (Dan is within earshot, Dan speaks English) even though they are strongly manifest, and so easily available, because they have little or no cognitive effect (she already knew this). On the other hand, she may find it a worthwhile effort to draw some weakly manifest inferences (Dan is belittling her intellectual staying power), because the cognitive effects are large (he is not so friendly after all). She remains tapping away at her keyboard.

   The most important consequence of relevance theory, for my purposes, is the new relation it proposes between the functions of relevance and truthfulness in communication. Relevance theory advances the idea that, for the purposes of communication, the propositional criterion of truth is a subordinate consideration to the contextual pragmatic criterion of relevance. This is not to say that the truth or falsehood of assumptions is a matter of indifference, or even that there are circumstances where it is a matter of indifference (as one might be tempted to say, precipitously, is the case with fiction): an assumption, to be an assumption at all, must be taken as true. But all assumptions are, to a greater or lesser extent, the products of inference, which is a pragmatic, relevance-driven process, and the truth of an assumption need not depend upon the truth of the encoded form of an utterance, or its literal meaning. Sperber and Wilson offer an extended account of metaphor and irony, which shares with speech act accounts the assumption that successful communication in such instances is dependent upon an inferential search for contextual relevance. It does not, however, present this search as a process resulting in a dichotomy between the literal sense of "what is said," which is false, and a recovered implicit meaning, which is true (1995: 242).

From a relevance theory perspective, the comprehension of figurative language (as all language) is understood as an inferential process of filling out the linguistic code until maximal relevance is achieved (that is, up to the point at which the cost in processing effort exceeds the benefit in contextual effect, for the reader concerned). Criteria of truth only enter into this process to the extent that truthfulness is a condition of the particular contextual effects involved, and only apply in relation to the assumptions producing those effects, which need not include the literal utterance, or any translation of it, as a proposition: truth criteria are applicable to successful communication only in the sense that the *output* of the inferential process, its cognitive effects, must qualify as information. Relevance to an individual is, definitionally, a measure of cognitive benefit, which Sperber and Wilson generally interpret as an "improvement in knowledge" (Wilson and Sperber 2002: 601), although they do expressly want to leave open the possibility of taking into account other kinds of benefit to cognitive functioning. The notion of "improvement in knowledge" itself, however, embraces a wide range of cognitive effects. For instance, Sperber and Wilson describe a category of cognitive changes they call "poetic effects": an utterance has poetic effects, in their sense, if it achieves most of its relevance through a wide array of weak implicatures (1995: 222). That is, the improvement in knowledge required to achieve relevance may be of an impressionistic or affective nature, yet also be the cumulative product of many minute cognitive effects, many weakly manifest assumptions, all of which are outcomes of the process of comprehension, and none of which is necessarily dependent upon the propositional truth of the input to that process.

On this basis I want to argue that the problem of fictionality is not, after all, a problem of truthfulness but a problem of relevance. It is the presumption of relevance, not any expectation of literal truthfulness, that drives the reader's search for an appropriate interpretative context. Relevance theory allows for inference, and the generation of implicatures, to proceed from an utterance that is clearly false in the same direct way as for one that is taken as true: evaluations of truth only come into play in consequence of that process. So the fictionality of a narrative only compromises the relevance of those assumptions that are contingent upon its literal truth. The relevance theory model allows for a view of fiction in which fictionality is not a frame separating fictive discourse from ordinary or "serious" communication, but a contextual assumption: that is to say, in the comprehension of a fictive utterance, the assumption that it *is* fictive is itself manifest. The main contextual effect of this assumption is to relatively subordinate implicatures that depend upon literal truthfulness in favor of those that achieve relevance in more diffuse and cumulative ways. Fiction does not achieve relevance globally, at one remove, through some form of analogical thinking, but incrementally, through the implication of various cognitive interests or values that are not contingent upon accepting the propositional truth of the utterance itself; and upon the deployment, investment, and working through of those interests in narrative form.

There is, certainly, a global, retrospective sense in which narrative can be understood as the suspension of relevance along the line of action, and narrative closure figures less as the resolution of plot in itself (though it is an effect usually achieved in terms of plot), than as the resolution of suspended evaluations of relevance. In this straightforward sense, irrespective of questions of fictionality, narrative form in itself responds to certain expectations of relevance. K.'s death, at the end of *The Trial*, is not just a very emphatic terminal plot event, but also the "answer" to several kinds of questions raised by the narrative, and in that respect it occasions a range of possible overall assessments of relevance from the reader (relating, for example, to K.'s moral desserts and models of justice, whether legal, cosmic, or poetic; to the balance of power between state and individual, or between structure and agency; to the psychological mechanisms of guilt, and the authority of the superego, and so on). Such global, thematic relevance is by no means the only kind offered by narratives, nor is it necessarily the most important; though in fiction, such interpretative logic is likely to dominate over the kind of factual enrichment of the reader's cognitive environment for which nonfictional narratives are better suited. Still, the investment of interpretative effort in the process of reading a fiction requires an ongoing sense of relevance: there are limits to everyone's tolerance of delayed gratification, and no ultimate resolution alone could plausibly justify the effort of reading Proust's *Recherche*, or *War and Peace*, or *Clarissa*. The narrative force of fiction depends upon assumptions carried forward, enriched, modified, reappraised, overturned in the process of reading: even in fiction, narrative development is only possible on the basis of an *established* sense of relevance.

Relevant information, in fiction, is supplied by assumptions with the capacity to inform a cognitive environment that includes the assumption of fictionality itself, as well as a set of general assumptions that might be collectively labeled "narrative understanding" (which would include logical, evaluative, and affective subsets), and more specific assumptions relating to, for instance, generic expectations of the text in hand, and the particulars of its subject matter. In this cognitive environment, the contextual effects that constitute relevance may be produced by new assumptions informing the project of narrative understanding in general (and the further kinds of understanding this may facilitate), or by assumptions enabling further inferences from the narrative particulars, which will themselves contribute to an ongoing cumulative experience of relevance (such cumulative effects being analogous to those that Sperber and Wilson term "poetic effects" in their discussion of how impressions may be communicated). So a reader of *The Trial* may find relevance in constructing some of the subtle hypotheses about psychological motivation needed to comprehend K.'s behavior; or such comprehension may contribute to an emotional investment of interest, for which K. becomes the vehicle. In either case, the narrative coherence that provides for these effects rests upon more manifest assumptions, of a sort that relates to the familiar idea of what is "true in the fiction." Such assumptions have the status of information irrespective of the literal truth value of the utterance, because their validity, their "aboutness," is contextual, not referential (though this is not to exclude the possibility that some of the assumptions made available by fictive discourse may indeed be referential: as, for instance, in the case of a *roman à clef*, or a historical novel, or the many modern forms of documentary fiction).

The notion of truth "in the fiction" does not imply an ontological frame, but a contextual qualification: assumptions of this kind provide information relative to a context of prior assumptions. We do not generally attempt to resolve the reference of fictive utterances because we know in advance that, in the absence of any evidence to the contrary, their literal truth value will probably be of too little relevance to be worth determining. But this does not compromise the narrative coherence of fictions, because successful reference resolution is not necessary for coreference to occur (think of algebra: we do not need to know the value of x to know that, in $x^2 = 2xy$, each x refers to the same value, which is also the value of 2y). The communicative efficacy of multiple references to fictional characters, places, and events is a pragmatic matter, not a semantic one. As a fictional narrative progresses, further assumptions become manifest not because earlier assumptions have projected a fictional world within which the fictional truth of new assumptions can be established, but because the achieved relevance of the earlier assumptions itself becomes a contextual basis for maximizing the relevance of subsequent related assumptions.

A relevance-driven pragmatic account of inference in fiction does not need to proceed by way of a referential world beyond the discourse, or a denotative "de re" semantics beyond the attributive "de dicto" relations between referring expressions. Everything we can explain by conceiving of fictions as referential constructs projecting fictional worlds, we can explain as well, without cumbersome detour, restrictive norms, paradox, or redundancy, by understanding fiction as the serious use of a language's representational capacity for fictive (imaginary, not literally assertive) purposes: by thinking in terms of the pragmatics rather than the semantics of fictionality. If we do so, the communicative criterion of relevance is primary rather than deferred or indirect, and unitary rather than internal or external to a fictional frame.

A more developed example from Kafka's novel might help to clarify the view of fictionality I am proposing. In what follows, however, I am not advancing a critical methodology, only illustrating a theoretical model. Relevance theory can help explain the principles underlying the experience of fictive communication, but it doesn't lend itself to the eloquent articulation of sophisticated instances of such experience, and still less to the production of striking new interpretations. In my Penguin Classics edition, the first sentence of *The Trial* is translated as follows: "Someone must have made a false accusation against Josef K., for he was arrested one morning without having done anything wrong" (Kafka 1994: 1). In elaborating the inferential processes invited by this sentence, I shall deal only with possible assumptions relating to K., who is clearly its focus, if not its subject. Without any pretension to analytic precision or completeness, then, these four possible assumptions immediately present themselves:

1   Josef K. existed.
2   Josef K. was arrested.
3   Josef K. had not done anything wrong.
4   Someone had made a false accusation against him.

The contextual assumption of fictionality also informs the processing of this sentence (because we found the book in the fiction section of the bookstore, or we are reading it for a course on the modern novel, or we have a prior general knowledge of Kafka). How does that affect our processing of these assumptions?

First, it diminishes the relevance of assumption 1. This is an existential assumption, contingent upon the possibility of resolving the reference of "Josef K." in the real world. The assumption of fictionality doesn't rule this out, but it does create a presumption that it is of negligible relevance, and therefore, within the economy of effort and effect that drives the process of comprehension, it is not worth processing. Note that this is a quite different matter from that of K.'s "existence" in his world, which is either a fictional worlds concept, or (in its more general looser usage) a form of participatory collaboration between critical discourse and fictive discourse. An existential assumption adds nothing to the latter perspective, because (following Kant) existence is not a predicate: it is not in itself a quality of any concept (here, the concept "K."). There are other kinds of characters, of course, for whom the existential assumption would indeed be relevant: it would be an impoverished reading of *War and Peace* that failed to recognize any reference to a historical figure in the character of Napoleon. Assumptions 2 to 4 fare differently, because they provide information about K. presupposing rather than asserting the proposition in assumption 1; their coherence is provided for by coreference, not reference resolution, and so they are not in direct conflict with the assumption of fictionality. Clearly, though, they cannot achieve relevance merely as information about K., but they can help to flesh out several possible narrative schemata, each of which is a potential explanatory framework for information of this kind. Processing these assumptions in accordance with our assessments of their relative strength, and in relation to such schemata, involves the testing and development of our narrative understanding: in those terms alone it offers a degree of relevance that we may well find worth the effort involved.

This prospect is enhanced by another effect of the assumption of fictionality, which is to license imaginary extensions of the scope of knowledge – specifically, here, in the form of internal focalization. The representation of another's mental perspective is not in itself a categorical indicator of fictionality, but it is certainly a possibility that the assumption of fictionality makes much more readily available to interpretation. So here, "somebody must have..." is, in a fiction, unnecessarily conjectural unless it reflects K.'s perspective (or it is the voice of a represented narrator – but no other evidence emerges to support that inference). This is enough to make manifest the further assumptions

5   Josef K. thought that someone had made a false accusation against him.

And, on the same basis,

6   Josef K. did not think he had done anything wrong.

The interpretative basis for assumption 6 is more explicit in the original German than in this translation, but it is available here nonetheless (and there is further confirmation of internal focalization in the following sentence, in which the cook who normally brought K. his breakfast did not come "this time" – the deictic focus conveying K.'s experiential perspective rather than that of the narration).

These assumptions qualify the manifestness of assumptions 3 and 4, and introduce a fundamental ambiguity. Internal focalization belongs within the class of utterances that Sperber and Wilson term "echoic": utterances that interpret another person's thought or speech (this class also includes direct speech and first person narration). They achieve relevance not only by providing information about what that thought was, as in assumptions 5 and 6, but also by taking an attitude towards it (Sperber and Wilson 1995: 238). But what attitude? Internal focalization embraces many shades of irony and sympathy, and under different interpretations, this particular echoic utterance may allow either of the following assumptions to be inferred:

7   Josef K. was the victim of an injustice.
8   Josef K. was ignorant of the law to which he was subject.

And of course further assumptions become manifest in the light of the reader's evaluation of these two: that K. had been framed, or was a paranoid victim (7); that he had been justly reported, or was a paranoid and ignorant offender (8). The evaluative nature of these inferences involves an affective investment of some degree, ranging from judgmental detachment to sympathetic involvement, which will be informed by the reader's emotional and ideological predispositions toward the relation between the individual, self or subject and the law, with all its connotations. Given that the ambiguity of the case inhibits a decisive preference for any one subset of the available competing assumptions, the affective investment (in any nonreductive interpretation) will be complex. This, of course, is fundamental to the effect of the narrative to come, not least because K.'s own attitude toward his predicament is complex: in a wonderful passage a few pages later, Kafka has him "trying to see it from his own point of view" (1994: 7). There is a nice equilibrium between evaluative detachment and imaginative involvement here: the reader's uncertainty in relation to the evaluative import of the internal focalization has an effect of detachment, yet its congruence with K.'s own anxiety about his standing before the law also invests it with the quality of affective involvement.

As the inaugural sentence of a fiction, this one achieves its effects within a relatively simple context. Nonetheless the inferences available here already (necessarily) tend to extrapolate narratively from the utterance itself; and the subsequent narrative development will carry forward the investment of interpretative effort already made, along with the effects that secured a sense of relevance from the process, so that the context for subsequent utterances will furnish many more possible inferences of all kinds. The inferences actually drawn will vary from reading to reading, according to cognitive environment and interpretative agenda, because these contextual factors will qualify the specific expectations of relevance in each case. But in all cases, the satisfaction of those expectations will require some prioritizing of lines of inference: the pragmatic nature of the process of comprehension dictates that it is hardly ever exhaustively logical. The goal of relevance does not require it, which is as well, not because it allows for the assumption of fictionality (that, indeed, secures the logic of fictive utterance), but because it renders inconsequential the many possible inferences from most fictional narratives that would throw their representational logic into disarray.

In contrast with extant accounts, a pragmatic theory of fictionality does not require any detachment of fictive discourse from its real-world context. There is no need for a principle of minimal departure to supply a background for the narrative particulars, because this role is filled by contextual assumptions. These are not part of a fictional world, but of the communicative situation. In this respect as in others, the point is that fictionality is best understood as a communicative resource, rather than as an ontological category. Fictionality is neither a boundary between worlds, nor a frame dissociating the author from the discourse, but a contextual assumption by the reader, prompted by the manifest information that the authorial discourse is offered as fiction. This contextual assumption is a preliminary move in the reader's effort to maximize relevance. It amounts to a rhetorical orientation: an expectation that the relevance of the discourse will be most profitably pursued, not by deriving strongly informative implicatures that depend upon successful reference resolution, but by deriving a large array of weaker implicatures which cumulatively produce affective and evaluative effects, and which are not vitiated by any degree of literal reference failure, but do indeed, ultimately, constitute a cognitive benefit, and an improvement in knowledge. Nothing in this model excludes the possibility of gaining factual information from fiction: fictionality does not admit of degree as a rhetorical set, but fictions do as representations. This distinction, between mutually exclusive communicative intentions (the fictive and the assertive) and the relativity of informative intentions, can accommodate the range of borderline cases that vex definitions of fiction: historical novel, *roman à clef*, fictionalized memoir, historiographic meta-fiction, hoax. The knowledge offered by fiction, however, is not primarily specific knowledge of what is (or was), but of how human affairs work, or, more strictly, of how to make sense of them – logically, evaluatively, emotionally. It is knowledge of the ways in which such matters may be brought within the compass of the imagination, and in that sense understood. A pragmatic theory of fictionality does not *confine* the value of fiction to an improvement in knowledge, even in the broadest senses I have suggested; but it claims that fictions do offer directly communicated cognitive benefits, foregrounded by the contextual assumption of fictionality itself.

There is room for dispute about the scope of the properly cognitive in our experience of fictions, but I am not seeking to characterize that experience, or its value, in wholly cognitive terms. Nor do I think that the cognitive view of communication here implies a restrictive view of authorial intention in fiction.[1] My argument is specifically directed against the entrenched idea that fictive discourse entails a formal, intentional, or ontological frame. All current approaches to fictionality invoke some such frame, and literary criticism negotiates with the fact by a kind of equivocation, doublethink, or fudge: that is, even while its raison d'être is arguably to bridge the gulf between fiction and reality, it actually tends to oscillate between views from either side. It collaborates with, participates in, the fiction; or else it detaches itself, in the process often opening up a gap between the enlightened critic and the naïve, deluded reader. The first, inside, view dominates in most close reading and representationally oriented criticism (by which I mean criticism focused upon the narrative particulars); the second, outside, view is often apparent in formalist and reader-response critical orientations (at least insofar as they project stories of reading), and symptomatic modes of criticism that bring to bear (for example) Marxist, feminist, psychoanalytical, queer, or postcolonial perspectives upon the text. While I do not think there is anything fundamentally wrong with either approach, neither actually explains what is going on in fictive discourse: the first takes it for granted that we are already familiar with fiction (which of course we are); the second tends to bracket fictionality in pursuit of other interests for which the fictional text provides occasion. By refusing this inside/outside dualism, a pragmatic approach to fictionality identifies the issue it effaces: it does not, and should not, conflict with what we currently do as readers and critics, but it identifies something we are not doing that I suggest would be worthwhile. It challenges us to explain the force and effect of fictionality itself in our experience and understanding of fiction.

NOTE

1   For a perspective upon authorial creativity that
    lends itself to redescription in relevance theory
    terms, see Walsh (2000).

REFERENCES AND FURTHER READING

Abbott, H. P. (2002). *The Cambridge Introduction to Narrative*. Cambridge, UK: Cambridge University Press.

Genette, G. (1990). "The Pragmatic Status of Narrative Fiction." *Style* 24, 59–72.

Grice, H. P. (1989). *Studies in the Way of Words*. Cambridge, MA: Harvard University Press.

Kafka, F. ([1925] 1994). *The Trial*, trans. I. Parry. Harmondsworth, UK: Penguin.

Kearns, M. (1999). *Rhetorical Narratology*. Lincoln: University of Nebraska Press.

Kearns, M. (2001). "Relevance, Rhetoric, Narrative." *Rhetoric Society Quarterly* 31, 73–92.

Margolin, U. (1991). "Reference, Coreference, Referring, and the Dual Structure of Literary Narrative." *Poetics Today* 12, 517–42.

Ohmann, R. (1971). "Speech Acts and the Definition of Literature." *Philosophy and Rhetoric* 4, 1–19.

Pavel, T. G. (1986). *Fictional Worlds*. Cambridge, MA: Harvard University Press.

Pratt, M. L. (1977). *Toward a Speech Act Theory of Literary Discourse*. Bloomington: Indiana University Press.

Ryan, M.-L. (1991). *Possible Worlds, Artificial Intelligence and Narrative Theory*. Bloomington: Indiana University Press.

Searle, J. R. (1975). "The Logical Status of Fictional Discourse." *New Literary History* 6, 319–32.

Sperber, D. and Wilson, D. (1995). *Relevance: Communication and Cognition*, 2nd edn. Oxford: Blackwell.

Walsh, R. (1997). "Who is the Narrator?" *Poetics Today* 18, 495–513.

Walsh, R. (2000). "The Novelist as Medium." *Neophilologus* 84, 329–45.

Wilson, D. and Sperber, D. (2002). "Truthfulness and Relevance." *Mind* 111, 583–632.

PART II
Revisions and Innovations

10

Beyond the Poetics of Plot: Alternative Forms of Narrative Progression and the Multiple Trajectories of *Ulysses*

Brian Richardson

While a detailed examination of discussions of plot in the twentieth century would reveal some significant disagreement (e.g., the structuralist emphasis on a grammatical order of events versus the neo-Aristotelian stress on the affective consequences of a trajectory of action), stepping back from specific divergences reveals substantial areas of general agreement, even among theorists who otherwise have little in common. The analysis offered by a proto-structuralist like Vladimir Propp is entirely compatible with the formulation of Paul Ricoeur, writing from the rival perspective of hermeneutics: for Ricoeur, plot is "the intelligible whole that governs a succession of events in a story. . . . A story is made out of events to the extent that plot *makes* events *into* a story" (1981: 167); Propp similarly postulates a connected series of events that leads to a resolution of the problem or conflict with which the story began. These stances are not only congruent with Peter Brooks's post-structuralist psychoanalytic approach, both are actually cited by him in support of his own position (1984: 13–17). Brooks's use of plot as a term to embrace "the design and intention of narrative, a structure for those meanings that develop through succession and time" (1984: 12) is in turn consonant with the other major strand of theorizing plot: the emphasis on unity, design, completion, and effect produced by the neo-Aristotelians associated with the University of Chicago, beginning with R. S. Crane. Distilling these different discussions leads to this conception of plot: an essential element of narrative, plot is a teleological sequence of events linked by some principle of causation; that is, the events are bound together in a trajectory that typically leads to some form of resolution or convergence.[1]

The problem with such a notion, however, is that many narratives resist, elude, or reject this model of plot and its explicit assumption of narrative unity, cohesion, and teleology. This is especially true of twentieth-century texts that remain insistently fragmentary, open-ended, contradictory, or defiantly "plotless." The definition just set forth is of little use in describing the trajectories, or what I will call narrative progressions, traced by *Ulysses* or *The Waves*, to say nothing of the still more experimental work of Gertrude Stein, Raymond Roussel, Samuel Beckett, or Alain Robbe-Grillet.[2] (I might add that this assertion is not altered by the fact that we need to draw on this definition of plot in order to comprehend the specific violations made by such authors.) In what follows, I will identify the most salient varieties of nonplot-based narrative ordering in recent fiction, point out relevant historical antecedents, and note how these strategies supplement or supersede more traditional modes of sequencing. This inventory will have its own sequencing principle, moving from the most familiar to the most outrageous orderings, that is, from those that almost invisibly accompany the movement of story to those that most spectacularly over-throw it. It is striking how many different nonplot-based methods of producing events there are, and surprising that these have not been more thoroughly examined and discussed by narratologists. I will also look for the presence of each strategy in *Ulysses*, a novel that employs a rather large number of ordering techniques other than those of conventional emplotment.

Ulysses is particularly interesting in this regard. On the one hand, the work seems to lack what might seem to be the minimal necessary plot: event after event appears to occur more or less randomly; the first linear progression (Chapters 1–3) is interrupted and the clock is reset as we meet Bloom in Chapter 4; the two main storylines often approach each other but never fully meet in any significant way; and the final chapters resist any mechanism that will tie the events together as Stephen and Bloom part ways like two ships passing in the night, as a common description of the book's inconclusive ending avers. Many shorter sequences seem adventitiously con-joined and are certainly unconnected by any large causal chain; "The Wandering Rocks" episode, which traces the essentially noninteractive movements of several spatially adjacent Dublin citizens, can even be seen as a kind of quintessence of the work's refusal of traditional plot.[3] The book's frequent use of interior monologue and free indirect speech makes the sequencing of still shorter passages seem even more adventitious; to say that sentence B follows sentence A because that thought just popped into the character's mind is not much of an explanation at all. Todorov goes so far as to state that "the most striking submission to the temporal order is *Ulysses*. The only, or at least the main, relation among the actions is their pure succession" (1981: 42).

One obvious method by which these ostensibly gratuitous events and episodes are patterned is by their reproduction of the order of an earlier text.[4] The dual linear progressions just noted appear in *Ulysses* because the same sequence occurs in the *Odyssey*: Joyce puts Stephen's otherwise unmotivated and inconsequential encounter with the Protean ocean (Chapter 3) after his meeting with the Nestor figure (Chapter 2) because Homer's Telemachus speaks with Nestor (Book Three) before doing battle with Proteus (Book Four). Homer's largely causal sequence becomes the template for Joyce's otherwise random conjunctions. This ordering continues for much but not all of Joyce's text: his Lotus Eaters, Aeolus, Lestrygonians, Sirens, and Oxen of the Sun episodes follow the same order as that used by Homer; other episodes, however (Cyclops, Circe), are rearranged to suit different purposes.

Sheldon Sacks has provided another useful way in which we may think about narratives organized in a manner largely independent of the customary qualities of plot. Discussing the genre of the apologue, or fictional exemplification of a thesis or worldview such as *Candide* or *Rasselas*, he points out that the episodes are "related to each other in a rhetorical order," rather than a probabilistic one. "There is no fictional 'probability' that Rasselas, after he leaves the haunts of gay young men, will meet a sage committed to controlling the passions" (Sacks 1964: 56); such a sequence, however, does follow from the demands of the novella's argument. This kind of rhetorical sequencing is found in the more ideologically charged turns of many novels. Joyce, being resolutely antididactic, does not normally use rhetorical progressions in this way. Nevertheless, we can see numerous miniature and oblique rhetorical sequences in the dialectical progression of the events in "Scylla and Charybdis," in which the idealistic theses propounded by the figures in the library are followed by the crassly materialistic positions of Buck Mulligan, whose entry into the room is synchronized with the model of thesis/antithesis. In a related manner, the catechistic structure of "Ithaca" is minimally narrative and is sequenced instead by the linked series of questions and answers; as C. H. Peake observes, this "is not naturally a narrative method; it implies a static situation which is being examined and analyzed rather than the unrolling of a concatenated series of events" (1977: 283).[5] Aspects of the progressions common to apologues also appear in the numerous rhetorical trajectories present in the "Aeolus" chapter that is set in a newsroom and thematizes the art of rhetoric.

It is easy to move from a sequence of events that exemplifies an argument to more general motif-based alternation or progression. But while these modes of composition are similar, their motives may be opposed. Rhetorical sequencing is an intentional arrangement set forth as advantageously as possible to produce a particular effect: to bring the mind of the reader into closer conformity with the beliefs of the author. In this sense, it is every bit as "functional" as traditional emplotment, whose purpose is to impel the reader from chapter to chapter observing how sympathetic protagonists attempt to overcome adversity and attain their desires. Motif-based, architectonic, numerological, or geometrical kinds of sequencing are primarily formal designs that have little function other than that of satisfying a desire for symmetry. I will refer to these forms as "aesthetic" orderings. We may start by looking at the growth of the "little phrase" of music by Vinteuil in Proust's *In Search of Lost Time*. The phrase appears in a number of scenes in different incarnations, but, following a general trajectory, ever more elaborate instantiations. It begins as a musical phrase heard by Swann, and then is identified as part of a sonata by a man named Vinteuil. As the work continues, the composer's identity is fully disclosed, and the theme, once a token of Swann's love for Odette, becomes an emblem of the disintegration of Marcel's love for Albertine. Finally, the discovery of a full-length septet by Vinteuil is made.[6] The development of this motif has its own independent trajectory; in response to the question, "Why does the discovery of the Vinteuil septet occur late in the work?" it is as plausible to say, "Because it is the culmination of the expanding theme of the musical phrase" as to aver that it discloses again the achievement of the neglected composer at a strategic point of the narrative. After a certain point, the theme does not merely accompany the narrative; instead, the narrative events are produced to accommodate the development of the motif.

Numerous other such aesthetic progressions may be enumerated, including the familiar circle pattern that returns important aspects of the narrative to their starting points; another is that which E. M. Forster described as the hourglass shape of Henry James's *The Ambassadors* (Forster 1927: 153–62). We may also point to Tolstoy's insistent alternation of light and dark scenes throughout *Anna Karenina*, and further note James's perhaps unfair castigation of Tolstoy for producing "fluid puddings" and "large loose baggy monsters" from the perspective of formal design (James 1972: 267, 262). When examining any of the many scenes that do not obviously impel the plot forward, one may explain its placement in terms of its motif function rather than as part of any causal chain of events. Joyce is quite adept at these kinds of progressions: each of the final 15 chapters of *Ulysses* thematizes a different organ of the human body; similarly, a different art or science is foregrounded in each. The specifically generative functions of these themes occur more at the level of individual events than of the chapter – Joyce did not add the Aeolus episode because he wanted to dramatize a specific organ (lungs) and discipline (rhetoric) – though several smaller events (including mental events) take place for the primary purpose of illustrating these themes ("The door of Ruttledge's office whispered: ee: cree. They always build one door opposite another for the wind to. Way in. Way out" [Joyce 1986: 97].)

Still other kinds of symmetrical arrangements of chapters and events can be adduced; these do not merely provide a structure for an otherwise unorganized conglomeration of events but at times go on to actually *produce* some of those events. Viktor Shklovsky (1990) identified a number of formal arrangements of narrative materials, including repetition, parallelism, antithesis, and triadic patterns, and pointed out that much of the *Chanson de Roland* is composed around dual and triple repetitions of the same set of scenes and events. In fact, many of these actions are present *only* because they complete the formal pattern that animates the rest of the text, in contravention of other compositional principles like causal connection, verisimilitude, or rhetorical efficacy. William W. Ryding carries this kind of analysis much further, describing how a number of medieval narratives eschew narrative unity in favor of "artistic duality, trinity, or some other form of multiplicity" (1971: 116), including the multiplication of parallel or antithetical story lines exclusively for this effect. Thus the second part of *Beowulf*, which takes place 50 years after his victory over Grendel and the hag, is an entirely new (though fully symmetrical) story of the aged Beowulf's battle with the dragon. This work, like the *Chanson de Roland*, "has in fact two beginnings, two middles, and two ends. The central discontinuity that seems so clumsy to us appears to have served the medieval writer as a means to a particular esthetic end – it was, we may suppose, a special grace in story-telling" (Ryding 1971:

43).[7] Other comparable methods of production and ordering of narrative segments are common in numerous periods of literary history.[8] These various architectonic progressions are no doubt understudied because in many cases they may seem to be less important than, or a mere appendage to, the unfolding of the progression of the story's main events; so powerful is the pull of the plot in the perception of narrative that plot may need to be abandoned or suppressed for alternative ordering systems to become visible. Nevertheless, these methods of sequencing do help explain why a given narrative has the events and arrangement it does. Even if Dante's story were largely completed halfway through the *Paradiso*, he would have had to stretch his material out until he had reached the structurally requisite 33 cantos.

As the example from Proust suggests, the arrangement of a cluster of literary motifs may be modeled on or borrowed from standard musical progressions. For his entire novel Proust employed the structure of a Wagnerian opera; others have utilized the general structure of the sonata (Strindberg) or the symphony (Gide, Andrei Biely), the framework of jazz (Ralph Ellison, Toni Morrison), or the prescriptions of the classical Indian musical form, the *raga* (Amit Chaudhuri's 1993 *Afternoon Raag*). A trajectory provided by the fugue has at times proven irresistible, as evidenced by Thomas Mann's "Death in Venice" and the *fuga per canonem* that orders the "Sirens" episode of *Ulysses*.[9] These last two examples point to an important distinction in nonplot-based ordering devices: often, these are unobtrusive, working in tandem with more conventional modes of story sequencing, producing a trajectory of otherwise largely unmotivated sequences or (as in the case of Mann) an overdetermined narrative progression (that is, Aschenbach dies in Venice *both* because he has chosen to stay in the city as the plague spreads *and* because it is the final expression of the bass theme, death, as it merges with its contrapuntal theme of sexual desire). Many of the sequences in Joyce's "Sirens," however, make little or no sense if approached from the traditional perspectives of story or plot; indeed, the episode's first set of words make virtually no sense from almost any conventional framework: "Bronze by gold heard the hoofirons, steelyringing./ Imperthnthn thnthnthn./ Chips, picking chips off rocky thumbnail, chips./ Horrid! And gold flushed more./ A husky fifenote blew./ Blew. Blue bloom is on the./ Goldpinnacled hair. A jumping rose on satiny breast of satin, rose of Castille./ Trilling, trilling: Idolores./ Peep! Who's in the . . . peepof-gold?" (p. 210, Joyce's ellipsis). As an overture that previews the primary versions of the major themes and motifs to follow (and roughly approximating the order of their appearance), it is an accurate and useful compendium that performs the same function as a musical overture – especially a very daring one which offers such disparate motifs that we are unsure whether they can in fact come together in the development of the music that follows.

One might designate the presentation of the opening phrases of "Sirens" as foreshadowing or announcing the material to follow, but one may equally effectively view them as generating the rest of the chapter. This type of oscillating perspective is frequently relevant to narratives that are or seem to be generated by (fictional) pictures within the text. Longus's second-century novella, *Daphnis and Chloe*, begins with the partial description of a narrative painting, which the narrator finds so wonderful that he decides to narrate in prose the story it depicts. In Goethe's "Novelle," we are presented with drawings of an abandoned castle, the story of a marketplace fire, and the picture of a tiger leaping on a person. As the tale unfolds, the protagonist visits the castle, observes a fire break out in the marketplace, and witnesses a real tiger leaping on a person. Such unlikely repetitions may be properly viewed as uncanny coincidences or an overactive display of irony; however, one might also read them as a cunning, proto-Borgesian play with narrative sequencing in which simulacra come to engender the objects and events that they had represented.

For a Joycean example we may turn to the phantasmagoric "Circe" chapter, in which images Bloom has seen earlier in the day now come alive, such as the Greek nymph in the painting in his bedroom (pp. 444–51). This kind of "pictorial genesis" is also found in many *nouveaux romans*, perhaps most memorably in Robbe-Grillet's *In the Labyrinth*, in which a number of shapes described at the beginning of the book go on to generate objects having a similar shape which then become foci of unfolding narratives. Thus the layer of dust in the room engenders the snow that appears in the story that grows from it, the image of the cross-shaped object on the desk is transformed into the bayonet of the soldier in the inner story, and the painting, "The Defeat at Reichenfels," after being described in impossible detail, comes alive and turns into a narrative, as a description becomes through metalepsis a sequence of events, and the opposition between temporal and spatial art forms dissolves.[10]

Other forms of text generation are common in the *nouveau roman* and its various antecedents; a particularly seminal type is the way in which a few select words go on to generate the object or actions they depict. This is an important and fascinating method of engendering a narrative and deserves to be far better known. Jean Ricardou (1972) has called it a structural metaphor, and describes it as a trope that is made literal and takes on life in the text. I will refer to it as a "verbal generator" and use it to refer to a practice that names an object or event which then appears or occurs in the narrative. In a traditional work, there may well be an ironic foreshadowing by an event before it occurs; in the *nouveau roman*, this becomes an alternative principle of narrative progression as words or images produce the events of the text. Thus, in Robbe-Grillet's *Project for a Revolution in New York*, the concept "red" in all its permutations and variations generates many of the events (including murder and arson); still more primary is the juxtaposition of contraries, as Thomas D. O'Donnell (1975) has explained. Noting further narrative proliferation, O'Donnell traces the avatars that produce the rat in the book. "Very early in the novel, the narrator informs us that Ben Said is wearing black gloves; when writing in his notebook, Ben Said tucks the gloves under his armpit. Another glove appears on the cover of Laura's detective story," this in turn suggests that

> Ben Said may be responsible for the fate of the girl on the story's torn cover. Upon closer examination, it is noted that the "glove" is in reality an enormous furry spider. Laura

found the book on top of the bookcase while trying to escape from a giant spider or a *rat*; henceforth, spider and rat form an elementary combination that may not be dissociated.

(O'Donnell 1975: 192)

These examples, O'Donnell points out, "illustrate Robbe-Grillet's thematic generative technique to provide a long range 'plot' for his novel" (1975: 192). In Joyce's "Circe," we find a clear example of a verbal generator producing a substantial stretch of text. As Bloom denigrates tobacco, Zoe retorts: "Go on. Make a stump speech out of it." What immediately follows in the narrative is the figure of Bloom in working-man's overalls, giving an oration on the evils of tobacco before an adoring populace (1986: 390–3), as the phrase "make a stump speech" precedes the event it simultaneously names and produces.

In many of the compositions of Jean Ricardou, on the other hand, individual French words produce slight lexical variants which go on to generate the newly named objects or relations in the text as it unfolds. Even the name of the press that appears on the title page ("*Les Éditions de minuit*") can serve as a textual generator: thus, in *La Prise de Constantinople*, the word *Éditions* engenders the characters Ed and Edith, as well as the idea of the hill of Sion, while *Minuit* determines the book will open at night (Ricardou 1972: 384).[11] Though it may appear the exclusive demesne of the avant-garde, such "lexical generators" can actually be traced back as far as Sterne's *Tristram Shandy* if not in fact to Dante.[12]

Somewhat less dynamic is the comparable ordering principle of alphabetical patterns. Such a progression, as Roland Barthes once remarked at the beginning of one of his own such compositions, has all the order and arbitrariness of the alphabet itself. This kind of progression, which probably traces its descent from Raymond Roussel, is not inherently a fictive one, and can be readily found in nonfiction and nonnarrative forms (e.g., Barthes's *A Lover's Discourse*) as well as works that straddle the line between narrative and nonnarrative, such as Michel Butor's *Mobile*, which Sherzer describes as "semiotic catalogue" and states (certainly debatably), that it "is without narrative" (1986: 46, 50). An interesting elaboration of this stratagem can be found in Milorad Pavić's *Dictionary of the Khazars*, a novel in the shape of three dictionaries. A narratologist might object that alphabetical composition is merely a different way to rearrange the *sjuzhet* and does not really affect the *fabula*; however, in some works, like Walter Abish's *Alphabetical Africa*, the ordering principle is clearly generating that which is depicted (see Orr 1991: 113–16). Other transpositions of familiar verbal ordering principles onto narrative fiction (critical commentary in Nabokov's *Pale Fire*, the crossword puzzle in Pavić's *Landscape Painted with Tea*) may be included here. Though Joyce delights in the play of individual letters and is intrigued by the alphabet ("Ahbeesee defeegee kelomen opeecue rustyouvee" [p. 48], I don't find any strictly alphabetical orderings in *Ulysses* of any scale (though the letters of the last word of the book –"yes" – are contained, in reverse order, in its first word, "Stately").[13]

Another generating mechanism used by many recent French authors is based on repetition of events rather than on a progression from one event to another. The classic instance of this practice is probably Robbe-Grillet's *Jealousy*, in which approximately the same set of events is presented nine consecutive times, with each version containing significant variations. As Robbe-Grillet has explained, in a traditional narrative, "what follows phenomenon A is a phenomenon B, the consequence of the first," while in a *nouveau roman* like *Jealousy*, "what happens is entirely different. Instead of having to deal with a series of scenes which are connected by causal links, one has the impression that the same scene is constantly repeating itself, but with variations; that is, scene A is not followed by scene B but by scene A', a possible variation of scene A" (Robbe-Grillet 1977: 5). This technique is variously designated by its theorists; the most useful term is probably that employed by Dina Sherzer, who calls this kind of progression "serial constructs" (1986: 13–36).[14] Serial constructs may be further sequenced according to other patterns of progression: the repeated, contradictory depictions that constitute Robbe-Grillet's "The Secret Room" are shaped in the form of a temporal spiral; the obsessively reenacted scene in Robert Coover's *Spanking the Maid* gradually rises to a peak of physicality before rapidly subsiding at the end of the book. That this technique continues to thrive in other genres is evidenced by the success of the recent German film *Run, Lola, Run*. In each episode of *Ulysses*, Joyce includes echoes of other episodes, some of which can feel quite out of place, and seemingly present only for their echoic function, but other than this cannot be said to generate the text. Miniature reproductions of the string of events of the entire book (that is, *mises en abyme*) are also present at several points in Joyce's text (e.g., pp. 543, 552).

A related technique is "collage" composition, in which several key elements are recombined in a number of different arrangements and contexts and which constitute the nexus that connects the different units.[15] This order may be present (and is no doubt less jarring) in nonnarrative texts; it is also more of a principle of coherence rather than progression *per se*, since after a certain amplitude is reached, there is no inherent reason for the text to continue. Nevertheless, to answer the question "How are the third or fourth sections related to the opening units?" a plausible response is that they are recombinations, analogues, or variations of some of the elements present in the earlier segments; the collage technique, that is, necessitates such a progression. As Dina Sherzer remarks, such texts "are open in that no one referential or morphological element brings about the sense of an ending or a feeling of completion; other variations and repetitions could be added to the existing ones, lengthening the text but not changing it otherwise" (1986: 14). This observation is a fairly good depiction of Lyn Hejinian's text, *My Life*, a partially autobiographical collage that was originally published in 1978, when the author was 37. At this time, the work consisted of 37 sections, each with 37 sentences. The second edition, published eight years later, has eight new sections of 45 sentences, and eight new sentences were added to all of the previously published sections. Here, *Ulysses* can function as a model for such practices, as its central figures, motifs, tropes, and elements are recombined in successive chapters, sometimes in ways that violate the book's mimetic stance, as Hazard Adams (1986) has pointed out in his study of these deviously "wandering rocks."

Before leaving this arena we need to engage with two other kinds of transgressive orderings: those that may seem to have too much plot and those that have too little. The "forking paths" principle articulated by (though not really embodied within) Borges's story "The Garden of Forking Paths" can lead us directly to a genuinely new kind of multiple, mutually exclusive, orderings of a text. A good instance is found in Ana Castillo's *The Mixquiahuala Letters*, a text that offers three different sequences for reading the book: one for conformists, one for cynics, and one for the quixotic reader. None of these recommended sequences includes the entire group of the letters, or even begins with letter number one, with which the book opens; this arrangement necessarily suggests yet another possible progression, the numerical one. In this work, like Julio Cortázar's *Hopscotch*, whose techniques it extends, the suggested *sjuzhet* is largely linear; the different possible trajectories do not result in radically different *fabulas*, though the interpretation of the basic fabula will alter depending on which version is followed. More radical in this regard are the popular children's "pick your own adventure" books, where different readerly choices result in quite different sequences.

The "forking paths" kind of composition is not unrelated to hypertext narratives, and indeed may be usefully thought of as a simple prototype of the latter. Such examples are now fairly common on the web, where *afternoon, a story* is achieving a certain eminence. Intriguingly, Margaret Atwood has written a kind of quasi- (or, indeed, anti-) hypertext in her story, "Happy Endings," in which some 10 available narrative options all lead sooner or later to the same story of the death of the protagonists. Atwood's piece may provide a useful metacommentary on hypertext generation: these may well be entirely containable within traditional concepts of plot; the primary difference would be that it is the reader rather than the protagonist or the author who chooses which event will happen next (or, more precisely, the reader chooses from a set of limited options made available by the author). *Ulysses* has regularly been described as a kind of hypertext due to its difficulty of being comprehended on a first reading (one must know the whole book to understand any part), as well as the innumerable patterns and correspondences that extend across chapters and, indeed, across Joyce's other works.

A final aspect of narrative unfolding needs to be mentioned, and that is the move toward a relatively pure sequence that has few connectors and still fewer textual generators, whether conventional or avant-garde. A number of feminist works move in this direction, starting with Dorothy Richardson's fiction, the first works of literature to which the critical term "stream of consciousness" was applied, and which Virginia Woolf critiqued for lacking "unity, significance, or design" (1980: 190). Woolf would herself experiment with pure linearity in the "Time Passes" section of *To the Lighthouse*, a section that may have inspired Eva Figes's novel *Waking*, a chronicle of seven awakenings into consciousness by the central character, each of them separated from the others by about a decade, and so loosely conjoined that there is fairly little to connect them all to the same individual. Such an "excessive" linearity also appears in other works that fall under the rubric of *écriture féminine*, such as Clarice Lispector's *Agua Viva* (*The Stream of Life*) or Molly Bloom's soliloquy.[16] An even greater challenge to the notion of a single narrative line is the kind of narrative with a collective subject dispersed over three continents and 250 years in Caryl Philips's novel/novellas of the African diaspora in *Crossing the River*. These radical examples show how much traditional plot is actually present in episodic or picaresque novels; after all, Lazarillo de Tormes "is a character who is modified and molded by his adventures and his ambience. The innocent child who has his head smashed against the bull is quite different from the vengeful child who makes his blind master smash his head against the pillar" (Fiore 1984: 84).

This analysis leads now to our last category, or rather anticategory, of narrative progression: the aleatory. Popularized by Dadaists who would select phrases that had been cut out of newspapers and thrown into a hat, a number of authors and composers including William Burroughs and Karlheinz Stockhausen have utilized this technique. Beckett's "Lessness" is a short text said to be randomly assembled, though the numerous interconnections among its elements tend to make any order they may appear in seem purposive. There are no aleatory elements in *Ulysses* – Joyce once wondered whether it wasn't too meticulously structured – and it may be that there is only a single aleatory phrase in all Joyce's works. As Richard Ellmann recounts, Joyce was dictating part of *Finnegans Wake* to Samuel Beckett.

> In the middle of one such session there was a knock at the door which Beckett didn't hear. Joyce said "Come in." and Beckett wrote it down. Afterwards he read back what he had written and Joyce said, "What's that 'Come in'?" "Yes, you said that," said Beckett. Joyce thought for a moment, then said, "Let it stand." He was quite willing to accept coincidence as his collaborator.
>
> (Ellmann 1982: 649)

What conclusions are we to draw from the preceding analyses, a cluster of examples that at times no doubt threaten to turn into an episodic collocation of entries devoid of all the basic elements of a good plot: unity of design, inescapable development, and definitive conclusion? We may begin by observing the curious fact that the full range of mechanisms for the development and progression of narrative fiction in all its varieties has, to my knowledge, never been systematically set forth (though I hasten to add that theorists like Monika Fludernik [1996: 269–310] and Brian McHale [1987] have approached many of these issues from somewhat different perspectives).[17] Nevertheless, I find this vast theoretical gap quite surprising and hope this essay will help to begin to rectify this unusual situation.

Looking back over the various sequencing practices discussed above, we may attempt some general observations on narrative progression. It is clear that a thorough analysis of nonplot-based forms of narrative progression reveals how prevalent they are and how significant they can be. Some of these, like rhetorical or aesthetic ordering, can be complementary to more conventional kinds of emplotment; they add an additional though rarely discussed motivation for the exact narrative trajectory that emerges. Traditional emplotment often or even typically works in a kind of un-acknowledged counterpoint with other methods of progression. At times these diverge or come into collision, a situation most evident when ideological trajectories displace probability in a realist work.[18] I suspect it is where these modes clash most visibly that we may find ideological work being done in the most undisguised fashion, as in ideologically imposed closures that do violence to a work's mimetic economy. By contrast, radical aesthetic ordering techniques, such as verbal generators, are quite disruptive in a different, more obviously deliberate, manner and regularly defy conventions of mimesis and supplant plot altogether.

Nevertheless, I suspect that all of the more vigorous nonplot or antiplot mechanisms of narrative sequencing are ultimately dependent on a prior notion of emplotment, and work in a dialectical way to negate the conventional pattern that the new arrangements nevertheless presuppose. Thus, while the concept of plot alone cannot describe the various sequencing patterns present in many recent works of fiction, most of those patterns can only be fully comprehended in relation to plot. Even chance compositions are interesting not for any intrinsic reason but for the ways they appear to mimic or contravene the kind of order produced by emplotment. The symbiotic between plot and other antithetical orderings is especially pronounced in the arrangement of the collection of nine contradictory versions of essentially the same set of events in Robbe-Grillet's *Jealousy*. The shifting intensity of these descriptions, as Jean Ricardou has pointed out, nevertheless traces the traditional structure of slowly rising and rapidly falling action typical of the conventional novel. Similarly, the sequence of variants that compose the experimental film *Run, Lola, Run* follow the general pattern of comedy, with a successful conclusion at the end of the final sequence.

We may affirm that narrative progression is a protean, dynamic process, with multiple sources of narrative development operating at different points in the text, as *Ulysses* exemplifies so clearly. The concept of plot alone is not adequate to explain all the sequences even of many plot-driven compositions, let alone the more experimental textual generators identified above. We would do well to think of plot as a component of narrative sequencing that is independent of, and working in varying degrees of complementarity with or opposition to, other kinds of progres-sion, especially rhetorical and aesthetic orderings. Looked at from the vantage point of literary value, it may well be that the most compelling narrative sequences are those that seamlessly interweave two or more strategies of progression, making the independent orderings seem to be coextensive and unobtrusive. In any event, it is clearly the case that the more simple and streamlined the mode of progression, whether mere allegory, facile verbal generation, overly predictable plot, or an unmotivated concatenation of adventures, the easier it is for experienced readers to lose interest in the work. We may conclude by urging that the theoretical study of plot should be subsumed within the logically more capacious category of narrative progression. Such a more extensive framework is essential if we are to have a thorough account of the way narrative fiction actually unfolds in time.[19]

NOTES

1   As Peter Brooks states, "The very possibility of meaning plotted through sequence and through time depends on the anticipated structuring force of the ending" (1984: 93, cf. 90–112).

2   I wish to point out that James Phelan's flexible and very useful account of narrative progression as a dynamic event that treats its subject as a developing whole does not suffer from the limitations of the concepts of plot noted above and partly for this reason I use his term (1989: 14–22). Ralph Rader (1973) presented another important earlier attempt to move beyond what he terms "the realism-plot-judgment" model of narrative he identified with the earlier Chicago School theorists; his account, while disclosing three very different forms a realistic narrative progression may take, nevertheless remains grounded in a mimetic framework and thus cannot encompass antimimetic patterns.

3   Timothy Martin observes that "many of the later episodes betray principles of wholeness independent of *Ulysses* as a whole" (1998: 208); the rest of his essay provides an impressive study of the unity and disunity of the events and other aspects of the text.

4   Though this strategy is a favorite of modernist and postmodern authors, its origins stretch back to antiquity. An early, playfully self-conscious example can be found in Aristophanes' *Thesmophoriazusae*. Toward the end of this drama, Euripides' cousin finds himself captured by those he fears will harm him. In order to escape, he tries to imitate analogous roles of characters similarly stranded in different plays by Euripides. After two false starts, he enacts the scene from *Andromeda* that most closely resembles his situation and is then able to escape.

5   For an analysis of the nonnarrative nature of "Ithaca," see Monika Fludernik (1986).

6   E. M. Forster (1927: 165–9) has a deft account of the development of this motif.

7   Such a concern for symmetrical presentation may explain in part some of the contradictions in biblical narrative noted by David Richter in this volume.

8   For a comprehensive overview of symmetrical and numerological progressions in narrative literature, see R. G. Peterson (1976). For a study of symmetries in chapter sequencing in the traditional novel, see Marshall Brown (1987).

9   There is still some disagreement on just how closely this episode approximates a fugue. For a recent approach that employs Schoenberg's 12-tone system to explicate Joyce's sequencing, see Herman (1994).

10 For other examples of this kind of text generation, see Julio Cortazar's "Blow Up" and Claude Simon's *Triptych*. For the opposite movement, in which a narrative progresses only to end up as a painting, see Alejo Carpentier's *Explosion in a Cathedral*, in which the metaphor of spatial form becomes literalized, as it were. Emma Kafalenos (2003) has compellingly discussed the intriguing narrative status of "Blow Up" and other ekphrastic works.

11 For additional discussion of these important yet insufficiently known modes of generation, see Sherzer (1986: 13–36) and Hayman (1987: 104–46).

12 Tristram's father, Walter Shandy, actually writes a book that attempts to prove that the name one is born with strongly influences one's fortunes in life; or in his words, "that magic bias which good or bad names irresistibly impress upon our characters and conducts" (Bk 4, Ch 8). This is certainly true for Tristram's sad fate. For Dante's use of this strategy, see the 30th canto of the *Purgatorio*.

13 There is, however, plenty of alphabetical play in "Ithaca" (anagrams, acrostics, etc.).

14 Rather less felicitously, David Hayman refers to this as "nodality" (1987: 73–104).

15 Dina Sherzer discusses this type of work under the rubric of "multidimensional montages" (1986: 37–76).

16 For a brief discussion of some of these texts, see my article on linearity (Richardson 2000).

17 For additional discussion of many of the issues raised in this essay, see my introductions to the sections on "Plot and Emplotment," "Narrative Progressions and Sequences" and "Narrative Temporality" in *Narrative Dynamics* (Richardson 2002: 9–14, 64–70, 159–63).

18 An example that comes readily to mind is the ending of D. H. Lawrence's "The Fox," in which Lawrence is so determined to show that two women cannot live happily together without a man that, in violation of the realism that governs the events of the rest of the text, his hero chops down a tree that falls on and kills the more pushy woman. Other readers can no doubt supply their own favorite such examples.

19 I wish to thank many individuals at the "Contemporary Narrative Theory" conference for a number of excellent comments, including Wayne Booth, Royal Brown, Melba Cuddy-Keene, David Richter, and Dan Shen; special thanks go to James Phelan and Peter Rabinowitz for numerous helpful observations and suggestions.

REFERENCES AND FURTHER READING

Adams, H. (1986). "Critical Construction of the Literary Text: The Example of *Ulysses*." *New Literary History* 17, 595–619.

Brooks, P. (1984). *Reading for the Plot: Design and Intention in Narrative*. New York: Random.

Brown, M. (1987). "Plan vs. Plot: Chapter Symmetries and the Mission of Form." *Stanford Literature Review* 4, 103–36.

Ellmann, R. (1982) *James Joyce*, revised edn. Oxford: Oxford University Press.

Fiore, R. L. (1984). *Lazarillo de Tormes*. Boston: Twayne.

Fludernik, M. (1986). " 'Ithaca' – An Essay in Non-Narrativity." In G. Gaiser (ed.), *International Perspectives on James Joyce* (pp. 88–105). Troy, NY: Whitsun.

Fludernik, M. (1996). *Towards a "Natural" Narratology*. London: Routledge.

Forster, E. M. (1927). *Aspects of the Novel*. London and New York: Harcourt, Brace and World.

Hayman, D. (1987). *Re-Forming the Narrative: Toward a Mechanics of Modernist Fiction*, Ithaca, NY: Cornell University Press.

Herman, D. (1994). " 'Sirens' after Schoenberg." *James Joyce Quarterly* 31, 473–94.

James, H. (1972). *Henry James: Theory of Fiction*, ed. James E. Miller. Lincoln: University of Nebraska Press.

Joyce, J. ([1922] 1986). *Ulysses: The Corrected Text*, ed. H. W. Gabler. New York: Random.

Kafalenos, E. (2003). "The Power of Double Coding to Represent New Forms of Representation: *The Truman Show, Dorian Gray,* 'Blow Up,' and Whistler's *Caprice in Purple and Gold*." *Poetics Today* 24(1), 1–33.

Martin, T. (1998). "*Ulysses* as a Whole." In R. Frehner and U. Zeller (eds.), *A Collideorscape of Joyce* (pp. 202–14). Dublin: Lilliput.

McHale, B. (1987). *Postmodernist Fiction*. London: Methuen.

O'Donnell, T. D. (1975). "Thematic Generation in Robbe-Grillet's *Projet pour une révolution à New York*." In G. Stambolian (ed.), *Twentieth Century French Fiction: Essays for Germaine Brée* (pp. 184–97). New Brunswick, NJ: Rutgers University Press.

Orr, L. (1991). *Problems and Poetics of the Nonaristotelian Novel*. Lewisburg, PA: Bucknell University Press.

Peake, C. H. (1977). *James Joyce: The Citizen and the Artist*. Stanford, CA: Stanford University Press.

Peterson, R. G. (1976). "Critical Calculations: Measure and Symmetry in Literature." *PMLA* 91, 367–75.

Phelan, J. (1989). *Reading People, Reading Plots: Character, Progression, and the Interpretation of Narrative*. Chicago: University of Chicago Press.

Rader, R. (1973). "Defoe, Richardson, Joyce, and the Concept of Form in the Novel." In

W. Matthews and R. Rader, *Autobiography, Biography, and the Novel* (pp. 31–72). Los Angeles: William Andrews Clark Memorial Library, UCLA.

Ricardou, J. (1972). "Naissance d'une fiction." In J. Ricardou and F. van Rossum-Guyon (eds.), *Nouveau Roman: hier, aujourd'hui*, vol 2: *Practiques* (pp. 379–92). Paris: 10/18.

Richardson, B. (2000). "Linearity and its Discontents: Rethinking Narrative Form and Ideological Valence." *College English* 62, 685–95.

Richardson, B. (ed.). (2002). *Narrative Dynamics: Essays on Time, Plot, Closure, and Frames.* Columbus: Ohio State University Press.

Ricoeur, P. (1981). "Narrative Time." In W. J. T. Mitchell (ed.), *On Narrative* (pp. 165–86). Chicago: University of Chicago Press.

Robbe-Grillet, A. (1977). "Order and Disorder in Film and Fiction." *Critical Inquiry* 4, 1–20.

Ryding, W. R. (1971). *Structure in Medieval Narrative.* The Hague: Mouton.

Sacks, S. (1964). *Fiction and the Shape of Belief.* Berkeley: University of California Press.

Sherzer, D. (1986). *Representation in Contemporary French Fiction.* Lincoln: University of Nebraska Press.

Shklovsky, V. (1990). "The Relationship between Devices of Plot Construction and General Devices of Style." In *Theory of Prose*, trans. B. Sher (pp. 15–51). Elmswood Park, IL: Dalkey Archive Press.

Todorov, T. (1981). *Introduction to Poetics*, trans. R. Howard. Minneapolis: University of Minnesota Press.

Woolf, V. (1980). *Women and Writing.* New York: Harcourt Brace Jovanovich.

11

They Shoot Tigers, Don't They?: Path and Counterpoint in *The Long Goodbye*

Peter J. Rabinowitz

The Long Goodbye is Raymond Chandler's longest and most serious novel – and, to many, his darkest: a meditation on failure and despair, ending in what Frank MacShane has called a "blank" and a "void," almost as if he were describing the finale of Flaubert's *l'Éducation Sentimentale* (MacShane 1976: 207). I'm going to challenge, or at least complicate, that standard reading here, but I'm going to do so circuitously. So let me start out in a different forest of the night altogether, John Tavener's 1987 choral setting of Blake's "The Tiger." It's not, to my mind, a particularly effective setting, but there is a moment of heightened attention on the line "Did he who made the Lamb make thee?," where the music's dense texture – a rich polyphony over a long drone – abruptly resolves into simple harmony, creating a sense of suddenly clarified vision. I mention it here not because Chandler, in his dreadful early poetry, showed a partiality for Blake.[1] Nor do I bring it up because Tavener's decision is musically ingenious or interpretively subtle. Rather, the moment is valuable for my purposes because it demonstrates an extremely elementary contrapuntal effect that's readily available even to a fledgling composer, but that written narrative, even in the hands of an expert, can't reproduce. Or can it?

As someone who divides his life between literary narrative and music, I've long been intrigued with the ways in which creators in one medium in fact do manage to find analogues for techniques and effects that would seem, on the surface, limited to the other.[2] In the past, I've worked mostly on musical analogues to literature – in particular, on the ways in which absolute music, even without referentiality (and hence with no immediate way of distinguishing the true or the real from the false or the imaginary), can nonetheless manage to play games with fictionality or irony. But spurred by my recent experiences teaching a series of seminars on time and narrative, I've been turning to literary analogues to music – in particular, the ways in which the single line of narrative prose can engage in contrapuntal games.

The problem facing would-be contrapuntal writers, of course, comes from the difficulty of expressing simultaneity in words, with their unavoidable one-after-the-other order. One key insight generating Borges's famous story "The Garden of Forking Paths" is that the only way for a writer of prose narrative to express temporal simultaneity (in this case, "parallel" times in which different choices are made by the characters) is to project it onto spatial contiguity (here, consecutive versions of a "single" chapter), leaving it up to the reader to reconceptualize the relationship between the events.[3] Thus, for instance, the double time frame of Horace McCoy's Depression downer *They Shoot Horses, Don't They?* – which presumably represents the protagonist's memories of events as he is listening to the judge's pronouncement of the verdict in his murder trial – is indicated by alternating chapters and interchapters; Joyce Carol Oates, in her short story "The Turn of the Screw," tries to convey simultaneity by using columns; Carol Shields's *Happenstance* binds together two separate novels that cover the same time period from different perspectives.[4] Yet as became increasingly clear to me during my time seminars, narrative fakes simultaneity in more ways than I had realized, many of which have little to do with simultaneous events in the physical world. There are, for instance, techniques for representing simultaneous thoughts on a variety of different levels of consciousness and reality (memory, fantasy, whatever). Narrative writers have also figured out ways to represent simultaneity (or, perhaps more accurately, "copresence") in visions of a sedimented present which contains several layers, a present that is "caused by" or is a "repetition" or an "echo" of a past, real or imagined, that continues to linger, somehow, in the present: whether in Brontë's *Wuthering Heights* or Faulkner's *Absalom, Absalom!* or more radically in Borges's claim that any human proposition implies "the entire universe; to say 'the jaguar' is to say all the jaguars that engendered it, the deer and turtles it has devoured, the grass that fed the deer, the earth that was mother to the grass, the sky that gave light to the earth" (Borges 1998: 252).

More generally, we have the contrapuntal intertwining of the authorial and narrative audiences (Rabinowitz 1998: 93–104), of tensions and instabilities (Phelan 1996: 30), and of the mimetic, synthetic, and thematic dimensions of characters (Phelan 1989: 2–3); we also have the counterpoint of perspectives in any ironic discourse, and the kind of polyphony celebrated by Bakhtin (see also Richardson, this volume). Indeed, one can argue that narrative is, for all its apparent reliance on a single line, linearity, *fundamentally* contrapuntal because it is founded on the duality of story and discourse (or *fabula/ sjuzhet* or whatever alternative terms you want to use) (e.g., Chatman 1978). I'd like to start from that fundamental premise and develop it further, suggesting that the story/ discourse distinction is too simple, and that narratives actually get quite far beyond the two-part inventions that scheme would suggest.

More specifically, my argument is that we need to supplement the story/discourse distinction with a third term: *path*. Seymour Chatman once claimed that "time passes for all of us in the same clock direction" (Chatman 1978: 98) – and in a certain sense, that's true. But the Theory of Relativity makes it clear that the order of events is, under certain circumstances, dependent on the situation of the observer;[5] and that's the case even in our everyday Newtonian lives. Different people (or, in literature, different characters) experience events in different orders. In other words, a character's order of experience may conform to neither the story order nor the discourse order.

Let me exemplify the problem with a concrete example from a novel: as happens in so many narratives, a character takes a trip (**Event A**), returns from the trip (**Event C**), and gathers his friends together to tell them what adventures befell him while he was away (**Event E**). In this case, the text we're reading (a report of the traveler's narration by one of those friends) includes the following anecdote about a woman the traveler met while on his journey, an anecdote that occasions a brief interruption in the traveler's story:

> [She] ran along by the side of me, occasionally darting off on either hand to pick flowers to stick in my pockets…[**Event B**] And that reminds me! In changing my jacket I found…[**Event D**]
> [He] *paused, put his hand into his pocket, and silently placed two withered flowers, not unlike very large white mallows, upon the little table* [**Event F**]. *Then he resumed his narrative.*

At first, this looks like a standard kind of anachronic zigzag (nearly a rondo): although the discourse order is ACEBDF, experienced readers will know how to reconstruct the underlying story order, ABCDEF. In fact, though, that's not the story order at all. For this passage comes from H. G. Wells's *The Time Machine* ([1895] 1934: 49–50, first ellipsis added, italics in original), and Event B occurs in the distant future.[6] The story order is thus ACDEFB. So what do we call the structure ABCDEF? It clearly has a significant role in the novel, for it's the order of the events as experienced by the protagonist, the Time Traveler. But it's neither the order of events as they happen(ed) nor the order in which the narrator presents them – no surprise, since the essence of time travel is that you experience things "out of order." I call this order the *path* of the protagonist. And the more time travelers there are, the more paths there are.[7]

Were this kind of multiplicity simply a characteristic of time-travel narratives, it would be at best a minor narratological blip. In fact, though, it has broad implications for narrative more generally. Standard narratology encourages us to think of "discourse" from the perspective of the author or narrator. That is, to the extent that we're talking about "order" (and it's order rather than, say, focalization or voice that I'm concerned with here), discourse is usually considered to involve, in Gerald Prince's terms, "the order of *presentation* of situations and events" (Prince 1987: 21, emphasis added). But if we think as reader critics, it's possible to reconceptualize discourse order as the order in which the situations and events are *received* or experienced by the reader. And once we're talking about the order of reception, why so privilege the reader's that we're unable to recognize other orders that emerge in texts? After all, characters, too, "receive" the events, either by experiencing them directly or by hearing about them second hand, sometimes from the narrator as a narratee but more often in some other way. Rarely do they all do so in the same order or from the same source. Indeed, we could easily reconceptualize dramatic irony as a clash of paths: the clash between Oedipus's path and Tiresias's, for instance, or the clash between the paths of Grace Ansley and Alida Slade, the main characters of Edith Wharton's "Roman Fever." As a result, most narratives turn out, on closer examination, to be gardens of fuguing paths.

So what's at stake here? What happens if we take the existence of the multiple paths seriously? There are, I believe, both theoretical and interpretive payoffs to the consideration of path as a third term. To begin with theory: the notion of "path" points out some of the blind spots in our traditional terms. Let me just point to two biases introduced by the traditional thinking of order through the story/discourse dyad, as a distinction between "order of events" and the "order of presentation."

First, as I've said, the binary distinction tacitly assumes that those two orders cover the ground – as if it weren't possible for the order of experience or perception to be quite different. And that assumption tends, if only subtly, to place more stress on event than on experience or perception. Now given all the attention paid to focalization, especially in analysis of James and post-Jamesian fiction, it would be hard to justify the claim that experience has been erased. Still, our terminology encourages us to think of event as somehow prior to or more significant than or more basic than experience. Thus, while Gerald Prince's invaluable *Dictionary of Narratology* and the forthcoming *Routledge Encyclopedia of Narrative Theory* include entries for "event," there are no parallel entries for "experience." Of course, experience isn't entirely expunged: David Herman's excellent discussion of "event-types" in the *Routledge Encyclopedia* does talk about "states of mind" and "processes of reflection." But events, in the sense of "time- and place-specific transitions from some source state . . . to a target state," are surely primary (Herman forthcoming).

Second, to the extent that narrative theory *does* highlight experience, the story/discourse distinction tends to privilege either the narrator's or the protagonists' experience or else – as, say, in James Phelan's valuable notion of "progression" (Phelan 1996) – the reader's experience. Even if you throw in unreliable narration, you end up with a triad: (implied) author, narrator, (implied) reader. My approach, in contrast, makes us take the experiences of other characters more seriously on the level of the narrative audience. Or, more accurately, it encourages us to take them seriously *in a different way* than the way promoted by classical narratology: specifically, if we take the notion of path (and experience) seriously, we might want to consider a narratology that included not only "actants" but also "passants" – those (especially including those beyond the narrator and his or her chosen focalizers) on whom impressions are registered.[8]

Since our categories influence the way we read, this theoretical shift to include "path" as a third term also has consequences on interpretation. For instance, taking other characters seriously encourages a kind of *refocalization*, a rethinking of a narrative in terms of how it's experienced from positions other than those focalized by the narrator. Needless to say, most narratives invite us to follow one path – or one limited set of paths – that's presented as more relevant to its purposes than others. At the same time, however, most narratives of any complexity offer other paths that, when pursued, offer significant illuminations of the literary landscape.

Sometimes, these paths are simply potentials that the text does not fully develop. Take Chekhov's story "Lady with a Dog." It's a classic "experience-saturated" text, one in which there are few real "events." But even readers ready to focus on inward experience are likely to consider only Anna's and Dmitri's experiences. That is, even though (unusually for Chekhov) the story begins with a reference to public knowledge ("People were saying that someone new had shown up on the promenade: a lady with a dog") (Chekhov 1964: 173, my translation) – and even though the first part of the story takes place largely in public places – few of us are apt to ask ourselves how the nameless gossips are viewing Anna once her relationship with Dmitri begins. (In fact, we're not even apt to ask ourselves how their spouses are viewing the affair, although Anna's husband suspects that something is going on.) An analysis that took "passants" seriously might well give us new perspectives from which to reflect on the story. Likewise, what happens if we take seriously Sonia's path in *Crime and Punishment*, a path that's quite different from that of the reader, who knows of Raskolnikov's crime from the beginning? What can thinking about the book this way teach us about Dostoevsky's formal artistry, about Sonia's psychology, about Dostoevsky's philosophy of acceptance? I didn't choose those three areas – artistry, psychology, philosophy – at random; they are of course aspects of what Phelan (1989: 2–3) calls the synthetic, mimetic, and thematic dimensions; and path opens up our understanding of all three.

Sometimes, in contrast, these new paths are more actively discouraged – and following them results in "counterreadings" that resist or undermine those most clearly invited by the text. What happens if we try to read Hammet's *The Maltese Falcon* in terms of Brigid O'Shaughnessey's path – or if we take seriously Albertine's path in *In Search of Lost Time*? There is, in fact, a whole genre of "rewritings" – best typified, perhaps, by Jean Rhys's *Wide Sargasso Sea* – that recenter familiar novels by following new paths.[9]

Even beyond this, however, there are novels where the concept of path opens up *fundamental* features of the narrative structure in a way that uncovers what the narrative itself is depending on. In these cases, I'd argue, attending to path doesn't simply enrich the intended meaning – much less resist it. Rather, it makes that meaning available in the first place. Let me demonstrate in more detail by returning to *The Long Goodbye*.

Now, in a sense, nearly all detective stories make a gesture toward the importance of path by engaging an "If I had but known" structure – but *The Long Goodbye* gives that generic gesture unusual psychological and thematic weight, since the consequences of lack of knowledge are finally so detrimental to the well-being of the protagonist, detective Philip Marlowe. Marlowe sets up this structure toward the beginning, saying of his friend Terry Lennox, "He would have told me the story of his life if I had asked him. But I never even asked him how he got his face smashed. If I had and he told me, it just possibly might have saved a couple of lives. Just possibly, no more" (Chandler 1992: 22). And Marlowe's on-again off-again friend Bernie Ohls, a lieutenant working out of the LA Sheriff's office, recapitulates the gesture toward the end:

> "If you had connected up Wade and the Lennox frail for me the time Wade got dead I'd have made out. If you had connected up Mrs. Wade and this Terry Lennox, I'd have had her in the palm of my hand – alive. If you had come clean from the start Wade might be still alive. Not to mention Lennox."
>
> (Chandler 1992: 337)

This kind of knowledge-curve is heightened by a stylistic tic: Marlowe, as narrator, often postpones giving us the information we need in order to understand his position. It's not simply that he doesn't tell us what he knows at the discourse-moment of his narration; he often keeps us in the dark about what he knows at the story-moment, too.[10] He does this not only in ways that heighten the mystery; often, it's just a brief twitch that has little to do with the question of who-dun-it. Thus, Marlowe first describes the gangster Mendy Menendez as if he were a complete stranger (Chandler 1992: 74); but we learn two pages later that Marlowe knows exactly who he is.[11]

As I've said, Chandler's novel is traditionally read as a story of failure and frustration, chronicling how Marlowe's friendship with Terry Lennox – a friendship for which he has had made serious sacrifices – unravels under what Marlowe calls Terry's moral defeatism. To return to Frank MacShane's description: "At the end there is just a blank, a void that has to be filled with something, even a code of behavior that sounds sentimental" (MacShane 1976: 207). Or in Fredric Jameson's words,

> The form of Chandler's books reflects an initial American separation of people from each other, their need to be linked by some external force (in this case the detective) if they are ever to be fitted together as parts of the same picture puzzle. And this separation is projected out onto space itself: no matter how crowded the street in question, the various solitudes never really merge into a collective experience.
>
> (Jameson 1970: 633)

But if we look at the odd showdown between Marlowe and gangster Mendy Menendez toward the end of the novel in terms of story/discourse/path, we cast some doubt on these by now canonical interpretive claims.

The scene is itself problematic – indeed, many critics skip over it entirely. Thus, McCann gives a plot summary that leaves it out, calling the events revealing Eileen's guilt the novel's "climactic scenes" (McCann 2000: 178). R. W. Lid's summary (Lid 1969: 173–6) similarly ignores this scene, as do MacShane's (1976: 199–200) and Hiney's (1997: 207–9). And even those who take it into account miss much of the (counter)point: Johanna Smith says simply that Ohls "sets up Marlowe as a decoy so that he can capture the gambler Menendez" (Smith 1995: 197); Marling also mentions it, but leaves much out: "He … goes home, where Menendez is waiting to beat him up. But it is Menendez who gets beat up: his hired thugs turn out to be disguised policemen sent by Lieutenant Ohls" (Marling 1986: 134).

I suspect these critics treat the scene cavalierly because they consider it simply filler. After all, thematic resonances aside, Chandler's title has a formal meaning as well: the novel takes longer to say goodbye than most of its generic siblings. In the Vintage edition, the unmasking of the killer comes on page 313. That's already long for a detective novel of this era – but Chandler gives us a Beethovenian coda, taking another 66 pages to wrap things up. And this scene between Marlowe and Menendez, which occurs between pages 343 and 352, can seem like simply another delay to keep the novel from ending.[12]

What happens during this coda? To summarize – and summarizing a Chandler novel is never an easy task – the "solution" to the mystery comes when Eileen Wade commits suicide, and takes responsibility for the murder of her novelist husband Roger (until then considered a suicide) and for that of Sylvia Potter Lennox (a murder for which Terry Lennox had taken the rap in a self-sacrificing suicide note of his own). The powers that be want to suppress Eileen's confession, since it will only create bad publicity for the wealthy and influential Potter family and for the District Attorney, who had botched the case from the beginning. But Lieutenant Ohls lets Marlowe steal a photostat of Eileen's confession. Marlowe delivers it to the press because he wants to clear Terry's name – even though he knows that publication will anger not only the powers that be, but also the mobster Menendez. Menendez, along with Las Vegas casino operator Randy Starr, had been saved by Terry's heroic action during the war – he has been indebted to Terry ever since, and has consistently asked Marlowe to stop stirring things up. Marlowe ignores warnings that he's acting rashly, even when Linda Loring (Sylvia's sister) tells him that he's being set up: " 'Do you know how they shoot tigers?,' " she asks. " 'They tie a goat to a stake and then hide out in a blind. It's apt to be rough on the goat' " (Chandler 1992: 342). And she urges him not to imitate Terry, who has been a fall-guy himself.

Sure enough, shortly after that conversation, Marlowe returns to his house to find himself facing Menendez and a trio of "hard boys." Marlowe is punched and pistol-whipped, and just as he thoughtlessly starts to fight back – an act that threatens to get him killed – Lieutenant Ohls appears, like a *deus ex machina*, to confirm the tiger-shooting scenario. Ohls's reasons for letting him take the photostat had nothing to do with the murders. Rather, he is using Marlowe as bait for Menendez, who had previously crossed the line of acceptable mobster conduct by beating up a crooked vice-squad cop named Magoon. Menendez's apparent bruisers are, in fact, Nevada cops supplied by casino operator Starr, who, we're told, is just as angry as Ohls that Menendez has upset the delicate balance of power: " 'Somebody in Vegas don't like the way you forget to clear with them' " (Chandler 1992: 349), Ohls remarks as the hard boys lead Menendez away, presumably to his death. As Marlowe coolly puts it, " 'The coyotes out in the desert will get fed tonight' " (Chandler 1992: 350).

Why is this scene here? One might argue that it is plot-driven: after all, Chandler needs to clear up the Magoon subplot. But in fact that subplot is very sketchy, and introduced late in the novel. If anything, it seems more likely that Chandler introduced the Magoon subplot in order to set up the tiger-trap scene – which only adds force to the question of why it's included. One might argue, alternatively, that the scene is simply the result of Chandler's famous difficulty with plot: he often had trouble keeping things from getting away from him. In that regard, it's roughly analogous to a climax-postponing episode in *The Postman Always Rings Twice* (Chandler might cringe at the comparison [Chandler 1981: 26]) – Frank's brief liaison with Madge, a woman who, by a bizarre coincidence, raises tigers and other big cats. But I'd like to propose that the scene burns a lot more brightly than this – especially when we consider how it ends. For the tiger-trap scene has its own long goodbye, which occurs 25 pages later, during Marlowe's last conversation with Terry (whose suicide, we learn, has been faked), a conversation facilitated by Starr. Almost as an afterthought, we're told that Menendez is alive and well in Acapulco, leaving us to infer a key shadow-event that's never explicitly mentioned in the book: Starr has set up Ohls just as Ohls has set up Marlowe, planning the whole scene as a way to spirit Menendez away from the police.

So much for the events. But what about the experiences? Let me outline the story, the discourse, and the various paths in a chart:

STORY	1 Ohls sets up trap
	2 (Shadow event: Starr sets up Ohls)
	3 Photostat stolen by Marlowe
	4 Linda warns Marlowe
	5 Scene in the house
	6 Marlowe's final conversation with Terry

DISCOURSE	3	4	5	1	6 (implies 2)
OHLS	1	3	5		
MARLOWE	3	4	1	5	6 (implies 2)
or	3	4	5	1	6 (implies 2)
MENENDEZ	3	5	1	2	
or	1	2	3	5	
or	2	1	3	5	
STARR	1	2	3	5	6

The variety of paths has synthetic, mimetic, and thematic significance. First, and perhaps least important, looking at the paths gives us an appreciation for the formal intricacy of Chandler's plotting. I'd argue that the moment we learn that Menendez is in Mexico is comparable to the moment of resolution in Tavener's "The Tiger" – a moment where the dissonant clashes of the novel's contrapuntal lines give way to a piercing clarity in which everyone understands what the tiger-trap scene was really all about. But even if you don't accept that particular analogy, it would be hard to deny that Chandler's handling of the contrapuntal paths reveals considerable technical ingenuity.

On the mimetic level, working out the paths clarifies just how much we don't know about the characters' experiences – in particular, Menendez's and Marlowe's. Their heated exchange is based on illusion – whatever the apparently deadly terrors of this scene, neither is actually in danger. But here we have another of the knowledge twitches – one, in this case, that's postponed indefinitely. Does either of them know that he's not in danger, and if so, does he know whether the other knows it or not? We never find out, so the psychological energy of the scene has a curious resonance – although it only has that resonance if we think carefully in terms of path. Geoffrey Hartman (1975: 216) has argued that in Chandler (and Ross Macdonald) "the only person . . . whose motives remain somewhat mysterious, or exempt from this relentless reduction to overt and vulnerable gestures, is the detective." This scene suggests something more complex: it's impossible to reconstruct either Menendez's or Marlowe's path.

But it's on the thematic level that the analysis in terms of path pays its most significant rewards. At first glance, Starr is a background figure, someone who barely shows up in the novel, and even then at the other end of a telephone. But the chart suggests that, in this climactic scene at least, he's the *cantus firmus* or the drone around which the other figures are swirling – or, to put it less metaphorically, Starr is the one who knows (and controls) the story that everyone else is trying to reconstruct. Marlowe, in contrast, is the last of the major characters to understand that story, suggesting that our notion of center and periphery may be skewed. What happens if we reconsider the tiger-trap scene from Starr's perspective? Refocalized in this way, it emerges as a replay of Terry's fake suicide, which was an elaborate hoax set up by Starr and Menendez to fashion Terry with an escape. But although Linda Loring has worried (and thus warned the reader) that Marlowe will become another Terry, although the pistol-whipping numbs Marlowe's face in a way that mimics the disfigurement of Terry's own face (the result of Nazi torture during the war), in fact it's Menendez, not Marlowe, who takes Terry's role in this scene.

Most important, the refocalized tiger-trap scene, like Terry's suicide, gives the lie to Marlowe's final observation. In one of Chandler's more memorable endings, the novel concludes with the hero in despair, saying, "I never saw any of them again – except the cops. No way has yet been invented to say goodbye to them" (Chandler 1992: 379). Chandlerians know that Marlowe is technically wrong *in fact* here because his next novel *Playback* ends with his plans to marry Linda Loring.[13] But if we look at the world from Starr's perspective, we see that Marlowe is wrong *in principle* at a more profound level. No way has yet been invented to say goodbye to the cops? But that's precisely what Terry and Menendez, with Starr's help, have been able to do. And they've been able to do so in part because of their absolute, unquestioning, unbreakable friendship.

The end of the novel, then, doesn't suggest that friendship is impossible, much less that without the detective, as Jameson puts it, the various solitudes fail to merge. Rather, it reveals *Marlowe's* inability to break away from his solitude, his inability to join this trio, this clique that manifests, in its actions, precisely the commitment he so clearly values. And reading in terms of path allows us to reconceive the long war of words between Marlowe on the one hand and Menendez and his minions on the other, not as Marlowe's distaste for his hoodlum flash, but as Marlowe's envy for his tight circle of friendship. The ending is all the more poignant to readers familiar with Chandler's earlier work, especially *The Big Sleep*, where Marlowe's hard-boiled approach gives him a reliable, even privileged, vision of the world. In *The Long Goodbye*, one senses that he has so exaggerated his persona that he's lost his ability to interpret the world around him.

Now I'm not so naïve as to believe that my interpretation of the novel would not be available without my terminological meddling; there is, as they say (for reasons I've never understood), more than one way to skin a cat, and that probably goes for tigers, too. Still, the terminology illuminates it, makes it easier to see. Certainly, I had never seen the ending of *The Long Goodbye* in this light until I decided, more or less arbitrarily, to see what would happen when I applied this theoretical perspective. And that seems sufficient justification for adding path to our categories of analysis.[14]

NOTES

1 How close are the ties between Chandler and Blake? It's hard to tell. But by some quirk of fate, when I opened Chandler's book of verses to see if anything relevant caught my eye, the poem that appeared at random was "A Lament for Youth," which centers (as *The Long Goodbye* does) on "sweet and long" yearning — and which begins with the line "From the forests of the night" (Chandler 1973: 36).

2 For a fuller discussion of the relationships between absolute music and written narrative, see Fred Maus's essay in this volume.

3 The same need for projection haunts Joseph Frank's notion of "reflexive reference" in his influential essay on "spatial form" (Frank 1963).

4 Film has it easier in this regard, although even so, films like *Time Code* are the exception, simultaneity more often being represented through alternation, as in *24*, than through long-term use of a split screen.

5 Specifically, when two spatially separated events occur in such a manner that no beam of light can get from A to B before B occurs (and vice versa), the order of those events will vary according to the frame of reference of the observer.

6 See also the temporal confusion in the following sentence: "It was here that I was destined, at a later date, to have a very strange experience — the first intimation of a still stranger discovery — but of that I will speak in its proper place" (Wells [1895] 1934: 24).

7 For a truly Bachian, well-temporaled experience of multiple paths, I'd recommend Hilary Brougher's dizzying time-travel film *Sticky Fingers of Time*.

8 The "receiver," whose function is to receive the object sought by the "subject," is quite a different category; so, of course, is "ficelle."

9 Gerry Brenner's "performative criticism" — in which the critic writes from inside a literary text by "becoming or impersonating a character in or close to a text" — can be seen as a way of using path as a critical tool, too (Brenner 2004: 2).

10 For that reason, this is not an instance of what Phelan calls "paradoxical paralepsis" (Phelan 1996: 82–104). For further discussion of paradoxical paralepsis, see Alison Case's essay in this volume.

11 Similarly, Marlowe knows the connection between Endicott and Eileen well before we do (Chandler 1992: 96).

12 For an excellent appreciation of the form of this novel – in particular, the way Chandler uses "background action" to convey its ideology – see Richter (1994).

13 Chandler never finished the novel in which they are actually married.

14 Thanks to Hilary Dannenberg, Elizabeth Jensen, Jessica Kent, James Phelan, Haley Reimbold, and Brian Richardson for their assistance and their valuable suggestions.

References and Further Reading

Brenner, G. (2004). *Performative Criticism: Experiments in Reader Response.* Albany: State University of New York Press.

Borges, J. L. (1998). *Collected Fictions*, trans. A. Hurley. New York: Penguin Books.

Chandler, R. (1973). *Chandler Before Marlowe: Raymond Chandler's Early Prose and Poetry, 1908–1912*, ed. M. J. Bruccoli. Columbia: University of South Carolina Press.

Chandler, R. (1981). *Selected Letters of Raymond Chandler*, ed. F. MacShane. New York: Columbia University Press.

Chandler, R. ([1953] 1992). *The Long Goodbye.* New York: Vintage.

Chatman, S. (1978). *Story and Discourse: Narrative Structure in Fiction and Film.* Ithaca, NY: Cornell University Press.

Chekhov, A. P. ([1899] 1964). *Izbrannye Proizvedeniia: Tom tretii.* Moscow: Izdatel'stvo Khudozhestvennaia Literatura.

Frank, J. ([1945] 1963). "Spatial Form in Modern Literature." In *The Widening Gyre: Crisis and Mastery in Modern Literature* (pp. 3–62). New Brunswick, NJ: Rutgers University Press.

Hartman, G. (1975). *The Fate of Reading and Other Essays.* Chicago: University of Chicago Press.

Herman, D. (forthcoming). "Events and Event-Types." In D. Herman, M. Jahn, and M.-L. Ryan (eds.), *The Routledge Encyclopedia of Narrative Theory.* London: Routledge.

Hiney, T. (1997). *Raymond Chandler: A Biography.* New York: Atlantic Monthly Press.

Jameson, F. (1970). "On Raymond Chandler." *Southern Review* 6(3), 624–50.

Lid, R. W. (1969). "Philip Marlowe Speaking." *Kenyon Review* 31, 153–78.

MacShane, F. (1976). *The Life of Raymond Chandler.* New York: E. P. Dutton & Co.

Marling, W. (1986). *Raymond Chandler.* Boston: Twayne Publishers.

McCann, S. (2000). *Gumshoe America: Hard-Boiled Crime Fiction and the Rise and Fall of New Deal Liberalism.* Durham, NC: Duke University Press.

Phelan, J. (1989). *Reading People, Reading Plots: Character, Progression, and the Interpretation of Narrative.* Chicago: University of Chicago Press.

Phelan, J. (1996). *Narrative as Rhetoric: Technique, Audiences, Ethics, Ideology.* Columbus: Ohio State University Press.

Prince, G. (1987). *Dictionary of Narratology.* Lincoln: University of Nebraska Press.

Rabinowitz, P. J. ([1987] 1998). *Before Reading: Narrative Conventions and the Politics of Interpretation.* Columbus: Ohio State University Press.

Richter, D. (1994). "Background Action and Ideology: Grey Men and Dope Doctors in Raymond Chandler." *Narrative* 2, 29–40.

Smith, J. M. ([1989] 1995). "Chandler and the Business of Literature." In J. K. Van Dover (ed.), *The Critical Response to Raymond Chandler* (pp. 183–201). Westport, CN: Greenwood Press (originally in *Texas Studies in Language and Literature* 31(4), 592–610).

Wells, H. G. ([1895] 1934). *The Time Machine.* In *Seven Science Fiction Novels of H. G. Wells.* New York: Dover.

12

Spatial Poetics and Arundhati Roy's *The God of Small Things*

Susan Stanford Friedman

Space is not the "outside" of narrative, then, but an internal force, that shapes it from within.

(Franco Moretti 1998: 70)

Every story is a travel story – a spatial practice.

(Michel de Certeau 1984: 115)

In 1967, Michel Foucault presciently observed: "The great obsession of the nineteenth century was, as we know, history. . . . The present epoch will perhaps be above all the epoch of space" (Foucault 1986: 22). In citing Foucault's "Of Other Spaces," geographer Edward W. Soja charged that by 1989 "no hegemonic shift has yet occurred to allow the critical eye – or the critical I – to see spatiality with the same acute depth of vision that comes with a focus on *durée*. The critical hermeneutic is still enveloped in a temporal master-narrative, in a historical but not yet comparably geographical imagination" (Soja 1989: 11). But since Soja's call in *Postmodern Geographies* for a compensatory emphasis on spatiality to counteract the hegemony of temporal modes of thought, there's been a sea change in cultural theory, a veritable flood of spatial discourses proliferating across the disciplines in the 1990s, as an effect (I believe) of the intensified form of globalization in the late twentieth century.

Narrative theory, however, has largely continued its privileging of narrative time over narrative space, with a few notable exceptions. In spite of M. M. Bakhtin's insistence in the 1920s and 1930s on *topos* as coconstituent of narrative along with *chronos*, prominent narrative theorists from Paul Ricoeur and Gérard Genette to Peter Brooks mute or altogether delete considerations of space in their analysis of narrative discourse and narrative as a mode of human cognition. Space in narrative poetics is often present as the "description" that interrupts the flow of temporality or as the "setting" that functions as static background for the plot, or as the "scene" in which the narrative events unfold in time. Even when theorists acknowledge that particular settings such as Thomas Hardy's Wessex or William Faulkner's Yoknapatawpha County are charged with signification, these acknowledgements do not disrupt the prevailing view of the relation between space and time in narrative. I want to challenge this prevailing view by first reviewing some standard theoretical formulations, then exploring some alternative views, and finally testing a revisionist emphasis on space in narrative poetics with a brief reading of Arundhati Roy's prize-winning and controversial novel, *The God of Small Things* (1997).

Space, Time, and Narrative Poetics

As a form of telling, narrative exists in time: a narrative takes time to tell and tells about a sequence of events in time. It is perhaps understandable, therefore, that temporality has dominated discussions of narrative poetics. Ricoeur, the preeminent theorist of narrative temporality, writes, for example: "My first working hypothesis is that narrativity and temporality are closely related.... [I]ndeed, I take temporality to be that structure of existence that reaches language in narrativity and narrativity to be the language structure that has temporality as its ultimate reference" (Ricoeur 1981: 165). In *Reading for the Plot*, Brooks's challenge to structuralist narratology takes the form of giving priority to temporality in narrative: "We might think of plot as the logic...that develops its propositions only through temporal sequence and progression.... And plot is the principle ordering force of those meanings that we try to wrest from human temporality" (Brooks 1984: xi). H. Porter Abbott in *The Cambridge Introduction to Narrative* similarly focuses on time as the key property of narrative. "Narrative," he writes emphatically, "*is the principle way in which our species organizes its understanding of time*" (Abbott 2002: 3). "Narrative," he sums up aphoristically, "gives us what could be called the shape of time" (Abbott 2002: 11). As "*the representation of an event or series of events*," narrative is distinct from "description" (Abbott 2002: 12).

Genette's magisterial *Narrative Discourse* identifies three main components of narrative discourse for analysis: tense ("temporal relations between narrative and story"); mood ("modalities [forms and degrees] of narrative 'representation'"); and voice ("the narrative situation...: the narrator and his audience, real or implied") (Genette 1980: 30–1). Three of the five chapters are devoted to the temporal dimension of narrative, and space hardly enters into his account of narrative discourse at all. He mentions in passing only the way in which "narrative exists in space and as space," by which he means the pages of a book that require "the time needed for 'consuming' it [as] the time needed for *crossing* or *traversing* it, like a road or a field" (Genette 1980: 35). He is interested in "the narrating situation, the narrative matrix – the entire set of conditions (human, temporal, spatial) out of which a narrative statement is produced," but his chapter on "voice" – that is, the narrative situation – does not develop the spatial dimension of "situation" (Genette 1980: 31).[1]

This prevailing privileging of time over space in narrative poetics is evident as well in a fascinating thread of exchanges on the Narrative listserv in 1997 in response to Ruth Ronen's article in *Narrative* on the canonical binary of "description" and "narration" in narrative studies.[2] Monika Fludernik observes, for example, that "characters (agents) require a setting (description), whereas narrative (plot) is configured most in terms of actions (chronology)" (December 1, 1997). This posting elicited from prominent narratologist Gerald Prince the comment that "description itself can be narrative, of course; but it has very low narrativity because it stresses the spatial rather than temporal, the topological rather than chronological existence of events" (December 1, 1997). In reply, Marie-Laure Ryan suggests that in many writers "the description is reasonably free from narration" and that "Descriptions...can be skipped by the reader without serious damage for the understanding of the plot" (December 4, 1997), a practice that is particularly prevalent in the reading of description-rich Victorian novels.[3] In such formulations, Bakhtin's concept of narrative chronotope shifts subtly into narrative chronotype, with the time–space axes of story morphing into a figure–ground binary. What happens to characters in time is the "figure" we pay attention to; where the plot happens in space is the "ground" we can ignore at will. In this view, narrative is the function of temporal sequence and causation that take place against a static background of spatial setting.

It is worth returning, I believe, to Bakhtin's resonant definition of *chronotope* in his essay "Forms of Time and of the Chronotope in the Novel" in *The Dialogic Imagination*. He acknowledges his debt to Einstein's theory of relativity and then writes:

> We will give the name *chronotope* (literally, "time space") to the intrinsic connectedness of temporal and spatial relationships that are artistically expressed in literature.... What counts for us is the fact that it expresses the inseparability of space and time.... Time, as it were, thickens, takes on flesh, becomes artistically visible; likewise, space becomes charged and responsive to the movements of time, plot and history. This intersection of axes and fusion of indicators characterizes the artistic chronotope.
>
> (Bakhtin 1981: 84)

Bakhtin's sense of the mutually constitutive and interactive nature of space and time in narrative has largely dropped out of narrative poetics. Following Soja, I suggest that we need a compensatory emphasis on space in order to bring back into view Bakhtin's continual attention to the function of space as an active agent in the production of narrative. We need a *topochronic* narrative poetics, one that foregrounds *topos* in an effort to restore an interactive analysis of time with space in narrative discourse.

Walter Benjamin's essay "The Storyteller" offers an implicitly topochronic account of narrative, one that anticipates the compelling spatial homonym in James Clifford's "Traveling Cultures," in which he identifies "roots" and "routes" as opposing but interrelated spatialized dimensions of culture (Clifford 1997: 88). In tracing the roots of modern narrative to archaic forms of storytelling, Benjamin divides early narrative into two "archaic types" whose defining nature is based on the storyteller's relationship to space. The first type is the story told by the seaman, the man "who has come from afar" and "has something to tell about" (Benjamin 1969: 84). The second type is told by the tiller of the soil, the "man who has stayed at home . . . and knows the local tales and traditions" (Benjamin 1969: 84). "The realm of storytelling in its full historical breadth," he continues, "is inconceivable without the most intimate interpenetration of these two archaic types" (Benjamin 1969: 85). Home and elsewhere – both spatial locations – are for Benjamin the coconstituents of story, not incidental to it, as narrative tradition has evolved through time and across many societies.

In "Spatial Stories," Michel de Certeau theorizes narrative as a "practice of everyday life" for which the building blocks are the spaces that enable various kinds of cultural practices or movements in time. To repeat the epigraph, "Every story is a travel story – a spatial practice" (Certeau 1984: 115). For him, "narrative structures have the status of spatial syntaxes." Like buses and trains, "every day, they traverse and organize places; they select and link them together; they make sentences and itineraries out of them. They are spatial trajectories" (Certeau 1984: 115). For Franco Moretti in *Atlas of the European Novel*, the spatial trajectories of narrative not only establish linkages, but also actively *enable* narrative. For him, space is not incidental to narrativity, but rather generative of it.[4] "Geography," he writes, "is not an inert container, is not a box where cultural history 'happens,' but an active force that pervades the literary field and shapes it in depth" (Moretti 1998: 3). Mapping the locations of novels, he explains, helps to identify what has been submerged in literary studies, how space "gives rise to a story, a plot" (Moretti 1998: 7).

Space restored to its full partnership with time as a generative force for narrative allows for reading strategies focused on the dialogic interplay of space and time as mediating coconstituents of human thought and experience. In this sense, space is not passive, static, or empty; it is not, as it is in so much narrative theory, the (back)-ground upon which events unfold in time. Instead, in tune with current geographical theories about space as socially constructed sites that are produced in history and change over time, the concept of narrative as a spatial trajectory posits space as active, mobile, and "full."[5] This is in part what Lawrence Grossberg calls for in positing a "spatial materialism": "space as the milieu of becoming" allows for understanding reality as a "question not of history but of orientations, directions, entries and exits. It is a matter of a geography of becomings . . . ; it refuses, not only to privilege time, but to separate space and time. It is a matter of the timing of space and the spacing of time" (Grossberg 1996: 179–80). For Grossberg, the separation of space and time is itself an illusory construct of human thought, one that results from the privileging of the temporal. Perhaps a debatable assertion, this view nonetheless suggests that a re-visioning of space in narrative poetics can lead to a new understanding of how space and time interact as constitutive components of story, what Grossberg calls "the timing of space" and the "spacing of time." It fosters comprehension of the dialogic interplay of location and action in the *topochrone* of the narrative.

Space within the story told – the space through which characters move and in which events happen – is often the site of encounter, of border crossings and cultural mimesis. For Certeau, narrative establishes "frontiers" (that is, borders) that both mark difference and establish relations across it. "A narrative activity," he writes, "continues to develop where frontiers and relations with space abroad are concerned.... [Narrative] is continually concerned with marking out boundaries.... On the one hand, the story tirelessly marks out frontiers. It multiplies them" (Certeau 1984: 125–6). But on the other hand, the story continually makes "bridges" – it "welds together and opposes insularities" (Certeau 1984: 128). Narrative is built out of a contradiction of interactions in space: a "complex network of differentiation" and "a combinative system of spaces" (Certeau 1984: 126). Certeau likens this spatial practice to the contact of two bodies: "Thus, bodies can be distinguished only where the 'contacts' ("*touches*") of amorous or hostile struggles are inscribed on them. This is a paradox of the frontier: created by contacts, the points of differentiation between two bodies are also their common points. Conjunction and disjunction are inseparable in them" (Certeau 1984: 126–7).

Moretti's claim about borders is more modest, but nonetheless suggestive. He theorizes first that the locations of the novel – at least the European novel from 1800– 1900 – are entwined with the national imaginary, with the "imagined community" that was being formed in conjunction with the modern nation-state. "The novel," he writes, "functions as the symbolic form of the national state ... and it's a form that (unlike the anthem, or a monument) not only does not conceal the nation's internal divisions, *but manages to turn them into a story*" (Moretti 1998: 20). As the imagined space of history, the nation is in one sense *"the sum of all its possible stories"* (Moretti 1998: 20). Borders – both external and internal – play a particularly important role in the formation of these stories, he argues, particularly in the historical novel. As a *"phenomenology of the border"* (Moretti 1998: 35), the historical novel narrates the confluence of space and time by telling stories about "external frontiers" where opposites or enemies collide, and "internal borders" as sites of treason and rebellion (Moretti 1998: 35–6).

Although I have learned to be suspicious of claims about "all narrative," I wish to hypothesize provocatively that all stories require borders and border crossings, that is, some form of intercultural contact zones, understanding "culture" in it broadest sense to incorporate the multiple communal identities to which all individuals belong (Friedman 1998: 134–40). Isn't it borders that make movement through space/time interesting, suspenseful, agonistic, reconciliatory? Borders insist on purity, distinction, difference, but facilitate contamination, mixing, and creolization. Borders of all kinds are forever being crossed; but the experience of crossing depends upon the existence of borders in the first place. Borders function symbolically and materially around the binaries of pure and impure, sameness and difference, inside and outside – polarities that set in play spatially enacted oscillations, migratory movements back and forth that I have elsewhere called an intercultural *fort/da* (Friedman 1998: 151–78). Identity is unthinkable without borders, whether individual or communal.

Bodies too are border sites, marking the distinction between inside and outside, self and other. Bodies are a flesh and blood upon which the social order marks its hierarchies based on boundaried systems of gender, race, ethnicity, class, caste, religion, sexuality, and so forth. In all these modes and functions, borders are sites and social locations that generate and shape narrative in conjunction with time.

Spatial Poetics in *The God of Small Things*

Spaces – particularly border spaces – generate and shape the stories of caste and gender division as they unfold in the palimpsestic sequence of colonial, postcolonial, and postmodern time in *The God of Small Things*. While it ultimately interweaves the poetics of space *and* time, the novel's narrative discourse privileges space over time, tropes locations as "figures" on the "ground" of time, and thus illustrates more than many narratives the compensatory emphasis on space that cultural theorists like Soja and Grossberg have called for. An architect, screenwriter, and political activist, Arundhati Roy won the Booker Prize for her worldwide best-selling novel. Like Salmon Rushdie's *Midnight's Children*, Roy's novel is a political allegory about the newly formed nation-state of India and the silences it needs to confront in order to fulfill the promise of freedom. But more than Rushdie, Roy preeminently calls attention to the borders *within* the nation-state – power relations of gender and caste, in particular – as an inseparable element of the postcolonial dilemma. Like a number of non-Western feminist writers and activists, Roy situates her writing at the contradictory conjuncture of gender, race/caste/class, and nation. Attacked as a traitor to the national cause of postcolonial liberation, she nonetheless insists that future freedoms depend on painful interrogations of social inequities at home as these mediate and are mediated by national and transnational histories.[6]

In setting the novel in her home state of Kerala on the southwestern tip of the subcontinent, Roy features a region of India that is highly anomalous and provides the novel's political allegory with a complexly doubled reference, first to Kerala and then more generally to India. Kerala is the only state ruled for most of the post-Independence period by elected communist officials. Kerala prides itself on its rates of literacy, network of social welfare programs, strong labor movement, and the status of its women – all among the highest in India. Less attention has been paid to its stagnating economy and to its having among the worst records in India for land reform directed at the Dalits, that is, the unscheduled castes also known as the "untouchables." Kerala is also distinctive for its relatively large Christian population – about 20 percent, some of whom descend from the conversions made by British missionaries in the nineteenth century, but most of whom are upper-caste Syrian Christians who trace their ancestry back to the conversion of one hundred Brahmins by St Thomas the Apostle in the first century of the Christian era. As Indians allied with Eastern Orthodox Christianity, they have traditionally formed the social and economic elite of Kerala, thus marking the region's difference from the rest of

Hindu-dominated India. Kerala's status as uncharacteristic anomaly in India's already heterogeneous landscape makes it an unlikely setting for political allegory for India as a whole. Nonetheless, close attention to the novel's spatial poetics reveals ways in which Roy uses this locale to address the politics of regional, national, and transnational landscapes through time.

The novel moves back and forth between two brief time periods in the life of three generations of the Ipe family, members of the Syrian Christian elite: 13 days leading up to catastrophe in December of 1969 and one day in June of 1992, when the youngest generation, the twins Rahel and Estha, are reunited for the first time in 23 years. The narration of trauma and its disastrous effects unfolds out of temporal sequence, in fragments of the story that keep emerging as returns of the repressed. Spatially oriented memories mark the porous border between the conscious and unconscious, the remembered and the forgotten, the forbidden and the desired.

At the core of this resisted remembrance of things past lies a series of dystopic and utopic border crossings that transgress material, social, psychological, sexual, and spiritual frontiers. It starts when the orangedrink man in the Abhilash Talkies movie theater forces seven-year-old Estha to rub his sticky penis. Then, the twins' cousin, Sophie Mol, just arrived from England and treasured for her white Englishness, drowns in the dangerous waters of the Meenachel River. Ammu, the twin's divorced mother, crosses the river every night to touch and be touched by Velutha, the charismatic and tender untouchable who had left the area with the new nation's abolition of untouchability, returned with an education to be the engineer and foreman at the Ipe's Paradise Pickles & Preserves factory, and played the part of the twins' surrogate father. Velutha's father betrays his son to Ammu's mother and aunt, Baby Kochamma, who denounce him to the police as a rapist and child kidnapper. Comrade Pillai, the town's communist leader, refuses Velutha's plea for help. The twins secretly watch the police beat Velutha nearly to death. Baby Kochamma locks her niece Ammu in her room and manipulates Estha into supporting her false accusation to the police to save his mother. Velutha lives just long enough to hear Estha's betrayal, but not long enough to hear Ammu's affirmation of her love to the police. Ammu's brother Chacko banishes her from the Ipe home, and she later dies, unable to support herself or reunite her family. Estha is returned to his dissolute father in Calcutta, and Rahel is sent to boarding school, never to see her twin again until 1992.

The events of 1969 are 13 days of doom that leave the children emotionally frozen in time. Estha hardly speaks again, obedient and servile, performing a kind of exaggerated femininity as penance in contrast to the loud, unruly, and rebellious Rahel, who wanders the globe, finally to return home when her twin is "re-returned" to Kerala with his father's migration to Australia. The day of remembrance in 1992 ends in the incestuous embrace of the twins, the connection of souls figured in the anguish of forbidden touch.

The story is convoluted, melodramatic, sensationalist – borrowing from the conventions of "Bollywood," India's hugely profitable film industry in Bombay. But the events in *The God of Small Things* are not narrated in the kind of chronological sequence I have provided. Exhibiting its own form of the narratological distinction between *fabula* and *sjuzhet* (Propp 1968), "story" and "narrative" (Genette 1980), or "story" and "discourse" (Chatman 1978), the novel refuses the foregrounding of temporality that my summary embodies and demonstrates instead an emphasis on narrative as a spatial practice. Rather than history containing space, different spaces in the novel contain history. The novel moves associationally in and out of these spaces, rather than sequentially in linear time, with each location stimulating different fragments of events, often lyrically rendered through motif, metonym, or image. Each of these spaces contains multiple borders of desirous and murderous connection and separation, borders that are continually erected and transgressed in movement that constitutes the kinetic drive of the plot.

Reflecting, no doubt, Roy's profession as an architect, each space is troped in a building that is a charged site of historical overdetermination. These buildings are more than settings or backgrounds. Instead, they embody the social locations that concretize the forces of history. They are places that palimpsestically inscribe the social order as it has changed over time. Containing history, they set in motion the identities of the people who move through them. No mere backgrounds for plot, they embody narrativity. They make things happen. They contain the borders that juxtapose sharp edges of different cultures – the communal differences of nation, gender, caste, class, religion, sexuality. They trope contact zones where these differences clash and blend, where borders get crossed.

Foucault would call these spaces of narrativity "heterotopic." His neologism appears in "Of Other Spaces," where he defines *heterotopias* as "real places" that bring into focus the interrelationship of other spaces and "slices of time" as structures of the social order (Foucault 1986: 24–7). Cemeteries, prisons, theaters, brothels, museums, libraries, fairgrounds – these are some of his examples of heterotopic sites that relate to larger cultural structures of crisis, deviation, incompatibility, juxtaposition, compensation, or continuity. What I take from his term is the notion that certain real spaces contain by inference other spaces and the spatial trajectories of the disciplinary social order. I would add to his notion a psychoanalytic concept of spatial cathexis, the powerfully magnetic drawing into a given site other geographical and geopolitical formations. In *The God of Small Things*, various buildings function metonymically as heterotopic places that bring into focus the social, cultural, and political systems that form identities; set in motion the transgression of borders; and, in effect, generate the story, the unfolding of events which cannot, because of their anguish, be told in sequence and can only be apprehended in fragments attached to specific locations.

The Abhilash Talkies movie theatre, for example, is just such a heterotopia that contains the history of colonialism, postcolonialism, and the growing American cultural and economic hegemony. The faded opulence of the movie palace built in the provincial capital of Cochin after the advent of the "talkies" recalls the period just before the demise of the Raj. The Ipe family journeys from Ayemenem to Cochin in

1969 to see *The Sound of Music*, the Hollywood movie about the escape of the Von Trapp family from the clutches of the Nazis. The "clean white children" in *The Sound of Music* make Estha and Rahel feel irreparably dirty and naughty as they nervously anticipate meeting their half-English cousin for the first time. It is a moment of postcolonial angst complicated by the conflation of the British Raj with America's growing postwar dominance (Roy 1997: 101). But the (post)colonial plot generated by Abhilash Talkies turns "domestic," when the orangedrink man violates Estha's body border at least in part out of class and caste resentment of the borders between himself and the privileged boy who have been brought together in the space of the Abhilash Talkies theater. To echo Bakhtin (1981: 84), "Time, as it were, thickens, takes on flesh, becomes aesthetically visible" in the ornate building that both contains many stories of the past and generates stories of the future, specifically the first transgression in a chain of events leading to disaster.

Many other buildings function heterotopically as generators of story in *The God of Small Things*. Ayemenem House is the ancestral home of the Ipe family, where the mixture of Anglophilia and Anglophobia passes down through the generations and ends in decay by 1992. Their nearby factory, Paradise Pickles & Preserves, is another, as a hybrid masala of Mammachi's local business acumen and the Western practices that Chacko introduces and that eventually ruin the factory. The factory's spatial trajectory incorporates Velutha's rise as foreman and the opposition from lower-caste workers to this once-unthinkable position of authority for an untouchable. As a contact zone, the factory brings together not only East and West, touchables and untouchables, but also manager and communist leader; for Comrade Pillai, who wants both the votes of the lower-caste workers and the money of the factory's owner, needs to maintain his contract with Chacko to print the factory's advertising fliers. The corruption embedded in the factory as heterotopic space is a critical component of Comrade Pillai's betrayal of Velutha.

Velutha's family home, a squatter hut built long ago on the grounds of the Ayemenem House, is still another heterotope, highlighting the patronage relationship that Velutha transgresses in touching Ammu and that his father fulfills in betraying his son. The Kottyam police station embodies the power relations of the state, guards the borders of caste and gender, and empowers the "touchable" police to violate the bodies of the dying Velutha and the desperate Ammu, who has come too late to save him with her public avowal of her affair and must withstand Inspector Thomas Mathew's lecherous gaze and baton as he taps her breasts. In 1992, the nouveau riche house of Comrade Pillai contains the history of his rise in the new India, a success built on his alliance with the lower-caste workers against the untouchables. The temple is the building in front of which Kathakali dancers perform full sections of the *Mahabharata* after doing "truncated swimming-pool performances," packaged for tourists at the Heritage Hotel in 1992. And so forth.

The buildings of the novel are crucial to the topochronic dimension of the narrative because they bring into focus the social structures that built them, the history of their change over time, and the identities of the people whose lives are inseparable from the structures into which they are born. The buildings further bring into focus Roy's complex politics – on the one hand, unveiling the geopolitical structures of colonialism, postcolonialism, and multinationalism; on the other hand, turning a critical searchlight onto India's internal affairs. As a site of theatrical spectacle for the "true" *Mahabharata*, for example, the temple opposes the spatial trajectories of both the Abhilash Talkies movie palace and the stage at the Heritage Hotel. But the temple also enables the stratification of Hindu society. As members of an unscheduled caste, the Kathakali dancers are not allowed inside the temple, and the epic they perform represents an India destroyed by internal family feuding. Where the novel's buildings contain distinct stories of multiple borders, the Meenachal River meanders in between them as a figural representation of the dangers and allure of fluidity, of transition and transgression. It is the river that gets crossed and recrossed on the days leading up to the day of everyone's doom, the day that changes life forever.

More than all the other heterotopic buildings, the Akkara house is the place that serves as "an active force" that "gives rise to a story, a plot," to cite Moretti again (Moretti 1998: 7). Troped repeatedly by the twins and the narrator as the "History House," Akkara sits at the center of a rubber plantation around the bend and down river from Ayemenem House. Invoking India's colonial past, Akkara had belonged to Kari Saipu: "The Black Sahib. The Englishman who has 'gone native.' Who spoke Malayalam and wore mundus. Ayemenem's own Kurtz. Ayemenem his private Heart of Darkness. He had shot himself through the head ten years ago, when his young lover's parents had taken the boy away from him" (Roy 1997: 51). Akkara is Roy's indigenized answer to Conrad's *Heart of Darkness*, one that attacks the colonialism he reflected in spite of the anticolonial dimensions of his novel, but also one that borrows his project of critique to point a finger at the politics at home. The History House is a metonym for what Benjamin regards as the basis of narrative poetics: "the most intimate interpenetration of these two archaic types" – the intertwined stories of home and travel (Benjamin 1969: 85). The structure of the house mines the structures of history, embodying in a spatial figure what Grossberg calls "the timing of space and the spacing of time" (1996: 179–80).

Historical change over time is marked on the face of the History House. In the postcolonial India of 1969, Akkara is empty: the Englishman's Heart of Darkness has become India's own. For Chacko – Oxford-educated, married briefly to a white woman, back in Kerala, and unlike his sister Ammu, invited by his mother to run the factory and have sex with lower-caste women – India is doomed to postcolonial angst, loving and hating its former rulers. "History," he tells the twins, "was like an old house at night. With all the lamps lit. And ancestors whispering inside" (Roy 1997: 51). The problem with India, he expounded to them in his spatialized allegory of British colonial rule and the lingering effects of Anglophilia, is that:

> we can't go in...because we've been locked out. And when we look in through the windows, all we see are shadows. And when we try and listen, all we hear is a whispering. And we cannot understand the whispering, because our minds have been

invaded by a war. A war that we have won and lost. The very worst sort of war. A war that captures dreams and re-dreams them. A war that has made us adore our conquerors and despise ourselves.

(Roy 1997: 52)

What the children, and by extension the readers, learn is that colonialism cannot explain all of India's "darkness." For, in spite of Chacko's insistence, the children do, in some sense, enter the History House, at least as far as the verandah, as least far enough to see unfold before them "History in live performance" (Roy 1997: 293). Here, they watch as the "Dark of Heartness tiptoed into the Heart of Darkness" (Roy 1997: 290). Here, Velutha and Ammu broke the Love Laws against touch. Here, Velutha retreats after the Ipe family and Comrade Pillai betray him. Here, the children watch as the "posse of Touchable Policemen acted with economy, not frenzy. Efficiency, not anarchy. Responsibility, not hysteria. They didn't tear out his hair or burn him alive. They didn't hack off his genitals and stuff them in his mouth. They didn't rape him. Or behead him. After all they were not battling an epidemic. They were merely inoculating a community against an outbreak" (Roy 1997: 293). Velutha the untouchable has polluted an upper-caste woman through his touch, and the police, those "patrolling the Blurry End," must contain his desire by methodically beating him to the borderlands between life and death, in effect condemning Ammu to exile and slow death, a modern immolation of the woman with the "Unsafe Edge" (Roy 1997: 5, 44). The History House is, in Certeau's terms, the "frontier" where "the 'contacts' (*"touches"*) of amorous or hostile struggles are inscribed" on the walls and bodies that move through it (Certeau 1984: 126). For Roy, the body is the initial site upon which the spatial meanings of the social order are written. The body is the primal border, the first space of passionate connection and violent disconnection.

By 1992, when Rahel returns to the History House where the caste laws had polluted her life ever after, she finds the Heritage Hotel, reborn through an infusion of multinational millions into a playground of the past: "Toy Histories for rich tourists to play in" (Roy 1997: 120). "So there it was," the adult Rahel realizes, "History and Literature enlisted by commerce. Kurtz and Karl Marx joining palms to greet rich guests as they stepped off the boat" (Roy 1997: 120). While the Ayemenem House "on the Other side" decays, the History House morphs into a postmodern space, burying in its playful facade the sedimented layers of desire and trauma that characterized the erection and dissolution of colonial, postcolonial, caste, and sexual boundaries. Postmodernity, the age of representational play and transnational corporations, has supplanted the (post)colonial age of modernity metonymically present in the novel through the allusions to Conrad's *Heart of Darkness*, Forster's *A Passage to India*, and Hollywood's *The Sound of Music*.

As much as colonial domination, postcolonial angst, and transnational corporate tourism are central to the History House of Roy's border narrative, they constitute only a part of the Heart of Darkness. And, for someone like Chacko, and the Indians whom he represents in contemporary India and its diaspora, the power exerted *over* the nation by outside forces becomes all too easy an excuse for suppressing the history of gender and caste inequities that preexisted the arrival of the Muslims and the British and have continued to evolve in the complex contact zones of a heterogeneous subcontinent and through interaction with colonial, postcolonial, and transnational historical formations. As a political allegory, the novel asks that attention be paid as well to the "Dark of Heartness," that is, not only to the legacy of Western imperialism and late twentieth-century transnationalism, but to the dark borders erected in the "heart" of India – the laws of love and touch that regulate relations between genders and castes *within* the nation. In Moretti's terms, *The God of Small Things* "functions as the symbolic form of the nation state . . . [,] a form that . . . not only does not conceal the nation's internal divisions, *but manages to turn them into a story*" (Moretti 1998: 20).[7]

Roy tells her story through buildings, through spatial entities that heterotopically draw within their walls the geopolitical and domestic structures that have taken shape through time. As Bakhtin writes about space in the novel, these buildings become "charged and responsive to the movements of time, plot and history" (Bakhtin 1981: 84). In Roy's narrative, space and time exist in Einsteinian relativity, each understood only in relation to the other, its discursive forms fulfilling Grossberg's call for the "timing of space" and the "spacing of time." At the same time, the discursive form of Roy's narrative foregrounds spatiality. The narrative's structural reliance on buildings to move the narrative forward gives a compensatory emphasis to space over time as constitutive of narrative discourse. A tale of many borders, *The God of Small Things* narrativizes story as a spatial practice, one that doesn't erase time, but rather constitutes space as the container of history and the generator of story. Roy narrativized what Certeau theorizes when he writes: "On the one hand, the story tirelessly marks out frontiers. It multiplies them" (Certeau 1984: 126). Such borders, frontiers, are not the background of narrative, mere description where time unfolds its plot. They are, instead, the generative energy of narrative, the space that contains time.

NOTES

1   See also Ricoeur's *Narrative Time*; Chatman's "Story: Events" in *Story and Discourse* for his discussion of sequence, causality, and time (1978: 45–95); Scholes and Kellog's *The Nature of Narrative*, in which they argue that "Plot can be defined as the dynamic, sequential element in narrative literature" (1966: 207) and ignore the spatial element of narrative entirely; and Martin's *Recent Theories of Narrative*, where he rejects the notion of setting, scene, or description as merely static, but follows Genette in emphasizing the modes of narrative temporality (1986: 122–5, 229–30). Chambers' *Story and Situation* and *Room for Maneuver*, as their titles suggest, pay considerable attention to the context of narration – the narrator as the teller to an audience; but he doesn't directly address the function of space within the story told. Joseph Frank's ([1945] 1963) essay, "Spatial Form in Modern Literature," which spawned decades of debate, deals only with the formal techniques developed to interrupt chronological sequencing and give the illusion of simultaneity; see also

Frank's *The Widening Gyre* and Frank (1978) and Smitten and Daghistany (1983). In *Mappings*, I discuss the predominance to time in narrative studies (Friedman 1998: 137–40).

2 Ronen responds in part to the special issue of *Yale French Studies*, "Towards a Theory of Description" (Kittay 1981), importantly challenges the "almost canonical description of description as non-narrative" (Ronen 1997: 275), and argues that description is a part of narrative, not its opposite. But, like the articles in *Yale French Studies*, she does not discuss description as spatiality.

3 A recent thread on the Narrative listserv is more spatially oriented, answering Christine Junker's inquiry about "narratives of place and the relationship between narrative and place" (October 13, 2003); various answers from Jim Holm, George Perkins, Alison Booth, Rick Livingston, and others continue to assume that place is the backdrop of plot, not a part of it.

4 In *Mappings* (Friedman 1998), published in the same year as Moretti's *Atlas*, I made a similar point; see chapters 5 and 6 for my earlier efforts to shift the emphasis in narrative poetics from time to space. For a discussion of spatialization as a reading practice, see my "Spatialization" (Friedman 1993) which does not take up the question of how the space that characters inhabit and move through works in the narrative.

5 In addition to Soja, see for example Lefebvre (1991), Massey (1994), Keith and Pile, and Bourdieu's concept of "habitus" (esp. 1990:

52–65). In this essay, I make no distinction between "space" and "place," primarily because such distinctions (rampant in geography and social theory) vary considerably and are often contradictory. For some different formulations of space/place, see Tuan and Hoelscher (2001), Sack (1997), and Certeau (1984: 117–18). My concern is spatiality as an aspect of human cognition and as a component part of narrative discourse, both of which incorporate space as place or location.

6 For fuller discussion of the production and reception of the novel, its status as political allegory, its relation to feminism, and its setting in Kerala and the debates about the "Kerela model" of development, see my "Feminism, State Fictions, and Violence" (Friedman 2001). For other discussions of Roy's novel, see Dhawan (1999).

7 In reading *The God of Small Things* as a political allegory of the nation state, I do so outside the framework of Fredric Jameson's (1986) much-critiqued "Third-World Literature in the Era of Multinational Capitalism," where he hypothesizes preposterously (in my view) that "all third-world cultural productions seem to have in common" a quality that "distinguishes them radically from analogous cultural forms in the first world" – namely, that "all third-world texts are necessarily ... allegorical, and in a very specific way" – as "national allegories" (Jameson 1986: 60). I would suggest in contrast that Roy's novel is a national allegory in much the same way as *Heart of Darkness* and *A Passage to India*. See Ahmad's stinging critique of Jameson's argument (1987: 3–25).

REFERENCES AND FURTHER READING

Abbott, H. P. (2002). *The Cambridge Introduction to Narrative*. Cambridge, UK: Cambridge University Press.

Ahmad, A. (1987). "Jameson's Rhetoric of Otherness and the 'National Allegory'." *Social Text* 17 (Autumn), 3–25.

Bakhtin, M. M. (1981). *The Dialogic Imagination: Four Essays*, ed. M. Holquist, trans. C. Emerson and M. Holquist. Austin: University of Texas Press.

Benjamin, W. ([1936] 1969). "The Storyteller." In *Illuminations: Essays and Reflections*, ed. H. Arendt, trans. H. Zohn (pp. 83–110). New York: Schocken Books.

Brooks, P. (1984). *Reading for the Plot: Design and Intention in Narrative*. New York: Vintage.

Bourdieu, P. ([1980] 1990). *The Logic of Practice*, trans. R. Nice. Stanford, CA: Stanford University Press.

Certeau. M. de. ([1974] 1984). "Spatial Stories." In *The Practice of Everyday Life*, trans. S. Rendell (pp. 115–30). Berkeley: University of California Press.

Chambers, R. (1984). *Story and Situation: Narrative Seduction and the Power of Fiction*. Minneapolis: University of Minnesota Press.

Chambers, R. (1991). *Room for Maneuver: Reading Oppositional Narrative*. Chicago: University of Chicago Press.

Chatman, S. (1978). *Story and Discourse: Narrative Structure in Fiction and Film*. Ithaca, NY: Cornell University Press.

Clifford, J. ([1992] 1997). "Traveling Cultures." In *Routes: Travel and Translation in the Late Twentieth Century* (pp. 17–46). Cambridge, MA: Harvard University Press.

Dhawan. R. K. (ed.) (1999). *Arundhati Roy: The Novelist Extraordinary*. New Delhi: Prestige Books.

Foucault, M. ([1984] 1986). "Of Other Spaces," trans. Jay Miskowiec. *Diacritics*, 16(1), 22–7.

Frank, J. ([1945] 1963). "Spatial Form in Modern Literature." In *The Widening Gyre: Crisis and Mastery in Modern Literature* (pp. 3–62). New Brunswick, NJ: Rutgers University Press.

Frank, J. (1978). "Spatial Form: Some Further Reflections." *Critical Inquiry* 5, 275–90.

Friedman, S. S. (1993). "Spatialization: A Strategy For Reading Narrative." *Narrative* 1 (January), 12–23.

Friedman, S. S. (1998). *Mappings: Feminism and the Cultural Geographies of Encounter*. Princeton, NJ: Princeton University Press.

Friedman, S. S. (2001). "Feminism, State Fictions, and Violence: Gender, Geopolitics, and Transnationalism." *Communal/Plural* 9(1), 112–29.

Genette, G. ([1972] 1980). *Narrative Discourse: An Essay in Method*, trans. J. E. Lewin. Ithaca, NY: Cornell University Press.

Grossberg, L. (1996). "The Space of Culture, the Power of Space." In I. Chambers and L. Curti (eds.), *The Post-Colonial Question: Common Skies, Divided Horizons* (pp. 169–88). London: Routledge.

Jameson, F. (1986). "Third-World Literature in the Era of Multinational Capitalism." *Social Text*, 15 (Autumn), 65–88.

Keith, M. and Pile, S. (1993). *Place and the Politics of Identity*. London: Routledge.

Kittay, J. (ed.) (1981) "Towards a Theory of Description." Special Issue, *Yale French Studies* 61.

Lefebvre, H. ([1974] 1991). *The Social Production of Space*, trans. D. Nicholson-Smith. Oxford: Basil Blackwell.

Martin, W. (1986). *Recent Theories of Narrative*. Ithaca, NY: Cornell University Press.

Massey, D. (1994). *Space, Place, and Gender*. Minneapolis: University of Minnesota Press.

Moretti, F. (1998). *Atlas of the European Novel, 1800–1900*. London: Verso.

Propp, V. (1968). *The Morphology of the Folktale*, 2nd edn., trans. L. Scott. Austin: University of Texas Press.

Ricoeur, P. (1981). Narrative time. In W. J. T. Mitchell (ed.), *On Narrative* (pp. 165–86). Chicago: University of Chicago Press.

Ricoeur, P. (1983, 1985). *Time and Narrative*, 2 vols. Chicago: University of Chicago Press.

Ronen, Ruth. (1997). "Description, Narrative and Representation." *Narrative* 5(3), 274–86.

Roy, Arundhati. (1997). *The God of Small Things*. New York: Random House.

Ryan, M.-L. (1997). Posting on Narrative Listserv. December 4.

Sack, R. (1997). *Homogeographicus: A Framework for Action, Awareness, and Moral Concern*. Baltimore, MD: Johns Hopkins University Press.

Scholes, R. and Kellogg, R. (1966). *The Nature of Narrative*. Oxford: Oxford University Press.

Smitten, J. R. and Daghistany, A. (eds.) (1983). *Spatial Form in Narrative*. Ithaca, NY: Cornell University Press.

Soja, E. (1989). *Postmodern Geographies: The Reassertion of Space in Critical Theory*. London: Verso.

Tuan, Y.-F. and Hoelscher, S. (2001). *Space and Place: The Perspective of Experience*, 2nd edn. Minneapolis: University of Minnesota Press.

13

The "I" of the Beholder: Equivocal Attachments and the Limits of Structuralist Narratology

Susan S. Lanser

A piece by Ann Beattie in the November 5, 2001, *New Yorker* begins like this: "True story: my father died in a hospice on Christmas Day" (Beattie 2001: 84). The "I" who tells this story is a writer of fiction named Ann. Is this narrator then Ann Beattie or some other Ann, and am I reading a short story that's playing with conventions or a piece of autobiography? When Ann tells us she is superstitious, is Beattie confessing her frailties? When Ann gives us her views about writing, are these also Beattie's views? Did Beattie's own father die on Christmas Day, or die at all?

As the history of literary reception has made dramatically evident, there is simply no way to resolve these questions from the text "itself." Because autobiography and homodiegetic fiction deploy the same range of linguistic practices, the ontological status of most I-narratives cannot be proved by citing any part or even the whole of the text. Techniques of omniscience and focalization conventionally signal the fictivity of a heterodiegetic (third-person) narrative,[1] but homodiegetic texts provide no such formal index of their status as fiction or fact. Indeed, writers and publishers have exploited this ontological ambiguity for centuries, passing off fictions for histories and hiding autobiographies beneath claims of fictitiousness; the "rise" of the novel is indebted to just such practices. Nor is modern literature exempt: Maxine Hong Kingston, for example, has said that she wrote her acclaimed *The Woman Warrior: Memoirs of a Girlhood Among Ghosts* as a novel but let her editor market it as autobiography. That the book has continued to be read as the true story of Kingston's childhood not only reveals the conventional rather than essential distinction between fiction and autobiography, but casts both the historicity *and* the fictivity of *The Woman Warrior* into doubt.

Most of the time, the generic identification of I-narrative hinges on the single and frail signifier of the proper name – that is, upon the narrator's "identity or non-identity with the author in whose name the narrative has been published" (Cohn

1999: 31–2). But if I want to distinguish between the author Ann Beattie and the narrator-character Ann, I am quite dependent on someone else's word for it. That word usually comes in the rather flimsy and accidental form of a narrative's placement within categorical space: the "fiction" or "nonfiction" shelves in a bookstore, the blurb on a book cover, the information in the library catalog, the table of contents of a magazine. I myself would have taken Beattie's story for memoir had not the *New Yorker* placed the word "fiction" on its first page.

The question should be settled, then: the announcement of "fiction" opens a chasm between the life and opinions of the author "Ann Beattie" and the life and opinions of the character "Ann." For, as all good students of narrative have learned, the cardinal rule for reading fiction is that the narrating "I" is not the author, and thus the claims made by the narrating "I" are not to be taken for the author's claims. Structurally speaking, the "I" who speaks in a fiction is simply and wholly a fictional "I": that is indeed, as narrative theorists from Wolfgang Kayser to Dorrit Cohn have argued, what makes fiction fiction. Fiction defines itself by the pretended quality of its speech acts: thus Gérard Genette argues that even when names and histories are parallel, as in a novel such as *A la recherche du temps perdu*, "*no* speech acts belong to Marcel Proust, for the good reason that Marcel Proust never takes the floor... no matter how the narrative content may happen to relate to the biography, the life and opinions, of its author." Genette concludes, therefore, that "we are just as entitled to set aside the discourse of first-person fictional narrative as to set aside that of fictional characters themselves" (Genette 1993: 34). Under these strictures, Ann is not Ann Beattie, and that is that.

Or so it seems. I will argue, however, that the impossibility of linguistic distinction opens a seductive bridge across the structural chasm between a first-person narrator-character and the author of the text. Against the demurrals of authors and the onto-logic of narratologists, although we are "*entitled*" to take fiction as nothing but fiction, I-narrative taunts us with the possibility that the "I" of the fiction has some relation to the author's "I" even when the I-character is not also a writer or does not share the author's first name. Dorrit Cohn says as much when she recognizes that the readerly inclination to blur the lines between I-narrator and author "must be acknowledged, even if it is nowadays severely frowned upon." But for Cohn, the essential chasm remains: while in theory some "indeterminate" fiction "condemns us to vacillate, or allows us to oscillate, between referential and fictional readings" (Cohn 1999: 34), in the end, ambiguous I-narratives require us to read referentially *or* fictionally, and not both at once.

I will take a contrary stance: that readers *routinely* "vacillate" and "oscillate" and even double the speaking voice against the logic of both structure and stricture. I want to ask, therefore, not *whether* unauthorized crossings happen, but *under what circumstances* they are likely to occur. Since homodiegetic texts cannot effectively demonstrate their own status as fiction or history, exploring this question from within a structuralist narratology keeps us immured in precisely the rules of separation that I believe have failed to address the ways in which readers actually apprehend first-person texts. I want, rather, to proceed pragmatically by mapping a larger field of I–I relationships that I think are available to texts, and by locating fiction in general, and homodiegetic fiction in particular, upon that broader field. Such a project reveals some of the complicated and transgressive ways in which the "I" of the beholder – the "I" a reader constructs according to what we might call his or her intelligence, in every sense of that term – is not always the singular "I" of a fictional speaker but the "I" of an author as well. Understanding this equivocal I–I relationship may provide new insights into the project of literature in general and narrative fiction in particular.

Attachments and Detachments

My map divides all discourse into three parts, each inhabited by a cluster of genres that we usually separate, and each representing a different set of conventions for apprehending a text's enunciating "I." The first encompasses works as diverse as Mary Karr's *The Liars' Club*, Foucault's *Discipline and Punish*, a letter to the editor of the *New York Times*, any history of the French Revolution, and the essay you are reading now. All these texts evoke an "I" who is conventionally assumed to be the author of the work. Foucault does not have to utter the first person pronoun for *Discipline and Punish* to function as his words. The acclaim given to the painful and powerful *Liars' Club* is rooted in the belief that the "I" is recounting a very close approximation of Mary Karr's own history: Karr's thanks to her mother for "bravery" and "support," the photographs that divide the book's three sections, and the thematization of truth and lying that generate the book's title, all lend authentication to what would become an outrage if discovered untrue. If my colleague writes a letter to the *New York Times* opposing a presidential policy, I will be startled and perhaps resentful if she tells me the letter does not really represent her views. While histories of the French Revolution will vary in their selection, narration, and interpretation of events, I read them with the assumption that to the best of her or his knowledge, each author has attempted a factual account, compromised perhaps by errors but not by lies. By the same generic compact, you have a right to assume that the person named as the author of this essay is indeed its author and that at least while I am writing, I believe what these pages assert.

I thus call works in these genres *attached* or *contingent*: they depend for their significance – that is, for their value and arguably also for their meaning – on the equation of the work's presumptive author with the text's primary "I." Readers may deconstruct this "I," may argue that it utters meanings the author did not "intend," may challenge its assertions, may charge it with various misprisions – for every "I" is ultimately the beholder's "I," by which I mean the "I" that the reader constructs in the process of reading. Readers may of course question the attribution of a text to a certain author, contest the legitimacy of a particular edition of a text, seek out the truth behind a pseudonym. If the text presents itself as its author's own story, I may even allow for the ways in which the narrative fashioning of a life stretches or complicates the autobiographical compact whereby, to use Philippe Lejeune's (1980) formulation, author = narrator = character. But in practice, I suggest, not even the most postmodern reader treats a work of history or philosophy or scholarship, a letter to the editor, or an autobiography as if the author *in* the text were not also the author *of* the text. That may be why we so rarely use the term *"implied* author" for attached texts (with the singular exception of "creative nonfiction"); for example, I've not yet heard anyone allude to the "implied author" of *Discipline and Punish* rather than alluding simply to Foucault. It might of course be quite useful to speak of a Foucauldian "implied author" as a way of understanding the complicated relationship of writing persons to written words. But readers do not typically make this distinction between author and implied author of attached texts.

The effects can be explosive when the authorial and textual "I" do not cohere in this expected way. In 1983, a work called *Famous All Over Town* by "Danny Santiago" was hailed as the first "authentic" account of a Mexican-American adolescent's life in the Los Angeles *barrio*. The book was later revealed to be a pseudonymous novel written by an elderly white social worker and Yale graduate named Daniel James. The author's achievement underscores the power of writers to inhabit subject positions far different from their own. But the readers' outrage underscores the investment in the compact of contingency that relies on the connection between presumed author and textual "I." An even more infamous case is *The Education of Little Tree* (Carter 1976), touted as the "memoir of a Cherokee boyhood" and later identified as a novel by a former Klan leader and white supremacist. Henry Louis Gates's argument that all writers are "cultural impersonators" (Gates 1991: 26) did not stem the tide of protest *or* re-evaluation in light of the text's "new" authorship. In a more complicated vein, the 1996 publishing events known as the "Alan Sokal/*Social Text* Affair" worked similarly on an outraged academy: when physicist Sokal submitted a bogus essay on the "hermeneutics of quantum gravity" and *Social Text* published it, some scholars reveled in the alleged exposure of postmodern theory, but others argued that scholarship must operate on conventions of trust that preclude a parodic distance between the textual voice and the author-scientist.[2]

My second group of texts carries no such suppositions. Even more diverse in genre than the first, it includes "The Star Spangled Banner," a stop sign, the Apostle's Creed, the *Bhagavad Gita*, a joke about the President, and an advertisement for AT&T. All of these texts are conventionally read in detachment from and usually in indifference to their authors' – though not, of course, their culture's – identities. I doubt that more than a handful of people could name the advertising firm, let alone the writers, who taught the United States to reach out and touch someone, and the significance of "The Star-Spangled Banner" is rarely dependent on its connection to Francis Scott Key. The *Bhagavad Gita* is read and revered despite its unknown authorship, and most of the believers who recite the Apostle's Creed probably neither know nor care who composed the declaration of their faith. When an "I" matters in such instances, it is not the author's but the beholder's or performer's "I," the "I" who sings the anthem, recites the creed, or tells the joke. What I am calling "detached" texts simply don't derive their meaning from a link between any textual voice and its authorship. Often these texts are specimens or signifiers of a particular culture, but their significations are not anchored by any person (other than the reader) who has a speaking part within the text.

Although I've been speaking of texts as attached and detached, the distinction is at least as much a matter of context as a matter of form. Käte Hamburger reminds us that generic distinctions are themselves pragmatic ones: thus Novalis's "Sacred Songs" would be read as lyric "when we encounter this work in a collection of poems," but as hymn, with the "I" referring to the collective congregation, "when we encounter it in a Protestant hymnal" (Hamburger 1973: 242). Different cultures are differently invested in contingent and detached writings; it is possible, for example, that Finns hear in "Finlandia" the "I" of Sibelius, himself a cultural icon, in ways that people do not hear in "The Star Spangled Banner" the "I" of Key. Conversely, if a Democratic candidate were known to be the author of a joke about a Republican President, the joke would become an attached text for which its author would doubtless pay. A detached "I," moreover, can be merely a convenient fiction referring to "no one" at all: if I join a songfest in a pub and belt out "I'm in love with you, honey," my "I" is quite detached from both myself *and* any author. Robert Griffin (1999) has noted that anonymous writings pervade our daily lives; what I call *detached* genres are *functionally* even if not technically anonymous because the "I" who wrote them is not connected to any specific enunciating entity that the text inscribes.

This mapping of texts according to the attachment or detachment of a textual speaker to the text's (putative) author offers a pragmatic axis that cuts across conventional generic groupings. In "Literature as Equipment for Living," Kenneth Burke reminds us, however, that textual categories are "neither more nor less 'intuitive' than *any* . . . classification of social events. Apples can be grouped with bananas as fruits, and they can be grouped with tennis balls as round." But if "the range of possible academic classifications is endless," Burke continues, the most salient classifications are those that "apply both to works of art and to social situations outside of art" (Burke 1941: 302–3). Recognizing authorial attachment as a significant aspect of any text's "social situation" challenges us to return to literature, and particularly to homodiegetic fiction, as a place or set of places on a larger discursive map.

The Equi-vocation of Literature

Somewhere between attachment and detachment sit the imaginative genres that we call "literature" in its *constitutive* rather than *evaluative* sense, the sense that encompasses those genres, loosely identified in classrooms as poetry, fiction, and drama, "that impose [themselves] essentially through the imaginary character of [their] objects" (Genette 1993: 21).[3] I call these genres *equivocal* – literally *equi-vocal*—for they not only manifest but, I submit, *rely for their meaning on* complex and ambiguous relationships between the "I" of the author and any textual voice. The "I" that characterizes literary discourse, in other words, is always potentially severed from *and* potentially tethered to the author's "I." I would go so far as to propose that the condition of "literature" (again, in the constitutive rather than evaluative sense) resides precisely in this equivocality – this vocation, as it were, to evoke voices ambiguously related to their historical origins, and that from this equivocality derive many of the liberties and liabilities of literature along with some of the interpretive dilemmas that underlie our scholarly debates.

I want to emphasize, however, that when I speak about the equivocality of literature I am not concerned with either implied or biographical authorship. The sense of an authorial presence "behind" the text that Wayne Booth has famously called the "implied author" (Booth 1961) may be constructed for *any* text, attached or detached, although I have already suggested that the *need* for the term "implied author" may be diminished for attached texts because "the" author is *already* being associated with the text's enunciating "I." Nor do I mean here the commonplace practice of reading texts in relation to the historical persons who wrote them – a practice that despite postmodern proclamations of "the death of the author" still dominates literary scholarship (as a glance at the names of academic societies, journals, and conference panels makes evident). Both the concept of implied author and the reading of texts as extensions or embodiments of the historical writer entail attaching to the author the *whole* of a text. While such critical methods may intensify the likelihood that readers will also attach authors to specific textual "I"s, practices of authorial reading are not dependent on aligning any *textual* speaker with the author's "I."

My concern here, by contrast, is specifically with the ways in which *specific* voices inscribed in literary texts may – at once, or in oscillation – be both attached to *and* detached from the author's "I." When I speak about the equivocality of literature, then, I am speaking pragmatically about whether readers link a voice *within* the text to the actual author's voice, even when they "know" that a speaking "I" is fictional and "ought" to be considered purely as such. That is, against the claims of imaginative literature to be purely imaginative, the ontological status of literary speech acts as fictions, and the efforts of narrative theorists to enforce boundaries between fiction and "reality," under what circumstances might readers nonetheless attach a speaking voice within a literary text to the (presumptive) author of that text? What textual signals might lead us to take a formally fictional voice for the author's against our instructions to do otherwise?

Terms of Attachment

The likelihood that readers will form some attachments between the "I" of an author and an "I" in the text seems to me to be in large measure generically contingent in ways that map surprisingly well onto the broad distinction of lyric, narrative, and dramatic modes. Strictly speaking, of course, all three of these genres are constructed on the premise of imaginative content and thus of putative fictivity. But I will claim that this fictivity does not extend identically for all three genres to the identities and the assertions of speakers within texts. Not only are the three equivocal genres not identically equivocal, but within any given literary work, both attachments and detachments may occur. As a starting point for what must be a much more extensive project of parsing out the terms of attachments, I want to speculate that readers will make attachments between an author and a textual "I" according to five criteria which I will call *singularity, anonymity, identity, reliability*, and *nonnarrativity*. Together, these criteria help to explain why, in normative cases, lyric is the most attached, drama the most detached, and narrative the most equivocal of the equivocal genres.

By *singularity* I mean the presence of one rather than many voices at the highest diegetic level of the text. It is my hypothesis that readers are significantly more likely to attach an "I" to the author when there is only one "I" to attach and that the introduction of a second voice at the same diegetic level disturbs this tendency. Lyric poetry is nearly always characterized by a singularity of voice, while drama – except in the case of dramatic monologue or performance art – is, conversely, characterized by a multiplicity of voices at the same diegetic level. Narrative fiction, of course, lends itself to a great diversity of diegetic modes. "Third person" (hetero-diegetic) fiction is likely to deploy a single narrator at the highest diegetic level, but Dickens's *Bleak House*, which places the omniscient narrator and the I-narrator Esther Summerson at the same diegetic level, is only one of many complicating cases in point. And homodiegetic fiction may use any number of first-person voices, just as fully focalized third-person fiction may limit itself to the consciousness of a single character or shift among characters. Thus narrative fiction occupies a spectrum of possibilities *between* the singular "I" of most lyric poetry and the multiple "I" of most dramatic works.

Anonymity and *identity* are somewhat interrelated if technically distinct. By *ano-nymity* I mean the absence of a proper name for the textual speaker, as is the case with a surprising number of homodiegetic novels and nearly all lyric poems. I hypothesize that it is easier to attach an unnamed than a named "I" to its author except perhaps when, as in Beattie's story , the "I" shares the author's name. The term *identity*, as I use it here, encompasses all (perceived) social similarities between a narrator and an author: of name, gender, race, age, biographical background, beliefs and values, or occupation as writer, and I suggest that textual voices closely allied in identity to that assumed voice of the author provide readers with encouragement to attach. I would go farther, and suggest that when a fictional narrator is unnamed, it may take clearly marked *differences* in identity to deter readers from imposing the identity of the author onto an anonymous textual voice, for historically speaking, and perhaps especially in the case of women writers, even when a textual "I" has differed from the author in name, the convergence of the author's known identity with that of the narrating character has promoted attachment: nineteenth-century critics read *Jane Eyre* as Charlotte Bronte's autobiography just as twentieth-century critics have read *The Bell Jar* as the autobiography of Sylvia Plath.

Identity is one index of a fourth criterion, *reliability*, by which I mean a reader's (complex) determination that the narrator's values and perceptions are consistent with those of the author – that is, with the values and perceptions the reader believes the author holds. I would claim that a reader is very unlikely to attach an author to a narrator whom that reader has already deemed unreliable. This judgment of reliability does not require the reader to agree with the author's values, but it does mean that the reader thinks the author shares the narrator's values. If, for example, I consider Robinson Crusoe's presumption of cultural and religious superiority to Friday to be a presumption that Defoe would share, I will take Crusoe as a reliable "I" even if I myself abhor the views I believe Defoe to be endorsing through Crusoe, and I will not be deterred from attaching the "I" of Defoe to the "I" of Crusoe. If, on the other hand, I have reason to think Defoe critical of missionary colonialism, I might question Crusoe's reliability and consider a detached ironic relationship between author and narrator-character. While reliability does not in itself determine attachment, in other words, unreliability does tend to keep attachment from happening.

I will explore *nonnarrativity* or *atemporality* more fully below. Here I'm simply noting that I mean this criterion to distinguish speech acts that do not recount the actions, words, or behaviors of characters or events as these unfold in time. I believe readers are more likely to make attachments between narrators and their author when the narrating "I" is *not* reporting or enacting events. I am more likely, in other words, to believe that Ann Beattie shares the homodiegetic narrator Ann's views about writing than to believe that Ann Beattie's own father died on Christmas Day. I will suggest, indeed, that equivocal genres are most likely to enact their now-attached and now-detached character along lines of narrativity. That is, a literary text's potential for detachment stems from the pretended nature of some or most – though not necessarily all – of its *temporal* speech acts, while the same text's potential for attachment stems from the potentially nonpretended nature of at least some of its *atemporal* or *nonnarrative* acts, *even when these appear within fictional discourse*. Indeed, James Phelan has suggested that what I'm calling attached discourse (and what he calls "mask narration") might be a particularly persuasive rhetorical device, for by "draw[ing] upon the character narrator's experiences as the ground for the utterance," the author can "not only make the direct communication plausible but also make it even more forceful" (Phelan 2005: 201).

These five criteria combine to help explain the very different tendencies of specific literary genres. Lyric poetry, with its conventional singularity, its commonplace anonymity, its almost axiomatic reliability, its likelihood of evoking aspects of its author's identity, and its relatively low narrativity, is primed for authorial attachment. Drama is, conversely, primed for detachment: apart from the provider of stage directions, who "disappears," as it were, in performance, the highest diegetic level in a play usually entails a multiplicity of named characters engaged in a high level of temporal behavior, so that unless criteria of *identity* are applied, no voice typically calls out to be connected with an author's "I." Epistolary fiction, for example, seems to me by virtue of its multiplicity of characters on the same diegetic level to resemble drama in its detachment of all voices from the author's voice; certainly I have never known a reader to attach any voice in *Les Liaisons dangereuses* to the "I" of Laclos. Conversely, "third person" (heterodiegetic) narration by a single and unnamed public voice encourages attachments similar to, if arguably more fragile than, the attachments conventional to lyric modes. Thus, even though heterodiegetic narrators are technically fictional, some narrative theorists have acknowledged that readers have very little incentive to distinguish the narrator of *Northanger Abbey* from Austen, *Le Père Goriot* from Balzac, or *Song of Solomon* from Morrison. Homodiegetic fiction emerges as the most equivocal of the equivocal genres, always technically detached and yet sometimes readily attachable.

Attachment and Narrativity

In order to understand the kinds of transgression that I believe are possible in the reading of homodiegetic fiction, it is useful to begin with the lyric as an extended case in point, for as Käte Hamburger noted decades ago in *The Logic of Literature*, "the question of the identity or non-identity of the lyric I with the empirical I of the poet" has "not yet been answered by our structural analysis of the lyric statement" and remains "the topic of much debate" (Hamburger 1973: 272).[4] Let me take, for example, John Keats's "Bright Star." Whether or not I read this sonnet as expressing the author's longing for Fanny Brawne, in which case I have surrounded the poem with narrative elements to create fully attached autobiography, I am likely to make some equivalence of vision between the poem's unnamed persona and the "I" of John Keats. That is because, as I have been suggesting and as Brian McHale has stated outright, "the assumption of autobiographical authenticity, of an identity between the poem's 'I' and the poet's self, is something like the 'default setting' for lyric poems" (McHale 2003: 235). Were I to read the "I" of "Bright Star" as wholly detached from the "I" of Keats by positing an unreliable speaker and thus an ironic rendering of the sonnet, I would not only be changing the meaning of the sonnet but, in transgressing the conventions of lyric reading, turn "Bright Star" into a detached dramatic monologue.

What I am proposing as the conventional reading of lyric would be relatively unconcerned with the poem's narrative elements, in this case with the hope to be "pillowed" and with the identity or even the real existence of the "fair love." Let me make this key point with a stronger example. Sharon Olds's short poem "Son" begins with an event: "Coming home from the woman-only bar,/ I go into my son's room." The poem goes on to describe the sleeping child, and it ends with the exhortation, implicitly addressed to other feminist women, that "Into any new world we enter, let us/take this man" (Olds 1984: 68). For the final line to have significance, it must count as the author's position in the same sense as does a letter to the editor; the poem's point of view must be guaranteed by a person, and the person the poem evokes must be not a fictitious speaker but "Sharon Olds." At the same time, however, I do not think this poem requires me to accept as a *narrative* truth that the writer Sharon Olds came home from a woman-only bar on a particular evening and gazed upon her sleeping son. Whether Olds actually experienced this moment or only imagined it does not compromise my attachment of the poem's thoughts and feelings to Sharon Olds. That is, I may recognize the narrative elements as a convenient *fiction* – attached therefore to a purely fictional *narrator* – while still attaching to Olds the *author* the viewpoint of the final words.[5]

We can explain this readerly practice by recalling Peter Rabinowitz's concept of the "rules of notice." Rabinowitz reminds us that readers, unable to remember and attend to the signification of *everything* in a text, must create a "hierarchy of importance" to distinguish what matters to their reading from what does not (Rabinowitz [1987] 1998: 44). Such rules of notice "tell us where to concentrate our attention," and those elements on which we concentrate "serve as a basic structure on which to build an interpretation" (Rabinowitz 1998: 53). Certain textual elements – titles, first and last sentences, primary narrators, central characters – conventionally receive greater attention than other elements. But Rabinowitz recognizes that the grids of notice also vary from genre to genre. I suggest that readers of lyric poetry so privilege non-narrative thought, feeling, and vision that events can slide "beneath notice" when they are not central to our understanding of the poet's thought. Or, put differently, I can attach the *lyric* "I," as it were, to the author while rendering the *narrative* "I" fictional, *even though technically this "I" is a single entity*. I can do so because I recognize that the narrative apparatus of the poem exists in the service of nonnarrative purposes. On somewhat different grounds but through a similar logic, I can detach as a fiction the eye-witness claims George Eliot's narrator makes in *Scenes of Clerical Life* – for example, about being a member of "Shepperton Church as it was in the old days" (Eliot [1858] 1973: 42) – while attaching quite firmly to the author the philosophical generalizations this same narrator makes about the world.

In the case of lyric, then, readers probably do make attachments and detachments on more than technical grounds, *overriding* the technical singularities about "who's speaking" that structuralist narratology holds dear. I want to propose an inverse and even more equivocal readerly behavior with respect to homodiegetic (and possibly also fully focalized figural) fictions, in neither of which can one technically identify any "voice" that is authorial and thus "supposed" to be attached. It is important to acknowledge that narrative fiction presents a tougher case. Brian McHale rightly notes that if the "default setting" for lyric is "autobiographical authenticity," the "default setting" for the relationship between fictional narrator-characters and their authors is just the opposite: "impersonation," not "authenticity" (McHale 2003: 235). I would affirm this axiom, which is also held by nearly all narrative theorists: impersonation, and thus what I am calling detachment between authorial and textual "I," is indeed the *default* condition of narrative fiction. But I am also arguing that this default position is frequently transgressed, and transgressed most often through the same criteria that link author and voice in the lyric. In the case of narrative fiction, of course, the story cannot quite fall beneath notice as it might with respect to Olds's poem. Yet readers may ignore the technical boundaries of fictional voice, in effect *doubling* the "I" so that the narrator's words sometimes belongs to the author *as well as* to the narrating character and sometimes do not. Most commonly, as I have suggested, this doubling occurs through a split between the text's narrative and nonnarrative textual elements, so that narrative elements are relegated purely to the fictional narrator-character, while nonnarrative elements may be tied to the author as well as to the narrator-character. If, however, readers believe that a fiction is autobiographical, they can enact this doubling for most or all of a text without splitting the temporal from the atemporal: if I have reason to believe that Ann Beattie's own father died in circumstances similar to those her character Ann narrates, even if not precisely on Christmas Day, then I might read many elements of the text as potential autobiography. For as Dorrit Cohn admits in spite of her own admonitions to maintain boundaries, "the distance separating author and narrator in any given first-person novel is not a given and fixed quantity but a variable" that gives readers enormous "interpretive freedom" (Cohn 1999: 34). The most likely scenario, I suggest, is that readers will detach many or all of the narrated events from the author but weigh nonnarrative elements according to the other criteria I have set forth.

Transgression: *The Human Stain*

Let me take as an example Philip Roth's novel *The Human Stain*, which uses the first-person voice of the writer Nathan Zuckerman to tell the story of Coleman Silk, a black man who passes for Jewish and whose distinguished academic career is ruined by a misguided accusation of racism. As I read *The Human Stain*, I know that Nathan Zuckerman is not Philip Roth. I do not assume that Roth has prostate cancer just because Zuckerman does – though Norman Podhoretz does raise this question in a review of the novel in which he notes that although the facts of Zuckerman's life may differ from the author's, it has become "harder and harder… to distinguish" Roth from Zuckerman (Podhoretz 2000: 36). But when Zuckerman the narrator writes a several-line paean to male friendship, I do attach that paean to Philip Roth. When, in the next moment, the same narrator re-enters narrative time with "This probably isn't usual for him, I was thinking" (Roth 2001: 27), I cease to align Nathan Zuckerman with Philip Roth – or rather, Philip Roth dips once again beneath my notice *as* an "I". In the space of a paragraph, I have split the narrative from the nonnarrative discourse of the *same "I" narrator*, attaching one to, and detaching the other from, "Philip Roth." Later in the novel, I find myself associating with Philip Roth the words of yet another character, the woman Faunia Farley, because it is by way of Faunia's musings, focalized through free indirect discourse, that the novel offers us the meaning of its title phrase, "the human stain." At that moment, in other words, I am attaching together Nathan Zuckerman (who is allegedly "writing" Faunia's story), Faunia herself, *and* Philip Roth, even though a piece of me may want to resist the connection between this female character and an author with a history of misogyny.

(A similar process leads me, when I read Defoe's *The Fortunate Mistress, or Roxana*, to attach to Defoe – perhaps even *more* than to Roxana – the extensive critique of marriage as the source of women's miseries, a critique that Roxana herself does not precisely heed.) But the split I'm suggesting readers of lyric make between temporal and atemporal discourse is not always clear-cut: what Bakhtin has described as the "dialogism" of language, exploited especially in the novel, can arguably commingle atemporal and temporal discourse, and attached and detached voices, in the same sentence and even the same word.

Seeing "I" to "I"

I have been claiming, then, that our reading of textual voice does not simply follow the rules of discourse; it adheres to another logic that is not only formal and structural but pragmatic and contextual, "staining" the divide between fiction and the real. The farther a homodiegetic narrator wanders from the demands or details of story, I speculate, the *more* likely that voice is to get authorially attached. I would even hypothesize that when a narrator is exercising what Marie-Laure Ryan calls the "testimonial" function of narrative, only a perception of *un*reliability actively prevents readers from attaching the author to the homodiegetic narrator's voice. That is perhaps one reason why unreliability preoccupies narrative theorists as it does not preoccupy theorists of lyric or drama, and why it is usually homodiegetic rather than heterodiegetic voice whose reliability worries us.

This perverse propensity for attachment may also help to explain why the inability to attach an autodiegetic "I" to the "I" of an identifiable author can leave readers quite adrift; I have discussed elsewhere (Lanser 2003) an anonymous work of 1744, *The Travels and Adventures of Mademoiselle de Richelieu*, for which two sophisticated scholars, Carolyn Woodward and Susan Lamb, have produced quite oppositional readings. Woodward sees the work as a subversive lesbian and feminist novel; Lamb considers it an antifeminist satire. Each scholar anchors her reading through a claim not simply about the autodiegetic narrator but about the author's politics and indeed the author's sex: Woodward's imagined author is a feminist woman, Lamb's a misogynist man. Both scholars attach the narrator's ideological pronouncements to their imagined author, and yet both treat the *events* narrated by the autodiegetic narrator as pure invention.

When it comes to the equivocal project of fiction, then, the beholder has a queer and shifty eye, attaching and detaching by turns, and doing so *despite* the "fact" that all fictional voices are fictions or that each "I" can technically represent only one speaking entity. The Ann Beattie story with which I began offers metafictional support for such behavior. The plot focuses on the narrator's widowed mother, whose involvement with another man after her husband's death is viewed as tantamount to insanity by the daughter-narrator still mourning her father's death. The story's title, "Find and Replace," suggests the daughter's bitterness at the mother's substitutionary act. But the narrator also proposes "Find and Replace" as a recipe for composing fiction and thus arguably also for reading it. In conversation with a stranger, Ann explains the mechanism by which writers turn autobiography into fiction: "you just program the computer to replace one name with another. So, in the final version, every time the word 'Mom' comes up, it's replaced with 'Aunt Begonia,' or something" (Beattie 2001: 88). Later in the story, in order to avoid a speeding ticket, the character herself enacts such a replacement when she tells a police officer that her mother is dying. Her reasoning is arguably a program for fiction as well: "After all, it was a terrible situation. The easiest way to express it had been to say that my mother was dying. Replace 'lost her mind' with 'dying'" (Beattie 2001: 89). But this one act of replacement leads Ann to other permutations of her story in order to tell what she insists to the reader is nonetheless "the truth." When I then reread her opening sentence – "True story. My father died in a hospice on Christmas Day" – I can, without a sense of contradiction, accept the claim "true story" as Ann Beattie's along with Ann's (admittedly glib) comment on the project of fiction, while (at least until I have reason to believe otherwise) attributing "My father died in a hospice" and all that follows upon this assertion to the fictive "Ann."

I am not suggesting that the watchword of fiction, if I may pervert a phrase of E. M. Forster, should be "only attach." But I do think it worth probing further how, when, and why attachment might happen despite formal imperatives against it, and revising our narrative theories to allow for the ways in which readers may be breaking the rules of structure as a way to give literary speech acts their fullest significance. In "What Is an Author?" Foucault imagines a time when "who's speaking" would no longer matter and "discourse would circulate without any need for an author [. . .] unfolding in a pervasive anonymity" (Foucault 1977: 138). This world of wholly detached genres may seem more dystopic than Foucault envisioned in an age of anonymous websites and anthrax-laced letters with no return address. Yet complete attachment is surely equally disturbing in an age of internet "cookies" and finger-printing at airports. This may be just the moment to revel in the equivocality of literature, with its attached and detached visions and the imaginative space to "find and replace," and in that process to behold multiple others, real and invented, "I" to "I."

NOTES

1   Biographies and histories sometimes adopt these same techniques of omniscience and focalization, but these methods are fictional liberties taken with historical material, and are usually recognized and often deplored as such.

2   For a fuller sense of the debate surrounding the *"Social Text* Affair," see Professor Sokal's website: <http://www.physics.nyu.edu/faculty/sokal/>.

3   I do not mean to suggest here that nonfictional genres are not *worthy* of the designation "literature." The *constitutive* definition of literature that I draw from Genette recognizes literature as a set of genres that rely for their construction, for their very existence, on *fictive* or *imaginary* objects. In this constitutive sense, "pulp" fiction is literature, but autobiography and essay are not. When literature

is taken in its evaluative sense, however, Rousseau's *Confessions* and Montaigne's *Essais*, both attached texts, of course become literature, as indeed does Mary Karr's *The Liar's Club*.

4   I am of course not using "lyric" to be synonymous with "poetry," which runs the generic gamut from, say, Pope's quite attached and authorial "Essay on Man" to Browning's quite detached and dramatic "My Last Duchess."

5   It is possible that the poem would be compromised were I to learn that Sharon Olds did not have a son. In a modest way, such knowledge might lead me to see the poem as a kind of "lyric hoax" of the sort that Brian McHale describes (McHale 2003).

References and Further Reading

Beattie, A. (2001). "Find and Replace." *The New Yorker*, November 5, 84–9.

Booth, W. (1961). *The Rhetoric of Fiction*. Chicago: University of Chicago Press.

Burke, K. (1941). "Literature as Equipment for Living." In *The Philosophy of Literary Form: Studies in Symbolic Action* (pp. 293–304). Baton Rouge: Louisiana State University Press.

Carter, F. [A.] (1976). *The Education of Little Tree*. New York: Delacorte Press.

Cohn, D. (1999). *The Distinction of Fiction*. Baltimore, MD: Johns Hopkins University Press.

Eliot, G. ([1858] 1973). *Scenes of Clerical Life*. Harmondsworth, UK: Penguin.

Foucault, M. (1977). "What Is an Author?" In *Language, Counter-Memory, Practice: Selected Essays and Interviews*, ed. D. F. Bouchard, trans. D. F. Bouchard and S. Simon (pp. 113–38). Ithaca, NY: Cornell University Press.

Gates, H. L., Jr. (1991). " 'Authenticity,' or the Lesson of Little Tree." *New York Times Book Review*, Nov. 24, 26.

Genette, G. ([1991] 1993). *Fiction and Diction*, trans. C. Porter. Ithaca, NY: Cornell University Press.

Griffin, R. (1999). "Anonymity and Authorship." *New Literary History* 30, 877–95.

Hamburger, K. (1973). *The Logic of Literature*, trans. M. J. Rose. Bloomington: Indiana University Press.

Lanser, S. (2003). "The Author's Queer Clothes: Anonymity, Sex(uality), and *The Travels and Adventures of Mademoiselle de Richelieu*. In R. J. Griffin (ed.), *The Faces of Anonymity: Anonymous and Pseudonymous Publication from the Sixteenth to the Twentieth Century* (pp. 81–102). New York and Basingstoke, UK: Palgrave Macmillan.

Lejeune, P. (1980). *Le pacte autobiographique*. [The Autobiographical Compact.] Paris: Seuil.

McHale, B. (2003). " 'A Poet May Not Exist': Mock-Hoaxes and the Construction of National Identity." In R. J. Griffin (ed.), *The Faces of Anonymity: Anonymous and Pseudonymous Publication from the Sixteenth to the Twentieth Century* (pp. 233–52). New York and Basingstoke, UK: Palgrave Macmillan.

Olds, S. (1984). *The Dead and the Living*. New York: Knopf.

Phelan, J. (2005). *Living To Tell About It: A Rhetoric and Ethics of Character Narration*. Ithaca, NY: Cornell University Press.

Podhoretz, N. (2000). "Bellow at 85, Roth at 67." *Commentary*, July/August, 35–43.

Rabinowitz, P. J. ([1987] 1998). *Before Reading: Narrative Conventions and the Politics of Interpretation*. Columbus: Ohio State University Press.

Roth, P. (2001). *The Human Stain*. London: Vintage.

Santiago, D. [D. James] (1983). *Famous All Over Town*. New York: Simon & Schuster.

14

Neonarrative; or, How to Render the Unnarratable in Realist Fiction and Contemporary Film

Robyn R. Warhol

In 1988, in the first special issue of *Style* devoted to "Narrative Theory and Criticism," Gerald Prince published a typically ambitious brief essay called "The Disnarrated." That issue of *Style* (the same number where Susan Lanser and Nilli Diengott held their notorious debate over the possibility of bringing politics and narrative theory together in a feminist narratology) did for narrative studies in 1988 what the present volume is to do for the early twenty-first century, showing the current state of the field. I find myself still intrigued with Prince's contribution to that issue, and with the fate of the term he coined there, "the *disnarrated*," which means "those passages in a narrative that consider what did not or does not take place" (Prince 1988: 1). Prince concluded his essay by allying himself with us feminist narratologists, on the one hand, and, on the other hand, with Ross Chambers or Marie-Laure Ryan (who, Prince says, were insisting on taking narrative situation always into account), pulling our work together under the heading of "Pragmatics." Calling this emphasis on pragmatics "the most striking difference between what might be called the classical narratology of the 1960s and 1970s and what might be designated as modern narratology," Prince asserted that narratology turned toward pragmatics because of the repeated (sociolinguistic) reminders about the importance of communicative contexts, because of the great interest among literary critics and theorists in the receiver and his or her decoding strategies, because of the growing number of cognition-oriented studies, and because of the (renewed) awareness that narrative must be viewed not only as an object or product but also as an act or process, as a situation-bound transaction between two parties, as an exchange resulting from the desire of at least one of these parties (Prince 1988: 7).

I believe that we are still practicing Prince's "modern narratology," and that the concerns he cites still motivate what has evolved into a fundamentally pragmatic approach to texts. In this spirit, I am returning to the topic of "the disnarrated," a term which fell into disuse soon after Prince coined it.[1] I concur with Prince's claim that "the nature and content of the disnarrated ..., the level at which it functions ..., the relative frequency with which it appears, and the relative amount of space it occupies can be a useful tool for characterizing narrative manners, schools, movements, and even entire periods" (Prince 1988: 6). Although Prince does not mention them, literary genres can also be characterized by the degree to which they use disnarration, and the nature of the material their narrators explicitly omit. I will draw here on examples from literary narratives for the purposes of defining terms, then look at a narrative form Prince did not consider – fictional film – for insight into the role the disnarrated, as well as its associated tropes, "the unnarrated" and "the unnarratable," have played in filmic form. If the "disnarrated" describes those passages in a narrative that tell what did not happen, what I call the *"unnarrated"* refers to those passages that explicitly do not tell what is supposed to have happened, foregrounding the narrator's refusal to narrate. While Prince's work describes "the disnarrated" as an object in itself, I am interested in viewing disnarration and unnarration as narrative acts, much in keeping with Prince's vision of the pragmatics-focused future of narratology.

I examine the disnarrated, as well as its affiliated figure, the unnarrated, and the larger category to which they both belong, the unnarratable, for the ways they serve as distinctive markers of genre. Narrative genres are known as much by what they do not or cannot contain as by what they typically do contain: a novel or film belongs to a particular genre as much for what it does not say or do as for what it does. The limits of narratability vary according to nation, period, and audience as well as genre, but they also stretch and change as genres evolve. Indeed, shifts in the category of the unnarratable are, I would say, significant indicators of generic change itself, and they both reflect and constitute their audiences' developing senses of such matters as politics, ethics, and values. The "disnarrated" along with "the unnarrated" are instances of narrators' making explicit the boundaries of the narratable; sometimes disnarration and unnarration also become strategies for moving the boundaries outward, and changing the genre itself. When disnarration and unnarration lead to genre change, they are participating in what I will call *"neonarrative,"* or narratorial strategies for making narrative genres new.

Varieties of the Unnarratable in Classic Realist Fiction

First, I want to make some terminological distinctions that Prince himself never got around to making, although both his *Narratology: The Form and Functioning of Narrative* and his *Dictionary of Narratology* do offer definitions upon which I can build. Prince never defined "the unnarratable," collapsing it instead with "the nonnarratable" in defining his term, "disnarration"; nor did he make the noun forms he coined into verbs, that is, "to unnarrate" or "to disnarrate." Starting with his definition for the positive term, "narratable," then, I will build a vocabulary for talking about what is *not there* in fictional narratives, both novelistic and filmic.

Drawing on the work of Peter Brooks and D. A. Miller from the early 1980s, Prince's *Dictionary of Narratology* defines "the narratable" as "that which is worthy of being told; that which is susceptible of or calls for narration" (Prince 1987: 56). If *"unnarratable"* (which Prince does not define in the dictionary) is to be the antonym for this term, then it would mean "that which is unworthy of being told," "that which is not susceptible to narration," and "that which does not call for narration" or perhaps "those circumstances under which narration is uncalled for." Prince does define the "unnarratable" as "that which, *according to a given narrative,* cannot be narrated or is not worth narrating either because it transgresses a law (social, authorial, generic, formal) or because it defies the powers of a particular narrator (or those of any narrator) or because it falls below the so-called threshold of narratability (it is not sufficiently unusual or problematic)" (Prince 1988: 1). Because I think there are significant pragmatic differences between that which "cannot be narrated" and that which "is not worth narrating," I will reorganize these definitions of the unnarratable to highlight this distinction. For the sake of analysis, I will classify my illustrative examples of the unnarratable from classic realist fiction in four categories. This is not meant to be an exhaustive list of all possible forms of the unnarratable; indeed, I offer these categories as four among many possibilities: that which, *according to a given narrative,* (1) "needn't be told (the *subnarratable*)," (2) "can't be told (the *supranarratable*)," (3) "shouldn't be told (the *antinarratable*)," and (4) "wouldn't be told (the *paranarratable*)." While that which is unnarratable may sometimes simply be left implicit in a narrative (Prince 1982: 135), the "unnarratable" does not always lead to a textual silence or to what Meir Sternberg has called "blanks" and "gaps"[2]: in the instances I will cite, it becomes explicit. I focus in my definitions on two narrative strategies for representing the unnarratable: *"disnarration"* – telling what did not happen, in place of what did – and *"unnarration"* – asserting that what did happen cannot be retold in words, or explicitly indicating that what happened will not be narrated because narrating it would be impossible.

The subnarratable: what needn't be told because it's "normal"

The first definition, "that which is unworthy of being told," is the equivalent of what Prince calls "the non-narratable," or the "normal" (Prince 1987: 52). These are events that fall below the "threshold of narratability" because they "go without saying," events too insignificant or banal to warrant representation. As Prince remarks, "If I told a friend what I did yesterday, I would most probably not mention that I tied my shoelaces" (Prince 1987: 1). Depending on the genre, however, the boundaries around what is worth saying may cover a wide range of normal territory. I think of the scene in the Richard Lester-directed Beatles' movie, *Help!* (1965), in which Victor Spinetti rolls his eyes and grimaces while Leo McKern tells him over the walkie-talkie, "I am moving my left foot. I am moving my right foot." In realist Victorian fiction, as in the mind of McKern's character, the threshold for this kind of narratability is low indeed. Novels such as Anthony Trollope's are filled with narration detailing "the normal" at a seemingly minimal level of significance, for example:

> Lady Lufton got up and bustled about; she poked the fire and shifted the candles, spoke a few words to Dr. Grantly, whispered something to her son, patted Lucy on the cheek, told Fanny, who was a musician, that they would have a little music; and ended by putting her two hands on Griselda's shoulders and telling her that the fit of her frock was perfect.
>
> (Trollope [1861] 1987: 158)

Trollope's narrator tells us that Lady Lufton was trying to make everyone comfortable at her party, going about it the long way. Still, even in this passage, such details as the motion of Lady Lufton's feet as she bustles about, the blinking of her eyes, the beating of her pulse "go without saying" – these details, along with myriad others that Trollope does not include in sketching out the action of the scene, are not narrated because they are taken for granted. So are the sequences of action that got Lady Lufton from her bed that morning to the party that evening, all of which are absent from the text. They are literally unremarkable – they need not be told. For this category, I would substitute for Prince's "nonnarratable" my new term, "subnarratable," in order more clearly to distinguish it, as Prince does not, from the larger term, "unnarratable." In realist fiction, the subnarratable is not marked by either disnarration or unnarration; like Prince's "nonnarratable," its presence is typically marked by its absence.

The supranarratable: what can't be told because it's "ineffable"

The second variety of the unnarratable, "that which is not susceptible to narration," comprises those events that defy narrative, foregrounding the inadequacy of language or of visual image to achieve full representation, even of fictitious events. The supranarratable is the category that often forms the occasion for what I am calling "unnarration" in classic realist texts, beginning with Tristram Shandy's recourse to an all-black page as the antiexpression of his grief for "poor Yorick's" death (Sterne [1759–67] 1967: 232) and carrying over in the sentimentalist tradition to narrators' assertions that "I don't think I have any words in which to tell" the specifics of highly charged emotional scenes (Alcott [1868] 1983: 187). Louisa May Alcott's sentimentalist narrator habitually unnarrates such moments, with comments such as "the shock she received can better be imagined than described" (p. 359) or "Beth ran straight into her father's arms. Never mind what happened just after that, for the full hearts overflowed, washing away the bitterness of the past and leaving only the sweetness of the present" (p. 206). This is the unnarratable as the ineffable: events that simply cannot be retold. The supranarratable is the one of these four types of the unnarratable that most consistently carries a textual marker in the form of the explicit disclaimer I am calling "unnarration."

The antinarratable: what shouldn't be told because of social convention

The antinarratable transgresses social laws or taboos, and for that reason remains unspoken. This is the unnarratable as "that which does not call for narration," in the specific sense that it might prompt a response of "that's uncalled for." (I am thinking of the phrase some people use to scold others for making impertinent or inappropriate remarks.) Sex in realist Victorian novels, for instance, is always antinarratable, and can only be known by its results as they play themselves out in the plot (for instance in the presence of new babies, disillusioned hearts, or ruined reputations). As I have written elsewhere, Victorian narrative uses euphemism, allusion, metaphor, and especially metonymy to signify sexual connection between characters, but never narration – and not even unnarration of the kind premodernist novels use to represent sentimental affect.[3] The same is true in Victorian fiction for most bodily functions, not just copulation but especially excretion, so that when James Joyce places Leopold Bloom on a toilet in *Ulysses*, he is making perhaps his most radical break with Victorian limits of unnarratability by changing the boundaries of the antinarratable.

Twentieth-century novels like William Faulkner's *Absalom, Absalom!* or Toni Morrison's *Beloved*, to give just two prominent examples out of many possibilities, challenge the unnarratability of another kind of taboo, the silence that results from trauma. These novels can be said to be about the struggle to tell what supposedly shouldn't be told, that which has been repressed both from history and from the characters' own consciousnesses. The much-commented-upon ambiguity of *Beloved*'s narrator's assertion that "It was not a story to pass on" combines, as Shlomith Rimmon-Kenan says, "acceptance and rejection, an injunction to remember and a recommendation to forget" (Rimmon-Kenan 1996: 123), thus pointing to the difficulties of embarking on a narrative of the antinarratable taboo. While Abdellatif Khayati has quite persuasively written that *Beloved* traffics in the "unaccountable language of the ineffable" (Khayati 1999: 315), which would imply that it *can't* be told (or that it is supranarratable), I would argue that Sethe's story, and Beloved's too, eventually does get told in the course of the narrative: what has been repressed or suppressed because it *shouldn't* be told, gets expressed before the novel's end because it *must* be told for healing to occur and, for that matter, for the novel to get written. As Khayati rightly argues, "Morrison's grappling with the 'unspeakable' for her characters – namely, the fear that to evoke a past degradation may diminish them, humiliate them, and shame them – is clear from the way in which they try to force forgetting into a willed activity" (Khayati 1999: 319). Many commentators, Khayati among them, have shown that what began as the unnarratable trauma in Morrison's novel ultimately becomes narratable, in a narrative process moving toward wholeness for the characters and for the text itself.

Trauma in Victorian realist fiction can also be figured as antinarratable, as belonging beyond the bounds of what should be told, but the boundaries of this kind of narratability are stricter in Victorian than in twentieth-century texts. Many traumatic experiences of characters in Victorian fiction – even in the sensation novels of Wilkie Collins, for instance – happen outside the diegesis, and are narrated second-hand if they are told at all. First-hand or focalized accounts of trauma in Victorian novels are rare, making trauma the kind of antinarratable experience represented mainly by silence or gaps in realist texts. Charles Dickens's David Copperfield unnarrates the childhood trauma of laboring in Murdstone and Grinby's warehouse: "No words can express the secret agony of my soul as I sunk into this companionship.... and felt my hopes of growing up to be a learned and distinguished man, crushed in my bosom. The deep remembrance of the sense I had of being utterly without hope now... cannot be written" (Dickens ([1849–50] 1981: 210). Charlotte Brontë's *Villette* presents an interesting instance of a *dis*narrated trauma, in the famous passage where the evasive narrator Lucy Snowe accounts for her teenage years:

> I betook myself home, having been absent six months. It will be conjectured that I was of course glad to return to the bosom of my kindred. Well! The amiable conjecture does no harm, and may therefore be safely left uncontradicted. Far from saying nay, indeed, I will permit the reader to picture me, for the next eight years, as a bark slumbering through halcyon weather, in a harbour still as glass – the steersman stretched on the little deck, his face up to heaven, his eyes closed: buried, if you will, in a long prayer.... Picture me then idle, basking, plump, and happy, stretched on a cushioned deck, warmed with constant sunshine, rocked by breezes indolently soft. However, it cannot be concealed that, in that case, I must somehow have fallen over-board, or that there must have been wreck at last. I too well remember a time – a long time, of cold, of danger, of contention. To this hour, when I have the nightmare, it repeats the rush and saltness of briny waves in my throat, and their icy pressure on my lungs. I even know there was a storm, and that not of one hour nor one day.... In fine, the ship was lost, the crew perished.
>
> (Brontë [1853] 1979: 94)

I call this disnarration because Lucy tells what did *not* happen, in two different ways: first she asserts that she will not contradict the "amiable conjecture" that she was happy to return home, strongly implying that the conjecture is mistaken, though it "does no harm." She says she will, in other words, not deny what did not happen. The passage then moves into a more elaborate disnarration, as Lucy plays out the metaphor of the storm. If she had been floating comfortably along (as she has implied she was not), then she must have fallen overboard – the description of the shipwreck is only an analogy for what is supposed to have "really" happened to Lucy. The metaphor (which turns out to be drawn from a nightmare referring to the unspeakable trauma) is at the same time a narrative, telling the story of a shipwreck that did not happen, which Lucy offers in place of a narrative of what did happen. This is disnarration, a Victorian novelistic solution for narrating the antinarratable, or what shouldn't be told.

The paranarratable: what wouldn't be told because of formal convention

This last category of the unnarratable comprises that which transgresses a law of literary genre without being recognizable as sub-, supra-, or antinarratable. For example, in the feminocentric nineteenth-century novel, as Nancy K. Miller (1980) so memorably pointed out, the heroine can in the end only get married or die. Laws of literary generic convention are more inflexible, I believe, than laws of social convention, and have led throughout literary history to more instances of unnarratability than even taboo has led. My students always look puzzled when I tell them that there were many more possibilities for the life-stories of real Victorian women than there were for Victorian heroines: it's counterintuitive, because fiction would seemingly be limited only by imagination, while "real life," as the students call it, is bound to follow the dictates of what undergraduates like to call "society." I explain to them that many, many, young women neither got married nor died, but (like Jane Austen, the younger Brontë sisters and George Eliot, whose own lives followed trajectories very different from their heroines') found other ways to pass out of youth into maturity. For an early to mid-nineteenth-century heroine, however, to find a different end from marriage or death is unthinkable: how many of them publish a novel, or cheerfully set up housekeeping with an unmarried sister, or pursue a professional career? As feminist commentators have frequently observed, the influence of dominant ideology on fictional form is too powerful. Such a story is paranarratable in that period: although it certainly could happen "in life," "in literature" it wouldn't have been told.

For a Victorian novelist to choose an alternate outcome to a heroine's marriage plot, then, would be to attempt to narrate the paranarratable. Again *Villette* presents an example of how Charlotte Brontë renders the unnarratable, this time not just by disnarrating, but also by unnarrating it. Describing how she has waited for M. Paul's return by ship from South America, Lucy brings the narration to the point when he is to set sail. She embarks on another description of a storm (metaphorical? literal? It could be either and is probably both), but backs off from positively killing her hero, for his death would be paranarratable, according to the laws of the genre in which she writes:

> Here pause: pause at once. There is enough said. Trouble no quiet, kind heart; leave sunny imaginations hope. Let it be theirs to conceive the delight of joy born again fresh out of great terror, the rapture of rescue from peril, the wondrous reprieve from dread, the fruition of return. Let them picture union and a happy succeeding life.
>
> (Brontë [1853] 1979: 596)

That's Lucy's last word on the fate of her marriage to M. Paul, and if Charlotte Brontë wrote the conclusion this way to please Patrick Brontë – whose dismay at Lucy's unconventional ending led him to beg his daughter to leave some room for hope – most commentators agree that the narrative provides little doubt that M. Paul is indeed to be presumed dead. As in the example of the antinarratable above, Lucy disnarrates the ending, telling what did not happen ("the rapture of rescue from peril, the wondrous reprieve from dread, the fruition of return"). This time, though, the disnarration is introduced by unnarration, "There is enough said." The unnarration states what is not to be told, in this case not because it is insignificant, ineffable, or taboo, but because in the Victorian novel it is paranarratable; it would not be told: it simply would not do.

Neonarrative in Film: Stretching the Boundaries of the Unnarratable

For a set of examples of how this vocabulary for the unnarratable might be useful in describing shifts in generic form, I turn now to popular films that circulated in the United States around the turn of the twenty-first century. Film makes literally graphic the changes and developments in its form, and sometimes a particular film's experiments with widening the boundaries of the narratable can make us conscious of unnarratability we hadn't realized was previously there. The following are examples of instances where films' management of three of the categories of the unnarratable draws attention to a genre's limits and, in many cases, actually pushes those limits out to widen the possibilities for filmic narration.[4]

The subnarratable

The threshold of narratability varies greatly among filmic genres, just as it does for novelistic ones, and certain experimental films (Andy Warhol's first film, *Sleep* [1963], for instance, or Jim Jarmusch's *Stranger than Paradise* [1984]) challenge the idea that anything at all should be outside the realm of the narratable. Nothing on the level of plot ever happens in these films, so every gesture, every breath or flick of an eyelid becomes an event worthy of narrative representation. Such challenges to norms of the subnarratable have been finding their way lately into popular film, sometimes for a specifically aesthetic purpose – as in the scene in Sam Mendes' *American Beauty* (1999) where the camera lingers for 60 long seconds on a plastic bag being blown up against a brick wall by a gusty wind, described by the young filmmaker in the movie as "the most beautiful thing I've ever filmed" – and sometimes for more explicitly ethical or political ends. An excellent example is *Three Kings*, the anti-Gulf War film David O. Russell directed in 1999. As one character asks another to think seriously about what happens when you shoot a gun at someone, the film shows a soldier being fatally shot, but instead of focusing conventionally on the external view of the body falling and hitting the ground, the frame jumps to a computer-animated internal image of the flesh and organs being torn apart by the intruding metal, complete with sound effects. The interior damage done by a bullet has up to this point been, for Hollywood film, a subnarratable set of details, something that goes without saying. By violently anatomizing "the normal," Russell's technique broadens the range of the narratable for contemporary film, calling into question what needn't be told. As this technique for imaging the injured body has been picked up on network television's *CSI*, it has become increasingly familiar, eventually losing the consciousness-raising value it holds in *Three Kings*. When it happens in *Three Kings*, it is neonarrative; by the time it has become a familiar feature of a network TV series, it is one of the conventions of a newly changed genre.

The antinarratable

Examples of ways in which contemporary film has broken social conventions or taboos by representing subjects previously considered beyond the pale are too numerous to elaborate – so, for the purpose of illustration, I will cite only the most vivid example I can think of, *Boogie Nights*, directed in 1997 by Paul Thomas Anderson. After a long and complicated story hinging always on the reputed largeness of the porn-star protagonist's penis, the film concludes with a mirror-view of the organ itself: a rare instance of making literal the phallic engine that propels not only this action film, but the majority of Hollywood films in its genre. Since so much of this movie, like other action films before it, is about the fact that the film cannot show the audience "how big it is," the visual revelation at the end comes with a shock. That moment in *Boogie Nights* functions as neonarrative for Hollywood film, but it would be unremarkable in, for example, a porn film, as it would in a photograph by Robert Mapplethorpe. In stretching the boundaries of the antinarratable in one genre (in this case, mainstream action film), neonarrative can borrow from another genre (here, porn or gay art), and appropriate images or elements of story that represent a more radical anticonventionality in their earlier forms. Once the phallus has made its appearance in *Boogie Nights*, it enters the vocabulary of convention for Hollywood films. It shows up again two years later, for example, in a locker room scene in Oliver Stone's 1999 football film, *On Any Given Sunday*.

The paranarratable

More interesting, for my present purposes, are those films that defy formal convention by visually narrating incidents that may not be socially remarkable, but have been hitherto unimaginable as filmic images. I read Spike Lee's first feature-length movie, *She's Gotta Have It* (1986) as a formalist exercise in narrating scenes that had been paranarratable for mainstream film up to that point: Lee's film shows in detail a black woman oiling a black man's scalp, an African-American couple performing a Fred Astaire/Ginger Rogers-style dance in 1950s Technicolor romantic movie style, and a black man's rape of a black woman, among many other images that mainstream films had not previously framed. The introduction of these images into Lee's movie is neonarrative (or it becomes neonarrative when Lee's film-school project gets released as a mainstream feature film), as it introduces them also into the realm of the narratable for Hollywood film at large.

Conventions governing plotline and closure form another boundary of the narratable in mainstream film. The "narratable," in this sense, is what can be imagined as possibly happening within the plot of a given genre produced in a specific time and place; as its opposite, the "paranarratable" could be defined as "the unthinkable." For example, in a classical Hollywood romantic comedy, it is not possible for the heroine to die at the end, or for the romantic male lead to ditch her; nor is it possible for her to decide to leave him at last for a better job in another city. Such outcomes are paranarratable: they *wouldn't* be told, because the conventions governing the genre have proven too strong to allow them to be told without disrupting the genre altogether. Several contemporary Hollywood comedies in this genre have pushed at the boundaries of paranarratable endings (for instance, P. J. Hogan's 1997 *My Best Friend's Wedding*, and Nicholas Hytner's 1998 *The Object of My Affection*) by introducing gay male characters into the relationship mix and resolving the heroine's story with alternatives to marriage. When neonarrative enables a paranarratable plot closure to become narratable in this way, the distinguishing characteristics of the genre of romantic comedy have changed.

Disnarration and Unnarration in Film

If disnarration is simply telling of something that did *not* happen, many familiar filmic conventions might qualify as disnarration, including fantasy or dream sequences and subjective points of view. Arguably, though, a fantasy sequence in a film is a piece of ordinary narration: the film tells that the character is having this fantasy or this dream, and the film signals (by the character's suddenly jolting awake, for instance) that the sequence is not to be taken as an authoritative set of actions within the diegesis. Often, too, the focalization of events through a protagonist's point of view leads to implicit conclusions about what is "really" happening that are false, but get corrected by the film's end: Richard Rush's 1980 Peter O'Toole vehicle, *The Stunt Man*, for instance; or Francis Ford Coppola's *The Conversation* (1974), starring Gene Hackman; or, more recently, *The Usual Suspects*, directed in 1995 by Bryan Singer. In each of these films, the first-time viewer realizes – with a jolt – along with one of the focal characters that the diegetic world is not what it has seemed to be. These films are not employing disnarration, though – the filmic narrative has presented the same story all along, while the difference comes in interpretation of what happened, not in presentation of what happened.

I would reserve "disnarration" to refer to the technique used in several recent films which tell alternate versions of the same story, without marking one version or the other as "what really happens" diegetically until the end. Examples would include *Run Lola Run*, Tom Tykwer's 1998 German film released in the United States in

1999, in which the titular character's being late for a rendezvous leads to a sequence of disastrously violent consequences adding up to a tragic ending. As in a video game constantly reset by a persistent player,[5] the action rewinds and plays out more than once, and as the last version of the narrative concludes, the disasters most closely touching the protagonist are ultimately averted. A similar structure based on the contingent relationship of events governs the narration of Fisher Stevens's *Just A Kiss* (2002), in which an act of unfaithfulness leads to multiple suicides, accidents, brutalizations, and murders before a reversal of time erases the unfaithful kiss, resulting in a much less violent and happier ending. In both *Run Lola Run* and *Just a Kiss*, I am arguing that the violent versions are disnarrated because the film gives priority to the happier closure which comes at the movies' end. Other, similarly structured films (such as Peter Howitt's *Sliding Doors* from 1998 and Spike Jonze's *Adaptation* from 2003) test the limits of my definition of disnarration, as they do not offer a privileged narrative to choose from among the various versions of the diegesis they present. Their postmodern technique more closely resembles alternate world or parallel universe narratives typical of science fiction films and novels, in which the question of what "really" is supposed to have happened is ultimately unresolvable, even within the terms set out by the text.

The category I find most fascinating, and also most elusive, in this grammar of the unnarratable in film, is "unnarration," or the narrator's assertion that what happened cannot be rendered in narrative. The only clear examples I have found of unnarration in film come from Hollywood classics of an earlier era, such as Leo McCary's 1957 romance, *An Affair to Remember*. In that movie, the hero and heroine share a kiss off-screen while the camera frames their bodies up to mid-torso. The kiss itself is left to the viewer's imagination; the aggressively odd framing of the gesture is tantamount to an assertion that the experience cannot be captured in narrative. This exemplifies the supranarratable, or the unnarratable as the ineffable, that which cannot be told. Here the kiss outside the filmic frame is being "unnarrated," not out of prudery or squeamishness or Hollywood censorship codes, but as a narrative means of indicating that the emotion of the moment transcends representation. Alfred Hitchcock's *Frenzy* (1972) presents a similar case, in the scene where the camera tracks up a staircase, stopping outside the door of the apartment where a woman is being brutally murdered; so does John Ford's 1956 *Searchers*, when John Wayne looks through a window at the devastation wrought by an Indian raid on a settler's household, the camera focusing on his back rather than tracking with his gaze. In both cases, the unnarration asserts that the scenes themselves are too horrific, supranarratable: they can only be told by being not-told. The supranarratable in contemporary film seems to reside primarily in horror movies, where the inability to see the terrifying object can still be scarier than even the most vivid special effects, as in *The Blair Witch Project*, directed by Daniel Myrick and Eduardo Sánchez in 1999. Using the hand-held camera and the fictional documentary situation to misdirect the audience's generic expectations, *The Blair Witch Project* expands the genre of the horror film by refusing to narrate the source of the horror.

As I hope these examples from Victorian novels and contemporary film have shown, a vocabulary for discussing the varieties of the unnarratable can be helpful in identifying specific changes in genre over time. Passages of disnarration and unnarration are signposts pointing to the supranarratable, the antinarratable, and the paranarratable in a given genre at a given moment, marking what cannot, shouldn't, or wouldn't be told while still maintaining its unnarratability. My aim has been to provide a way to talk about what narratives do not tell.[6]

NOTES

1   Brian Richardson addressed a similar topic in "Denarration in Fiction" (2001) but he was coining a new term for the phenomenon he observed there.

2   See *The Poetics of Biblical Narrative* (Sternberg 1985, especially pp. 235–58).

3   See "Narrating the Unnarratable" (Warhol 1994: 85–8).

4   For examples of the supranarratable in film, see the section on unnarration in film, below.

5   Tom Whalen (2000) has pointed out the parallels between the narrative of *Run, Lola, Run*, and video game structure, seeing the audience, along with Lola, as players. I thank Alan Nadel for pointing me in the direction of this article.

6   I am grateful for substantive help on this project from Emma Kafalenos, Peggy Phelan, Jay Clayton, Todd McGowan, James Vivian, Peter Rabinowitz, and Jim Phelan.

REFERENCES AND FURTHER READING

Alcott, L. M. ([1868] 1983). *Little Women*. Toronto and New York: Bantam.

Brooks, P. (1985). *Reading for the Plot: Design and Intention in Narrative*. New York: Vintage Books.

Brontë, C. ([1853] 1979). *Villette*. Harmondsworth, UK: Penguin.

Dickens, C. ([1849–50] 1981). *David Copperfield*. Harmondsworth, UK: Penguin.

Khayati, A. (1999). "Representation, Race, and the 'Language' of The Ineffable in Toni Morrison's Narrative." *African American Review* 33(2), 313–24.

Miller, D. A. (1981). *Narrative and Its Discontents: Problems of Closure in the Traditional Novel*. Princeton, NJ: Princeton University Press.

Miller, N. K. (1980). *The Heroine's Text: Readings in the French and English Novel, 1722–1782*. New York: Columbia University Press.

Prince, G. (1982). *Narratology: The Form and Functioning of Narrative*. Berlin, New York, and Amsterdam: Mouton.

Prince, G. (1987). *A Dictionary of Narratology*. Lincoln and London: University of Nebraska Press.

Prince, G. (1988). "The Disnarrated." *Style* 22(1), 1–8.

Richardson, B. (2001). "Denarration in Fiction: Erasing the Story in Beckett and Others." *Narrative* 9(2), 168–75.

Rimmon-Kenan, S. (1996). *A Glance Beyond Doubt*. Columbus: Ohio State University Press.

Sternberg, M. (1985). *The Poetics of Biblical Narrative: Ideological Literature and the Drama of Reading*. Bloomington: Indiana University Press.

Sterne, L. ([1759–67] 1967). *Tristram Shandy*. Harmondsworth, UK: Penguin.

Trollope, A. ([1861] 1987). *Framley Parsonage*. Harmondsworth, UK: Penguin.

Warhol, R. R. (1994). "Narrating the Unnarratable: Gender and Metonymy in the Victorian Novel." *Style* 28(1), 74–94.

Whalen, T. (2000). "Run Lola Run." *Film Quarterly* 53(3), 33–40.

15

Self-consciousness as a Narrative Feature and Force: Tellers vs. Informants in Generic Design

Meir Sternberg

Self, Action, and Transmission: Unifying the Narrative Field

In the narrative of human agency – the generic mainstream – private discourse is a condition of narrativity itself. Strictly, the characters needn't talk to each other at all but must think in the acting. Typically, they do both, changing voices (along with arenas, priorities, behaviors) on the social/secret axis. Most narrative texts, further, combine the characters' public and private life, verbal as otherwise, if only because action logic involves psychologic, and vice versa. Definitionally so, hence even across media, within any teleological model of agency: from Aristotle's end-directedness at large to cognitivism's problem solving. The agent then doubles as subject, mimesis plots embodied minds, self-address elucidates and/or counterpoints the overt dealings with the world, dialogues not least. Just think of the role played in causal enchainment by the doer's viewpoint – hope, fear, goal, motive, planning, knowledge, ideology – as either cause or effect of doing. From the reader's side, consider how the emergence or opacity or timing of such hidden views and forces on the narrative surface affects our processing of the enacted dynamics: between certitude and gap-filling hypothesis, irony and ignorance, suspense and curiosity or surprise, closure and open-endedness, for example.

The manifestations of the secret life alone vary and its, or their, relations to the social arena, the world in flux, the entire narrative text. Besides sequential disclosure, the manifestations widely vary in the object rendered, as among private thought, speech, and writing, or among the types of thought itself, including the operative psychic model; likewise with the form of rendering: direct, indirect, free indirect, telescoped, or latent in the external world or the artful design. (Some finer variants will come later.) The relations, again, vary in the traffic or balance or hierarchy between the public and the private domains, all the way to reverse subordinacies: as with the *Odyssey* versus *Ulysses*. Throughout, however, acting twins – even merges – with reflecting, emplotment with perspective, due to their joint anchorage in the self.

It is on such a fundamental ground, and across such a range of variability, that narrative, known as the most "dialogic" of genres, typically includes "monologic," or, better, what I call *unself-conscious* discourse. By self-consciousness I mean the discourser's awareness of addressing an audience, transmitting a message. In this basic sense, the term is independent of further traits associated with it in some common usages, looser or value-laden.[1] Sophistication, tight control, literariness, fictionality, reflexivity, for instance, may but needn't go with self-consciousness, nor are they definitionally precluded from unself-consciousness. By this feature, instead, discoursers in narrative polarize (or shuttle) between tellers and informants: those who communicate with another about the world, as against those who lead their secret life and unwittingly mediate in the process another's higher-level communication.

On the one hand, we have Fielding's persona in *Tom Jones*, Rousseau in his *Confessions*, Humbert in *Lolita*, or for that matter, any dialogist within their world and the dramatic monologist elsewhere; on the other hand, there is the secret diarist, like Samuel Pepys in real life or Bridget Jones in fiction, the vocal soliloquist, usually less regular, and the interior monologist, from sentence- to work-length. Where the issue turns on transmission-mindedness, no paradox attaches to the fact that other-oriented discourse is self-conscious, self-discourse unself-conscious. But if the apparent paradox of selfhood in and out of touch with alterity troubles you, then replace the terms by cognizant vs. uncognizant or addrecentric vs. egocentric (Sternberg 1983b).

In face of this polarity, we all sense, I believe, that the difference makes quite a difference – if only from our knowledge of the chasm between what we tell and what we keep to ourselves, or even from ourselves, complete with the respective modes of presentation. It is therefore strange that, as narratologists, we have done so little to act, or reflect, upon this tacit difference, regarding either our likes in everyday (hi)storytelling or fictional creatures denied our privilege of keeping the secret life secret, thanks to the bounds of human insight.

I have long tried to bring this feature into the prominence it deserves, but with limited success thus far. In my first book on telling/reading in time, I introduced self-consciousness as a key factor in the interplay between two omnipresent axes of viewpoint, the discourser's potential (or competence) and performance; hence also as a key factor in the still larger, generic relation between point-of-view system itself and temporal structure or even the entire narrative text.[2] What with the self's twin plot-role, therefore, the very integrity of the field is at stake.

In a nutshell, all discourse choices are ultimately motivated (determined, justified, patterned, explained) in terms of the author's silent communicative design; the author in turn motivates those choices via the chain (as well as the object) of transmission interposed, or mediating, between the authorial and the readerly end; and the transmissional work done by each of the links in the chain crucially depends for its rationale and shape and impact on their own awareness of transmitting, if only to an audience other than the author's.

From the reader's side, everything goes in reverse. Faced with the data as transmitted, we progressively infer (and if necessary, remake) some line of transmission along which they assume operative shape: the one presumably designed by the ultimate, reticent yet self-conscious, communicator, our opposite number. Originated for this purpose, the in-between line we puzzle out alternates or crosses tellers with informants to suit, among various functional relays (e.g., writing/speaking/thinking, knowledgeable/unenlightened, right-/wrong-minded). Just as we motivators invest the transmission with forms en route – down to the smallest, like pockets of direct, indirect, free indirect quoting – so we endow the transmitters with features: by whatever makes the wanted purposive sense, if only provisionally, of the text in context. Reading, subtle or simple, thus constitutes a trial-and-error process of motivating the givens to yield their best intermediate fit under the likeliest authorial rules and goals.

Accordingly, with point of view understood as a (re)constructed end/means or indeed end/mediacy system, the feature at issue gravitates from constancy at the ultimate transmissional source to variability, even reversibility, along the mediating chain. In fictional narrative, these options most proliferate between extremes, and most invite crossing or enchainment, even of the extremes themselves. At one extreme, a narrator is created in the author's own image, endowed with all the relevant powers, including equal audience-mindedness as well as omniscience, artistry, reliability, sense of communicative purpose. At the extreme opposite to omnicompetence, the creaturely transmitter receives none of these authorial privileges – least of all, the awareness of transmitting that makes (or here, in absentia, breaks) narratorhood. And without such awareness, there also evaporates the drive toward interesting, moving, guiding, persuading any outsider, let alone the implicit readership. Reduced to the lowest potential, even below communicating humans in life and art, the informant then mirror-images the superhuman teller as well as the originator of both.[3]

Such a gulf in competence will bear on the respective performances, notably their distance from the powers delegated and from the delegating author behind the scenes. Nothing in the text escapes these polar bearings, yet the handling of the event sequence is the most fundamental of them all, because generic: the interaction of narrated with narrating time distinctively constitutes narrative. It has therefore the strongest claim to illustrating the principle at diametric work.

How, then, does enabled relate to encountered transmission, possible to actual as well as to authorial stance, and what's the role of (un)self-consciousness in their (mis)match? Apropos temporal strategy, for example, the author-like narrator can by virtue of omniscience tell us everything in time, just as things happened and as would best serve their fullness, development, intelligibility in the reading self-consciously managed. Omnicompetence indeed strategically matches and produces omnicommunicativeness, hence orderly sequencing, throughout a narration like Trollope's, and for exactly these reasons. But then, given a diametric enterprise, the quasi-author becomes suppressive instead: temporal performance runs counter, not true, to the same narratorial powers in Fielding or Dickens. Bent on ambiguity instead of lucidity – on the artful disclosure rather than the natural-looking development of knowledge or judgment about the world – the narrator there will exploit the very highest privileges to twist the event-line into the wanted surprise and curiosity dynamics of reading.

In stark contrast to the omnicompetent narrator, the diarist quiet at the desk and the monologist in thought are by nature *un*self-conscious, usually also liable to ignorance and the rest of human fallibility. Here, therefore, it is all-round powerlessness that readily translates into a Fielding-like time performance, confronting us with a multigap sequence to fulfill much the same generic ends – a reading unsettled all along by curiosity or surprise – only from within the world, and the secret arena at that. Having nobody but themselves to consider, Molly Bloom and Bridget Jones plunge *in medias res*, then proceed toward further discontinuities, as befits the workings of psychic license twinned with epistemic limitation. Midward, backward, forward, sideward: the jumps reflect their mental state from moment to moment, while newly forcing us into uneasy progressive closure, ever vulnerable to lingering riddles or belated discoveries.

By a remarkable yet reasonable coincidence, superhuman and all too human qualifications, public and private viewpoint, sheer world-representing and represented discourse, ironic teller and self-betraying informant, all meet here, in the transmission of a winding, elliptic, ambiguous narrative. So they meet, but, against appearances and current opinion, not necessarily. Even when the thinking or soliloquizing or journal-keeping informant could and would do otherwise in outbound telling, it may appear, why do it in the free egocentricity of self-address?[4] But, given the will to Trollope-like lucidity, the author will nevertheless always find a way to have the unwitting as well as the addrecentric transmitter begin at the beginning and proceed in step with the world's time, more or less, even from exposition through complication toward resolution. Among narrative's universal effects, future-bound suspense dynamics will accordingly outweigh the backward-looking curiosity or surprise to transform the entire reading experience. The very time-scheme of the diary encodes this linear march *between* entries and enables it *within* each. Pepys thus describes the relevant states of affairs (his own, his family's, the nation's) "at the end of the last year," with Cromwell gone and nothing certain, before recording the first particular day, 1/1/1660, from morning to bedtime. Also, a review of one's life, with a view to making honest sense of its flow, will explain the retracer's adherence to chronology in solitary thought. "Just as it happened. In the right order": so the widower in Dostoevsky's "A Gentle Creature" understandably chooses to recall, *ab ovo*, his catastrophic marriage.

Across the gulf, then, either perspectival extreme freely correlates with any temporal strategy; either form of mediacy can serve either basic set of narrative interests, as with means and end in general. To the author, as to the reader, therefore, the most high-powered and the most disempowered transmissions contrast not in the range of time effects open to performance but in their logic of motivation: aesthetic and mimetic, functional and fictional, respectively.[5]

At the heart of this contrast, adjustable to either logic, self-consciousness operates as a prime motivating factor. Endowed with it, omnicompetent telling, whether arrowlike or crooked, is thus motivated in purely effective, aesthetic terms: the "communication has no existence, hence no role and reason, on the level of the fictive reality... but takes place exclusively within the framework of the rhetorical relationship between narrator and reader" (Sternberg 1978: 247), author's deputy and author's target. Even when less than immediate – outside metanarrative – their dealings need only pass through the generic object, which the one renders and the other reads as a first-order reality (un)made for some end, like the world of *Tom Jones* plotted for comedy. In the absence of any lifelike subjective mediation, and so motivation, to interrupt this contact, the discourse addresses itself to us straight – often indeed against time, but always in line with authorized narratorial teleology. The ordering of events goes by an order of sheer artistic priorities, with, say, lucidity *or* ambiguity, development *or* disclosure, at their head.

Under the mimetic logic of transmission, however, equivalent (dis)orderings stand at some further, substantial remove(s) from the author's frame cum priorities. They no longer reach, affect, enlighten, or trouble us virtually firsthand, objectified on the highest communicative authority, but through the mediation of characters who appear to be leading an independent existence in a world and discourse world other than ours as frame-sharers. The characters' very speaking, narrating, reflecting, writing, belong to that existence, can always get it wrong and, as activities, change it: transmissional joins with physical agency or eventhood, figural life-imaging with living itself, under the umbrella of mimesis. The dynamics of the reading process, orderly or tortuous, is then propelled not just in the guise of the dynamics of the world-in-action but also of enacted discourse.

Like all enactment, the characters' discursive acts, public or private, narratorial or self-oriented, *mediate* the author's artful design by interposing some lifelike pattern that embodies, camouflages, distances it: that both realizes and removes the operative poetics. Here lies the key to the overdue theorizing and branching of this elusive concept.[6] Mediation, I would suggest, amounts to mimetic motivation, namely, representation for an end beyond itself, below the worldlike surface. Russian war-and-peace thus mediates Tolstoy's ideology; Wonderland, Carroll's nonsense; Gulliver's narrative of his travels, Swift's satire; Emma Woodhouse's unshared thoughts, self-willed or contrite, Austen's precarious rhetoric.

So the mediating fiction always stands to the mediated function as carrier and cover at once, vehicle and veil. Only, when the characters join discursive to physical agency – Gulliver or Emma style – mediacy extends accordingly from the world in flux to some world-bound perspective on the world: the transmissional chain lengthens, the transmitted event-chain humanly wavers, and the object in general darkens, along with the authorial intent governing them all at a commensurate remove. The mimesis overlying the poesis is then not first- but second-order. It represents not (fictional) existence proper but a (figural, vocal, silent, written) representation thereof, a subjective image of what counts as the tale's objective reality.

Therefore, I further argue, all such re-presentational mediacy entails quotation: discourse within discourse, discourse about another's discourse about the world originally made from a viewpoint independent of the enclosing narrative frame that transmits it at second hand, orchestrates it by remote control to new effect. The inset as given has its artistic motivation (e.g., why work-length or piecemeal, why verbatim-looking or edited or obliquely echoed, why more reliable or less) in the quoting frame's teleology; the frame owes its mimetic motivation (for whatever arts designed) to the subjectivity (e.g., blindness) of the quotee's inset discoursing. And nowhere does this subjective, perspectival mimetic guise so thicken as with quoted discoursers whose unself-consciousness runs to the limit of not even addressing their fellow creatures: they think, speak, write along self-propelled lines, unmindful of outsiders, let alone us readerly intruders on privacy by the frame's courtesy.

By nature, all quotees remain ignorant of their framing between other parties for other purposes. However, if acutely self-conscious narrators, once inset, turn informants relative to the higher-level discourse around and about them, then such informanthood will *a fortiori* characterize quoted voices that are egocentric. These informants can therefore deploy broken time-lines too erratic and enigmatic for would-be communicators, whether equally quoted or telling in propria persona. Contrast Bloom's stream of associations with the disciplined twists of a mystery narrated by Watson or Fielding's surprise plot. Nor need the egocentric transmitter show more reader-friendliness when inclined toward chronological ordering – elsewhere notoriously judged too simple, dull, artless, but here assuming subjective interest as well as cover. Thus a life unself-consciously recorded seriatim, or retraced. Either way, given pure informanthood, the master effects built into the genre's twofold happening/reading dynamics arise by a logic of motivation polar to the omnicompetent narrator's. Among eligible rationales, the mimetic now always overlies the aesthetic or otherwise communicative, and within mimesis itself, the perspectival displaces the objectively existential line of accounting for surface (e.g., sequence) givens.

As with the interplay of times that defines narrativity, moreover, so with each and every aspect of the narrative text. The polarized rule stretches from the (im)mediacy of causal, analogical, thematic, ideological, intertextual sense-making down to the given language: how the option between, say, well-formed and ungrammatical, even incoherent, discourse gets motivated by appeal to the respective transmitters. Compare the Dickens spokesman truncating his sentences for sheer expressive impact with Pepys's or Molly Bloom's verisimilar private shortcuts.[7]

Again, beyond temporality, the motivation for the author's designs and effects may change guises, even logics in sequence, as between narrated reality and some quoted perspective on it. The mimesis overlying Carrollian nonsense thus gravitates, in late retrospect, from an apparently first-order Wonderland to Alice's dream of Wonderland. And as with global, story-length mediated transmission, so with local frame/ inset shifts. At will, Fielding's deputy mimeticizes ad-hoc any artful choice by changing roles and voices from narrator to quoter, toward enacted speech and thought, inset talk and inside view: whatever emerges or stays hidden to whatever effect, it's the current quotee's (e.g., the soliloquizing Tom's) responsibility, as it were. Indeed, given the teleological action represented, its communicator *must* interpose and enchain some re-presentations of agentive private views and scenarios: the plotters within the plot necessarily double as informants to this extent, event line as relay line. For global informants, again, changing tacks is easier still. Under some lifelike pressure, the monologist or diarist (e.g., Dostoevsky's Underground man) can break into and out of chronology, well-formedness, soul-searching, other-echoing, or even address to an imagined audience.

The ever-available shifts of or within the dominant logic of perspectival motivation, (un)self-consciousness and all, cannot be emphasized too strongly. Nor, inversely, can the systematic, often work-length interweaving of the two rationales in further well-defined perspectival configurations. There, neither merging nor breaking with the chief transmitter all along the line, the author rather fictionalizes the narrative art by depriving that transmitter either of omniscience and the like *or* of self-consciousness.

In the one instance, there arises the dramatized narrator, autobiographer, eyewitness. We encounter a representer re-presented at work, naturally limited but communicating (e.g., sequencing) well or ill inside the represented world, at some distance from the author's own artistic frame and accordingly manipulable, even exposable in its service. By remote control, therefore, the narration operates, shuttles, wavers, divides, evolves between incompetence and authority, or what we read as such for the best fit. Monologist-like self-betrayal itself persists – a Watson's, Holden's, Humbert's – now amid occupational, if always lower-level, self-consciousness, as well as an apparent monopoly on discourse. When novelistic, such inset forms an enormous direct quote of a public narrative, oral or written, which freely encloses in turn quotes of all kinds, styles, levels, voices, beginning with the narrator's experiencing self. But direct quotation that runs and recounts and relays from cover to cover, minus title page, is a quotation under a director still.

In the other instance, the Jamesian paradigm emerges: a self-conscious omniscient narrator self-restricted to a humanly *un*self-conscious "reflector" or "vessel of consciousness," figural, fallible, thinking and observing, and so mediating the world for us in multiple (discursive cum epistemic) lifelike ignorance, as wanted by the framing communicator. A human mediator quoted (typically nondirectly, preferably free indirectly) by a superhuman mediator, that vessel, like its (directly) speaking fellow, can in turn quote ad lib to remove the artist's design further – only with the greater latitude and naturalness kept for egocentricity. James's Lambert Strether, monologist-like, reflects in every sense; Holden also tells, not least self-conscious in telltale defiance of autobiographical decorum.

The variety-in-unity of these two interpolar forms of transmission should leap to the eye by now, what with their (over)privileged status in modern writing and theory.[8] Instead, let us move toward a higher vantage point, a more comparative research program trained on this feature and its fortunes.

Some Obstacles and Further Ramifications: A Comparative Balance Sheet

The original theory as just outlined has since been taken up by some narratologists, with notable results. For example, David Bordwell (1985: 57ff.) and Kristin Thompson (1988) have boldly extended this idea of self-consciousness to cinematic narrative, where narratorhood itself is in question. Again, in redefining (un)reliability as a text-integrating measure, Tamar Yacobi (e.g., 1981, 2000, 2001) has located the unreliable narrator vis-à-vis the author at the poles of giveaway information and goal-directed communication. Symptomatically, though, her own followers on the inferred status of the narrator's (un)reliability have often overlooked this rudiment, to the limit of erasing the authorial reference-point itself. (But see Cohn 2000: 73, 89, 148.) Reducing mediators instead, the author-oriented Booth (1961: especially 149–54), with parallels before and since, erases the narrator/informant line, as a mere technicality of "person." Inversely, the few analogues to our transmissional divide, though better than the common oblivion, or erasure, leave more holes and oddities than they repair.

So the task ahead is twofold. On the widest front, there remain both a great deal of misunderstanding, even resistance, to be overcome and still more work of exploration, pulling together, finer line-drawing to be carried out on the topic itself. A condition and test of the advance proposed, moreover, uncovering the impediments to it also freshly illuminates the nature, centrality, and range, or subgrouping, of the phenomena at issue. So the levels of analysis will intercross below. But I don't have the space now for going into both the metatheory and the theory required, except on a programmatic scale. Let me therefore critically adumbrate the former and, constructively, suggest in the process how the latter may develop the opening argument.

What tendencies, then, have conspired against this key feature? First, the partitioning of the generic whole. Recall the basics of narrative economy with which I started: the actional value of the subjective life, and vice versa, as well as their protean manifestations. In E. M. Forster's bare "plot" exemplar, "The king died and then the queen died of grief," (Forster 1962: 93) how to separate the public from the psychic, or enchainment from mind-imaging? The uncommon effect of the one death on the survivor not only generates the other death but also individuates the sufferer, via miniature thought-quotation: the widow's collapse is the action's coherence. (Contrast "of grief" with "of typhus".)

Note also that, with every mimetic perspectival guise assumed by the author's designs on us, big or small, another agent, another force for and possibly object of change, enters the represented arena. A quotee leads a life, a dramatized subject (mouth, hand, eye, ear, mind) is dramatizable at all levels, to all purposes. So the slightest move or shallowest motive of a doer necessarily reflects a viewpoint on the world; the barest viewpoint of an observer refracts, impels, or itself enacts some movement in the world. Beyond twinship, either operates as a two-in-one. Yet the former, *if* registered, would traditionally be consigned to the sphere of "action," or character in action; the latter, to "narration" or "focalization."

Such compartmentalizing issues from an age-old split in theoretical agenda between plot and perspective, doing and discourse, representation and communication, even *fabula* and *sjuzhet* – down to what defines narrative, hence where its study should center. For the respective camps along history, think of Aristotle and Plato; E. M. Forster or Vladimir Propp and Percy Lubbock; Ronald Crane and Wayne Booth; Claude Bremond and Gérard Genette; cognitivist and pragmaticist story analysis. Recent narratologies, despite increasing gestures toward holism, still cut asunder what narrative joins together. Lately, the above miniature plot, interlinking the two royal deaths from within, has even been found wanting by zealots of both parties. It counts as underplotted in Ryan (1991), because driveless, planless, unconflictual; and as short on "experientiality" (i.e., underquoting, overobjective), by modernist standards, in Fludernik (1996). With narrativity itself barely allowed to the exemplar on either ground, at that, the convergent negatives alleged only radicalize in little the persistent split.

The losses suffered, and the challenges posed, largely mass at this juncture, namely, the interplay of transmissional feature with actional force, either way. Unselfconscious discourse, where treated at all, has got partitioned between the camps. The less classifiable or elaborate or prestigious forms (e.g., the telescoped inside view latent in Forster's queen dying "of grief") are assimilated to emplotment; the more determinate or expressive or just novel-looking (e.g., interior monologue, free indirect thought, however causative) are assigned to perspectivity, specifically mind representation. Forms of *private happening* like these cry out for treatment as such or as a whole, always in their two-in-one re(-)presentationality. Inversely, for that matter, with selfconsciousness. Despite theory's heavy investment not only in narration but also in speech representation, what do we know about the kinds and movements and workings of enacted dialogue, from local communicative interaction among speakers in and viewpoints on the world to plot value and oblique rhetoric within the authorial frame? A staple of narrative, it would appear to have fallen between the discipline's stools.

However, even in the perspective-oriented camp, especially that born of Structuralist narratology, this hole-ridden compartmentalizing goes with a second obstacle. I refer to the influence of the linguistic model. Here it compounds other, betterknown restrictive effects in privileging not simply communication, but face-to-face communication. Such talk exchange, with the partners changing roles between speaker and addressee, marks of course the antipole to unself-conscious discourse, *a fortiori* if soundless and wordless as well as addresseeless.

Since Saussure, this oblivion to the noncommunicative half of our experience, lived or lifelike, has become the rule in various fields – pragmatics, discourse analysis, philosophy of language, as well as linguistics and semiotics – with repercussions on Structuralist narratology and beyond. Unparalleled in impact is Emile Benveniste's notorious opposition of tellerless "(hi)story" to subjectivity-flaunting "discourse";

but, for its lesson and lineage to be duly appreciated, we must trace them back to the roots.

Throughout Benveniste's important work on person deixis as/and the subjectivity of language, note first the extreme interpersonal bias of his master coinage "'instance of discourse,' ... by which language is actualized in speech by a speaker" (1971: 217). More insistently yet, "discourse is language put into action, and necessarily between partners": from primordial time, we find "man speaking to another man," so that "language provides the very definition of man" (pp. 223, 224).

This forcing of a speech partnership on language use to constitute person(ality), subjectivity, even humanity itself, on top of discoursivity, artificially restricts the whole lot. Oddly, "subjectivity" comes down to humans at their least subjective (least private, hence least freely egocentric, individual, off-guard). Surface-deep, it then invests us at our most other-minded, because communicative, hence most disinclined to express or reveal our hidden selves, best forearmed against self-exposure as inform-ants. The theory accommodates only the self-conscious "enunciatory" half of our discourse activity, or rather the social tip of the iceberg, for even the most talkative among us think more (and frequently, of course, other) than they speak, not least in speaking. Everything else drops out by fiat.

Thus, where is all silent self-communion, which eludes an outsider's access in reality but not one's own introspection? Oblivious to empirics, further, the linguist also typically blanks out at least two ranges of accessible unself-consciousness, one lived and spied upon, one lifelike and reportive. One absentee is all spoken and written private discoursing, given in principle to overhearing and, as it were, overreading, respectively. If you don't listen at keyholes, you look over Pepys's shoulder. The other is our licit second-order experience – all everyday and literary re-presentations of all modes of privacy in all quoting forms. With Benveniste's "discourse is language put into action ... between partners," contrast my inclusive threefold definition of (verbal) discourse, as a piece of language that renders, or relays, a piece of world from a certain standpoint.

In turn, the narrow scope leads to outright misconception of the forms in play, especially the personal deictics and the situational roles they encode. False Gordian knots are tied between the partners supposed to coform the instance of discourse. Thus the knot of role-reversibility: "the one whom 'I' defines by 'you' thinks of himself as 'I,' and 'I' [then] becomes 'you'" (Benveniste 1971: 199). An invariant of two-way communication alone, however, such turn-taking grows variable in commu-nication at large – a novelist's audience can't speak back – and wholly avoidable out of it. There, in ego-land, real or represented, our own or a storied informant's, no "you" has to be faced and defined, much less inverted into "I." Even where present, this "you" remains optional, interior, self-made and self-voiced *or* self-silenced. Discourse, thus remodeled, would join bipolarity and flexibility to inclusiveness: the systemic gains compound, proportionately to the opposite minuses.

Likewise with the alleged mutual implicativeness of the deictic terms, as contrast-ing members of Benveniste's "correlation of personality," exclusive of the "he," the nonpresent nonperson. Now, from the tolerable premise that "'I' designates the one who speaks," it does *not* follow that "'you' is necessarily designated by the 'I'"(Benveniste 1971: 197), so that "neither of the terms can be conceived of without the other" (p. 225). For unself-conscious discourse may keep out even the self-made "you" altogether: either to focus on the ego as ego, the usual way, or to correlate instead with a "he," allegedly outside the deictic circle. In this opaque third-person guise, Blazes Boylan haunts the mind of the cuckolded Bloom. The principle holds even on the belief, often enacted in literature since antiquity, that thought is the soul discoursing with itself: the self-discourse may well remain unaddressed to any psychic entity, as always in the Bible's inner speech. By a logic that accommodates discourse as a whole, therefore, it is rather "you" (exterior *or* interior to the self) that necessarily designates an "I," self-conscious or otherwise, but not vice versa. The "correlation of personality" needn't work both ways, just the one least in keeping with Benveniste's rationale and paradigm. In turn, this one-way implication brings home the true universal dependency-relation. It confirms and explains precisely the dispensability of the "you" in our mental representations, as the special, secondary term of the pair, hinging on whether the "I" opts for or against address, self-address to a countervoice in private dialogue included.

Last but not least fallacious among the package deals is that of superficial, especially pronominal, reflex with underlying situational role. The linguist occupationally adheres to the surface – as if it were freezable outside Utopia's regimented Unispeak – often conflating the variable, multiform, even dispensable pronouns I/you with the universal and protean discourse-roles speaker/addressee. Conflating reflex with role, indexical with indexed, worsens the earlier imbalance between the two discourse-situations. Even in terms of this very fallacy, the two's shared repertoire of person-deictic indicators, headed by the fancied I/you "correlates," renders the monopoly given in theory to one sharer all the less tenable, visibly so. Why ignore private expression, if copronominalized for role-playing? And with the fallacy overcome, the difference made by (un)self-consciousness to the roles (from their obligatory number upward, as just argued) springs into higher relief against the surface pronominal commonalities.

Now, within social language itself, the same formalist reflex/role conflation also breeds Benveniste's impossible "(hi)story" – purely objective, tellerless, noncommunicative – to invalidate the dichotomy with so-called "discourse." His otherwise mandatory correlates I/you (here, referred to narrator/narratee) abruptly turn contingent in, or on, the language of narrative: present in "discoursed," absent in "(hi)storied," events. Yet the incongruous genre-specific binarism just splits the theory's overall package dealing, and so founders in turn, now on public realities. Briefly, suppose a historical account dispensed with any visible "correlation of personality," how would it follow that events would then unroll "without any intervention of the speaker in the narration" (Benveniste 1971: 206), "so that there is then no longer even a narrator" (p. 208)? How, in reason, would events "narrate themselves" and to whom but a narratee?

Ironically, these rhetorical questions become genuine only with the polar change of rationale to our secret life. There alone can (e.g., perceived) events find (in the mind's unreflective or camera eye) an image both unknowing and unknown: a limit of unself-consciousness imageable in turn, though never reachable, via story's mimesis of that world-reflecting yet unreflective mind as an inset advisedly quoted between discoursive knowers.

Even so, the rationales polarize by awareness of self and other in event-imaging, not by person-deixis. The most impersonal-looking history, with no I's and no you's, like the Bible from Genesis to Kings, still entails, if public, both a speaker and an addressee, and may indeed pronominalize their roles at any turn. Just as the surfacing of the pronouns does not establish interpersonal contact, so their burial never precludes it: the manifest/latent variants rather enrich the cross-typology of self-consciousness and transmission or, regarding "history," narration itself, *within* (narrative) discourse.

Echoes and parallels and follow-ups to Benveniste abound in narratology: little wonder, since even the more critical references (e.g., Culler 1975: 197–200) generally fail to target and redress the discursive imbalance. The field, instead, is torn between comparable alternative extremes (often – on which later – between theory and practice as well). Apropos public storytelling itself, witness the throwback to pseudo-Jamesian immediacy of transmission, under fresh disciplinary auspices. Benveniste's reifying of surface deixis has revived, or reinforced, the modernist belief in the logical monster of "history"-like, narratorless linguistic narratives – and within written fiction at that. This revival has not passed unopposed, of course, especially when putative addressee-lessness in these narratives (Banfield 1982) followed suit. But then, among the very opponents, the genre is alternatively theorized *by* its public discourse, correlated roles and all. Less a mistheorizing, this, than an undertheorizing, deficient in scope and power rather than downright illogical.[9] Unlike mine, the sundry communication models of narrative are invariably symmetrical throughout: real author corresponds to real reader, implied author to implied reader, narrator to narratee, dialogist – if mentioned – to interlocutor. So, instead of replacing Benveniste's illusory noncommunicative form ("history," with precursors and offshoots) by the genuine, secret-life article, they reject it only to reimpose, actually multiply his speech partnership between exterior subjects. The transmitter/receiver symmetry all along the chain officially neither allows nor accounts for the varieties of asymmetrical, egocentric, receiverless, unself-conscious discourse incorporated in narrative – not even those somehow cropping up in the narratology.

It's like omitting motive from the action chain. How, where, why do sheer informants enter, and at times apparently replace, the official line of communicators? Or how do so-called focalizations (especially if internal, or if coming and going) enter the flow of narration? Once the question arises, the answer enforces itself to reconceptualize the whole narrative model. They enter, as explained, the way all intermediate transmitters do and must, the only possible way: via quotation by the anterior higher frame, with all the built-in choices and montages and subordinacies available to it, except that the inset concerned quotes an informant, re-presents an originally private single-party discourse event.

At the receiving end, likewise, standard typologies of reader, audience, narratee omit to mark the polar extreme of absence (i.e., addresseelessness) for two-way comparison. To enlarge and refine the comparison, as already noted apropos Benveniste, an inclusive typology will also embody the modulations within unselfconsciousness itself toward self-discourse proper: from "no addressee" to "no outside addressee," to private dialogue, to the surfacing, even alternating of "you" forms, always self-made.

Furthermore, such reconceptualizing can alone accommodate the intermediate, mixed variants of narrative awareness that apply to both transmitter and receiver, often in significant contrast to their absolutely or comparatively (dis)privileged mates. Otherwise, at discourse's either end, the gradability of viewpoints (hence of contrast) that we outlined in between the poles will then also escape notice, or at least systematic reference to this feature. Nabokov outreaches the telling Humbert as well as opposes the experiencing Humbert in self-consciousness, while his reader enjoys more protection against novelistic ironies than any dramatized addressee within the novel's world.

Again, the wanted rethinking in the light of this feature, with new gains in coverage, discrimination, and explanatory power at once, stretches to the very *what's* of quoted privacy. Theories of reported discourse have long opposed speech to thought as objects of report, subjective objects in effect, but without due attention to the reported vis-à-vis the reporting subject's self-consciousness. From life to narrative, from inset to frame, the divide between vocal speech and mental thought does not entail that between social and secret re(-)presentation, as perhaps appears, but flexibly correlates with it. Crosses and compounds result and alternate, as do the two obvious pairings, all enchainable in sequence.

Thus Elizabeth Bennet, holding a dialogue framed within Jane Austen's large novelistic dialogue, indeed polarizes with Molly Bloom in silent thought vis-à-vis Joyce's communication. Clean against such automatic fourfold sorting, however, Elizabeth in equally vocal *self*-address (e.g., in exclamatory response to Darcy's letter) polarizes with herself as the Austen-like dialogist, and groups instead with Molly the silent monologist reported to us in Joyce's novel. The differences in transmitted expression – from world-making to ordering to wording – regroup to suit: privacy, as always, motivates discursive egocentricity. Further, the very reporter may turn unself-conscious, even interior: we witness those heroines looking back or forward *in* private speech or thought *to* speech or thought – or for that matter, writing – with a freedom denied to their inventors and higher-level reporters, never mind their own public selves. Apart from signifying along the traditional outer/inner line, our feature multiply cuts across it to diversify the genre's resources and record.

So does another, still more principled, breach of that line. It is time to appreciate the uniqueness of the hearing act, first-order or reported, as a cross between speech and thought: an operation on the former public utterance in the latter's privacy. Given a reported encounter, between every two turns of dialogue there lurks a pocket of monologue – usually gapped, elsewhere surfacing in "x heard that" form, but always an eventful subjective nexus. In that pocket, the hearer (mis)perceives and (mis)interprets the foregoing utterance with a view to a vocal response, one possibly, sometimes advisedly, divergent from what has just been heard, let alone spoken. As an emplotted inside view, hearing within an interpersonal speech-event thus corresponds to motive between two physical events.

Much the same holds for every two letters exchanged in a correspondence, and, on a wider scale, for every dramatized narratee, whether responsive or formally reticent. All along, then, what I call "the world from the addressee's viewpoint" (Sternberg 1986) extends the range of unself-consciousness opened by addresseeless discourse to the very heart of self-consciousness territory. Just like goal-directed action in general, dramatized communication itself subsumes, provokes, and enacts reflection, inset telling multiplies informants of its own. Another revealing measure, this, of the power of a unified theory to encompass, indeed to enrich the narrative field, while both integrating and differentiating the parts in systematic operational terms: largely by appeal to our feature-cum-force.

Among further obstacles to such a versatile approach, another array runs through two books contemporaneous with mine (Sternberg 1978), and apparently informed for a change by a distinction analogous to self-consciousness. In Franz Stanzel's *A Theory of Narrative* ([1979] 1984), the first constitutive element of narrative situations is "mode," opposing "narrator" (Cid Hamete in *Don Quixote*, Zeitblom in *Doctor Faustus*) to "reflector" (Strether, Molly). The Jamesian terminology augurs well for its theorizing. Dorrit Cohn's more specialized *Transparent Minds* (1978) traces the narrative rendering of "consciousness," as against outer affairs and accounts. Either work also rightly criticizes Booth's grouping of minds with mouths under narratorhood. Between them, however, the promised distinction gets so mishandled as to confuse the issue and its wider implications in various respects: some peculiar, some already more familiar, some newly typical and beyond German scholarship. (Thus Genettian Mood/Voice, focalizing/narrating.) Sorting out this tangle will redraw, even retest, the difference the negative way, on a broad front. Especially, (un)self-consciousness will prove resistant to marriage, *a fortiori* to interchange, with other narrative attributes; *a fortiori* with its own binary; *a fortiori* where such attempts on it either load its typology or force some type(s) into or out of mediacy, even narrativity, regardless.

This ascendant order of distinctiveness gains relief, point by point, from the opposite analyses cited. Regarding the customary narratological split, both analysts favor transmission over action. Stanzel even defines narrative by its (undefined) "mediacy of presentation" alone (1984: 4ff.). Within the favored half, therefore, you would at least expect a sharp polarizing of "teller" and "reflector" modes, to suit with Jamesian usage:

A *teller-character* narrates, records, informs, writes letters, includes documents, cites reliable informants, refers to his own narration, addresses the reader, comments on that which has been narrated . . . By contrast, a reflector-character reflects, that is, he mirrors events of the outer world in his consciousness, perceives, feels, registers, but always silently, because he never "narrates," that is, he does not verbalize his perceptions, thoughts and feelings in an attempt to communicate them.

(Stanzel 1984: 144)

James would hardly approve. Far from being criterial – necessary *or* sufficient – the two bundles of traits put forward are mostly sharable by the alleged binaries. Thus, except for the circular or tautological "narrates, records, informs" and the equivocal "addresses the reader" (overtly?), none of the activities associated here with the "teller" (letter-writing, documenting, quoting, self-reference and self-commentary) is in fact obligatory, much less as a set. Or else Hamsun's *Hunger*, or Joyce's *Portrait*, remains untold. Nor does reflection, least of all written, Pepys style, bar any of these discourse activities.

Inversely, a reflector like Strether indeed "mirrors . . . perceives, feels, registers," but will the same necessarily apply to his vocal or journal-writing counterparts? Or to the (day)dreamer? Mirroring, perception, emotion, registration itself, anything beyond private world-making, are all dispensable to the reflector mode at large. ("Informant" is duly noncommittal.) And even where vessel or soliloquist or diarist indulges in all these activities, doesn't the same mental repertoire extend to the narrator proper (as, elsewhere, to the crossmodal focalizer)?

Hence also the falsity of the categorical "always silently," imposed on the reflector's discourse as such, yet again geared to the nonspeaking, nonwriting variety alone. But then, "does not verbalize" is hardly the law of even this reflectorial variety – Strether, Molly, Faulkner's Benjy – which famously ranges over the axis of mute self-expression, as between word and image.

So the one relevant distinction ("attempt to communicate" present or absent) gets lost in the mishmash on and between the modal flanks. No wonder taxonomic incongruities abound. Beckett's Malone swings from "interior monologue" to "first-person narrator" and back to "reflector" (Stanzel 1984: 61, 94, 145), then "oscillates" between the roles (pp. 150, 226). Across the same barrier, "epistolary and diary novels" are lumped together, the second being mediated by a "teller" amid self-address (pp. 202, 211, 225–6). Inversely, "the dramatic monologue is non-narrative" (pp. 225–6), though both addrecentric and actional by definition. The nonnarrativity verdict is even generalized for all direct quoting, as if "first person narrative" itself didn't manifest this form in large. Wavering, contradictory bracketing, arbitrary exclusion from the genre: a signal negative lesson. Together with the overemphasis on interiority – abetted by the very term reflector – it highlights both the cutting edge and the scope of our (un)self-consciousness model.

If this lust for feature-clustering already defeats itself, worse ensues. The uttermost package-dealer in narratology – witness his entire "typological circle" – Stanzel proceeds to conflate the two modes with an assortment of further binarisms, mainly presentational and all in truth independent, crosspolar, reversible. Narrator vs. reflector allegedly goes with:

1 Telling vs. showing;
2 Commentary present vs. absent;
3 Account explicit, generalized, and purportedly complete vs. implicit, specific and conspicuously incomplete;
4 Indeterminacy in communication vs. built into the human condition;
5 Preliminaries first vs. none;
6 Beginning with identifiable "I" vs. referentless "he";
7 Reference to hero by name vs. opaque pronoun;
8 Stable vs. open ending;
9 Unreliability (if character) definitional vs. irrelevant;
10 Past tense having vs. shedding past meaning; and so forth

(Stanzel 1984: 146–70).

Never mind consistency, or the persistent bias for interior unself-consciousness, or the bizarre idea of reliability: the packaging of these 10 extra oppositions with the modal one at issue is again all demonstrably wrong in reason and fact alike. So indeed my argument already predicts about the lot, or has even demonstrated regarding the majority, concerned in effect with temporal structure between lucidity and ambiguity. Just recall how omnicompetent narrators, Fielding's suppressor *or* Trollope's all-communicator, meet their operational equivalents among unprivileged informants, dechronologizing *or* chronologizing, with a view to either basic time experience. Poles apart in aesthetic/mimetic motivation, crucially hinging on self-consciousness, the respective transmitters yet co-implement the desired authorial strategy via the means appropriate to it: Stanzel's assorted opposites, inter alia.

Worst of all, these false concomitants in Stanzel not only overload and defocus the pertinent feature, to the loss of cutting edge, but may even substitute for it to metamorphic effect both ways: either polar discourser transforms into the other, regardless of self-consciousness itself. And this beyond the plainer, if symptomatic, oversights that befall Malone or the diarist, the dramatic monologist, the direct quoter. Incredibly, the theory boasts the logical (typological, *a fortiori* teleological) monster of "reflectorization," whereby the "teller temporarily assumes certain characteristic qualities of a reflector-character" (Stanzel 1984: 173).

Even an authorial narrator will become "reflectorized" by dint of what is actually nothing but intermittent, ever-eligible, at most reportive shifts in communicational tactics or posture or distance. If we look back to the gratuitous tenfold opposition above, these reflectorizers involve a switch of discourse from left to right column - all amid ongoing self-consciousness, clean forgotten by the taxonomist (Stanzel 1984: 156–200 passim). So much so that reflectorizing, down to free association, overtakes the very highest communicator, and nowhere else than in *Ulysses*, taken as "the interior monologue of the author" at "composition" (pp. 178–80).

Author apart, were such "transformation" conceptualized as devolving from omniscient to humanly fallible *narrator*, it would at least avoid sheer unreason, if only inconsistency with the distinctive feature of their shared narratorhood vis-à-vis reflectorhood. So, late in Nabokov's *Pnin*, the impersonal teller emerges as the hero's earthly opponent, while remaining self-conscious, unreflectorized. Again, were the "transformation" described as a narrator fronting and framing some reflector, instead of "temporarily becoming" one, it might even fit the case here and there, even if nothing like news, let alone a general explanatory rule: not even for the listed discourse breaches. Transmissional motivating options would still extend from, say, bare narratorial games of withholding or code-switching to inset reflectorial peculiarities of style, judgment, knowledge, beholding, thinking, hearing. So Fielding's narrator pretends human ignorance at will, and James's systematically limits himself to rendering the vessel's human outlook – limited and secret by nature – without any metamorphosis in either teller's absolute powers, whether omniscience, however suppressive, or audience-mindedness, however disguised. Nor does such metamorphosis attend even an unexpected overall shift of motivation: from Wonderland told to Wonderland dreamed, with the teller removed intact, frameward, and the tale alone, if you will, reflectorized in the dreaming, via Alice.

As it is, instead, Stanzel's transmitter abruptly changes poles, complete with realm of existence, across a qualitative barrier impassable on his own premises. With self-consciousness forgotten in favor of its imaginary correlates, the artistically motivated devices of the most author-like of tellers (and, in *Ulysses*, also the most knowing of authors), at will operating under subjective guise, veer round into the perspectival lapses and liberties betrayed by the most creature-like, disempowered, egocentric of reflectors. Discourse surface gets mistaken for discursive reality, contrivance for self-exposure, performance for (in)competence.

Similarly with "first-person narrative." Changes in pronominal, I/he self-reference (though, Benveniste fashion, never affecting speech role), or in distance from the experiencing self, will reflectorize it (Stanzel 1984: 104, 208–9). Conversely, the interior monologue turns "narrative" – though "of course" still unaddressed to any listener – where its reflector changes tenses from present to past (pp. 207–8, 227). Reminiscing monologists or soliloquists, most nondirectly quoted vessels, and diarists at large would thus collocate, by force of tense, with the standard retrospective narrator.

Either way, the polar modes transform into each other on the strength of their noncriterial features – if theirs at all - against the one that makes the difference: self-consciousness present or absent. It is like saying that, as a woman eats and plays and menstruates and reasons, an eating or playful or reasoning man becomes womanized.

So the attack on Booth's modal indifference boomerangs with a vengeance. Yet the narrator/reflector miscorrelations and the reflectorizing illogic circulate nevertheless, even in the better hands of Cohn (1981: 170–4) or Fludernik (1996). The allure of package-dealing dies hard, the oblivion to self-consciousness comes easy, given the ongoing taxonomic spirit unmindful of the Proteus Principle: the living interplay of features with forces, re(-)presentational forms with communicative functions, that makes and make sense of discourse as transacted, varieties included. If teller and reflector can interchange as alternative perspectival means to a narrative end – mediators, hence motivators, of generic (dis)ordering, above all – they can neither stand opposed nor change to each other by force of any adjoinable superficiality.

Indeed, as well as endorsing Stanzel's typological fallacies here, Cohn (1978) outspecifies them in her reflector-focused study, otherwise the best of its kind. Just observe the tendentious packaging drive that runs, on various scales, through the book's Part II to overdiscriminate among narrative forms, all in honor of one idealized private mode. Common options specialize, harden, and bunch into constants, may's into pseudo-differential must's, some already encountered.

Thus, the monologist vs. first-person narrator divide is reyoked with variables beyond communicativeness, especially present vs. past tense and anachrony vs. chronology. On the monologic flank, in turn, such overlinkage apparently rationalizes Cohn's (likewise standard, here titular) bias for unvoiced self-discourse, as against written journal and spoken thought. Besides their alleged past-reference, these inferiors willy-nilly gather further narration-like markers, or forfeit their "properly" monologic opposites: randomness, emotivity, ellipsis, pronominal opacity. All, again, counter to the expressive freedom shared perforce by all egocentrics. Last, within unvoiced self-discourse itself, her specialty, Cohn even outdoes Stanzel. She invents otherwise useful types like the orderly retrospective "autobiographical monologue" (Dostoevsky's "A Gentle Creature") and the disorderly, free-associational yet still past-oriented "memory monologue" (*The Sound and the Fury*), not as variants of, or at least parallels to, but as variants *from* "genuine interior monologue." Note the essentialist rhetoric enlisted in "genuine" to valorize and purify, hence reify, the latter monologue form – exclusive of its nearest equivalents in unself-consciousness, plus inner speech, plus work-length "autonomy," plus temporality.

Monologism, then, progressively reduces to privileged contingencies. So, by the end of the road, at a prohibitive cost rising with each fork, the monologic – instead of encompassing the secret life, or even the hushed kind, or the directly quoted subkind thereof, or the extended subsubkind – finds its rare quintessence in Molly Bloom, as desired. No interpretive finesse can save this web of fissures and (con)fusions by fiat, either; nothing short of the reorientation outlined, via (un)self-consciousness, will do justice to the private domain as such, and to the transparent mind within it.

The less so because the macromonologue loses in Cohn its generic tellerliness (reminiscent of modernism's "dramatized" tale, or Benveniste's "history," or structuralism's "reproductive" quoting below) along with its informant-specific unity. Even the disfavored types, once grown text-length, count here as equally "autonomous": *im*mediate, single-voiced, directly quoted yet narrator-free to the point of "antinarrative," *sui generis*. This intersects afresh with Stanzel, who generalizes the vanished mediacy of narration in narrative for all direct citation of speech and thought: passing echo, scene, text, interior and dramatic monologue. (Compare

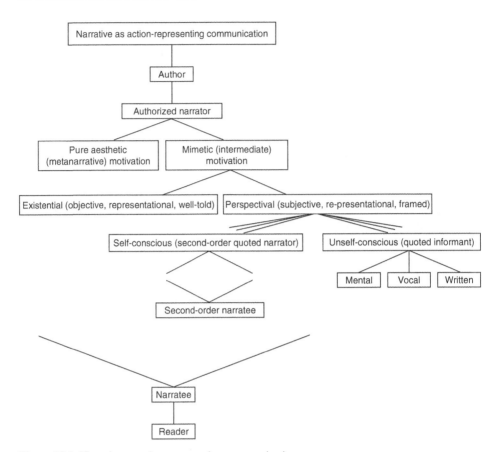

Figure 15.1 Narrative as action-representing communication

Genette denarrativizing such formal directness into "pure mimesis" or "immediate discourse," again literally and hermetically reproductive of the original. Elsewhere, the narratorless purity has long subsumed free indirectness and the "third-person" Jamesian model.) Inconsistently selective to boot, Cohn and her followers would keep the vanishing narrative act for "autonomous" quoted self-discourse, as though sheer extent made all the difference in transmissional, hence generic, kind.

So the contradiction in terms only sharpens, along with the counterevidence. Logically, direct quotation entails a quoter, regardless; and the quoter must be acknowledged to re(con)textualize, reperspectivize, subordinate the original utterance or thought in the framing, however quietly, on pain of what I call the direct speech fallacy. Indeed, how else, if not through the narrator turned quoter, do we gain access to the monologist's consciousness, deemed here "the special preserve of narrative" vis-à-vis "dramatic and cinematic" fictions (Cohn 1978: vi, 5) at that? Again, who else decides where to begin, or end, re-presenting the secret flux? And if you would attribute both access and cutoffs to the author instead – already in breach of putative autonomous monologic univocality – there still remain in the inset marks of framing textual (rather than arguably contextual) interference that are definitionally given to a performing narrator alone. Who else verbalizes nonverbal mentation? Who segments the interior speech or thought continuum with written aids to understanding like chapters, paragraphs, sentences, punctuation? Who introduces and deciphers and annotates (let alone expurgates) Pepys's self-writing, or, in effect, the episode-length Molly paradigm itself set within the *Ulysses* whole?

Here, therefore, incurring the direct speech fallacy means that the unself-conscious mind somehow, by wondrous default, quotes, inscribes, edits, publishes, as well as expresses itself; the self-centered reflector also plays self-teller to us outsiders. By this *self*-contradiction, moreover, the theories (Genette included) divide against themselves, joining their very targets of attack: from Booth et al.'s insideviewee-as-narrator to Banfield et al.'s narratorless subjectivity.

Inset experience, like all re(-)presentation, never displaces but unknowingly mediates the framing communication on every axis. Taken together, the consequences, for good or for ill, are radical. To dovetail my argument's constructive and critical thrusts, Fig. 15.1 will serve. (You'll recall that the generic branching increasingly enables in practice crosses, shifts, enchainments, further ramifications, unrealized possibilities.)

Notes

1 In Booth (1961: 155), it thus depends on the narrator's awareness of composing a literary work and reference to the problems involved: these stipulations exclude Huck Finn and the barber in Lardner's "Haircut," both self-conscious, as addressors, within my framework. Likewise restrictive is the common phrase "self-conscious artistry," echoed in, e.g., Cohn (1978: 152, 180, 187, 199, 265).

2 Sternberg (1978: 246–305, 1983a: esp. 172–86; also, e.g., 1986, 1991, 2001: esp. 167ff.), on how the same functional, holistic (re)construction produces in little the quoting forms of speech and thought, or indeed speech vs. thought.

3 Narrative (in)competence defines itself relative to the author – across all exterior value judgments – as its linguistic parallel does to the relevant speech-community.

4 Accordingly, below we will find Stanzel packaging the reflector, and Cohn the interior monologist, with anachronic deployment, a miscorrelation that goes as far back as Edouard Dujardin.

5 Again, these two logics govern all representation – across kinds, arts, media, ontologies, truth claims – but we'll proceed with the exemplary, because most protean, case of narrative fiction.

6 Never defined, often unstable, where most invoked: in Lubbock, Stanzel, Genette and company.

7 Interestingly, *Ulysses* imitates Pepys's style in Oxen of the Sun.

8 Details in Sternberg (1978: 276ff.), and below.

9 Illogic ensues, as will appear, when certain discourse types, often private ones (above all, interior monologue) get officially excepted from narrativity.

REFERENCES AND FURTHER READING

Banfield, A (1982). *Unspeakable Sentences*. Boston: Routledge.

Benveniste, E. (1971). *Problems in General Linguistics*. Coral Gables: University of Miami Press.

Booth, W. C. (1961). *The Rhetoric of Fiction*. Chicago: University of Chicago Press.

Bordwell, D. (1985). *Narration in the Fiction Film*. Madison: University of Wisconsin Press.

Cohn, D. (1978). *Transparent Minds: Narrative Modes for Presenting Consciousness in Fiction*. Princeton, NJ: Princeton University Press.

Cohn, D. (1981). "The Encirclement of Narrative: On Franz Stanzel's *Theorie des Erzählens*." *Poetics Today* 2, 157–82

Cohn, D. (2000). *The Distinction of Fiction*. Baltimore: Johns Hopkins University Press.

Culler, J. (1975). *Structuralist Poetics*. London: Routledge.

Fludernik, M. (1996). *Towards a "Natural" Narratology*. London: Routledge.

Forster, E. M. (1962). *Aspects of the Novel*. Harmondsworth, UK: Penguin.

Ryan, M.-L. (1991). *Possible Worlds, Artificial Intelligence, Narrative Theory*. Bloomington: Indiana University Press.

Stanzel, F. K. (1984). *A Theory of Narrative*. Cambridge, UK: Cambridge University Press.

Sternberg, M. (1978). *Expositional Modes and Temporal Ordering in Fiction*. Baltimore: Johns Hopkins University Press.

Sternberg, M. (1983a). "Mimesis and Motivation: The Two Faces of Fictional Coherence." In J. Strelka (ed.), *Literary Criticism and Philosophy* (pp. 145–88). University Park: Pennsylvania State University Press.

Sternberg, M. (1983b). "Deictic Sequence: World, Language and Convention." In G. Rauh (ed.), *Essays on Deixis* (277–316). Tübingen: Gunter Narr.

Sternberg, M. (1986). "The World from the Addressee's Viewpoint: Reception as Representation, Dialogue as Monologue." *Style* 20, 295–318.

Sternberg, M. (1991). "How Indirect Discourse Means: Syntax, Semantics, Pragmatics, Poetics." In R. Sell (ed.), *Literary Pragmatics* (pp. 62–93). London: Routledge.

Sternberg, M. (2001). "Factives and Perspectives: Making Sense of Presupposition as Exemplary Inference." *Poetics Today* 22, 129–244.

Thompson, K. (1988). *Breaking the Glass Armor: Neoformalist Film Analysis*. Princeton, NJ: Princeton University Press.

Yacobi, T. (1981). "Fictional Reliability as a Communicative Problem." *Poetics Today* 2, 113–26.

Yacobi, T. (2000). "Interart Narrative: (Un)Reliability and Ekphrasis." *Poetics Today* 21: 708–47.

Yacobi, T. (2001). "Package-Deals in Fictional Narrative: The Case of the Narrator's (Un)Reliability." *Narrative* 9, 223–29.

16

Effects of Sequence, Embedding, and Ekphrasis in Poe's "The Oval Portrait"

Emma Kafalenos

Edgar Allan Poe's initial consideration when beginning to write, he says in "The Philosophy of Composition," is the effect, or impression, he wants the story or poem to have on its readers. Only after he has chosen the effect, he continues, does he "consider whether it can best be wrought by incident or tone...afterward looking about me (or rather within) for such combinations of event, or tone, as shall best aid me in the construction of the effect" (Poe 1977: 550). "The Philosophy of Composition," published in 1846, is the essay in which Poe offers a description of how he wrote "The Raven." For that poem, Poe says, he chose "a novel, first, and secondly a vivid effect" (1977: 550). Poe's stories, too, often produce vivid and novel effects, and, like "The Raven," may have been written to do so.

The strong effect that Poe's stories and poems produce is often, in part, the result of supernatural elements. But even in his stories that include the supernatural, the effect that the supernatural produces is often heightened by narrative strategies that, unlike the supernatural, can be explained through analysis. Poe's story "The Oval Portrait," published in 1842, takes its title from a portrait that in the story is represented through ekphrasis, the rerepresentation in words of a visual representation. Poe's use of ekphrasis draws attention to the power of language to guide interpretations by what is omitted as well as by what is said. The embedding in the story of both the oval portrait and a document that purportedly describes how it was made demonstrates the power of narratives to shape interpretations of causality by controlling the sequence in which information is revealed.

"The Oval Portrait" is very short – a mere six paragraphs. For the purposes of the present analysis I think of the story as made up of three sections of about the same length: the first two paragraphs, the next three paragraphs, and the final long paragraph. In the first of the three sections an intradiegetic narrator introduces himself and his situation. In the second section the narrator recounts his experience viewing the oval portrait. The final section is a quotation, set off by quotation marks at the beginning and the end, of a paragraph describing how the portrait was made, which the narrator reports that he is about to read. Thus readers read the quoted paragraph as if at the same time that the narrator does, and with knowledge of the narrator's situation and of the experience that has led him to pick up the volume and turn to this specific passage. I begin my analysis by looking at this quoted paragraph, to consider how we would interpret the causal relations among the events it reports if we encountered the paragraph as an independent text, complete in itself. At the end of this essay I will compare this interpretation with our interpretation of exactly the same text when we read it as an embedded segment in Poe's story. The difference in the two interpretations illustrates the degree to which narrative strategies can guide readers' interpretations of an event's causes and effects.

To be able to talk about and compare interpretations, I draw upon a vocabulary I have developed, primarily from work by Tzvetan Todorov (1969a, 1969b) and Vladimir Propp (1968), for naming interpretations of causal relations. The set of 10 functions that I have defined names stages in a causal sequence that leads from one equilibrium to another equilibrium. Readers can use these names to express their interpretations of causal relations in a story or in part of a story.

I list here the five functions that provide the necessary vocabulary to formulate and compare interpretations of the quoted paragraph at the end of Poe's story, when read by itself and when read in the context of the complete story. These five functions represent stages from the disruption of an equilibrium to the establishment of a new equilibrium:[1]

Five functions, with definitions
EQUILIBRIUM

A	destabilizing event that disrupts an equilibrium
C	decision by C-actant (the character who performs function C) to attempt to alleviate the function-A event
C′	C-actant's initial act to alleviate the function-A event
H	C-actant's primary activity to alleviate the function-A event
I *or* I$_{neg}$	success (*or* failure) of the function-H activity

EQUILIBRIUM

Turning to the quoted paragraph at the end of Poe's story and reading it by itself as if it stood alone, most readers would probably interpret the initial situation as a moment of equilibrium. The first sentence reads: "She was a maiden of rarest beauty, and not more lovely than full of glee" (1977: 105). Because this first sentence describes an ongoing situation in which unsurpassable beauty and pleasure coexist, readers are guided to interpret that all is well in the narrative world – that the narrative world is in a state of equilibrium. As we read on, because the first character to whom we are introduced is the girl, we are guided by the primacy effect to interpret what follows in relation to how it affects her and her situation.[2]

For many readers, the combination of superlative beauty and pleasure that the first sentence describes will suggest that something disruptive is about to occur. In fact, the second sentence immediately introduces a destabilizing set of events that disrupts that equilibrium: "And evil was the hour when she saw, and loved, and wedded the painter." Soon the "evil" is specified; the painter has "already a bride in his Art" (1977: 105). My interpretation – and, I suggest, most readers' interpretation – of the causal relations among the reported events can be represented by these functions:

Analysis 1 (quoted paragraph, first three sentences)
EQ   maiden is full of glee
A   she marries a painter who is already married to his art

Once we have understood that it is the painter's devotion to his art that disturbs the girl's otherwise unqualified happiness, probably most of us read on wondering how, or whether, the painter will reassure his wife that she is as important to him as his art is. But as the story continues we learn that she "dread[s] only the pallet and brushes and other untoward instruments which deprived her of the countenance of her lover. It was thus a terrible thing for this lady to hear the painter speak of his desire to portray even his young bride" (1977: 105). Because the girl is made so unhappy by the painter's desire to paint her, most readers probably interpret his request as a second function-A disruptive event:

Analysis 2 (quoted paragraph, first four sentences)
EQ   maiden is full of glee
A_1 she marries a painter who is already married to his art
A_2 painter requests that the girl sit for a portrait (for the girl, his request is "a terrible thing . . . to hear")

Moreover, as the weeks pass during which the girl sits for her portrait, she grows "daily more dispirited and weak" (1977: 106), a third function-A event. And then, although some who saw the unfinished portrait "spoke of its resemblance in low words, as of a mighty marvel," the painter "*would* not see that the tints which he spread upon the canvas were drawn from the cheeks of her who sate beside him" (p. 106, Poe's italics), a fourth event that disrupts the initial equilibrium. Probably most readers continue to think about how, and by whose efforts, the disruptive situation can be resolved. We wonder whether there isn't someone who can point out to the painter how damaging painting her portrait is to the girl he is painting.

But then at last the painter applies the final brushstrokes. The quoted paragraph – and Poe's story – conclude:

. . . and, for one moment, the painter stood entranced before the work which he had wrought; but in the next, while he yet gazed, he grew tremulous and very pallid, and aghast, and crying with a loud voice, "This is indeed *Life* itself!" turned suddenly to regard his beloved: – *She was dead!*

(1977: 106, Poe's italics)

Reading the quoted paragraph in its entirety and considering it as an entity complete in itself, without reference to the story in which it is embedded, I interpret (and assume that most readers interpret) the causal relations among the reported events according to these functions:

Analysis 3 (quoted paragraph, read as an entity complete in itself)

EQ   maiden is full of glee
A_1 she marries a painter who is already married to his art
A_2 painter requests that the girl sit for a portrait (for the girl, his request is "a terrible thing . . . to hear")
A_3 the girl grows dispirited and weak
A_4 painter won't recognize that he is killing the girl by painting her
A_5 upon completion of the painting the girl is dead

In the quoted paragraph an initial equilibrium is followed by one event after another that disrupts the girl's previously happy life. These disruptive events destabilize the situation and culminate in the death of the girl at the very moment that the painting is completed. The girl's death is the awful final event, the event we learn about even after we learn that the painting has been successfully completed. We interpret the death of the girl as the concluding tragic event in a series of disruptive events. The quoted paragraph offers an example of a narrative that traces only a part of a complete sequence – in this case the move from an equilibrium to a disruptive situation, a pattern that is relatively uncommon in narratives and that most readers probably find dissatisfying.

Narratives guide readers' interpretations of the function of events in a number of ways, including ways that make even tragic concluding events seem less thoroughly disruptive than the quoted paragraph makes them seem. One way is to encourage readers to align their interpretations of the function of events with the interpretations of one character rather than another, for instance, by providing information from the perspective of one character rather than another. In the quoted paragraph we are given information about how the girl responds – to seeing that her husband is already married to his art, to being asked to sit for her portrait, to being painted. As a result, readers tend to interpret the function of events according to their effect on the girl, that is, as a series of function-A occurrences.

These same events that the quoted paragraph reports could have been told instead from the perspective of the painter. It is much more common, in fact, in narratives in which one character accomplishes something and a character that that character cares about dies, that the story be told in a way that guides readers to interpret the function of events in accordance with the character who accomplishes something (in this case, the painter who paints a marvelous painting) rather than, or as much as, with the character who dies (in this case, the girl). We can imagine the events that the quoted paragraph reports told in a way that would guide readers to admire the painter's accomplishment and, yes, to recognize the tragedy of the girl's death, but at the same time to appreciate the complexity of the concluding situation in which the painter recognizes simultaneously his success as a painter and his failure as a husband. Readers might interpret the conclusion of this imagined story as offering a balance between the two simultaneous final events: the function-A death of the girl and the function-I successful completion of the painting.

Analysis 4: (imagined retelling of the events that the quoted paragraph reports)

A   painter desires to portray his bride
C   painter decides to ask her to sit (the painter is the C-actant – the character who performs function C)
C′   painter asks her to sit
H   painter paints her portrait
I   painter completes the painting, but
A   the girl is dead

Another way that narratives guide readers' interpretations of the situation at the end of a story is by appending a concluding comment by a character or the narrator. In some cases these comments reveal the character's or the narrator's interpretation of what has occurred; in other cases such comments may merely indicate that life in the narrative world is continuing. The quoted paragraph offers an example of a narrative in which the events that have occurred make the resolution of the motivating function-A situation impossible. After the death of the girl there is no way to bring her back to life and make her happy again. In this situation, in some narratives, a character or a narrator will say something that guides readers to recognize that the narrative world is again in equilibrium. At the end of the quoted paragraph, for instance, one further sentence could tell us that the painter regretted for the rest of his days his blindness to his wife's deteriorating condition. That one sentence would draw our attention from the final function-A event (the girl's death) to the stability – the new equilibrium – of the resultant ongoing situation. If readers find the quoted paragraph dissatisfying when read as if it stood alone, I suggest, it is largely because the paragraph guides readers to interpret the function of events from the perspective of the girl, to whom nothing good happens to balance the bad, and because it withholds all comment about the state of the narrative world after her death.

But the quoted paragraph, which thus far we have analyzed as if it were a separate entity, is the final section of Poe's story. Poe's story ends with the same words – "She was dead" – and the same event – the girl's death – that the quoted paragraph does. I want now to look at Poe's story in its entirety, ultimately to show how differently readers interpret the causal effects of the girl's death when we read about it in the larger context of the complete story, which shifts readers' primary attention from the short life and the death of the girl to the context in which Poe's narrator views (presumably) her portrait and to the questions the portrait raises in his mind and in ours.

Poe's story begins at what can be called an achieved equilibrium: an equilibrium that is the result of events that we learn about at least in broad outline. The opening sentence reports a set of events that trace an entire sequence. The sentence reads:

> The château into which my valet had ventured to make forcible entrance, rather than permit me, in my desperately wounded condition, to pass a night in the open air, was one of those piles of commingled gloom and grandeur which have so long frowned among the Apennines, not less in fact than in the fancy of Mrs. Radcliffe.
>
> (Poe 1977: 103)

Once we organize in chronological sequence the events this sentence reveals, we will probably interpret the causal relations according to these functions:

Analysis 5 (how the initial equilibrium came about)

A   the narrator is too desperately wounded, his valet thinks, to spend the night outdoors in the Apennines

C   the narrator's valet decides to locate shelter for the narrator (the valet is the C-actant – the character who performs function C)

C′   the valet breaks into a chateau

H   the valet establishes the narrator in a room inside the chateau

I   the valet succeeds in finding shelter for the narrator

EQ   the narrator is now ensconced indoors for the night

In the rest of the first two paragraphs (the initial section of the story), the further information reinforces readers' initial interpretation that the opening situation is an equilibrium. The narrator describes the "remote turret" (1977: 103) to which his valet has brought him. He is in a bed that has black velvet curtains. A candelabrum provides enough light that he can contemplate his surroundings.[3] The walls, in his words, "were hung with tapestry and bedecked with manifold and multiform armorial trophies, together with an unusually great number of very spirited modern paintings." A "small volume" he found on his pillow "purported to criticise and describe" the paintings (p. 103). For hours, the narrator explains, he gazed at the paintings and read from the book, until finally it was midnight. In this first section of the story, readers have been given only one piece of information that suggests that the ongoing equilibrium is less stable than it otherwise would have seemed. The narrator has mentioned that his "incipient delirium" (his words) perhaps explains his "deep interest" in the paintings (p. 103).

In the next section of the story (the third, fourth, and fifth paragraphs), the prevailing equilibrium is disrupted when the narrator moves the candelabrum. With the resultant change in lighting, he is able to see a painting he had not previously noticed: the oval portrait to which the story's title refers. About the painting, after this first glimpse, the narrator tells us no more than that it is "the portrait of a young girl just ripening into womanhood" (1977: 104). His own response, however, he describes in some detail. After glancing at the painting, he says, he immediately closed his eyes, then began to analyze why he had done so. In his words, "It was an impulsive movement to gain time for thought – to make sure that my vision had not deceived me – to calm and subdue my fancy for a more sober and more certain gaze" (p. 104). Since the narrator has previously mentioned his "incipient delirium," and since he now describes "the dreamy stupor which was stealing over [his] senses" (p. 104), readers probably gather that his initial view of the portrait has led him to fear that he has in fact been overtaken by delirium and that he cannot trust his sensory perceptions. We may interpret his response to the portrait according to these functions:

Analysis 6 (narrator's first response to the portrait)
EQ   narrator is ensconced in the chateau
A   narrator fears he has become delirious
C   narrator decides to determine whether he is delirious (the narrator is the C-actant)
C′   narrator "calm[s] and subdue[s] [his] fancy for a more sober...gaze"
H   narrator studies the painting at length

Thus far, all that we know about the portrait is that it has made a strong impression on the narrator and that its subject is a young girl. We have no additional information beyond what the narrator tells us, of course, because we cannot see the portrait, which is embedded in Poe's story through ekphrasis. As Tamar Yacobi has discerned, when an artwork (or other document) is embedded in another work, two media need to be considered if we are to understand how the embedded artwork is perceived by readers or viewers in our world. On the one hand there is the medium we would perceive if we could enter the narrative world and experience the artwork there – in the case of the oval portrait, paint. On the other hand there is the medium in which the embedded artwork is represented in the work in which it is embedded – in this case (as always in the case of ekphrasis), words.[4] Readers' response to Poe's story is affected by the interplay between the two media: the visual representation (for which, on the basis of our prior experience with paintings, we can conceive certain characteristics, but not others) and the verbal rerepresentation that at best can convey to us one among other possible descriptions.[5]

The narrator, after looking again at the painting, now judges that he "saw aright" (1977: 104). But because readers cannot see the portrait, we cannot gauge whether the narrator's initial shocked response was the result of something unusual about the portrait, or whether his perceptions are less trustworthy than he now thinks they are. In other words, at this point in our reading, some readers may be unsure whether to analyze the causal relations among the events we have thus far learned in accordance with Analysis 7 below (the narrator is in full control of his faculties and now understands his earlier response) or Analysis 8 (the narrator's shocked response to the portrait may be an effect of his delirium).

Analysis 7 (the interpretation the narrator proposes)

EQ   narrator is ensconced in the chateau
A   narrator fears he has become delirious
C   narrator decides to determine whether he is delirious
C′   narrator "calm[s] and subdue[s] [his] fancy for a more sober... gaze"
H   narrator studies the painting at length
I   narrator decides he "saw aright"

Analysis 8 (some readers' interpretation)

EQ   narrator is ensconced in the chateau
A   narrator may have become delirious; readers cannot trust his perceptions

Once the narrator judges that he "saw aright," he devotes a few words to describing the painting before analyzing why he had been "so suddenly and so vehemently moved" (1977: 105). The portrait, which is set in an oval frame, depicts no more than a head and shoulders, the body disappearing into the deep shadow of the background. Without the frame, the head and shoulders disappearing into the shadows might well have been understood as an apparition. Here Poe's story flirts with the supernatural. It is because of the frame, the narrator says, and because only a part of the body is depicted, that he decides that even though his "fancy [had been] shaken from its half slumber," he could not have "mistaken the head for that of a living person." Continuing to stare at the painting for perhaps another hour, he at last concludes: "I had found the spell of the picture in an absolute *life-likeliness* of expression, which at first startling, finally confounded, subdued and appalled me" (p. 105, Poe's italics).

The word "appalled" guides us to recognize that the narrator is interpreting viewing the painting as a function-A disruptive event. Because the narrator describes the "life-likeliness" of the depicted girl's expression as appalling, we understand that, for him, deciding that he has viewed the painting "aright" does not re-establish the equilibrium established in the first section of the story. Rather, the narrator has now explained, at least to his satisfaction, why seeing the painting has been so disturbing an event:

Analysis 9 (narrator's interpretation of his experience in response to the portrait)

EQ   narrator is ensconced in the chateau
A_1 narrator fears he has become delirious
C   narrator decides to determine whether he is delirious
C′   narrator "calm[s] and subdue[s] [his] fancy for a more sober... gaze"
H   narrator studies the painting at length
I   narrator decides he "saw aright" – that the "life-likeliness" of the depicted expression is appalling (the resolution of the function-A_1 situation creates a new function-A situation)
$I = A_2$ the "life-likeliness" of expression is appalling: the equilibrium is again de-stabilized

Because the painting is represented in the story only through ekphrasis, which makes it impossible for readers to envision it except through the double lens of the narrator's perceptions and the narrator's words that describe his perceptions, some readers may question whether visual representation can ever be sufficiently lifelike to be considered appalling. For these skeptical readers, the narrator's finding the "life-likeliness" of expression appalling may corroborate and extend their earlier worry that the narrator is delirious and that his perceptions – and now his conceptions also – cannot be trusted.

Analysis 10 (skeptical readers' interpretation)
EQ   narrator is ensconced in the chateau
A   narrator may have become delirious; readers may not be able to trust his perceptions
A   visual representation so lifelike as to be appalling is impossible; readers cannot trust narrator's conceptions

It is exactly because skeptical readers question the accuracy of the narrator's perceptions and conceptions, however, that they share his desire to understand why the depicted girl's expression has seemed to him appallingly lifelike. For this reason, at this point in the story, the narrator himself, readers whose interpretations agree with the narrator's, and skeptical readers are similarly motivated to investigate the causes of the narrator's experience. Immediately after being told that the narrator finds the portrait's "life-likeliness" of expression appalling, we read:

> With deep and reverent awe I replaced the candelabrum in its former position. The cause of my deep agitation being thus shut from view, I sought eagerly the volume which discussed the paintings and their histories. Turning to the number which designated the oval portrait I read there the vague and quaint words which follow.
>
> (1977: 105)

Although the narrator and skeptical readers are attempting to resolve different issues, readers make the same decision that the narrator does: to read on to resolve the questions that the narrator's experience has raised.

Analysis 11 (Poe's story, the first two sections)
A   (for the narrator) the "life-likeliness" of the portrait is appalling
A   (for the skeptical reader) the narrator's incipient delirium may have affected his perceptions and conceptions
C   a decision is made – by the narrator and by readers – to look for an explanation through reading (narrator and readers are C-actants)
C′   narrator picks up book; readers read on
H   the narrator and readers read the quoted paragraph simultaneously and for the same purpose: to find out why the narrator has found the portrait so appallingly lifelike

Thus readers read the quoted paragraph not only as if at the same time the narrator does, but also with the same function-C motivation that the narrator has: to look for information that explains the narrator's response to the painting. As a result, most readers as they read, I suggest, devote more attention to the painting than to the painter, and to the painter than to the girl – a reversal of the attention we pay to the girl when we read the quoted paragraph as if it stood alone.[6] In fact, when we reach the final words and hear the painter, looking at his painting, say "'This is indeed *Life* itself!' [before] turn[ing] suddenly to regard his beloved: – *She was dead!*'" we find the explanation we sought. Even skeptical readers recognize that a painting with the history of the one in question is no ordinary painting and that the circumstances in which the painting had been made lend support to the accuracy of both the narrator's perception of the depicted girl's lifelike expression and his conception that that "life-likeliness" was appalling. After reading the complete story, most readers, I propose, interpret the function of the reported events according to these functions:

Analysis 12 (Poe's story in its entirety)

EQ	narrator is ensconced in the chateau
A_1	narrator fears he has become delirious
C	narrator decides to determine whether he is delirious
C'	narrator "calm[s] and subdue[s] [his] fancy for a more sober . . . gaze"
H	narrator studies the painting at length
I	narrator decides he "saw aright" – that the "life-likeliness" of the depicted expression is appalling
$I = A_2$	the "life-likeliness" of expression is appalling
C	both the narrator and readers decide to look for an explanation through reading (narrator and readers are C-actants)
C'	narrator picks up book; readers read on
H	the narrator and readers read the quoted paragraph simultaneously and for the same purpose: to find out why the narrator has found the portrait so appallingly lifelike
I	the circumstances in which the painting was made can be understood to explain the narrator's experience

Because the quoted paragraph is the concluding section of Poe's story, both the paragraph and the story end with the same words and the same event: the completion of the painting and the subsequent death of the girl. Let us now contrast analysis 12 to analysis 3. When we read the paragraph by itself as if it stood alone (analysis 3), we interpreted the death of the girl at the moment when the painting was completed as a major disruptive event – in my terminology a function-A event. When we read the identical paragraph in the context of Poe's story (analysis 12), we interpreted the death of the girl at the moment when the painting was completed as a successful outcome to our efforts to explain why the narrator found the portrait so lifelike – in my terminology a function-I event. Function analysis demonstrates the magnitude of the effect that the way events are told can have on interpretations of the causes and effects of those events, in this case the death of the girl.[7] I draw attention to five narrative strategies that help to explain these very different interpretations that the girl's death elicits in the two contexts.

First, and perhaps most obvious, there is the primacy effect. The quoted paragraph introduces the girl in the first sentence, whereas in the first sentence of Poe's story the narrator introduces himself.

Second, the primacy effect is reinforced in both cases by the perspective from which information is presented. In the quoted paragraph, the information comes to us through a lens that is positioned near the girl. When we read the quoted paragraph by itself, as we saw at the beginning of this essay, the information we are given about how the girl responds to the events in her life guides us to align our interpretation of the function of the events with hers. Our interpretation stops at function A because, from the perspective of the girl, after her death there is nothing more to interpret. In the first two sections of Poe's story, in contrast, it is the narrator himself whose perceptions and thoughts we learn. As a result, we tend to align our interpretation of the function of events with his interpretation. When we reach the quoted paragraph, knowing that we are reading it as if at the same time that he is, we tend to align our interpretation with what we presume is his interpretation. From his perspective, we know him well enough to assume, the juxtaposition of the girl's death and the painting's completion will provide reassurance that he was correct (function I) in analyzing the painting's "lifelikeliness" as the cause of its strong effect.

Third, in addition to which character is introduced initially we need to consider the sequence in which events are reported. In the quoted paragraph the events in the girl's life are told chronologically. We are introduced to her, then told that she meets, falls in love with, and marries the painter, and then that he paints her portrait. The first and second sections of Poe's story too, after the opening flashback, are told more or less chronologically. The narrator lies in his bed, looks about the room, reads, then looks at the oval portrait, then reads about the oval portrait. But in Poe's story the quoted paragraph that the narrator reads provides information about events that are chronologically prior to, rather than subsequent to, the night during which the narrator is reading it.[8]

As Meir Sternberg has shown, the sequence in which information is provided to readers affects the form of attention readers accord to it. The quoted paragraph, when read by itself as if it stood alone, exemplifies *suspense*. We read it with the expectation that we are going to learn what lies ahead: what is going to happen as the events continue to unroll. Given this expectation our attention is focused on the outcome – in this case the completion of the painting and the subsequent death of the girl. When the quoted paragraph is read as a part of Poe's story, on the other hand, it exemplifies *curiosity*. We read it with the expectation that we are going to learn about some previous occurrence that will help to explain the present situation in the narrative world. Given this expectation, our attention is focused primarily on the relation between the earlier events and the present situation – in this case the relation between, on the one hand, the completion of the painting and the subsequent death of the girl, and, on the other hand, the narrator's appalled response to the portrait.[9] The sequence of the telling establishes the temporal relation between a present situation in the narrative world and the events of another time period, previous or future, to which readers' attention may be drawn.

Fourth, in *Metahistory*, Hayden White (1973) recognized that the historian chooses a segment of the historical record to narrate, and that the choice of one segment rather than another segment influences interpretations of the events the historian reports. White gives as an example the death of a king: the "death of the king may be a beginning, an ending, or simply a transitional event in three different stories" (1973: 7). In other words, whether an historical event is interpreted as a beginning, as a transition, or as a concluding event depends on its chronological position in the set of events being told, which depends on which segment of the historical record the historian chooses to treat. In fiction, as in accounts of historical events, interpretations of causal relations among reported events are influenced by the chronological position of the event in the set of events being reported. In the quoted paragraph at the end of Poe's story, when read by itself as if it stood alone, the segment of time that is reported extends from the girl's period of happiness to her death. Because her death is chronologically the final event in the set of reported events, we interpret it as the consequence of the earlier events and even as the culminating event that explains why the events that lead up to it have been reported.

In the complete story as Poe tells it, however, the events that are reported scenically take place during a segment of time that includes only a few hours. In the opening paragraphs the narrator is lying in bed, looking at and reading about paintings. He views the portrait, then reads about it in the book. During this temporal segment the girl exists only as a portrait and as the subject of a paragraph. By limiting the scenic representation to these few hours, Poe shifts the emphasis from the girl's short life and early death, as well as from the violence the narrator has previously suffered, to the narrator's experiencing the girl's portrait, which is the only event that disturbs the equilibrium during this temporal segment.

If we consider not just the events that are reported scenically but the entire set of events that the story reveals about the narrator, the temporal segment that is reported extends from the narrator's being wounded somewhere in the Apennines to his being brought for shelter to the château, to rest and recuperate. In the context of this temporal segment, which Poe could have chosen to represent scenically in its entirety, beginning with the wounding and the breaking into the château, the girl is again only a portrait and a paragraph, and even the narrator's shocked response to the portrait is no more than a minor distraction during the period of his recovery.

Fifth, from the perspective of contemporary interarts studies, the apparition of a head and shoulders that in Poe's story is contained in a frame draws attention to parallel temporal, ontological, and epistemological issues that embedded artworks and literary representations of the supernatural both raise. Just as any artwork can be thought of as a conduit to the earlier time in which it was made, and any portrait as a link to the time in the life of the person that is portrayed, the shock that the appearance of a ghost creates is surely in part the result of the clash between two temporal periods, the present in which it is perceived and the earlier time in which the apparition is presumed to have been alive.

In addition to bringing into the present the prior temporal period in which both the painted person and the ghostly apparition once presumably lived, both the portrait and the ghost further complicate perception by introducing a tension between contradictory interpretations of the ontology of the image. When a portrait is thought of as an artwork, we assume an ontological boundary that we cannot cross. We cannot enter a painting and, for instance, have dinner with the painted figure. When a portrait is thought of as comparable to a photograph, a representation of someone who once lived, then logically only the temporal gap – but not the ontological gap – separates the person portrayed from the person viewing the painting.[10] Nonetheless, experience teaches us that we respond with different emotions to a painting that represents a person in pain, even when we know that the representation is of an historical figure, than we do to a living person in front of us who is in pain, or, arguably, even to a photograph of a person who is in pain. Part of the difference is presumably the result of the temporal gap; there is nothing we can do in our time period to relieve the suffering the painted figure once endured. But part of the difference is the effect of the ontological separation indicated by the medium; oil paint does not feel pain. Similarly, the continuing fascination with ghosts is in part the effect of the tension between considering an apparition as an image of someone who once lived among us and from whom we are separated only by time, or as an emanation from an extraworldly realm to which we have no access.

The epistemological tension that the ontological issue introduces is compounded by ekphrasis, which, as we saw earlier, allows readers to know only what the viewer of the artwork in the narrative world sees and chooses to describe. In contrast to the portrait that readers see only through the narrator's words, the quoted paragraph is in the same medium in the narrative world as in the story we read: language. Because we read the very same account that the narrator does about the girl whose husband paints her to death, we are more ready to accept than we would be if the information were rerepresented to us by the narrator, that in the narrative world an unusual relation of near-identity exists between the object of representation (the girl who gives herself entirely to her husband's art), the representation (the portrait that conveys her "life-likeliness"), and its perception (the narrator's response as if to a living person).

As a function analysis demonstrates, Poe's complete story shapes readers' interpretations of the effects of the girl's death very differently than the quoted paragraph does. The narrative strategies in the complete story that guide our interpretations include the selection of the very short temporal segment that is scenically represented and the sequence in which information is provided, both of which are made possible by embedding the events pertaining to the girl. The two media through which the girl's story is represented contribute too. Because the portrait is represented only through ekphrasis, readers can question the accuracy of the narrator's scarcely believable perceptions and conceptions – a questioning that for readers is a function-A disruption that motivates us to read the quoted paragraph to resolve it. Then, because readers can join the narrator in reading the words of the quoted paragraph, we can substitute our experience for his and read the passage as he presumably does: as evidence of the accuracy of his perceptions.

Notes

1 These five functions are selected, for the purposes of this essay, from the set of 10 functions I use to analyze causal relations in any narrative (Kafalenos 1995, 1999).

2 Both Meir Sternberg (1978: 93ff.) and Menakhem Perry (1979: 53ff.) have summarized and analyzed psychologists' studies that document the primacy effect: our tendency to accept as valid the information we are initially given, even when that information is contradicted later in the same message.

3 Similarities between this turret and the turret in which the painter paints his wife permit interpreting the quoted paragraph as a *mise en abyme* – a contained work that mirrors or duplicates aspects of the work that contains it. Moshe Ron (1987: 427) proposes that the repetition of the word "turret" in this story can in itself "prompt readers to posit a *mise en abyme* relation with very little additional substance." J. Hillis Miller drew my attention, in conversation in response to an earlier version of this essay, to the parallel between the candelabrum that lights the painting in the narrator's turret and the light in the painter's turret that "*dripped* upon the pale canvas" (1977: 106, italics added). I am grateful to Brian McHale, who was the first to point out to me that the quoted paragraph could be read as a *mise en abyme* and who brought Ron's essay to my attention.

4 Yacobi perceives that

In ekphrasis . . . the represented as well as the representing domains are representations of an object. . . . Like all "quotation," therefore, ekphrasis bundles together no less than three, rather than two, domains: one first-order, strictly "represented"; one second-order, "representational" in the visual mode; one third-order, "re-presentational" in the linguistic discourse. From the side of the reader of literature, we encounter the original object [in Poe's story, the girl] at a twofold remove . . . mediated by the pictorial image that the language itself mediates, re-images, *quotes* for us. (1997: 36, her italics).

In Poe's story (1) the girl is (2) represented in a portrait, which is (3) rerepresented in words. For analysis of the rerepresentation in one medium of a representation in another medium, other than the visual-to-verbal move of ekphrasis, see Kafalenos (2003).

5 Roland Barthes (1985: 150) describes "a picture [as] never anything but its own plural description," effectively suggesting the limitless ways a given visual depiction can be described. Further, Barthes argues, "the identity of what is 'represented' is ceaselessly deferred . . . the analysis is endless; but this leakage, this infinity of language is precisely the picture's system: the image . . . is not the repository of a system but the generation of systems." See also Spence (1982), particularly chapter 3, "Putting Pictures into Words."

6 Alan Nadel pointed out in conversation, in response to an earlier version of this essay, that some readers when they begin to read the quoted paragraph still expect (and want) to be told how the narrator became wounded. Unlike skeptical readers, for whom the story of how the painting was made offers information that helps them gauge the validity of the narrator's perceptions and conceptions, these readers will not have their question answered. But these readers' curiosity about the narrator's earlier adventure – like skeptical readers'

interest in gauging the narrator's perceptions – by focusing their attention on something other than the girl and her fate will lead them to interpret the girl's death differently when they read the quoted paragraph as part of Poe's story than when they read it as if it stood alone.

7 Functions name interpretations of causal relations among events in the narrative world; the comparison I am drawing is between interpreting the death of the girl as a major disruptive event that ends her life (analysis 3) and as an event that successfully resolves an enigma (analysis 12). For both the trusting reader and the skeptical reader, however, learning about the girl's death produces a stronger emotional response when we read the quoted paragraph as part of Poe's story than when we read it as if it stood alone. Stating the case for the trusting reader (in a response to an earlier version of this essay), James Phelan points to the significance of

> the way that the context intensifies the horror of the embedded story. "The Oval Portrait" seems to me to work by constructing a reliable witness to the effect of the horror narrated in the embedded story. The whole thing builds to the last two lines, and the punch packed within those lines depends on our having seen the result of the

painter's effort in the narrator's prior account of the painting's effect.

For the skeptical reader too, whose position I more comfortably share, the amazement that a portrait can possess the "life-likeliness" that the last two lines suggest that in fact it does, is similarly intense.

8 Menakhem Perry discerns that one of the common ways in which accounts vary from the chronology of external events is by including "a block of information transmitted from one character to another" (1979: 39–40).

9 Meir Sternberg describes the interplay between the two sequences of narrative (story and discourse, a told and telling/reading sequence) as the source of "the three universal narrative effects/interests/dynamics of prospection, retrospection, and recognition – suspense, curiosity, and surprise, for short" (2001: 117). In this essay I draw attention to two of the three, suspense and curiosity.

10 See Marie-Laure Ryan's analysis of "boundaries within the representing discourse, and boundaries within the represented reality (the 'semantic domain' of the text); boundaries with gates to get across, and boundaries with only windows to look through" (1990: 873).

REFERENCES AND FURTHER READING

Barthes, R. ([1969] 1985). "Is Painting a Language?" In *The Responsibility of Forms: Critical Essays on Music, Art, and Representation*, trans. R. Howard (pp. 149–52). New York: Hill and Wang.

Kafalenos, E. (1995). "Lingering Along the Narrative Path: Extended Functions in Kafka and Henry James." *Narrative* 3, 117–38.

Kafalenos, E. (1999). "Not (Yet) Knowing: Epistemological Effects of Deferred and Suppressed Information in Narrative." In D. Herman (ed.), *Narratologies: New Perspectives on Narrative Analysis* (pp. 33–65). Columbus: Ohio State University Press.

Kafalenos, E. (2003). "The Power of Double Coding to Represent New Forms of Representation: *The Truman Show, Dorian Gray*, "Blow-Up," and

Whistler's *Caprice in Purple and Gold*." *Poetics Today* 24, 1–33.

Poe, E. A. (1977). *The Portable Poe*, ed. P. A. D. Stern. New York: Penguin.

Perry, M. (1979). "How the Order of a Text Creates its Meanings (With an Analysis of Faulkner's 'A Rose for Emily')." *Poetics Today* 1, 35–64, 311–61.

Propp, V. ([1928] 1968). *Morphology of the Folktale*, revised and ed. L. A. Wagner, trans. L. Scott, 2nd edn. Austin: University of Texas Press.

Ron, Moshe (1987). "The Restricted Abyss: Nine Problems in the Theory of *Mise en Abyme*." *Poetics Today* 8, 417–38.

Ryan, M.-L. (1990). "Stacks, Frames and Boundaries, or Narrative as Computer Language." *Poetics Today* 11, 873–99.

Spence, D. P. (1982). *Narrative Truth and Historical Truth: Meaning and Interpretation in Psychoanalysis*. New York: W. W. Norton.

Sternberg, M. (1978). *Expositional Modes and Temporal Ordering in Fiction*. Baltimore, MD: Johns Hopkins University Press.

Sternberg, M. (2001). "How Narrativity Makes a Difference." *Narrative* 9, 115–22.

Todorov, T. (1969a). *Grammaire du* Décaméron [The Grammar of the *Decameron*]. The Hague: Mouton.

Todorov, T. (1969b). "Structural Analysis of Narrative," trans. A. Weinstein. *Novel: A Forum on Fiction* 3, 70–76.

White, H. (1973). *Metahistory: The Historical Imagination in Nineteenth-Century Europe*. Baltimore, MD: Johns Hopkins University Press.

Yacobi, T. (1997). "Verbal Frames and Ekphrastic Figuration." In U.-B. Lagerroth, H. Lund, and E. Hedling (eds.), *Interart Poetics: Essays on the Interrelations of the Arts and Media* (pp. 35–46). Amsterdam and Atlanta, GA: Rodopi.

17

Mrs. Dalloway's Progeny: The Hours as Second-degree Narrative

Seymour Chatman

Michael Cunningham's *The Hours* was a great critical and popular success when it appeared in 1998, winning the Pulitzer and the PEN Faulkner prizes. When it was turned into a movie, directed by Stephen Daldry, in 2002, sales of the novel and of *Mrs. Dalloway* skyrocketed. This enthusiasm once again demonstrated the permeability of the borders between high and popular culture. Quite apart from its merits as a novel, the popular reception of *The Hours* must be counted an important cultural event, one that justifies an interest in the formal dimensions of Cunningham's project.

What kind of a narrative is *The Hours?* How best to describe its relation to *Mrs. Dalloway* — narratologically, stylistically, thematically? And what does that description tell us about both novels' aesthetic and thematic achievements? Answering these questions may shed light on the current popularity of the derivative or imitative text, a kind of text that some critics believe especially characterizes the postmodern era.

The reviewers of *The Hours* could not agree on how to classify it. One thought it a "sequel." Others evoked a musical metaphor, likening it to "variations on a theme," or "extended riff." More matter-of-factly, it was called a "retelling" or a "reworking." Cunningham himself (in a question-and-answer session at a bookstore reading) said he intended not an "imitation," an "annex," or a "pastiche" but a "rewriting." Still others settled for "emulation," "replay," "echo," or "parallel." Clearly our critical vocabulary lacks distinctive terminology for what Gérard Genette has dubbed "second-degree" narratives, those bearing a more than passing resemblance to some original. To situate novels like Cunningham's, we need to understand the complex varieties of second-degree texts. Fortunately, we have Genette's excellent guide *Palimpsests*, which sifts eruditely through literary tradition. Genette (1997) identifies five major types, which, as is his custom, he distinguishes with daunting combinations of classical morphemes: (1) "Intertexts" – these are older texts encapsulated within newer, as in quoting, plagiarizing, and alluding; (2) "Paratexts" – the framing elements of a core text, like titles, prefaces, notices, and forewords; (3) "Metatexts" – literary criticism and other kinds of external commentary; (4) "Architexts" – "the entire set of . . . categories – types of discourse, modes of enunciation, literary genres – from which emerges each singular text"; and (5) "Hypertexts" – the products of "any relationship uniting a text B, the 'hypertext,' with an earlier text A, the 'hypotext,' upon which it is grafted in a manner that is not that of commentary." Unfortunately, as users of the internet know, "hypertext" has come to mean something quite different, namely, "nonlinear" or "linked." So I'll use "original" and "imitative" to refer to these different texts.

Of course, every text arguably imitates one or more originals. But of principal concern to this essay are those which are massively imitative. *The Hours*, like Max Beerbohm's parodies, or what Genette calls "serious transformations," like *Ulysses*, imitates another text on sustained and explicit grounds. It announces a contract with Woolf's novel: not only are some of its chapters entitled "Mrs. Dalloway," one character named "Virginia Woolf" and another "Mrs. Brown" (presumably after that elusive ordinary person whom, Woolf argued, Arnold Bennett could never capture), but "The Hours" was the original working title of Woolf's manuscript.

The vagaries of traditional usage tend to muddy rather than clarify discussion. Especially in English, different kinds of imitation are lumped indiscriminately together. If it does nothing else, Genette's taxonomy usefully clarifies what *The Hours* is *not*. It distinguishes among texts that are satirically, playfully, and seriously derivative. It further divides satires into three subtypes: (1) "strict parody," (2) "satirical pastiche" or "caricature," and (3) "travesty." A strict parody is very short; it makes fun of the original through wordplay, sticking as closely to it as possible: Thomas Gray's line becomes "the short and simple flannels of the poor"; Hemingway's stories are retitled "The Snooze of Kilimanjaro," "The Crullers," or "A Clean-Well-Sighted Ace." Strict parody is but a rhetorical figure, a one-liner, and so tells us little about extensive second-degree texts.

Satirical pastiche goes beyond minimal alteration. For instance, an elevated style may be applied to trivial or wildly inappropriate events, as in "The Rape of the Lock." And whereas "parody . . . deforms a text . . . pastiche . . . *borrows* a style – and all that goes with it" (Genette 1997: 78). The opposite also occurs: a lowbrow style may be used to convey "noble" events. This is "travesty" or "burlesque travesty" (a type rarer today than in the eighteenth century). A modern English example is the reconstruction of the letter from Goneril to Regan (*King Lear* I, iv) as it might have been written by a twentieth-century society matron: "Dearest Regan . . . We have been having the most trying time lately with Papa . . ." (by Maurice Baring, reprinted in Macdonald 1960: 307–11).

Pastiches need not be caricatural: they may be merely "playful," a stylistic imitation aiming "at a sort of pure amusement or pleasing exercise with no aggressive or mocking intention . . . it [is] the *ludic* mode of the imitative text" (Genette 1997: 27). Classic examples appear in Proust's *Pastiches et Mélanges*. The line between satire and play is fine but perceptible: the satirist means to deride the original, its author, or someone else; the nonsatiric *pasticheur* means only to tease without really challenging the value of the original. Both kinds entail critique, but ludic pastiche also implicitly offers homage. It is gentle and shows evident respect for the original. In "The Guerdon" and "The Mote in the Middle Distance," for example, Max Beerbohm teases Henry James's excessively delicate representation of characters' states of mind, but clearly does not seriously deride the Master's manner or content. Sometimes, as in Proust, the motive for pastiche seems a mere flex of stylistic muscle.

Clearly, *The Hours* is neither caricature nor travesty: the reader will find no ridiculing of Virginia Woolf, of her novel *Mrs. Dalloway,* or of Cunningham's own major characters (though it does satirize minor characters with satirized counterparts in *Mrs. Dalloway* – Walter Hardy is Cunningham's version of Hugh Whitbread, Oliver St. Ives of Lady Bruton, Mary Krull of Miss Kilman). But *The Hours* profusely imitates aspects of the style of *Mrs. Dalloway,* and to that extent entails pastiche. Still, a novel whose intention were *mere* pastiche – satiric or playful – would not win a Pulitzer Prize.

So we must turn to Genette's category of the "serious" derivative, a category heretofore unnamed by literary criticism. Genette distinguishes between serious imitation and serious transformation. Serious imitation is *forgerie,* a word obsolete in French which Genette's translators render as "forgery." Unfortunately, in English that term connotes an illicit text which passes itself off as a newly discovered work by a famous author or source, like James Macpherson's Ossian poems or Thomas Chatterton's ballads. But *forgerie* can also mean simply "that which is wrought or crafted" (the actual French equivalent of English "forgery" is *falsification.*) An English example of this more neutral sense is the James Bond novels written after Ian Fleming's death by Kingsley Amis (pseudonym "Robert Markham"), John Gardner, and Raymond Benson.

But *The Hours* does not fit into that category either: it does not turn on further adventures of Clarissa Dalloway – hence the inappropriateness of the term "sequel." (Another novel published in 1999, *Mr. Dalloway,* by Robin Lippincott, *is* such a sequel. It retains many of the characters, and its events occur in 1927. Additionally, it "transfocalizes" Woolf's novel, in other words, tells the story from the perspective of an erstwhile minor character, Richard Dalloway [as *Rosencrantz and Guildenstern Are Dead* transfocalizes *Hamlet*]). The category most appropriate to *The Hours,* rather, is "serious transformation" or "transposition," the category of *Ulysses, Doktor Faustus,* and *Mourning Becomes Electra.* These are texts that do not continue the lives of the original characters, but rather use them as patterns for new characters whose experience is somehow parallel. They preserve important elements of the *story,* but move it to a new spatiotemporal world, a new *diegesis* (Genette 1997: 295). Genette finds transposition the most important kind of hypertext, both historically and aesthetically. Paraphrasing and expanding his definition, we can say that transposition is an "imitation in a serious mode, usually signed by its real author and often marked 'contractually' (e.g., by a name) whose dominant function is to pursue or extend a preexisting literary achievement while proclaiming itself as a new effort."

The Hours is indeed an "extension," in particular, what Genette might call a *complement* of *Mrs. Dalloway*. It makes a new whole with its original, not merely allusively but formatively. The engaged common reader of *The Hours* (and not only the scholar studying second-degree texts) will (re)read *Mrs. Dalloway* for a fuller comprehension of how both novels work. *Mrs. Dalloway* then becomes an explanatory source for what motivates Mrs Brown, why Clarissa Vaughan should be happy despite the death of Richard, how gay marriages can be as ordinary as straight ones. *The Hours* fits into the category of complement because it presupposes its readers' familiarity with *Mrs. Dalloway* and also their tacit agreement that the structure and style of the original permit an alternative sexual ethos.

Obviously, declaring *The Hours* a "complementary transposition" is only a categorization, not an explanation or analysis. How precisely does it adapt Virginia Woolf's novel, and what are the aesthetic and thematic consequences? Does it constitute an independent classic? I suggest that Cunningham's failure to capture one important aspect of Woolf's technique limits his novel's scope and so misses something of the universality of *Mrs. Dalloway*'s appeal.

Let us first consider the obvious similarities of content. These are to be found exclusively in the chapters that Cunningham labels "Mrs. Dalloway." A generalized plot summary fits both the original and Clarissa Vaughan's story: on a given day in a large metropolis, a female protagonist plans a party. A mentally ill man with whom she feels close kinship kills himself in despair. The heroine is deeply shocked, but, with the support of a stable partner, finds that this death has given her courage to live on. (*Mrs. Dalloway*: "She felt somehow very like him – the young man who had killed himself. She felt glad that he had done it; thrown it away... He made her feel the beauty; made her feel the fun" [Woolf 1925: 186]; *The Hours*: "Clarissa Vaughan thinks: 'It is, in fact, a party, after all. It is a party for the not-yet-dead; for the relatively undamaged; for those who for mysterious reasons have the fortune to be alive'" [Cunningham 1998: 226].)

At a more detailed plot level, the correspondence is equally close. At the outset each Clarissa feels playfully exhilarated as she goes out shopping for flowers ("What a lark! What a plunge!" [Woolf 1925:5]/"What a thrill, what a shock..." [Cunningham 1998: 10]). Each is observed sympathetically by a neighbor, a walk-on who never reappears (Scrope Purvis/Willie Bass). Each reminisces fondly about adolescence in a country home (Bourton/Wellfleet), and recalls a boyfriend's playfully cynical response to her love of natural beauty (Peter Walsh: "I prefer men to cauliflowers" [1925: 3]/ Richard Brown: "Beauty is a whore, I like money better" [1998: 11]). On their errands, each runs into a bluff, well-known, and well-connected male friend (Hugh Whitbread/Walter Hardy), men who do good works but who are more facade than substance, men who normally reside in the country but are in town today for the sake of a sickly partner (Evelyn/Evan). Each visits the shop of a female florist who is an old friend (Miss Pym/Barbara). Each hears a noise out in the street associated with "a face of the greatest importance" (the Prime Minister? the Queen?/Meryl Streep? Vanessa Redgrave? Susan Sarandon?). Throughout the "Mrs. Dalloway" chapters,

Clarissa Vaughan thinks the same thoughts as Clarissa Dalloway, sometimes in the very same words ("Heaven only knows why we love it [the city] so" [1925: 4/1998: 226]). What goes oddly unexplained, however, is why Clarissa Vaughan, despite her manifold associations with Clarissa Dalloway, including Richard's calling her by that name, should be oblivious of these parallels. Are they supposed to be coincidental? If not, what was Cunningham's purpose in exercising this artistic license?

The parallelism among other characters is equally patent: Clarissa Vaughan also has her faithful mate, Sally Lester. Like Peter Walsh, Richard Brown has been left by a Clarissa who cannot handle his tumult; like Septimus Smith he commits suicide after suffering an illness that causes him to hear voices. Richard's lover Louis's plight also resembles Peter Walsh's: rejected, he has gone off to San Francisco (as Walsh has gone off to India), returning a bit the worse for wear and agonizing about an affair he is having with a young person. Both Peter and Louis have nervous tics: Peter plays with his pen knife, Louis counts his steps. Like Clarissa Parry, Clarissa Vaughan has chosen a more stable if less exciting partner over a teenage sweetheart. Ms. Vaughan's choice can be read as the fulfillment of the (only latent) lesbian desire evident in Clarissa Dalloway's and Sally Seton's kiss. (Both Clarissas remember that passionate kiss – to the "wrong sex" – as the happiest moment of their lives.) Sally Lester, like Richard Dalloway, attends a luncheon to discuss a silly project with Oliver St. Ives, the counterpart of Lady Bruton. And so on.

Of course, these parallels concern only one of the three stories in *The Hours*; Mrs Brown's and Mrs Woolf's stories are newly minted. So the novels really have quite different structures and themes. *Mrs. Dalloway* turns on two main story threads – Clarissa Dalloway's preparations for her grand party, and Septimus Smith's drift toward suicide. Woolf joins these protagonists only contingently. Except for a critical moment in Mrs Dalloway's consciousness, the stories do not intersect. Clarissa never meets Septimus but only hears about his suicide at her party.

Clarissa Vaughan, on the other hand, personally witnesses Richard Brown's suicide. Until the end, *The Hours* seems to be weaving three story threads. But the plot is not really tripartite. The "Mrs. Brown" and "Mrs. Dalloway" chapters, in a surprise (and rather un-Woolfian) twist, belong to the same story, since Richard, the adolescent lover and lifelong friend of Clarissa, is revealed to be the son of Mrs Brown. Further, the characters reflect two aspects of Clarissa Dalloway's character. Laura Brown, who prefers a good book to the company of her doting husband and apprehensive child, corresponds to the retiring, "nun-like" Clarissa Dalloway constrained by fatigue and illness. Conversely, Clarissa Vaughan's busy life in New York corresponds to Clarissa Dalloway's activity as accomplished hostess. We are led to believe that Laura is frustrated by unrequited lesbian desires, desires which she suppresses for a solitary life in Canada – as opposed to Clarissa Vaughan, who has acknowledged her lesbianism, achieved liberation, and enjoys a satisfying domestic relationship. The chronology here is relevant: the gray 1950s of the Mrs. Brown chapters is still closet-time, the time of repression, while the 1990s generally accepts more diverse roles for women and is witnessing a waning of homophobia.

But what role do the "Mrs. Woolf" chapters play in Cunningham's complementary novel? The biographical fragment is not popular with some Woolfians, who argue that Virginia was not dominated by Leonard, that she was not mean to her servants, that Vanessa's children did not make fun of her, and so on. Of course, the novel is not a biography. The "Mrs. Woolf" sections seem designed less to reconstruct the actual genesis of *Mrs. Dalloway* than to draw situational parallels with Cunningham's protagonists – Virginia's "entrapment" in Richmond with Laura Brown's entrapment in a Los Angeles suburb, and her yearning for an active metropolitan life of the sort enjoyed by Clarissa Vaughan. Indeed, the juxtaposition of Mrs Woolf, Mrs Brown, and Ms Vaughan appears more admonitory than historical. Though acknowledging that the world is a vale of tears (AIDS corresponds to World War I shell-shock), *The Hours* suggests that a degree of salvation and happiness can be achieved by being true to one's sexual inclinations. Cunningham's "Virginia Woolf" sublimates her lesbian impulse, creates a novel, and the novel solaces a reclusive woman ill-suited to conventional marriage but unready to move to a different sexual orientation. For Laura, the consequence is celibacy. Clarissa Vaughan is clearly the happiest of the three: growing up in a more tolerant age, she finds contentment with another woman, and can celebrate life and Richard's poetic achievements even with the mother whom he publicly reviled.

The explicit connection between the plots, of course, isn't Mrs Woolf but Virginia Woolf's Mrs Dalloway, a fictional character seemingly projected as a "working out" of Woolf's suicidal depressions, a projection crystallized in her decision to kill off not Clarissa but Septimus ("a greater mind than Clarissa's" [Cunningham 1998: 154]). Insofar as they recount the *writing* of *Mrs. Dalloway*, the "Mrs. Woolf" chapters presumably relate to the *sjuzhet* or discourse of *The Hours*. Here the "real" author is portrayed as deciding just how to tell a story, a story which inspires one reader, Mrs Brown, to change her life and somehow serves (mysteriously) as a pattern for Clarissa Vaughan. These two threads presuppose an earlier, generative, part, a moment in the life of Virginia Woolf and her evolving creature, Clarissa Dalloway. There is, of course, nothing new about using a real historical figure as a character in a fiction. Indeed, the technique occurs frequently. One reviewer, Jonathan Dee (1999), cites the recent "torrent of such novels, by Russell Banks (on John Brown), Pat Barker (Wilfred Owen and Siegfried Sassoon), Jay Parini (Walter Benjamin), Thomas Pynchon (Mason and Dixon), Susan Sontag (Lord Nelson), John Updike (James Buchanan)."

At the level of style, that is, of *homage* pastiche, *The Hours* (and Lippincott's *Mr. Dalloway* too) offers a plenitude of Dallowayisms. Here are a few examples:

- Exclamations, especially of *joie de vivre*: Mrs. Dalloway: "What a lark! What a plunge!/*The Hours*: 'What a thrill, what a shock' (but without exclamation *points*: Woolf uses them to mark at least 25 of Clarissa's thoughts in the first 10 pages of the novel; Cunningham is mostly content with a simple period).
- Interruptions of the flow of thought – marked by commas, parentheses, or dashes – as each Clarissa tries to recover a memory, searches for a word, feels uncertain.

(The self-questioning tic is prominent in Woolf's diary, e.g., "All my nerves stood upright, flushed, electrified (what's the word?) with the sheer beauty [of nature]," August 19, 1924, Woolf 1996: 64). A favorite form is "Was that it?" – *Mrs. Dalloway*: "Peter Walsh said 'Musing among the vegetables?' was that it?" (1925:3); *The Hours*: Clarissa wonders what to buy Evan, like Richard an AIDS victim: "Not flowers; if flowers are subtly wrong for the deceased they're disastrous for the ill. But what?" (1998: 21). (About these parentheses, see John Mullan's (2003) review "But I digress . . . ").

- Repetitions that register the full implications of what each Clarissa has just thought or perceived, a form that would be otiose in ordinary prose: *Mrs. Dalloway*: "Clarissa read on the telephone pad, 'Lady Bruton wishes to know if Mr. Dalloway will lunch with her today.' 'Mr. Dalloway, ma'am, told me to tell you he would be lunching out'" then: "Lady Bruton, whose lunch parties were said to be extraordinarily amusing, had not asked her" (Woolf 1925: 29); *The Hours*: "Clarissa pushes the rewind button. If Sally forgot to mention her lunch with Oliver St. Ives it's probably because the invitation was made to Sally alone. Oliver St. Ives, the scandal, the hero, has not asked Clarissa to lunch" (Cunningham 1998: 93–4).
- Frequent "near" deixis through words like "here," "now," "this," to highlight the immediacy of the characters' (rather than the narrator's) immediate presence on the scene rather than the narrator's. *Mrs. Dalloway* : [about the air at Bourton] "How fresh, how calm, stiller than this, of course" (1925: 3)/*The Hours*: "New York . . . always produces mornings like this" (1998: 9); *Mrs. Dalloway*: Peter thinks: "Life itself, every moment of it, every drop of it, here, this instant, now, in the sun, in Regent's Park, was enough" (1925: 79)/*The Hours*: "If she were to express it publicly (now, at her age), this love of hers would consign her to the realm of the duped and the simpleminded" (1998: 12).

But there are important nuances of *Mrs. Dalloway*'s style which Cunningham seems to miss or ignore. Their absence affects the degree and nature of our immersion in his characters' psyches. Cunningham's are too often depicted from an outside, narrator's, perspective (or "slant"). Perhaps Cunningham did not grasp the extent of Woolf's internalizing method, or perhaps he had other goals. Whatever the reason, he made quite different (and, I believe, technically less interesting) lexical and syntactic choices.

The principal differences concern syntactic focus. Woolf studiously avoided presenting Clarissa from an external narrator's vantage, in the manner she associated with Arnold Bennett's fiction. How Clarissa gets around town is syntactically minimized, a mere frame for her musings – her memories of Bourton and of Peter Walsh's sarcastic remarks, her sense of the hush that follows Big Ben's sound, her love of the bustle of London. When Woolf does provide an external view of Clarissa she embeds it in the consciousness of another character, often a walk-on, a personage who, despite his or her irrelevance to the plot, could function as "chorus": "She stiffened a little on the kerb ... A charming woman Scrope Purvis thought her" (Woolf 1925: 4). In her notebook Woolf tells herself: "no chapters," and then "possible choruses." Scrope Purvis is such a chorus. Deep into Aeschylus at the time, Woolf decided to use observing bystanders instead of the narrator to describe aspects of the protagonists' appearance and behavior: "Why not have an observer in the street at each critical point who acts the part of chorus – some nameless person?" (1996: 419). Equally explicit is her diary entry of September 5, 1923: "Characters are to be merely views: personality must be avoided at all costs ... Directly you specify hair, age, etc. something frivolous, or irrelevant gets into the book." "You" here clearly refers to an external narrator. Since she was writing a novel, not a play, she did not need to have these walk-ons literally speak; she could simply enter their minds. Henry James had already questioned narratorial omniscience; Woolf was going a step farther in minimizing the narrator's independent spatial vantage on the scene. As I shall argue below, the device has important thematic implications.

Cunningham's sentences, however, more regularly feature Clarissa as the subject of a visualizable predicate, and hence the narrator as interpreter of the spectacle: "Clarissa ... runs out, promising to be back in half an hour" (1998: 9), "She delays for a moment the plunge" (p. 9), "As Clarissa steps down from the vestibule her shoe makes gritty contact with the red-brown, mica-studded stone of the first stair" (p. 10), "Clarissa crosses Eighth Street" (p. 13). By Woolf's standards, these sentences presuppose a narrator who moves Clarissa from place to place, instead of letting her thoughts simply flow along, without much concern for her whereabouts. We see Woolf erasing such expressions from her manuscript. For instance, from the original sentence "she had burst open the French windows ... & stepped out on to the terrace of Bourton" she deletes everything after "&." Assigning the narrator the task of tracking Clarissa's stroll (Woolf would say) interferes with our immersion in her mind. Cunningham's syntax, by Woolfian standards, excessively features his protagonist's occupations at the expense of her preoccupations. At the very beginning of the "Mrs. Dalloway" section, for example, Vaughan is the subject of a stream of active predicates evoking an externally observable scene: "Clarissa feigns exasperation ... leaves Sally cleaning the bathroom, and runs out, promising to be back in half an hour" (1998: 9).

A related stylistic detail: Woolf often prefers *-ing* verb forms – both present participles and gerunds – to completed predicates. These emphasize the continuing flow of experience and the co-occurrence of events inside and outside the mind, the to-and-fro of memory, opinion, perception (fittingly, as we learn, since Clarissa Dalloway has a life-and-death interest in continuation). Typical is the novel's third paragraph, which, after the exclamations, moves to a participial string that could, theoretically, go on forever: "How fresh ... the air was ... solemn, feeling as she did, standing there at the open window, that something awful was about to happen; looking at the flowers, at the trees with the smoke winding off them and the rooks rising, falling; standing and looking ..." (1925: 3). Actually, in her diary Woolf expressed some uneasiness about her penchant for present participles: "It is a disgrace that I write nothing, or if I write, write sloppily, using nothing but present participles" (September 7, 1924). But Clarissa's need to *live*, even if in a state of sensation and dread, could not have been more effectively represented. Present participles enabled Woolf to highlight meditation and minimize banal movements through the streets – "'Such fools we are,' she thought, crossing Victoria Street" (1925: 4). Absorbed self-communing remains the focus; *-ing* forms, casually attached, are only there to mark Clarissa's physical progress.

Although he does of course use some present participles, Cunningham regularly favors a verb form we don't find in *Mrs Dalloway* – the historic present tense: "The vestibule door opens onto a June morning" (1998: 9), "Clarissa pauses at the threshold" (p. 9), "Clarissa crosses Eighth Street" (p. 13) and so on. Whether the historic present suggests a greater immediacy than the simple preterite is debatable, but its use is clearly less evocative of the eddying dynamics of the protagonist's inner life than Woolf's present participles.

The Hours generally differs from *Mrs. Dalloway* in its treatment of time. Of course, both novels rely on temporal unity: the whole of *Mrs. Dalloway* takes place on a single day – the day of Clarissa's party – while *The Hours* lasts a single day in each of the lives of the protagonists. But the movement through "the hours" of these days varies noticeably. In *Mrs. Dalloway* the exact diegetic moment is frequently stated or implied, providing a detached real-life chronological armature for the multiplicity of consciousnesses. A nexus is formed by clocks, which figure significantly in the background and at moments of transition – not only the city-wide booms of Big Ben but also the registrations of local clocks, like that above the shop of Rigby and Lowndes (1925: 102). Clocks tangibly demarcate the thought flows of characters. As a clock strikes, the discourse often seeps from Scrope Purvis to Clarissa, from Regia to Hugh Whitbread, from Sir William Bradshaw to Peter Walsh. The clocks facilitate daringly unpredictable shifts from one consciousness to another.

A larger purpose underlies this scrupulous fixing of chronology: Woolf is preoccupied with the whole life of London and beyond it, the British Empire. Her city is more than just background. *The Hours*, on the other hand, concerned as it mostly is with Greenwich Village, uses the "hour" as a thematic leitmotif. It contrasts the despair that Richard Brown feels about how he will fill the few hours of life left to him with Clarissa Vaughan's optimism about the future – "there will be ecstatic hours and darker hours, but still we cherish the city, the morning; we hope, more than anything for more" (1998: 225).

Woolf's innovative contribution to fiction is a great fluidity of mental representations, in indirect or direct style, to form a path among unrelated as well as related characters. Chance proximity is sufficient to trigger one. A typical example: Peter Walsh, consoling himself in Regent's Park, watches a little girl, Elise Mitchell (given a name but only a momentary presence), who "scudded off again full tilt into a lady's legs," a sight which makes him laugh out. Not missing a beat, the next paragraph enters a totally different mind, Lucrezia's, preoccupied as it is with the unfairness of her plight – until the same Elise ran "full tilt into her, fell flat, and burst out crying."

"That was comforting rather. She stood her upright, dusted her frock, kissed her" (Woolf, 1925: 65).

Spatial proximity can even facilitate telepathy:

> For Heaven's sake, leave your knife alone! [Clarissa] cried to herself in irrepressible irritation; it was [Peter's] silly unconventionality, his weakness; his lack of the ghost of a notion what any one else was feeling that annoyed her, had always annoyed her; and now at his age, how silly!
>
> I know all that, Peter thought; I know what I'm up against, he thought, running his finger along the blade of his knife.
>
> (Woolf 1925: 46)

In *Mrs. Dalloway*, shifting mental filters through chance proximity has important political as well as aesthetic implications. The technique emphasizes the democracy of the city street (in the face of England's official class rigidity), a place where everyone, even the youngest or most modest denizen, enjoys the dignity of a name and even a partial view of the scene. The aesthetic effect, early perceived by David Daiches (1942), is to make Woolf's art impressionist. What is important is not how things are in themselves but how they *appear* to characters. The novel registers these impressions virtually simultaneously but from different angles. To use Woolf's own word, though in a different sense, the novel moves through "haloed" mental registrations, through a space that is permeable among agents regardless of their importance to the plot. The narrator does not independently concretize how things look, sound, or feel "out there." Rather she travels from one character's angle to another — that of Peter, Rezia, Edgar J. Watkiss, Sarah Bletchley, Maisie Johnson, Mrs Dempster — whoever the random witness is. The nexus between politics and aesthetics is implicit in Daiches's observation that characters are "introduced whose sole function is to have fleeting impressions of the principals . . . yet not solely, for this sudden flash of light reveals him [or her], too, as an independent person with a life of his own somewhere in the background, with experiences, prejudices, a texture of living" (Daiches 1942: 56). "Independent" is worth repeating: the technique democratically reminds us that there is more to the vibrant world of London than Clarissa's party and Septimus's death. The crowd in the street jumbled together without regard to class distinction is not mere background. It represents, not only bodies brushing past each other, but also minds and plights. By the same token, British history, no longer locked behind dusty academic doors, opens out into this microscopically examined hour of city life.

Woolf enhanced this sense of psychic fluidity among her characters by forgoing chapter breaks, separating the novel's parts only by gaps in the space on the page. *The Hours*, on the other hand, is divided into a prologue and 22 chapters clearly labeled with one of the three major characters' names. Further, it attenuates the number and abruptness of shifts among consciousnesses. Most of the book is confined to the consciousnesses of the protagonists or to major characters like Richard Brown,

Louis Waters, or Sally Lester. Except for that of Willie Bass, no consciousness from the outside world is followed. When Clarissa Vaughan shares diegetic space with random minor characters, there is usually no corresponding shift in filter. Compare, for example, the "unknown famous face" sequences in both novels. In *Mrs. Dalloway*, named individuals vividly experience this "face of the very greatest importance" (1925: 14), this symbol of Empire. They hear the "voice of authority, the spirit of religion." This face, this "greatness," the narrator predicts, as if speaking for the crowd, "will be known to curious antiquaries, sifting the ruins of time, when London is a grass-grown path and all those hurrying along the pavement this Wednesday morning are but bones with a few wedding rings mixed up in their dust and the gold stoppings of innumerable decayed teeth" (Woolf 1925: 16). Anyone who knows Woolf's essays, diaries, and letters, of course, cannot believe that the real author unironically endorses the narrator's effusions. The paratextual evidence alone – the author's very name – calls into question any rosy prognosis of the British empire's future. And as if to corroborate our skepticism, the crowd's awed attention quickly moves to the smoke letters of the skywriting airplane. (Woolf's diary entry of June 19, 1923: "I want to give life and death, sanity and insanity; I want to criticise the social system and to show it at work, at its most intense," [Woolf 1996: 56]).

In the corresponding scene in *The Hours*, however, we stay only in Clarissa's consciousness. Two young bystanders are mentioned, but we learn neither their names nor their unspoken thoughts. We hear only the dialogue between them, through Clarissa's ears. The one with hair dyed canary yellow is arbitrarily named "Sun" by Clarissa and the other, the platinum, "Moon." The only mind entered is Clarissa's, as she silently agrees with Sun that the famous face belongs to Meryl Streep and not Susan Sarandon. It is true that Cunningham also puts the episode in historical perspective: Sun and Moon

> will grow to middle age and then old age, either wither or bloat; the cemeteries in which they're buried will fall eventually into ruin, the grass grown wild, browsed at night by dogs; and when all that remains of these girls is a few silver fillings lost underground, the woman in the trailer, be she Meryl Streep or Vanessa Redgrave or even Susan Sarandon, will still be known. She will exist in archives, in books; her recorded voice will be stored away among other precious and venerated objects.
>
> (Cunningham 1998: 50–1)

But since his novel lacks Woolf's breadth of social and political resonance, it is difficult to know precisely what it is satirizing. Is it the adoration of celebrity? Is it archivists? Since *The Hours* seems so much less a social critique than *Mrs. Dalloway*, does the author even mean this sentence ironically?

Certain of Woolf's "choruses" converge at Clarissa Dalloway's party (not only in the novel but in various short stories written during this period). Clarissa reflects upon her guests, upon her own past, and upon the world outside her window; and the characters who know her best – Sally Seton, her husband Richard, and Peter

Walsh – reflect upon *her*. The last to do so is Peter, for whom Clarissa remains . . . in-describable: "For there she was." The words that end *The Hours* are only superficially similar, their force is quite different. Despite his consistent usage of indirect free style to represent characters' thinking, Cunningham seems uninterested in Woolf's concept of character as "chorus." It is Clarissa, not some outsider, who thinks "here she is, herself, Clarissa, not Mrs. Dalloway anymore; there is no one now to call her that. Here she is with another hour before her" (1998: 228). Quite apart from the difference in content, that's a significant alteration of *Mrs. Dalloway*'s overall point-of-view strategy and the implications about history and culture that it engenders.

Judging Cunningham's overall success is not the task of this essay, but placing it in the universe of second-degree texts would be arid without drawing some critical inferences. Despite his successful transposition of many features of *Mrs. Dalloway*, we see important significant stylistic differences that bear on Cunningham's project, a project which might be characterized as transferring the spirit, and, indeed, much of the letter of Woolf's 1923 London to 1998 Greenwich Village. Cunningham says he was inspired by Woolf's ability to "write the epic stories of ordinary people." The word shows up at a critical moment in his "Mrs. Woolf" section when Virginia decides that Septimus should die instead of Clarissa, who shall spend her life "loving her life of ordinary pleasures" (Cunningham 1998: 211). But despite his apparent range – the evocation of Woolf in Richmond, of a lost housewife in a 1950s Los Angeles suburb (in some ways the most achieved part of the book), and of a book editor in Greenwich Village – Cunningham does not achieve the broad cultural sweep of *Mrs. Dalloway*. His Village has been likened to Woolf's Bloomsbury. But *Mrs. Dalloway* is not set in Bloomsbury; it is not concerned with a colony of artists and intellectuals; its purview is the whole of London's population, indeed the whole of a British empire in decline. It is a design finely etched, as we've seen, by devices like the "chorus." Both explicitly and implicitly, Woolf conjures up a simulacrum of English society of the 1920s – from the Prime Minister to the "veriest frump" in the street. Cunningham's limitation to a small segment of American culture, to a group of professionals in the entertainment industry living in Greenwich Village – however accurate the depiction – against its achieving the pantheon of transposed novels, a pantheon dominated by *Ulysses*. It is true that the equivalencies work – that Richard's suicide is made plausibly comparable to Septimus's, and that the tension between Clarissa Dalloway's and Sally Seton's kiss and the humdrum domestic contentment of the Dalloways is satisfyingly reflected in the relationship between Clarissa Vaughan and Sally Lester, that, in short, Cunningham has gone beyond gender questions to address the commonality of human emotions, to what James Phelan aptly calls his characters' "responses to the wonder and chaos and pain of existence" (private correspondence, 2003). To that extent, *The Hours* can be accounted a small "epic of ordinary lives."

But what circumscribes the novel is its apparent lack of engagement with the rest of the American, even of the New York, world, a world with which gay intellectuals, like everybody else, must interface. *The Hours* seems too sealed off. Like her counter-part, Clarissa Vaughan feels, at least occasionally, anxiety and a sense of failure. But

Mrs Dalloway's plight has an important social cause – the exclusion of women, including those of the upper-middle class, from matters of national significance. And while it may be true that the AIDS epidemic has been as great a scourge as World War I, it has not led to the sort of political and social consequences that afflicted Britain in the 1920s.

The Hours persuasively offers a "postcloset" American rewriting of *Mrs. Dalloway*, addressing an implied reader with enlightened attitudes about same-sex relationships. For such readers – and happily they are increasingly numerous and mainstream – the correspondences with *Mrs. Dalloway* are quite happy. But to match the scope of the original, Cunningham needed a broader canvas and a set of Woolfian techniques that he didn't utilize.[1]

NOTE

1 I am grateful to the editors and to Emma Kafelanos, Gerald Prince, and Alex Zwerdling for help with this essay.

REFERENCES AND FURTHER READING

Chatman, S. (2001). "Parody and Style." *Poetics Today* 22, 25–39.

Cunningham, M. (1998). *The Hours*. New York: Picador USA.

Cunningham, M. (2002). "Talk at Kelly Writers House Fellows Seminar (February 11, 2002)." <http://www.english.upenn.edu/~whfellow/cunningham.html>.

Daiches, D. (1942). *Virginia Woolf*. Norfolk, CT: New Directions.

Dee, J. (1999). "Review of *The Hours*." *Harper's Magazine* 298 (June), 76.

Genette, G. ([1982] 1997). *Palimpsests: Literature in the Second Degree*, trans. C. Newman and C. Doubinsky. Lincoln and London: University of Nebraska Press.

Lee, H. (1997). *Virginia Woolf*. New York: Knopf.

Lippincott, R. (1999). *Mr. Dalloway*. Louisville, KY: Sarabande.

Macdonald, D. (1960). *Parodies: An Anthology from Chaucer to Beerbohm – and After*. New York: Random House.

Mullan, J. (2003). "'But I digress...': a review of *The Hours*." *The Guardian* 22 February.

Wood, M. (1998). "Parallel Lives." *The New York Times Book Review* 22 November, Section 7, Column 1, p. 6.

Woolf, V. (1925). *Mrs. Dalloway*. London: Harcourt.

Woolf, V. (1996). *Virginia Woolf "The Hours": The British Museum Manuscript of Mrs. Dalloway*, ed. H. Wussow. New York: Pace University Press.

Zwerdling, A. (1986). *Virginia Woolf and the Real World*. Berkeley: University of California Press.

PART III
Narrative Form and its Relationship to History, Politics, and Ethics

18

Genre, Repetition, Temporal Order: Some Aspects of Biblical Narratology

David H. Richter

The term "biblical narratology" is an oxymoron, particularly if we come to biblical narrative not from an ideological perspective but from the angle of the formal features that are peculiar to it. Contemporary narratologies, both rhetorical and structuralist, in the style of Phelan and the style of Fludernik, were created to operate on the complexities of works like *Absalom, Absalom!* rather than the book of Samuel. That is, their analyses were designed for works of narrative artistry that are wholes rather than totals, that are written by identifiable authors about whose lives and attitudes information can be discovered, or – in the case of anonymous works – by authors who can be placed with some confidence both geographically and historically. They presume that the texts of these works can be established, that omissions, transpositions, and additions imposed by later redactors have not warped them almost beyond recognition. They presume that we can easily intuit whether a given narrative is intended to be read as fiction or as fact or an intricate combination of the two.[1] They further presume that we can understand in at least a rough and ready way the system of genres within which a given narrative text has its place. And they presume that we are free to locate the meaning of a text using rules of notice, signification, configuration, and coherence, that is, the usual rules for the interpretation of secular narratives identified and elucidated by Rabinowitz, rather than special rules of interpretation that derive from exterior systems of belief. None of these things is true of biblical narrative – which is kind of scary. Here I would like to focus on three of these interconnected issues: genre, repetition, and temporal order.

Genre

Let me take as my first text the familiar story of Jonah, who, summoned to prophesy the doom of Nineveh as punishment for its wickedness, attempts to flee his mission by taking ship in the opposite direction. God thwarts this escape by causing a tempest, and Jonah, admitting that the tempest is his own fault, is thrown overboard, and swallowed by a fish who, three days later, vomits him up on the seashore. Sent by God once more to Nineveh, Jonah fulfills his mission. His prophecy is believed by the inhabitants, who repent, fast and pray, so that God relents and does not destroy them.

This is the first three-fourths of the story, the part that has entered orthodox Judaism, Christianity, and Islam, each of which has different ways of accounting for the one rough patch in that part of the story, Jonah's refusal of his mission. The Jewish reading of Jonah is, by and large, one that accords with its role as the prophetic book read on the day of Yom Kippur, often ignoring Jonah's questionable behavior and concentrating instead on the Ninevites who avert divine judgment by repentance, fasting, and prayer.[2] Christian commentaries on Jonah take off, as they must, from Jesus's identification of himself with Jonah in Matthew and Luke. In Matthew 12: 38–41, Jonah primarily prefigures the death and resurrection of Jesus by descending into the depths and rising after three days; in Luke 11: 29–32, Jesus reads Jonah as a sign for the prophet of God whose word compels spiritual change. Jonah is thus a messianic antetype in ways that have been endlessly elaborated.[3] In the Qur'an the prophet Yunus teaches several moral lessons: Yunus was "one of those who are cast off" who would have been left in the belly of the fish till the last judgment, save that he redeems himself through confession and prayer, to which Allah responds with deliverance.[4]

What all these interpretations have in common is that they have agreed to ignore the last chapter of Jonah, which finds the prophet camped outside Nineveh, waiting to witness its destruction, made so miserable by the success of his mission that he wishes he were dead. Jonah spells out his point to YHWH: didn't I tell you why I was refusing to come here? "Didn't I already say before I fled for Tarshish that you are the God of grace and compassion, slow to anger, full of kindness, repenting of evil?"[5] Then, since the Ninevites seem to have learned their lesson, God directs his mighty acts toward Jonah, who has not. He creates a gourd to shade Jonah from the fierce Assyrian sun, and once Jonah is glad of the shelter, makes a worm to destroy the gourd, calling up at the same time a hot dry east wind. And when Jonah once more rages and wishes he were dead, God asks: how could you care about a gourd, which came up in a night without your labor and perished in a night, and not care about my other creations, those thousands of inhabitants of Nineveh?

As Meir Sternberg argues persuasively in *The Poetics of Biblical Narrative*, this story's operation depends upon our jumping to exactly the wrong conclusion, as we read Chapter 1, about the reason Jonah is fleeing God's mission – we assume that "Jonah is too tender-hearted to carry a message of doom to a great city" (Sternberg 1985: 318). Jonah's honesty in admitting to the sailors that the tempest is his own fault, and his self-sacrificial willingness to be thrown overboard for their sake, feeds this misunderstanding of his character. The information we are given at the start of Chapter 4 "shatters the entire model of the narrative world and world view. . . . Not that the plot and the participants are suddenly transformed but they are suddenly recognized for what they always have been..." (Sternberg 1985: 319). Sternberg asserts that the story moves generically from "a punitive affair between God and Nineveh" to "a story of a prophet's education" (p. 320).

Sternberg's reading is thus in radical contrast with the edifying readings demanded by the various orthodoxies, which evade any contact with the reversal that follows the reader's discovery of Jonah's motives. I suspect that the orthodox readings have already hijacked the public meaning of the book of Jonah beyond all repair by wise narratologists, but even Sternberg's reading may be more edifying than it needs to be. That is, Sternberg posits that Jonah is educated by his experience, but since Jonah makes no reply to God's final question, there is not a shred of textual evidence that anyone but the reader learns a thing. What explodes into view, in contrast to the mercy of God, is Jonah's narcissistic ruthlessness. Jonah raises none of the usual theological and moral issues of the prophetic books, like Israel's infidelity to God or their exploitation of their fellow humans, and the only prophecy Jonah utters ("Yet forty days and Nineveh shall be destroyed") takes up exactly five Hebrew words.[6] If this makes Jonah unique among the prophetic books, it is because, as Tom Paine pointed out over two centuries ago, Jonah is not a prophetic book at all but an antiprophetic book, a satire on bloodthirsty prophets.[7] Prophets are probably the most popular object of satire in the Hebrew Bible, from Balaam in Numbers 22, cursing for pay, to the petty revenge of Elisha on the children who mock his baldness in 2 Kings 2, and so here. It would not be necessary for the author of Jonah to have had a specific prophet in mind, but if he did, Joel might be a strong candidate.[8] There are linguistic links between Joel and Jonah – lots are cast in both books with unpleasant results for the winner – and Jonah's characterization of YHWH seems to come word for word out of Joel.

Be that as it may, the antiprophetic satire in Jonah is, if anything, more light-hearted and goofy even than Elisha's bears or Balaam struck dumb by his speaking ass. And it is the animals here too that contribute crucially to the outrageous atmosphere. I'm thinking of that wonderfully excessive moment when, after the people have fasted and put on sackcloth, after the King of Nineveh[9] has himself fasted and put on sackcloth, the King issues an edict that the fast shall include "man and beast, flocks and herds, none shall taste food or drink water, all shall be covered with sackcloth and cry mightily unto YHWH" (Jonah 3: 7–8). One imagines all too easily the miserable bullocks and rams, bleating and bellowing their repentance. And it is to this scene that the author of Jonah alludes when, in the final verse, he has God refer to the creatures he has spared as "more than one hundred twenty thousand people who do not know their left hand from their right hand, *and also much cattle*" (4: 11, my italics).

If this reading of Jonah is far from wild or surprising, if configuring the story this way seems obvious, we need to explain the apparent reluctance, even among secular scholars, to read Jonah as a satiric fable,[10] as opposed to "a didactic story about a prophet" (Day 1990: 39), or "the story of a prophet's education" (Sternberg 1995: 320) or some other formulation. John Day questions "whether a distinct class of literature consciously dubbed 'satire' existed in ancient Israel, unlike say ancient Greece" (p. 39). But the issue cuts deeper than the lack of a biblical Hebrew word for "satire." I suspect that the real problem with calling Jonah what it is, a satirical fable, is that it implicitly classifies it as fiction. The allusion to Jonah in two of the Gospels may make the matter even more sensitive, although for Jesus to compare his mission to that of a fictional character well known from scripture would be by no means absurd.[11] Indeed one might think that the faithful would rejoice in not having to defend the veracity of a story that features a man who survives for three days and nights in the belly of a fish,[12] or a Bronze Age city so large that it would take a person three days to cross it on foot – roughly the size of Los Angeles County – or a God who brings into existence on cue gourds, worms, and huge fish as well as several varieties of bad weather.[13] But characterizing a biblical book as fiction can enrage, with something like Jonah's rage, that large segment of Bible readers who believe in its literal truth.[14] And the particular satire in Jonah – on ruthless prophets of doom – may be even more rebarbative to evangelicals for whom predictions of imminent disaster can be pleasure as well as good business.

For me, insisting that biblical narratives must be nonfictional is far too limiting. I think the world has a great deal to gain from the notion that some biblical narratives that have been absorbed into the Deuteronomistic "sacred history" that runs from Joshua to 2 Kings may at some point have been designed to be read as fictions. I have argued that the story of the concubine of Gibeah that ends the book of Judges may have originated as a lampoon against King Saul, that, for instance, the faithless concubine from Bethlehem in Judah may represent David, who sold his services first to King Saul and then to his enemy, the Philistine King Achish of Gath.[15] Other stories in the book of Judges show similar patterns.[16] And I would argue more generally that, given how little we can know about the generic system that characterized Israelite narratives two or three thousand years ago, our default position should be to assume that they had the same mix of fictional and factual genres we find in other cultures of the period, including lampoons and satires, whether or not they had names for these genres, as the Greeks did.

Similarly, I would argue that, absent discoveries not yet made about rules of reading in use two or three millennia ago, we should be willing to assume that textual juxtapositions that generate suspicious readings today might well have done so in the intended authorial audience of historical texts.

Repetition

In 1 Samuel the relationship of Israel's last judge, Samuel, and its first king, Saul, is roiled by Samuel's deep ambivalence about giving up the power he has wielded as the charismatic leader of Israel for a position as second fiddle, the prophet channeling the word of God for the direction of the anointed monarch. This ambivalence is expressed directly, as when Samuel resists giving Israel a king, but it is also enacted in episodes in which Samuel puts Saul into a double bind. If Saul interprets what Samuel has commanded in the name of God in one way, he can be condemned for not interpreting them the other way. Saul of course never understands this. Trusting in Samuel, he always responds as a sinner grateful to have had his errors pointed out and eager for forgiveness. We too can be trusting readers of the literal word of the text, just as Saul is a trusting reader of Samuel, but to do that we would have to ignore what we already know about Samuel's rancor against monarchy in general and Saul in particular. So it is difficult to avoid suspicious readings of these episodes.

That is, the trusting reader understands that Saul has shown his unworthiness to be King of Israel by failing to carry out the will of YHWH not once but twice, but a suspicious reader might understand that Samuel revenges himself upon the king he never wanted to crown by placing him in a pair of double binds, once by giving him inadequate instructions, and once by giving him too many contradictory instructions, so that whatever he does he can be put in the wrong.[17] Interestingly, the reader's dilemma – to read as the trusting reader or the suspicious reader – places him or her in the same double bind in which Samuel places Saul, who is forced to infer an intention from ambiguous language.

We also need to point out that the reader's stance, in the hermeneutic duel between Samuel and Saul, will be opposed to that of the character whose position we support. That is, those who adopt with respect to the narrative the "trusting" reading associated with Saul will agree with Samuel that Saul has transgressed and should be deposed as king, while those who adopt toward the narrative the hermeneutic of suspicion characteristic of Samuel (who refuses to take at face value the professions of Saul) will be more likely to view Saul as the victim of Samuel's machinations.[18]

If the reader of sacred history is likely to start in a trusting frame of mind, the mere fact of the doublet may in itself foster a suspicious mode of interpretation. Just as people who give us a whole series of reasons for taking a given action may thereby suggest they are concealing the true one, the fact that there have to be two depositions of Saul may make his inadequacy seem less plausible than if there had been only one. Especially since, despite having been deposed twice, Saul continues to rule Israel for what is apparently many years, until his death in battle some 15 chapters later. Indeed, a son of Saul's succeeds to his throne, so that it is not until several years after Saul's death that David comes into his kingdom, at 2 Samuel 5.

But at the next turn of the screw, the suspicious readings of 1 Samuel begin to raise questions, not only about what the text says but about how the text was composed. That is, unless we refuse to notice them, we are likely to become puzzled by the endlessly reduplicated events of 1 Samuel. For there are not only two depositions of Saul, those depositions follow three different acclamations of Saul as king, which themselves follow at least two different versions of Samuel resisting the demand of Israel to be ruled by a king. And following Saul's deposition are two different stories about how David becomes a part of Saul's entourage, two daughters of Saul who become David's brides and then are sundered from him, the two flights of David from Saul, the two brotherhood oaths of David with Jonathan, the two approaches by David to King Achish of Gath, the two occasions when Saul takes an army to hunt David, who spares Saul's life when he is most vulnerable, and so on, including two versions of the death of Saul. Doublets occur elsewhere in the Bible – Genesis begins with two inconsistent accounts of the Creation – but nowhere else are so many collected together.[19]

Some of these doublets are events that could quite easily happen twice in succession. Saul could throw his spear at David and miss him on Tuesday and repeat the same performance on Wednesday, could offer David marriage with one daughter in March and another daughter in April. Other doublets seem clearly to be offered as alternative stories: we are told one version of the death of Saul by the narrator of Samuel, an authoritative story, though one that, taken literally, could have had no possible witness; the other version is the eyewitness account of an Amalekite – and we all know how reliable those Amalekites are – who is attempting to curry favor with David by bringing him Saul's crown and bracelet.

In the case of some doublets it is clear that an attempt has been made to reconcile contradictions: the two stories about David's first meeting with Saul are harmonized at 1 Samuel 17: 15: "But David went and returned from Saul to feed his father's sheep at Bethlehem." With this redactorial smoothing, David can be the shepherd boy freshly come with a food parcel from Bethlehem even though we have already seen David as the personal attendant of Saul, his musician, and his armor-bearer.[20] But other doublets defy any usual mode of reconciliation, such as the two very different episodes that are presented as the origin of the proverbial saying "Is Saul too among the prophets?"

These peculiarities can be resolved in at least three ways. In one trusting reading, we can become reconciled to the fact that we are in a world in which everything happens twice, where we are not to be bothered by repetitions or apparent contradictions. Or we can naturalize the contradictions of the lifeworld by thinking of 1 Samuel as a nouveau roman like those of Robbe-Grillet, in which things happen once but are narrated multiple times in inconsistent ways, a narrative that problematizes the way the world of events can be mapped by language. Or we can naturalize the contradictions yet another way, by viewing the authorship of 1 Samuel as residing in a redactor who has gathered materials from sources that include alternative versions of most of the significant events, and, helpless to decide which of two accounts may be the true one, has fashioned a narrative that allows him to include both, but who intends for us to notice the contradictions.[21] As the history becomes less transparent and as the conflicts between the various versions of events begin to focus the interest of the suspicious reader upon the redactor rather than the agents within the narrative, 1 Samuel begins to turn into a precursor of *Rashomon*, or of the historical novel by Faulkner that is only too aptly named (*Absalom, Absalom!*), where the interest in the story of Thomas Sutpen shifts in the course of the various tellings from the actions of the tragic or demonic figure at the center of the tale to the motivations of the various narrators for constructing the inconsistent versions we are offered.[22]

Temporal Order

With the accession of David this elaborate parade of doublets comes to an end but not the occasions for suspicious readings. In the case of 2 Samuel, some of these issues have to do with when in David's reign things are done, and by whom. I want to acknowledge that not all the chronological anomalies generate questions. Meir Sternberg (1990) has worked out the basic mechanisms of representing time in the Bible, and most of the anomalies come under his general exceptions to the basic rule of first things first.[23]

But just as there are doublets that are impossible to make sequential (like David's two first meetings with King Saul) there are episodes whose problematic chronological relation to the rest of 2 Samuel forces a reconfiguration of our understanding of King David's reign. Consider the dark episode recounted in 2 Samuel 21. After three years of famine David asks God why Israel is being punished, and is told that it is on account of the bloodguilt on the House of Saul, who slew or attempted to slay the Gibeonites out of zeal for Judah and Israel. It may seem strange that the episode of Saul slaying the Gibeonites was not mentioned in its proper place during his reign, stranger that God should have caused a famine in Israel for the sake of mere Gibeonites,[24] and that the famine should be delayed until what looks like late in the reign of David, and strangest of all that atoning for Saul's crime should involve executing his entirely innocent descendents. But after a brief negotiation, King David agrees to hand over seven blameless men to the Gibeonites who crucify them in Saul's home town of Gibeah and leave their bodies for the birds to peck at: two sons of Saul's concubine Rizpah bat Aiah and five sons of Michal, Saul's daughter, David's wife.[25]

But one stray remark during this revolting vengeance – that David "spared Mephibosheth, the son of Jonathan the son of Saul" (21: 7) – gives us a clue about the time frame by linking this episode to Chapter 9: 1, where David asks, 'Is there yet any that is left of the house of Saul, that I may show him kindness for Jonathan's sake?' David's question, isolated and unmotivated where it sits, leads to David making generous provision for Mephibosheth at the royal court. But that scene only makes sense if David had already sent off every other male descendent of Saul to the Gibeonites for execution.

Once we make this connection, we see that the Gibeonites' vengeance at the end of 2 Samuel is chronologically out of place. It doesn't come late in David's reign over unified Israel, as we might expect from its textual position, but in its earliest days. But seeing this raises two other questions. The easy question is what rhetorical purpose is served by telling it where it is told, in Chapter 21. David has himself suffered grievously from the deaths of the nameless child of Bathsheba, his firstborn

Amnon, and his favorite Absalom. Lately he barely survived the civil war fomented by his own son. Coming after all this, the horror of David's action, undertaken as it is for the sake of public welfare, is moderated. Told in its proper position, at the beginning of David's reign, it would have a different valence. 2 Samuel begins with what seem to be a series of lucky breaks that leave David on the throne with his hands relatively clean. He has profited by the deaths in battle of Saul and Jonathan, and the assassinations of Saul's general Abner, and Saul's son and successor Ishbosheth, but he has had nothing personally to do with these deaths. Told here, the Gibeonite episode would expose the bloodbath with which David's reign began, the way he got rid of every male descendent of Saul except for the lame, and thus harmless, Mephibosheth.

The harder question is why it was included at all, since this is not an episode that anyone would miss if it were not here. Its presence suggests that the redactor[26] wants to force the audience to reconfigure retroactively their understanding of David's character and reign just as it comes to a close. Those whose minds are shaken by the Gibeonite episode may be struck dumb by the single shocking verse later in the same chapter (21: 19), stuck amid a catalog of the mighty acts of David's warriors: "There was again war with the Philistines at Gob; and Elhanan . . . the Bethlehemite slew Goliath of Gath, the staff of whose spear was like a weaver's beam." This verse has evident textual corruptions[27] but it seems to state that the great deed of the lad with slingshot and five smooth stones, that immortal moment from 1 Samuel 17 we can all envision, may have happened at some other time and may have been accomplished by somebody else entirely. A summary verse at the end of the chapter tells us that all the monstrous enemies of Israel "fell by the hand of David and his servants" as though every legendary deed somehow belongs to the monarch, no matter who actually performed it, as though legend must triumph over history.[28] But saying so deflates legend, and indeed our last look at David, in the second chapter of Kings, shows the decrepit former warrior, shivering in bed, croaking out his final instructions to Solomon, a mixture of general pious cant about obedience to the commandments of YHWH and a specific list of the people he wants his son to dispose of after he is gone. It's a chilling farewell, disgusting in its hypocrisy and more horrifying than anything in *The Godfather*.

Biblical Narrative vs. Bible Stories

Given the temptations to suspicious readings and the ungovernable complications that arise out of such readings, one can well understand why the religions that have adopted Samuel and Jonah as two of their holy books have avoided reading the text as a continuous narrative but have instead read it as pericopes (as biblical scholars call the chunks of text that can be extracted for study or for preaching). Individual pericopes can be coherent and morally edifying, as Jesus found the book of Jonah, even though the narrative as a whole is not. We know Bible stories, that is, rather than biblical narrative, because Bible stories are safer things, safer both for Jews who look to David as the model of the righteous king whose lineage will return in the end of days, and for Christians who look to David as one of the antetypes of Christ the King, who came and who will come again. Within these broader cultural narratives, the tragic story of Saul, doomed by the malice of Samuel and the contradictions of his own nature, and the horrific tale of David, God's anointed monster, have become stories we can read as wholes only with the greatest difficulty.

NOTES

1 I am using "factual" to cover stories meant to be taken for true, regardless of actual truth (including lies and propaganda).

2 This picture can be complicated if one goes into the midrashic details. The early midrash *Mekilta de Rebbe Ishmael* argues at Pesiqta Bo that Jonah was trying to protect the Israelites from God's anger. If the Ninevites heeded Jonah's prophecy and repented, would not God punish the Israelites who ignored God's prophets even more severely for their sins? The *Mekilta* considers Jonah wrong to defend the honor of the child (Israel) against the honor of the father (God), but his flaw lies in his priorities, not in his character. Ibn Ezra's commentary (1951) defends Jonah by thematizing the heavy burden of prophecy, comparing Jonah's reluctance to go to Nineveh with Moses's reluctance to return to Egypt and take the Israelites out of slavery.

3 For example, Faussett, Jamieson, and Brown's nineteenth-century commentary emphasizes the multiple allegorical dimension of Jonah as "living symbol": Jonah's engulfment by the fish is "the emblem of death" which is "a present type to Nineveh and Israel of the death [of the soul] in sin, as his deliverance was of the spiritual resurrection of repentance." And in addition to the symbolic significance of Jonah to his contemporaries, he is a "future type of Jesus's literal death" as atonement "for sin and resurrection by the Spirit of God."

4 *Qur'an*, Sura 10 (Yunus): 96–8; Sura 21 (The Prophets): 87–8; Sura 37 (The Rangers): 139–48; Sura 68 (The Pen): 48–50.

5 The phraseology here goes back to pre-exilic documents like Exodus 34 (and also found in Nehemiah 9 and Psalms 86, 103, and 140), but it exactly parallels Joel 2: 13, especially with the key phrase "*v'nachem al ha-ràah*" which is found nowhere else. (The verse goes: "And rend your heart, and not your garments, and turn unto the LORD your God: for he [is] gracious and merciful, slow to anger, and of great kindness, and repenteth him of the evil.") This link may be more than just coincidence – Jonah may be satirizing Joel.

6 "Yet forty days and Nineveh shall be destroyed"; in Hebrew:`od arba'im yom v'Nin' ve nehapecheth*.

7 See *The Age of Reason* (1795), Part II, chapter 1: As the book of Jonah, so far from treating of the affairs of the Jews, says nothing upon that subject, but treats altogether of the Gentiles, it is more probable that it is a book of the Gentiles than of the Jews, and that it has been written as a fable to expose the nonsense, and satirize the vicious and malignant character, of a Bible-prophet, or a predicting priest.

8 Joel's subject emerges as a final battle among the nations after which those like Egypt and Edom that have plundered Israel, that have "cast lots for my people, given a boy for a harlot, sold a girl for wine" (Joel 3: 3) shall be judged and punished, while Judah and Jerusalem shall be restored to fruitfulness and beauty. The dates of both Jonah and Joel are held by the orthodox to be pre-exilic, but secular scholars are more apt to place both books in the postexilic period.

9 An off-kilter title like "The Queen of London" or "The President of Cincinnati."

10 Contemporary secular scholars who have con-
    figured Jonah as a satire include E. M. Good
    (1965), M. Burrows (1970), J. C. Holbert
    (1981), and J. S. Ackerman (1981).
11 No more strange rhetorically than for the
    newly elected governor of California to
    speak of his political program in terms of
    characters he has enacted in the movies.
12 Ibn Ezra (1951) ambiguously refers to
    Jonah's survival in the fish as a *"neis,"* which
    literally means "sign" – either a miraculous
    sign from God or, as I think likely, a sym-
    bolic event not meant to be taken literally.
13 Terry Eagleton (1990: 236) refers to
    YHWH's performance as being like a magi-
    cian "having a ropy night on a stage in
    Blackpool."
14 There is agreement even among the orthodox
    and the fundamentalist Christians that the
    Bible contains *meshalim* (parables), stories
    whose literal truth is not guaranteed, as
    long as these pericopes are bracketed off
    from the main narrative, ascribed to an indi-
    vidualized speaker, and given a rhetorical
    situation (e.g., Jotham in Judges 9, Nathan
    in 2 Samuel 12, the Wise Woman of Tekoah
    in 2 Samuel 14, as well as the many parables
    of Jesus in the gospels). The problem with
    reading Jonah even as a didactic fable is that
    none of these features obtains here.
15 I argued (Richter 1999) that other narrative
    elements of the story travestied or satirized
    major events of Saul's reign: his cutting up of
    oxen to initiate his first campaign, his insist-
    ence on risking the entire tribal army to save
    the frontier town of Jabesh-gilead while more
    important areas of Canaan were not under
    Israelite control, his superstitious reliance
    on oracles, his listless lingering under the
    pomegranate tree before the battle against
    the Philistines, his fatal combination of rash-
    ness and inanition.
16 For example, the story of Micah in Judges
    17–18 is an alternative version, almost car-
    toon-like in its extravagant breaches of both
    secular morality and sacred tradition, of how
    an alternative temple with a graven image
    happened to wind up at the northern bound-
    ary of Israel at Dan. The story of Jephthah's
    rash vow in Judges 11 (to sacrifice to

YHWH whatsoever comes out to meet him
on his return home from battle) parallels
Saul's rash vow to fast before and during the
battle of Michmash and to slay anyone who
breaks the fast, a vow that, except for the
intervention of the people, should have
resulted in the execution of Jonathan.
Jephthah's obscure origins in Gilead link
him to Saul who has an equally obscure connection to Gilead on the other side of the
Jordan. The stories of both Gideon and Samson may allude to the monarchy under Solomon. Like Solomon, Gideon amasses huge
amounts of gold, enjoys many wives and
fathers dozens of children, making an ephod
which leads the Israelites to idolatry, and has
a royal reign of 40 years. Samson, like
Solomon, has a weakness for wine and for
non-Israelite women who lead him into sin;
Samson destroys a heathen temple while
Solomon builds the temple to YHWH.
17 Saul is given the contradictory instructions at
    1 Samuel 10: 7–8: verse 7 tells him to "do as
    occasion serve thee" while verse 8 tells him to
    wait seven days for Samuel, who will come to
    perform sacrifices before Saul's battle with
    the Philistines. Saul waits the seven days,
    but since Samuel has not appeared, and
    since the army with which he is supposed
    to defeat the Philistines is deserting before
    his eyes, he follows the "do as occasion serve
    thee" part of the instructions and performs
    the sacrifices preliminary to the battle by
    himself. No sooner has he done so than Sam-
    uel appears, and tells Saul that he has already
    blown his mission and the monarchy:
    "Thou ... hast not kept the commandment
    of the LORD thy God ... [N]ow thy king-
    dom shall not continue: the LORD hath
    sought him a man after his own heart, and
    the LORD hath commanded him to be cap-
    tain over his people, because thou hast not
    kept that which the LORD commanded
    thee."
        The inadequate instructions are in 1 Sam-
    uel 15, where Saul is commanded to smite
    the Amalekites and "devote them to destruc-
    tion" (*hecharamtem*). Saul defeats and destroys
    the Amalekites, slaying all except the king,
    coming in triumph with the king and the

best of the cattle "to sacrifice to the Lord thy God at Gilgal." Samuel treats this as a poor excuse for taking spoils in a holy war – implying that Saul should have killed the king and slain all the cattle right on the battlefield – and deposes Saul for the offense. But if that is what Samuel meant, perhaps he should have said so, since Joshua is described as doing exactly what Saul did (with full apparent approval by the Deuteronomic narrator) at Joshua 11: 10–14, after which Joshua and the people return, just as Saul has now done, to Gilgal.

18   This chiastic relation between characters and their hermeneutic has been pointed out before in Shoshana Felman's (1977) analysis of *The Turn of the Screw* and by Barbara Johnson's (1985) analysis of *Billy Budd*.

19   Some of the doublets in the story of King Saul – the references to 1 Samuel unless otherwise marked:
The Israelites demand a king; Samuel harangues them on their sin in so doing: 8: 5–20;
The Israelites having demanded a king are harangued by Samuel on their sin in so doing: 12: 6–18
Saul chosen as ruler (*nagid*) by the LORD: 9: 16, Saul anointed as ruler (*nagid*) 10: 1
Saul chosen as king (*melech*) by the divination ritual of the ephod: 10: 26
Saul is made king by the people (*yimlichu*): 11: 15
Saul prophesies, the origin of the saying: "Is Saul among the prophets?": 10: 11–12
Saul prophesies, the origin of the saying: "Is Saul among the prophets?": 19: 23–24
Saul deposed as king by Samuel before the battle of Michmash: 13: 8–14
Saul deposed as king by Samuel after the battle with the Amalekites: 15: 16–31
David joins Saul's court as musician and armor-bearer: 16: 18–21
David joins Saul's court as warrior after slaying Goliath: 17: 57–58
Saul throws a spear at David but misses: 18: 10
Saul throws a spear at David but misses: 19: 10

Saul throws a spear at Jonathan but misses: 20: 33
Saul gives David his daughter Merab as his wife: 18: 17; then gives her instead to Adriel: 18: 19
Saul gives David his daughter Michal as his wife: 18: 27; then gives her instead to Phalti: 25: 44
Saul's daughter helps David flee Saul's assassins: 19: 11–12
Saul's son helps David flee Saul's assassins: 20: 41–2
Fleeing from Saul, David seeks the protection of King Achish of Gath: 21: 10
Fleeing from Saul, David seeks the protection of King Achish of Gath: 27: 2–3
Saul, pursuing David but in a vulnerable position, is spared by David, who cuts his robe: 24: 3–4
Saul, pursuing David but in a vulnerable position, is spared by David, who takes his spear: 26: 12
Saul, wounded, asks his armor-bearer to slay him, but is forced to kill himself: 31: 3–4
Saul, wounded, asks a passing Amalekite to slay him, who does so: 2 Samuel 1: 9–10

20   See 1 Samuel 16: 18–23. This reconciliation only partly reconciles, it would seem, for in the aftermath of the slaying of Goliath in Chapter 17, Saul asks after David's identity as though he had never laid eyes on the lad before. The harmonizer has not entirely gone on strike, though, since there is a final note at 1 Samuel 18. 2 that "Saul took [David] that day and would not let him go back to his father's house."

We might speculate that the language in which Saul asks Abner about David ("Who is the father of that lad?" at 17: 55, repeated literally at verses 56 and 58) may be deeply meaningful in context, because Saul has been told that his successor as king has already been chosen and will not be of his own family. Given that Saul has already met David twice for the first time, his insistent question about the identity of David's father may be taken metaphorically, as expressing the desire to be the father of David, which he accomplishes, in the only way he can do so retroactively, by marrying one of his daughters to David. Saul's insistent question "*Mi*" (who?) as a form of wishful thinking may be connected to the biblical idiom "*Mi yiten li*" – literally "Who will give me" but best translated as the optative "Would that I were . . .") This posited desire of Saul's to be David's father is of course highly ambivalent, as one might expect from a man welcoming his already anointed successor into the royal family: Saul first offers his elder daughter Merab, then gives her to Adriel, then his younger daughter Michal, who becomes David's first wife until she too is taken away from David after his defection from Saul's court and given to Palti ben Laish. Nevertheless Saul several times refers to David at key episodes as "my son" (24: 16, 26: 17 and 25) but David reciprocates by calling Saul "my father" only once, at 24: 11. We may want to question just how affectionate David's expressed filial attitude toward Saul is, because in the next chapter, when David is shaking down a rich farmer named Nabal for blackmail, David has his messengers refer to him as "thy son David" (1 Samuel 25: 8).

21   Many biblical commentators, including Robert Alter (2000), have argued that readers knew that the historical books of the Bible contained alternative versions of events and that they were read the way we would read a documentary political history that gives space to different accounts whose contradictions cannot be resolved. It is tempting to think that people a few millennia ago read Samuel differently from the way we do, but the actions of the Samuel redactor in attempting to reconcile discrepant accounts would seem to work against this view. But we cannot tell at what stage prior to the tenth-century Masoretic recension these reconciliatory comments were inserted into the text, and so Alter could be right: the original historian may have assumed the "alternative version" mode of reading while a later redactor, after this mode of reading had passed away, sensed a genuine contradiction and inserted glosses. Harmonizing the contradictions in the book of Samuel begins as early as the book of 1 Chronicles.

One keen reader of 1 Samuel, Ken Gordon, has suggested to me (personal communication) that the doublets are not placed in the text at random but function to highlight the episode that separates them. The two depositions of Saul, for example, flank the episode in which both Saul's heroism and his quixotry hit their high point at the battle of Michmash. The two episodes in which David spares Saul when he has him in his power flank the episode of David and Nabal, which highlights David's crude extortions as a local warlord. But sometimes doublets come so far apart that a doublets-as-highlighter theory seems difficult to sustain.

22   In "The Grand Chronology" Meir Sternberg feels that, while from the genetic perspective of source criticism, doublets present alternative versions of a single event, "when we switch from the genetic to the poetic perspective . . . each compels . . . a successive reading. In the finished narrative they have all been linearized into stages within a well-plotted chronology" (Sternberg 1990: 126).

23   For example, it is during the siege of the Ammonite city of Rabbah that King David begins his affair with Bathsheba, and it is under the wall of Rabbah that her husband Uriah the Hittite perishes. Then the domestic story shifts to David's marriage to Bathsheba, Nathan's condemnation, the king's repentance, the death of the couple's first son, and the conception and birth of Solomon. Finally, Joab sends David word that Rabbah has been taken and advises him to be present at the victory. Are we to think that Joab and his army have been waiting under the walls of Rabbah throughout the many months of Bathsheba's two pregnancies? Sternberg rightly suggests that the chiastic structure is formal rather than chronological, that ending the war story is a way of indicating that the domestic drama of David's household, as far as it has come, is complete.

24   The Gibeonites first appear in Joshua 9, as Canaanites who pretend to be allies of the Israelites from a distant land, and make

a covenant with them. When found out, they cannot be slain because of the treaty but are turned into a permanent underclass –"hewers of wood and drawers of water."

25 Thus the Masoretic text, but this is inconsistent with Michal's barrenness stated at 2 Samuel 6: 23. Editors speculate that "Michal" is a scribal mistake here for "Merab" her elder sister, whom Saul married to Adriel, who is named here as the father of those children, and as Merab's husband at 1 Samuel 18: 19. Another conjecture is that, despite the word "bore" here (*yaldah*), Michal for some unstated reason had raised her sister's children and would for that reason have been considered their mother. The King James Bible and other translations translate what the Gibeonites did to the descendents of Saul as "hanged," but the verb *v'hoqàanum* refers to a slow method of execution involving impalement, where the body once dead remains exposed, so I have translated it perhaps anachronistically as "crucified" (the Vulgate has "*crucifixerunt*").

26 Many scholars argue that the so-called 2 Samuel epilogue (Chapters 21–4, containing two narrative episodes, two lists of David's warriors, and two Davidic psalms, arranged in chiastic order) is from a different "hand" than the rest of Samuel. From a source-critical point of view, it is often seen as shoveling a batch of unrelated documents and episodes at the end of a book, just before the narrative close, which is also done elsewhere in the Bible (for example the end of Deuteronomy). The narrative close of 2 Samuel actually comes at 1 Kings 2: 12, when the succession of Solomon is assured. Robert Alter, who is generally dismissive of source-critical readings, and insistent on taking a redactorial standpoint, here finds he needs to reverse course and discuss "alternate source" theories because of the harm these episodes do not just to the unity but to the coherence of his "David Story."

27 Elhanan's patronymic here (son of Yaare-oregim) has somehow picked up the word for "weavers" (*oregim*) repeated in "weavers' beam" further down in the verse; later in a catalog of David's 30 picked warriors, the same Elhanan is referred to as Elhanan ben Dodo of Bethlehem. Chronicles picks up the story and revises it so that Elhanan kills Goliath's brother Lahmi (1 Chronicles 20: 5), a name that seems to be made up (from Elhanan's birthplace – in Samuel Elhanan is a Bethlehemite, in Hebrew "beth-ha-*lahmi*"). The revision in Chronicles underlies the King James Version's translation of the verse, which goes "Elhanan ... slew *the brother of* Goliath the Gittite." (The italics on the words "the brother of" mean that they are supplied by the translators but are missing from the original text.) Some rabbinic commentators including Rashi rescue the situation by claiming that "Elhanan" (meaning "God is gracious") is the throne name of David.

28 The 3,000th anniversary of the birth of David, celebrated recently, has been the occasion for dozens of "debunking" biographies (e.g., Steven L. MacKenzie's (2000) *King David: A Biography*; Baruch Halpern's (2001) *David's Secret Demons*, David Rosenberg's (1997) *The Book of David*). What I find endlessly amusing about these books is their common stance of unvarnished truth – that they will heroically tell the real story about David that the book of Samuel doesn't tell. But aside from a few factual references that can be inferred from early psalms, and the highly complimentary account of David in Chronicles (which whitewashes David by simply eliminating any story that shows his blemishes), there just aren't any sources about David except the one in Samuel. And all the ugly things the biographers tell about David that he began his career as a freebooter who lived by shaking down local landowners, that he hired himself and his guerrilla band out to the Philistines, the national enemy, that he came to power by getting rid of Saul and all of his descendents, that he was an adulterer and a murderer, that he was a terrible father, husband, and leader – all these things are plainly written in the book of Samuel for those who know how to read it, and few of them need to be read "between the lines."

REFERENCES AND FURTHER READING

Ackerman, J. S. (1981). "Satire and Symbolism in the Song of Jonah." In B. Halpern and J. Levenson (eds.), *Traditions in Transformation* (pp. 214–46). Winona Lake, WI: Eisenbrauns.

Alter, R. (2000). *The David Story: A Translation with Commentary of 1 and 2 Samuel.* New York: W. W. Norton.

Burrows, M. (1970). "The Literary Character of the Book of Jonah." In H. Thomas Frank and W. L. Reed (eds.), *Translating and Understanding the Old Testament* (pp. 80–107). New York: Abington Press.

Day, J. (1990). "Problems in the Interpretation of the Book of Jonah." In A. S. Van de Woude (ed.), *Quest of the Past. Studies on Israelite Religion, Literature and Prophetism* (pp. 32–47). Leiden: Brill.

Eagleton, T. (1990). "J. L. Austin and the Book of Jonah." In R. Schwartz (ed.), *The Book and the Text: The Bible and Literary Theory* (pp. 231–6). Oxford: Blackwell.

Fausset, A. R., Jamieson, R., and Brown, D. (1871). *A Commentary, Critical and Explanatory, on the Old and New Testaments.* Hartford, CT: Scranton. <http://blueletterbible.org/Comm/jfb/Jon/Jon001.html>

Felman, S. (1977). "Turning the Screw of Interpretation." *Yale French Studies* 55–6: 94–207.

Good, E. M. (1965). *Irony in the Old Testament.* Philadelphia: Westminster Press.

Halpern, B. (2001). *David's Secret Demons: Messiah, Murderer, Traitor, King.* Grand Rapids, MI: Eerdmans.

Holbert, J. C. (1981). "Deliverance Belongs to the Lord: Satire in the Book of Jonah." *Journal for the Study of the Old Testament* 21, 59–81.

Ibn Ezra, Avraham ben Meir (1951). Commentary on Jonah in *Mikraot Gedolot: Nevi'im u-Ketuvim.* New York: Pardes.

Johnson, B. (1985). "Melville's Fist: The Execution of Billy Budd." In *The Critical Difference. Essays on the Contemporary Rhetoric of Reading* (pp. 79–109). Baltimore and London: Johns Hopkins University Press.

McKenzie, S. L. (2000). *King David: A Biography.* New York: Oxford University Press.

Mekilta de-rebbe Ishmael (1961). ed. and trans. J. Lauterbach, 3 vols. Philadelphia: Jewish Publication Society of America.

Paine, T. (1794–5). *The Age of Reason.* <http://libertyonline.hypermall.com/Paine/AOR-Frame.html>

Rabinowitz, P. J. ([1987] 1998). *Before Reading: Narrative Conventions and the Politics of Interpretation.* Columbus: Ohio State University Press.

Richter, D. H. (1999). "Farewell My Concubine: The Difficult, the Stubborn, and the Outrage of Gibeah." In M. L. Raphael (ed.), *Agendas for the Study of Midrash* (pp. 101–22). Williamsburg, VA: William and Mary Press. <http://www.qc.edu/ENGLISH/Staff/richter/concubine.html>

Rosenberg, D. (1997). *The Book of David.* New York, Harmony.

Sternberg, M. (1985). *The Poetics of Biblical Narrative: Ideological Literature and the Drama of Reading.* Bloomington: Indiana University Press.

Sternberg, M. (1990). "Time and Space in Biblical (Hi)story Telling: The Grand Chronology." In R. Schwartz (ed.), *The Book and the Text: The Bible and Literary Theory* (pp. 83–145). Oxford: Blackwell.

19
Why Won't Our Terms Stay Put? The Narrative Communication Diagram Scrutinized and Historicized

Harry E. Shaw

I would hazard the guess that few teachers and few students of narratology or narrative poetics have failed to use the Narrative Communication Diagram, in one of its familiar guises or another – for instance, the one proposed by Seymour Chatman (Chatman 1978: 151) many years ago, which runs as follows:

Real Author → | Implied Author → (Narrator) → (Narratee) → Implied Reader | → Real Reader

Versions of the diagram differ, but in whatever form, it has proven its usefulness.[1] Perhaps for that very reason, it seems fitting to subject it to some scrutiny. I believe that the diagram has gained wide acceptance and use in part because its terms are malleable. Critics with quite different views of narratology and of narrative itself can avail themselves of the diagram, simply by giving its various terms rather different meanings.

Some, echoing a familiar criticism of narratology, might conclude that such critics are simply finding devious ways around a system that is too abstract and constraining. This, however, is not my own view, even though I do not hope to find a way of ironing out the differences and coming up with a definitive, all-purpose diagram. My hope instead is to uncover the conditions of possibility for disagreements, overt and latent, about the diagram and in doing so to suggest what is at stake in different ways of imagining its terms. Along these lines, I'll make two local suggestions: first, that users of the diagram bring to it two different implicit models of the communication situation; and second, that the terms the diagram seeks to describe necessarily become hazier as we move from left to right. On a more general level, my argument will be that we are likely to imagine the diagram in one way and not another depending on our pre-existing beliefs about some large and fundamental matters involving the scope of narratology itself, and also – and this is the heart of my argument – on the kind of fiction we think of as normative. (To say this is to say that our use of the diagram turns out to be historical in several senses.) I will therefore conclude my essay, not with a definitive version of the model, but with the admission that the version of the model I recommend in these pages reflects my own critical priorities on both these scores.

The notion of a narrative communication diagram evokes a simple underlying image, the image of someone telling a story to someone else. But this image is susceptible to different emphases, and I think that in practice those who have developed and employed its components have tended to rely on two significantly disparate ways of imagining what's central about situations in which communication occurs. If you observe two people conversing, you can take an objective stance in which you concentrate on what they are saying, on who is talking and who is listening, on whether the person who is telling the story is recounting his or her own experience or that of another (and in the latter case, if he or she does so by enacting the other person's words and actions or summarizing them), and so on. We might call such an emphasis, which looks on from the outside and gauges the flow and the parameters of the narrative situation, an emphasis on the modality of "information." (Here I echo Genette, who consistently speaks in terms of the transfer or flow of information in his seminal discussions of narrative focalization.) The external observation that characterizes the information perspective begins with immediate perceptions, but it need not be confined to them. We might, for instance, wish to go beyond immediate perceptions in an attempt to assess the reliability of a tale-teller by measuring what he or she says against other evidence we observe in the text.

It would, however, also be possible to engage differently with two figures in a story-telling situation in a different way. Instead of focusing on the flow of information as seen from outside, we might adopt a role familiar to all of us when we ourselves participate in such situations, the role of imagining what the person addressing you has in mind as he or she tells you the story, what effects and purposes the teller wishes to achieve. Does the story-teller seem to be crafting a version of the story designed to appeal to the particular listener being addressed? Might the story-teller even be attempting to inveigle the listener into adopting a certain kind of role and thereby acquiescing in certain beliefs and values? And what do the story-teller's intentions reveal about his or her own values? When we connect with the narrative situation in this way, we have moved from issues of information to issues of "rhetoric." Both approaches are and must be based on the reading of signs; the latter, however, attempts to use its reading of signs to reconstruct and indeed to inhabit a world of internality.

I believe that the terms contained in the communication diagram that have caused most controversy have done so because their nature changes according to whether one thinks of them in terms of information or of rhetoric. The most dramatic example is the category of the implied author. This category seems clearly to belong to the rhetoric mode, and not only because it was invented (by Wayne Booth) in a book entitled *The Rhetoric of Fiction*. The implied author is a critical reconstruction of the mind behind the rhetorical purposes informing a work of narrative. It serves to focus the question "What would you have to have believed and valued to have created this work?" by constructing an anthropomorphic agent of belief, and thereby invites those who use it to employ the vast and subtle panoply of techniques, most of them unformulated and hardly conscious, that we draw upon in everyday life when we try to assess the values and intentions of others. It has the particular pedagogical virtue of allowing this cornucopia of hermeneutic expertise to be focused on a work of art, but at the same time preventing it from flowing over (as it would naturally be inclined to) into a scrutiny of the agent we all know actually made the work of art, namely its author; instead, the focus stays on the work itself. Given these manifest virtues, it is unsurprising that the category of the implied author has gained wide acceptance, and it is hard to feel that there isn't something perverse about the insistence of Genette (and others) that it is a mere redundancy. But if we shift from issues of rhetoric to issues of information, the perversity vanishes, for there it *is* redundant. We never, the information argument would go, read the implied author's words, or hear his or her voice telling the story. (I myself believe that this is not entirely true, but I work from the rhetoric perspective.) When we assess, say, the narrator's reliability, the information critic would continue, we respond to all kinds of objective cues we hear in the narration. There is, however, no necessity for creating an anthropomorphic source for these cues and for any discrepancies we find among them: we can simply note and assess them, without having to concoct a special agent from which they proceed. We know that someone wrote the story; we know that we are hearing a narrator tell the story. That (if you inhabit the information camp) is all we know, and all we need to know. Thus if we think for the moment only of the terms that fall on the left side of the narrative communication diagram, we can see that the implied author is different in kind from the others. The real author and the narrator harmonize with both the information and the rhetoric views of the diagram. The implied author fits only the rhetoric view.

I move now to a perturbing force that affects the diagram as a whole in a more systematic way, a force described by what I have come to call "Genette's Law." (I call it a "law" to stress the fact that what is at issue here depends not on the presuppositions one brings to the diagram, but on an inherent property of the diagram itself.) Genette identifies what he calls "the *vectorality* of narrative communication. The author of a narrative, like every author, addresses a reader who does not yet exist at the moment the author is addressing him, and who may never exist. . . . the implied reader is the idea, in the real author's head, of a *possible* reader" (Genette 1988: 149). The implications of this seemingly innocuous, commonsensical observation are significant, for it tends to destroy the symmetry of the communication diagram, rendering "audience" terms on the right side of the diagram less substantial than "narrator" terms on its left side. It is amusing that Genette's own formulation, made from the information camp, echoes the hallmark of what I've called the rhetoric camp, by raising the question of what is "in the head" of a narrative entity – to be sure with a difference, since entering the head is viewed an inescapable plight, not a useful and illuminating hermeneutical procedure. Such is the power of a general perspective to alter the force of individual terms and locutions.

Genette's Law suggests that the items in the narrative communication diagram will become more diffuse as we move from left to right. How should we act on this insight? I believe that it is possible to obtain a high degree of solidity and specificity for the terms "narratee" and "implied reader" if we define those terms from the information perspective, but that the effects of Genette's law cannot be evaded from the rhetoric perspective. Turning first to the information perspective, it is possible to stabilize both the terms "narratee" and "implied reader" by severely narrowing their scope. When narrowed in this way, the term "implied reader" becomes (as I think it already is for many analysts) a way of specifying matters buried so deeply in culture that they precede and undergird the realm of the conscious persuasion that characterizes the implied author. What level of linguistic competence does the narrative seem to assume? What level of cultural knowledge? What set of shared values? Talk about the implied reader would in this scheme of things contain a large element of the empirical: an attempt to define the implied reader in the classroom might well begin by suggesting that implied readers of older texts would already know the lore provided for modern students in the footnotes of modern editions.

The effect of restricting the narratee to the realm of objectively observable information would be more dramatic. Under such a scheme, narratees would need to be specifically described recipients of a narrative, palpably addressed by the narrator; a narratee could not simply be a figure the narrator has in mind in telling the story. Two kinds of narratees would then emerge. One would occur in frame tales, where one character acts as a narrator and addresses another character, who thereby becomes the narratee. The other would occur when a narrator suddenly addresses someone specific, as when the narrator in *Tristram Shandy* evokes a narratee by exclaiming, "How could you, Madam, be so inattentive in reading the last chapter?" (chap. 20). This sort of narratee is often a "scapegoat" narratee, singled out to exemplify traits the actual audience should avoid.

If we turn to the rhetoric perspective, the scene changes: we will find it impossible to stabilize and concretize the terms narratee and implied reader by restricting their meaning. (At least, I haven't been able to find a way to do so.) At first blush, this seems disconcerting. After the initial shock, though, it turns out not to be a problem, and indeed not to be surprising. This is because from the rhetoric perspective, what we're interested in anyway occurs in the mind of the implied author (or sometimes, as I'll argue more fully in a moment, in the mind of the narrator). To be sure, it is crucial that we keep in mind the possibility that a narrative may be addressed to different audiences simultaneously, and particularly the possibility that (guided by the implied author), the narrator may be addressing one kind of audience *through* another. But whether the best way to keep this vital distinction in mind is to reify it into set categories of audiences seems to me doubtful. I suspect that in the end, the sentences we write either to describe a given passage or to give a more general account of the narratological situation they exemplify will in any case involve what entities on the left side of the diagram have in mind with regard to audiences. If this is so, why not simply shift the focus back on those entities and their rhetorical attempts to imagine and move their audiences?[2] And as it happens, for *this* purpose, an attempt to specify different kinds of narratees and other audience entities can have a significant heuristic value. Robyn Warhol, for instance, helps clarify what she means by the "engaging" narrator by outlining different possible relationships between the narrator, narratee, and reader (Warhol 1989: 25–30). In such discussions, however, I would argue that the concept of the narratee functions most fruitfully precisely when the insights it enables fold back into insights about the purposes of the narrator. Warhol's contribution (and I consider it a very significant one) is, after all, to have added to our narratological discourse the figure, not of the engaged narratee, but of the engaging narrator.

Let me further solidify what I have in mind here by borrowing an example adduced by Warhol (1989: 34). When Stowe's narrator addresses the "mothers of America" in *Uncle Tom's Cabin*, urging them to put themselves in the place of slave mothers, the audience she actually has in mind includes the mothers of America, but extends beyond them: she is addressing all possible readers *through* the specific narratees she singles out, inviting them all to focus their feelings about slavery by imagining that they are mothers, even if they are not female, or not mothers, or not even Americans (one recalls the profound effect *Uncle Tom's Cabin* had on the male workers of England). It's important to realize that more than one audience is at issue here, and it is helpful toward this end to describe the "mothers of America," in information terms, as a (collective) narratee. So much is clear. But how much help could terms on the right side of the diagram give us in describing the nonmother non-American parts of the audience Stowe actually wishes to address? Do they constitute a second narratee group? To pursue this possibility, we would have to specify their difference from the first narratee group, and to do that we would soon find ourselves in the mind of the implied author. How many different groups do we wish to specify with the term narratee? Perhaps we should instead describe them by employing the term "implied reader." If we do so, however, that term will begin to splinter, because in fact what is in the mind of Stowe's implied author is a set of different audiences. For some members of the audience, she is preaching to the converted and thus needs only to encourage further solidarity. For others, her task is different: she needs to win them over. To discuss such possibilities, we will again find ourselves in the mind of the implied author. Perhaps that is where we should stay.

From the rhetoric point of view, then, there would appear to be no way to increase the solidity of the narratee and implied reader by limiting their scope, as we can from the information point of view; the only way to gain greater solidity and specificity is to turn to figures who reside on the left side of the diagram, untouched by the diffusive effects of Genette's Law. Normally, if we're working along these lines, we will interest ourselves in the mind of the implied author. Most attempts to discuss the rhetorical aims of a given passage or scene as they involve imagined audiences can be handled by considering what the implied author has in mind; indeed, the category of the implied author itself was invented as a way of describing the implications of the overall rhetorical intent of a given work. But there are novels in which the narrative presence is so fully developed that it will be necessary to shift our attention to the narrator's own rhetorical purposes. I have argued elsewhere that such a situation obtains in the novels of George Eliot. Eliot sometimes creates a narrator whom she self-consciously places in situations that seem constrained by history in just the same way as her readers are so constrained in their everyday lives (Shaw 1999: 236–55). Eliot does this partly because she wants her narrator's ethical judgments to affect real-world historical readers in a way that the words of a being exempt from such constraints simply could not. We tend to trust those who have "been there," who know from the inside what the difficulties of life feel like, more than those who have not, and for Eliot, those difficulties include being in history.

George Eliot's historicized narrator assumes a stance that allows her to wield ethical authority, as a result of accepting a definite and limited position in history. We find a similar situation in the novels of Thackeray, though what hems his narrator in is not quite the fully imagined historicity of Eliot, but instead a sense of the ethical situation all human beings face in a world which I think we can fairly identify as being that of urban modernity, but which Thackeray presents in more timeless terms, as the world of "Vanity Fair." Thackeray's narration is so multivalent and complex in its shifts of tone that our sense of what kind of narrative entity is addressing us makes a very great difference in how we interpret passages and even individual sentences. My own view is that we are likely to miss what Thackeray is up to if we do not keep our attention on what the narrator (not just the implied author) "has in mind." Thackeray's narrator is a figure who finds himself trying to mount an adequate response to a world characterized sometimes by nobility and kindness, but more often by cruelty, stupidity, blindness, self-absorption, and (outrageously, given the narrator's own feeling of inadequacy in reacting to all of this) ethical smugness. The narrator enacts a complex attempt, sometimes self-contradictory and at best only partially successful, at taking all this in and reacting to it in an adequate way, and by doing so tries to goad us into seeing just where we are in the world.

It matters a great deal that it *is* the narrator who tries to do this, not a disembodied implied author positioned somewhere above the ethical situation. The narrator's difficulties, and his authority, arise precisely from the fact that he finds himself in the same fix as that of the characters he is describing. To be sure, he appears to understand how the world of "Vanity Fair" works better than they do, and he is probably neither as good as the best of them nor as bad as the worst. Yet in his desires, motivations, and likely actions, he is just as "creatural" and limited as all of them are – and as we his readers are as well, if only we will admit it. Consider the following passage from *Vanity Fair*:

We must pass over a part of Mrs. Rebecca Crawley's biography with that lightness and delicacy which the world demands – the moral world, that has, perhaps, no particular objection to vice, but an insuperable repugnance to hearing vice called by its proper name. There are things we do and know perfectly well in Vanity Fair, though we never speak them: as the Ahrimanians worship the devil, but don't mention him: and a polite public will no more bear to read an authentic description of vice than a truly refined English or American female will permit the word breeches to be pronounced in her chaste hearing. And yet, Madam, both are walking the world before our faces every day, without much shocking us. If you were to blush every time they went by, what complexions you would have! It is only when their naughty names are called out that your modesty has any occasion to show alarm or sense of outrage, and it has been the wish of the present writer, all through this story, deferentially to submit to the fashion at present prevailing, and only to hint at the existence of wickedness in a light, easy, and agreeable manner, so that nobody's fine feelings may be offended. I defy any one to say that our Becky, who has certainly some vices, has not been presented to the public in a perfectly genteel and inoffensive manner. In describing this syren, singing and smiling, coaxing and cajoling, the author, with modest pride, asks his readers all round, has he once forgotten the laws of politeness, and showed the monster's hideous tail above water? No! Those who like may peep down under waves that are pretty transparent, and see it writhing and twirling, diabolically hideous and slimy, flapping amongst bones, or curling round corpses; but above the water-line, I ask, has not everything been proper, agreeable, and decorous, and has any the most squeamish immoralist in Vanity Fair a right to cry fie? When, however, the syren disappears and dives below, down among the dead men, the water of course grows turbid over her, and it is labour lost to look into it ever so curiously. They look pretty enough when they sit upon a rock, twanging their harps and combing their hair, and sing, and beckon to you to come and hold the looking-glass; but when they sink into their native element, depend on it those mermaids are about no good, and we had best not examine the fiendish marine cannibals, reveling and feasting on their wretched pickled victims. And so, when Becky is out of the way, be sure that she is not particularly well employed, and that the less that is said about her doings is in fact the better.

(Thackeray [1848] 1994: 637–8)

What is in the head of the narrator in this passage would appear to include a wish not simply to indicate Becky's downward spiral after Rawdon discovers her with Lord Steyne, but also and more centrally to ensure that the reader doesn't imagine that downward spiral too glibly. The passage condemns what Becky does and becomes, but it also directs anger and disdain toward those who enjoy glutting their prurience on spectacles they don't want fully represented, the better to enjoy them in an unhealthy half-light. When the narrator suggests that "those who like may *peep* down under [the] waves" he catches his readers' voyeuristic tendencies; when he adds that the waves are "pretty transparent" he among other things admits to a certain complicity on his own part in those tendencies. The element of prurient exaggeration likely to be present in our imaginings, and the sheer absurdity of male fear of the nether parts of females, is underlined by the parody into which the description of the "syren" descends, with its talk of mermaids "twanging" their harps, "fiendish marine" cannibals, and "pickled" (*pickled?*) victims. Becky is guilty, but our ways of imagining her guilt make us, all of us including the narrator, guilty too – which is one reason why Becky outrages us, which is not to say that certain aspects of what she does should not outrage us.

To take in the full tonal complexity of the "syren" passage, I am arguing, it is useful to impute it to the mind of an anthropomorphic narrative agent full of anger, sorrow, pity, and incredulity at the human spectacle, and particularly at the spectacle of those whose smug moralism would exempt themselves from its complexities and their own complicity in human weakness. If we as readers of *Vanity Fair* have been engaged in the process of imagining this sort of mind in action, we will have come to expect its workings to be ongoing and cumulative, as the narrator pursues an endless attempt to come to grips with life's complexities. As a result of this expectation, it will not come as a surprise when, in the second paragraph following the "syren" passage, the narrator tells us, in quite a different tone and with a significant transformation of the underlying imagery, that Becky's "*abattement* and degradation did not take place all at once: it was brought about by degrees, after her calamity, and after many struggles to keep up – as a man who goes overboard hangs on to a spar whilst any hope is left, and then flings it away and goes down, when he finds that struggling is in vain" (p. 638). This is a very different vision of drowning from the one in the "syren" passage, where women like Becky drag men down into the water, to their pickled doom. Here it is Becky who is the victim, and the metaphoric death is real. I will add in passing that, from our own historical vantage point, it is the more striking that at the moment of his greatest generosity toward Becky's plight, when he has left behind him the scapegoated female narratees with which the "syren" passage opens, the narrator dignifies that plight by imagining her as a drowning "man."

If we imagine Thackeray's narrator to be a dramatized ethical and rhetorical agent, then, taking in the "syren" passage means following the narrator's mind as he tries to meet the full ethical complexities of coming to grips with Becky's guilt, her society's guilt, and our guilt as readers of the passage. If we approach *Vanity Fair* through a version of the narrative communication diagram that posits a less substantial narrator, however, our reading of the passage is likely to change. A distinguished narratologist, James Phelan, has suggested that, far from assuming a stance of creaturality or of being "one of us," Thackeray's narrator in his "virtuosity" betrays "a fondness for ironic one-upmanship" and that as readers we are invited "to participate in the metavoice's smugness or snideness or superciliousness" (Phelan 1996: 55). The many voices and tones we hear in the passage are not for Phelan the complex attempt of the narrator to come to grips with a troubling reality; they reveal a different kind of purposefulness. Thus in speaking of "the monster's hideous tail" the narrator adopts a "melodramatic" voice that is "privileged" and thereby conveys "the Showman's clear condemnation of Becky as a hideous female creature." The "refined voice" we hear elsewhere in the passage "acts as a cover under which the Showman asserts that Becky is ugly, fiendish, and murderous" (1996: 57). Clearly enough, Phelan and I hear very different voices, and a very different orchestration of those voices, in the "syren" passage. A full explanation of why we perceive the passage so differently would doubtless have its interest; at the present, however, I'm most interested in the part that differences in how we imagine the narrative communication diagram may play in our disagreement. (Concentrating on this issue prevents me from registering the signal contributions Phelan's essay makes in two other areas: its exploration of the meaning of "voice" in narrative, and its connection of general narratology with feminist critique.) My view of Thackeray's narrator as substantial to the point of seeming human in his deployment of rhetorical agency leads me to grant that narrator and his intentions every benefit of the doubt. I locate, for instance, the narrator's sexism at a less conscious, more culturally ingrained level than Phelan does. Phelan takes a less forgiving view of Thackeray's narrator, and I believe one reason is that his image of the narrator is considerably less robust than mine: for him, the narrator is the "source" of the various ironies in the passage, but he is also Thackeray's "mouthpiece," and we must wonder how much mind and intention a "mouthpiece" can muster. The version of the narrative communication diagram Phelan employs (which also explicitly minimizes the presence of an implied author in the case of *Vanity Fair*) seems to me to discourage an attempt to imagine what might be in the mind of any narrative agent in Thackeray's novel; instead, we find ourselves resolutely in the information mode, in which we observe from the outside the various voices produced by the narrator. This enables a familiar kind of critique, very much in the mode of the hermeneutics of suspicion, which views narrators, and indeed human beings, as spoken by collections of cultural voices rather than as independent agents who speak those voices in the service of their subjective intentions with an efficacy dwarfing any subjective intentionality.[3] In such a scenario, it's not surprising to find, as Phelan does, that one voice carries the definitive ideological punch, with the other voices providing a "cover" for that voice.

Whether the reader agrees with Phelan or with me about the "syren" passage, I hope that we can all agree that how we imagine the figures in the narrative communication diagram matters not simply for interpretation but for how we register a fictional scene in the first place. I now turn to other, more global presuppositions that can perturb the meanings of the various terms that constitute the diagram. The version of the diagram that has been evolving in this essay, which aggrandizes the narrator at the expense of other occupants of the narrative communication diagram, and even explores what is in the mind of the narrator, reflects a wish to make the diagram as useful as possible for approaching a certain kind of prose fiction, the social novel of the nineteenth century. But such a choice suggests certain priorities, indeed certain views on the use and ultimately on the *scope* of narratology itself, and those with other priorities will make different choices. Chatman's version of the diagram, with which we began, is instructive in this regard:

Real Author → | Implied Author → (Narrator) → (Narratee) → Implied Reader | → Real Reader

Chatman wants to construct a diagram that will include filmed as well as verbal narratives; as a result, he makes the narrator and narratee "optional" in his diagram (that is the significance of the parentheses). This is proper and indeed indispensable for his purposes, but such an optionality would be most unlikely to occur to a critic focused on the nineteenth-century novel. In a similar fashion, as we've seen, Genette denies the usefulness of the term "implied author," demonstrating with meticulous logic that (in the context of the information perspective) the implied author adds nothing to the term "real author" and thus deserves to be lopped off by Ockham's razor as redundant. But the question arises, "redundant for what purpose?" The answer resides on a level that precedes logic. Genette believes that questions of ideology are outside the province of narratology, and he rightly identifies the implied author as an instrument for focusing signs of ideology. Both Chatman and Genette, then, inflect the diagram in one way and not another in response to their views of what narratology should include.

The issue of what sort of phenomena we should expect the communication diagram to bring into focus raises the question of how general we can expect narratology (and narratological terms) to be, and in doing so recalls the quarrel between philosophical realists and nominalists that arose among the scholastic philosophers in the Middle Ages. Nominalists, believing in the ultimate reality of particulars, might be tempted to argue in the present case that if narratological terms cannot fully account for the particularities of texts, so much the worse for the generalities. Realists, persuaded that general terms have a reality denied to particular instances, would be tempted to relegate to the realm of inconsequential "noise" the aspects of the particular texts that don't assort with a well-formed set of generalities. From this point of view, no problem should arise: it ought to be possible to construct a diagram that would cover what's important, narratologically speaking, about any and all narratives of whatever genre or period. The necessarily high level of generality of such a diagram would not be a problem, it would save us from distraction, allowing us to concentrate on the forest without losing what matters about the trees. The Curé of Combray (to be sure, an equivocal source of enlightenment, despite his impressive knowledge of etymologies) seems to me to give a truer picture of what we stand to gain, and lose, when we shift between levels of generality. He reports that from the steeple of his church:

> you can see at the same time places which you normally see one without the other, as, for instance, the course of the Vivonne and the irrigation ditches at Saint-Assise-lès-Combray, which are separated by a screen of tall trees, or again, the various canals at Jouy-le-Vicomte . . . Each time I've been to Jouy I've seen a bit of canal in one place, and then I've turned a corner and seen another, but when I saw the second I could no longer see the first. I tried to put them together in my mind's eye; it was no good. But from the top of Saint-Hilaire it's quite another matter – a regular network in which the place is enclosed. *Only you can't see any water*; it's as though there were great clefts slicing up the

town so neatly that it looks like a loaf of bread which still holds together after it has
been cut up.

(Proust 1981: 114–15; my emphasis)

That moving up and down the scale of generality without discernible loss can in the
right circumstances and in the right hands be entirely, even triumphantly, possible
in narratological discussion, was demonstrated some time ago by one of the
founding texts of narratology, Genette's *Narrative Discourse*, which moves from
framing general categories to considering the specifics of Proust's *Remembrance of
Things Past* with great ease and constant illumination. Or is this simply an illusion,
resulting from a hidden bias of some of Genette's formulations to fiction of a certain
kind and period? Whatever we decide about this matter, one thing seems certain (at
least to the nominalist who is writing these words): there is no justification for
allowing definitions suitable for a high-level view to legislate out of existence
phenomena visible closer to the ground. We ought not to deny that water is really
there in the river or the canals just because we can't see it from the top of the steeple.
Mutatis mutandis, this dictum applies to all the perturbing forces I have been
describing, inconvenient though they may be for the project of arriving at an all-
purpose version of the narrative communication diagram (or any other narratological
construct).[4] Which is not to say that we should frame and use terms in any way
we like.

My own inflection of the narrative communication diagram arises in part from the
use I wish to make of the narratological apparatus, and in particular from a "close-up"
focus on one subset of prose fiction, the realist novel produced in nineteenth-century
Britain. (I suppose that this has been evident to the reader all along, for instance in my
scandalous inclination toward anthropomorphizing the narrator, to whom I'm quite
happy to attribute a mind and a gender, attributes that suit the narrators I have
centrally in mind admirably but would fit less comfortably, if at all, with the
narrators of some other kinds of fiction.) In doing so, my use of the diagram reflects
the power of history, in a number of ways. I believe that all my comments about the
diagram (for instance, my recommendations regarding how the term "narratee"
should be used) are correct and helpful, and that none is more helpful and correct
than the suggestion that the narrator should be made as substantial a figure as
possible. And I trust that it goes without saying that I value attempts to define our
terms as clearly as we can, and to bring the intellectual choices and biases that
underlie our definitions into focus as crisply as we can, or I wouldn't have offered
my commentary in the first place. At the same time, I am fully aware that my view of
the narrator is particularly likely to seem self-evidently useful to a critic of nineteenth-century fiction, where narrators tend, to a greater degree than in the fiction of
other periods, to possess the kind of substantiality I have argued obtains with the
narrators of Eliot and Thackeray. (Consider the difference between the narrative
situation in *Vanity Fair* and the one that obtains in *The Sound and the Fury*, which
has plenty of narrators and voices, but none to which it is possible to attribute a

"mind" that has the scope of the mind of Thackeray's narrator.) As a result, I am also willing at least to entertain the possibility that, for modern fiction, it might turn out to be expedient to define the narratee more capaciously than my present recommendations allow. That I, like the narrators of Thackeray and Eliot, have historically inflected priorities may temper the universal applicability of some of my recommendations about how we should parse the narrative communication diagram. But it also reinforces my suggestion that the terms the diagram includes are, for good reason, unlikely to stay put, because they are part of history and refer to things that are part of history. This shiftiness needs watching, but it needn't pose insuperable problems so long as we keep its potential effects in mind – and also keep our prescriptive, tidying tendencies under check, allowing such constructs as the narrative communication diagram to function as devices, not of foreclosure but of exploration.[5]

Notes

1   My discussion presupposes a general familiarity with the diagram; those unfamiliar with it may wish to turn to Rimmon-Kenan (1983: 86–9), for a clear and useful introduction.

2   For a careful and influential attempts to define different rhetorical audiences, see Rabinowitz (1977). The end of this essay will qualify my disapproval of this tactic.

3   Reliance on such a model would tend to move Phelan toward the information camp, a place where the author of *Narrative as Rhetoric* is rarely to be found.

4   For a cognate argument, suggesting that assertions that narrators behave like characters in certain narrative works shouldn't simply be ruled out of order because they conflict with general narratological "laws," but instead might point to significant phenomena, see Shaw (1995). In that essay, I argue that *"the force of general narratological concepts undergoes modification when they are placed in subordination to broader cultural presuppositions"* (p. 113, emphasis in original). The present essay extends this attempt to place narratology in a historical context, by arguing that narratological terms themselves contain an inescapably contextual element.

5   I am grateful for the incisive commentary I received as this essay took shape from James Phelan, Peter Rabinowitz, and Jonathan Culler.

References and Further Reading

Chatman, S. (1978). *Story and Discourse: Narrative Structure in Fiction and Film*. Ithaca, NY: Cornell University Press.

Genette, G. ([1972] 1980). *Narrative Discourse: An Essay in Method*, trans. Jane E. Lewin. Ithaca, NY: Cornell University Press.

Genette, G. ([1983] 1988). *Narrative Discourse Revisited*, trans. Jane E. Lewin. Ithaca, NY: Cornell University Press.

Phelan, J. (1996). "Gender Politics in the Showman's Discourse; or, Listening to *Vanity Fair*."

In *Narrative as Rhetoric: Techniques, Audiences, Ethics, Ideology* (pp. 43–58). Columbus: Ohio State University Press.

Proust, M. ([1913] 1981). *Remembrance of Things Past*, vol. I, trans. C. K. Scott Moncrieff and Terence Kilmartin. New York: Random House.

Rabinowitz, P. J. (1977). "Truth in Fiction: A Reexamination of Audiences." *Critical Inquiry* 4, 121–41.

Rimmon-Kenan, S. (1983). *Narrative Fiction: Contemporary Poetics*. London: Methuen.

Shaw, H. E. (1995). "Loose Narrators: Display, Engagement, and the Search for a Place in History in Realist Fiction." *Narrative* 3, 95–116.

Shaw, H. E. (1999). *Narrating Reality: Austen, Scott, Eliot*. Cornell University Press.

Thackeray, W. M. ([1848] 1994). *Vanity Fair*, ed. Peter L. Shillingburg. New York: Norton.

Warhol, R. R. (1989). *Gendered Interventions: Narrative Discourse in the Victorian Novel*. New Brunswick, NJ: Rutgers University Press.

20

Gender and History in Narrative Theory: The Problem of Retrospective Distance in *David Copperfield* and *Bleak House*

Alison Case

Narratology gives us, among other things, the tools to identify and describe narrative techniques more precisely, and thereby to consider their implications and significance in more nuanced ways. In recent years, feminist critics have begun to make good use of these tools to examine the impact of gender ideology on the form as well as the content of literary narratives: asking, for example, how gender is encoded in the formal structures of novels, and in the dynamic of reading those structures produce. Hence Robyn Warhol defines "feminist narratology" as "the study of narrative structures and strategies in the context of cultural constructions of gender" (Warhol 1996: 21). Most commonly, this has meant examining the distinctive structures and strategies of women authors, individually or as a group, particularly when these appear to have been ignored, misperceived, or denigrated by a tendency to take male-authored texts as the norm. But feminist narratology can also help us to attend to gendered distinctions *within* texts, whether they are authored by men or women – as, for example, by looking at the ways narrative voices are gendered in homodiegetic narration.

Of course, as soon as we begin talking about "cultural constructions of gender," we are in the realm of history: "which culture?" we must ask, "when?" Unless its practitioners want to slip into gender essentialism, arguing, say, that women are biologically inclined to tell stories differently from men, feminist narratology requires that we ground our generalizations in some degree of historical and cultural specificity.

By way of illustration, I will examine some peculiar moments in Esther Summerson's homodiegetic narration in Dickens's *Bleak House*. These moments, I will argue, can usefully be explained by means of James Phelan's concept of "paradoxical" paralipsis (Phelan 1996: 82–104). But for reasons that have to do with both history and gender, Phelan's discussion of paradoxical paralipsis cannot fully account for the significance of its occurrence in *Bleak House*.

A paradoxical paralipsis is an omission or misrepresentation of information on the part of a retrospective homodiegetic narrator that appears to be inconsistent with the knowledge and perspective otherwise assigned to that narrator. Most commonly it occurs in the earlier portions of homodiegetic narratives that go on to recount a drastic change of perception – a revelation, a disillusionment, a change of heart – on the part of the narrating character. At such points, there ought to be a substantial perceptual gap between the knowing self who narrates and the still-naïve self whose experiences are being narrated. In paradoxical paralipsis, this gap is effaced, so that the narrator's *own* perceptions and judgments appear to match those of the naïve narrated self. For example, another character with whom the narrator has contact may be described *by the narrator* as admirable or trustworthy, despite the fact that she or he will later be revealed to the narrator as untrustworthy and despicable.

It is important to distinguish this phenomenon from the commonplace one whereby narrators of any kind keep their audience in the dark, or even subtly mislead them about revelations yet to come – by, for example, emphasizing some observations and de-emphasizing others. In a paradoxical paralipsis, the narrative voice itself appears to endorse beliefs or judgments that, by the time the story is narrated, the narrator knows to be inaccurate. The phenomenon is labeled *paradoxical*, then, because the narrative voice appears to violate mimetic logic. Because most readers are not in the habit of distinguishing strenuously between the "I" of a homodiegetic narrator and the "I" of the character, and because first-time readers will not necessarily be conscious of the impending change in the narrator's perspective, paradoxical paralipsis tends to be unobtrusive – to become apparent only retrospectively or on rereading – and even then often only to the narratologically aware (Phelan 1996: 104). When it occurs, especially in a highly wrought and artistically successful narrative, it is of interest in the way that narrative anomalies and contradictions often are: because its appearance suggests that there is something at this point more important to the author than producing a mimetically consistent narrative voice. In Phelan's account, this "something" is an artistic effect: by making the narrative voice share in the naïve perspective of the narrator/protagonist's earlier self, paradoxical paralipsis allows the reader to experience more fully the shock of the subsequent enlightenment or disillusionment, enhancing the story's emotional power. What I will suggest here is that this explanation applies predominantly to a twentieth-century fictional aesthetic, and that the use of the device in *Bleak House* has a different aim: that of reinforcing the femininity of Esther's narrative voice by means of a gendered literary code in place at the time.

The clearest examples of paradoxical paralipses in *Bleak House* occur in the opening chapter of Esther's narrative, when she describes her childhood with her godmother. I give the passage in full, with the relevant statements in italics:

> *She was a good, good woman!* She went to church three times every Sunday, and to morning prayers on Wednesdays and Fridays, and to lectures whenever there were lectures; and never missed. She was handsome; and if she had ever smiled, would have

been (I used to think) like an angel – but she never smiled. She was always grave, and strict. She was so very good herself, I thought, that the badness of other people made her frown all her life. I felt so different from her, even making every allowance for the differences between a child and a woman; I felt so poor, so trifling, and so far off; that I never could be unrestrained with her – no, could never even love her as I wished. It made me very sorry to consider how good she was and how unworthy of her I was; and I used ardently to hope that I might have a better heart; and talked it over very often with the dear old doll; but *I never loved my godmother as I ought to have loved her*, and as I felt I must have loved her if I had been a better girl.

(Dickens 1987: 15–16, my emphasis)

A similar example occurs a few pages later, describing her parting from the housekeeper: "*Mrs. Rachael was too good to feel any emotion at parting, but I was not so good, and wept bitterly*" (p. 22, my emphasis).

To accept these statements as sincere assessments by Esther the narrator – that is, Esther writing seven years after the close of the narrative recounted in the whole of *Bleak House* – is clearly nonsensical. *That* Esther has learned things about her godmother and Mrs Rachael, understands things about her own childhood, and has come to conclusions about what constitutes goodness, that would make these remarks simply absurd. If taken at face value, then, the remarks appear to violate the mimetic consistency of Esther's narration.

If we take mimetic consistency as an absolute virtue in a narrative, perceived instances of paradoxical paralipsis, like this one, leave us with two options as critics. First, we can simply choose to read the instance as an artistic mistake, a flaw. There is a long critical tradition, dating from the earliest reviews of the novel, that sees Esther's narration as precisely this: an experiment "not worth success, and certainly not successful" as John Forster famously put it (Forster 1907: 610) – and that see her as unsuccessful for reasons that have to do precisely with the unstable relationship between what Esther as narrator *ought* to know and what she appears or claims to know.

Alternately, we could try to somehow naturalize or psychologize an occurrence of paradoxical paralipsis – and there is, in principle, probably *no* narrative anomaly or contradiction that can't, with sufficient ingenuity, be attributed to a mimetically represented narrative consciousness. The most obvious way is simply to take whatever rhetorical function the paralipsis serves in the novel and attribute that rhetorical self-consciousness to the narrator – concluding, say, that the narrator is adopting a deceptively naïve voice for exactly the same reasons that the author might wish to adopt a mimetically inconsistent naïve voice. This move solves the problem of mimetic inconsistency by, in effect, creating an additional narrational entity: the seemingly naïve and abjectly self-critical persona who narrates this portion becomes a second-order fictional construction *by the narrator* (who is herself, of course, a fictional construction of the author's). If that logic fails, the limitless realms of mental illness are always open to us: for example, we can conclude that the narrator somehow neurotically reinhabits the earlier state of mind in narrating it, that she is traumatically bound to it in some way that precludes the distancing perspective of hindsight. Both of these options have also been pursued by numerous critics to account for these moments in Esther's narrative.

But there is a price paid to naturalize these narrative anomalies – the price of shifting the overall meaning of Esther's characterization further and further from the inspiring image of self-effacing feminine goodness Dickens's contemporaries all assumed he intended to create, whether or not they were impressed by the result. A rhetorically canny Esther who deliberately and deceptively crafts these sympathy-winning moments is a far less attractive figure, and raises the question of just how far her canniness extends: are the numerous instances of her simultaneously reporting and modestly disclaiming other characters' praises of her goodness similarly rhetorically self-conscious, for example? A reading of Esther as mentally ill or permanently emotionally damaged, while it certainly makes her more sympathetic, also makes the narrative trajectory of the book almost unrelievedly dark. Furthermore, both approaches wind up casting almost the entire Victorian readership of the novel as having completely missed the point of the novel in imagining that they were expected to admire Esther.

Phelan's analysis of the phenomenon of paradoxical paralipsis usefully moves us beyond these options by recognizing that mimetic consistency in the narrating consciousness may legitimately *not* be the highest priority even in a work of fiction, like *Bleak House*, that in other respects clearly aspires to produce a believably mimetic narrative voice. Instead, he suggests, literary convention in fiction allows for the localized splitting apart of the character functions and the narrator functions of the homodiegetic "I" when such splitting proves rhetorically effective for the telling of the story (Phelan 1996: 105). Paradoxical paralipsis is no more than an extreme case of the rhetorical unself-consciousness he sees as the "unmarked case" for homodiegetic narrative in general (p. 81).

To offer a less controversial example of such splitting from another Victorian novel: in reading *Wuthering Heights*, readers are clearly invited to form judgments about the character of Lockwood, the primary narrator, based on what we learn about his history, thoughts, feelings, and actions. But at the same time, the fact that Lockwood is apparently recording in his journal day by day every word Nelly Dean tells him of the lengthy story of the Earnshaw family – a fact that, if we encountered it in a real person, would suggest nearly superhuman powers of verbal memory as well as something like an obsessive-compulsive disorder – is obviously *not* intended to contribute to the novel's portrait of Lockwood. Lockwood's labors in recording Nelly's narrative are a fictional necessity for getting this story told, but as regards his character, they are simply irrelevant.

Similarly, in Esther's case, Phelan's account of how paradoxical paralipsis comes about does seem like the best explanation for what's happening in the narrative at this moment. The remarks highlighted above clearly reflect Esther's childhood perspective – specifically, her pathetic willingness to blame herself for the emotional cruelty both her godmother and Mrs Rachael subject her to – rather than the perspective of the more mature and enlightened Esther who has emerged by the end of the novel. Dickens includes them because he wants to immerse the reader sympathetically in Esther's childhood unhappiness. For readers who are so immersed, the fact that the comments are inconsistent with knowledge and views Esther will have adopted several hundred pages later — and, for the first readers of this serially published novel, over a year later — is likely to go unnoticed.

Significantly, though, this chapter does not operate consistently to identify Esther's narrative voice with the naïve perspective of the child. The bulk of the chapter — as in the unhighlighted portion of the passage above — does *not* rely on paradoxical paralipsis to present the child's viewpoint. It instead uses a method we might term "ambiguous distancing," in which past-tense tags like "I thought," "I wished," or "it made me very sorry to consider" assign the observations and judgments specifically to the earlier consciousness. Statements like these neither assert nor deny a gap between the narrating consciousness and the perceptions of the narrated self. But particularly in combination with other evidence — such as the actual details of the godmother's treatment of Esther, which clearly invite a more hostile judgment of her — they can subtly or not-so-subtly signal the narrator's awareness that that perspective should not be taken at face value. In other words, while statements like "I was not so good," invite us to identify the narrating consciousness with the naïve, self-blaming consciousness of the child Esther, conspicuous qualifiers like "(I used to think)" suggest, on the contrary, that the narrator now recognizes the limitations of that childhood perspective.

What is going on here? The very inconsistency of the oscillation between ambiguous distancing and paradoxical paralipsis in this passage suggests that this account is not intended, as in "My Old Man" (the Hemingway story Phelan 1996 uses as a key example), to convince the reader that we are dealing with a naïve narrator who still inhabits the perspective the character occupies at the beginning of the story. Nor, therefore, can they operate to enhance the emotional power of any subsequent disillusionment on the part of the narrator. In fact, no such explicit disillusionment ever occurs: over the course of the novel, the more mature consciousness hinted at here by ambiguous distancing simply comes gradually to predominate in Esther's narration. Instead, I would argue, the paralipses function primarily to dissociate Esther's narrating consciousness from the harsher, more judgmental reading of the godmother's "goodness" the chapter makes so readily available to a reader, and, more importantly, from the explicit recognition that the child Esther deserves sympathy and approval for her efforts to "love" her cold caretakers, rather than blame for her failure to elicit an adequate response from them.

In this respect, these paralipses are consistent with a number of other conspicuous points in Esther's narration that similarly operate to collapse momentarily the distinction between the narrating and the narrated self. For example, throughout the first half of the novel Esther as narrator frequently makes rather coy and embarrassed references to the dark young surgeon, Woodcourt, who has been paying attention to her; as here:

I have forgotten to mention – at least I have not mentioned – that Mr. Woodcourt was the same young surgeon whom we had met at Mr. Badger's. Or, that Mr. Jarndyce invited him to dinner that day. Or, that he came. Or, that when they were all gone, and I said to Ada, "Now, my darling, let us have a little talk about Richard!" Ada laughed and said –
But I don't think it matters what my darling said.

(Dickens 1987: 202)

Though there is no statement here that subsequent developments will prove to be unreliable, the hesitant, backtracking style of these remarks does appear to reflect the perspective of a young woman with little self-confidence, in the early stages of a romance, unsure whether to believe that the young man is attracted to her, ashamed of her own presumption in imagining he could be – Esther's state at the time she describes. By the time she *writes* this scene, though, Esther has been married to Woodcourt for seven years, and is presumably well aware that she was not imagining his attentions in the early days of his courtship. But a narration informed by this fact might risk implying a self-congratulatory consciousness of her own attractiveness and modesty at the time. As with the paradoxical paralipses in the opening chapter, these moments violate the mimetic consistency of Esther's retrospective narration in order to explicitly dissociate the narrating consciousness from forms of knowledge and judgment that, while implicit in the epistemological privilege of hindsight, might undermine the overall image of Esther as a virtuously modest and self-effacing woman.

There are of course also localized points where Esther signals her retrospectivity quite explicitly, but these are much more infrequent, and despite them many Victorian reviewers talked about Esther's story as if the telling of it and the experience of it were roughly contemporaneous – comparing her to the epistolary heroines of the eighteenth century and in one case referring to her narrative as a "diary" (Dyson 1969: 54). In my own experience also, with hundreds of first-time readers of *Bleak House*, students challenged to explain these and similar moments, even after finishing the novel, usually do so by making reference to what Esther the character was thinking and feeling at the time, without noticing that the retrospective status of the narrative means that the *narrator's* knowledge and feelings would be quite different.

We encounter a very different handling of the representation of a naïve childhood perspective in Dickens's previous homodiegetically narrated novel, *David Copperfield*, and the differences in many ways exemplify the points I want to make about the role of history and gender in narrative techniques. In that novel, as in *Bleak House*, the bulk of the work of presenting David's childhood perspective is carried out by ambiguous distancing, as in "I couldn't quite understand why Peggoty looked so queer, or why she was so ready to go back to the crocodiles" (Dickens 1989: 18). But in *Copperfield* this mode is punctuated at regular intervals with explicit reminders of the narrator's retrospective distance, as in, "my later understanding comes, I am sensible, to my aid here" (p. 18), or, more clearly, the following passage about David's feelings toward his future stepfather Murdstone:

I liked him no better than at first, and had the same uneasy jealousy of him; but if I had
any reason for it beyond a child's instinctive dislike, and a general idea that Peggoty
and I could make much of my mother without any help, it certainly was not *the* reason
that I might have found if I had been older. No such thing came into my mind, or near
it. I could observe, in little pieces, as it were; but as to making a net of a number of these
pieces, and catching anybody in it, that was, as yet, beyond me.

(Dickens 1989: 24, Dickens's italics)

What is striking about this passage is its assertion not only that this narrator knows
things about what will happen next that enrich his understanding of what was going
on then – the commonplace privilege of hindsight – but that he now possesses
analytic capacities that, had he had them then, would have enabled him to deduce
Murdstone's character even from the limited information then available to him, to
"make a net" from the "little pieces" of his observations and "catch" a character in it.
But it also signals that such ability is to come: "that was *as yet* beyond me." So this
statement both reminds us of the narrator's retrospective distance and alerts us that we
can anticipate watching David close that gap – in fact, the implication of this passage
is, in part, that in David's instinctive dislike of Murdstone we are to perceive the
embryo of the analytic capacity that is "yet" to come. The frequent reminders of
retrospection throughout the narration of David's early years can in fact be seen to
mark the gradual closing of that gap, so that in a certain sense we could summarize
the narrative of *David Copperfield* as: "this is the story of how I came to be able to tell
this story."

Dickens's underscoring of David's retrospective wisdom, and of the more self-
consciously authoritative account of others' characters, motivations, and relationships
it enables, is connected to a model of narrative authority that is to some degree
particular to nineteenth-century fiction. In *Telling the Truth*, Barbara Foley points
out that in fiction "mimesis is *constitutively* a social and historical phenomenon" (Foley
1986: 42). She argues that the conventions by which British and American novels
make claims to reference shift substantially from century to century. In the eighteenth
century, she suggests, the characteristic model is that of the "pseudofactual novel,"
in which claims to reference are founded on the likeness of the narrative to nonfictional narrative forms like the confession, the travel narrative, and so forth (1986:
107–8). In the main realist tradition of the nineteenth century, by contrast, she
suggests, claims to reference tend to be tied to the accuracy of the picture of society
the novel offers (pp. 143–5). To put her claims in slightly different terms, there is a
shift over time in the conventional *location* of verisimilitude – in where readers look
for "mimetic effects" – with the pseudofactual novel locating verisimilitude in the
form of the discourse as a whole, while the realist novel locates it in the content of
the story. In the early twentieth century, the conventional location of verisimilitude
shifts to the perceiving consciousness, so that what grounds claims to reference is
fidelity to the subjective experience of perception rather than, as in realism, to a
seemingly objective vision of the thing perceived (Foley 1986: 185–8).

What are the implications of these three models for the status of a narrative phenomenon like paradoxical paralipsis? Of the three, the last would seem to be by far the most fertile ground for generating instances of paradoxical paralipsis. If fidelity to the lived experience of perception is a value – or to the extent that it is a value – retrospective distance, the privilege of hindsight, will be at least as much an obstacle as a benefit to effective narration, and the benefits of conflating the narrating consciousness with the experiencing consciousness would far outweigh the cost of violating, unobtrusively, the "mimetic logic" of narration.

In the pseudofactual novel, though, that "mimetic logic" of narration is central to the novel's aims and claims, and violations of it would presumably pose severe problems. Certainly, when Moll Flanders narrates some of her early exploits with a relish for her nefarious accomplishments that seems more appropriate to her state of mind at the time than to the supposedly reformed and repentant condition she is in when she undertakes the narrative, this is not simply a rhetorically effective anomaly we pass silently over, as in Hemingway's "My Old Man," but a good reason to question the depth and sincerity of her final repentance – as the fictional Editor of the "confession" takes care to point out in his Preface.

In the nineteenth-century realist novel, in keeping with the value placed on accurate social portraiture, the characteristic narrative form is the uniquely epistemologically privileged heterodiegetic narrator usually termed "omniscient," for whom the category of paradoxical paralipsis is simply inapplicable. Homodiegetic narratives of this period do tend to retain closer ties with the conventions of the pseudofactual novel than either heterodiegetically narrated novels or later homodiegetic narratives. Nineteenth-century homodiegetic narrators, unlike many of their twentieth-century counterparts, will tend to make explicit their analogy to real-life autobiographers: they make reference to the project of writing – at the start of their respective narratives, Esther confesses to "a great deal of difficulty in beginning to write my portion of these pages," while David Copperfield makes reference to what "these pages must show" – the presence of an anonymous and public reader or readers, and so on. To the extent that these texts share the values of the pseudofactual novel, then, we might expect paradoxical paralipsis to be an infrequent and problematic technique.

But *David Copperfield* is not really meant to be a convincing imitation of a real-life autobiography; despite its technical limitation of perspective, the narrative voice actually has a great deal in common, rhetorically, with Dickens's heterodiegetic narrators. That is, while Dickens avoids actually violating the mimetic logic of an autobiography, he uses David as a narrator to tell the same kind of story he has told elsewhere with heterodiegetic narrators, and one which makes similar claims to reference. While the narrative voice is identified with a particular character, it aspires to the same scope and clarity of perception and judgment claimed by Dickens's other narrators. This aspiration is made more explicit, of course, by the fact that David eventually becomes a novelist bearing a striking resemblance to Dickens himself. To the extent that a homodiegetic narrator aspires to the status of a heterodiegetic realist narrator, then, paradoxical paralipsis poses a whole different problem, in that what it would violate is not so much the mimetic logic of the narration as the claim to narrative *mastery*: to the coherence and completeness of vision that would authorize such a narrator. The narrator's frequent reminders of his retrospective interpretive privilege in *David Copperfield*, then, rather than detracting from the mimetic effect by distancing us from the character's perceptions, enhances it by reassuring us that this narrator knows whereof he speaks.

This is clearly not the case for Esther. In *Bleak House*, comprehensiveness of vision, with the narrative authority it confers, belongs predominantly to Esther's heterodiegetic, "omniscient" conarrator, whose authoritative breadth of vision is contrasted with the more humble and limited perspective associated with Esther herself. On the strength of these two texts alone, of course, it is not possible to assert that the determining difference here must be that of gender. But placed in the broader context of English fiction of the eighteenth and nineteenth centuries, they do neatly exemplify a larger gendered pattern, in which self-conscious narrative mastery is coded as a masculine attribute, while credibility for female narrators tends to be associated with unself-consciously embodying or reflecting social truths (Case 1999: 4–34). Hence, for example, female narrative voices in the period are more likely to be represented in an epistolary or diary mode, a form which often relies for its effects on the narrator's ignorance of the trajectory and significance of her own unfolding story – as in Richardson's *Pamela*, or, later, Collins's *The Woman in White*.

Esther's affiliation with such narrators was implicitly recognized by the Victorian reviewers who compared Esther to Pamela, or referred to her narrative as a "diary." In keeping with this gendered pattern, in Esther's narrative, the underlying mode of ambiguous distancing is punctuated, not, as in *David Copperfield*, with explicit reminders of her epistemological privilege as a retrospective narrator, but instead with moments of explicit paradoxical paralipsis, and with other forms of verbal hesitation and self-corrections that similarly tend to collapse the distinction between the narrating consciousness and the narrated self. These work to create the impression of a narrator who is relatively unreflectively *immersed* in the feelings and experiences she recounts, because female credibility in the period tends to be linked to a lack of the kinds of rhetorical self-consciousness and critical distance retrospectivity enables.

The sharply contrasted solutions in these two novels to the same narrative problem – how to represent sympathetically a naïve prior consciousness by means of a retrospective homodiegetic narrator – should make clear that the instances of "paradoxical" statements by Esther in *Bleak House* should *not* be understood, as in twentieth-century instances, as an authorial reluctance to call attention to retrospective distance on the grounds that it might impede our engagement with the character's naïveté. It represents, instead, an authorial *eagerness* to call attention to a continuing *lack* of such distance. In other words, it is as important to Dickens to signal that Esther does *not* have a certain kind of narrative mastery, despite her retrospective position, as it is to signal that David *does*. A dehistoricized reading of paradoxical paralipsis as rhetorically effective in enhancing the mimetic effect of a homodiegetic narrative of disillusionment will not suffice to account for Dickens's employment of the technique in *Bleak House*, and his avoidance of it in *David Copperfield*, because it overlooks the roles of historically and culturally specific literary conventions that both construct and gender mimetic authority in fiction.

References and Further Reading

Case, A. (1999). *Plotting Women: Gender and Narration in the Eighteenth-and Nineteenth-Century British Novel*. Charlottesville: Virginia University Press.

Dickens, C. *Bleak House*. (1987). Oxford: Oxford University Press.

Dickens, C. *David Copperfield*. (1989). Oxford: Oxford University Press.

Dyson, A. E. (ed.) (1969). *Dickens's Bleak House: A Casebook*. London: Macmillan.

Foley, B. (1986). *Telling the Truth: The Theory and Practice of Documentary Fiction*. Ithaca, NY: Cornell University Press.

Forster, J. (1907). *Life of Charles Dickens*. London: Chapman & Hall.

Phelan, J. (1996). *Narrative as Rhetoric: Technique, Audiences, Ethics, Ideology*. Columbus: Ohio State University Press.

Warhol, R. R. (1996). "The Look, the Body, and the Heroine of *Persuasion*." In K. Mezei (ed.), *Ambiguous Discourse: Feminist Narratology and British Women Writers* (pp. 21–39). Chapel Hill: University of North Carolina Press.

21

Narrative Judgments and the Rhetorical Theory of Narrative: Ian McEwan's *Atonement*

James Phelan

As its title suggests, Ian McEwan's *Atonement* (2001) focuses on its protagonist's transgression and her effort at making amends for its disastrous consequences. Briony Tallis misidentifies her sister's lover, Robbie Turner, as the man who has sexually assaulted her cousin Lola, and then years later tries to do what she can to atone for her error. These events are themselves sufficient to make the issue of judgments – by Briony and of Briony – central to the novel and our experience of it. But McEwan also arranges the progression of his narrative so that it contains a startling twist in its last 20 pages, one that makes the issue of our judgment of McEwan as author equally significant. These pages, Briony's diary entry on the night of her 77th birthday, reveal that the previous 330 pages have been her novel as well as part of McEwan's. In other words, Briony's "Atonement," a straightforward and fascinating modernist novel, is Parts One, Two, and Three of McEwan's *Atonement*. McEwan's novel continues for this fourth section, "London, 1999," which, among other things, suddenly reveals that his *Atonement* is a self-conscious, self-reflexive novel employing a character narrator who is herself a novelist. Furthermore, Briony's diary entry reveals that her novel has mixed a factual account of her transgression with a fictional account of her atonement even as she now regards the novel itself as her major effort at atonement. How, then, do we judge (1) that novel and (2) McEwan and his novel for springing all this on us so suddenly?

I will offer answers to these questions before the end of this essay, but I want to argue first that *Atonement*, in highlighting the centrality of judgment to its narrative purposes, makes explicit something that, from a rhetorical perspective, is always implicitly central to narrative. I shall begin, therefore, by formulating six general theses about the importance of judgment in the rhetorical approach to narrative,[1] and I shall illustrate those theses by reference to the relatively uncomplicated case of Ambrose Bierce's "The Crimson Candle." I shall then return to the rich complexities of *Atonement*.

Six Theses about Narrative Judgments

Thesis one: narrative judgments are central for a rhetorical understanding not only of narrative ethics but also of narrative form and narrative aesthetics. The corollary of this thesis is that judgment functions as the hinge that allows each of these domains to open into the other two.

To substantiate this thesis I turn to a rhetorical understanding of narrativity, one that is tied (1) to the rhetorical definition of narrative as somebody telling somebody else on some occasion and for some purpose that something happened and (2) to the concept of narrative progression. From this perspective, narrativity is a double-layered phenomenon, involving both a dynamics of character, event, and telling and a dynamics of audience response. The phrase "somebody telling . . . that something happened" gets at the first layer: narrative involves the report of a sequence of related events during which the characters and/or their situations undergo some *change*. As I have discussed elsewhere (Phelan 1989), the report of that change typically proceeds through the introduction, complication, and resolution (in whole or in part) of unstable situations within, between, or among the characters. These dynamics of instability may be accompanied by a dynamics of tension in the telling – unstable relations among authors, narrators, and audiences – and the interaction of the two sets of dynamics, as in narratives that employ unreliable narration, may have significant consequences for our understanding of the "something that happened."

Turning to the second layer, the dynamics of audience response (or, in terms of the definition, the role of the "somebody else"), narrativity encourages two main activities: observing and judging. The authorial audience perceives the characters as external to themselves and as distinct from their implied authors, and the authorial audience passes interpretive and ethical judgments on them, their situations, and their choices.[2] The audience's observer role is what makes the judgment role possible, and the particular judgments are integral to our emotional responses as well as to our desires about future events. In short, just as there is a progression of events there is a progression of audience response to those events, a progression rooted in the twin activities of observing and judging. Thus, from the rhetorical perspective, narrativity involves *the interaction of two kinds of change*: that experienced by the characters and that experienced by the audience in its developing responses to the characters' changes.

To turn from this abstract theorizing to its practical consequences, consider the *relative narrativity* of the following two short narratives.

The Crimson Candle, by James Phelan
A man lying at the point of death said these words to his wife who had been constantly by his side throughout his long illness.
"I am about to say good-bye forever. I hope you know that I love you very much. In my desk you will find a crimson candle, which has been blessed by a High Priest. It

would please me if, wherever you go and whatever you do, you would keep this candle with you as a small reminder of my love." The wife thanked him, assured him that, because she loved him too, she would do as he asked, and, after his death, she kept her word.

The Crimson Candle, by Ambrose Bierce
A man lying at the point of death called his wife to his bedside and said:
"I am about to leave you forever; give me, therefore, one last proof of your affection and fidelity, for, according to our holy religion, a married man seeking admittance at the gate of Heaven is required to swear that he has never defiled himself with an unworthy woman. In my desk you will find a crimson candle, which has been blessed by the High Priest and has a peculiar mystical significance. Swear to me that while it is in existence you will not remarry."
The Woman swore and the Man died. At the funeral the Woman stood at the head of the bier, holding a lighted crimson candle till it was wasted entirely away.

(Bierce 1946)

Both versions of "The Crimson Candle" fit the rhetorical definition of narrative, since both involve a teller and an audience, a progression by instability (each husband seeks the promise, each wife gives it, and each fulfills it in her different way) and a series of developing responses by the audience. But Bierce's version has a higher degree of narrativity. What is striking to me, however, is that this difference is not simply because Bierce's version introduces a more substantial instability and resolves it with more ingenuity. The higher degree of narrativity in Bierce's version is also tied to two more substantial sets of judgments: one set made by the characters and the other set made by the audience. Furthermore, and this is my most basic claim, the set of judgments made by the audience is at least as fundamental to narrativity as the set involving the characters.

In other words, we can't locate the difference between Bierce's version and my version only by pointing to the presence or absence of the progression by instability itself. We get closer to locating the difference by noting that the progression by instability is accompanied by narrative judgments and that those judgments, in turn, significantly affect our emotive, ethical, and aesthetic engagements with the narrative. This point brings me to my second thesis.

Thesis two: readers make three main types of narrative judgment, each of which has the potential to overlap with or affect the other two: interpretive judgments about the nature of actions or other elements of the narrative, ethical judgments about the moral value of characters and actions, and aesthetic judgments about the artistic quality of the narrative and of its parts. This thesis has two corollaries: Corollary 1: a single action may evoke multiple kinds of judgment. Corollary 2: because characters' actions include their judgments, readers often judge characters' judgments.

In Bierce's version of "The Crimson Candle," for example, the man and the woman make different interpretive judgments about the nature of the commitment entailed by the wife's oath, and these interpretive judgments overlap with ethical ones. In fact, their interpretive judgments are about the ethical obligation the wife incurs with her sworn promise. The husband assumes that her promise binds her to remain unmarried indefinitely. The wife finds a loophole in the language, one that allows her to fulfill the letter of the promise at the funeral and then be liberated from it. We readers need to make an interpretive judgment about the characters' judgments; we need, that is, to decide about the validity of the wife's interpretation of her oath.

Not surprisingly, since the characters' interpretive judgments overlap with ethical judgments, the audience's judgments are also overlapping. Indeed, it is possible that the force of one judgment will determine the other. If, for example, we say that the wife has found a valid loophole in her promise, we may also be inclined to say that it is an ethically just fulfillment of that promise. And the other way around. Similarly, if we say that the wife's interpretive judgment is not valid, we may also be inclined to say that she is guilty of breaking her promise. And, once again, the other way around. However, since it is also possible to separate the legal and the ethical, we may separate the interpretive and the ethical judgments at least to some extent: we may decide that the wife's interpretive judgment is not valid because she knew that her husband would not regard her burning the candle at the funeral as a fulfillment of her promise. But we may also make a positive ethical judgment of her action because we see it as an appropriate response to the husband's ethically deficient action of insisting on her promise.

The decisions we make about these ethical questions will have consequences for our aesthetic judgments. Indeed, a large part of the difference in the aesthetic quality of Bierce's version of "The Crimson Candle" and my version of it stems from the relative blandness of the ethical judgments in my version when compared with Bierce's version. More generally, the question of which set of interpretive and ethical judgments we should make in Bierce's version takes me to my third thesis.

Thesis three: individual narratives explicitly or more often implicitly establish their own ethical standards in order to guide their audiences to particular ethical judgments. Consequently, within rhetorical ethics, narrative judgments proceed from the inside out rather than the outside in. It is for this reason they are closely tied to aesthetic judgments. The rhetorical theorist, in other words, does not do ethical criticism by applying a pre-existing ethical system to the narrative, however much he or she may admire the ethics elaborated by Aristotle, Kant, Levinas, or any other thinker; instead the rhetorical theorist seeks to reconstruct the ethical principles upon which the narrative is built. To be sure, the rhetorical theorist does bring values to the text, but he or she remains open to having those values challenged and even repudiated by the experience of reading.

Bierce reveals his ethical principles through his stylistic choices, his use of the narrator, and his management of the progression. The stylistic choices reveal that the man acts in violation of such basic values as love, generosity, and justice, as a comparison of his speech with that of the corresponding character in my version of the story indicates. To take just one prominent contrast, Bierce's character does not make requests; he issues commands: he "calls" his wife to his bedside and delivers a series of additional imperatives: "give me one last proof"; "swear that you will not remarry." The ethical subtext of his speech, which is also evident in the patriarchal religious "principle" he cites, is "because I am your superior and my fate matters more, you should do what I command regardless of the personal consequences for you." All of these elements of the language are reinforced by the inescapable phallic symbolism of the crimson candle. Consequently, we make – tacitly and automatically – a negative ethical judgment of him.

Bierce manages the progression so that we make no significant interpretive or ethical judgments of the woman until the last sentence, when the narrator's simple description prompts not only the unexpected resolution of the instability but also our simultaneous interpretive and ethical judgments of her and our aesthetic judgment of the whole. When we read, "The Woman stood at the head of the bier, holding a lighted crimson candle till it was wasted entirely away," we simultaneously recognize and endorse her unexpected interpretive and ethical judgment of her promise. The simultaneity of these responses gives the ending its kick and contributes substantially to our positive aesthetic judgment of the story. To put the point another way, given our ethical judgments about the husband, we approve of both the wife's insight and her values in finding the loophole and acting upon that finding so swiftly and dramatically. We may or may not decide that the loophole is technically valid – that is, whether she is fulfilling the promise in a legalistic sense or simply manipulating it for her own ends – but our negative ethical judgment of the husband allows us to leave this question open without detracting from the effect of the story.

The woman's acting out her release from the promise during the husband's funeral is also a telling commentary on her view of this promise and, we are invited to extrapolate, of the marriage itself. Indeed, the inferences packed into the final sentence are so many that we can't help moving from the wife's manipulation of the promise back to Bierce's management of the narrative. And that move brings me to thesis four.

Thesis four: ethical judgments in narrative include not only the ones we make about the characters and their actions but also those we make about the ethics of storytelling itself, especially the ethics of the implied author's relation to the narrator, the characters, and the audience.

Let's start with Bierce's relation to the narrator. While narrators typically serve three main functions – reporting, interpreting, and evaluating (see Phelan 2005) – Bierce restricts his narrator to the single function of reporting, and relies on his audience's being able to infer interpretations and evaluations through the progression and the style. As the sudden flurry of inferences surrounding the last sentence indicate, the technique is at once straightforward – the narrator is a reliable and efficient reporter – and coy: the narrator neither prepares us for the wife's maneuver nor gives us any inside view of her. This technique of restricted narration has consequences for Bierce's ethical relation to his characters and to his audience. He lets the characters speak and act for themselves, and he assumes that, through our inferential activity, we can stand with him and take satisfaction in the interpretive and ethical dimensions of his narrative. Identifying this assumption brings me to thesis five.

Thesis five: individual readers need to evaluate the ethical standards of individual narratives, and they are likely to do so in different ways.

Bierce's handling of the characterization and the progression, with its emphasis on the husband's selfishness and the wife's brilliant manipulation of her promise, may receive total approval of some readers while it may make others uneasy about the way Bierce treats the husband. For these readers, including me, the issue is not that Bierce may be unfair to his own creation but rather that he delights in exposing the husband's ultimate futility. This delight borders on a gleeful embrace of the impotence conferred by death that I find emotionally chilling and ethically deficient. And this point takes me to thesis six.

Thesis six: individual readers' ethical judgments are inextricably connected to their aesthetic judgments.

We have already seen how the interpretive, ethical, and aesthetic judgments to which Bierce guides us overlap – and reinforce each other – in the ending of his tale. But I want to emphasize that ethical judgments we make about storytelling have consequences for our aesthetic judgments and vice versa – even as the two kinds of judgment remain distinct. In my overall response to "The Crimson Candle," I find that my ethical judgment about Bierce's pleasure in the husband's futility detracts from my otherwise positive aesthetic judgment of the narrative. Similarly, aesthetic judgments can have consequences for ethical ones. If, for example, Bierce had employed an intrusive narrator who imposed explicit ethical judgments on the characters, he would not only have introduced an aesthetic flaw that reduced our pleasure in inferring those judgments but that flaw would also lead to a negative judgment about the ethics of his telling, since the technique would communicate his distrust of his audience.

Judgment in McEwan's *Atonement*: Briony's Misidentification

I start with the role of judgment in the representation of the transgression, Briony Tallis's misidentification of Robbie Turner as the man who raped her cousin Lola. I will look first at the judgments we make when we assume that Part One is only McEwan's novel and then at how those judgments get modified – if at all – once we learn that Part One is also Briony's novel.[3] Much of Part One of the novel is devoted to providing the context for the transgression through its careful recounting of the remarkable convergence of characters, circumstances, and events on the hot June day in 1935 when Briony's misidentification occurred. There are four sets of characters who come together on this day: Briony; her sister Cecilia and Robbie, who is the son of the Tallis's charwoman, and who, like Cecilia, has just graduated from Cambridge; Lola and her younger brothers, Jackson and Pierrot, who are at the Tallis estate because their parents' marriage is falling apart; and Paul Marshall, a friend of Briony and Cecilia's older brother, Leon. Marshall remains in the background in Part One as the narrative focuses primarily on Briony and secondarily on Cecilia and Robbie, though at dinner Robbie notices a two-inch scratch on Marshall's face, shortly after Lola has shown Briony scratches and bruises of her own.

Briony at age 13 is on the cusp between childhood and adolescence; she has written her first play, *The Trials of Arabella*, a romantic tale in which the eponymous heroine overcomes many hardships and eventually marries a prince, but Briony's hopes for a grand performance of it by her cousins and herself are dashed by the nonromantic realities of everyday life. Cecilia and Robbie discover that they have been repressing their mutual love and sexual desire after Robbie inadvertently gives Cecilia the wrong draft of a note, one containing the spontaneous overflow of his powerful feelings: "In my dreams I kiss your cunt, your sweet wet cunt. In my thoughts I make love to you all day long" (McEwan 2001: 80). What's more, Robbie asks Briony to deliver the note, and she reads it before passing it on; a little later, Briony interrupts Cecilia and Robbie in the library where they are on the verge of consummating their newly discovered love.

Briony, in an effort to ingratiate herself with her 15-year-old cousin, tells Lola about Robbie's note and then deems Lola's description of him as a "maniac" to be apt. Jackson and Pierrot, the nine-year-old twins, struggle so much in their new environment that during dinner they decide to run away, though they leave a note explaining their plans. It is during the ensuing search for them that Lola is assaulted. Briony comes upon Lola and her assailant in the dark and sees only his retreating shape, yet she makes the interpretive judgment that the shape is Robbie's. McEwan's representation of this judgment and the reasons that Briony holds fast to it are worth a longer look.

> Briony was there to help [Lola] at every stage. As far as she was concerned, everything fitted; the terrible present fulfilled the recent past. Events she herself witnessed foretold her cousin's calamity. If only she, Briony, had been less innocent, less stupid. Now she saw, the affair was too consistent, too symmetrical to be anything other than what she said it was. She blamed herself for her childish assumption that Robbie would limit his attentions to Cecilia. What was she thinking of? He was a maniac after all.
>
> (McEwan 2001: 158)

Strikingly, this passage details not just the interaction of Briony's interpretive, ethical, and aesthetic judgments, but the way her interpretive judgment is overrun by her ethical and aesthetic judgments. Briony is certain that the figure she saw retreating from the scene had to be Robbie not because she has ocular proof but because that interpretation fits the narrative she is scripting on the basis of her earlier encounters with Robbie. And that narrative fit is a consequence of her ethical judgments: any one who could write that sentence in the letter to Cecilia must be a "maniac," and, hence, Lola's rapist.

McEwan, however, clearly signals that each of these judgments is erroneous. Through several scenes dominated by the technique of internal focalization, McEwan presents Robbie as an admirable young man; what's more, McEwan shows that his letter to Cecilia functions to break through his and Cecilia's repressions and take them to a state of passionate love. Without the linchpin of Briony's ethical judgment, her aesthetic and interpretive judgments fall apart – though it is not until Part Three that we learn that the scratches and bruises on Lola and Marshall were from a preliminary skirmish in the house before he found her in the dark.

Although Briony's misjudgments of Robbie have the potential to be the basis of our strongly negative ethical judgment of her, McEwan carefully guides us to a more complex response, one that continues to underline her errors while also mitigating our judgment of them. On a macro level, McEwan relies on the careful tracing of the convergence of the different characters and events to show how Briony's transgression was overdetermined; on a micro level, he shows how difficult it was for Briony to change her narrative once she had articulated it.

> As early as the week that followed, the glazed surface of conviction was not without its blemishes and hairline cracks. Whenever she was conscious of them, which was not often, she was driven back, with a little swooping sensation in her stomach, to the understanding that what she knew was not literally, or not only, based on the visible. It was not simply her eyes that told her the truth. It was too dark for that.... Her eyes confirmed the sum of all she knew and had recently experienced. The truth was in the symmetry, which was to say, it was founded in common sense. The truth instructed her eyes. So when she said, over and over again, I saw him, she meant it, and was perfectly honest, as well as passionate. What she meant was rather more complex than what everyone else so eagerly understood, and her moments of unease came when she felt that she could not express these nuances. She did not even seriously try. There were no opportunities, no time, no permission. Within a couple of days, no, within a matter of hours, a process was moving fast and well beyond her control.
>
> (McEwan 2001: 158–9)

While this passage once again emphasizes her error ("It was not simply her eyes that told her the truth. It was too dark for that"), it also emphasizes how deeply she believes in her judgments ("she...was perfectly honest, as well as passionate") and how, once she'd spoken, it was impossible to qualify or otherwise add nuance to her testimony: "what she meant was rather more complex than what everyone so eagerly understood," but "there were no opportunities, no time, no permission" for her to express those complexities. Consequently, McEwan is asking us to understand and even be sympathetic toward Briony's misjudgments, even as he leaves no doubt that they are egregiously erroneous and likely to have major negative consequences for Cecilia and Robbie. Furthermore, this handling of our ethical judgments raises the aesthetic and ethical stakes of the novel: how will McEwan work through the difference between Briony's intentions (and his mitigation of our negative ethical judgment) and the terrible practical consequences of her misjudgment?

Once we learn that Part One is part of Briony's novel, we do not need to alter these judgments but rather add another layer to them. First, we see that the adult Briony has made a number of interpretive judgments that she was unable to make as a child, judgments that get expressed through her vivid representation of the inner lives of the other principal characters, particularly Cecilia and Robbie. This element of Briony's narrative also informs our aesthetic judgment of its quality: she is a novelist well in command of the techniques of modernist fiction, especially its many modes for representing consciousness. And by guiding us toward this aesthetic judgment of Briony's novel, McEwan helps guide us toward a more difficult ethical judgment of her self-representation. It is one thing to regard McEwan's mitigation of Briony's blameworthiness as a positive feature of the narrative, quite another to make that same judgment about Briony's own representation of her behavior, since as novelist she clearly has a conflict of interest. Nevertheless, because her narrative so sympathetically enters into the consciousnesses of the other characters, and because she so clearly signals how deficient her judgments were, McEwan invites us to admire her now clear-eyed reconstruction of what she later calls her "crime."

Judgments of Briony's Effort to Atone

More complex questions of judgment arise from the surprise disclosures of the novel's final section, "London, 1999," especially that we have been reading a novel within a novel and that Briony's novel has seamlessly combined the historical events of Part One with her mixtures of fact and invention in Parts Two and Three. Part Two tells the story of Robbie Turner's experiences as a British soldier involved in the retreat to Dunkirk (he becomes a soldier in order to be released from prison) in late May and early June of 1940. Part Three tells the story of Briony's work as a nurse during the war (an indirect effort at making amends) and of her pledge to Cecilia and Robbie shortly after the retreat to atone for her crime by making a full confession. Briony's 1999 diary entry, however, reveals that Robbie and Cecilia are never reunited, that he dies during the retreat and that she dies a few months later when a German bomb blows up the Balham Underground station in London. Consequently, we are faced with the discrepancy between Briony's novelistic invention of being on the verge of some atonement and her actual inability to atone. We are also faced with the discovery that McEwan has asked us to invest our emotions and desires in Briony's quest for an atonement that he and she both knew in their different ways was impossible.

In her diary entry, Briony explains that, though she did her first draft of the novel in 1940, it is only in her final draft that she decided to alter history – to make, in effect, another judgment that is simultaneously interpretive, ethical, and aesthetic. More precisely, she explains her interpretive judgment to alter the historical record as a consequence of her aesthetic and ethical judgments. No one would want to believe the historical facts, she writes, except in "the service of the bleakest realism," and she decided it was important that her novel provide some "sense of hope or satisfaction"

(McEwan 2001: 350). Furthermore, "I like to think that it isn't weakness or evasion, but a final act of kindness, a stand against oblivion and despair, to let my lovers live and to unite them at the end. I gave them happiness, but I was not so self-serving as to let them forgive me" (p. 351).

But Briony also realizes that her alteration of history for these reasons has consequences for her relation to her original purpose for writing the novel: to use the power of narrative itself as a way to atone for her crime.

> The problem these fifty-nine years has been this: how can a novelist achieve atonement when, with her absolute power of deciding outcomes, she is also God? There is no one, no entity or higher form that she can appeal to, or be reconciled with, or that can forgive her. There is nothing outside her. In her imagination she has set the limits and the terms. No atonement for God, or novelists, even if they are atheists. It was always an impossible task and that was precisely the point. The attempt was all.
>
> (McEwan 2001: 350–1)

To paraphrase, the novelist's power is also her limitation: since Briony's writing brings into being the novel's world, including both the crime and its aftermath, her decisions about the fates of her characters, whether they conform to history or not, cannot atone for what she has done to real people. There is no one external to the fiction who can serve as judge of whether her effort is sufficient to achieve atonement. Nevertheless, Briony thinks, the effort to seek the atonement is necessary, since attempting the impossible demonstrates the sincerity and depth of her desire to atone. This conclusion allows Briony, 64 years after the original crime, to come to terms with the impossibility of atoning for it, with the necessity of her 59-year effort, and with its result.

But Briony's judgments here exist within the frame of McEwan's novel, and that frame leads us to assess her judgments as inadequate – indeed, almost as inadequate as the judgments she made at the age of 13. Briony's diary entry includes a description of the Tallis family's present to her on her 77th birthday: a performance of *The Trials of Arabella* by the younger generation. The entry quotes the final couplet Arabella and her prince address to the audience:

> Here's the beginning of love at the end of our travail.
> So farewell, kind friends, as into the sunset we sail!
> (McEwan 2001: 348)

More than simply rounding off the novel, this return by McEwan to 13-year-old Briony's romance implicitly comments on the romantic impulses governing her novel. It ends with the "continuation of love" for Robbie and Cecilia at the end of their travail and with the possibility of Briony's atonement. Briony's question, "who would want to believe that [Cecilia and Robbie never reunited] except in the service of the bleakest realism?" reminds McEwan's audience that her romantic impulses fueled her misidentification of Robbie. Had she been more interested in realism then, she would have required far more evidence before fingering Robbie. Had she been more interested in realism here, she would have followed through on revealing the grim consequences of her transgression. Her failure to do that, in a sense, is to turn away from her quest to atone.

McEwan also signals the inadequacy of Briony's judgments through her commentary about Lola and Paul Marshall. In Part Three, we learn that although Marshall was, in fact, Lola's assailant, she "saved herself from humiliation by falling in love, or persuading herself she had, and [she] could not believe her luck when Briony insisted on doing the talking and blaming. And what luck that was for Lola – barely more than a child, prized open and taken – to marry her rapist" (p. 306). In the final section, we learn that Lola and Paul have become Lord and Lady Marshall and have enjoyed living in the luxury made possible by the success of his candy company.[4] Briony reflects:

> There was our crime – Lola's, Marshall's, mine – and from the second version [of my novel] I set out to describe it. I've regarded it as my duty to disguise nothing – the names, the places, the exact circumstances – I put it all there as a matter of historical record. But as a matter of legal reality, so various editors have told me over the years, my forensic memoir could never be published while my fellow criminals were alive. You may only libel yourself and the dead. The Marshalls have been active in the courts since the late forties, defending their good names with a most expensive ferocity.... To be safe, one would have to be bland and obscure. I know I cannot publish until they are dead. And as of this morning I accept that will not be until I am.
>
> (McEwan 2001: 349)

Briony's reflections, however, actually call attention to the fact that her long delay in finishing her novel has also been a way to avoid taking the one concrete step toward atonement available to her: the public admission of her crime – not in a novel but in some nonfictional form, including letters to all who were present at the Tallis estate in June 1935 – and the effort to clear Robbie's name. Her reflections show how difficult and uncertain that step would be, since the Marshalls would obviously deny Briony's account and even sue for libel, but, in failing to take it, Briony perpetuates her crime against Robbie. In sum, looked at within the frame of McEwan's novel, the best we can say about Briony's efforts to atone through her novel are much like her efforts during the transgression: her intentions are good but her execution leaves a lot to be desired. (It is also possible to judge her even more harshly, as seeking the pleasure of having atoned without having done so.) These conclusions invite us to reflect on McEwan's purpose in framing Briony's judgments this way, reflections that are part and parcel of the judgments we make about his larger construction of the novel.

Judgments of McEwan's Misidentification

McEwan's delayed disclosure that Parts One, Two, and Three are Briony's novel and that her novel combines fact and fiction pulls the rug out from under many of our previous judgments and especially many of our emotional investments during Parts

Two and Three. Many of our judgments, we suddenly learn, have been misguided because we based them on misinformation. The satisfaction we took in the reunion of Cecilia and Robbie after the horrific retreat and in Briony's promise to recant her testimony about Robbie are significantly altered because we suddenly learn that these events, as part of Briony's novel but not part of her life, exist on a different ontological level than her transgression. In this respect, McEwan's delayed disclosure is analogous to Briony's misidentification of Robbie: since we have no signal that Parts One, Two, and Three are Briony's novel, he has implicitly misidentified the nature of his narrative up until this point. To be sure, McEwan is aware – and expects his authorial audience to be aware – of the significant difference between the consequences of the two misidentifications. Nevertheless, when Briony finally decides in her diary entry that her effort at atonement via narrative has been both impossible and necessary, we need to ask whether McEwan is speaking directly through her about his own narrative as well, since that narrative both involves its own transgression and explores the possibility of atonement.

Briony writes, "[H]ow can a novelist achieve atonement when, with her absolute power of deciding outcomes, she is also God? There is no one, no entity or higher form that she can appeal to, or be reconciled with, or that can forgive her. . . . No atonement for God or novelists, even if they are atheists." Seen within the frame of McEwan's novel, these comments have significantly different implications than Briony could possibly be aware of. First, they invite us to add another layer to our understanding of the novel's central concerns: what is the relation between art and atonement? Second, they raise some more specific questions: (1) the delayed disclosure is an instance of McEwan's playing God, his using his novelist's absolute power not only to decide the outcome but to reveal that decision suddenly and, from the perspective of our emotional engagement in Briony's novel, violently. After playing God this way, does McEwan need to atone and, if so, how can he? (2) There is an entity to which McEwan can appeal for atonement and forgiveness: the audience that he has misled. Has McEwan also included some grounds upon which we can achieve reconciliation? Has he has ultimately "set the limits and the terms" of the novel in such a way that his transgression also carries within it the seeds of his atonement? (3) Finally, what light does this dynamic between transgression and atonement in the telling shed on the similar dynamic in the represented action?

The first two questions come together in our interpretive and aesthetic judgments about the relation between the surprise disclosure and the previous three Parts of *Atonement*. Effective surprises are ones in which the audience begins by being taken aback and ends by nodding their heads as a result of recognizing that the surprise has been prepared for (see Phelan 2004). Preparing the audience of *Atonement* is an especially delicate operation because the terms and limits of the novel stipulate that McEwan must write Parts One, Two, and Three as Briony's novel, and Briony of course has no conception that she is a character in McEwan's novel and thus no conception of McEwan's audience. McEwan carries out the operation in two main ways: (1) he includes in Briony's representation of the events details that, when seen retrospectively, function as clues to her introduction of fictionalizing elements; (2) he includes in Briony's novel meta-level communications about its modernist techniques, communications that function for Briony as elements in the story of her evolution as a writer but function for McEwan as a way to establish a tension about the techniques of Briony's novel – and by extension of his own.

The main clues in the representation of events occur in Parts Two and Three. At the end of Part Two, Robbie, though close to being evacuated from France to Britain, is wounded, exhausted, and only intermittently aware of his environment. Furthermore, his last utterance – and the final sentence of Part Two – is "I promise, you won't hear another word from me" (p. 250). In short, this section of the novel ends without McEwan's audience being able to determine whether Robbie gets evacuated or dies. Part Three appears to disambiguate that ending by showing Robbie reunited with Cecilia. But in retrospect we can see that the end of Part Two is a subtle preparation for the revelation that Robbie did not survive the retreat. This conclusion is reinforced by a passage in Part Three that, in retrospect, we can understand as functioning for both Briony and McEwan as marking the seam between history and fiction.

> [Briony] left the café, and as she walked along the Common she felt the distance widen between her and another self, no less real, who was walking back toward the hospital. Perhaps the Briony who was walking in the direction of Balham was the imagined or ghostly persona. This unreal feeling was heightened when, after half an hour, she reached another High Street, more or less the same as the one she had left behind.
>
> (McEwan 2001: 311)

In other words, the historical Briony returns to the hospital while her ghostly persona continues her wish-fulfilling journey to Cecilia and Robbie.

Turning to McEwan's meta-level communications, we find the most dramatic example in McEwan's inclusion of a response from Cyril Connolly to Briony's submission to *Horizon* of an early version of a section of Part One: Connolly finds that it "owed a little too much to the techniques of Mrs. Woolf" (p. 294) and that "its static quality does not serve [Briony's] evident talent well" (p. 295). Although Briony revises in light of these comments, they function for McEwan as a way to raise questions about *Atonement*'s own extensive use of modernist technique. The tension generated by McEwan's meta-level communication can be put this way: what does it mean for an accomplished novelist writing in 2001 to construct a novel along modernist lines and simultaneously question such a construction? The surprise ending resolves the tension even as it provides an appropriate surprise: the accomplished novelist has been writing not a straight modernist novel in Briony's mode but a more self-conscious, self-reflexive, novel. In its self-reflexiveness, McEwan's surprise ending acknowledges *Atonement*'s postmodern moment, but, more important, it gives new weight to the elements of Parts One, Two, and Three that comment on Briony's evolution as a writer and new weight to the novel's theme of the relation between art and experience.

Turning to the relation between transgression and atonement in the represented action and in the telling, we can now recognize that McEwan's undercutting of our emotions through the delayed disclosure of Briony's diary entry is a strategy by which to engage with the problem of atonement even more deeply. The meta-message of McEwan's misidentification of our reading experience is that our emotional trajectory through the problem of the crime and its atonement, however intense and difficult, has been too easy: in retrospect, we must admit that we were too ready to believe that Robbie survived the retreat, that Briony's meeting with Robbie and Cecilia would lead to some atonement. McEwan's framing of Briony the novelist's judgments as severely inadequate reinforces this message. By encouraging our mimetic involvement in Parts One, Two, and Three, and then pulling the rug out from under that engagement in the final section, McEwan not only juxtaposes the hope held out by Briony's novel to "the bleakest realism," but he also makes us feel that bleakness.

Consequently, though our interpretive judgments of McEwan's strategies lead us to judge McEwan's misidentification as one for which he successfully atones both aesthetically and ethically, those strategies also heighten the contrast between his transgression and atonement and Briony's. His remain entirely within the boundaries of art; hers is an attempt to do in art what she failed to do in life. The meta-message is that, though art can carry out its own patterns of transgression and atonement, it cannot – and should not be expected to – atone for transgressions that occur beyond its boundaries.

Not surprisingly, these conclusions – both McEwan's and mine – are highly contestable. Some readers of *Atonement* will, I am sure, find that I have let McEwan off the hook too easily, that his atonement for the misidentification of our reading experience is insufficient, and, thus, their ethical judgment of his performance will ultimately be negative. Other readers will contest the idea that one can draw the boundary between art and life as neatly as McEwan's novel – or at least my account of it – does. Indeed, the layers of fiction in the novel – Briony's fiction existing within McEwan's fiction – open up another layer to the dialogue between art and atonement: since Briony, Robbie, and Cecilia are inescapably fictional, the dynamic of transgression and atonement among them is finally less important than that between McEwan and his readers. But such contestations, when carefully argued, are to be welcomed rather than turned away. Both McEwan's novel and the rhetorical approach to narrative judgment welcome the debates that follow from them. If this essay sets out an analysis of narrative judgments in *Atonement* that others deem worth contesting, I will judge it as an interpretive success. More generally, if this essay has such a result, it will implicitly support my larger case for the centrality of narrative judgment, and I will judge it as a theoretical success.

NOTES

1   Although I have not seen anyone formulate the significance of judgment as I propose to do here, other theorists of narrative form influenced by Aristotle and the neo-Aristotelians have influenced these proposals. See especially Booth ([1961] 1983), Sacks (1964), Olson (1976), and Battersby (2002).

2   The narrative audience typically makes such judgments as well, but the authorial audience's role is more crucial to the rhetorical understanding of narrativity.

3   For a complementary approach to the issue of how a late revelation of embedding provides a new frame for our understanding of a narrative, see Emma Kafalenos's chapter in this volume.

4   Peter J. Rabinowitz's chapter in this volume leads me to believe that a careful examination of the paths of Lola and Marshall would add a valuable dimension to our understanding of McEwan's construction of his novel.

REFERENCES AND FURTHER READING

Battersby, J. L. (2002). *Unorthodox Views: Reflections on Reality, Truth, and Meaning in Current Social, Cultural, and Critical Discourse*. Westport, CT: Greenwood Press.

Bierce, A. (1946). "The Crimson Candle." In *The Collected Writings of Ambrose Bierce* (p. 543). New York: The Citadel Press.

Booth, W. C. ([1961] 1983). *The Rhetoric of Fiction*, 2nd edn. Chicago: University of Chicago Press.

McEwan, I. (2001). *Atonement*. New York: Doubleday.

Olson, E. (1976). *On Value Judgments in the Arts and Other Essays*. Chicago: University of Chicago Press.

Phelan, J. (1989). *Reading People, Reading Plots: Character, Progression, and the Interpretation of Narrative*. Chicago: University of Chicago Press.

Phelan, J. (2004). "Narrative as Rhetoric and Edith Wharton's 'Roman Fever': Progression, Configuration, and the Ethics of Surprise." In W. Jost and W. Olmsted (eds.), *A Companion to Rhetoric and Rhetorical Criticism* (pp. 340–55). Oxford: Blackwell.

Phelan, J. (2005). *Living to Tell about It: A Rhetoric and Ethics of Character Narration*. Ithaca, NY: Cornell University Press.

Sacks, S. (1964). *Fiction and the Shape of Belief*. Berkeley: University of California Press.

22

The Changing Faces of Mount Rushmore: Collective Portraiture and Participatory National Heritage

Alison Booth

On October 21, 2003, I happened to turn on the cable TV channel C-Span around 5:30 in the afternoon, and encountered Mike Pence, Republican Congressman from Indiana, addressing the camera in an empty chamber on behalf of the bill to ban so-called partial birth abortion. My attention was riveted when he began an excursion into biographical history by way of an anecdote. He asked his audience to imagine that he took a short stroll, between congressional duties, through the National Statuary Hall into the Rotunda of the Capitol in Washington, DC, where he stopped to admire a statue honoring three great women of American history (Figure 22.1). I can imagine it: passing the *Portrait Monument to Lucretia Mott, Elizabeth Cady Stanton, and Susan B. Anthony,* Pence leaned forward to read the names that identify the women represented by those carved heads and shoulders, looked again at the distinctive personalities sculpted there, reflected on what little he or most of us would recall about why they were remembered in history, and sent a staff member to research their lives. Names and faces may be effective mnemonics in the public eye, but life narratives usually are needed to keep the record alive.

Pence did his part in the exchange begun by the sculptor, Adelaide Johnson: he received the exemplary impression of these early feminist leaders and passed it on. On camera, he delivered short eulogies of Anthony (1820–1906) and Stanton (1815–1902). He made no reference to the prominent figure in the foreground, Lucretia Mott (1793–1880), perhaps because this leader of an earlier generation is less renowned today, or because Mott's Quaker abolitionism still rankles among the largely-Southern Christian right. As readers of honor rolls or visitors to pantheons often do, Pence not only willed one person out of the picture but also added another: he told the story of Alice Paul and her campaign for the Equal Rights Amendment (which Pence admitted he would have voted against). Each of these heroines was a

Figure 22.1 Portrait Monument to Lucretia Mott, Elizabeth Cady Stanton, and Susan B. Anthony, Architect of the Capitol.

champion of the rights of women, and according to Pence's logic each was therefore also "prolife."

Pence's speech followed an ancient narrative form, the collection of worthies, in which names, faces, and narratives combine to represent a national heritage. Nationhood as "imagined community" constructs its ancestry in the form of selected group portraiture (Anderson 1991, Booth 2004a, 2004b). What such collections omit or belie is as important as what they figure. In Joseph Roach's terms, collective representations require a "process of surrogation" or deletion and substitution of subjects, a "doomed search for originals by continuously auditioning stand-ins" who will perform community (Roach 1996: 2–3). The selection and replacement of representatives may, in modern societies, adopt the procedures of democratic elections or free markets, though the process remains kin to ritual sacrifice. Representations of the chosen, moreover, expose a gap between the framing interpretation – a published volume, a monument, a presentation or display in the media – and the variegated detail of the chosen personalities and their lives, much as Pence's invocation of "prolife" foremothers conflicted with the antipatriarchal activism of Anthony, Paul, Mott, and Stanton. Pence also followed convention in making anachronistic claims of unity and allegiance, both among the represented figures and between that cohort and the present observer.

The hot-button issues and historical blunders of Pence's speech engage me less here than its demonstration of the uses of visual and verbal portraiture in prosopography, or collective biographical history. His citation of that triple statue in the Rotunda also nicely illustrates the way that dominant collections of personified heritage are under perpetual revision, demanding supplements. The US Capitol, I have argued, is a monumental collection of life-narratives concentrated in the friezes, paintings, and sculptures (Booth 2004a: 15–16). Pence may not know that his heroines almost went missing from the pantheon. Three of Adelaide Johnson's separate busts of women from the World's Columbian Exposition of 1893 were compiled and unveiled on Susan B. Anthony's birthday in 1921 (Weimann 1981: 289–94), but until this three-headed monument was lifted from the Capitol crypt in 1997 there were no named historical women featured prominently in the Rotunda other than Pocahontas.[1] Pence, however hostile to feminism post-Roe v. Wade, evidently approves of the feminist practice of recovery.

In one illuminating moment, the congressman praised the marble statue of three women as a "miniature version of Mount Rushmore." The Mount Rushmore National Memorial in Keystone, SD (Figure 22.2) was formed by Gutzon Borglum and nearly 400 workers between 1927 and 1941, almost entirely with federal funding. (It is unlikely that Pence knew of legislation proposed in 1937 to add Susan B. Anthony to Mount Rushmore [Taliaferro 2002: 312–18].) Like viewers of the Rotunda portrait monument, visitors to the full-scale memorial reiterate the names associated with magnified models of famous heads, and presumably feel admonished to recall the heroic lives of the originals as well as the shared history formed by placing this selection together. Pence's TV audience lacked the visual cues, but had to draw on their memories of the personified rockface, so indelible from travel ads, postage stamps, political photo opportunities, and Hitchcock's Cold War allegory, *North by Northwest*. The monstrous cluster of heads has come to seem a providential design as old as those hills.[2] But of course the site is on shaky ground, with its selection of these four presidents as protagonists of the narrative of manifest destiny, its fusion of sacred iconography and ecological violence, and its suppression of the histories of the displaced peoples and laborers who made the presidential vision possible. Similar ideological trouble disturbs Johnson's statue, the Rotunda and the Capitol's iconography as a whole (Fryd 1992: 1, 177), and indeed collective biographical representation in general. The series of iconic subjects as surrogates for a narrative of national heritage is so familiar as to go unremarked, but it warrants careful examination.

How does collective portraiture commemorate a national heritage? What are some of the conventions of representation of historical persons in groups? What are the interdependent functions of the name, the face or bodily image, and the verbal

Figure 22.2 Mount Rushmore.

narrative? I will address these and related questions through instances of competition to supplement monumental biographical collections, from Mount Rushmore to canons of great writers to the first Hall of Fame. In each instance, commercialism and civic self-improvement conjoin, as members of the audience are interpellated or inducted into their roles as voting citizens, tourists, or buyers of books. Not all prosopographies actually conduct opinion polls, as these do, to select new surrogates in the series. A memorial or biographical tradition always conveys a sense of both preserved presence and conspicuous lacunae. Similarly the representation, whether in words, images, or a combination, both appears to recapture the person alive and inevitably fails to do so. Thus, the representations simultaneously confirm the ineffable absence of that desired being, and urge you to revisit the sites – and vote – to fill that void.

Inquiring into the association of biography and portraiture, I propose neither a new theory of visual narrative (Heehs 1995: 211–14) nor another history of the sister arts. The correspondence between poetry and painting has been debated since before Horace pronounced "*ut pictura poesis*" (often translated "as a painting, so also a poem," Mitchell 1986: 43). Even the relation between life-narrative and portraiture, a special instance of this word–image, temporal–spatial intercourse, would elude a definitive theory (Wendorf 1983: 98–9, Piper 1982, Adams 2000). I will explore the conventions of prosopography – the verbal–visual mode of collective biographical history – by way of examples of exemplification. It should be clear from the conservative use that Pence made of the sole feminist intervention in the Rotunda that such forms of representation may support mainstream or tributary constituencies and interests. They have persisted in all eras of literate culture, carrying different ideological freight in different contexts. Biographical or "particular" history, the kind of catalog that I call prosopography, has been a recognized counterpart to "universal" or political history since Plutarch, and was revived in seventeenth-century France to honor galleries of authors rather than royalty (Stedman 2000: 130–1). Commentators on life-writing usually note its memorial and civic functions (Wendorf 1990: 10), its origins in panegyric and hagiography, but rarely note the customary presentation of exemplary personae in series or groups.

Prosopography

Mount Rushmore is a fitting emblem of prosopography as I define it. I favor the term over alternatives, multibiography or collective biography, because its etymology encodes both the persona and the rhetoric of mourning, while at the same time signaling multiplicity rather than individual life narrative. *Prosopon*, persona or mask, suggests an ancient association of the self with the face (Aird 1996, Le Guin 1983: 338–9), or of personhood with the appearance of the perceiving head in lieu of the remainder of the body. Face-to-face encounter with the difference of the other person is arguably fundamental to subjectivity, as the Lacanian concept of the Mirror Stage suggests.[3] Language is said to arise as the infant experiences the absence of the desired object, the need for the word to represent or perform the object's return. Psychoanalytic accounts tend to imagine this fall into the Symbolic Order as a one-on-one face-off with the perceived other – *"I"* am *"not-You"* – and an apostrophe: *"O, Thou, be all-sufficient to me as you once were."*

Related to the concept of such an address to the persona of the other is the rhetorical trope *prosopopoeia*, whereby that persona talks back. That is, prosopopoeia attributes name, voice, face, animation to an absent or dead entity, as though the monument were to come alive, the epitaph to speak. Paul de Man construes prosopopoeia as the trope of lyric and autobiography (de Man 1979: 926), still in the mimetic dyad of self and other. I suggest that biography, which is at least a triad (a third-person narration that presents the subject to the audience), is similarly prosopoetic, similarly naming and reviving ancestral personae or figures for the desired parent. In general, life-narrative should be conceived as a three-way narrative exchange among presenter, subject(s), and audience, in which each position is occupied not by an autonomous individual but by constituencies. I further suggest that social groups multiply such figurations of identity in series of mismatched reanimations. For a nation, a group of founding fathers or mothers may seem to restore our own faces. Thus, uniting the concepts of the *prosopon* and *prosopopoeia*, *prosopography* is an appropriate designation of the sets of personae that represent a nation's history.

The term has been employed for different purposes. At the turn of the twentieth century, eugenic social science and positivist historiography developed interest in the prosopography of elites, from men of genius to members of parliament. Something of the belief in genetically determined leadership animated Gutzon Borglum's design of a monument in the Black Hills to the great men of the young empire. Even today the spirit of Francis Galton's eugenics resurfaces in a prosopographical study, Charles Murray's *Human Accomplishment*, which identifies the 4,002 best artists and scientists of all civilizations by polling encyclopedias (Murray 2003). But the focus on measurable groups of life-histories could be used to challenge prevailing historiography, as Lewis Namier's prosopography of biographical data about sets of men in the ruling elite was an alternative to the history of individual ruler-heroes and wars (Colley 1989: 72–8). The most common use of the term today occurs in classical and medieval studies, as a method of reconstructing populations and social systems by culling large samples of remains in diverse media, including coins and trade marks, ruins, and record books.[4] Lists of names, nameless images of people in anonymous manuscripts, cemeteries – these begin to document segregated groups such as the military or the church.

I would adapt *prosopography* for less specialized use and as a means of interpreting modes and uses of life narratives. In prosopographies, the representation of a national heritage slips from the apotheosis of a single Father into a sequence of representatives, whether in printed collections or in monuments on the scale of Westminster Abbey. Group portraits may form synchronic associations or diachronic genealogies, in monuments or anthologies that emulate a convention in painting, the "conversation piece." In such paintings, the artist would gather depictions of the faces and figures of well-known cultural leaders in an imaginary moment in actual or imaginary surroundings: a "generic rather than historical" symposium that leaves space for the spectator to join in, or to imagine what the voices of ghostly familiars (favorite authors) might say to each other (Brilliant 1991: 98). Prosopography, in short, refers to the many forms of memorial personification that resemble the temporal and spatial structure of a conversation piece.

Mount Rushmore

Mount Rushmore, then, is a prosopography in that it presents a group or series of *personae*, its personae represent a *collective* history, and it serves as a *memorial* that ritually reconstitutes the community. The monument in South Dakota, moreover, shows the primacy of visual portraiture. It would not have served the purpose to carve into the rock the words, "George Washington, Father of Our Country," with a short biography in smaller font. This would certainly have added to the American landscape as national heritage, much as the naming of many towns after Washington has done. A representation of the man's person invites a more compelling veneration, like an effigy that implies the saints' continuing presence even though the bones are buried far away. (Borglum thought the obelisk of the Washington Monument was too abstract and uninformative; the future would forget what it commemorated.) A solitary statue of George Washington might have overcome the arbitrariness of the location, which has no link to the life of any of the presidents, but it would have constituted a shrine to one man, not to democracy. Completed first, the head of Washington alone was dedicated in 1930 (Boag 2003: 42), but in order to tell a national story Mount Rushmore needed to be a prosopography.

Just which prosopography it would be was a matter of continuing negotiation. The origin of the Mount Rushmore project was a proposal in 1923 by South Dakota historian Doane Robinson to carve Native American leaders and other western heroes on a series of local rock formations (American Park Network 2001), partly to attract tourists to the state. When Lorado Taft declined the position as sculptor, Robinson asked Borglum, who insisted that the figures be of national rather than regional significance. Korczak Ziolkowski, a sculptor hired and soon fired from the Rushmore project in 1939, later carved Crazy Horse at another location in the region (American Experience 2002). These facts confirm that the decision to honor a few male leaders from the east was not inevitable, but rather the outcome of Borglum's criteria of national scale and historical significance.[5] Initially, Borglum planned full-length statues of George Washington and Abraham Lincoln, but then he decided to extend the series to include Thomas Jefferson and Theodore Roosevelt, leaders who expanded American dominion through the Louisiana Purchase and the Panama Canal. In 1937, the Congressional proposal to add Susan B. Anthony to Rushmore was defeated when the funding appropriation was restricted to completing the existing plans (American Experience 2002). As the series of four men was confirmed, the figures were reduced to torsos only. In 1941, after Borglum's death, his son Lincoln Borglum declared the monument complete with only the 60-foot heads, omitting the torsos planned on the models. The famous faces of these four presidents, without names, appeared sufficient to compile a narrative of a community.

Yet Borglum had worried that faces would not be enough. On his timeline the pyramids were a recent scheme, and any image of the empire must address many generations hence. Therefore he planned to add narrative to the monument. "You might as well drop a letter in the postal system without an address or signature as to send that carved mountain into the future without identification."[6] The plan was to carve a history of the United States, in 500 words, with three-foot-high lettering: an "Entablature" on the mountain where Lincoln's face now looms. (This text would have been supplemented at the site by a fuller inscription in English, Latin, and Sanskrit, in a strangely antique address to the archeologists of the future, as well as by a Hall of Records containing copies of key documents of American history.) These plans had to be revised because of the fragile quality of the rock where the carving of Jefferson had begun, to the left of Washington; moving Jefferson to the right meant displacing the "Entablature" to the back of the mountain (American Experience 2002). Portraiture took precedence over narrative, in part because it is much easier to arrive at consensus about the likeness of a face than about a written summary of over a century of history.

The contention over the inscription on the mountain ultimately left the monument without words, though possible texts are continually offered. President Calvin Coolidge was originally to write the text, but Borglum disputed Coolidge's version and prompted the Hearst newspapers to run a national contest to select the best synopsis of the nation. None of the more than 100,000 submissions was ever carved due to the lack of funds, though in 1975 the winner in the college category erected his "history" on a plaque near Borglum's studio, by then a museum on the grounds of the park. In 2002, American Experience, a website of PBS and WGBH Boston, ran another contest for children to write a 500-word history appropriate to Mount Rushmore. The National Park Service regularly polls the more than two million visitors who come to Mount Rushmore each year to name the most popular president. Neither contest nor poll promises that citizens (or foreign tourists) can place their marks on the mountain the way Borglum did, but there is a widespread notion that it would be possible to choose – by democratic vote – another face to add to the group that represents US history. (Apparently the eroding mountain would never sustain another personifying assault.)

As of July, 2001, according to the virtual tour of Mount Rushmore on the American Experience site, Ronald Reagan was second to Abraham Lincoln as the favorite president of the visitors polled at the park. Since Reagan's death on June 5, 2004, there has been a flurry of acclamation of the 40th president as the fit fifth man for Rushmore. Some in Congress have also proposed placing Reagan's name and face on a currency denomination (Waller 2004), as Lincoln serves on the penny and the five dollar bill, Jefferson on the nickel and the two dollar bill, and Washington on the quarter and the dollar. I have not heard anyone demanding Teddy Roosevelt's face on any legal tender, though surely Reagan should wait his turn till the last of the Rushmore eminences gets coined. Or perhaps he should let Susan B. Anthony go first. And here again the age-old association of currency with the prosopography of rulers recurs (some of the earliest surviving portraits appear on coins). Of all famous American women, only Susan B. Anthony was minted – on the dollar coin – until she was supplanted by Sacajawea. The process of surrogation has been more severe for women than men. From a portrait monument to the money of the nation is not such a shift in theme; two figures for what is missing on Mount Rushmore trade places on a coin more collected than used.

Biographical Portraiture and Literary Canons

Mount Rushmore is one of many projects of collective portraiture that link commercialism with the progress of national civilization and that enfranchise as well as entertain and instruct. Before I turn to a less renowned monumental project, the first Hall of Fame, I want to consider related traditions of biographical portraiture that further a comparison of visual and verbal representation. In printed as well as monumental prosopographies, the visual portrait may dominate; in some books written words annotate the pictures instead of images illustrating the verbal text. Clearly verbal and visual media have different capacities to represent a person (Wendorf 1983, Le Guin 1983). The painted, sculpted, or photographed portrait imagines one moment in the existence of an embodied human being as though it epitomized an entire character and career; artists are often urged to imitate not only the exterior appearance but also the spirit and intentionality of the person. Prose narrative provides the advantage of extension through time as it forfeits the sense of embodied shape in space. Words may more readily elaborate a subject's family, environment, development, actions and manners, ideas, or even feelings, but that indispensable signal of identity, the face (Wallen 1995: 55, Schoug 2001: 103), is difficult to describe without an obsessive blazon of each feature. Sensing the advantages of each mode of representation, individual and collective biographies almost always include portraits (Wendorf 1983: 106), as though the prose were an ekphrasis of the image and the image were an epitome of thousands of words.

A work of visual art, like a written text, attains the status of a portrait because of the stated intention of the portrait-maker to represent a given original. Although students are often taught to put away as childish things all the data of authorial intention, biography, and accurate mimesis when they interpret belles lettres and fine arts, in biographical portraiture these are the first questions to answer. According to Richard Brilliant, "resemblance" is the subject of a portrait; when the name and identity of the original have been lost, works of art lose the status of portraits (1991: 70, 55). Yet neither the accurate likeness nor the name is truly essential to a portrait. The representation of named persons in paintings, statuary, and manuscripts or books long predates the aim of "faithful imitation of external appearances" (Piper 1982: 2, 11). And peculiar faces of individuals, nameless to us, appear in some classical statuary before Donatello is said to have invented the portrait bust (Brilliant 1991: 127). Portraits moreover usually distort the appearance and character of the original (D'Israeli 1932: 50), at times with the conscious approbation of the subject, the presenter, or the audience. The demands that biography be fully documented and that portraiture be photographically accurate seem to have arisen quite late and concurrently in the nineteenth century. Lucretia Mott's Quaker cap and Teddy Roosevelt's spectacles are symptomatic of this trend, though details of contemporary dress or imperfections of feature were still controversial in sculpture into the twentieth century. Artists were always free to invent the looks of subjects long dead, who never sat for a daguerreotype or photograph, though traditions built up a characterization of such figures as Aristotle or Homer (Brilliant 1991: 80–1).

Representation of a face or body, with the implied reference to a real original, seems crucial to portraiture even if the proper name, the facts of the life, or a confirmed likeness may be waived. Although "portraits partake of the artificial nature of masks" (Brilliant 1991: 115), they nevertheless announce a greater degree of referentiality than fictional representations. The presenter's claim to represent a real subject authorizes the audience to test that claim with further evidence, and to prefer one representation over another (Wendorf 1990: 8, Brady 1984: 424), much as in biography or history. In group portraits or collective biographies names take on the additional service of differentiating the members of the series. An unknown "group of noble dames" might remain anonymous representatives of the type, but the beauties of the court of Charles II would need to be cataloged by their renowned names in order to serve as collective portraiture of a phase of national history (Jameson 1833, Booth 2004b).

If these are some of the interrelations of the name, face, and narrative in collective biographical portraiture, how have they played out in the developments of literary history and canons of national literature? Since the ancients, portraits have been assumed to inspire emulation in the young and to aid memory, while they have served as tutelary spirits guarding the written tradition. In Roman libraries or the Renaissance revivals of them, busts of eminent philosophers might personify the categories of thought shelved in their name, or copies of portrait busts might illustrate collected lives of exemplary men or the collected writings of one author (D'Israeli 1932: 44–5, Piper 1982: 4–8, 52–3). In the early modern "art of memory," human figures or other images might be arranged like a collection of "treasures" in a building or an illustrated book might resemble a "gallery" of "statues and paintings" (Bolzoni 2001: xxiv, 205–7). Modern Europeans regarded a portrait as the "memory-image of a biography" (Bolzoni 2001: xxiii, Wendorf 1990: 7) – a visual rendition of a narrative. Biography in turn was a means to place a model inside the reader, and thus to "mould behaviours and thought" (Bolzoni 2001: 225–6). To learn the skills of reading prosopography was thus an induction into humanist self-discipline.

Perhaps the world of letters affords the broadest scope for modern reconstructions of the pantheon, calendar of saints, or gallery of worthies. The prosopoetic animation of the absent author seems an inevitable attendant of reading (Wallen 1995: 54), and the construction of literary history as a genealogy of figures of genius has been presumed to be an inevitable practice, even though particular figures may be challenged as they are in any list of heroes or stars (Schoug 2001: 99). Almost as soon as the English began to produce "naturalistic" portraits rather than "generic images" of individuals, they portrayed poets as personifications of national heritage (Piper 1982: 9). A portrait of Chaucer is nearly the first known "likeness" in England, and the monument to Chaucer (without portrait) erected in Westminster Abbey in 1555 was one of the first to commemorate a writer ("the real peopling of Poets' Corner with images" occurred between "1720 and 1740" [Piper 1982: 9, 79]). The author of a prosopographical pilgrimage (and of a biographical collection of good women), Chaucer helps to launch the practice of literary pilgrimage and enshrinement of authors.

The image and biographical "notice" of the author adorning the printed book – an aid to reader identification not unlike the images of musicians on the covers of their CDs – has a venerable tradition. By the eighteenth century, a conjunction of the professionalization of the man of letters, the expansion of publishing, and the increased demand for portraits and biographies as likenesses of individuals generated some of the first English prosopographies of authors – after 1750, of women as well as men. One of the lasting figureheads of biographical portraiture is Samuel Johnson, memorialized in Joshua Reynolds's numerous portraits and James Boswell's classic biography. Although Johnson distrusted the ability of prose or paint to capture complete character, his Boswell sought to construct "'an Egyptian Pyramid in which there will be a compleat mummy of Johnson that Literary Monarch'" (quoted in Wendorf 1990: 11, n. 36, see Folkenflik 1978). To this day, Reynolds's paintings of Johnson adorn paperback editions of his works, and the spirit of Boswell is never far to seek, as though the three men and their extended coterie occupy each others' works. Such memorials emulate the great man's own contributions to national commemoration in *The Lives of the Most Eminent English Poets*, a much-reprinted prosopography of authors. In later abbreviated editions, the portraits have vanished, and some of the poets have been erased altogether. No one has quite dared to add on biographical portraits of Wordsworth or Tennyson by "Dr. Johnson" speaking from the grave. But surrogation is far easier in print than in stone; generations of critical anthologies succeeded Johnson's. Only by the 1830s, amid illustrated magazines and gift annuals, were the collections of portraits inevitable counterparts to the prose sketches of literary characters.

The idea of a gallery of literary figures is of course alive and well today. Many anthologies of literary personalities circulate in the classroom and on the Web. Unlike the celebrities of visual media, authors may "have a name" without "'hav[ing] a face,'" as Fredrik Schoug observes (2001: 101–2). Yet for some famous authors, the image is enough: the portrait invokes the name, a recollection of the works, and a narrative of the career. On t-shirts, mugs, or shopping bags, the tilted classic head with twisted bun of dark hair of the young Virginia Woolf is instantly recognizable without any other aid to memory. But again, even the most heroic icon serves as metonymy for a whole series of writers' images, anachronistically grouped, as in the conversation pieces on the walls of national bookstore chains imagining a kind of café in paradise. If only Zora Neale Hurston, Woolf, William Faulkner, and D. H. Lawrence had indeed been friends out on the town!

The personification of literature has multiplied and spread from small circles of writers in London, New England, or other centers to highly mobile networks across many borders. In book tours and magazines and on websites, the author must exhibit and perform an attractive persona and lifestyle to complement the text. Canons of the more enduring national poets and authors may not be carved on mountainsides, but they are imaged on maps and in anthologies as *genii loci* and tourist destinations. Accordingly, in one representation of "The English Romantic Poets" (Figure 22.3) three oval painted heads hover over Mont Blanc, Shelley the large centermost figure gazing at us, Byron on the lower left, Keats on the lower right with averted gazes, chin on hand; the poses echoing traditional representations of poets (Sullivan 2004a, Piper 1982). Such a display constructs a historical argument and locates personae in a landscape for veneration, much as does Mount Rushmore. Since at least the 1840s, tours of countries have been designed as pilgrimages to authors' homes or haunts, and today it is not uncommon to superimpose the portraits of writers upon national maps.

Figure 22.3 The English Romantic Poets, used with kind permission of James Sullivan of Ard Ri Design.

As though writers have replaced saints in their capacity to sanctify ground, regions become associated with their patrons and protectors, and literary history may be read as a travelogue: "From Robert Frost's New England farms to John Steinbeck's California valley to Eudora Welty's Mississippi Delta" (Library of Congress 2004). An image of Irish writers, for example (Figure 22.4), appears as a prosopography upon a map (Sullivan 2004b). In this display as elsewhere, the writers seem so famous as to need no name, but they have a country and a cause. The flag and the harp signal the viewer to pursue tourism as well as reading to supply the memories for this prosopography.

If biographical portraiture of literary canons solicits veneration of an idealized cultural heritage, it also induces tourism and book purchases. Literary canons even engage in the kind of miniaturization of democracy that I noted in the contests and polls associated with Mount Rushmore. Judges for literary prizes stand in for an electorate, as did the editors that chose Modern Library's 1998 lists of the "100 Best" novels and "100 Best" works of nonfiction of the twentieth century. The Random House subsidiary now claims to have intentionally provoked outrage by its selections to "get people talking about great books." Modern Library quickly solicited readers' votes on their own favorites, and today it posts the incompatible lists side by side on its website (Modern Library 2003, Wood 1998). In Britain, BBC 4 runs continual

Figure 22.4 Irish Writers Montage, used with kind permission of James Sullivan of Ard Ri Design.

contests to entice readers (or the BBC audience and book buyers), including a series of weekly votes on pairs of famous novels, such as *Bridget Jones's Diary* and *Pride and Prejudice* (the latter preferred by 82%), or *Brideshead Revisited* and *The Great Gatsby* (the latter preferred by 54%). The link for "More About the Books and Authors" provides the necessary exhibit of personae: beside each novel's cover and description, a portrait and three-sentence biography of each author. Such populist canon-building is not strictly national, but there are signs of the government's effort to construct a citizenry of readers. *The Lord of the Rings* was recently elected winner of The Big Read: "the nation's favourite book."[7] The popular series of films of Tolkein's novels may lead these British fans to seek Middle Earth in New Zealand. Anglophone culture has gone global, and is ever more open to local substitutions, even as it is more conspicuously tied to commerce and consumption. Collected biographical portraiture constructs literary canons and histories, and solicits the public to participate in the rites of selection.

National Prosopography at the Hall of Fame

Literary prosopography is dispersed in a dizzying range of visual and verbal media. I close with a more grounded form of competitive collection of portrait and narrative in a national prosopography, the first Hall of Fame. As do Borglum's portrait monument and the literary biographical portraits, anthologies, and contests, the Hall of Fame for Great Americans stands for many similar instances of collective portraiture of national heritage. Each of these is an entry in an international competition for greatness, though the rules and prizes are never stated clearly. By the later nineteenth century, the United States was eager to trump Britain, Germany, and France as an international power, as demonstrated in the World's Columbian Exposition of 1893. (It was there that Adelaide Johnson displayed her sculptures of Stanton, Anthony, and Mott in the Woman's Building [Weimann 1981: 545–7].) Less than a decade after the celebrations at the White City on Lake Michigan, the Hall of Fame for Great Americans, designed by Stanford White, was dedicated on the campus of New York University, avowedly to rival Westminster Abbey, Munich's Temple of Fame, and the Pantheons in Paris and Rome. (It was a private, nonprofit enterprise, whereas Rushmore and the US Capitol were funded by taxpayers.) Like other galleries or exhibitions, this yielded a prosopographical catalog, *The Illustrated Story of the Hall of Fame: Lives and Portraits of the Elect and of Those Who Barely Missed Election* (Banks 1902), which recounts the elaborate process of selection: almost a thousand nominations of great Americans' names were gathered nationwide, aided by newspaper contests; these were pruned by the University Senate to 234 (including nine women). A panel of 97 judges then voted to select the 29 white men inducted into the Hall of Fame, including George Washington (97 votes), Abraham Lincoln (96), and Thomas Jefferson (91); Borglum could rely on the popularity of the subjects he choose a quarter century later, though Theodore Roosevelt, not yet President in May 1901, could not be elected to the Hall because he was still alive. Space was built for 150 panels, with future elections to fill them; the plan prescribed that the names represent a variety of vocation, and today authors slightly outnumber politicians, both well ahead of other categories (Lehman College Art Gallery n.d.). Of course the short, all-male list was a travesty of representation: many other famous men and women deserved note, and contemporaries felt entitled to propose substitutions and additions. The Hall of Fame, though in expensive concrete form (it cost $250,000), was far more open to surrogation than the remote mountain carving of four president's heads.

Like the Rotunda, the Hall of Fame at first seemed dedicated to a race of white men, though some women encroached. An art-nouveau image of Lady Fame rules on the cover of the Hall of Fame memorial volume, much as Liberty tops the dome of the US Capitol. "A list of America's most eligible women" supplements the volume (Banks 1902: 398–409), and Banks suggests that the "regulations" for selection should be changed so that eminent women might be elected to "the Immortals" (p. 409). The frontispiece shows George Washington, "who alone was unanimously elected to the Hall of Fame." Other illustrations consist of the chosen men – images of heads and shoulders grouped by number of votes – interspersed with biographies; thus Lincoln's life story is illustrated with a page of oval portraits of Lincoln and three other men with similar scores: U. S. Grant, Daniel Webster, and Benjamin Franklin, as though what is being portrayed is collective fame more than individual character. Other illustrations in Banks's book display the colonnades of the Hall and samples of the prosopoetic "memorial tablets" that give the man's name, dates of birth and death, and an excerpt of his writing. As the pages of the book turn and become more crowded, fame necessarily declines; apparently therefore it's gentlemen first. Clusters of portraits of those who received fewer than the necessary 51 votes, as well as of "famous women who were nominated but not elected" (Lucretia Mott, who received 11 votes, appears with four other women [p. 278]). The final chapter, "Some Famous Women," indicates that there was another election, for the missing women, sponsored by *The Christian Herald* in 1902. Again Mott is presented, but there is no sign anywhere of Stanton or Anthony.

The rugged individualism celebrated in the legend of Mount Rushmore makes it appear that the artist, with the aid of a few politicians, his son, and nameless workers, summoned four pre-eminent spirits out of the vast rock. The Hall of Fame in contrast is a high-society pageant that honors all the collaborators, women included, along with numerous named personae. The memorial volume for the Hall of Fame features large "galleries" of participants in the selection process, as in "some famous professors of history and scientists who acted as judges" (Banks 1902: 333). The female judges form a distinctly small group, three leaders in higher education who posed standing in academic regalia. Women in fact participated from beginning to end of the project. The prime benefactor was Miss Helen M. Gould (later Mrs. Finley J. Shepard), who was much celebrated at the opening festivities in spite of withholding her name. At the dedication ceremonies associated with Memorial Day, 1901, women representing the Colonial Dames, Daughters of the American Revolution, United Daughters of the Confederacy, and nearby girls' high schools unveiled specific tablets. These groups of women assisted in one of the main tasks of the project, a consolidation of a united American history in the name of world power. Today, opponents of the Neo-Confederate movement attack the Hall of Fame as a shrine to the genocide and hate crimes of slavery and Jim Crow (Sebasta n.d.).

Comments on the opening of the Hall make its nationalist purpose clear. *The New York Tribune* marked the event in an editorial, "The Nation's New Shrine," celebrating the reconciliation of North and South symbolized by the presence of both U.S. Grant and Robert E. Lee in the Hall of Fame (Banks 1902: 31–2), and praising the Hall's superiority to British and German equivalents in its democratic synthesis of all representative types (pp. 32–3). New York Senator Chauncey M. Depew's oratory included a collective elegy for plural names (Booth 2004a: 13):

> We have now no Tennysons, nor Longfellows....Perhaps it is because our Michael Angelos are planning tunnels under rivers...our Hawthornes and Emersons have abandoned...revelations of the spirit...to exploit mines and factories. Reserve the Temple of Fame for those only whose deeds and thoughts are the inheritance, education, inspiration and aspiration of endless generations.
>
> (pp. 28–9)

Borglum's project two decades later seems symptomatic of this view of the United States as a feat of engineering more than of genius, addressed to future ages.

The first of many American Halls of Fame, the site near the Hudson River has been a bit of a bust. In the century since, it has struggled financially (without walls, it does not charge admission). Now a registered historic landmark at Bronx Community College, it receives only scattered visitors, whereas in the 1920s and 1930s as many as 50,000 arrived annually (McShane 2004). In 2001, Governor Pataki created the I Love New York Halls of Fame Passport program to encourage tourism to all 18 of the state's halls of fame, but the press release names the Baseball Hall of Fame and the National Women's Hall of Fame without note of the original hall in the Bronx (New York State Governor's Office 2001). Like Mount Rushmore, most such prosopographical collections have a commercial as well as patriotic inspiration, but the Hall of Fame was not designed as a tourist attraction, and indeed is badly located in today's geography of the boroughs (NYU gave up its northern campus in part because of crime in the Bronx). Perhaps the intensification of celebrity in the age of film and video decreased the public's interest in eminent names of the past. The Hall of Fame resembles a history lesson in the round more than an arena for sports heroes or stars of popular entertainment. The impact of biographical portraiture relies on recognition, and few other media besides school curricula are reinforcing the renown of Eli Whitney or Daniel Webster. Perhaps, too, the concrete prosopography in the Bronx is too miscellaneous and inclusive to have the shrine-like appeal of the Mall in Washington, DC, or Mount Rushmore.

The United States is still addicted to choosing lists of the top or greatest or best, and a new magazine contest might get many submissions of great names. The Hall of Fame did continue its project for some decades: after 1920, statues were commissioned to accompany the tablets along the colonnade, with additions of newly elected names every five years until 1973; today, a total of 98 of the 102 subjects have busts (Bronx Community College 2004). Although now more diverse, with George Washington Carver, Booker T. Washington, Harriet Beecher Stowe, and Susan B. Anthony (Lehman College Art Gallery n.d.), it may still have an aura of an age of eugenics and hero-worship. And so the Hall of Fame becomes itself something of a relic, a site of interest to architects, art historians, preservationists, school groups, and the odd collector of prosopographies. It generates websites that identify the contributing sculptors with brief lives and portraits; present digital images of the portrait bronzes, a Java Run Time 360-degree panorama of the "630-foot open-air Colonnade," or a QuickTime "Virtual Reality Movie" in which, really, nothing happens: the busts continue to gaze toward each other, their features and the plaques illegible to the virtual visitor (Bronx Community College 2004, Lehman College Art Gallery, n.d.). The edifice with the affirmation "BY WEALTH OF THOUGHT/THEY LIVE FOR EVER MORE" carved on two of its pediments can now be found by consulting a guide book called *City Secrets – New York* (Bronx Community College 2004). The Hall becomes a link on walking tours of "Public Art in the Bronx." Regional material culture may be more inspirational today than saints, gods, or even national heroes. Still, prosopography personifies spirits of place to represent a community's heritage.

The instances of prosopography that I have presented above suggest some of the ways that collective portraiture has constructed and memorialized national heritage. Exchanging our cash or reading our literary anthologies, we may seem far removed from tours of literary landscapes or national monuments, though the interaction of names, faces, and narratives take similar forms in each context. Yet we may vote with our feet as well as with the click of a mouse to preserve the systems of veneration. Perhaps we are surrounded by miniature Mount Rushmores with figures of ancestry that may be appropriated, as Congressman Pence appropriated Stanton, Anthony, and Mott, to justify new agendas. Such prosopographies engage the presenters as well as the audience in collective memorial representation, claiming a certain kinship in cultural heritage, forming a conjunction of biography and history, and leaving a palpable after-image of what is missing. Martin Luther King Jr. has a bronze bust in the Rotunda, but that scarcely takes care of the question of race in that prosopography. When someone votes to add Teddy Roosevelt to Adelaide Johnson's statue, then I'll know that the rules have really changed.

NOTES

1   In the adjacent Hall of Statuary (begun in 1864), each state is represented by a statue, of which five represent women. Most states have contributed a second statue to the Capitol building.

2   Cecilia Tichi interprets the design of Mt Rushmore, set in Oglala Sioux sacred land, in a context of nineteenth-century readings of American geography as a series of natural monuments to white male disembodied "heads" of state and industry. Teddy Roosevelt disrupts chronology and adds a threat of mock epic (Tichi 2001: 15–43). Dubbed the "Shrine

to Democracy" in 1930, the sculptures were said to tell the story of liberty and territorial expansion; the lives of the heroes themselves also encode gender indeterminacy in spite of the dominant heterosexual masculinity of the West (Boag 2003: 42–3, 52–3).

3   Face–name association is an ongoing topic of psychological research into memory and learning. Eugene Winograd and Vaughan E. Church, for example, find that "a constant spatial location" in which subjects see a face "is more conducive to learning associations" between the name and the face than when a

face is encountered in various places (Winograd and Church 1988: 1). Schweinberger, Burton, and Kelly (2001) examine the "tip-of-the-tongue" phenomenon in which people recognize faces and even "semantic information" (biographical facts) about another person far more reliably than the proper name (pp. 303–4).

4 In 2004, the Modern History Research Unit at Oxford University announced the opening of the Oxford Prosopography Centre to promote and disseminate such research, which has been facilitated by advances in computer data processing. It features a fragmented group portrait on its website: <users.ox.ac.uk/~prosop/>.

5 Gutzon Borglum "created more statues for . . . the [US] Capitol Building than any other sculptor," including his "marble portrait" of Lincoln (Shaff and Shaff 1985: 369). Usually a political reactionary, he allied himself with members of the United Daughters of the Confederacy and the Ku Klux Klan in producing a memorial to the Southern cause at Stone Mountain in Georgia (Shaff and Shaff

1985: 149–51); the project had collapsed when Borglum was hired for Mount Rushmore. He was an outspoken antisemite yet close friends with a number of Jews, and he publicly denounced Hitler and the Nazis (1985: 3–6, 103–5). A child of western states, he wrote of early fantasies of "killing off the whole Sioux tribe," yet expressed his sense of confidence among "wild Indians," and a number of his works represent Native Americans (pp. 22–3, 60). For a perceptive account of Borglum's adventurous career, politics, and negotiated representation of great men, women, Native Americans, see Taliaferro (2002).

6 Borglum's own immortality would be in the work itself. "Weeks after I am gone, they will start to forget me. A decade and most people of South Dakota will be unable to even recall my name. . . . but ten thousand years hence, the people of the earth will know Gutzon Borglum" (American Experience 2002).

7. See BBC4 website <www.bbc.co.uk/bbcfour/books/battle/> and BBC2 Big Read website <www.bbc.co.uk/arts/bigread/>.

References and Further Reading

Adams, T. D. (2000). *Light Writing and Life Writing: Photography in Autobiography*: Chapel Hill, NC: University of North Carolina Press.

Aird, C. (1996). "Read that Countenance." In D. Salwak (ed.), *The Literary Biography* (pp. 41–6). Iowa City: University of Iowa Press.

American Experience (2002). "Mount Rushmore." PBS Online/WGBH. <www.pbs.org/wgbh/amex/rushmore/index.html>.

American Park Network (2001). "Mount Rushmore History." <www.americanparknetwork.com/parkinfo/ru/history/carve.html>.

Anderson, B. (1991). *Imagined Communities*, revised edn. London: Verso.

Banks, L. A. (1902). *The Illustrated Story of the Hall of Fame*. New York: Christian Herald.

Boag, P. (2003). "Thinking like Mount Rushmore: Sexuality and Gender in the Republican Landscape." In V. J. Scharff (ed.), *Seeing Nature Through Gender* (pp. 40–59). Lawrence: University Press of Kansas.

Bolzoni, L. (2001). *The Gallery of Memory*, trans. J. Parzen. Toronto: University of Toronto Press.

Booth, A. (2004a). *How to Make It As a Woman: Collective Biographical History from Victoria to the Present*. Chicago: University of Chicago Press.

Booth, A. (2004b). "Bibliography of Collective Biographies of Women in English, 1830–1940," <etext.lib.virginia.edu/WomensBios/>.

Brady, F. (1984). *James Boswell, the Later Years, 1769–1795*. New York: McGraw Hill.

Brilliant, R. (1991). *Portraiture*. Cambridge, MA: Harvard University Press.

Bronx Community College (2004). "Hall of Fame for Great Americans." City University of New York. <www.bcc.cuny.edu/HallofFame/>.

Colley, L. (1989). *Lewis Namier*. New York: St. Martin's.

De Man, P. (1979). "Autobiography as Defacement." *MLN* 94, 919–30.

D'Israeli, I. ([1791–1834] 1932). *Curiosities of Literature*, abridged and ed. E. V. Mitchell. New York: Appleton.

Folkenflik, R. (1978). *Samuel Johnson, Biographer*. Ithaca, NY: Cornell University Press.

Fryd, V. (1992). *Art and Empire*. New Haven, CT: Yale University Press.

Heehs, P. (1995). "Narrative Painting and Narratives About Paintings: Poussin among the Philosophers." *Narrative* 3, 211–31.

Jameson, A. (1833). *Memoirs of the Beauties of the Court of Charles II. With Their Portraits, after Sir Peter Lely and Other Eminent Painters: Illustrating the Diaries of Pepys, Evelyn, Clarendon, and Other Contemporary Writers*. London: Bentley.

Le Guin, C. A. (1983). "The Language of Portraiture." *Biography* 6, 333–41.

Lehman College Art Gallery (n.d.). *Public Art in the Bronx*. Susan Hoeltzl, Project Director. <bronxart.lehman.cuny.edu/pa/>.

Library of Congress (2004). "Language of the Land – Exhibition Overview." <www.loc.gov/exhibits/land/landover.html>.

McShane, L. (2004). "The Original Hall of Fame: Are its 15 minutes up?" The JournalNews.com. May 30. <www.thejournalnews.com/newsroom/053004/B4web4travelhallof.html>.

Mitchell, W. J. T. (1986). *Iconology*. Chicago: University of Chicago Press.

Modern Library (2003). "100 Best Novels." <www.randomhouse.com/modernlibrary/100best.html>.

Murray, C. (2003). *Human Accomplishment*. New York: HarperCollins.

Office of the Governor of New York (2001). "Governor: I Love New York Halls of Fame Passport Program Under Way." Press Release, June 20 <www.state.ny.us/governor/press/>.

Piper, D. (1982). *The Image of the Poet: British Poets and Their Portraits*. Oxford: Clarendon.

Roach, J. (1996). *Cities of the Dead: Circum-Atlantic Performance*. New York: Columbia University Press.

Schoug, F. (2001). "Public Face, Respected Name: The Conditions of Fame." *Ethnologia Scandinavica* 31, 99–108.

Schweinberger, S. R., Burton, A. M. and Kelly, S. W. (2001). "Priming the Access to Names of Famous Faces." *British Journal of Psychology* 92, 303–17.

Sebesta, E. H. (n.d.). "Hall of Fame: A Favored Shrine of the United Daughters of the Confederacy." <www.templeofdemocracy.com/Hall-Fame.htm>.

Stedman, A. (2000). "A Gallery of Authors: The Politics of Innovation and Subversion in Monpensier's *Divers Portraits*." *Genre* 33, 129–49.

Shaff, H. and Shaff, A. K. (1985). *Six Wars at a Time: The Life and Times of Gutzon Borglum, Sculptor of Mount Rushmore*. Sioux Falls, SD: Center for Western Studies.

Taliaferro, J. (2002). *Great White Fathers: The Story of the Obsessive Quest to Create Mount Rushmore*. New York: PublicAffairs.

Tichi, C. (2001). *Embodiment of a Nation*. Cambridge, MA: Harvard University Press.

Wallen, J. (1995). "Between Text and Image." *Auto/biography Studies: a/b* 10, 50–65.

Waller, D. (2004). "Reagan Bills? Not Yet." *Time* June 21, 18.

Wendorf, R. (1983). "Ut Pictura Biographia: Biography and Portrait Painting as Sister Arts." In *Articulate Images: The Sister Arts from Hogarth to Tennyson* ed. R. Wendorf (pp. 98–126). Minneapolis: University of Minnesota Press.

Wendorf, R. (1990). *The Elements of Life: Biography and Portrait-Painting in Stuart and Georgian England*. Oxford: Clarendon.

Weimann, J. M. (1981). *The Fair Women*. Chicago: Academy.

Winograd, E. and Church, V. E. (1988). "Role of Spatial Location in Learning Face-Name Associations." *Memory and Cognition* 16, 1–7.

Wood, J. (1998). "Bookdumb." *New Republic* August 17/24, 14.

23

The Trouble with Autobiography: Cautionary Notes for Narrative Theorists

Sidonie Smith and Julia Watson

Of course, the distinction between "fictional" and "nonfictional" is notoriously problematic these days.

(Shlomith Rimmon-Kenan 2002: 25, n. 5)

The problem with fiction is that it must seem credible, while reality seldom is.

(Isabel Allende 1994: 299)

The two of us have spent several decades theorizing the autobiographical, individually and collaboratively, in a wide range of life narrative modes – verbal and visual, literary and everyday, women's and men's, (post)colonial and Western. But neither of us is a narratologist, though we admire, and have some conversancy with, the work of narrative theorists. Consequently, we write from one side of what Rimmon-Kenan suggests is a shifting but stubbornly tenacious divide. That divide places the autobiographical on the side of nonfiction, though distinct from biography and history in its greater use of fictional strategies such as dialogue, interior monologue, autodiegetic narration, and its address to readers. Our purpose here, however, is not to explore the differences between fictional and nonfictional narrative in a schematic sense.[1] Like Rimmon-Kenan, we think there are reasons to *assert* the difference of the autobiographical, despite its permeable and fluid character, not least because both writers and theorists negotiate that boundary in multiple ways. Asserting this difference, we explore four problematics of autobiographical practice – impersonation, withholding of autobiography, the ethical call to witness, and materiality – to point to issues that are central to autobiographical studies but that have yet to fully inform narrative theory, with its primary focus on the novel and fiction.

Many decades of work on life writing have complicated our initial understanding of the autobiographical as such and revised our conceptualization of what happens and what is at stake in autobiographical acts. Self-representations and acts of self-narrating are always located, historical, subjective, political, and embodied. Stories don't just "come" from a life, although readers imagine that autobiographical narrators just tell life stories that articulate unified coherent selves. Rather, storytellers rework and improvise upon established forms, such as the slave narrative, apprenticeship story, or narrative of political consciousness, to compose identities. Moreover, no coherent "self" predates a story about identity – about "who" one is. It is impossible to construct a single unchanging self capable of remembering and reciting the totality of the past because each of us lives in time and takes ever-changing perspectives on the moving target of our pasts.

Theoretically speaking, both the storytelling and the self constituted by it are narrative constructions of identity.[2] Autobiographical telling is performative; it enacts the "self" that it claims has given rise to the "I."[3] Furthermore, an "I" is neither unified nor stable; rather, it is split, fragmented, provisional, a sign with multiple referents. And those various identities presented by a narrator are directed to disparate addressees or audiences. They make diverse calls to identity that do not align neatly. Instead, the tensions and contradictions in representing an "I" to various audiences, for various occasions, by various means, produce gaps, fissures, and boundary trouble within the narrative.

Furthermore, autobiography is not a single genre but an "umbrella" term for widely diverse kinds of life narrative (the term we prefer), literally dozens, that engage historically situated practices of self-representation.[4] The field of autobiography studies, as it has developed across multiple theoretical and methodological approaches, has consistently troubled single definitions as inadequate to account for its myriad genres and the rich complexities of acts of self-narrating and self-representation. The autobiographical exceeds attempts to pigeonhole it, in terms of generic aesthetics, forms, usages, and receptions. Both the importance and the excesses of this theorizing call those of us in the field to return repeatedly to how the autobiographical exceeds our efforts to fix its aesthetic, ethical, political, and sociocultural meanings across histories and geographies.

In what follows, we set out some difficult but fascinating theoretical issues that have troubled those of us working in the field. We do so for two main reasons: (1) to encourage greater exchange between life writing theorists and theorists dedicated to narrative theory or narratology; (2) to contribute to a more comprehensive account of narrative, which in our view would be enriched by engaging the kinds of theoretical issues raised by life writing. We have chosen four foundational issues that currently challenge theorists as we read, teach, and think about life narratives, whether those are composed in the first, second, or third person; individual or collective; contemporary or of an earlier moment; canonical or counterstories. These issues speak to the special status of the autobiographical and tease out particular aspects of that special status. Each issue highlights a feature or question that has emerged, since the memoir boom of the 1990s, as pivotal for theorists negotiating complex practices of autobiographical writing. They are:

- autobiographical hoaxes and the status of the autobiographical pact;
- the politics of reading postcolonial writers who efface distinctions between the autobiographical and the fictive and the status of marking the withholding of autobiography as an "out-law" rhetorical move;
- the ethics of narrative witnessing to suffering, loss, and survival and the status of witness narratives for narrators and readers;
- the materiality of the narrator's body and the status of materialized self-representation in the autobiographical.

All of these aspects of autobiographical narration propose a relationship between text and (material) world that its theorists find both important and challenging. In examining each issue we turn to specific texts as sites of "trouble" that nonetheless have potential to inform the contemporary scene of theoretical debates about the nature of narrative – its aesthetics, politics, and ethics.

Issue 1. Impersonation and the Affect of Reading

What difference does it make if a writer impersonates someone else or appropriates another's experience in an autobiographical hoax?

To whom and when do hoaxes matter? Of course, there are many different kinds of hoaxes; and many literary genres have been implicated in hoaxes. A novelist, for instance, might try to pass off a work he or she has written as the work of another, perhaps more famous, novelist. In this instance, we as readers would question the ethics of the author. But we would not question the veracity of the representations within the text since in fictional verisimilitude the likeness of possible worlds is sufficient, as Allende suggests in the epigraph at the beginning of the chapter. Although its representation of reality may be bad, morally reprehensible, unconvincing, inept, or tedious, the story narrated cannot be labeled "a hoax," even if the event and the claims of authorship are willful misrepresentations.

But an autobiographical hoax raises different issues and these are illuminating for the nature of autobiographical narrative. When readers and the general public discover that a story promoted and sold as autobiographical is entirely "made up," it is highly troubling because of the perceived violation of an autobiographical pact between narrator and reader.[5] In 1975 Philippe Lejeune introduced this concept productive for subsequent theorizing of autobiographical acts to describe the double contract of life writing: an author guarantees that the name on the book's cover corresponds to the "life" narrated within; it is a "contract of identity...sealed by the proper name" (Lejeune [1975] 1989: 19). In making this claim to the "real," life narratives solicit a particular mode of reading, since they are claiming not verisimilitude, but the "truth" of lived experience, however elusive that may be. Of course, critics of life writing acknowledge that the autobiographical cannot reveal the "truth" of the flesh-and-blood author, which is an inaccessible and constantly reconstructed truth. In its representation of subjectivity and rhetorical staging of truth claims, the autobiographical engages with multiple conflicting discourses of truth, experience, and authority in ways that require unpacking. Nonetheless, the idea of an autobiographical pact helps us understand why autobiographical hoaxes are so troubling to readers. An autobiographical hoax troubles expectations about the ethics of self-referentiality because readers expect autobiographical writing to refer to a "real" experienced world that, however remembered, they can imagine as compelling and immediate.

The nineteenth-century slave narrative composed by Harriet Jacobs and published as *Incidents in the Life of a Slave Girl* in 1861 is an example of a life narrative thought to be a hoax but then later validated as authentic. Life narratives chronicling life in the slave system, at times produced with and circulated by abolitionists, were often challenged as fraudulent by defenders of slavery. Jacobs's text fictionalized several names, including her own, and downplayed the editorial help she received from abolitionist editor Lydia Maria Child. This collaboration led critics in the 1860s and throughout much of the twentieth century to dismiss her narrative as fictional.[6] That is, they contested the truth claims of the autobiographical and shifted the text's generic designation to novel, strategies that discredited it despite its popularity. Effectively, this fictionalizing undermined its claim to be read and registered as a painful history. Over a hundred years later, the archival and editorial research of scholar Jean Fagan Yellin authenticated the narrative in different terms and for different reading publics. As a result of Yellin's scholarship, critics now recognize the truth claims of its "experience" of brutality, attempted rape, and self-imprisonment as more compelling than the juridical accuracy of its particular terms and facts of self-reference. Its fictionalizing has been validated and valued as necessary to tell a life narrative that lacked both literary model and social sanction. Now, audiences credit the historian's claim that ex-slaves used various rhetorical strategies to protect loved ones left behind. Jacobs's turn to fiction, then, was strategic. Her case shows that some kinds of fictionalizing, some maskings of facticity, are necessary responses to time, place, circumstance, and purpose rather than evidence of violations of the autobiographical pact.

The question of hoaxes became a central issue in a different way during the memoir boom of the 1990s. A widely publicized autobiographical hoax involved *Fragments: Memories of a Wartime Childhood*, translated into English in 1996 and alleged to be by "Binjamin Wilkomirski."[7] G. Thomas Couser recounts the history of counterevidence, including Wilkomirski's refusal of DNA testing, that led to his publisher's subsequent withdrawal of the book and his literary agency's investigation of its claims. The investigator, Stefan Mächler, published a biography in 2001 that exposed *Fragments* as a fictional collage weaving memories of survivors together with various literary and historical sources. But the question of whether this fraud was intentional is more complex, in that Wilkomirski's painful memories of a Swiss foster home may have contributed to his sense of persecution. He continues to insist that his identity is that of a Jew and a survivor of the Holocaust (Couser 2004: 174–5).

Fragments originally garnered attention in Europe and the United States as a compelling act of first-person witnessing to the horrors of the Nazi genocide. It appeared at a historical moment when the number of Holocaust survivors was dwindling and the possibility of first-person witness was giving way to what Marianne Hirsch terms "postmemory."[8] But when Wilkomirski's *Fragments* was exposed as false witness, it was immediately withdrawn from bookstores, condemned as being either delusion or opportunistic identity theft, and later republished as fiction.

In Australia, Wanda Koolmatrie's *My Own Sweet Time* also created a scandal involving cross-cultural impersonation. *My Own Sweet Time*, published in 1994, told the story of an indigenous woman's itinerant wandering from her hometown of Adelaide to the urban world of Melbourne. Critics hailed *My Own Sweet Time* as representative of the voices of a hip new generation of indigenous Australian writers, a mixed-blood generation cut off from traditional community but at ease in urban Australia's multicultural maze. When the book won a literary award a year later and the publisher requested a meeting with Koolmatrie, the hoax was revealed. Wanda Koolmatrie was the fictional persona of a young white man named Leon Carmen. Annoyed because he felt white men could no longer find publishers for their work, Carmen decided to cash in on the popularity of personal narratives told by indigenous Australians.[9]

Our three examples of alleged autobiographical hoaxes point to several overlapping issues involved in impersonation. In the case of Jacobs's slave narrative, the charge of "hoax" was used to undermine the story told and challenge the authenticity of the narrator. Readers and critics in the 1860s contested Jacobs's authenticity because racist discourses and the slave system – even as that system was collapsing – located slaves and ex-slaves as fundamentally less-than-human, uneducable, and incapable of either free agency or narrative authority. Some apologists for slavery were dismissive of the narrative's content, some skeptical that an escaped slave could write so eloquently, some hostile to the abolitionist movement. Proslavery advocates and antebellum apologists, recognizing the cultural stakes of Jacobs's narratives, raised the specter of "hoax" to great effect. Abolitionists, by contrast, were concerned to provide authenticating prefaces to support the narrative's claim to authenticity. Thus the sociopolitical context of production and reception rendered the narrative suspicious and made its external verification necessary. The text's truth claims could easily be shifted from truthful to fictional because of the vulnerable social location of the narrator.

The second case, *Fragments*, underscores how an historical event may be particularized and re-presented as a fantasy of cultural belonging. For someone like Wilkomirski, close to the traumatic event, but not in it as a survivor, the desire to claim a shared past of victimhood offered a personal way to understand the past and situate himself inside world memory. What this apparent delusion illustrates, as Ross

Chambers (2002) argues, is that certain traumatic stories become so much a part of world memory shared across cultures that an individual can imagine himself "truly" in that story. Had it been released as "fiction," *Fragments* would not have garnered the attention, awards, or eventual notoriety it did. This aspect of the hoax suggests how certain kinds of autobiographical narrative become culturally believable rather than suspicious, and underscores the potency of asserting the autobiographical.

The author of *My Own Sweet Time*, by contrast, deliberately exploited the contemporary commodification of aboriginal life narratives. During the 1990s publishers in Australia sought stories by indigenous Australians for several reasons: partly because of the increasing national engagement with the stories of the "stolen generation," partly because the UN Decade of Indigenous Peoples was calling attention to indigenous rights movements around the world, and partly because the marketing of "victim" stories played to the insatiable desire of the more privileged for stories of those who suffer. Leon Carmen recognized that there would be cultural receptiveness to the story of Wanda Koolmatrie told, not as a white man's novel, but as an indigenous woman's life narrative. This example shows a violation of the autobiographical pact between narrator and reader. Carmen's claiming an identity he did not have led to allegations of autobiographical bad faith. When an autobiographical narrator claims that the memories and experiences narrated are those of the authorial "signature," when the publisher classifies the narrative as "memoir" or "autobiography," readers attribute the events narrated within the book's pages to a flesh-and-blood person identical with that signature. And when readers discover that the story is entirely "made-up," they feel betrayed. Although the flesh-and-blood person and the textual "I" are never identical, publishers and readers make a distinction between the self-representation in storytelling of actual persons and the "entirely made-up" appropriation of another's story.

Readers engage autobiographical narratives on multiple levels. They approach them as a source of information about other peoples' lives, even historical documents. Readers are also drawn to the promised intimacy and immediacy of the first-person voice. And they find themselves responding to narratives empathetically, as stories that release charges of affect, intensities registered in the body – fear, anger, rage, shame, or horror. When an autobiographical narrative that feeds reader desires and spurs affective and cognitive response is revealed to be a fabrication, readers feel betrayed. Their experience of reading, identifying, and empathizing has been undermined.

Issue 2. Outsider Histories and the Politics of Reading

How does the sociocultural location of an author affect the way that a narrative is read? That is, what calls to a different politics of reading can an "out-law" narrative that "withholds" the autobiographical exert?

The title or credit pages of books often announce them either as autobiography or as fiction, with repercussions for readers, particularly contemporary readers. Certainly novels, such as *David Copperfield, Jane Eyre*, or *Wilhelm Meister's Apprenticeship*, invite readers to read them autobiographically, while indicating in the discrepancy between the author's and protagonist's names that they are not autobiography but *Bildungsromane*. Thus they observe the "law" of autobiography and do not violate its pact. But some postcolonial writers in recent years have troubled the fiction/nonfiction boundary by both calling on readers to read their narratives against autobiography and asserting authoritative witness to subjective truth through a – usually first-person – narrator. They are, in Caren Kaplan's term, "out-law" life narratives that violate the norms of autobiography as a genre and present versions of subjective experience excluded from its master narratives and official histories of the West.[10] And they play on the different readerly expectations of fictional and nonfictional texts in ways that admit of no easy resolution.

Gayatri Spivak addresses this effacing of the fiction/nonfiction distinction by arguing that postcolonial writers at times conceive their narratives as "withheld autobiography" (Spivak 1998: 10). In its place their apparently fictionalized narratives inscribe the voices of subjects without access to writing, converting an autobiographical discourse of subjectivity into testimony, which she defines as "the genre of the subaltern giving witness to oppression, to a less oppressed other" (p. 7). By theorizing this reworking of autobiography as a narrative mediating multiple accounts of silencing *that cannot be voiced directly*, Spivak suggests that such narratives rework the terms of life narrative rather than willfully impersonating another's experience, like the hoaxes discussed in Issue 1.

For example, Jamaica Kincaid's *The Autobiography of My Mother* announces itself as an "autobiography" but is classified on the back cover as a novel. Its tropic claim to be the autobiographical narrative of another, a narrating subject whose access to her Carib language and history has been erased, asserts the relational subjectivity that we have discussed above. But it complicates that model in two ways: the narrating I, though she speaks in a first-person autobiographical voice, is of the generation of Kincaid's mother and recalls *her* mother, analogous to Kincaid's grandmother; and that narrator situates herself as not knowing her mother, who died giving birth to her. Thus the narrative can *only* be a "novel." Kincaid, in this fable of embodied subjectivity, interrogates the claims made by both autobiography and novel as master narratives, suggesting the inadequacy of either to tell the excluded history of subjects for whom agency was outlawed. Her narrative, focused on preliterate women of African descent whose histories were erased, negotiates a kind of cultural authority and agency for them by an act of narrative "impersonation." And it suggests the difficulties certain subjects or collectivities have had in making claims to personhood. As Françoise Lionnet (1995) has usefully pointed out, reading such postcolonial narratives for their "autobiographicality" shifts the reader's focus to orality and the *métissage* or braiding of incommensurate discourses and languages as multiple dissonant voicings.

Kincaid's complex location between the autobiographical and the novelistic, sustained throughout several narratives in what Leigh Gilmore has called "endless autobiography," is hardly unique.[11] Postcolonial narratives may also intervene in modes of the autobiographical that constitute legacies of what Aijaz Ahmad terms "capitalist modernity" (1995: 7). The *Bildungsroman*, for instance, is a novelistic form often taken up by autobiographers to narrate the journey from outsider childhood through education to participation in society and incorporation in normative social identities. As a form, it calls its narrative subject to an individualist accumulative engagement with past experience framed through the modernist notion of progress. But when the formerly colonized subject narratively occupies the *Bildungroman*'s "I" as a site of remembrance and knowledge, she or he can become complicit with colonialism's asymmetries of power and projects of othering.

Engaging narrative modes of the autobiographical, however, can also be an occasion for interrogating, contesting, and reframing history, memory, culture, and power. The Jamaican writer Michelle Cliff, in autobiographical works explicitly called novels – *Abeng* and *No Telephone to Heaven* – troubles dominant modes of autobiographical inscription in the West through her story of the pseudonymous Clare Savage. As she tells her story/Clare's story, Cliff invokes, inhabits, ruptures, and challenges several aspects of coming-of-age narratives: family genealogy (querying genealogical pedigrees' penchant for eliminating "unusable" ancestors); the adolescent diary (contesting its privatization of experience and its project of self-surveillance); and the autobiographical *Bildungsroman* (questioning its normative notion of identity and history and the costs of misidentification for the postcolonial subject).

The practice of framing an autobiographical narrative as a novel to distance it from the "law" of autobiography occurs in many other contemporary postcolonial life narratives, such as Nawal-El-Saadawi's *Woman at Point Zero*, Ken Bugul's *The Abandoned Baobab*, Tsitsi Dangarembga's *Nervous Conditions*, Maryse Condé's *Hérémakhonon: A Novel*, Myriam Warner-Vieyra's *Juletane*, Norma Cantú's *Canícula: Snapshots of a Girlhood in La Frontera*. They employ the strategies and complex relationship of narrated and narrating "I"s to embed the individual subject in a collective identity overwritten by the process and legacies of colonization. In both incorporating and resisting the autobiographical, such narratives attest to the damage of that past.

Why, if these texts have obviously autobiographical features, do their authors announce them as novels that refuse or divert an autobiographical reading? When these writers trouble generic borders to subvert a fiction/nonfiction distinction, they call attention to the historical focus of canonical autobiography as a master narrative for political legitimacy by invoking other discursive regimes, such as occluded oral histories and testimonies of violence and violation. Marking the autobiography/fiction difference by withholding the marks of autobiography and placing a text to the other side of that difference is a way of interrogating the complicity of the autobiography canon and its critics with dominant modes of self-representation and truth-telling. By recasting the presentation of subjectivity through fictionalized testimony, such writers call the myth of individual self-production sharply into question.

In our view narrative theory needs to take up this ambivalent relationship of postcolonial texts such as Kincaid's and Cliff's to traditions of autobiographical representation that elicit competing claims about personhood, experience, and authority. When narratives written by those formerly refused access to cultural authority are situated as fictional, their interrogation of the relationship of alternative storytelling traditions – testimony, oral witnessing, family history, and the like – to dominant conventions of life writing becomes crucial to the act of reading. To read such texts only as the "novels" they claim to be elides larger debates about the stakes and rhetorics of subaltern subjectivity, the political uses of life stories, and the ethics of naming, framing, and responding.

Issue 3. Witnessing: The Ethics of Recognition

How are readers differently addressed in narratives of witness than in other first-person modes?

Since World War II, and more particularly in the last two decades, the literature of personal witness has become a globally recognized and broadly circulated mode of personal narrating.[12] The practice of witnessing informs such autobiographical genres as Holocaust narratives, identity movement narratives of rights, narratives of incest and violence in the family, disability narratives, and narratives of exile and displacement. It emanates from Western publishers, but also from the dispersed global sites of national storytelling such as the Truth and Reconciliation Commission in South Africa and the Inquiry into the forced removal of indigenous children (the Stolen Generation) from their families in Australia (The National Inquiry into the Separation of Aboriginal and Torres Strait Islander Children from Their Families). In fact, personal storytelling has become central to the international regime of human rights and is being employed increasingly in the service of nation-building and national projects of reconciliation.

Narratives produced and circulating within the regime of human rights confront readers with emotional, even overwhelming, episodes of dehumanization, brutal and violent victimization, and exploitation. They call the reader to an ethical response through their affective appeals for recognition. Thus, while there can be many unpredictable responses to the publication, circulation, and reception of personal narratives of suffering and loss, scenes of witness are ones in which the narrator, the story, and the listener/reader are entwined in an ethical call to empathic identification, recognition, and oftentimes action.

How has this ethical call to recognition intervened in notions of the autobiographical with which we began this essay? The insistence that the history of suffering and abuse experienced and remembered by the speaker or those for whom she or he speaks can no longer go unnarrated compels the telling of witness narratives. Witnesses often understand and position themselves as members of a collectivity whose story can and must be told. Readers and listeners are asked to recognize the risks of witnessing, to validate suffering and survival, to confer a different status on those who have been disparaged by history, to play a role in protecting the humanity and dignity of the other. Narratives of witness thus make an urgent, immediate, and direct bid for the attention of the reader/listener.

Reading narratives of autobiographical witness educates readers, cognitively, emotionally, and/or rationally, about the subjective and bodily effects of rights violations and the particular sufferings of individuals. These appeals of witness narratives are of a different sort from other kinds of life narratives; but they are also different from those that fictive narrators can possibly exercise. The discursive contexts of witness narratives have consequences beyond the aesthetic pleasure and individual moral education traditionally understood as the purposes and effects of the novel. Thus these are appeals with consequences for the narrators.[13] At times, the act of witnessing may open traumatic wounds for the narrator rather than offer healing and reconciliation. Often the narratives are enabled but also constrained by the institutional setting in which storytelling takes place, such as the need to conform stories to communal and contextual expectations and frames; in such instances the narrator may have to make his or her appeal through the subject position of victimhood that fixes the narrator in the past, or that erases incommensurable differences between narrator and reader. Sometimes, acts of personal witnessing bring further violence and suffering. Inescapably, witnesses lose their stories as they enter into global circuits of reproduction far beyond their immediate contexts of telling, there to be put to different, sometimes adversarial, uses, as the example of Rigoberta Menchú's narrative *I, Rigoberta Menchú* makes clear.[14]

If the witness has an investment in making autobiographical claims, others may be invested in disputing those claims. Narratives of witness are often received with suspicion by individuals or groups (often acting within institutional settings) that challenge the speaker's claim to an authoritative story. This aura of suspicion that hovers over witness narratives points to the different stakes in producing and disputing the truth-claims of survivors of human rights violations. The demand for verifiable truth cannot be directed to the novel or the novelist in the way it can to the witness and his or her narrative. Though a reader might reject the truth of history or of character or of fable represented in a fictional narrative, that rejection does not carry the same consequences for those making appeals about rights violations and validation of the truth of their suffering and loss.

The affective call made to the reader by witness narratives thus differs significantly even from that of novels that sympathetically and imaginatively portray similar situations. To read testimonial accounts such as Maria Rosa Henson's *Comfort Woman* (1999) or Jan Ruff-O'Herne's *Fifty Years of Silence* (1996) – narratives of personal witness to the degrading history of sexual slavery during the Pacific War – next to novelistic narratives by contemporary writers such as Nora Okja Keller's *Comfort Woman* (1997) and Simone Lazaroo's *An Australian Fiancé* (2000) is to understand more fully the radically different stakes of fictive and testimonial versions of stories of suffering and loss. On the one hand, the novels offer more latitude for exploring the psychic costs of a silenced past as a former World War II sex slave and greater aesthetic and affective license to imagine alternative forms of experiencing and surviving structures of feeling under the duress of the silenced past. They can render imaginary worlds of interiority for those who suffer and for those involved with those who suffer. Moreover, they are unbounded by the imaginative horizons and cultural tropes of the survivor of profound degradation, of the "victim" of abuse. On the other hand, the novels' appeals for recognition of the subjectivity of the survivor and the truth claims of the suffering can lose the immediacy and the raw power of the appeals of actual sex prisoners who had been shamed into silence for over 50 years.

Nor can the witness narrator depend upon readers to respond ethically. Some readers may be exhausted by yet another call to shame; some may choose to recuperate the other's suffering into their own recognizable forms of experience. Some may feel inadequately informed to act as witness to the other's witnessing. Some may be uninterested in stories told by particular witnesses. Ruff-O'Herne's witness narrative, as it tells the story of that silenced past, entered into a global rights context in which it played a significant role in calling international attention to the plight of those women from Southeast Asia forced into state-sponsored prostitution by the Japanese military. Ruff-O'Herne recognized that her story, told by a white Western woman, would draw significantly more attention to the fate of these women, joined in their activism across their radical differences, than a story told by an impoverished Korean woman living a life of destitution in North or South Korea.

Fictive and testimonial narratives as modes of intervention for social change have existed in a complex relationship at many historical moments. The novelistic treatments of the history of World War II sex prisoners come in the aftermath of public activism on behalf of the survivors of sexual slavery. In this instance, novelistic tellings become possible because witnesses have come forward, at great personal cost, to tell their stories of sexual degradation publicly. The historically specific relationship of fictive and witness discourses at once foregrounds and confounds distinctions between the fictive and the autobiographical.

Autobiographical theory thus raises questions about narratives of witness, about who is authorized to tell stories, why, and when, of what kinds, and to what ends. Attending to how a narrator establishes the authority and legitimacy of truth claims and how she or he asserts an affective call are crucial critical practices for readers, ones that narrative theorists might benefit from investigating further.

Issue 4.   Multiple Modes of Subjectivity

What do autobiographical practices in diverse media reveal about the material embeddedness of narrative?

The autobiographical migrates across media and material sites of production, expanding our understanding not only of the materialities of narrative but also of the space of potential self-reference in visual works or performances that only obliquely announce themselves as self-referential. Less bounded than the novel, with its generic history and canon, the autobiographical, as a modality of self-representation and self-inspection, ranges across disciplines and intervenes in the above sites, which were formerly closed to the intervention of minoritarian subjects. Some theorists, notably Mieke Bal and Peggy Phelan, have brilliantly mobilized the resources of narrative theory in critical acts of reading the visual and plastic arts through rhetorical categories. Placing multiple modes of self-representation in complex relationship to their maker entails categories and tropes of self-representation, implicating the issues we have already discussed as well as some particular to the materiality and media of presentation.

Attending to narrative acts of self-representation in material form enables us to trace imprints of subjectivity registered in matter or light, or, in the case of performance art, dispersed in gesture, voice, and body. Consider the extraordinary series of 784 representations in gouache, words, and imagined music that comprise the narrative of *Life? or Theatre?* by German artist-autobiographer Charlotte Salomon. Salomon, killed in Auschwitz in 1943 at age 26, near the end of her life created a story of intertwined familial, national, and cultural histories. They are in dialogue with the self-reflexive story of her growth as an artist, her melancholic meditation on loss and injury in the family's generations of women, her embodiment of language in and as painting. Reading this text only as a biography, play, novel, or series of visual experiments would ignore how its intermixing of media articulates a proliferation of self-images as an intervention in the erasure of women's agency in her family.

The autobiographical, then, can be a multimedia site that insists on the inextricable connection of narrative and the materiality of the body. It invites a reading that engages autobiographical narrative as embodied and attends to several issues: when and where the body becomes visible in the narrative; how the narrator's body and its visibility are tied to various communities; which cultural meanings are attached to the narrator's body outside the text; whether the body is ritualized and eroticized as a locus of desire or viewed as an impediment to its circulation; the relationship between the material body of the narrating "I" and the body politic; and the body as a site of knowledge and knowledge production, labor, disease, disability, and the possibility of therapeutic recuperation.

The intertwining or imbrication of autobiographical narrative and materiality, as evidenced in the textual/visual modes cited above, suggests that the autobiographical can be malleable and capacious. If we think of installations such as Janine Antoni's *Gnaw: Lard* or *Gnaw: Chocolate*, first exhibited in 1992 at the Luhring Augustine Gallery, New York, the need for autobiographical reading becomes clear. In these installations Antoni placed a 300-pound (136 kg) cube of chocolate and a 300-pound cube of lard in a gallery. After hours in the gallery she would gnaw at the cube, spitting up her gnawings and reforming the chocolate gnawings into large chocolate boxes to be displayed on shelves installed in the gallery. The lard gnawings she formed into large lipsticks to be displayed near the chocolate boxes. In this complicated and rather alarming installation Antoni enacted on the materials of sculpture a desire for consumption and the aesthetics of anorexia, putting female desire and appetites alongside the aestheticized object of the cube. Approaching Antoni's installation as a material mode of self-inscription – as vanishing matter – opens up the interstices of visual and verbal domains of the autobiographical.

Conclusion: The Troubling Differences of the Autobiographical

We began with a set of questions about what distinguishes the reading – and arguably the writing – of autobiographical narratives from explicitly fictional forms such as the novel. While boundary issues between fictional and nonfictional forms cannot be fixed absolutely, autobiographical negotiations of that boundary make troubling differences for the politics and ethics of writing and reading a life. Our discussions of four issues in autobiographical difference explored several cases that trouble, or make trouble for, theorizing the autobiographical. We considered the valance of the "real" narrator, the politics of reading for withheld autobiography in postcolonial novels, appeals to readers made by witness narratives, and the materiality of self-narration in multimedia presentations. And we suggested that narrative theorists who engage autobiographical texts may encounter different reading practices, expectations, and effects than in first-person fiction. At the least, they will want to pose additional questions.

Thinking about the autobiographical as a practice and act, rather than one genre, undermines the notion that there is a polarizing boundary between fiction and nonfiction. At the same time it urges narrative theorists to attend to differences of the autobiographical from the novel in the specific, yet different, claims each makes on audiences. When a narratological critic such as Rimmon-Kenan (2002) reads autobiographical narratives of disability as "nonfiction," she may helpfully call attention to a blind spot in narrative theory that obscures how theorizing the autobiographical may productively trouble the limits of narrative theory.

While autobiographical theorists have redefined questions of genre, authorship, audience, ethics, kinds of cultural stories, and the fiction/nonfiction boundary, there are ongoing debates on each of these questions. And these debates are increasingly informed by the work of narrative theorists raising similar issues about first-person narrative, autofiction, and autodiegetic narration. No longer regarded as the mono-logic retrospective narrative documenting a lived past, life narrative is being re-thought in relation to different subjects, sites, kinds, and modes of representing experience and constructing identity. As theorists now situate autobiography troub-lingly, as at once fictive, self-referential, and experienced by readers as nonfictional, referential, or "real-world," our sense of how life narratives engage the "real" may persuade narrative theorists to attend more extensively to the contexts of reading and the locations and positions of narratives. Autobiographical texts may be a minefield for the unwary reader, but they can also be a field of play and an occasion for critical reflection on changing reading practices, audiences, and ethics.

Notes

1 In Chapter One of *Reading Autobiography* (Smith and Watson 2001) we have argued that the autobiographical has aspects of both fictional and nonfictional narrative and is reducible to neither. Although Marie-Laure Ryan's essay on "panfictionality" attempts to theorize the fiction/nonfiction borderline, her essay is problematic because she makes no reference to autobiographical theorists (e.g., Lejeune's concept of the autobiographical pact), and she sets the novel on one side of a divide and biography and history on the other side (Ryan 1997: 166). Ryan classifies biography as a kind of nonfiction that can be evaluated by its "external verification, potential falsity, and textual competition," criteria that are insufficient for *auto*biography (p. 167). Such a schema occludes the complexity of intersubjective discourse in autobiographical narrative and harks back to an archaic notion of it as subsumed in biography.

2 "Narrative construction," a theory of the autobiographical still disputed in the field, is associated with Jerome Bruner, among others. Bruner's many books and essays, as well as his autobiography, explore how stories call selves into being. He asserts: "there is no such thing as a "life as lived" to be referred to . . . a life is created or constructed by the act of autobiography" (Bruner 1993: 38).

3 See Sidonie Smith, "Performativity": "There is no essential, original, coherent autobiographical self before the moment of self-narrating" (Smith 1998: 108).

4 Our Glossary in *Reading Autobiography* (Smith and Watson 2001) lists 52 terms, but the number is important only as an indication of the ongoing permutations of life narrative forms.

5 Consider the trouble politicians get into when the press exposes the falsity – or fictiveness – of a biographical story. Early in the 2004 presidential campaign, for instance, Howard Dean was criticized for representing his brother – lost in Laos during the Vietnam War – as a member of the US military.

6 See Jean Fagan Yellin's discussion of how Jacobs came to write her narrative for herself, using the melodramatic style of the sentimental novel, and her struggles over years to get it published. Yellin cites Child on her limited role in editing and writing an introduction to the narrative: "I abridged and struck out superfluous words sometimes, but I don't think I *altered* fifty words in the whole volume" (Jacobs 1987: xxii).

7 Following G. Thomas Couser (2004), we place the name "Benjamin Wilkomirski" in quotation marks because the Swiss citizen using this "signature," who alleged he had a Latvian-Jewish father and was imprisoned in Nazi concentration camps before adoption, has the birth name of Bruno Grosjean and the adoptive name of Bruno Dössekker.

8 Hirsch defines postmemory as the memory of a second generation, a belated displaced form of cultural memory in tension with personal memory (Hirsch 1997: 21–3). Postmemory, then, is witnessing by those who cannot offer direct witness; rather it is the witnessing of witness by children whose lives were haunted by the specter of that traumatic past and the parental struggle of traumatic remembering.

9 Recently, another international hoax hit the headlines. On July 23, 2004, the *Sydney Morning Herald* alleged that the best-selling memoir *Forbidden Love* (entitled *Honor Lost* in the USA), by the self-proclaimed Jordanian in exile Norma Khouri, is a fraud. Published by Random House Australia in 2002, *Forbidden Love* had been widely acclaimed as the true and horrifying story of Khouri's friend Dalia, a young Jordanian woman who was stabbed to death by her father when he learned of her secret relationship with a Christian army officer named Michael. Khouri recounted her life

after escape from Jordan and her struggle to write her story in internet cafés in Athens. With the book's publication, Khouri became an instant celebrity, hailed as a defender of the human rights of Muslim women.

The Australian newspaper exposé presented evidence that Norma Majid Kjouri Michael Al-Bagain Toliopoulos had emigrated to the United States at age three, become a citizen, and spent 27 years in Chicago, where she married and had two children, before disappearing in 2000. To this point neither Khouri nor Random House has admitted the hoax. This controversy suggests how a sensational story of suffering may be commodified and circulated in a Western world eager for stories that reproduce Western stereotypes of Muslim tradition. (The full story is available in the *Herald* at <http://www.smh.com.au/articles/2004/07/23/1090464851895.html>. The *Lebanese Daily Star* for August 29, 2004, has a summary at <http://www.zmag.org/content/showarticle.cfm?SectionID=22& & ItemID = 6129>.)

10 Kaplan's essay (1992) argues that many postcolonial writers have resisted the "law" of genre in autobiography by interweaving life narrative with such discourses as ethnography, psychobiography, or testimony, to create hybrid forms such as Audre Lorde's "biomythography."

11 Gilmore argues that Kincaid's narratives are a limit case that extends the autobiographical into an intertextual system of meaning (Gilmore 1998: 211). Thus the autobiographical becomes an "expansive, extendible system of meaning" (p. 214) that breaches division between the genre and first-person fiction in its nonmimetic capacities and takes as its focus the interrogation of problems in autobiography (pp. 214–15).

12 The argument of this section is adapted in part from Kay Schaffer and Sidonie Smith's (2004) *Human Rights and Narrated Lives: The Ethics of Recognition*.

13 Hilde Lindemann Nelson, in *Damaged Identities, Narrative Repair*, also considers the importance of personal storytelling in reworking trauma, but primarily as a personal and interactive process.

14 The challenge to the narrative's veracity and authenticity issued by David Stoll in his book on *I, Rigoberta Menchú* is a complex case of claims and counterclaims about the collective *testimonio* of the Quiché. For a thorough discussion of issues in this ongoing debate, see Pratt (2001).

REFERENCES AND FURTHER READING

Ahmad, A. (1995). "The Politics of Literary Postcoloniality." *Race and Class* 36 (3), 1–20.

Allende, I. (1994). *Paula*. New York: HarperCollins.

Bal, M. (2002). "Autotopography: Louise Bourgeois as Builder." In S. Smith and J. Watson (eds.), *Interfaces: Women, Autobiography, Image, Performance* (pp. 163–85). Ann Arbor: University of Michigan Press.

Bruner, J. (1993). "The Autobiographical Process." In R. Folkenflik (ed.), *The Culture of Autobiography* (pp. 38–56). Palo Alto, CA: Stanford University Press.

Cantú, N. E. (1995). *Canícula: Snapshots of a Girlhood en la Frontera*. Albuquerque: University of New Mexico Press.

Chambers, R. (2002). "Orphaned Memories, Foster Writing, Phantom Pain: The Fragments Affair." In N. K. Miller and J. Tougaw (eds.), *Extremities: Trauma, Testimony, and Community* (pp. 92–111). Urbana: University of Illinois Press.

Cliff, M. (1984). *Abeng: A Novel*. Trumansburg, NY: Crossing Press.

Cliff, M. (1987). *No Telephone to Heaven*. New York: Dutton.

Condé, M. (1982). *Hérémakhonon: A Novel*, trans. R. Philcox. Washington, DC: Three Continents Press.

Couser, G. T. (2004). *Vulnerable Subjects: Ethics and Life Writing*. Ithaca, NY: Cornell University Press.

Dangarembga, T. (1988). *Nervous Conditions*. London: Women's Press.

El Saadawi, N. (1983). *Woman at Point Zero*, trans. S. Hetata. London: Zed Press.

Gilmore, Leigh. (1998). "Endless Autobiography." In A. Hornung and E. Ruhe (eds.), *Postcolonialism and Autobiography* (pp. 211–31). Amsterdam: Rodopi.

Henson, M. R. (1999). *Comfort Woman: A Filipina's Story of Prostitution and Slavery Under the Japanese Military*. Lanham, MD: Rowman & Littlefield.

Hirsch, M. (1997). *Family Frames: Photography, Narrative, and Postmemory*. Cambridge, MA: Harvard University Press.

Jacobs, H. A. (1987). *Incidents in the Life of a Slave Girl: Written by Herself*, ed. and with introductions by L. M. Child and J. F. Yellin. Cambridge, MA: Harvard University Press.

Kaplan, C. (1992). "Resisting Autobiography: Out-Law Genres and Transnational Feminist Subjects." In S. Smith and J. Watson (eds.), *De/Colonizing the Subject: The Politics of Gender in Women's Autobiography* (pp. 115–38). Minneapolis: University of Minnesota Press.

Keller, N. O. (1997). *Comfort Woman*. New York: Viking.

Kincaid, J. (1996). *The Autobiography of My Mother*. New York: Farrar Straus Giroux.

Koolmatrie, W. (1994). *My Own Sweet Time*. Broome, Australia: Magabala Books.

Ken Bugul (1991). *The Abandoned Baobab: The Autobiography of a Senegalese Woman*, trans. M. de Jager. Brooklyn: Lawrence Hill Books.

Lazaroo, S. (2000). *The Australian Fiancé*. Sydney: Picador.

Lejeune, P. ([1975] 1989). "The Autobiographical Pact," trans. K. Leary. In P. J. Eakin (ed.), *On Autobiography* (pp. 3–30). Minneapolis: University of Minnesota Press.

Lionnet, F. (1995). "Logiques Métisses." In *Postcolonial Representations*. Ithaca, NY: Cornell University Press.

Menchú, R. (1984). *I, Rigoberta Menchú: An Indian Woman in Guatemala*, ed. E. Burgos-Debray, trans. Ann Wright. London: Verso.

Nelson, H. L. (2001). *Damaged Identities, Narrative Repair*. Ithaca, NY: Cornell University Press.

Phelan, P. (1993). *Unmarked: The Politics of Performance*. New York: Routledge.

Pratt, M. L. (2001). "*I, Rigoberta Menchú* and the Culture Wars." In A. Arias (ed.), *The Rigoberta Menchú Controversy* (pp. 29–48). Minneapolis: Minnesota University Press.

Rimmon-Kenan, S. (2002). "Illness and Narrative Identity." *Narrative*, 10 (1), 9–27.

Ruff-O'Herne, J. (1996). *50 Years of Silence: Comfort Women of Indonesia*. Singapore: Toppan Company.

Ryan, M.-L. (1997) "Postmodernism and the Doctrine of Panfictionality." *Narrative* 5 (2), 165–87.

Salomon, C. (1998). *Charlotte Salomon: Life? or Theatre?*, trans. L. Vennewitz, introduction by J. C. E. Belinfante et al. Zwelle: Waanders/London: Royal Academy of Arts.

Schaffer, K. and Smith, S. (2004). *Human Rights and Narrated Lives: The Ethics of Recognition*. New York: Palgrave/St. Martin's Press.

Smith, S. (1998). "Performativity." In S. Smith and J. Watson (eds.), *Women, Autobiography, Theory: A Reader* (pp. 108–15). Madison: University of Wisconsin Press.

Smith, S. and Watson, J. (2001). *Reading Autobiography: A Guide for Interpreting Life Narratives*. Minneapolis: University of Minnesota Press.

Spivak, G. C. (1998). "Three Women's Texts and Circumfession." In A. Hornung and E. Ruhe (eds.), *Postcolonialism and Autobiography* (pp. 7–22). Amsterdam and Atlanta: Rodopi.

Stoll, D. (1998). *Rigoberta Menchú and the Story of All Poor Guatemalans*. Boulder, CO: Westview.

Warner-Vieyra, M. (1987). *Juletane*, trans. B. Wilson. London: Heinemann.

Wilkomirski, B. (1996). *Fragments: Memories of a Wartime Childhood*, trans. C. B. Janeway. New York: Schocken Books.

24

On a Postcolonial Narratology

Gerald Prince

As Michel Mathieu-Colas (1986) once emphasized, the boundaries of narratology have evoked considerable discussion. The definition of the discipline (or perhaps "undiscipline") varies widely depending on whether one believes in "getting it all in" or getting it all out, "only connecting" or always disconnecting, always historicizing or only abstracting, theory or science, expansiveness or restraint. No real consensus has obtained and, in recent years, there has been an increasingly frequent recourse to modified and "hyphenated" expressions (structuralist narratology, postclassical narratology, postmodern narratology, socionarratology, psychonarratology) or to the adoption of a plural (as in "narratologies"). There are now formalist modulations of narratology but also dialogical and phenomenological ones; there are Aristotelian approaches to it as well as tropological or deconstructive ones; there are cognitivist and constructivist variations on it, historical, sociological, ideological, and anthropological views, feminist takes, queer speculations, and corporeal explorations (cf., e.g., Herman 1999, 2002, Mezei 1995).

In spite of this proliferation of discourses pertaining to (the systematic study of) narrative, there have been few proposals for or elaborations of a postcolonial narratology (see, e.g., Fludernik 1996, Gymnich 2002). Maybe it is because the very domain and boundaries of the postcolonial are at least as problematic as those of narratology: maybe the postcolonial is (always already) everywhere but maybe it is never (yet) anywhere. Perhaps too, specialists feel that examining, exposing, or contesting the values and consequences of the postcolonial or the (neo)colonial represent more urgent tasks than considering narratological modalities. Still, narratology can be useful (and it has been used) in the accomplishment of these very tasks: even the simple characterization of the points of view selected, the speeds adopted, the modes of discourse exploited, the actantial roles foregrounded, the transformations favored in particular narratives can help to shed light on the nature and functioning of the ideology those narratives represent and construct (see, e.g., Caldwell 1999). Besides, and more important from a narratologist's standpoint, narratology itself certainly profits from engagements with postcolonial realizations or potentialities since, at the very least, such engagements test the validity and rigor of narratological categories and distinctions.

In what follows, I will sketch a postcolonial narratology which would basically adopt and rely on the results of (post)classical narratology but would inflect it and perhaps enrich it by wearing a set of postcolonial lenses to look at narrative (cf. Herman 1999, Punday 2000). Note that this postcolonial narratology does not aim to identify postcolonial narratives or capture their distinctiveness. Note also that, contrary to Marion Gymnich's version, it does not propose to show "how concepts of identity and alterity or categories such as ethnicity, race, class and gender are constructed, perpetuated or subverted in narrative texts" (Gymnich 2002: 62). Similarly, though indebted to Susan Lanser's work on feminist narratology, it does not quite purport to "study narrative in relation to a referential context that is simultaneously linguistic, literary, historical, biographical, social, and political" (Lanser 1986: 145). It is not even bound to a specific corpus or primarily constituted through the study of particular texts and it does not chiefly depend on inductive procedures. Rather, it is sensitive to matters commonly, if not uncontroversially, associated with the postcolonial (e.g., hybridity, migrancy, otherness, fragmentation, diversity, power relations); it envisages their possible narratological correspondents; and it incorporates them.

Let us assume that, for an entity to constitute a narrative, it must be analyzable as the representation of one (or more than one nonrandomly connected and noncontradictory) transformation of a state of affairs, one (or more than one) event which does not logically presuppose that state and/or does not logically entail its transformation. However cumbersome, this definition, which is at once flexible and limiting, has, I think, several virtues (beside agreeing or at least not conflicting with widely held views about the nature of narrative). For example, it allows for a distinction between narrative and nonnarrative (a single linguistic sign or the repetition of the same sign, a series of nonsensical syllables, a purely phatic utterance, a simple existential statement, but also the mere description of an action like "John opened the window" or "Mary closed the door," a syllogism, an argument, and so on). The definition further allows for distinguishing between narrative and antinarrative (e.g., Alain Robbe-Grillet's *Jealousy*) by assigning consistency to narrative representations. Most generally, perhaps, and to use Emile Benveniste's (1974) terms, the definition evokes the *semantic* rather than *semiotic* character and mode of signification of narrative entities: unlike a sign, a narrative is not *recognized* but *understood* (which, no doubt, helps to explain the differences of opinion regarding the narrative status of many entities).

If the definition points to a number of boundaries and makes a number of conditions or restrictions explicit, it also leaves room for a considerable amount of diversity. For instance, it does not specify the medium of narrative representations (oral, written, or sign language, still or moving pictures, gestures, or a combination thereof). Nor does it specify their truth or falsehood, their factuality or fictionality, their traditionalism or modernity, their ordinariness or literariness, their spontaneity or deliberateness. Nor does it detail the nature of their content and its relation to anthropomorphic experience, the kinds of topics addressed and themes developed, the types of situations and events represented, or the qualities of their many possible links. Furthermore, it puts no limits on the maximal dimension of narratives; it barely indicates the degree of cohesion or the kind of closure they (ought to) possess; and it hardly constrains modes of narration (different ways of representing the same situations and events) or modes of narrativity – what Marie-Laure Ryan describes as the "various textual realizations of plots, the various ways in which a text relies on a narrative structure (or plot, or story) and suggests this structure as a model of coherence" (Ryan 1992: 369).

Just as it endeavors to trace explicitly the definitional boundaries of narrative (to specify what all and only narratives have in common), narratology tries to account for narrative diversity (for what allows narratives to differ from one another *qua* narratives). As suggested above, it already partly does this by providing a large repertoire of questions to ask of narratives (a large number of descriptive tools with which to capture the distinctiveness of any narrative and found or support interpretive conclusions).[1] Granting particular consideration to postcolonial concerns may, of course, affect the size of that repertoire, its economy, or its exploitation. For example, as Monika Fludernik remarks in her discussion of potentially productive links between postcolonial narratives and narratology, or as Marion Gymnich emphasizes in her study of the relevance of linguistics to a postcolonial narratology, the (kinds of) languages used by the narrator and by the characters constitute a fruitful area of narratological inquiry. They may be quite similar or very different, standard or nonstandard, positively or negatively marked, and so forth. In her discussion, Fludernik mentions as well the use of innovative or unconventional techniques as another fertile area of investigation. "Odd" pronouns in "one," "you," or "we" narratives would offer pertinent illustrations; and a narratorial "we," say, might represent a homogeneous or a heterogeneous group, designate a discordant rather than harmonious collectivity, or include certain communities but not others. Now it is true that, regardless of their interest in postcolonialism, students of narrative have examined and, to some extent, codified many of the (temporal, spatial, moral, intellectual, but also linguistic) distances between narrator, narratee, and characters. They have, likewise, done extensive work on the category "person" (second-person narration, first-person-plural narration, multipersoned narration, etc.). It is also true that formal innovation and technical daring are neither distinctive of nor integral to postcolonial texts. They may, in fact, be more common in (post)modern or feminist texts. But many postcolonial texts are (post)modern or feminist too and (postcolonial) narratology studies possibilities rather than only actualities. In any case, without altering any definitional boundaries, the accentuation – for the purposes of a postcolonial narratology – of characteristics like the linguistic power or the communal representativeness of the narratorial voice would foster the (classificatory) study of texts in terms of the ways they utilize such characteristics. Indeed, the (re)consideration of any narrative trait or category in a postcolonial light could yield different modulations in narratological accounts of (the syntax, semantics, and pragmatics of) narrative.

On the level of the narrated, for instance, narratologists consider whether space is explicitly mentioned and described, prominent or not, stable or changing, perceiver-dependent or, on the contrary, autonomous, characterized by its position or by its constituents. They further consider the paths that traverse it and their orientations, the ways it is segmented, the proximity or distance of the various segments from deictic centers and their relative importance, the (backgrounded or foregrounded) entities occupying these segments and the events animating them. Given the boundaries, crossings, transfers, dispersions, marginalizations, decks and holds, fields and jungles created by or related to colonialism, they might pay particular attention to the extent of multitopicality – here (and here and here) as opposed to there (and there and there) or to somewhere, everywhere, nowhere – as well as to the degree of heterotopicality, to the kinds of mixtures and inconsistencies, of gaps, breaches, and cracks within spaces or between them, to the nature of frames or limits, and to spatial alignments along such semantic axes as natural or artificial, familiar or strange, independent or colonized, rhizomatic, cybernetic, chaotic, and so on and so forth (see, e.g., Louis-Ferdinand Céline's *Journey to the End of the Night*, Linda Lê's *Voix*, or Henri Lopes's *Sur l'autre rive*).

Similarly, apart from taking notice of the relative explicitness, precision, and prominence of temporal anchorings, narratologists are attentive to the nature of time as well as to its action: straight, cyclical, or looping, regressive as opposed to progressive, flowing irregularly instead of regularly, subjective rather than objective, characterized by duration or by date, segmented according to artificial or perhaps natural measures, close or distant from deictic focuses, curative, energizing, paralyzing, degrading. Because of such postcolonially marked themes and preoccupations as the old, the new, nostalgia and hope, authentic and fake beginnings and ends, or memory, amnesia, and anamnesis, they might concentrate on datelessness, quasi- or pseudo-chronology, heterochronology, multichronology – now (or now or now) in contrast with a past or future then (or then or then) or with always, never, at times, at some time – as well as on the (partial or total) simultaneities, (immediate or proximate) continuities, and (weak or strong) inconsistencies between temporal segments, the relative magnitude of those segments, and the nature of their borders (see Raphaël Confiant's *L'allée des soupirs*, Ahmadou Kourouma's *Monnew*, or Leila Sebbar's *Le Chinois vert d'Afrique*).

Of course, like other narratologies, a postcolonial narratology would aim to account for the kind of characters inhabiting these spatial and temporal settings and to supply instruments for the exploration and description of their significance, their complexity, the stability of their designation and identity, or the actantial slots they occupy and the actantial functions they fulfill. In addition, it would allow for the study of their perceptions, their utterances, thoughts, and feelings, their motivations, their interactions, and their position with respect to such commonly exploited semantic categories as goodness and badness, class and power, sex, gender, or sexuality. But it might also make provisions for focusing on the exploitation of particularly pertinent features like (formerly or newly) colonizing or colonized, race or ethnicity, otherness and hybridity, collaboration, (forced) assimilation, resistance, or ambivalence, and, obviously, linguistic and narrative capacity.

Last but far from least, a postcolonial narratology would characterize the kinds of events (goal-directed actions and mere happenings, processes, accomplishments, or achievements) that can involve these participants and occur in these settings. It would distinguish kernel events from satellites as well as interventional from noninterventional or productive from preventive ones. It would specify the (syntagmatic and paradigmatic, spatiotemporal, logical, transformational) relations between these events and the types of change the latter can bring about (spatial transfer, physical modification, information transaction, object acquisition, etc.). It would also show how narrative sequences can belong to one or more narrative domains (one or more sets of actions pertaining to given characters), each of which is governed by (alethic, epistemic, axiological, or deontic) modal constraints, and how they can be combined into ever more complex sequences and story lines through operations like conjunction, embedding, and alternation. Furthermore, it would detail the kinds of story structures that can be elaborated (loose or tight, involving one or several lines, openended, partially closed, or totalizing, circular, repetitive, fugal, digressive, spiraling, or irreversible); and it would describe the kinds of narrativities that can obtain (e.g., simple or complex, multiple, braided, proliferating, or diluted) as well as such pragmatically conditioned features as foreshadowings, backshadowings, or mirrorings, the (situationally, actionally, instrumentally) scripted nature of sequences, and the discreteness or positivity of events and states of affairs. Above all, and in keeping with its postcolonial orientation, it might grant special consideration to the possibility of gaps, indeterminacies, and inconsistencies within a sequence (or domain), of contradictions between two sequences, and of metaleptic infractions, contaminations, and migrations between them: frame breakings, for example, transgressions of ontological boundaries, confluences and transfers across distinct domains, or "strange loops" whereby a given sequence embeds the sequence it is itself embedded in (see Nabile Farès' *La découverte du nouveau monde*, Edouard Glissant's *Tout-Monde*, Kateb Yacine's *Le polygone étoilé*). It might be extra sensitive to the possible multifunctionality of events and the dissimilarities between the functions they fulfill in different sequences or domains. It might promote not only the tracking of disnarrated elements and their distribution but also those of merely potential narratives (which the narrator or a character promises to recount but never does) or those of rudimentary ones, which the narrator or a character begins to recount but never gets to finish (cf. Maher 2002). It might, finally, help to focus on the meetings, contacts, and interactions represented, the kinds of confrontations and conflicts depicted, opponents involved, and forces deployed (equal or unequal, well-matched, ill-balanced, or incommensurable) as well as the types of alliances or agreements, of communications, negotiations, dialogues, and exchanges described.

Like the level of the narrated, the level of the narrating has been much studied by (post)classical narratology. For instance, narratologists have described the temporal orders that a narrative can follow, the anachronies that it can exhibit, the achronic structures that it can accommodate. Moreover, they have characterized narrative speed and its canonical tempos. They have investigated narrative frequency, scrutinized distance and point of view, examined the types of discourse that a text can adopt to present the utterances and thoughts of characters, and analyzed the major temporal kinds of narration (posterior, anterior, simultaneous, intercalated) as well as their modes of combination. They have also explored the distinctive features of first-, second-, and third-person narrative; they have isolated (some of) the signs referring to the (more or less overt, knowledgeable, reliable, self-conscious) narrator and to the narratee, and they have delineated the situation of these narrational actants. Once again, a narratology mindful of postcolonial issues might involve the recasting of the narratological means that indicate narrative roads (not) taken and it might therefore provide a different sort of optic with which to view these roads. Thus, following the lead of feminist narratology with regard to categories like sex, gender, and sexual orientation, it could make the narrator's postcolonial status (neo-colonizer, formerly colonized, etc.) as important a variable as intrusiveness, self-consciousness, or knowledge, and it could classify narrative texts according to their specification of that status and its linkage with the other variables. It could even make room for some "poco bending" (with the colonizers narrating as the colonized or vice versa). Similarly, following the suggestions and investigations of Fludernik or Gymnich, special attention could be given to the nature of the narrator's language in order to specify whether that language is (supposed to be) written, uttered, signed, or unexpressed, whether it is the same as that of the narratee and the characters, or whether it is that of the colonizer, that of the colonized, a creolized compound of the two, or none of the above. One might, in addition, concentrate on whether it is native to the narrator; whether it contains regionalisms, dialectal turns, neologisms, nonstandard or incorrect forms; whether, to what extent, and in what circumstances it involves code-switching, using words or phrases from a different linguistic code; and whether these words or phrases are (indirectly) translated or left untranslated (see, e.g., François Rabelais's *Third Book* or *Fourth Book*, Amadou Hampaté Bâ's *The Fortunes of Wangrin*, Patrick Chamoiseau's *Texaco* and *School Days*, Ousmane Socé's *Karim*, or Aminata Sow Fall's *L'appel des arènes*).

The question of narratorial language and of the kind of (oppressive, apologetic, hesitant) mediation it institutes and signifies is related to the question of the discourse types featured and to the way they accentuate or downplay that mediation. One possibility that has been neglected and that a postcolonial narratology might focus on and explicitly allow for is that of immediate discourses (whereby characters' utterances and thoughts are free of any narratorial introduction, mediation, or patronage) issuing from a group or collectivity rather than a single individual, from a (more or less homogeneous) "we" instead of an "I." Clearly, similar kinds of pluralities might obtain in other discourse types. It would be easy in a film, for example, to blend the utterances of a voiceover with those of several characters speaking simultaneously.

Given the hybridities and inconstancies, tensions, rifts, and shifts in the status, expression, and character of postcolonial entities and their contexts, extra consideration might likewise be granted to the narrator's diegetic situation (and to the narrating instance as a whole). Beside cases of oddly disframed narrators, metaleptically transgressing diegetic boundaries and stabilities, or cases of odd pronouns and odd persons, there can be cases of "counterpersonal" narration, where the antimimetic utilization of an unsteady, inconsistent, or heterogeneous narrative voice makes it difficult to ascertain the type of narrative person operating. Moreover, there can be cases of "personless" narration, where the feature "person" is absent rather than undecidable or undeterminable. Consider, for instance, a narrative written in the present participle (or one eschewing verbal forms altogether) and using no other marks of person.[2]

Verbless narratives can render nonpertinent several categories other than "person." For example, they can make it impossible to situate temporally the act of narrating vis-à-vis the events narrated and to speak of, say, simultaneous or posterior narration. Though such accounts are admittedly rare and though they seldom (if ever) constitute texts of significant length, they must be taken into account by a (postcolonial) narratology aspiring to universality. After all, such a narratology would regard any narrative (rather than merely existing, attested, or postcolonial ones) as part of its domain. Besides, the narratological relevance of any number of features does not depend on their being integral to or even important in narrative but, instead, on their capacity to be linked with or to raise narratively interesting questions (cf. Prince 1995).

Sometimes, in what may be more characteristic of postcolonial explorations of different temporalities, the detours of remembrance, the plays of desire and regret, the turns and returns of loss, discovery, and recovery, it is not so much that features like simultaneous or posterior narration are nonpertinent but that they are very much problematized. Certain uses of the present tense, for instance, or certain kinds of tense alternations and certain multiplications of deictic shifts make it hard to distinguish between "now" and "not now" or lead to inconsistent deictic centers (cf. Maurice Roche's *Compact*, Linda Lê's *Voix*, or Kateb Yacine's *Nedjma*).

Other temporal questions pertaining to the narrating act are similarly evoked by the postcolonial. Apart from narrations in which a chronological ordering is adopted and from narrations in which, on the contrary, anachronies abound, there can be cases of achronicity (in which events are deprived of all temporal connections with other events), antichronicity (in which events are dated in erratic and contradictory ways), and polychronicity (whereby the narration involves and exploits a multivalued system of temporal ordering, including such values or concepts as "indeterminately situated vis-à-vis temporal reference point x"). As Herman (2002: 213–14) emphasized, situations and events can be temporally ordered in a full and unequivocal manner; but they can be ordered randomly as well (all possible temporal orderings are equally probable); they can be ordered alternatively or multiply (two or more temporal orderings are (equi)probable); and they can be ordered partially (some events are unequivocally and uniquely situated relative to the other events in the narrative but some events are coded inexactly).

In general, every category at the narrating level should be reviewed in the light of postcolonial affinities and, if necessary, revised to accommodate narrative structures and configurations which these affinities might call for or suggest. Perhaps the category "point of view" can serve as a last example. A postcolonial narratology would obviously detail the standard types of point of view (i.e., unrestricted or "omniscient," internal, external). In addition, it would characterize more eccentric cases like compound point of view (when a set of elements is perceived simultaneously – and identically or differently – by more than one focalizer), unspecified point of view (when no particular focalizer is identified), undecidable point of view (when it is impossible to determine which one of two or more specific entities functions as the focalizer), or maybe even split point of view (when one focalizer yields two or more different but equally adequate presentations of the same existents and events).

The future of narratology lies partly in its past and my discussion has allowed me to mention a number of (well-established) narratological concepts and achievements that prospective narratologies will likely take into account. My discussion has further allowed me to point to what I consider the domain of the discipline. It may be worth stating again that, though (postcolonial) narratology can benefit from the examination of specific (sets of) texts, it is not tied exclusively to them. Rather, it is concerned with all and only possible narratives, including nonverbal, nonliterary, nonfictional, and nonextant ones. Finally, my discussion has given me the opportunity to insist on some important traits and functions of narratology. As a theory (or science, or poetics) of narrative, (postcolonial) narratology differs from (postcolonial) narratological criticism. The first characterizes and articulates narratively pertinent categories and features in order to account for the ways in which narratives are configured and make sense; the second uses these categories and features in order to specify the configuration and sense of particular narratives. Of course, apart from constituting a tool kit for criticism and because it explores the potentialities of narrative, (postcolonial) narratology can not only permit the (re)assessment of indefinitely many texts; it can also, perhaps, function as a rhetoric and indicate hitherto unexploited narrative forms.

The future of narratology lies in the future too and in a number of endeavors that narratologists should continue to pursue or that they ought to undertake. To conclude my remarks, I would like to mention a few of these endeavors. The first one is evident enough and I have already stressed it frequently. It consists, with the help of new tools, expanded corpora, and fresh inflections (let a thousand narratologies bloom!), in identifying or examining various aspects of narrative and in (re)defining them, reconfiguring them, and eliminating possible incoherences among them. I have myself pointed in passing to some narratologically neglected categories like pluralized immediate discourse and I could have noted Marie-Laure Ryan's revisionist view of the narrator (in Ryan 2001) or other efforts at breaking down theoretical units, like Dorrit Cohn's reanalysis of unreliability as misinformation or discordance (Cohn 2000). I could have referred to the very considerable work that continues to be done on point of view or to the re-explorations of figures like the implied author (see, e.g., van Peer and Chatman 2001); and I could have evoked Manfred Jahn (1997) on frames or Françoise Revaz (1997) on narrativity. Moreover, I could have underlined the increased affection, in much recent narratological work, for distinguishing narrative features or configurations in terms of continuums rather than strict binaries (or ternaries) and the increased concern for incorporating a "voice of the receiver" in accounts of narrative functioning. A second, not unrelated, task consists in undertaking (experimental, cross-cultural, or cross-media) studies of the role and significance of (problematic or uncontroversial) narrative features or narratological claims and in grounding narratology empirically. Indeed, the development of an explicit, complete, and *realistic* model of narrative competence (the ability to produce narrative texts and to process texts as narratives) ultimately constitutes the most important narratological task and it is the third and last task I will mention. After a number of (early) intoxicating proposals, the modeling impulse appears to have abated. But it seems clear to me that the construction of such a model will promote the coherence of the discipline and facilitate the systematic study of its object. Perhaps proposals for and elaborations of distinctly modulated narratologies – like, say, some postcolonial ones – will provide a stimulus for narratological modeling.[3]

NOTES

1   In my discussion of these tools, I rely on many works and, in particular, on Fludernik (1996), Herman (2002), Ireland (2001), van Peer and Chatman (2001), and Richardson (2000).

2   In nonlinguistic narratives, the category person simply does not apply (what would consti-

tute a wordless, "titleless" first-person narrative painting?). A distinction should therefore be made between the possible absence of a feature or category and its inapplicability.

3   I thank Lydie Moudileno for her insightful comments.

REFERENCES AND FURTHER READING

Benveniste, E. (1974). *Problèmes de linguistique générale. II.* Paris: Gallimard.

Caldwell, R. C., Jr. (1999). "*Créolité* and Postcoloniality in Raphaël Confiant's *L'Allée des soupirs.*" *The French Review* 73, 301–11.

Cohn, D. (2000). "Discordant Narration." *Style* 34, 307–16.

Fludernik, M. (1996). *Towards a "Natural" Narratology.* London: Routledge.

Gymnich, M. (2002). "Linguistics and Narratology: The Relevance of Linguistic Criteria to Postcolo-

nial Narratology." In M. Gymnich, A. Nünning, and V. Nünning (eds.), *Literature and Linguistics: Approaches, Models, and Applications. Studies in Honour of Jon Erickson* (pp. 61–76). Trier: WVT Wissenschaftlicher Verlag Trier.

Herman, D. (ed.) (1999). *Narratologies: New Perspectives on Narrative Analysis.* Lincoln: University of Nebraska Press.

Herman, D. (2002). *Story Logic: Problems and Possibilities of Narrative.* Lincoln: University of Nebraska Press.

Ireland, K. (2001). *The Sequential Dynamics of Narrative: Energies at the Margins of Fiction*. London: Associated University Presses.

Jahn, M. (1997). "Frames, Preferences, and the Reading of Third-Person Narrative: Toward a Cognitive Narratology." *Poetics Today* 18, 441–67.

Lanser, S. F. (1986). "Toward a Feminist Narratology." *Style* 20, 341–63.

Maher, D. (2002). "Precious Time: Pushing the Limits of Narrative in the Seventeenth Century." *Narrative* 10, 128–39.

Mathieu-Colas, M. (1986). "Frontières de la Narratologie." *Poétique* 17, 91–110.

Mezei, K. (ed.) (1995). *Ambiguous Discourse: Feminist Narratology and British Women Writers*. Chapel Hill: University of North Carolina Press.

van Peer, W. and Chatman, S. (eds.) (2001). *New Perspectives on Narrative Perspective*. Albany: State University of New York Press.

Prince, G. (1995). "On Narratology: Criteria, Corpus, Context." *Narrative* 3, 73–84.

Punday, D. (2000). "A Corporeal Narratology?" *Style* 34, 227–42.

Revaz, F. (1997). *Les textes d'action*. Metz: Université de Metz.

Richardson, B. (2000). "Narrative Poetics and Postmodern Transgression: Theorizing the Collapse of Time, Voice, and Frame." *Narrative* 8, 23–42.

Ryan, M.-L. (1992). "The Modes of Narrativity and their Visual Metaphors." *Style* 26, 368–87.

Ryan, M.-L. (2001). "The Narratorial Functions: Breaking Down a Theoretical Primitive." *Narrative* 9, 146–52.

25

Modernist Soundscapes and the Intelligent Ear: An Approach to Narrative Through Auditory Perception

Melba Cuddy-Keane

In E. M. Forster's *Howards End*, during an animated conversation about pictures and music, Margaret Schlegel protests, "What *is* the good of the arts if they're interchangeable? What *is* the good of the ear if it tells you the same as the eye?" (Forster [1910] 1973: 36). Surrounded by listeners who, in their various ways, make Beethoven's Fifth Symphony something *other* than sound, Margaret alone listens to music as music. Forster makes no attempt to convey what Margaret hears (and narrative always faces the difficulty that as soon as sounds are put into words, we are left with the sound of the word, not the sound of the sound); nevertheless, his famous symphony scene signals a distinctive new focus, in the modernist period, for humanists and psychologists alike: the act of auditory perception. In narrative, this perceptual "turn" can be traced in both a consciousness of expanded sounds and a heightened sense of sound as something perceived. I propose here that the city plays a formative role in stimulating this increased auditory awareness – an hypothesis that I pursue through an analysis of urban soundscapes in Virginia Woolf's short fiction and novels. Yet if one of my objectives is to explore the way listening functions in modernist narrative, another equally important and indeed inseparable goal is to promote the development of a critical methodology and a vocabulary for analyzing narrative representations of sound.

Sound has always played a significant role in literature, but generally in forms that are narrativized (converted, like program music, into a running scenic description), or thematized (used to represent or "stand for" a nonaural meaning or experience), or spiritualized (treated as yielding access to a transcendent suprasensual world).[1] Formalistically, allusions to specific sounds can function as leitmotifs, giving structural shape to a narrative; aurally, sound is ubiquitously present in the enunciated words of the text as we read them out loud or sound them silently in our minds.[2] Finally, dialogue – a fundamental element of narrative – is something voiced that is heard. But at the beginning of the twentieth century, a further dimension of sound appeared in the immediate and concrete way that narrative began mimetically to record a vast repertoire of sound, and to transcribe the actual process of listening. New sensory experiences – many of them occasioned by technology and the modern city – and a growing interest in cognitive perception gave rise to a new aurality, which in turn made its mark upon narrative, in new inscriptions of sound.

Modern approaches to sound originate in the late nineteenth century, with the birth of the science of acoustics and the advent of modern sound technology: Hermann von Helmholtz's ground-breaking work, *On the Sensations of Tone*, was translated into English in 1875; Alexander Graham Bell sent the first words through a rudimentary telephone in 1876; and Thomas Edison inaugurated the phonograph in 1877 (Picker 2003: 85, 100–1, 113). John Picker convincingly argues that the impact on literature is a heightened interest in "close listening" (p. 9), yet the conclusion we are likely to draw from his analysis is that nineteenth-century narratives generally treat acoustical science as metaphor and analogy. In Picker's examples, George Eliot's rendering of psychologically sympathetic vibration is *analogous* to Helmholtz's resonance theory of hearing; the nightmarish underside of the phonographic voice manifests itself, in Bram Stoker's *Dracula*, in the *parallels* between the engravings on the recording cylinder and the indentations of the vampire's teeth or, in Joseph Conrad's *Heart of Darkness*, in the hauntingly lingering cry of Kurtz, which echoes *like* a phonograph stuck in its groove. While the Victorians do show an increasing imaginative response to reproduced and amplified sound, attention shifts, in the modernist period, to the precise physical characteristics of sound and the complex processes of auditory perception.

A new perceptually based approach to sound appears in public controversies about the nature of music. The traditional idealist view still lingers – upheld, for example, by the literary and art critic Arthur Clutton-Brock, for whom *The Magic Flute* was a "religious work" by a "philosopher who spoke in music" with "depths and depths of meaning beyond our full comprehension" (Clutton-Brock 1916: 301), and by the historian of science, J. W. N. Sullivan, who likened music to mathematics in its freedom from any necessary correspondence to actual reality and in its "spiritual profundities" more expressible in the language of mysticism than common sense (Sullivan 1922: 562). But Sullivan was roundly rebutted by the poet and music critic W. J. Turner, who argued that "both music and mathematics are mental processes; they are the creation of the mind of man, therefore to say they are independent of the world is nonsense" (Turner 1922: 46). Music, he asserted, is part of the reality of human consciousness. Such realist views were furthered by I. A. Richards who, in his influential *Principles of Literary Criticism* (1925), similarly repudiated claims for the exalted uniqueness of music, arguing that what has yet to be analyzed is not therefore unanalyzable. Like Turner, Richards stressed the need for further knowledge, noting that music theory had found ways to discuss form, but had devised no way to deal with affect. Richards argued that affect can only be understood in terms of the relations of sounds to each other and that advances had to be made in neurology before such analysis could really take place.[3]

In narrative, modernism also "turned" to the experiencing subject, and the approach to sound was no exception. Elsewhere, I have related this development to the emergence of new sound technologies, exploring the parallels between Virginia Woolf's inscriptions of sound and the new approaches evident in broadcasting, recording, and early experimental music composition (Cuddy-Keane 2000). In *The Senses of Modernism: Technology, Perception, and Aesthetics*, Sara Danius goes further to posit that "technology is in a specific sense *constitutive* of high-modernist aesthetics" (Danius 2002: 3). Like a growing number of critics today, Danius rejects the commonly hypothesized split between modernism and modernity, arguing that that such a binary relies on a deterministic understanding of technology which opposes it to the human and the corporeal, and ignores the human body as perceiver and user.

Although Danius focuses more on seeing than on listening, she demonstrates the way that the "ever-closer relation between the sensuous and the technological" results in "a shift from idealist theories of aesthetic experience to materialist ones" (2003: 2). Detailing what she considers the turn of the twentieth century "crises of the senses" in the works of Thomas Mann, Marcel Proust, and James Joyce, Danius finds an increasing abandonment of knowing for perceiving until, in Joyce, we arrive at the purity of "everyday life in its lived immediacy" (p. 187), and perception becomes an aesthetic end in itself. For Danius, the ultimate assimilation of technology is achieved in Joyce's representation of the human body as a "sensorium" or all-perceiving inscription device. As convincing as this conclusion is, it seems to me to overlook both what a complex act human perception is, and the significance of what, precisely, the human body is observing. Another way to describe the changes taking place is to say that modernity occasioned new experiences for the "human sensorium," stimulating both a new perceptual knowledge and a new apprehension of perception.

The sense of perception as an active form of engagement with one's surroundings is heightened by the interaction of the modernist listener with the modern city. Although the city has been in many ways a disruptive force in human experience, we have perhaps overemphasized its stressful and alienating effects, forgetting that it can be an immensely productive stimulus as well. Individual writers and artists of course manifest mixed and varying responses, ranging from fears of isolation and dehumanization to enlivened attentiveness and a sense of expanded life. As the modern city evolved, the clashing and discordant sounds of its technological and mechanized environment challenged the ear with greater disparities and contrasts but, paralleling and reinforcing the impact of broadcasting and recording, the new sound relationships often prompted more acute and attentive listening. Not all writers recoiled from the "shock of the new."

The crowds of the city have for centuries disturbed those desirous of silence, as illustrated in Hogarth's 1741 engraving of "The Enraged Musician," in which an outraged German violinist looks out a window in horror, plugging his ears against the noisy assault of the London street. By the nineteenth century, the outdoor clamor that disturbed the indoor playing of Hogarth's musician had escalated into a cacophony that prompted, as John Picker explains, an antistreet-noise movement directed against itinerant musicians and organized to defend middle-class private space and quiet for work. By the end of the century, the predominantly human and animal sounds of the city were overlaid by the sharpened timbres of metallic noises and the higher decibels and constancy of vehicular traffic. While street noise would still offend the ear longing for quiet, the sounds of the city also came to be taken as a distinctive mark of a city's character. While the title of W. D. Howells's *London Films* augurs a visual description of the city, reinforced by its opening image of a "mental kodak," Howells also offers a verbal recording of the city's sound. Anticipating what the composer Murray Schafer would later call the city's "keynote sound" – the ubiquitous, underlying hum of traffic – Howells differentiated the "quality of the noise" heard in London from that in New York. London's "specialized noises" were the "dull, tormented roar of the omnibuses and the incessant cloop-cloop of the cab-horses' hoofs," whereas New York was characterized by the "harsh, metallic shriek" and "grind of trolley wheels upon trolley tracks" (Howells 1905: 52).[4] Despite his objections to the relentless intrusiveness of such noise, Howells's clear fascination evidences the way the modern urban soundscape stimulated what the composer Barry Truax (1984) calls "attentive listening."[5] The sounds of the city have furthermore fostered a wide array of art forms. In 1919, Dziga Vertov's inspiration for the *kino-glaz* or camera-eye – the foundation of *cinéma-vérité* – began in his desire to "photograph" the disparate and cacophonous sounds in a railway station; John Cage attributed his aleatoric and pluralistic compositions to an epiphanic experience of the multiplicity of sights and sounds on a street corner in Seville.[6]

New sound technologies, the sounds of the modern city, and an interest in auditory perception together form the backdrop of a new narrative inscription of the listening subject. But to understand narrative's new aurality, we need an appropriate language for its analysis. Previously, I proposed the terms auscultation, auscultize, and auscultator to parallel the existing terminology of focalization, focalize, and focalizer (Cuddy-Keane 2000). My motive was not to assert that hearing is a fundamentally different process from seeing – although there may be significant and distinctive attributes – but to signal the way a specialized terminology can help us to discriminate the sense-specific elements in the text. Our analysis of narrative acoustics can also be enhanced by employing the sonic vocabulary developed in the 1970s by the World Soundscape Project at Simon Fraser University: soundmark instead of landmark, soundscape instead of landscape, sound signal and keynote sound in place of figure and ground (Schafer 1974). Finally, we can usefully draw upon terminology employed in the study of auditory perception: auditory streaming, stream segregation and integration, and auditory restoration. New insights might well follow upon our efforts to emancipate our vocabulary from an excessive dependence on the visual. As Douglas Kahn asks, "How can listening be explained when the subject in recent theory has been situated . . . in the web of the gaze, mirroring, reflection, the spectacle and other ocular tropes?" (Kahn 1992: 4).

To pursue the development of an auditory typology, I begin with two different possibilities in the relation between sound source and listener, using, as examples,

Virginia Woolf's narratives set in urban environments. In one mode of representation, evident in Woolf's short fiction "Kew Gardens," sound is emitted from multiple sound sources widely separated in space but auscultized through one stationary perceiver. In the other mode, notably captured in the striking of Big Ben in *Mrs. Dalloway*, sound is emitted from a stationary source and broadly diffused to auscultators positioned in diverse and broadly scattered locations. For the reader of the text, the dynamics are different. The first mode invokes the activity of the narrative ear in processing and relating disparate sounds; the second, the reader's process of tracking and relating different auscultators. The different approaches yield two different acoustical mappings and two different experiences of the city.

"Kew Gardens," hand-set and printed by the Woolfs in 1919, is one of Virginia Woolf's earliest experimental fictions. Though set in a garden, the garden is embedded in city space; while intensely visual, the sketch is also a dense notation of voices. Diverse fragments of sound become the narrative thread: voices of people we see before we can hear what they are saying and which pass out of earshot before the conversations are over, the voice of the summer sky murmuring in the drone of an aeroplane passing overhead, and the voices of the flowers heard by an old man who babbles on about a conductive machine that operates by a battery and uses a rubber-insulated wire to transmit the spirit voices of the dead. The effect is of narrative auscultized from the position of a stationary microphone, its membrane vibrating to the sounds of a summer day. Although we hear only snatches of conversation, the absence or interruption of semantic content prompts us to read the narrative sonically: "Voices. Yes, voices. Wordless voices, breaking the silence." And the wordless voices are sounded against the keynote sound of the city: "But there was no silence; all the time the motor omnibuses were turning their wheels and changing their gear." While disjunctive and disparate, these multiple sounds are integrated by the narrative ear: "like a vast nest of Chinese boxes all of wrought steel turning ceaselessly one within another the city murmured; on the top of which the voices cried aloud and the petals of myriads of flowers flashed their colours into the air" (Woolf 1985: 89). City sounds and sounds of technology, while different in timbre from sounds of nature, are thus not different as objects of aural perception. Human voices, ambient noise, and environmental sound form an intricate polytextural acoustic web.

At least two features inform Woolf's notation: the first is the auscultation of discrete and specific rather than generalized sounds; the second is the inclusion of all sounds in a comprehensive soundscape.[7] But perhaps even more important is the centrality, to the narrative, of listening. Thematically, the sketch conveys the integration rather than the traditional opposition of the pastoral and the urban but, sonically, the significance is that the integrative pattern is apprehended by the narrative ear. Sounds are auscultized through an invisible narrating consciousness, and sound is inscribed as something perceived. Auscultation also goes further than focalization, since from the stationary position in the garden, the traffic is heard but not seen. Not only is listening the activity that constructs a meaningful representation of the narrative world, but hearing is the more inclusive, more integrative sense.

The second mode presents the reverse pattern, in which the sound source is single and stationary and the auscultators are multiple and diverse. And if, in my first example, the city augments the auditory spectrum for the ear by introducing new timbral dimensions, in my second example, the chiming of Big Ben in *Mrs. Dalloway,* urban space scatters and extends the locations of auscultation.

London's Big Ben is a classic example of a soundmark – what Murray Schafer defines as a "prominent feature of the soundscape, possessing properties of uniqueness, symbolic power or other qualities which make it especially conspicuous or affectionately regarded" (Schafer 1974: 37). And like another soundmark, the bells of a parish church, the audible zone of Big Ben defines a community. As Schafer notes, "The parish used to be defined as that area over which the parish church bells may be heard; when you can no longer hear the bells you are in another parish – or none at all" (p. 41). Traditionally, the notion of London as an aural community was well ensconced in the definition of a cockney as one born within the hearing of the bells of Saint Mary-le-Bow. In a similar sound mapping, Woolf uses the striking of Big Ben to redraw London with a significantly expanded geographical range. For the single sound source of Big Ben brings into temporal harmony a multiplicity of listeners positioned in a variety of locations. It is heard by Clarissa throughout the day in her home in Westminster, by Peter in Clarissa's home, by Richard entering Dean's Yard, by Rezia in Harley Street, and by an anonymous auscultator who traces the stroke as it wafts "over the northern part of London" until it mixes with "clouds and wisps of smoke" and dies up in the air "among the seagulls" (Woolf [1925] 2000: 80). In the farthest reaches of the auditory trajectory, the narrative shifts from literal to notional auscultation. Physically the sound would not be audible at that distance to the human ear, but theoretically the sound waves would continue, past the seagulls, out into space. Here, the full comprehension of sonic diffusion – the repeated phrase is "the leaden circles dissolved in the air" – must be performed in the imaginative ear of the reader. At the level of the characters, Woolf's notation maps a new, modern, urban community delineated, not through visual connection or physical proximity, but through shared aural experience. At the narrative level, the reader's auditory imagination performs a further integrative act, using sound as the thread to connect the city dwellers not only to each other, but also to nature, and ultimately to the universe beyond. Auscultation here leads to a perception of a complex whole, but it is not the suprasensual music of the spheres. The paratactical juxtapositioning of different auscultized perceptions generates a comprehensive human experiencing, rather than a transcendent and unified experience.[8]

Although auscultation functions differently in these two examples, both make us acutely aware of the inclusiveness of auditory perception. Geographical range may indeed be one of the chief differences between seeing and hearing. Peripheral vision generally operates within the range of 140–80°, with the area of acute central vision being significantly less (often functioning within a range of 5°), whereas we can, at any one moment, detect sound sources within the full circumference of 360°. In addition, we can more easily shut our eyes against unpleasant scenes than, lacking earlids, shut our ears against uninvited sounds. Hearing is our warning sense, which evolution does not allow us to shut off; it works at night, and works when our eyes are closed.[9] Hearing is arguably more inclusive and comprehensive than seeing, and it thus lends itself to narrative inscriptions of integrative perceptions – in "Kew Gardens," of the imbricated urban and pastoral and, in *Mrs. Dalloway*, of the interwoven urban community.

Not surprisingly, the increased inclusiveness of sound produces a heightened awareness of separate and disparate events, with the result that part of the crucial work of hearing is perceiving, or trying to perceive, relationships. What, then, is hearing's relational work, and how does narrative record it? To pursue such questions, we need to draw upon cognitive approaches to hearing, as captured in the title of Reinier Plomp's *The Intelligent Ear*, and consider the way "sounds presented to the ear are translated by the hearing process into sounds as percepts" (Plomp 2002: 1). We tend to naturalize audition as a "passive quality" rarely if ever "aware of our ears, nerves, and brain interceding between the world and ourselves" (Handel 1993: 180). But, as Plomp emphasizes, everyday listening, in the midst of our crowded soundscapes, is particularly dependent on highly sophisticated and complex perceptual acts. So, to rephrase our question, we might ask: what insights can we gain about the way auscultation functions in narrative by understanding more about the intelligence of the ear?

Numerous and complex cognitive processes underlie Virginia Woolf's representation of listening. It is not my claim that Woolf understood these intricate workings of the ear, yet her novels are intensely engaged with subjective perception and her descriptions of aural scenes clearly depict sound *as it is heard*. What we now understand about the activity of human consciousness underlying these auditory events suggests that Woolf intuitively conceived the act of listening not as mere passive sensation, but as active perception. Auscultation in her narratives reflects at least three complex processes at work: differentiating individual sounds according to their sound source, combining a variety of discrete sound events to form a collective continuous sound, and superimposing different sound events to "restore" the original simultaneity to the perceived acoustic scene.

One of the remarkable complexities of hearing is that, before we can consider the relations among different sound events, we first need to distinguish individual sounds. For although sound can be, and generally is, emitted simultaneously from numerous sound sources in a single environment, the input to the ear is one continuous (though complex) acoustic waveform, which the brain must then decode to *interpret* as separate sounds. Even the perception of a single sound requires us to disentangle the various frequencies in the input wave and to decide which, for example, are harmonics and reverberations of that sound and which are components of other sounds. And this process is increasingly recognized as a complex interdependent blend of passive physiological response and active perception and cognition: while the peripheral auditory system in the cochlea begins to partition the incoming sound into its various frequency components, these are then transmitted through electrical impulses by the nerve cells and interpreted by the brain, which must sort and reassemble them into single sound events, continuing sounds, and overlapping sounds. The activity of *creating* "percepts" of distinct and separate sounds, as it were to reconstitute the original sound sources, has been variously termed auditory streaming, auditory scene analysis, parsing, and perceptual or auditory grouping.

In Virginia Woolf's narratives, precisely detailed descriptions of sound reflect the processes of auditory streaming at work. Even the seemingly disembodied narration of the "Time Passes" section in *To the Lighthouse*, set inside a deserted house, is clearly auscultized through a listener. The sharply demarcated individual sounds, along with the shift in perceptual attention from silence near at hand, to sharply articulated sounds in the distance, and back again to silence reflect the activity of the intelligent ear, perhaps revealing why the scene conveys such an intense *human* response to the environment:

> Nothing it seemed could . . . disturb the swaying mantle of *silence* which, week after week, in the empty room, wove into itself the falling *cries* of birds, ships *hooting*, the *drone* and *hum* of the fields, a dog's *bark*, a man's *shout*, and folded them round the house in *silence*.
>
> (Woolf [1927] 1992: 176–7, italics added)

The ear is attending to and identifying sounds beyond the range of vision, and positioning those sounds in space. Silence is immediate, within the house; the articulated sounds are external and remote. A drama is thus played out between silence (suspension of life) and sound (life's activity), in which the player is perceptual attention. Here the pull of the immediate sound environment is stronger, and ultimately the ear shifts its attention to the close and unbroken silence. But later, the attraction of distant sounds returns, and a further struggle occurs between the ear's segregation of sounds and the effort to relate them to each other. Listening now involves two conflicting strategies of interpretation: decoding the continuous wave-form into the individual sound sources that produced it, versus attending to the similar and overlapping qualities of the composite stream:

> And now . . . there rose that half-heard melody, that intermittent music which the ear half catches but lets fall; a bark, a bleat; irregular, intermittent, *yet somehow related*; the hum of an insect, the tremor of cut grass, dissevered *yet somehow belonging*; the jar of a dor beetle, the squeak of a wheel, loud, low, *but mysteriously related*; which *the ear strains* to bring together and is always on the verge of harmonizing . . .
>
> (p. 192; italics added)

Although silence helps the ear to isolate and hence intensify the external sounds, the very clarity of articulation heightens their fragmentation and disconnectedness, baffling the ear's attempts to bring the separated sounds perceptually together. The sentence continues: "but they are never quite heard, never fully harmonized, and at last, in the evening, one after another the sounds die out, and the harmony falters, and silence falls."

It is as if the ear has been listening to the individual instruments in the orchestra, and is unable to grasp the music as a whole. But such double listening is at the heart of Woolf's theme: auditory perception participates in the fundamental narrative quest to capture the individual and the collective nature of reality at the same time.

If the quiet island in the Hebrides baffles this paradoxical attempt, what of the noisy city? The urban soundscape is usually regarded as noise pollution; sheer loudness of the whole can overwhelm our attention to individual sounds. But in Woolf's late novel *The Years*, urban sound acts as a stimulus to acute listening. The ears of her Londoners are constantly parsing individual sounds, with an increasing variety of timbral character; furthermore, several characters attend to another more complex auditory stream, merging the disparate noises of the street into an urban keynote sound. Whereas the silence in a deserted house seduces the ear away from the attempt to harmonize disparate sounds,[10] in *The Years*, the city enables a new composite percept. As opposed to the violence of city noise, traffic is perceived as meaningful sound.

The Years, as Rishon Zimring has expertly shown, is "a novel *about* urban heterogeneity" – a novel moreover in which "the aural sense, rather than the visual, links the reader to multiple worlds" (Zimring 2002: 132, 133). Acoustically, as Zimring points out, the narrative presents a "cacophony of urban and other sounds," which function in different ways. They frustrate desires for private space, disrupt attempts at communication, yet also offer a positive and expansive experience of multiplicity. Traffic can thus be intrusive noise, or it can be, perhaps surprisingly, comforting sound. In the 1917 chapter, following an air raid, the characters within a quiet drawing room perceive the return of life outside as a transformation from separate to collective sounds: "The rush of wheels and the hooting of motor cars had run themselves into one continuous sound" (Woolf [1937] 1992: 281). And the narrative has already established such merging as a perceptual process when, at a party in the 1914 chapter, Martin Pargiter experiences first the discomfort of attending only to individual sounds, and then the release of blending the more distant sounds into one. First, he experiences the acoustic environment as perceptual fragmentation:

> No, it's not going to work, Martin thought as they talked about horses. He heard a paper boy calling in the street below, and the hooting of horns. He preserved clearly his sense of the identity of different objects, and their differences. When a party worked all things, all sounds merged into one.
>
> (p. 237)

Then, sitting with the other guests around the dinner-table, his perceptions change:

> He listened to the sounds in the street. He could just hear the cars hooting; but they had gone far away; they made a continuous rushing noise. *It was beginning to work.* He held out his glass.
>
> (p. 239, italics added)

Martin has been able to shift his auditory attention here in the way the ear in the "Time Passes" section in *To the Lighthouse* could not, to perceive a relational continuity among disparate sounds. The muffled quality of the traffic – Martin has moved from the drawing room to the dining room – is in part what enables the change, but he perceives the merging as something that *happens as a change in the human perceiver*, not as a pre-existent acoustical state. His shift from hearing individual car horns to hearing traffic is still part of the process of auditory scene analysis, but it is a more complex operation than segregating sounds according to the original sound sources. Hearing "traffic" depends on fusing sounds with similar timbres, but this in itself is a complex operation since there is no one constant that constitutes timbre in a sound that changes over time (Handel 1995). And Martin is shifting from an individual to a composite percept – rather like shifting from listening to individual conversation at a cocktail party to listening to the generalized sound of voices in the room. Although Woolf herself would not have known the specific cognitive acts being performed, her narrative representation grasps the way attention *shapes* what is heard.

In this scene, Martin experiences a change in perception from one mode of attention to the other; a yet further auditory complexity in *The Years* is the *simultaneous* perception of individual and collective sound. Earlier in the day, Martin shares an idyllic moment with his cousins in Kensington Gardens and the soundscape, auscultized through his perception, echoes the polytextural acoustic web of Woolf's "Kew Gardens": "The birds made a fitful chirping in the branches; the roar of London encircled the open space in a ring of distant but complete sound" (Woolf [1937] 1992: 230).[11] Not only has Martin separated the acoustic wave into two streams, he has organized the streams into a figure–ground relationship (Moore 2003: 294–6). The sophistication of listening here is comparable, in the words of Reinier Plomp, to "the difficulty of reading a text from a sheet of paper on which a second text had been written" (Plomp 2002: 34). Woolf approaches listening as reading an acoustical palimpsestic text of the world, and the message of the urban soundscape here is unifying and consoling; the continuousness of the traffic roar and its spatial placement as circular "surround-sound" provide a stable and secure ground under the figures of individual voices in the auditory scene.

The acoustical drama, however, continues to be played out between individualized and collective perceptions. When North and Sara are dining together before the final party, their conversation is interrupted by sounds in both the street and the lodging-house across the way. The two auditory streams are experienced as conflicting, but the listener, instead of retreating as in the "Time Passes" section, is pulled out into an engagement with different readings of the world:

> She broke off; for now a trombone player had struck up in the street below, and as the voice of the woman practising her scales continued, they sounded like two people trying *to express completely different views of the world in general at one and the same time*. The voice ascended; the trombone wailed.
>
> (pp. 299–300; italics added)

Moments later, North Pargiter moves to the window and, having recently arrived from a farm in Africa, he is even more challenged by the onslaught of sound. Yet he is beginning to relate and compose the different sounds of the city, merging vehicular sounds into the keynote sound of traffic, and perceiving simultaneously, over the background sound, a variety of individual voices, all spatially distributed in different geographical locations:

> Against the dull *background* of traffic noises, of wheels turning and brakes squeaking, there rose *near at hand* the cry of a woman suddenly alarmed for her child; the monotonous cry of a man selling vegetables; and *far away* a barrel-organ was playing. It stopped; it began again.
>
> (p. 301, italics added)

Auscultation here relies on an extremely complex interaction of listening strategies: parsing individual sounds, merging individual sounds together into one complex sound, and superimposing and spatially locating different sounds to build up a polyphonic polytextural acoustic scene. And, as an act of reading a palimpsestic acoustic text, auscultation leads to a sensory knowledge of the fundamental paradox of life: conflicting diversity and interrelated continuity.

The auditory construction of this scene involves yet one more complexity. The perception of continuous sound, like the keynote sound of traffic, depends on the cognitive ability to fill in missing sounds. We are generally able to attend only to one auditory stream at a time (although we can monitor a second stream for change); we *think* we are hearing two sounds at the same time, but our attention is more likely rapidly shifting back and forth (a short auditory memory buffer assists in this process). In addition, on-going sounds are usually masked by louder sounds or are even broken or interrupted. In this latter instance, if the gaps are filled not by silence but by other sound, we will hear the interrupted sound as steady and continuous rather than as a series of intermittent segments. If, for example, a smoothly rising tone is interrupted and replaced by intervening noise, "the glide is heard as continuous even though certain parts of the glide are missing" (Moore 2003: 294). A similar effect occurs if a weaker tone is masked by louder tones: "The auditory system . . . perceptually restores the parts 'covered up' by the louder tone bursts – in other words there is a perceptual *(re-) creation* of sounds on the basis of probability" (Plomp 2002: 37). In this second process, termed auditory restoration or continuity effect, "when parts of a sound are masked or occluded, that sound will be perceived as continuous, provided there is not direct sensory evidence to indicate that it has been interrupted" (Moore 2003: 297).

The characters' ability to perceive the distant sound of traffic as a steady ground bass to city life depends on their ability to bridge the acoustic gaps, to perceive that the distant hum continues even when masked by sharp cries and bursts of sound in closer proximity. Primarily implicit in *The Years*, auditory restoration is rendered explicit in Woolf's next novel *Between the Acts*. Set in the country, this novel lacks the keynote sound of city traffic; however, when, at the end of the villagers' pageant, the minister stands to offer his closing remarks, his speech is masked, not precisely by urban sound, but by the technological sound of modernity intruding on the country scene:

> So that each of us who has enjoyed this pageant has still an opp..." The word was cut in two. A zoom severed it....
> "...portunity," Mr. Streatfield continued.
>
> (Woolf [1941] 1998: 174)

The audience's unbroken perception of Streatfield's speech shows the process of auditory restoration at work, as the listeners supply the missing sounds that the low-flying planes have masked. And although they are reading *past* the technological sound to *human* speech, it is significant that the interruption of speech by a loud *sound* allows them to do so. If sound were interrupted by silence, as in the "Time Passes" section of *To the Lighthouse*, auditory restoration would not occur.

Woolf's treatment of sound suggests both that what we hear is dependent on our cognitive processes and, at the same time, that whatever we hear is actually present in the acoustical scene. Thus, in *Between the Acts*, Lucy Swithin fantasizes the possibility of an ideally intelligent ear able to hear all divergent sounds and to restore all underlying continuity – able to grasp, that is, the contrasts, conflicts, and continuity of the world:

> "Sheep, cows, grass, trees, ourselves – all are one. If discordant, producing harmony – if not to us, to a gigantic ear attached to a gigantic head. And thus... we reach the conclusion that *all* is harmony, could we hear it."
>
> (p. 157)

Failure to perceive the ultimate harmony is due to imperfect audition: cacophony is merely our inability to relate segregated sounds to each other; disjunction is our inability to restore continuity. The supreme, though hypothetical, auscultizer would parse the complex waveform into separate auditory streams, restore the interrupted or masked sounds, and hear percepts of individual and collective sounds simultaneously together.

Lucy's fantasy of the ideally intelligent ear articulates what *The Years* implies throughout. Listening, at the final party, to the reiterative phrases that characterize people's speech, Eleanor Pargiter thinks,

> Does everything then come over again a little differently? Is there a pattern, a theme, recurring, like music, half-remembered, half foreseen?... a gigantic pattern, momentarily perceptible?... But who makes it? Who thinks it?
>
> (Woolf [1937] 1992: 351)

But if Woolf then implies "a gigantic pattern" perceived by a "gigantic ear," have we returned to the idealist mode in which sound offers a spiritual entry into a transcendent reality? The pattern that Woolf evokes, however, is located in *this* world, and in a *physical* soundscape. Challenged to define what she means, Eleanor responds, "But I meant this world! . . . I meant, happy in this world – happy with living people" (p. 368). And although Eleanor's more pessimistically minded niece, Peggy, finds in the "sounds of the London night" a harsher reminder of "other worlds, indifferent to this world," these worlds too are in the earthly sphere.

Since auscultation, in Woolf, leads to *this*-worldly knowledge, it does not imply that hearing is in any way a more spiritual or more irrational sense than sight. Although Vincent Sherry (1993), in his study of Ezra Pound and Wyndham Lewis, argues that a prevalent modernist construction associates the eye with rational clarity, individualized perception, and hierarchical orderings, and the ear with empathetic mergings and mass sympathy, such a division does not characterize Woolf. Nor does Woolf assert the primacy of the visual, as Danius argues is true for Joyce, or – another of Danius's Joycean claims – differentiate the senses only to tend toward synesthesia. The senses in Woolf are distinct, but in an interactive, co-operative relation. Woolf's answer to Margaret Schlegel's question would appear to be this: that the ear may give us a more inclusive knowledge of the world than the eye, but it perceives the same reality. The advantage of having different senses is that they can help each other out, in a way that is epitomized in a passage excised, for reasons of length, from the initial galleys of *The Years*.

The original galleys for *The Years* were massive and, by her own account, Woolf reduced this version by more than a third. The cuts, urged strongly by her husband Leonard, have been a subject of critical controversy, as has the novel itself. Shortening the novel seems to have been largely a pragmatic decision, but we know that Woolf was also making the effort to exclude all didacticism and propaganda. She may have considered two large "chunks" that she cut too vulnerable to the charge of communicating a "message," but they make fascinating parallel chapters, when read synchronically with the published work.

The second of these episodes depicts the adventure of a woman alone in the city, as, in 1921, Eleanor Pargiter enters a restaurant to have dinner on her own. The place she chooses is one of a chain, and therefore part of a developing urban network that could promise safe venues for women alone. The English conventionality of the menu and the diners annoys the free-spirited Eleanor but, as acoustic scene, it offers a vital experience. Auscultized through Eleanor, the "roar of the street" first transposes to the "roar" of "human voice[s]" within ([1937] 1992: 457); then, as she waits for her meal, she strains to hear – over the clatter of conversation and the thud of the swinging kitchen door – a group of musicians who are obscured, by a column, from her view. But the "scramble of bungled notes" seems only to reinforce her impression of the "odd assembly of objects" on the table before her (p. 460). Yet, like Lucy Swithin, she wonders, "If accidentally scattered[,] objects, were yet in order? If to a mind outside her mind they meant something?" (p. 461). When the orchestra then breaks into a new piece, she experiences a sudden perceptual change:

Listening to music, even to cheap music, always until it became boring, ran things together. For a moment as she looked at the table[,] it seemed to her that the connection she had half grasped now ran between the different things; as if she could live from the fork, to the flower – from the flower – she put out her hand and touched it – to the spoon.

(pp. 461–2)

Sound initiates the experience, but what Eleanor *hears* leads her to connect what she *sees*, and the circuit is completed by *touch*.[12] Each sense contributes its own perceptual knowledge, but together they bring Eleanor's insight to birth. And the "noisy" city restaurant is both context for, and continuation of, her mental journey: Eleanor's ongoing quest is for a way simultaneously to perceive both the atomized individuality and the continuous collective being of the modern world.[13]

I invoke this passage not because it tells us what the novel means, but because it encapsulates the way we need to read it. *The Years* is *about* perception, and it calls for a shift in the way that we as readers perceive. By reading for sonics rather than semantics, for percepts rather than concepts, we discover new forms of making narrative sense. Listening to the sounds around her, Eleanor builds up a model of reality, and the reader of these modernist texts needs to imitate that partially passive, partially active process, segregating and integrating the novel's voices to create a model of its complex world. In *The Years*, auditory perception is a paradigm for such model building, and sensory knowledge emerges as a way of understanding the world.

It remains to be "seen" how far other modernist works depict the kind of auditory acuity that emerges in Woolf's texts, or how central we will ultimately find the auditory sense to be. Certainly in writing this paper, I became acutely aware of the difficulty of avoiding visual terms, even in a discussion of sound: we *see* or *observe* how something works, *focus* on issues, seek *insight*, offer *views*, and explain how one idea *illuminates* another. Yet it is worth remembering that scientists are only now on the brink of discovering the true complexity of the "hearing brain," especially as it operates in what Plomp calls the "dirty" conditions of the everyday as opposed to the purified conditions of the laboratory. And the point Plomp argues is one he first encountered in Wolfgang Metzger's classic 1953 work on vision – a passage still so relevant that Plomp calls upon it again today:

The achievements of the ear are indeed fabulous. While I am writing, my elder son rattles the fire rake in the stove, the infant babbles contentedly in his baby carriage, the church clock strikes the hour, a car stops in front of the house, next door one of the girls is practicing on the piano, at the front door her mother converses with a messenger, and I can also hear the fine scraping of the point of the pencil and my hand moving on the paper. In the vibrations of air striking my ear, all these sounds are superimposed into a single extremely complex stream of pressure waves. Without doubt the achievements of the ear are greater than those of the eye. Why do the psychologists, particularly the Germans, stick so stubbornly to *vision* research?

(Metzger, trans. and abridged by Plomp 2002: 10)

This passage, written by a scientist at the end of the modernist period, bears a striking resemblance to the auditory descriptions I have analyzed in the works of Virginia Woolf, and it leads me to ponder what further kinds of crossovers might be made between auditory research and studies of narrative. Studies of auscultation and auditory scene analysis might reveal that hearing plays a considerably more crucial role in narrative than has been thought. And there may well be more for us to learn from narrative about the knowledge of the intelligent ear.[14]

NOTES

1   In Western culture, as Grant Sampson (1974) has indicated, earthly music was initially thought to imitate the music of the spheres – a tradition whose lingering effects are found in romantic idealizations of synesthesia, following Pater's dictate that "all art constantly aspires to the condition of music" (Pater 1877: 135), or – despite his skepticism about metanarrative – in Jean-François Lyotard's supreme fiction that all genuine music "aspires to the condition in which all sounds collapse into one sound," where "the differentiation of the one and the multiple would not have place or time" (Lyotard 1991: 163).

2   A complex approach to this auditory aspect of literature has been advanced by Garrett Stewart, who argues that the ambiguous space between the phonemes of the words creates a perceptual ripple sound – named a "phonotext" – that synchronously parallels and troubles the closure of the semantic meaning of the text.

3   Even Sullivan (1922) – despite his claims about music's independence from experience – referred to "a logic of the emotions as well as of the mind" (p. 561) and suggested that, "if we prefer scientific jargon to the mystical," we could substitute for "the soul of man," "the normally subconscious rather than the normally conscious" (p. 562). Paralleling Virginia Woolf's essay "Modern Fiction" ([1925] 1984) critics of music seem also to be seeking a new language for the work of the perceiving subject.

4   In a further aural differentiation, Howells labelled the omnibus sound "epic," but the hansom sound, "lyric" (Howells 1905: 49).

5   Truax distinguishes two forms of listening on a passive/active continuum, which he terms distracted and attentive, the first in which we relegate sound to background noise, the second where we focus on detail. The first form is obviously more difficult to convey in written narrative.

6   For Vertov, see Kahn (1992: 10); for Cage, see Hines (1994: 81).

7   If we adopt the definitions that noise is sound that is unwanted, and music is sound that is perceived as having meaningful patterns (a distinction in perceptual attention), then auscultation in Woolf can be understood as soundscape composition. For the correspondences with Cagean aleatoric music, see Cuddy-Keane (2000).

8   On parataxis as a key trope of modernism, see Susan Stanford Friedman (2001).

9   I am indebted to Dr Roy Patterson (private communication) for this comment.

10 In both "Kew Gardens" and *Between the Acts*, Woolf demonstrates a more Cagean sense that silence is always filled with sound.

11 To test Martin's perception, I visited Kensington Gardens on June 22, 2004, and determined that I could stereophonically balance the sound of traffic on Bayswater Road to the north and Kensington Gore to the south, at a point on Lancaster Walk between Watts's statue of "Physical Energy" and the Speke Monument. By facing east, I could blend the sounds on my right and on my left into a percept of circling traffic. It was, I should say, a particularly windy day; the traffic (reduced by the new congestion charge) was moving more smoothly than,

according to Woolf's description, it did in 1914; and the engines – particularly of double-decker buses – are considerably quieter than at that time. Auscultation in her novel is not, I conclude, merely hypothetical.

12 In the published version, a similar relation between hearing and touch is enacted when the underlying sound of city traffic becomes transposed into a circuit of touching underlying the conversation in the final party. In the "Present Day" chapter, there are approximately 40 instances of touch, including 10 gestures in which someone pats, or lays a hand on, or brushes against another person's knee, five gestures where a hand taps or is laid on an arm, and eight where hands are placed on another's shoulders.

13 In one of the most stimulating recent discussions of the novel, Robert Caserio reads it as fragmentary stochastic composition, arguing that the "collective, itself another name for unity or solidarity, is reimagined by Woolf in terms of dispersal" (Caserio 1999: 71). Although Caserio does not focus on sensory perceptions, the dynamics he perceives strongly accord with the processes of the novel's acute listening.

14 I would like to thank the editors of this volume, and my graduate student Sarah Copland, for their helpful comments on an earlier draft of this essay. Also, while absolving all concerned from any blame for my follies, I am indebted to my years on the peripheries of psychoacoustic experimentation and electroacoustic music composition for my continuing fascination with this field.

REFERENCES AND FURTHER READING

Caserio, R. (1999). *The Novel in England, 1900–1950: History and Theory.* New York: Twayne.

Clutton-Brock, A. (1916). "The Magic Flute." *Times Literary Supplement* June 29, 301–2.

Cuddy-Keane, M. (2000). "Virginia Woolf, Sound Technologies, and the New Aurality." In P. Caughie (ed.), *Virginia Woolf in the Age of Mechanical Reproduction: Music, Cinema, Photography, and Popular Culture* (pp. 69–96). New York: Garland.

Danius, S. (2002). *The Senses of Modernism: Technology, Perception, and Aesthetics.* Ithaca, NY: Cornell University Press.

Forster, E. M. ([1910] 1973). *Howards End*, ed. O. Stallybrass. London: Edward Arnold.

Friedman, S. S. (2001). "Definitional Excursions: The Meaning of Modern/Modernity/Modernism." *Modernism/Modernity* 8, 493–513.

Handel, S. (1993). *Listening: An Introduction to the Perception of Auditory Events.* Cambridge, MA: MIT Press.

Handel, S. (1995). "Timbre Perception and Auditory Object Identification." In B. C. J. Moore (ed.), *Hearing* (pp. 425–61). San Diego, CA: Academic.

Hines, T. S. (1994). "'Then Not Yet "Cage"': The Los Angeles Years, 1912–1938." In M. Perloff and C. Junkerman (eds.), *John Cage: Composed in America* (pp. 65–99). Chicago: University of Chicago Press.

Howells, W. D. (1905). *London Films.* New York: Harper and Brothers.

Kahn, D. (1992). "Introduction: Histories of Sound Once Removed." In D. Kahn and G. Whitehouse (eds.), *Wireless Imagination: Sound, Radio, and the Avant-Garde* (pp. 1–29). Cambridge, MA: MIT Press.

Lyotard, J.-F. ([1988] 1991). *The Inhuman: Reflections of Time*, trans. Geoffrey Bennington and Rachel Bowlby. Cambridge, UK: Polity.

Moore, B. C. J. (2003). *An Introduction to the Psychology of Hearing*, 5th edn. San Diego, CA: Academic.

Pater, W. (1877). *The Renaissance: Studies in Art and Poetry*, 2nd edn. London: Macmillan.

Picker, J. M. (2003). *Victorian Soundscapes.* Oxford: Oxford University Press.

Plomp, R. (2002). *The Intelligent Ear: On the Nature of Sound Perception.* Mahwah, NJ: Erlbaum.

Richards, I. A. (1925). *Principles of Literary Criticism.* New York: Harcourt, Brace and World.

Sampson, G. (1974). "Mimetic Relationships Between Music and Literature in England." *The Humanities Association Review* 25, 197–210.

Schafer, R. M. (ed.) (1978). *The Vancouver Soundscape.* Vancouver: A.R.C. Publications.

Sherry, V. (1993). *Ezra Pound, Wyndham Lewis, and Radical Modernism*. New York: Oxford University Press.

Sullivan, J. W. N. (1922). "Music and Other Arts." *Times Literary Supplement* Sept. 7, 561–2.

Stewart, G. (1990). *Reading Voices: Literature and the Phonotext*. Berkeley: University of California Press.

Turner, W. J. (1922). "The False Isolation of Music." *The New Statesman* Oct. 14, 45–6.

Truax, B. (1984). *Acoustic Communication*. Norwood, NJ: Ablex Publishing.

Woolf, V. ([1925] 1984). "Modern Fiction." In *The Common Reader: First Series*, ed. A. McNeillie (pp. 146–54). London: Hogarth.

Woolf, V. (1985). "Kew Gardens." *The Complete Shorter Fiction of Virginia Woolf*, ed. S. Dick (pp. 84–9). London: Hogarth.

Woolf, V. ([1927] 1992). *To the Lighthouse*, ed. M. Drabble. Oxford: Oxford University Press.

Woolf, V. ([1937] 1992). *The Years*, ed. H. Lee. Oxford: Oxford University Press.

Woolf, V. (1992). *A Passionate Apprentice: The Early Journals, 1897–1909*, ed. M. Leaska. London: Hogarth.

Woolf, V. ([1941] 1998). *Between the Acts*, ed. F. Kermode. Oxford: Oxford University Press.

Woolf, V. ([1925] 2000). *Mrs. Dalloway*, ed. D. Bradshaw. Oxford: Oxford University Press.

Zimring, R. (2002). "Suggestions of Other Worlds: The Art of Sound in *The Years*." *Woolf Studies Annual* 2, 127–56.

26

In Two Voices, or: Whose Life/Death/Story Is It, Anyway?

Shlomith Rimmon-Kenan

Collaborative compositions have become a subgenre of illness narratives. A few examples are Sandra Butler and Barbara Rosenblum's *Cancer in Two Voices* (1991), Jerry Arterburn and Steve Arterburn's *How Will I Tell My Mother?* (1990), and Joseph Heller and Speed Vogel's *No Laughing Matter* (1986). The three narratives differ from each other in the illness experienced, the relationship between the narrators, and the tone of the telling. The first narrates Rosenblum's struggle with advanced breast cancer, terminating in death, in alternation with her lesbian partner's journal entries, conveying her process of mourning as well as her resentment against the total subordination of her life to the needs of her dying partner. The second text is an AIDS story, told by Jerry Arterburn, the protagonist, and his brother Steve, with a foreword by their mother and a postscript by their father. It is a "conversion" story, relating Arterburn's renunciation of homosexuality, as a result of contracting AIDS, and his reaffiliation with his nuclear family. *No Laughing Matter*, the third book, is written by Joseph Heller, author of *Catch-22*, and the friend who took care of him, Speed Vogel. Heller suffered from Guillain-Barré syndrome, a neurological auto-immune illness, from which he later recovered. He and the caregiver, who took over his autonomy, his apartment, and his checkbook, both write about the illness in a tone of black humor. In spite of these, and other, differences among them, the three narratives share a concern with personal autonomy and the problematic role of narration in relation to it.

In this essay, I would like to discuss a narrative written in my own country (Israel) by Ilana Hammerman and her husband Jürgen Nieraad, *Under the Sign of Cancer: A Journey of No Return* (in Hebrew; my translation of the title). Through an analysis of this recently published book (2001), that is both documentary and literary, I wish to address the double telling and double perspective of such narratives and the main ethical question they give rise to: whose life/death/story is it, anyway? I shall structure my exploration as a series of concentric circles: the relations between the dying husband and his wife, the twofold act of narration, the appropriation of both husband and wife by the medical "system," published responses to the narrative by doctors and other readers, and my own appropriation as evidenced in this essay.

Jürgen Nieraad, a professor of German literature at the Hebrew University of Jerusalem, was diagnosed on March 21, 2000 as suffering from acute myeloid leukemia, with a predicted two to three months lifespan. He, who has always believed in suicide as an ultimate act of freedom, decides to take an overdose of sleeping pills and freeze to death, in total isolation, on a snowy mountaintop in the Alps, the beloved landscape of his childhood. Having made the decision, he experiences the euphoria of an exemption from all responsibility: the following year's courses will not take place, his participation in a conference planned for May is thereby annulled, the lecture he had intended to give in two weeks will be canceled, and even an imminent appointment with the dentist will not materialize. The one responsibility he cannot shirk is that of the love bond with his wife and son. On the way from Israel to his final destination, he stops in Berlin, where his wife, Ilana Hammerman, a well-known literary translator and editor, is residing temporarily in order to translate Kafka's letters into Hebrew. He tells her his news and, at least consciously, wants her to accept his decision. At a later stage, he speculates that, coexistent with this wish, there was also knowledge, perhaps even an unconscious desire, that his wife would not agree to the course of action he has chosen. Thus, turning to her may have been a way of letting her take the decision for him (Hammerman and Nieraad 2001: 192–3). And she does. She says they must return to Israel, undergo additional tests, explore possible treatments. Reinforcing his own ambivalence is the realization that putting an end to his life without his wife's consent will not only poison her future but also destroy for her the value of their shared past, based as it was on a belief in a partnership of equals. With the help of modern biotechnological medicine, they embark on a harrowing journey, including chemotherapy and two bone marrow transplants – all in vain. Both record their suffering and illuminations in two separate narratives which, together, form the doubly-titled book.

Their narratives differ in many ways. Nieraad wrote *Under the Sign of Cancer: A Concentrated Bildungsroman* in his mother tongue, German. Hammerman wrote *A Journey of No Return*, in *her* mother tongue, Hebrew. She also translated his part of the book into Hebrew, and – to the best of my knowledge – the German original has not yet been published separately. Nieraad's journey is mainly inward, while Hammerman finds herself struggling against medical institutions as much as against the fatal illness. They attribute this to a dissimilarity in temperament, but it probably also reflects the difference between their positions in the situation, that is, the unbridgeable gap between a person who is going to die and a loving partner who shares the suffering, mourns, but will nevertheless remain alive. From the perspective of my discussion, the most interesting differences are of a narratological order. I shall first describe the main formal features of the narrators, narration, and narratees, and then discuss their ethical implications.

Narrators, Narration, Narratees

Nieraad's part is told during the excruciating process of his illness, and it is divided into two sections, differing in both their genre and the grammatical person informing the narration. The first, written between March 21 and June 30, 2000, consists of 11 chapters and narrates the events that took place between the diagnosis and the bone marrow transplant. However, it is not written in the first person, as an autobiographical account, but in the third, as what seems at first to be a fictional narrative about a character named "Georg." In structuralist-Genettian terms, this is heterodiegetic narration (Genette 1972: 256–7). The second section of Nieraad's part, written between July 6 and September 30, 2000, narrates the period between the bone marrow transplant and a short remission in the illness. It consists of nine chapters and is told in the first person, partly as an autobiographical narrative, partly as diary entries. The narration here is homo- or autodiegetic. The very last period of Nieraad's life is not narrated by him, probably because he was too weak to write. We thus learn about the end only from Hammerman's narrative.

That the fictional mode of the first section of Nieraad's part is a fairly transparent device is made clear by a self-conscious pseudonarratological discussion which opens Ch. 2: "The character whose story is told here could not have existed without a narrator, even though the latter pretends to efface himself: a well-known device. The narrator, in turn, would not have existed without the author, sitting right now at the computer, typing these words [. . .] Clearly, the story is about the author, in a thin disguise" (p. 176).[1] Even after exposing the device, however, Nieraad continues with "Georg" and a narration in the third person until the period of the bone marrow transplant, where he switches to the first person for the rest of the narrative. What are the functions of the pseudofictional Georg? Some are more or less explicitly suggested by Nieraad as narrator, while others – to be discussed later – may be construed in a re-exploration of the whole book from an ethical perspective. The figure of Georg, it transpires during the process of reading, allows Nieraad to keep his distance from his own condition, and simultaneously to dramatize the split between "before" and "after," between his past – which he "now" sees as living inauthentically – and his present journey toward death and authenticity (hence the term "Bildungsroman"). It also manifests his self-ironic awareness of playing a role, the role of a hero in the shadow of death, "the dying gladiator," in the words he borrows from Heine.

Whereas Nieraad's narration is largely simultaneous with the narrated events, Hammerman's is retrospective, allowing for a shaping and an elaboration of the experiences from diverse temporal positions. Her translation of his German text is also, in a sense, an act of shaping, making her almost a coauthor of his text. Consequently, it is perhaps not surprising that her narrative is written in the first-person plural ("we"), suggesting that the illness is shared by the afflicted person and his loving partner. At the same time, she is painfully aware of the inequality between them, thus problematizing the "we." Consequently, variations on "we – that is, you" or "we – that is, I" recur in her text. Two examples will suffice: talking about the unnecessary exacerbation of their suffering by the hospital staff, Hammerman complains about "...disorder and small injustices and unintended humiliations and trivialities, which embittered our life and our death – your approaching death..." (p. 34). Or:

> In the spiritual and emotional world we did not feel disabled at all; on the contrary, we have never been so well, so free, the freedom of inconsiderate egotism in which the illness allowed us to indulge.//Though I, I was nevertheless in a situation different from yours, I was still formally healthy and every evening I used to leave the hospital and drive home.
>
> (p. 46)

The recurrent use of pronouns of togetherness ("we"), followed by the expression of differentiation noted above, enacts not only her recognition of his approaching death but also her attempt to imagine a future life without him. Painful as it is, proleptic glimpses of her future alone appear not only under the guise of pronominal separation: "Did you know that I sometimes asked myself if I would ever ride the bicycle without you on these pathways? (Today, for example, Friday February 9, 2001, I am going to travel this way alone.)"

The last sentence is uncannily addressed to the deceased Nieraad. And so is the whole of Hammerman's part of the book. The first section of Nieraad's part contains addresses to "the reader," but that "reader" sometimes loses its anonymity when characterized in terms that evoke Hammerman: "Maybe every writer," says Nieraad in ch. 2, "even when intending to write for himself alone, actually addresses someone, polishes his words and thoughts for a given audience he envisions – but who cares? Whoever wants to read, may. And someone may realize that things were addressed to *her*, that *she* is the reader for whom the writing was intended" (p. 177, my emphases). The second section of Nieraad's part, in particular the diary entries, is addressed primarily to himself, but also – indirectly – to Hammerman, who is bound to find the file carefully saved in the computer under "*Krebs*" (cancer). Textually reinforcing their bond, the couple address each other. At the same time, they conjure up different implied readers, characteristic perhaps of the differences in their positions and temperaments: Hammerman's implied reader is empathic, while Nieraad's is a secret sharer of his self-irony.[2]

Ethical Complexities

The narrative features discussed so far both consciously convey and unconsciously perform one of the main ethical problems in *Under the Sign of Cancer*: to what extent are human beings masters of their own life and death? And does mastery over the story become mastery over a life? Influenced by Nietzsche and other philosophers,

Nieraad has always believed in the autonomy of human beings and their sovereignty over their own fate. Therefore, when he faces terminal illness, he is convinced that he is free to decide when and how he will end his own life. However, illness also makes him aware of a sense in which his death is not only his but also a decisive factor in the lives of those left behind. He therefore feels a responsibility to make the process of mourning as bearable as possible for those closest to him. Furthermore, he generously realizes that coping with illness is more difficult for the family of the ill person than it is for the ill person himself and that *he* should help his wife and son in this ordeal. Unlike Nieraad, Hammerman has always been terrified of death – her own as well as that of others – and has disagreed with Nieraad's position long before the question became pertinent to their own reality: "No. I have never agreed with you that your life is yours and mine is mine, neither your life nor your death, specifically not death" (p.19). In spite of his ambivalent compliance, she feels that, in some sense, she has robbed him of his chosen death, out of love and an uncontrollable need to have him alive. This happens not only at the time of his initial decision but also at various stages of the treatment, when she puts pressure on him to submit to one more test, one more medical experiment (see, for example, pp. 79, 93, 131, 157–8). True, both of them sometimes feel that in spite of the terrible suffering involved, the prolongation of Nieraad's life has also yielded them rare moments of intimacy. "Thus," she says, "we gained another short chapter of happiness, happiness Ltd. No - the word 'happiness' is no longer adequate here, not suitable at all, better perhaps is the word 'love'" (p.145). And he, still using the figure of Georg:

Now [. . .], even more than before, they could talk to each other frankly and openly about their feelings, their love, their thoughts, doubts, fears, hopes [. . .] the truth is that the change was mainly in him: the disaster has finally loosened his tongue, rendered him capable of expressing his feelings, relaxed him and freed him from inhibitions and restraints. [. . .] Their love was being renewed and becoming more profound.

(p. 216)

Nevertheless, Hammerman is mortified by guilt feelings about her "confiscation" of Nieraad's death. The retrospective mode of her narration makes it difficult to determine whether these feelings are projected back onto the past from the time of writing, after his death, or whether they accompanied her throughout. Recounting the initial meeting in Berlin in which she begs her husband to fight for his life, she collapses the past and the present (which was the future then): "And I don't know yet, don't even begin to know, what it is I am offering, what right I have to a life and a death that is mine and not mine, but I feel, know, am almost sure that I have the strength, that I will have the strength." Then she adds, in a new line, in the past tense of a retroactive realization: "Strength I had, for everything, almost everything – but a right?" (p. 22). Much later in the ordeal, Nieraad asks his wife to respect their agreement and bring him the pills needed to commit suicide, but she cannot fulfill her promise, continuing instead to watch him deteriorating and losing control over his body (p. 157). She feels his anger at the time, as well as his pity, and when he finally decides to stop all treatment, he conveys his wish to a male nurse, not directly to his wife. Hammerman's remorse about limiting her husband's freedom of choice is also crystallized in a more concrete aspect of the dilemma. During a week at home, in the course of the treatment, Nieraad explicitly says that he would like to die at home rather than in the hospital (p. 110). Out of love and a submission, in spite of herself, to the medical "system," Hammerman finds herself incapable of fulfilling this wish. She later writes: "You should have died here, at our home, not in the hospital. I knew it then and I know it now, and this knowledge, upon which I didn't have the power to act, will never give me rest" (p. 151).

The above quotations suggest that both love and contrition motivate Hammerman's need to narrate, to write her part of the book and address it to her dead husband. Her narration, and even more so her translation of Nieraad's text, are a way of asking his forgiveness and giving him back at least his voice after she had taken control of his freedom of choice. This gesture is sharply contrasted to a scene in the hospital, close to his death, when she discusses her husband with a doctor, in his presence, in the third person – a dehumanizing objectifying third person, which he experiences as appropriate for someone who is no longer himself. The deceased Nieraad cannot respond to his wife's address. Moreover, his section of the book expresses a certain acquiescence to Hammerman's taking over his right to decide. This suggests that the forgiveness she seeks is not only his, but also her own as well as that of the implied reader. Hammerman as narrator tries to justify her own behavior as participant in the action, to exonerate herself in her own eyes. An empathic implied reader, it transpires, would be helpful in the nearly impossible task of freeing her from the guilt that keeps tormenting her. The narrative presents a model of such a desirable reader in the figure of a friend, a professional nurse, who came over during a moment of crisis and intuitively knew how to help. This "friend, nurse, savior [. . .] heard what happened and immediately understood much more than that" (p. 68).

Are real readers bound by the construct encoded in the text? Is it ethically incumbent upon readers to fashion their reactions in accordance with those promoted by the narrative, or are they free to detect in it elements that go against the grain, or perhaps even let their own set of values influence their reaction? The second answer seems more acceptable in these days of resisting readers (see Fetterley 1978), but ethical problems still haunt reader-response. The writer of this essay, for one, read Hammerman's narrative with great empathy, but at the same time could not help detecting a gap between the conscious motivation propelling her narration and unconscious needs underpinning its execution, causing it to repeat the very wrong it was intended to right. My uneasiness, in turn, has its own burden of guilt, for – taking the events first – how can I be critical in relation to terminal illness – a situation which I myself have not faced? How can I know that I would have acted differently? And in relation to the manner of narration, isn't a certain degree of appropriation inevitable in any attempt to tell the story of another?

In full awareness of the complexity of the ethical issue, let me describe the rift I detect. Consciously, Hammerman makes every effort to write a book that will restore her husband's voice as well as his dignity. However, in telling his story and publishing his text in her translation, she also *transposes* his otherness into her language and perception. This unconsciously repeats, at the level of narration, the loving control, at the level of events, over his decisions in matters of life and death (and I emphasize both "loving" and "control").[3] Whether this unconscious repetition is an enactment characteristic of the posttraumatic situation in which she writes, or a manifestation of an aspect of her personality, or both, is hard (and perhaps unnecessary) to tell. The posttraumatic hypothesis may also bring to light an additional facet of the overall address to the dead Nieraad: an unconscious desire on Hammerman's part to make him present a little longer, at least in words, a melancholy resistance to letting go and accepting a full separation from him (on melancholy and mourning see Freud [1917] 1957: 237–58, Kristeva 1987: 104–23). My interest, however, is not in "diagnosing" Hammerman but in discussing the relation between formal narrative features and their complex ethical implications.

The title is a good place to begin. This jointly authored text appropriately has a double title: the major – *Under the Sign of Cancer* – was originally the name of Nieraad's narrative and appears on the cover in a larger format. The minor – *A Journey of No Return*[4] – is the title of Hammerman's narrative, appearing in a smaller size, though in the same font, under his. However, *her* narrative is placed first and is considerably longer than his (partly because, toward the end of his illness, he had no strength to write). The primacy effect thus gives her an aura of some authority. On the other hand, one may interpret the concluding position of his section as her attempt to give him the last word. Further complicating the delicate, and tense, balance between the narratives is the autobiographical mode ("I" or "we") of her part, often turning her from witness into protagonist: however much she tries to tell *his* story, to imagine the way *he* lived the harrowing ordeal, she can only tell it through *her* experience. The retrospective nature of her narrative also gives her power over time through knowledge, manifested in prolepses, of a future that was by definition unknown to him during his illness.

Hammerman tries to respect and give voice to her husband's otherness. She often emphasizes differences in temperament between them, expounds on his ideas about diverse subjects, and tries to imagine his feelings concerning his deterioration. However, his voice tends to merge into the uniformity of her style in her section. There are very few (if any) direct quotations of what he says, quotation being the maximum freedom given to the voice of the other. The paucity of quotations may be a result of the retrospective mode of her narration: one cannot remember dialogues *verbatim* from a temporal distance. It may also be a result of her decision to address her text to him, since it would be strange to quote him to himself. Be this as it may, in spite of the inner dialogue with her husband, the predominant voice in Hammerman's section is hers. Nieraad's speech is rendered mainly through her reports, in indirect discourse, in subordination to her narrating voice, for example, "that I should take a cup of tea, you suggested, and sit down to rest after the trip – as if I were coming back

from a business trip – there is no hurry, I can tell what I have to tell later..."
(pp. 68–9). This occurs when Hammerman returns from a consultation with a
specialist in Tel Aviv and finds her husband and son joking and roughhousing in
their flat. The sentence structure is peculiar (less so in Hebrew than in my English
translation) but it is the equivalent of indirect discourse: "You suggested that I should
take a cup of tea" and it is continuous with her comment and directly followed by her
own thoughts. In the sequel, she subordinates not only Nieraad's words but also his
unspoken thoughts to her perception: "and with a hasty look straight from your blue,
still fresh eyes into my tired ones *you led me to understand* that you know very well what
it is that preoccupies me" (p. 69, my emphasis). Free indirect discourse (FID),
somewhat closer in principle to the speech of the other, is also used, but it tends to
subordinate Nieraad's voice to the uniformity of Hammerman's. The linguistic
features of free indirect discourse in Hebrew are not the same as in English, because
of a difference in tense-structure and the absence of backshifting rules in Hebrew.[5]
Moreover, the fact that Hammerman's narrative is addressed to Nieraad reduces the
interplay between personal pronouns that usually accompanies free indirect discourse.
What remains are deictics and interjections. One example in my translation will have
to suffice as an illustration of their neutralization: "I wanted to live eternally, and you
said that if you knew this life would last forever, *no*, even until a ripe old age, you
wouldn't want to live one day more. And I wanted you to live until you die with me,
no, until we don't die at all" (p. 20, emphasis added). The first "spoken" "no" is
Nieraad's but it becomes part of a symmetrical structure characteristic of Hammerman's style when countered by a parallel "no" from her.

On the other hand, Nieraad's voice resonates in his section of the book, and the
differences between his style and hers are striking. However, his independent otherness is problematic even here, because his text comes to us mediated through her
translation – a shaping and an appropriation of sorts.[6] I fully realize that the
alternative, that is, *not* publishing a translation of his text, would have effaced him
almost completely, but this does not mean that the *traduttore/traditore* predicament is
not operative in her attempt to make him heard. Paradoxically, Hammerman's
endeavor to experience and make us experience Nieraad from within, her "we" as a
linguistic and translinguistic gesture, often swallows his otherness within her discourse. On the contrary, his distance from himself – his use of Georg and the third
person, for example – gives more room to his otherness and hence also to his new self-
as-other. While intimacy is usually valorized, it may also be engulfing; distancing –
Nieraad's narrative suggests – sometimes has the advantage of leaving more space for
the otherness of the other.[7]

Medicine and its Discontents

So far, my discussion of the relation between narrative features and ethical complexities has been confined to the private sphere. But *Under the Sign of Cancer* also has a

public agenda. It engages the ethics of modern medicine with the same sensitivity to the dangers of appropriation that emerged from the more personal predicament. To be precise, this concern is prominent in Hammerman's part of the book, whereas Nieraad, the patient, keeps a distance from the "system," passively resisting its control. In this context, the reader projected, or called for (although not directly addressed), is the medical community, sometimes more specifically the doctors who treated Nieraad at Hadassah Medical Center in Jerusalem.

"Chemical, biotechnological, nuclear, computerized" contemporary medicine, according to Hammerman, arrogantly denies death, pretending to be able to vanquish it and tempting patients – sometimes even putting pressure on them – to submit themselves to a torturing chain of treatments, installations, indignities. About the appropriation of the patient and his or her family by modern medicine, she says at a crucial point: "But now we were totally entangled by the cogs of this medical machine [. . .] a system whose arrogant aspiration to fight death at any cost [. . .] is incompatible with the axiological, ethical, and care-giving capacities of most of those belonging to it" (p. 77). Her general criticism of the denial of death by the medical staff, the families (including herself), and the patients is concretely dramatized when she sees the empty room of a patient who must have died a little earlier, with the monitor still standing there. She asks a nurse what has happened, but the latter looks away, "as if to teach me that this is not the place for such questions, that here, precisely here, death is a taboo. [. . .] The priests and servants of modern medicine do not learn how to cope with death and certainly not how to prepare those in their treatment for it" (p. 127). Hammerman is fully aware of the possibility that what she calls "medical arrogance" may have another side: the desperate attempt to give people a last chance, even though it is not always viable at the present stage of the development of the profession. She also admits that she and her husband got trapped in "the system," from choice rather than compulsion. At the same time, she is deeply frustrated by the insidious subordination of the individual to the "system," manifesting itself when ill people and their families can no longer distinguish between freedom of choice and inevitability. Hammerman characterizes this "catch" by the frequent use of oxymoron, such as "this narrow world into which I *stumbled* with you out of *choice*" (p. 90, my emphases), or the near-contradiction in her reference to "the man who finally *pushed us*, always leaving the decision to us, to *choose* the path of (bone marrow) transplant" (p. 78, my emphases).

The appropriative character of modern medicine is aggravated by the reduction of people to patients and patients to cases. Hammerman bitterly complains about the lack of consideration for the patient's time: the long waits, the delay in transmitting information from one department to another, the hours one has to spend on the phone until one reaches a specific doctor or nurse. Intertwined with her complaints is the equally bitter realization that in some sense terminal patients have "all the time in the world" (they are not in a hurry to go anywhere) while in another "their time is up" and should not be wasted on trivialities. But her main criticism is leveled at the condescending attitude of the medical staff, establishing a hierarchy in which the patient and his or her family are inferior by definition. This manifests itself in an unwillingness to answer medical questions, or a provision of information in terms that assume the patient's ignorance as well as lack of intelligence, for example, the recurrent description of the human body as a factory, with a defect in the production line in cases of illness. Condescension also manifests itself in an infantilization of the patient, for example, expressions like "time for an injection!" in a bright voice. The result is a devastating feeling of humiliation on the part of the patient – hard to fight when his sense of identity is already diminished by the illness. A telling symptom of the doctors' attitude is, for Hammerman, the way they address patients and their families by their first names while taking for granted that they themselves will be called "Prof." or "Dr." so-and-so by those under their care. Here is Hammerman's intentionally colloquial silent comment on one occasion of such pseudo-familiarity: "Who am I for you that you call me Ilana? Call your girlfriend Ilana, Miriam, or Hanna, while I remain for you in this world, perhaps also in the next, Dr . . . or at least Mrs [. . .] but I was very careful not to say these words out loud, not even jokingly" (p. 33).

In addition to condescension, she also resents the absence of empathy with the patient and his or her family. Having been given a document that announced that "the Hematology Department is at your service 24 hours a day," she once hesitantly allows herself to knock on the door of one doctor's office in a moment of unbearable distress, only to hear "that I can't allow myself to burst into her room this way any time I feel like it" (p. 99). Tactlessness and jocular, even cynical, comments also betray the same incapacity to imagine the other. Thus the posters on the Department's walls are all jarringly light-hearted, as are the humorous small cartoon figures printed on patients' name plates. The "magician" in charge of bone marrow transplant explains that the procedure "is not exactly an 'at your request' program," and another doctor describes the dependence on the system entailed by the treatment as a "Catholic marriage" – ironically the type of marriage from which Nieraad escaped with great difficulty before meeting Hammerman (p. 103).

The most that could be said to account for the doctors' upsetting behavior is that it is often a defence-mechanism without which they wouldn't be able to cope with the threat of death, as well as with the suffering they are trying to alleviate. On the other hand, one can well understand Hammerman's antagonism against the "system" in its own right and also as a displacement of her anguish about her husband's condition, her imminent loss of him, and her guilt-feelings about having forced him to embark on this journey of no return. It is also important to remember that she does speak of *some* doctors and nurses as wonderful human beings, and that she consistently avoids mentioning the names of "the priests of modern medicine" she mordantly criticizes.

Readers Write Back

One measure of the impact the book had is the public debate it gave rise to for weeks, perhaps even months, in the Israeli literary and daily newspapers. This "scene of reception" is an extreme actualization of the dialogic potential of all narrative, the way that telling both presupposes and calls for a listening and a response. In this case the listening/reading triggered an urge to write, and publish, on the part of both physicians and patients. Gaps between the responses of real readers and those attributable to the implied reader are very interesting. No less interesting, however, are commonalities between the reactions of real readers and processes occurring in the text itself. Of these, my discussion will emphasize the operation of unconscious performative repetition and the tension between respect for and appropriation of the other.

The first shot in the debate was fired by Prof. A. Reches, a senior neurologist at Hadassah Hospital, who is also the Chair of the Israel Medical Association's Ethics Committee. With the double aura of a highly respected member of the "institution" and a relative *enfant terrible* in it, one who publicly fights for patients' right to euthanasia, Prof. Reches rose to defend the "system." I quote here some excerpts from his longish review, in the (far from felicitous) English translation of the newspaper in which it appeared, *Ha'aretz*: "I read, and I found it difficult to understand what it was the couple fought the hardest – the terrible disease or the 'system,' and at its head, the doctors entrusted with the treatment of Jürgen Nieraad." He *can* understand Nieraad's desire to be a master of his own death; he even endorses it in support of his own admirable struggle for the right to passive euthanasia. But:

> the mind of Ilana (I hope she will forgive me the liberty of using this intimate language) remains sealed to me. I did not find the answer to the question that most disturbs me in her book: How does someone feel who remains behind in the realm of the living? Does she now have feelings of remorse or guilt because she forced her husband into a losing battle? [. . .] It is difficult for me to accept and agree with Ilana's war on the "system." After all, this is about the hospital where I work and the Hematology Department, which I know well. Though she has tried to conceal the identities of the doctors, I recognize some of them quite easily, with utter certainty [. . .] And I know that some of them have been deeply hurt by this book, and I feel hurt along with them.

That Hammerman's mind remains sealed to him is amply demonstrated by his response: he would have liked her to write a different book from the one she wrote, a book that would answer the questions *he* is interested in. Moreover, he does not read carefully enough to notice how explicitly Hammerman expresses her guilt and remorse about robbing her husband of the death he desired. Hasn't she complained about the lack of empathy on the part of the doctors, and isn't her "sealed mind" precisely a symptom of that? In defending the system, Prof. Reches thus duplicates the original blindness that made the defense necessary in the first place. He also repeats the gesture of pseudo-intimacy implied by the use of her first name (Ilana), knowing from the book that this is a sensitive point for her. Some readers of the review immediately noticed this, writing response-letters such as "Who allowed the professor to use this language of familiarity? Did he ask Hammerman's permission before addressing her this way in public? Does he encourage his patients to call him by his first name?" The same correspondent was also quick to remind the writer of the review that "it is easier to cope with problems of human relations in the ethics committee and public speeches than in daily life in the hospital." Sympathy for Hammerman's complaints was expressed not only by lay persons but also by physicians, one of whom argued that the book should be made part of the compulsory reading of every student of medicine. He, incidentally, had been Chair of the Ethics Committee before Prof. Reches.

Just as not all doctors agree with Reches, so not all patients agree with Hammerman. One former patient of the hematology department wrote a long response in its defense, of which I translate only a few points:

> We too [like Reches] got to know a department Chair who is primarily a human being and only then a doctor. A woman whose devotion, sensitivity, and availability are astounding. Her attitude is warm and human, she explains to patients how to reach her at any time of the day and meets them at all hours. From our experience, the behavior of the rest of the staff is the same. [...] Mourning for a loved person can understandably lead to a loss of equilibrium. Does the medical staff deserve a deflection of anger and frustration to them, especially when the rules of medical ethics prevent them from defending themselves and presenting things from their point of view?

These disagreements show what narrativists have always said, namely that narration is a subjective construction of reality. Moreover, many of the letters participating in the debate use the Hammerman–Nieraad narrative for one vested interest or another or, alternatively, to tell the writer's own story ("When I was..." "When our son was...").

Indeed, in retrospect I realize that I too am implicated in the dangers associated with narration. I now see that, as a result of my experience with an illness of my own, I have unwittingly used aspects of Hammerman's narrative for a free indirect venting of my personal frustrations.[8] I also realize that my experience may have caused a certain slant in my reading. As a patient in the same Israeli context, I share Hammerman's so-called "war on the system." In the same capacity, however, I also share Nieraad's desire to master his own life and death (though dying on a snowy mountaintop strikes me as a distinctly male fantasy). A slight resentment of Hammerman's "confiscation" of Nieraad's death may have made me extrasensitive to manifestations of appropriation both in her narrated behavior and in the execution of her narration. However, I could not have engaged with this issue had it not left linguistic and structural traces in her text. Furthermore, I have tried to remain as faithful as possible to the complexity of attitudes as it is presented in both their narratives. And I am also aware that Hammerman as narrator is the severest critic of Hammerman as participant.

Nevertheless, a new self-doubt arises: perhaps the foregoing autobiographical confession is not only an unveiling of a possible appropriation on my part but also – like Hammerman's narration, Reches's response, and those of the readers/writers – a re-enactment, a performative repetition of appropriation? If, on several levels, I have used *Under the Sign of Cancer* for my own purposes, do I thereby extend a license to my readers to appropriate this text for theirs? To be consistent with my own practice, I would have to answer in the affirmative – once published, a text is no longer the property of its author. But such an answer leads to an interrogation of the very notion of "appropriation." The title of my essay is thus not a disguised statement, but a question I propose to leave open: whose life/death/story is it, anyway?[9]

NOTES

1 Throughout the essay, the quotations in English are my literal translation from the Hebrew. They do not do justice to the book's beautiful and complex style.

2 On "narratees" see Genette (1972: 265–7), Prince (1973: 178–96), Chatman (1978: 253–61), Rimmon-Kenan (1983: 103–5). On the notion of the "implied reader" see Iser (1974), Rimmon-Kenan (1983: 87–90). On different types of audiences and their relation to author and narrator see Rabinowitz (1977).

3 On unconscious repetition, see Freud ([1914] 1958). On the performative aspect of repetition in relation to writing and narration, see Felman (1977), Johnson (1977), Rimmon-Kenan (1987).

4 In my translation. The English translation on the inside of the book's title page merges the two titles into one, and is weak in many respects: *Cancer Zone of No Return*.

5 For a survey of various theories of FID see McHale (1978).

6 Because his text is accessible only in her translation, it is impossible to make an illuminating comparison between their styles here.

7 I am grateful to my friend and colleague, Ruth Ginsburg, for pointing this out to me, and situating it in the context of Bakhtin's "Author and Hero in Aesthetic Activity" ([1920–3] 1990).

8 For details, see Rimmon-Kenan (2002).

9 An earlier version of this paper was presented at a colloquium on Narrative Medicine at Columbia University in May 2003.

REFERENCES AND FURTHER READING

Arterburn, J. and Arterburn, S. (1990). *How Will I Tell My Mother?*, revised and expanded. Nashville, TN: Oliver-Nelson.

Bakhtin, M. ([1920–23] 1990). "Author and Hero in Aesthetic Activity." In M. Holquist and V. Liapunov (eds.), V. Liapunov and K. Brostrom (trans.), *Art and Answerability: Early Philosophical Essays by M. M. Bakhtin* (pp. 4–256). Austin: University of Texas Press.

Butler, S. and Rosenblum, B. (1991). *Cancer in Two Voices*. Denver, CO: Spinsters Ink.

Charon, Rita (1989). "Doctor-Patient/Reader-Writer: Learning to Find the Text." *Soundings* 72, 137–52.

Chatman, S. (1978). *Story and Discourse*. Ithaca, NY: Cornell University Press.

Couser, T. G. (1997). *Recovering Bodies. Illness, Disability, and Life Writing*. Madison: The University of Wisconsin Press.

Felman, S. (1977). "Turning the Screw of Interpretation." *Yale French Studies* 55/6, 94–207.

Fetterley, J. (1978). *The Resisting Reader: A Feminist Approach to American Fiction*. Bloomington: Indiana University Press.

Frank, A. W. (1993). "The Rhetoric of Self-Change: Illness Experience as Narrative." *Sociological Quarterly* 34, 39–52.

Frank, A. W. (1995). *The Wounded Storyteller: Body, Illness, and Ethics*. Chicago: University of Chicago Press.

Freud, S. ([1917] 1957). "Mourning and Melancholia." In *The Standard Edition of the Complete Psychological Works*, ed. and trans. J. Strachey (vol. 14, pp. 237–58). London: The Hogarth Press.

Freud, S. ([1914] 1958). "Remembering, Repeating, and Working Through." In *The Standard Edition of the Complete Psychological Works*, ed. and trans. J. Strachey (vol. 12, pp. 145–56). London: The Hogarth Press.

Genette, G. (1972). *Figures III*. Paris: Seuil.

Hammerman, I. and Nieraad, J. (2001). *Under The Sign of Cancer: A Journey of No Return* (in Hebrew). Tel Aviv: Am Oved.

Heller, J. and Vogel, S. (1986). *No Laughing Matter*. New York: Putnam Group.

Iser, W. (1974). *The Implied Reader: Patterns of Communication in Prose Fiction from Bunyan to Beckett*. Baltimore, MD: The Johns Hopkins University Press.

Johnson, B. (1977). "The Frame of Reference: Poe, Lacan, Derrida." *Yale French Studies* 55/6, 457–505.

Kristeva, J. (1987). "On the Melancholic Imaginary." In S. Rimmon-Kenan (ed.), *Discourse in Psychoanalysis and Literature* (pp. 104–23). London: Methuen.

McHale, B. (1978). "Free Indirect Discourse: A Survey of Recent Accounts." *Poetics and Theory of Literature* 3, 249–87.

Rabinowitz, P. J. (1977). "Truth in Fiction: A Reexamination of Audiences." *Critical Inquiry* 4, 121–41.

Reches, A. (2002). "Dying Notes." *Ha'aretz*, 25 January.

Rimmon-Kenan, S. (1983). *Narrative Fiction: Contemporary Poetics*. London: Methuen.

Rimmon-Kenan, S. (1987). "Narration as Repetition: The Case of Gunter Grass's *Cat and Mouse*." In S. Rimmon-Kenan (ed.), *Discourse in Psychoanalysis and Literature* (pp. 176–87). London: Methuen.

Rimmon-Kenan, S. (2002). "The Story of 'I': Illness and Narrative Identity." *Narrative* 10, 9–27.

PART IV
Beyond Literary Narrative

27

Narrative in and of the Law

Peter Brooks

To the student of narrative, the place, role, and status of narrative within the law may be puzzling. On the one hand, the law appears to be shot through with narrative, and predicated on a narrative construction of reality. On the other hand, one searches in vain for any recognition within legal doctrine that narrative is one of law's categories for making sense of its affairs. One has the impression that narrative is in large measure the *impensé* of the law: its untheorized or even its repressed content. Or perhaps more accurately: one can detect that the law does in fact recognize its entanglements with narrative – but reacts to them with unease and suspicion, so that the neglect of narrative as a legal category is possibly an act of repression, an effort to keep the narrativity of the law out of sight.

The notion of "narrativity" postulates that there is some property or set of properties that makes a given discourse a narrative rather than something else (e.g., a lyric, a description, an essay). Narrative, while not wholly independent of its expressive medium (in words or in film or ballet, for instance, in French or in Chinese) can nonetheless be abstracted from that medium – as in the "plot summary" – since what makes it a narrative doesn't depend on the medium. That is to say, narrative isn't wholly defined by the plane of its expression: stories can be translated, they can be transposed to other media, they can be summarized, they can be retold "in other words" and yet still be recognizably "the same story." Narrativity belongs to our cognitive toolkit, it constitutes one of the large categories in which we understand and construct the world. What needs analytic attention, then, is the narrativity of the law, in an effort to understand the place and use of narrative in legal matters.

Now the concept of narrative in fact made its way into legal scholarship a little over a decade ago, but curiously only through one limited perspective: that of the counter-majoritarian or "oppositional" narrative, put forward to call attention to stories told by those traditionally slighted or marginalized by legal thinking and procedure. Storytelling, in this claim, embodies the concrete particulars of the experience of individuals or groups in a way that conventional legal reasoning excludes. Storytelling is the only way to gain a hearing, from legal advocates and decision makers, for kinds of experience – that of poverty victims, of minority groups, of certain religious communities, for instance – that the legal system, its language and rules of standing and evidence, tends to silence. These persons and groups must be allowed to speak in their own voice, to claim the right to hearing in the manner of Coleridge's Ancient Mariner, who holds the Wedding Guest with his "glittering eye" and forces him to hear his tale through to its conclusion.

"Oppositional storytelling" has made an undeniable impact in legal-scholarly debates, if not necessarily in the practice of law. It nonetheless raises three interrelated questions in my mind. First, it appears to promote a naïve positive valuation of narrative, assuming without further examination that stories are good, and represent the good cause, whereas in fact narrative is morally a chameleon that can be used to support the worse as well as the better cause. Secondly, this valorization of storytelling tends to beg the questions of what narrative is and how it works: it does not enter into the analytic study of the nature of narrative that has been the subject of literary narratology. Finally, it fails to recognize the pervasive presence of narrative through-out the law: the many layers of storytelling involved in any adjudication before the law, the way stories are told and retold to different effects, the omnipresence of narrative presented for both majoritarian and countermajoritarian purposes. Here is a social practice which adjudicates narratives of reality, and sends people to prison, even to execution, because of the well-formedness and force of the winning story. "Conviction" – in the legal sense – results from the conviction created in those who judge the story.

In fact, when one begins to reflect on the role of storytelling in the law in general, the topic begins to proliferate, and to show its pertinence on every head. It need not take an O. J. Simpson trial to remind us that the law is in a very important sense all about competing stories, from those presented at the trial court – elicited from witnesses, rewoven into different plausibilities by prosecution and defense, submitted to the critical judgment of the jury – to their retelling at the appellate level – which must pay particular attention to the rules of storytelling, the conformity of narratives to norms of telling and listening – on up to the Supreme Court, which must braid together the story of the particular case at hand and the history of constitutional interpretation, according to the conventions of *stare decisis* and the rules of precedent, though often – since dissents are allowed – presenting two different tellings of the story, with different outcomes.

Trial lawyers know that they need to tell stories, that the evidence they present in court must be bound together and unfolded in narrative form. Presumably legal advocates have known this for millennia, since in antiquity the discipline of rhetoric, including argumentation through narrative, was primarily training for making one's case in a court of law. But over the centuries the professionalization of law and legal education has tended to obscure the rhetorical roots of legal practice – which might now be viewed as something of a scandal in a field that wants to believe that it is rooted in irrefutable principles and that it proceeds by reason alone.

If the law rarely recognizes overtly how much it is intricated with narrative, it may nonetheless implicitly acknowledge the power of legal storytelling in its efforts at policing narrative: the ways in which it limits and formalizes the conditions of telling, in order to assure that narratives reach those charged with judging them in controlled, rule-governed forms. In modern judicial procedure, stories rarely are told directly, uninterruptedly. At trial, for instance, they are elicited piecemeal by attorneys intent to shape them to the rules of evidence and procedure, then reformulated in persuasive rhetoric to the listening jurors. The fragmented, contradictious, murky unfolding of narrative in the courtroom is subject to formulae by which the law attempts to impose rule on story, to limit its free play and extent. Should Nicole Simpson's 911 phone call be considered part of the story of her murder? Or is that part of another story which, brought within the sequence ending in homicide, takes on a misleading significance and force? All the "rules of evidence" – including the famous "exclusionary rule," barring illegally seized evidence – touch on the issue of rule-governed storytelling. The judge must know and enforce these rules. And when stories are culled from the trial record and retold on the appellate level, it is in order to evaluate their conformity to the rules. Appellate courts are not supposed to second-guess the "triers of fact" in the case, but to judge the frameworks in which the verdict was reached. At this level, all narratives become exemplary: they illustrate a point of law, a crucial issue in justice, a symbolic moment in the relations of individual and state. So it is that the law has found certain kinds of narrative problematic, and has worried about whether or not they should have been allowed a place at trial – or what place they should have been allowed. Yet the law's recognition of its repressed narrative content and form generally comes in a negative manner, as denial. The bar of repression keeps the narrativity of the law under erasure.

A clear, if grim, example of narrative at work in the law can be found in cases of rape, which pre-eminently offer competing stories with dramatically different outcomes and interpretations. Take a well-known case from Baltimore, Maryland, *Rusk v. State* (in the Court of Special Appeals of Maryland), and then *State v. Rusk* (in the Court of Appeals of Maryland). Rusk was convicted at trial; the conviction was reversed in the first appellate court, then reinstated in the higher court. In the decisions on each level of appeal, there was a majority and a minority opinion starkly opposed to one another. Thus we have four different retellings of what we know is the "same" story – the story of what happened between a man and a woman one night in Baltimore, the story then constructed at trial – with wholly differing results, results that send Rusk to prison for seven years or else release him. How can these four stories, based on the same "facts" – and none of the principal events of what happened that night was in dispute – have different outcomes? The answer, I think, is that the narrative "glue" is different: the way incidents and events are made to combine in a meaningful story, one that can be called "consensual sex" on the one hand or "rape" on the other.

The substance of this narrative glue depends in large part on the judges' view of standard human behavior, on what words and gestures are held to provoke fear, for instance. Any given narrative will be built to some extent on what Roland Barthes

liked to call *doxa*, that set of unexamined cultural beliefs that structure our understanding of everyday happenings. In this case, the judges who ruled against the rape
conviction at the two appellate levels tend to construct their narratives on the basis of
how they believe a woman ought to behave in certain circumstances. A key moment
of the story comes when Rusk, in the passenger seat of Pat's car, asks her to come up to
his apartment; when she refuses, he gets out of the car, walks to the driver's side
window, reaches in and removes the keys from the ignition, and says: "Now will you
come up?" Here Judge Thompson writes: "Possession of the keys by the accused may
have deterred her vehicular escape but hardly a departure seeking help in the rooming
house or in the street" (*Rusk v. State*: 626). One could go on at some length in analysis
of this sentence. "Deterred her vehicular escape"? A translation would be: Pat is
totally stranded in a deserted street in an unknown and sinister section of downtown
Baltimore in the middle of the night (a translation that is itself of course another
version of events). A phrase such as "vehicular escape" in its very pompousness should
alert us that we are faced with some avoidance maneuver. And "a departure seeking
help" is similarly obscuring: it translates into something like: running though a
deserted street screaming for help. The sentence is one of many that eschews narrative
precision in favor of an arch rendering of the story from a normative narrative
standpoint which is that of the judge. It is part and parcel of a narrative point of
view in which Pat is always referred to as "the prosecutrix," is described as "bar-
hopping," and characterized as "a normal, intelligent, twenty-one year old vigorous
female." It's a narrative with little apparent self-awareness on the part of the narrator.

It is on the basis of such a retelling of the story that the first appeals court reversed
Rusk's conviction. In the higher court, the conviction was reinstated, but over the
strong dissent of Judge Cole, who writes, for instance:

> She [the victim] may not simply say, "I was really scared," and thereby transform
> consent or mere unwillingness into submission by force. These words do not transform a
> seducer into a rapist. She must follow the natural instinct of every proud female to
> resist, by more than mere words, the violation of her person by a stranger or unwel-
> comed friend. She must make it clear that she regards such sexual acts as abhorrent and
> repugnant to her natural sense of pride.
>
> (*State v. Rusk*: 733)

What he means is made more specific toward the end of his opinion:

> I find it incredible for the majority to conclude that on these facts, without more, a
> woman was *forced* to commit oral sex upon the defendant and then to engage in vaginal
> intercourse. In the absence of any verbal threat to do her grievous bodily harm or the
> display of any weapon and threat to use it, I find it difficult to understand how a victim
> could participate in these sexual activities and not be willing.
>
> (*State v. Rusk*: 734)

The detail of this plot summary would deserve much closer attention than I can give
it here. The one word "participate," for instance, speaks volumes about Judge Cole's

views of sex, especially oral sex, of women, and of the world. "Participate" in itself conveys a whole conception of a narrative incident that needs to be unpacked and analyzed. The differing outcomes in the retellings of the *Rusk* cases offer a dramatic instance of how narratives take on design, intention, and meaning. Narratives do not simply recount happenings; they give them shape, give them a point, argue their import, proclaim their results.

If the competing stories of a rape trial offer an obvious instance of legal narrativity – both its presence and the lack of explicit recognition of its importance – other kinds of judicial narrative are equally important and unrecognized as such. Take, for instance, a case that every first-year American law student knows by heart, a classic torts case from 1928, *Palsgraf v. Long Island Railroad Company*, where the Court of Appeals of the State of New York, in a famous opinion by its Chief Judge, Benjamin Cardozo, reversed the lower court's finding that the railroad was liable for Helen Palsgraf's injuries. I begin with the "facts of the case" as stated by Cardozo:

> Plaintiff was standing on a platform of defendant's railroad after buying a ticket to go to Rockaway Beach. A train stopped at the station, bound for another place. Two men ran forward to catch it. One of the men reached the platform of the car without mishap, though the train was already moving. The other man, carrying a package, jumped aboard the car, but seemed unsteady as if about to fall. A guard on the car, who had held the door open, reached forward to help him in, and another guard on the platform pushed him from behind. In this act, the package was dislodged, and fell upon the rails. It was a package of small size, about fifteen inches long, and was covered by a newspaper. In fact, it contained fireworks, but there was nothing in its appearance to give notice of its contents. The fireworks when they fell exploded. The shock of the explosion threw down some scales at the other end of the platform, many feet away. The scales struck the plaintiff, causing injuries for which she sues.
>
> (*Palsgraf v. Long Island*: 340–1)

Legal commentators for decades clucked admiringly over the laconic clarity of Cardozo's presentation here. More recently, Judge John Noonan has pointed to some of the relevant ancillary facts we don't get, such as the nature of Helen Palsgraf's injuries, her income and family status, the financial resources of the Long Island Railroad, the number of injuries annually resulting from railway accidents, and so forth: facts that would tend to go into a modern torts settlement. But what interests me here is less those other facts than how the admirable concision of Cardozo's narrative of the accident controls that very narrative, limiting its reach as a story, keeping it within well-policed boundaries.

Cardozo, like most judges, only appears to tell the story of the event under adjudication. He recasts the story events so that they make a legal point, rendering it a narrative recognizable in terms of legal principle. He wants to demonstrate that the defendant, in the person of the railway guard, could not reasonably have foreseen the harm to the plaintiff:

> The conduct of the defendant's guard, if a wrong in its relation to the holder of the package, was not a wrong in its relation to the plaintiff, standing far away. Relatively to her it was not negligence at all. Nothing in the situation gave notice that the falling package had in it the potency of peril to persons thus removed.
>
> (341)

The alliteration of this sentence gives it a kind of conclusive panache. After running through a brisk series of hypothetical narratives intended to show that "prevision so extravagant" as to include the remote consequences of acts cannot be a basis for a ruling in favor of the plaintiff, Cardozo writes, "Negligence, like risk, is thus a term of relation" (345). It has to do with a relation of a legal duty of care and foreseeable harm, which Cardozo cannot find here. His concise narrative of the incident on the railway platform is an antinarrative in that it seeks precisely to destroy relation, to show that certain linkages of cause and effect are "extravagant." It works against the kind of connections we usually seek in narratives.

The eloquent dissent in *Palsgraf*, by Judge William Andrews, gives a narrative of the incident even more laconic than Cardozo's, which is strange since one would think it in Andrews' interest to elaborate on *this* story. Instead, Andrews meditates philosophically on kinds of relation established in stories, and presents us with a series of hypotheticals: a dam with faulty foundations breaks, injuring property far down stream; a boy throws a stone into a pond, "The water level rises. The history of that pond is altered to all eternity"; "A murder at Sarajevo may be the necessary antecedent to an assassination in London twenty years hence. An overturned lantern may burn all Chicago"; and:

> A chauffeur negligently collides with another car which is filled with dynamite, although he could not know it. An explosion follows. A, walking on the sidewalk nearby, is killed. B, sitting in a window of a building opposite, is cut by flying glass. C, likewise sitting in a window a block away, is similarly injured. And a further illustration. A nursemaid, ten blocks away, startled by the noise, involuntarily drops a baby from her arms to the walk. We are told that that C may not recover while A may. As to B, it is a question for court or jury. We will all agree that the baby might not.
>
> (*Palsgraf v. Long Island* 353)

In fact, says Andrews, there are no fixed rules to guide us here. "It is all a question of expediency" (354). The best guide he can offer is: "The court must ask itself whether there was a natural and continuous sequence between cause and effect."

How far do the Rube Goldberg-like consequences of the dynamite-laden car exploding extend? Where do you declare the story to be over? By the term "expediency," Andrews appears to point to the concrete, particularized, possibly ungeneralizable issues of a single narrative. Without saying so — and again, without unpacking this particular incident on the railway platform — he seems to detect a problem in the doctrine of "foreseeability" of harm. We know harm caused only after it has occurred, retrospectively. Narrative itself is retrospective, its meanings become clear only at the end, and the telling of a story is always structured by anticipation of that end, the "point" of the story, the moment at which its sequences and their significance become clear. It is only in hindsight, retrospectively, that one can establish a "chain of events," in the manner of Sherlock Holmes concluding one of his cases. "'You reasoned it all out beautifully,' I exclaimed in unfeigned admiration. 'It is so long a chain, and yet every link rings true'" – as Dr Watson admiringly exclaims at the end of "The Speckled Band" (Doyle 1965: 83). In this sense, there are no principles to guide you, there is only the causal and sequential linkage of events, the concrete particulars which narrative alone can convey.

Now, in the tellings and retellings of the *Palsgraf* story I can find nothing about the narrative particular that seems to me most deeply mysterious and important: those scales which, in Cardozo's account, were "thrown down" by the shock of the explosion, injuring Helen Palsgraf. Where and what were these scales? What did they look like? Were they attached to the wall, or freestanding? How did they become dislodged from their customary position in such a way as to strike Helen Palsgraf? And how did they strike her, and what kind of injuries did they cause? You seek in vain, in both the majority and the dissenting opinions, for any attempt to render this vital moment – the moment of the injury – in the story. (Torts scholar William Prosser years later decided the scales could not have been dislodged by the explosion, as claimed by Cardozo, but were likely knocked down by the panicked crowd on the platform [Noonan 1976: 119]). Any student in Creative Writing 101 would be sent to rewrite his or her draft for omitting this crucial information. The very clever student might of course, in detective story fashion, reserve it for the end. One can imagine Holmes and Watson in discussion: "So those scales, you see. . . . "

Cardozo once eloquently declared in a speech that as "a system of case law develops, the sordid controversies of the litigants are the stuff out of which great and shining truths will ultimately be shaped." The statement makes very clear the rationale for repressing the sordid story of Mrs Palsgraf on the railway platform, in order to transform its dross into something precious, the narrative of the law itself. But surely those great and shining truths in *Palsgraf* depend intimately on narrative construc- tions, on "sordid" story details, which the opinions in the case repress even as they recognize their importance. Cardozo and Andrews both recognize that there is a story to be told, and the dissent, in particular, notices that how it is constructed makes a difference. But they both then eviscerate the particular story at hand, indeed they spend more time and give more particulars in their hypothetical narratives. Their recognition of the importance of the story is denied by their determination that the story exists only to reach the "great and shining truths" of legal precedent and rule. The gesture of the judges here could almost be analogized to classic scenarios of denial and repression in Freud, for instance the child's simultaneous recognition and repression of sexual difference. Here, recognition of the need to narrate what happened is used to deny any real narrative – concretely particularized, finely detailed – of what happened.

One could adduce many other kinds of examples. "Searches and seizures," for instance, almost inevitably involve narratives: even the application for a search warrant entails a predictive narrative of what the search will have uncovered when it has been carried out. Distinguishing the permissible from the illegal search can be difficult, and some recognition on the part of legal actors of the distinction between actions and their recounting – their reformulation as narrative discourse – could be helpful. In a different kind of instance, a troubling problematic of narrative has arisen in the "Victim Impact Statement" (VIS), a relative newcomer to American law that intends to restore a place to victims of crime who, it has been argued, are often excluded in the adversary process of prosecution versus defense (since victims no longer bring their own cases, as they did in the medieval world). The VIS gives a detailed account of the harms suffered by the victim. Is it legitimate to introduce this kind of narrative at the sentencing phase of a capital case, where its effect is bound to be (and is intended to be) a harsher penalty, likely death, for the defendant? The US Supreme Court said no in *Booth v. Maryland* (1987), then four years later reversed itself (having undergone a significant change of in its membership) in *Payne v. Tennessee* (1991). The opinions in these cases implicitly argue the question of whether certain kinds of story – by their nature, tragic, inflammatory, and irrebuttable – can be told in certain crucial contexts: notably, when a jury is debating the question of life or death. They raise questions about narrative relevance (is the trauma of the surviving family members of a murder victim relevant to the guilt of the defendant?) and narrative closure (are the sequels to murder, in the sufferings of the survivors, part of the murder story?) Are VISs the wrong story, meaning the story in the wrong place?

Another example, one of continuing controversial interest in the law, concerns confessions made by criminal suspects under interrogation. Courts have long struggled with the problem of how we know a confession was made "voluntarily," and not "compelled" or "coerced." Are there enforceable conditions and contexts that assure that confession is freely given? The Supreme Court in *Miranda v. Arizona* (1966) attempted to set formal conditions that would allow courts to discriminate the voluntary from the involuntary confession by way of the by now well-known "warnings" that must be given to any suspect when he or she is taken into custody for interrogation. The warnings are supposed to ensure that the suspect be enabled "to tell his story without fear," as Chief Justice Earl Warren wrote in his *Miranda* opinion (*Miranda v. Arizona*: 466). Yet it is far from clear that formal rules on the production of confessions get to the heart of the matter, since confessional speech is so complex and multilayered a phenomenon, activating layers of guilt, shame, abjection, dependency, propitiation. Storytelling without fear may in this instance be a utopian construct.

A few years ago, one US Supreme Court opinion appeared to breach the bar of repression that keeps the notion of narrative from being articulated in legal doctrine. In *Old Chief v. United States*, decided in 1997, the question at issue is whether defendants with a prior conviction on their record should be allowed to "stipulate" to the prior conviction, thus disallowing the prosecution from presenting the facts of the earlier felony in making the case against them for their new alleged crime. Defendant Old Chief knew he had to admit to a prior crime and conviction – on an assault charge – but didn't want the prosecutor to be able to detail the prior crime, for fear that it would aggravate his sentence on the new crime (which in fact was quite similar to the prior one). The prosecutor refused to accept the stipulation, and the District Court judge ruled in his favor: the full story of the prior crime and conviction was offered as evidence. Old Chief was found guilty on all counts of the new charges of assault, possession, and violence with a firearm. He appealed. His conviction was upheld by the Ninth Circuit, which essentially restated the traditional position that the prosecution is free to make its case as it sees fit. When the case reached the Supreme Court, Justice O'Connor, in a dissenting opinion joined by Justices Rehnquist, Scalia, and Thomas, endorsed that traditional position.

But this claim was rejected by the majority (consisting of Justices Souter, Stevens, Kennedy, Ginsburg, and Breyer) in an opinion written by Souter that argues that introduction of the full story of the past crime could be unfairly prejudicial; it could lead the jury to convict on grounds of the defendant's "bad character," rather than on the specific facts of the new crime. The story of the past crime might "lure the factfinder into declaring guilt on a ground different from proof specific to the offense charged" (*Old Chief v. United States*: 180). The story of the past crime must be excluded, not because it is irrelevant, but because it may appear overrelevant: "it is said to weigh too much with the jury and to so overpersuade them as to prejudge one with a bad general record and deny him a fair opportunity to defend against a particular charge" (181). The story of Old Chief's past crime must be excluded because it risks creating too many narrative connections between past and present: risks creating that large inference from narrative that we call "character," and authorizing the jury to convict on the basis of "bad character" rather than the specifics of the present story.

Souter in this manner orders the exclusion of the past story, reverses Old Chief's conviction, and remands the case for further proceedings. But the most interesting moment of his opinion comes in his discussion of the dissenters' point of view, their argument that the prosecution needs to be able to present all the evidence, including the story of past crime and conviction, in its specificity. He concedes the need for "evidentiary richness and narrative integrity in presenting a case" (183). He goes on to say that "making a case with testimony and tangible things... tells a colorful story with descriptive richness." And he continues:

> Evidence thus has force beyond any linear scheme of reasoning, and as its pieces come together a narrative gains momentum, with power not only to support conclusions but to sustain the willingness of jurors to draw the inferences, whatever they may be, necessary to reach an honest verdict. This persuasive power of the concrete and particular is often essential to the capacity of jurors to satisfy the obligations that the law places on them.
>
> (*Old Chief v. United States*: 187)

It is almost as if Souter had been reading literary narratology, and been persuaded by the argument that narrative is a different kind of organization and presentation of experience, a different kind of "language" for speaking the world. In conclusion to this section of his opinion, he writes:

> A syllogism is not a story, and a naked proposition in a courtroom may be no match for the robust evidence that would be used to prove it. People who hear stories interrupted by gaps of abstraction may be puzzled at the missing chapters ... A convincing tale can be told with economy, but when economy becomes a break in the natural sequence of narrative evidence, an assurance that the missing link is really there is never more than second best.
>
> (*Old Chief v. United States*: 189)

Here, Souter turns back to the case of Old Chief, to argue that the prosecution's claim of the need to tell the story of the earlier crime is unwarranted because that is another story, it is "entirely outside the natural sequence of what the defendant is charged with thinking and doing to commit the current offense." Old Chief's stipulation does not result in a "gap" in the story, it does not displace "a chapter from a continuous sequence" (191).

Souter hence rules out the prosecution's longer, fuller narrative as the wrong story, something that should not be part of the present narrative sequence. It is interesting that in so doing he feels the need to discourse of the place and power of narrative in the presentation of legal evidence: its "richness," its "momentum," its "persuasive power." "A syllogism is not a story": in this phrase, Souter appears to recognize what a handful of scholars from outside the legal world have recently argued, that the law's general assumption that it solves cases with legal tools of reason and analysis that have no need for a narrative analysis could be mistaken. Souter thus breaches the bar over what you might call an element of the repressed unconscious of the law, bringing to light a narrative content and form that traditionally go unrecognized. Yet curiously, or perhaps predictably, he does it by way of an argument that in the present case the lower courts failed to guard against the irrelevant and illegitimate power of narrative, admitting into evidence story elements – the story of Old Chief's prior crime – that should not be considered part of the "natural sequence" of the present crime. The past story would give too much credence to the present story that the prosecution must prove. It is in defending against the power of storytelling that Souter admits its force. And his disquisition on narrative has not been cited in any subsequent Supreme Court opinions.

Law, one might say, needs a narratology. A legal narratology might be especially interested in questions of narrative transmission and transaction: that is, stories in the situation of their telling and listening, asking not only how these stories are constructed and told, but also how they are listened to, received, reacted to, how they ask to be acted upon and how they in fact become operative. What matters most, in the law, is how the "narratees" or listeners – juries, judges – hear and construct the story. As I noted earlier, people go to jail, even to execution, because of the well-formedness and force of the winning story. "Conviction" – in the legal sense – results from the conviction created in those who judge the story. So it is that a greater attention to the narrative forms given to the law might serve to greater clarity about what it is that achieves conviction.

Yet this plea for a formal analytic attention to narrative in the law meets an objection that has been flamboyantly presented by Alan Dershowitz. Dershowitz contends that the whole notion of a well-formed narrative – as exemplified in Chekhov's "rule" that a gun introduced in Act I of the drama must by Act III be used to shoot someone – is misleading in the court of law, since it leads jurors to believe that real-life stories must obey the same rules of coherence (see Dershowitz 1994: 100). If we allow into evidence the narrative of spousal abuse, then the eventual murder of former wife by former husband becomes a logical narrative conclusion to the story. Whereas, Dershowitz wants to argue, who's to say that life really provides such a narrative logic? Dershowitz offers here his version of a theory of narrative advanced by, among others, Jean-Paul Sartre, in his contention that telling – as opposed to living – really starts at the end of the story, which is there from the beginning, transforming events into indicia of their finality, their making sense in terms of their outcome.

It is indeed in the logic of narrative to show, by way of the sequence and enchainment of events, how we got to where we are. As I suggested in discussing *Palsgraf*, narrative understanding is retrospective. Dershowitz may be right to protest that life is blinder and more formless than that. And yet his protest may be in vain. For our literary sense of how stories go together – their beginnings, middles, and ends – may govern life as well as literature more than he is willing to allow. Our very definition as human beings is very much bound up with the stories we tell, about our own lives and the world in which we live. The imposition of narrative form on life is a necessary human activity; we could not make sense of the world without it. We seek to understand actions as intelligible units that combine into goal-oriented plots. Hence, if Dershowitz utters a significant caveat about putting too much trust in a preformed sense of how stories "turn out," it's not clear that we could even put together a story, or construe a story as meaningful, without this competence – acquired very early in life – in narrative construction. If narrative form were to be entirely banished from the jury's consideration, there could be no more verdicts.

One final point: in American law, all the issues – including those that concern the telling of and the listening to stories – find their ultimate commentary in the judicial opinion, especially the Supreme Court opinion. "It is so ordered," the Opinion of the Court typically concludes, letting us understand that the Court has delivered a narrative of order, one that itself imposes order, and, more generally, that narrative orders, gives events a definitive shape and meaning. "It is so ordered": this rhetorical *topos* inevitably fascinates the literary analyst, who normally deals with texts that cannot call on such authority. (Much literature, one suspects, would like to be able to conclude with such a line – to order an attention to its message, to institute a new order or a new point of view on the basis of the imaginative vision it has elaborated.) The court, in so ordering, must activate conviction that its narrative is the true and the right one. There is an eloquent statement on this point in the "Joint Opinion" of Justices O'Connor, Kennedy, and Souter in *Planned Parenthood v. Casey* (1992), the case that reaffirmed (with some modifications) the right to abortion first secured in *Roe v. Wade* (1973). The Joint Opinion, arguing the importance of *stare decisis* and the respect for precedent, notes: "Our Constitution is a covenant running from the first generation of Americans to us and then to future generations. It is a coherent succession" (*Planned Parenthood v. Casey*: 901). The "covenant," we might say, is a master narrative, into which each new narrative episode must be fitted. How does this work? In the words of the Joint Opinion, "the Court's legitimacy depends on making legally principled decisions under circumstances in which their principled character is sufficiently plausible to be accepted by the Nation" (866). The narrative of the covenant relies on precedent and *stare decisis* in order that change or innovation appear to be principled, so that sequence appear not random but an instance of consecution. The most apt words in the sentence quoted may be "sufficiently plausible." What does suffice here? Only that which is rhetorically effective, that which persuades, that which assures "conviction." "Sufficiently plausible" invites assent, but also a degree of awareness of how one is being worked on by rhetoric. "Sufficiently plausible" offers a pretty good definition of what we, as listeners, demand of any narrative proposed to our attention.

Attention to the role of narrative in the law can begin to open to thought some of the unthought assumptions, procedures, and language of the law. If, as Souter puts it in *Old Chief*, a syllogism is not a story, the law needs to become more conscious of its storytelling functions and procedures. Narratology in the courtroom? Yes, it is very much needed there.

REFERENCES AND FURTHER READING

Amsterdam, A. and Bruner, J. (2000). *Minding the Law*. Cambridge, MA: Harvard University Press.

Binder, G. and Weisberg, R. (2000). *Literary Criticisms of Law*. Princeton, NJ: Princeton University Press.

Delgado, R. (1989). "Storytelling for Oppositionists and Others: A Plea for Narrative." *Michigan Law Review* 87, 2411–41.

Dershowitz, A. (1994). "Life is Not a Dramatic Narrative." In P. Brooks and P. Gewirtz (eds.), *Law's Stories* (pp. 99–105). New Haven, CT: Yale University Press.

Doyle, A. C. (1965). *The Adventure of the Speckled Band and other Stories of Sherlock Holmes*. New York: Signet.

Miranda v. Arizona (1966). 384 US 436.

Noonan, J. T. (1976). *Persons and Masks of the Law*. New York: Farrar, Straus & Giroux.

Old Chief v. United States (1997). 519 US 172.

Palsgraf v. Long Island Railroad Co. (1928). 248 NY 339.

Planned Parenthood v. Casey (1992). 505 US 833.

Rusk v. State (1979). 43 Md.App. 476, 406 A.2d 624.

State v. Rusk (1981). 289 Md. 230, 424 A.2d 720.

28

Second Nature, Cinematic Narrative, the Historical Subject, and *Russian Ark*

Alan Nadel

The central problem of narrative cinema is that of using a severely limited, two-dimensional space, within a severely limited time span, to represent a temporally limitless, three-dimensional world. The task of narrative cinema, in other words, is to naturalize a counterintuitive experience by creating the illusion that the viewer has acquired a privileged window on reality, a window through which one is supposed to see not objects and actions, but see instead a story. This task, of course, is impossible, and one way (of many ways) to group films in terms of style, form, school, historical or national trends, would be according to the degree and manner that each film chooses to foreground or efface the difficulties that it encounters in confronting that problem, in other words, according to the conventions it adopts to render itself referential.

"Audiences come to recognize and interpret conventions by 'naturalizing' them," Seymour Chatman tells us. "To naturalize a narrative convention means not only to understand it, but to 'forget' its conventional character, to absorb it into the reading-out process, to incorporate it into one's interpretive net, giving it no more thought than to the manifestational medium, say, the English language or the frame of the proscenium stage" (Chatman 1978: 49).

What are the implications of this form of learning-as-forgetting? What are the consequences of naturalizing, that is, of *making* something natural? Even to survey with a minimal level of rigor the possible avenues of inquiry opened by such broad questions would require far more space than this essay allows. They would touch on, among other things, the intersection of narrative with developmental, cognitive, and psychoanalytic psychology; with phenomenology and epistemology; with cultural anthropology and material culture; with such concepts as "false consciousness," "the autobiographical subject," "commodification," and "social Darwinism," to name just a few. What follows will be a much more narrow discussion exploring some of the learning-as-forgetting associated with specific conventions of what David Bordwell, Janet Staiger, and Kristin Thompson (1985) have called the "Classical Hollywood Style" in light of the way the recent film *Russian Ark* calls into question that style and the history of cinematic narrative in which it participates. The more general issue that I also want to touch upon is how the process of rendering these conventions invisible acclimates us to specific notions of reality, and, further, how those notions of reality inflect our sense of ourselves as historical subjects. Certainly the tenets of the stories we tell ourselves and tell others incorporate us into a community connected by the ability we share to identify with a recognizable set of implied authors and implied readers. Being part of an interpretive community not only allows us to comprehend narratives but also to situate ourselves in relation to them. I am interested, therefore, not simply in how narratives work but in how specific narratives acquire referential cogency, that is, how they can be recognized as veracious, how for any group of people at any moment they delimit reality.

"What constitutes 'reality' or 'likelihood'," as Chatman points out, "is a strictly cultural phenomenon, though authors of narrative fiction make it 'natural'. But of course the 'natural' changes from one society to another, and from one era to another in the same society" (Chatman 1978: 49). Authors, storytellers, filmmakers, politicians, astrologers, or any makers of narratives, however, do more than simply take the cultural pulse or glean the social consciousness of a particular time and place; their iteration of conventions contributes to and reinforces the parameters of a culture's narrative cogency. Conventionalizing the structures that give narratives legibility allows specific activities to become events, and specific events to become points of reference.

Narrative film, particularly Hollywood-style film,[1] provides an especially clear example of this phenomenon, for in order to comprehend a film's narrative, we perform a large number of counterintuitive procedures as though they were natural. We construct a three-dimensional space, for example, by coordinating shot/reverse shot sequences that would replicate the view of "reality" available only to those with eyes in both the front and back of their head. We move from the outside of a multistoried office building, as seen from a significant distance, to a desktop ostensibly within that building, without any explanation of the change in size, proportion, distance, or perspective. A shot before our eyes dissolves and another appears, attached to sites and actions separated (and separated differently in the produced narrative than in the production of that narrative) by space or time or both.

The procedures by which we reconcile these visual discrepancies are inherent neither to film nor to narrative; they are historical conventions. Over the last one hundred years, moviegoers – with prior assistance, no doubt, from more than half a century of familiarization with photographic representation (and assisted to some degree, as well, by more than four centuries of perspectival painting) – learned to comprehend and to naturalize, among many other things, the proportions of the cinematic shot, the demands of the mobile frame, the disruption of the cut, and the interplay of edited moving images. With the aid of American television – that has long enjoyed prolific worldwide distribution – the conventions of cinematic representation, particularly those employed in Hollywood-style films, have been influential globally and exceptionally ubiquitous throughout the industrialized West. They have helped huge populations to learn-as-forgetting the formal procedures of cinematic narrative.

Particularly characteristic of the procedures specific to Hollywood-style film is their attempt to efface, as much as possible, the signs of artifice. The characteristics of that approach have been exceptionally well described by Bordwell, Staiger, and Thompson (1985), who have shown how the "Classical Hollywood Style," perfected during the silent era and normalized during the heyday of studio domination (from the early 1930s to the early 1960s), carefully coordinated all its elements to codify specific notions of cinematic reality. Space allows only the briefest listing of the prominent characteristics of the Classical Hollywood Style: the privileging of desires, goals, and deadlines; a hierarchy of human worth; a methodical redundancy; the elimination of loose ends and extraneous digressions; the use of music as destiny; the use of continuity editing; the minimizing of self-consciousness; and the normalizing of limited omniscience.

In his book on film narration, Bordwell (1985) further analyzes the process by which film effects its narrative ends. Drawing on elements of cognitive psychology, Bordwell describes narrative film as presenting a series of cognitive cues. Bordwell then indicates the kinds of cues that, historically, have been codified to make legible a narrative film's temporal and spatial relations, that is, that enable it to narrate. Although these cues are the means by which the viewer is led to construct the story, they are not innate to human cognition. Rather, they are the accumulated "wisdom" of historical conventions.

We should remember that in 1895, the Lumières' moving picture, aptly titled *Train Arriving at the Station*, sent audiences fleeing in fear of being crushed. Similarly, when, in *The Great Train Robbery* (1903), a cowboy fired a gun point blank directly into the camera, terrified audience members ducked and screamed. It is less important that these early audiences misperceived the visual cues than that their behavior refers us to a point at which the meaning of the cues was in play, for the effacement of a medium can only occur to the extent that its cues become naturalized. In the same way, for example, one can only be said to know how to "play" a musical instrument or to "type" (or "keyboard") or to "drive a car" when a variety of specific procedures no longer require conscious deliberation.

Their seeming automatic, however, is just another version of what Roland Barthes has called a myth, that is, as he put it, "Nature and History being confused at every turn" (Barthes 1972: 3). The historical conditions that created the conventions of Hollywood-style film and the historical conditions under which audiences were instructed in their codes disappear beneath the audience's transparent acquiescence to them. In this way, the codes of cinematic representation become performative. By reinforcing the norms of cinematic reality, they teach the audience how to read a film as if the process were natural, not just second nature.

But What is "Second Nature"?

The phrase "second nature" is so ubiquitous that its use, like many phrases and clichés, like language itself, is second nature to us, meaning that we are comfortable using the term. But what exactly is second nature but the evocation of nature in the interest of authorizing convention? It is the affirming of nature in the interest of seeing that affirmation return as practice. To second, as a verb, is to affirm, to add to the consensus, to echo. In this sense, to second nature is to echo affirmatively; it is more or less the act of mimesis that film itself has been lauded for performing since its inception, such that many of the theoretical debates about film in the first half of the twentieth century focused on which modes of cinematic representation were best suited to reflect reality. The seconding of nature entailed in responding to cinematic cues thus can be seen as the affirming of cinematic reality, the seconding of film's kinship to nature.

By the same token, to be of a second nature is to be not of the first order, to be something less than the thing itself. Second nature is not nature but its double, an alias, a falling off, such that employing second nature to view a film means neither viewing nature nor responding naturally. Rather, one is constructing a world as though it were natural and as though the process of constructing it were natural, even though that world exists elsewhere, is only partially available to the senses, and, being always inferential, constantly needs supplementation. In this sense, second nature is the source of simulacrum, the reproduction of a narrative for which there exists no original in nature.

This form of second nature is not inconsistent with Bordwell's theory of film narrative: adapting to his cognitive model the terminology of Russian formalism, Bordwell calls the amalgam of cinematic cues the *sjuzhet* that renders the story or *fabula*. Through the repeated and systematic integration of distance, proportion, angle, perspective, duration, and punctuation, the spectator is cued, to use Bordwell's term, not just to construct a specific fabula, but also to accept a specific mode of cueing as "natural."

But that natural response informs a supernatural experience, for all we know of the fabula is the sjuzhet, which, nevertheless, is a version of a fabula while the fabula itself exists in an imaginary elsewhere. Thus the sjuzhet does not actually render the fabula, but rather it produces it. "In fiction film," as Bordwell says, "narration is the *process whereby the film's sjuzhet and style interact in the course of cueing and channeling the spectator's **construction** of the fabula*" (Bordwell 1985: 53, italics in original, emphasis on "construction" added).

Although the viewer constructs the fabula from the sjuzhet, however, the fabula is also the authority for the sjuzhet. The point that I am making is that in Bordwell's scheme, as in any evocation of "second nature" (or for that matter of "natural selection"), the viewer's relationship to the fabula is not only structural but theological; the "true" story remains inaccessible through the senses, and our belief in it must be cued by a maker who understands how we codify and ritualize our experience, no matter how counterintuitive that experience may be. The viewer occupies the subject position that mediates between an idea of an unfolding reality and the authority of an imaginary elsewhere.

This is not to suggest that every mediation is the same, and my concern in this essay, in fact, is the implication of specific types and patterns of mediation, especially as their prolific practice becomes so automatic as to seem as though it were "second nature." My interest, in other words, is in attending to that moment when a practice passes for a perception. The practice of constituting the fabula, therefore, is not just theological but performative in that the spectator is practicing specific modes of construction that are inherent neither in nature nor in narrative; they are the products of history. And thus this activity valorizes historical conventions, that is, naturalizes them.

Cinematic Intimacy and the Face of Narrative

Let us consider one of these conventions, the close-up, a device endemic to most narrative cinema and certainly to Hollywood-style film. The convention of the close-up deftly enfolds incongruous intimacy into a continuity that makes it seem normal rather than grotesque, ordinary rather than disruptive, comfortable rather than rude. "If the close-up lifts some object or some part of an object out of its surroundings," Bela Balazs wrote, "we nevertheless perceive it as existing in space; we do not for an instant forget that the hand, say, which is shown by the close-up, belongs to some human being. It is precisely this connection which lends meaning to its every movement" (Balazs 1992: 260). Balazs particularly praised film's ability to capture facial expression: "This most subjective and individual of human manifestations is rendered objective in the close-up" (p. 262). Can we imagine, after all, not as a logical possibility but as a historical practice, a narrative cinema without faces? As viewers of narrative film, we've grown accustomed to the face: its expressions are second nature to us now. As filmgoers, we expect to see the inscription of history transcribed on the expression of individuals. Even Eisenstein, whose own aesthetics, especially in regard to film's representation of history, rejected Hollywood-style and continuity editing, exploited the close-up, especially the close-up of faces. In order, in *Potemkin*, to render the massacre on the Odessa steps "real," he presented us with a terrifying montage of close-ups, dominated by those of faces.

The face, in other words, is indispensable to film narrative as we generally know it. And yet the close-up requires imagining a degree of intimacy with strangers experienced nowhere else in life, except perhaps on a subway during rush hour, where one can stand sharing the grip on one stainless steel pole with nearly a dozen strangers, whose faces (not to mention other body parts) are in intimate proximity. Anyone who has had this experience knows that it demands resisting narrative, requires not turning the random companions into protagonists, not thinking about their motives, goals, desires, conflicts, past and future actions. When a wrist and sleeve protrude under my arm from a person whose nose is pressed against the back of my shoulder, the last thing I want to think about is where that sleeve has been or where it is going. And while I don't want to overgeneralize from my own experience, I think it is reasonably safe to say that normally when riding close up to people, as in rush hour subways, the tendency is to avoid intimacy.

The privileged intimacy of the cinematic close-up helps train us, I believe, in how to navigate these subway rides. I am not saying that people who do not watch movies have more trouble with rush-hour intimacy than those who do, any more than I am claiming that children whose mothers did not hold them in front of mirrors did not experience what Lacan calls "the mirror stage." Rather than err in the direction of the overly literal, I am arguing that the unconscious is historically specific, manifesting the conventions of the cultural conditions in which it was programmed. Thus, in a world historically informed by cinematic notions of reality, we participate as a culture in conventions that regularly naturalize the arbitrary expansion and collapse of distance in the same way that continuity editing undermines a stable point of view. We see someone in front of us who is very close, and next perhaps we see equally close to us the person who would occupy the space 180 degrees behind us. What is so remarkable about this shot/reverse shot sequence is that the distance between the two parties is irrelevant; we can be equally close to them, regardless of how close they are to one another. At the same time, we can be equally close to their extremities – the shot of a hand or foot – as to their face, to their possessions as to the objects of their gaze. Or equally far away. Or both. If the frame of the cinematic screen by definition must permit a limitless time and space, then it cannot logically limit the spatial integration of shots although it can employ an arbitrary logic for arranging them.

In his important study, *Theory of Film Practice*, Noel Burch (1969) has very effectively described the array of possible "articulations," as he calls them, between shots. Burch makes clear that the conventional articulations represent only a small percentage of those that are logically possible. In this way, Burch moves us away from regarding narrative film as allowing us to look through a window or, à la Bordwell, from regarding it as a set of cues that allow us to imagine the time and space of an unfolding story. "By virtue of its handling of time and space," Bordwell explains, "classical narration makes the fabula world an internally consistent construct into which narration seems to step from the outside" (Bordwell 1985: 160). Burch instead impels us to envision film as the orchestration of recorded material, and thus to engage an understanding of film composition that is not authorized by an imaginary elsewhere. By divorcing the fabulous presentation from the fabula, we are able to understand more clearly how specific articulations conform not to nature but to a hierarchical set of conventions.

In this context, the close-up does not represent an inherent logic, but rather creates some of the hierarchies requisite to developing a specific style of narrative: notice this detail, it tells us, privilege that person, attend to that expression. These instructions are not logically crucial to constructing a narrative. Bordwell, in fact, makes them ancillary by designating them as aspects of "style" rather than of narration. The instructions are crucial, in other words, to a specific style of narration, one that regards extreme privilege as a phenomenological given.

Even a story about the most deprived of protagonists at the same time endows that protagonist with extraordinary narrative privilege. First, it asserts unequivocally and relentlessly that the world of the narrative we are constructing revolves around that protagonist. If the viewer constructs the fabula, that fabula names, by definition, the story that houses the protagonist. In Hollywood-style film, "the principal causal agent is . . . the character, a discriminated individual, endowed with a consistent batch of evident traits, qualities, and behaviors . . . the most 'specified' character is usually the protagonist, who becomes the principal causal agent, the target of any narrational restriction, and the chief object of audience identification" (Bordwell 1985: 157).

In this model, every viewer is being called upon to be the contractor who not only custom-builds a home for the protagonist but also screens other characters at the door. The criteria for that selection process are defined in relation to a system of causality attuned to the protagonist's goals and desires. Deadlines tend, in this regard, to be particularly prevalent devices to structure the needs of the protagonist and hence of the plot. "The priority of causality within an integral fabula world," Bordwell explains, "commits classical [Hollywood-style] narration to unambiguous presentation. Whereas art-cinema narration can blur the lines separating objective, diegetic reality, characters' mental states, and inserted narrational commentary, the classical film asks us to assume clear distinctions among these states" (Bordwell 1985: 162). The construction of "reality," in other words, combines an explicitly objective presentation with an implicitly subjective set of needs consolidated around the image of the star (or stars) whose close-ups dominate.

If the close-up can thus be considered the site of the intimacy with characters and objects away from which the beacons of the plot's requisite causes radiate, it can also be deemed a diversion. It not only calls our attention to one item, but away from everything else. By filling the screen with a very small set of details, it suggests the plenitude that nature provides but film does not. In other words, it puts the eye in competition with the frame, even though this competition, in the Hollywood-style, remains largely unacknowledged. The frame thus simultaneously is an always present absence and an always absent presence. It signifies the presumption that there is more – a *lot* more – than we see. It signifies this because, implicitly, we see enough to know that there is more and to infer aspects of that abundance which resides elsewhere.

History and *Russian Ark*'s Take on It

The audience thus engages in the prolific practice of these formal procedures involved in ignoring the frame while attending to the plenitude that it signifies. The engagement in these practices as though they were natural, however, affects not only the comprehension of cinematic narrative but also the understanding of historical cogency. Is it reasonable to assume otherwise? We employ formal procedures facilely and pervasively to delimit cinematic reality. These procedures, while themselves remaining invisible, allow us to visualize a reality far more extensive than the images we actually see; they enable us, in other words, to give the images a history. In performing these invisible procedures, moreover, we are practicing – drilling ourselves, one could say – in the activity of constructing historical narrative. Hayden White, after all, has demonstrated extensively that the production and consumption of historical narrative is inextricably connected to the governing narrative forms of a specific moment and culture.[2] The codes of cinematic representation, thus, are doubly performative: they produce the film's narrative and, by ritualizing the procedures by which events acquire cogency, then produce the historical subject as spectator.

This too is the tricky problem of history. That which unfolds itself as history does so by the authority of everything that escapes its gaze. Of all that has happened, Michel de Certeau (2002) reminds us, how little gets written down. In both cinema and history, the frame is the necessary obstacle to everything that does *not* lie within its margins. The illusion of limited omniscience is vouchsafed by the frame that excludes the unknown, as though it were only accidentally omitted since, as the multifarious scope of continuity editing assures us, our knowledge of time and space, our mastery of distance, is potentially limitless and absolutely without cost.

America particularly, as a culture, and the twenty-first-century industrialized West, more generally, has adopted the conventions of Hollywood-style cinema and its derivatives as though they were second nature. Contemporary Western culture has more or less tacitly accepted the fact that the logic of Hollywood-style narrative construction is inherent to the organization of narrative itself. Accepting those premises, we can begin to consider some aspects of that viewer whose historical subjectivity is enacted by adhering to the conventions of Hollywood-style mainstream cinema. Among other things, that viewer is one practiced in viewing history as the mediation between the close-up and the imaginary elsewhere that gives that close-up its ostensive meaning, that is, between the intimate and the theological. The viewer, in other words, constructs a narrative in the absence of the events that comprise that narrative, through a set of historically specific cues that conform to accepted historically specific conventions for representing events and their significance.

In this light, I want to turn to the 2002 film *Russian Ark* in order to consider how it underscores some of the issues involved in comprehending cinematic narrative as second nature and some of the implications of those issues for the role we play as historical subjects.

The remarkable film, directed by Alexander Sokurov, begins with a voice – that of the director – speaking over a black screen: "I open my eyes and I see nothing," he states. There are faint noises, perhaps a woman's voice calling in a windy marble corridor, perhaps just the wind itself. "I only remember there was some accident. Everyone ran for safety as best they could." More noise over the black: wind, the echo of a woman laughing. "I just can't remember what happened to me." The laughing woman gets louder, and she appears on the screen – looking like a nineteenth-century Russian aristocrat, formally and festively dressed in cape, furs, feathers, and jewels. She is in the arms of a man gaily taking her from a coach in the winter.

"How strange. Where am I?" asks the director whose camera places him very close to this woman and her friends, all of whom take no notice of him. "Judging from the clothes it must be the 1800s," the voice of the camera/director states. The two couples dressed for a ball advance toward him rapidly in the cold. "Where are they rushing to?" the camera/director asks, as the camera backs up as if to avoid being trampled. The couples turn, joined by many others, and enter a crowded passageway that, as it turns out, is the basement of the Hermitage. And the camera/director follows.

Thus our camera/director gets swept up in the flow of an event, a nineteenth-century ball in the Hermitage, today a world-famous museum, but earlier the winter palace of the tzars. The film will conflate those periods, incorporating characters from the eighteenth century to the present, and artifacts from earlier centuries. Entering this historical setting through the back door and the basement, the camera/director encounters something that resembles aspects of history, or at least of a small segment of it, a few centuries of Russian history, or perhaps European history, or perhaps the history of Western art represented by the works collected at the Hermitage.

Space here does not permit me to elaborate on the film's multifarious engagement with many of the issues crucial to contemporary historiography: how the past is represented, how our pathway through it is emplotted, how cause is related to accident, who or what constitutes the historical subject, what defines the relationship between the historical text and its own historicity, to name just a few. Instead, I want at this point only to note that the way the film raises these questions suggests the similarities between the problems of historiography and the problems of narrative film. In narrative cinema, as in history, we must construct the representation of a time and space, the meaning of which awaits emplotment. Like film, history requires the construction of an elsewhere and the perspective from which that elsewhere may be viewed as though from the outside. No matter how familiar to the viewer, therefore, this elsewhere must be discrete from the perspective that authorizes it. This must be the case, moreover, despite the fact that, as White points out, narrative "is at once a mode of discourse, a manner of speaking, and the product produced by the adoption of this mode of discourse" (White 1987: 57). Therefore, as de Certeau explains, "modern Western history essentially begins with a differentiation between the *present* and the *past*.... This rupture also organizes the content of history within the relations between *labor* and *nature*; and finally, as its third form, it ubiquitously takes for granted a rift between *discourse* and the *body* (the social body)" (de Certeau 1988: 2–3). Both the mode of discourse and its object are foregrounded by *Russian Ark*, when it moves in one, uninterrupted 86-minute shot through the museum, encountering over 2,000 people, most in costumes from the nineteenth and early twentieth centuries, and, as well, through 86 minutes of our real time, that is of our real *screen* time.

Screen time, meaning the amount of time that expires when one is watching a film, is the most uniform of the three temporal dynamics at work in cinematic narrative.[3] While the story time (the full chronological scope of enacted, recounted, and *inferred* events) can range from hours to centuries, as can the plot time (the span from the earliest to the last *rendered* event), screen time in Hollywood-style films usually falls between 80 and 140 minutes, and only in very rare cases exceeds 200 minutes.

The general principle, especially in Hollywood-style productions, therefore, is that screen time is the shortest of the three dynamics, and story time the longest. This tends to be true even in films where the plot and the screen time seem simultaneous. Alfred Hitchcock's *Rope*, for example, is shot to give the appearance that it consists of one uninterrupted take. It presents in continuous action the committing of a murder, the hiding of the victim in a chest, the laying out the food for a buffet dinner party, the greeting of the guests, the entire dinner party from cocktails to dessert, the bidding farewell to each guest, the straightening up, and the postdinner confrontation that leads to the crime's revelation. This all happens in 80 minutes, making *Rope* the most vivid example of a Hollywood film in which the screen time seems as though it must be synonymous with the plot time and yet also clearly cannot be.

In *Russian Ark*, in contrast, plot time must be consistent with screen time, not because of the single take, but because the film's limited partial take on history is its plot and the camera/director is the protagonist. The events of the film are his efforts to make sense of his time and place, and they are represented by the film's singular path – by definition to the exclusion of any others – from the first image to the last. The crisis of the film is that he occupies the position of the historical subject, that is, the person who remains invisible to – even if always partially aware of – all the conditions that circumscribe his existence, that inform his understanding of the past, and that allow him to move through a defined time and space. His movement is the film's plot, in other words, because space in the film is not constructed cinematically; the space is not the alleged fragments of an imaginary elsewhere given their presence and coherence – the illusion of nature – by a set of historical conventions.

The camera/director also moves through an elaborately staged and choreographed representation of history, but, as the film makes clear, a representation of history no more elaborately staged than the museum's individual and collected works of art or in the history of the museum's collection. The man playing the nineteenth-century French diplomat (Sergei Dreiden) is a distinguished Russian stage actor who, in his role as the Frenchman, encounters actors playing the roles of actors. Early in the film he sees actors staging a performance for Catherine the Great. The Frenchman and the camera/director approach the performance from behind the stage, moving through the wings across the edge of the platform into the auditorium where Catherine watches the performance and approves. Whispering to one another, the camera/director and the Frenchman caution each other not to intrude too visibly. Instead of the play's action and dialogue, however, we see the actors in the moments just prior to their performance or hear the remarks, even during the performance, that the actors make to one another rather than those meant for the audience. "Bend towards me" an actor dressed in eighteenth-century garb, who seems to be playing the play's director says to an actress backstage, in a chariot, wearing classical regalia, "You are beautiful." When we move through the wings onto the stage where dancers are performing, we hear one dancer whispering to her partner "Why are you pushing me?" "Don't scratch me," he whispers back.

Because we are seeing the actors primarily as staging the performance rather than as characters in their staged narrative, the contexts are richly layered, such that we cannot forget that a play staged for Catherine the Great also comprised moments in the lives of the now forgotten actors, moments no less real, in some sense no less a part of history, than the Empress who shared their time and space. When she rushes out of the Frenchman's sight (in order to urinate), he notes the theatricality of her disappearance: "Where's the Empress?" he asks "Gone? Russia is like a theater. A theater." Despite the cautions of the camera/director to speak softly and not call attention to his (and the camera's) presence, the Frenchman continues to peruse the Russian aristocrats (that is, the actors in the film *Russian Ark* dressed as aristocrats), exclaiming: "Theater! . . . What actors! And those costumes!"

The Frenchman also engages in discussions about the artwork in the museum. He discusses it with the camera/director, and also discusses the quality of the artwork, the originality, the history of specific works and styles with contemporary twenty-first-century people he meets along the way. At one point, in response to the European's criticism of some of the art and of some of the building's derivative décor, the camera/director says "The tsars were mainly Russophiles, but sometimes even they dreamed of Italy. Wasn't the Hermitage created to satisfy those dreams?" The dialogue between the two thus probes "the place of art" as that phrase's literal and figurative meanings intersect the historicity of artwork and artifact as the historical fulfillment of a dream.

The Frenchman also discusses aesthetics and meaning. "Are you interested in beauty or just its representation?" he asks friends of the camera/director, a contemporary doctor and a contemporary actor. When the Frenchman shows them "one of the Hermitage's earliest acquisitions," obtained by Catherine II, in 1772, they tell him "such information is for specialists. For us detail is more interesting." They are more drawn to the symbolic significance of a chicken and a cat in the painting's foreground.

This contrast, one of very many in the film, dramatizes the conflicting perspectives contained at the intersection of the place of history and the place of art, or evoked by the historicity of artwork and the artistry of historical preservation, as the film frames in counterpoise art and historical re-enactment. The story of *Russian Ark* can thus be viewed as a conflict between competing versions of history, as suggested by the museum, the works of art, the costumed actors, the dialogue, and the uninterrupted visual record of a single spectacular performance. Many of these possibilities are foregrounded by a dialogue in which the camera/director engages the Frenchman, as bewildered – and as fascinated – as the camera/director by his surroundings and the inexplicable events that have situated him in this place and this time. Together the two protagonists comprise the duality requisite for the concept of history, which must represent a composite vision that subsumes individual agency at the same time that it must represent the cumulative activity of individual agents. Together this partnership of visible European and invisible camera/director engage art, artifact, allusion, rumor, and performance, the "stuff" of historical knowledge.

To put it another way, they examine the elements of history in terms of the competing frames they require. At the same time, because *Russian Ark* exists within one frame, it effects an inversion of the frame and the subject. The frame does not represent the limitless world of the diegesis but the limitations of the world that circumscribes the narrative, which is the shot itself – one motivated motion through time and space.

The voiceover is not the film's narrator but the camera/director who is also the audience; the director in other words is the surrogate for the historical subject, not for God. This is particularly clear in that *Russian Ark* precludes one of the most ubiquitous signifiers of Hollywood-style's limited omniscience, a visual knowledge of the protagonists that they cannot have of themselves. Even a Hollywood-style film such as, for example, *The Graduate*, that is completely focused on the experiences of one character with whom the audience is encouraged/expected to identify completely, a film that shows only scenes and episodes in which the central figure, Benjamin Braddock, is present, still persistently lets us see something Benjamin does not: Benjamin. In addition, we always see what is behind him, whether he is aware of it or not. And we see both of these things at no expense to our ability to identify with Benjamin or his centrality.

This is the case, perhaps, because Hollywood style cues us to imagine Benjamin as existing not in a physical reality shared by the camera, but in an imaginary elsewhere that is devoid of the camera while still retaining the gaze that camera allowed. That is the theological site of the fabula upon which Hollywood style's illusion of limited omniscience depends and which *Russian Ark* rejects.

While depriving himself of the omniscience – the alleged truth of an imaginary elsewhere – implicit in editing (especially continuity-style editing), the camera/director moves the frame without editing, so that the close-up is the function of a movement, not a cut. This may seem trivial, but it does leave us to speculate about the effect of learning to view a narrative film as though its "elsewhere" is physical rather than metaphysical. When we move close to someone or something, we know completely the cost of this intimacy in that we cannot suture it artificially to everything we abandoned in order to attain it. Suture – the process of stitching together a space by cutting back and forth between shots that reverse the perspective by (roughly) 180 degrees – creates the illusion of a coherent world by constantly deploying and filling an absent space. For Jean-Pierre Oudart (1977–8) this implies an "absent one," that is, a theological concept. In not only precluding suture but also denying the logic that would enable it, therefore, *Russian Ark* is denying to the "absent one" a presence in the film and thus *Russian Ark* is denying, as well, the possibility of the spectator's ability to share that implicit form of omniscience.

The physical space – the corridors, stairwells, rooms, and buildings – also limit the shot. So does the limited time we are allowed. In contrast, imagination is unlimited, evoked as it is by the contemplation of the works of art, by the staged theatrical and orchestral performances, by the discussions among the characters. The imagination is free to roam – *qua* imagination – where the gaze cannot, so that in *Russian Ark* the imaginary elsewhere is marked as imaginary, that is, as the product of human endeavor, not as the site of reality.

This form of imagination – quite distinct from the response to Bordwell's cognitive cues – does not authorize the narrative or frame the gaze; the 86-minute journey, therefore, is the sole version of itself. The time frames delimiting the film's narrative are not those of the fabula and the sjuzhet, but rather those of the enduring and the ephemeral. The film mediates between the two, moreover, in that it turns the ephemeral performance effected by the individual acts of 2,000 nameless bit players and extras – like the thousands of soldiers without whom the battle of Waterloo would not have been a battle – into a permanent record. The film thus becomes the history of a performance as well as the performance of history.

At the same time, it makes clear that for the individual, history is always unique and singular. Both formally and thematically the tenets of *Russian Ark* allow only one, temporally limited opportunity to encounter and, ultimately, to comprehend the amalgam of vision and allusion, commentary and contemplation, that comprise our experience as historical subjects.

Thus at the end of the massive ball that concludes the film, the expressed sadness of the camera/director that "It's over" is heightened when the Frenchman decides to part with the camera/director, choosing not to go forward into "the future." Alone, amid the flow of thousands of actors, dancers, and extras exiting simultaneously the ball, the winter palace, the museum, and the film, the camera/director turns aside from the crowd to an open set of glass doors, looking out on a grey vaporous world, and advances toward the apparent void. "Sir, Sir," he softly calls to his lost Frenchman, "It's a pity you're not here with me. You would understand everything. Look. The sea is all around us. We are destined to sail forever, to live forever." These vain hopes are expressed as the gray sea and grayer sky into which it seems to be evaporating both dissolve into blackness. The future as a *concept*, this closing sequence suggests, may be limitless, but as an *experience* it is temporal, regardless of whatever we say or do, during the solitary take we get of all the experience that makes the concept imaginable.

While I have barely begun to elaborate the array of issues evoked by this magnificent film, or investigate their formal and thematic implications, I have used the film to illustrate that the codes of cinematic representation are arbitrary and, more important, that they are inflected. A different mode of representation performs a different relationship between intimacy and omniscience, between experience and imagination, between the historical subject and the scope of history.

When we are deprived of the self-satisfying capacity to believe in the authority of a world beyond our senses, the road to truth, of course, becomes difficult, and we will certainly not easily find it in history, even if it is usually waiting for us at the movies.

NOTES

1 I will use "Hollywood-style" to refer to studio
   productions made in the "Classical Hollywood
   Style" and the derivates made in the poststu-
   dio era, as well as television series and made-
   for-television movies that tend to conform to,
   much more than deviate from, the governing
   principles identified by Bordwell et al. (1985)
   as constituting the Classical Hollywood Style.

2 White's groundbreaking book was *Metahistory*,
   but his theories have been further elaborated
   upon and developed in *The Content of Form* and
   Tropics of Discourse. The latter books are less
   heavily influenced by the (fanciful?) schematics of Northrup Frye's *Anatomy of Criticism*.

3 For detailed discussion of these dimensions,
   see Chatman (1978: 41–95) and Bordwell
   (1985: 74–98).

REFERENCES AND FURTHER READING

Balazs, B. (1992). "The Close-up." In G. Mast,
   M. Cohen, and L. Braudy (eds.), *Film Theory
   and Criticism*, 4th edn. (pp. 260–7). New
   York: Oxford University Press.

Barthes, R. (1972). *Mythologies*, trans. A. Lavers.
   New York: Noonday Press.

Bordwell, D. (1985). *Narration in the Fiction Film*.
   Madison: University of Wisconsin Press.

Bordwell, D., Staiger, J., and Thompson, K.
   (1985). *The Classical Hollywood Cinema: Film
   Style and Modes of Production to 1960*. New
   York: Columbia University Press.

Burch, Noel. (1969). *Theory of Film Practice*, trans.
   Helen R. Lane. Princeton, NJ: Princeton University Press.

Certeau, M. de (1988). *The Writing of History*,
   trans. T. Conley. New York: Columbia University Press.

Certeau, M. de (2002). *The Practice of Everyday Life*,
   trans. S. Rendall. Berkeley: University of California Press.

Chatman, S. (1978). *Story and Discourse: Narrative
   Structure in Fiction and Film*. Ithaca, NY: Cornell
   University Press.

Frye, N. (1957). *The Anatomy of Criticism*. Princeton, NJ: Princeton University Press.

Oudart, J.-P. (1977–78). "Cinema and Suture."
   Screen 18 (4), 35–47.

White, H. (1973). *Metahistory: The Historical Imagination in Nineteenth-Century Europe*. Baltimore, MD: Johns Hopkins University Press.

White, H. (1978). *The Tropics of Discourse*. Baltimore, MD: Johns Hopkins University Press.

White, H. (1987). *The Content of the Form: Narrative Discourse and Historical Representation*. Baltimore, MD: Johns Hopkins University Press.

29

Narrativizing the End: Death and Opera

Linda Hutcheon and Michael Hutcheon

Opera as Narrative

A decade or so ago, in conference sessions and journal issues, a debate raged about whether music could *be* narrative rather than just *use* narrativity as a kind of metaphor. Since Fred Maus, one of those debaters, addresses this question in this volume, we would like to consider, instead, a particular case that was not the focus of that debate: scripted music, or what Dr Johnson called the "extravagant and irrational" art of opera. Opera could be defined as sung staged narrative, but given the history of narratology's restrictions, the first two words of this definition would demand a redefinition of the third, or at the very least, an acceptance of the fact that drama is a multimedia narrative text type (Jahn 2003). We have chosen the second route. In arguing for a (less restrictive) view of narrative as rhetoric, James Phelan defines narrative as the telling of a story by someone to someone for some purpose and on some occasion (1996: 8). If this be so, then opera is literally the embodied telling of a story by a phalanx of performers and producers for a live audience on a public occasion.[1] Despite the frequent presence of narrators on stage – Captain Vere in Benjamin Britten's *Billy Budd* or Wotan, Erda, Waltraute, and the Norns in Richard Wagner's *Der Ring des Nibelungen* – opera's narratives appear, on the surface, to be "shown," rather than "told," to use the standard narratological distinction. But since this showing is multiply mediated, we will argue that it functions like a telling.

Unlike novelistic narratives, operatic ones exist in two different forms: in what Kier Elam would call "dramatic" texts (in this case, the musical score and the verbal/ dramatic libretto) and in "performance" texts – the various productions that at one and the same time interpret, visualize, and bring to aural and physical life those dramatic texts (Elam 1980: 3). In short, a staged opera production is a form of mediation of two dramatic texts, parallel in its semiotic complexity to that provided by the narrator in fiction. Many different people shape the diegesis as it is to be experienced by an audience – everyone from the initial librettist and composer to the entire production team. The director, the conductor, the musicians, the singers, the designers (lighting, costume, and stage), and many more individuals and groups work together to tell opera's narratives on stage, and they do so in many different ways in many different media. The task of the production team in an allographic art (Nattiez 1990: 74, Goodman 1968: 129) like opera is to stage its nexus of interpretive values through its selecting, ordering, and embodying of narrative elements in the dramatic texts. Often this process results in major changes at the narrative level. A director can add an embedding narrative frame, for instance, and thereby add a focalizing force not existent in the dramatic text. When Nikolaus Lehnhoff, the 1987 director of the Bayerische Staatsoper production of Richard Wagner's *Der Ring des Nibelungen,* has one character, Loge, write on an opening scrim: *"Es war einmal"* ("once upon a time"), he orients the next four operas of the cycle in ways that Wagner might never have intended. Not only are these words not in the libretto text, but a relatively minor character, Loge, is also moved to center stage to function as focalizer, indeed as controller, of the narrative action. Arguably, however, *all* production decisions could be said to function narratively, in that they determine the way the story is "told."

Staged narrative may lack prose fiction's descriptions of people and places, its explications, and its easy ability to shift time and place. But it offers instead direct visual and aural presentation of people and places, enacted action and interaction as explanation, and a strikingly vivid sense of time in the here and now. In short, it depicts as it narrates. To all this, however, opera adds a further mediating element: music. Like stories, music is said to be central to human ordering, shaping, and meaning-making needs. When stories and music interact, as they must in opera, they force us to adapt, rather than simply adopt, existing narratological models. Music has often been inspired by narrative – as in program music, that is, instrumental music that reproduces or suggests literary ideas or evokes mental pictures. Music has also often been compared to narrative because it proceeds through time toward closure and, on the way, generates expectations, tensions, and resolutions. But opera is scripted or "texted" music. Carolyn Abbate claims that such music is performative in that it "works to interpret literary texts" (1991: x). But for whom does it interpret the libretto text? As a mediating narrative dimension, operatic music speaks directly to the audience, not necessarily to the characters in the staged story. Only in what are called "phenomenal" songs – that is, self-consciously sung pieces like ballads, serenades, toasts, or lullabies – do characters share our ears and hear the music we in the audience experience. Donna Elvira's maid, serenaded by Don Giovanni, in Mozart's opera of that name, is presumably seduced by his song – as are we, who listen with her. Normally, though, characters do not hear the music (though, as Richard Taruskin [1992: 196] points out, they do *live* it). As Abbate memorably puts it, the characters are deaf to the "music that is the ambient fluid of their music-drowned world" (1991: 119).

The mediating and communicating function of music in opera is as semiotically complex as that of any narrator in fiction. In its narrative interaction with the text, music can reinforce the action and words or it can undermine them completely, telling the audience something the character does not know or has not yet consciously faced. It can support or undermine the staged narrative, creating ironies that the audience alone can savor. Luca Zopelli has argued that at moments like this, the opera composer speaks in the first person (1994: 27). But characters too can be made into focalizers of the musical narrative, as happens when a solo instrument is isolated to signal our entry into a character's psyche. The audience's attention is thus concentrated on that character (and his or her inner world), with the music functioning like an aural spotlight (Zopelli 1994: 93–100).

Richard Wagner developed to a high art the use of what others have called *Leitmotiven* to extend the narrative complexities of the music/text interaction. These bits of melody or harmony associated with a character, emotion, object, or event become structural elements that take on a life of their own as they are repeated and varied throughout his music dramas. Isolde may assert that she hates Tristan, but she sings it to music associated with her love for him. Abbate has developed the narrative potential of the interaction of words and music into a theory about disruptive diegetic moments in opera when uncanny narrative "voices" can be heard in self-reflexive instances of enunciation when the text and music are momentarily misaligned (Abbate 1991: xii-xiv). Like Lawrence Kramer (e.g., Kramer 1990), Abbate has brought the tools of narratology to opera with a special emphasis on the enunciation of narrative: who tells the tale? Who controls it? However, moving away from descriptive narratology toward a more rhetorical dimension, we are more interested in the other end of the production process: the *receiver* of operatic narrative who chooses to witness on stage what Peter Conrad (1987) has called a "song of love and death."

Operatic Narratives of Death and Dying

When opera was born as a new art form in sixteenth-century Florence, its most popular narrative was that of the Orpheus story, a story that set a pattern of love and loss that would haunt the genre for centuries. While death is a human universal, our contemporary attitudes toward it are not the same as those of Renaissance Italy. Audiences today will filter what they see and hear on stage through their own time and culture, as well as their own feelings about personal mortality, and this will depend on such things as age, personality, religious and philosophical perspective, and personal experience with death and dying. If our culture is indeed the death-denying one that everyone says it is, how do we explain the continuing strong attraction to operatic narratives that are obsessed with death – from the conventionally tragic operas of the nineteenth century to the less conventional death-inspired ones like Wagner's *Tristan und Isolde?* J. Hillis Miller reads Aristotle as suggesting that we need narratives "to experiment with possible selves and to learn to take our places in the real world, to play our parts there" (Miller 1990: 69). Our question, provoked by opera's thematic obsession, is: does this extend to playing the finale too? Recent work in a range of fields – from medical anthropology to sociolinguistics – attests to the growing realization outside of literary circles that, in Cheryl Mattingly's terms, narrative "constitutes a mode of thought and representation especially suited to considering life in time, shifting temporal shapes, and the human path of becoming where death is never far away" (Mattingly 1998: 1). This description, we shall argue, fits death-obsessed operatic narratives particularly well.

The fact that operas are *staged* narratives, of course, adds a significant shared public dimension. It is now received wisdom in the theater that the interpreting audience is always part of the creative process of dramatic art forms, always part of the active making of meaning. But Aristotle's early theory of tragic catharsis, of the pity and fear said to be experienced by audiences, reminds us that audiences *feel emotions* as well as *make meanings*. The implicit double pull, then, between emotional identification and intellectual distance that has been theorized by so many people, likely also lies at the heart of audience responses to dramatized narratives of death and dying, if with a twist. The fact that opera is sung – in other words, that its artifice is manifest and audible – both complicates and simplifies any discussion of artistic distancing. The unavoidable artifice is most likely a factor in composers' choices of operatic subjects. As Herbert Lindenberger suggests, in their hunt for suitable subjects composers will be attracted to those that might bring about a "higher and more sustained level of intensity" in order to balance the distancing conventions of the art form itself (1984: 53). Yet the moving and mediating power of operatic music also works effectively against distancing, bringing the audience squarely into the emotional domain of the work, but *not* through the words or action.

The tension between emotional engagement and critical estrangement always comes to the fore in discussions of audience response to staged sung narrative. As we sit in the dark, watching and listening, are we empathizing participants or objectifying voyeurs? Does the artifice of the singing, the lighting, the stage makeup, or perhaps the verse language work to make us feel less close to the story and the characters on stage? Although in the twentieth century, it was Bertold Brecht's "alienation effect" that most influentially articulated the idea of critical distance as a dramatic necessity, the concept goes back at least to Aristotle and was further developed by eighteenth-century British and nineteenth-century German theorists of aesthetic "disinterestedness." But what do we do with the fact that opera audiences weep? Do we need distance as a kind of psychic protection – especially when the theme of what we are witnessing on stage is the inevitable fate of us all, death? And what mediating role does the power of music play in aiding – or thwarting – distance?

Friedrich Nietzsche certainly felt that it was the (Apollonian) function of artistic form to keep the (Dionysian) forces of chaos and emotional energy under control: only then could the audience actually bear the experience of seeing and hearing Wagner's opera about the infinite yearning for death, *Tristan und Isolde* (Nietzsche [1895] 1967: 126). Even if we think in somewhat less extreme terms, however, we might well feel there to be a certain commonsense truth to the notion that artistic artifice can act as a kind of protective buffer. Freud ([1905] 1953) made the psychoanalytic case for this theory in these terms: the audience identifies with the suffering hero on stage, yet knows perfectly well that the suffering is feigned and not real, and that the person on stage is an actor in a play. This double distancing – through fiction and through impersonation – allows the audience to identify, but to do so without danger, and indeed even to experience pleasure at the representation of suffering and death. Opera audiences may feel the music's power, in other words, but they are also aware that characters are singing, not speaking, and that they are enacting, not living, a narrative about death and dying.

We choose to put aside, for the sake of argument, the familiar explanations given to account for the audience's pleasure in watching narratives of the suffering and death of others on stage: that is, voyeurism, sadism, and masochism. Even A. D. Nuttall's (1996) theory of why tragedy provides pleasure (the events are hypothetical and the audience identifies with the protagonist, and both these features allow the audience to "play the game of death") does not quite account for responses to both conventionally tragic works and also those other nontragic (but death-obsessed) operas, in part because of the complexity added by the reaction to the music. Instead of these explanations, we'd like to test out the hypothesis that the act of witnessing staged operatic narratives of death might well function in a very different way. Audiences – of any period – are varied and diverse, but the one thing they share is that they are composed of mortal beings. But why should they enjoy (or even attend) a performance of a work that foregrounds their very mortality? Among the possibilities we have considered is the fact that such a performance might act as a commemoration or even as a form of therapeutic reassurance in the face of bereavement, making us ponder our social roles in, and our emotional responses to, the death of *others*. But is it possible to watch the death of someone on stage without at least for a moment considering one's *own* demise?

We suspect not, even if each person will inevitably react differently. Elisabeth Bronfen has argued that narratives of death force us to confront our own end in a kind of "death by proxy": we know we are mortal and must submit to our mortality, yet because (as safely distanced audience members) we do not actually die, but only witness staged death, we can feel as if we are asserting some mastery over the End. She sees an ambivalence in all representations of death: "while they are morally educating and emotionally elevating, they also touch on the knowledge of our mortality" (Bronfen 1998: 510). For most of us, she claims, this is so disconcerting that we would prefer to disavow it. These narratives "fascinate with dangerous knowledge." Our question is: would this ambivalence be configured differently if the operatic narrative were openly and centrally about coming to terms with death?

We hypothesize, therefore, that watching and contemplating a performed narrative of death in an opera could be analogous to undertaking what the Early Modern period thought of as a pious devotional practice known as the *contemplatio mortis* (the contemplation of death). Essentially a formal meditation on mortality, this was a late addition to the medieval "art of dying" or *ars moriendi* tradition that developed in the context of a generalized social anxiety caused by plagues, wars, and famines. Interestingly and not irrelevantly, the flourishing of the *ars moriendi* in the late sixteenth and early seventeenth centuries coincides historically with the rise of opera as a new and distinct art form in Europe. An inherently theatricalized and performative form, the *contemplatio mortis* specifically involved imagining one's own death in great (and personalized) detail by means of an extended sequential dramatic narrative. Its purpose was to prepare oneself, spiritually and emotionally, for one's end. Yet, when the performance of the meditation was over, one in a sense "awakened" and (like an audience member leaving the theater) one reclaimed one's normal, active, healthy life. The dramatized narrative that had just been imagined and entered into did serve, nonetheless, as a means both to practice the art of dying and, thereafter, to appreciate life more fully in contrast. Jonathan Dollimore calls this a performative "social practice" – private yet gaining its meaning from an "existing cultural history" (1998: 87).

Shakespeare's *Measure for Measure* has been convincingly read by Michael Flachmann as a kind of *contemplatio mortis* in which Claudio becomes "an emblem of mortality for Shakespeare's audience, a surrogate sufferer who is systematically fitted for death and then miraculously rescued from its fatal grasp" (Flachmann 1992: 227). According to this interpretation, Claudio's victory becomes "the audience's victory and confers in the process moral and spiritual strength upon Shakespeare's viewers at a time of great anxiety in their lives" – a time of plague and social unrest (1992: 236). Similarly, could attending an opera that stages death and dying not function as a kind of *contemplatio mortis*? At the conclusion of both kinds of imaginative exercises, we can walk away, alive and well, but having "rehearsed" our own demise. We can console ourselves, as Freud pointed out, with the knowledge that our psychic identification has been a safe one, that someone else (indeed, an actor) was "suffering" on stage. We might even persuade ourselves that death, at least given its portrayals in many operas, is not always something to be dreaded or evaded, but instead something natural and even acceptable.

In order to explore this hypothesis, we have had to think about operatic narratives not as simple entertainments for a passive, if appreciative, audience. To use Richard Schechner's terms, we have had to make theater "efficacious" (1994: 625), in this case, by thinking about it in terms of ritual. Operas about human mortality are perhaps easier than others to cast in this way, for like all rituals they too deal with the narrative basics. They hang on what Schechner calls "life's hinges where individual experience connects to society" (1994: 613). Uniting music, dance, and theater, ritual performances, he argues, create an "overwhelming synaesthetic environment and experience" for their actively participating audience (p. 632). An analogy with the multisensory experience of opera is not hard to make. To continue with this anthropological line of thought, Victor Turner's theory of the close relationship between what he calls "social drama" ("where conflicts are worked out in social action" [1986: 34]) and stage drama (where they are mirrored in artistic forms and plots) also tends to focus on significant narrative moments such as marriage and death, events he refers to as "life-crisis ceremonies" (1986: 41). For audiences, these rituals are deemed "prophylactic" (rather than "therapeutic") (1986: 41) – and that is not a bad description of the function of the *contemplatio mortis* or of the act of witnessing narratives of our mortality on the operatic stage.

Narrative Closure and Operatic Death

Since we know we will die, that experiential certainty (or its denial) is unavoidably going to be a touchstone for all our responses to staged narratives of death. But those responses are also going to be conditioned by our satisfying sense that the chaos and confusion of living (and dying) has been transformed into the safe order of narrative art. Once made intelligible, the end feels probable, indeed inevitable. As Henry J. Schmidt puts it: "The ultimate anxiety addressed by an ending is the fear of death. Entering into a literary or theatrical experience means exposing oneself to the risk that the as-yet-unknown ending might turn out to be meaningless, or at least disappointing" (1992: 7). Even in opera where (thanks to program notes and memory of the repertoire) we likely know the plot ending, the existential risk is still real, because the ending might not "work" in this particular production on this particular night. There is no guarantee of catharsis, argues Schmidt, but that gamble is part of the pleasure of the theater, even (or especially, we would add) when the theme of the work is death itself.

As Frank Kermode famously argued in *The Sense of an Ending*, "the End" is a figure for our own deaths and as such is feared (1967: 7); yet we also have a deep need for "intelligible Ends" (1967: 8). While our own death is something we might not want to face, for Kermode, "the End is a fact of life and a fact of the imagination" (p. 58). And, indeed, for Peter Brooks too, all narrative is "in essence obituary" in that its meaning comes after death. In his words, "The further we inquire into the problem of ends, the more it seems to compel a further inquiry into its relation to the human end" (1984: 95). We need to confer significance on experience (including that of dying) and narratives offer what he calls "imaginative equivalents of closure" which accomplish this in ways we can never manage in our own lives. Calling on Walter Benjamin, Brooks suggests that representations of death give a story authority by granting us a knowledge of death denied us in reality. Closure in opera, however, involves not only the formal act of bringing the story to a narrative conclusion. There is also another kind of closure, the rhetorical one involved in the ongoing process by which we too, as audience members, complete the incomplete, making everything into ordered and satisfying wholes, creating a sense of significance and completion that is emotional as well as intellectual or formal. To recall our anthropological remarks earlier, the analogy here would be to the reintegration that occurs at the conclusion of a ritual. Despite the urge to deconstruct this humanist response to closure as a learned one, loaded with ideological freight, we have also come to admit its likely reality, especially when closure is attained by reinforcing the audience's sense of finality through the thematic content of death and dying.

George Steiner has claimed that in the last half of the nineteenth century, opera put forward "a serious claim to the legacy of tragic drama," but that, aside from Verdi and Wagner, this challenge was rarely sustained (1961: 284). Many would disagree. Although we have been using the Aristotelian term "catharsis" to discuss the audience response to operatic narratives of death, there is also a very real sense in which operas such as Wagner's *Tristan und Isolde* or his *Ring* cycle are not tragedies in the classical sense of the term, as used in the Western tradition. They may well offer narratives of personal suffering and heroism in the face of uncontrollable forces, as do more conventionally tragic operas. But their final moments are often different, revealing more of a move to moral, psychic, or spiritual transcendence. Death, in fact, is given a decidedly positive value. In Kermode's words, "In Tragedy the cry of woe does not end succession; the great crises and end of human life do not stop time" (1967: 82). In the operas we have mentioned, though, death *is* the final message; time *does* stop, in a sense, when the curtain falls. In twentieth-century works like Francis Poulenc's *Dialogues des Carmélites* or Viktor Ullmann's *Der Kaiser von Atlantis* (written in the concentration camp of Theresienstadt), narratives of death and dying tell – by showing – other meanings for the End. They teach that death can bring out the core of existential and spiritual personhood; it can restore social order and moral honor; it can offer final peace and even give meaning and value to life. Because the meaning of death has been altered (to a positive one), the response of the audience is different. Instead of feeling the pity and fear provoked by tragedy, the audience here experiences understanding and comfort.

In his *Contemplatio Mortis et Immortalitatis*, first published in 1631, Henry Montagu informed his readers that, through acquaintance, death would lose its horror and become familiar, indeed "comely." He preceded this confident assertion with the claim that meditation on death would help us die in ease, alleviate pain, expel fears, ease cares, cure sins, and "correct" death itself. While we shall not try to make you believe that certain operatic narratives can do quite this much, we would like to suggest that they can lay claim to being a form of the didactic "art of dying." Death, like love (opera's other major theme), is obviously an aspect of the human condition for which there are always many questions and never easy answers. Does this fact, combined with the inevitability of mortality, account for death's continuing fascination for audiences? We project our imaginations onto the narrative we witness being staged and sung in a peculiarly contradictory manner: we participate intensely in the world of the narrative, in part because of the emotive power of the music, but we are also consciously distanced from it by the conventions of the singing, the simulation of the acting, and by all the narrative work of the performance team. Here, there is none of the engrossing realism of film, in other words, and this is true even of productions in which the *mise en scène* aims at reducing distance. Paradoxically, both the emotional identification and the intellectual distancing are enhanced in opera. Therefore, when the subject is death and dying, we can experience its power – but safely – just as Montagu said one could during the *contemplatio mortis* exercise. Watching these operas is analogous to imaginatively experiencing the emotions associated with dying and, in a sense, even working through one's own death or that of a loved one.

Some have argued that it is the very form of this "working through" that helps us find not only consolation but also meaning in death – and therefore in life. It is narratives of the end that let us explore and even invent ways of dealing with our mortality. The modern narratives provided by science and technology can only go so far in guiding our understanding of incommensurables like death. And where they stop, the human imagination takes over, proffering order and meaning as needed. As Kermode put it, we "make considerable imaginative investments in coherent patterns which, by the provision of an end, make possible a satisfying consonance with the origins and with the middle" (1967: 17). How do narrative forms like opera achieve this, especially if we have to project ourselves "past the End, so as to see the structure whole, a thing we cannot do from our spot in time in the middle" (Kermode 1967: 8)?

To do this, we rehearse death, be it in the form of tragedy or those more positive narratives of mortality. We can experience aesthetic pleasure and moral understanding even in the kind of closure provided by disturbing operas like Benjamin Britten's *Peter Grimes* and Alban Berg's *Wozzeck* – closure in the form of the protagonists' suicides. Here that response is conditioned and even made possible not by pity and fear but by a sense of psychological comprehension and ethical completion that comes from the self-murder of someone who has been responsible for the death of another. A similar kind of comforting order is induced by all those operas over the centuries about Orpheus grieving Eurydice's death, for they both enact the pain of bereavement and offer us the balm of a ritual of mourning. Likewise, providing a lesson in the power and significance of narrative closure, the "undead" – from Wagner's Flying Dutchman to Janáček's 300-plus-year-old heroine in *The Makropulos Affair* – come to see death as release, as reunion, as the desired end. In this kind of narrativizing of the End, death is, quite simply, what gives meaning to life.

To contemplate death, even on the operatic stage, however, is inevitably to feel (and perhaps even to face) our mortal anxieties as well. This too, we would argue, is part of the appeal of watching operatic representations of death and dying, not only tragic ones but even those in which the End is presented as something positive, complete with the consolations of rhetorical and narrative closure. As Sherwin B. Nuland (1994: xv) explains: "To most people, death remains a hidden secret, as eroticized as it is feared. We are irresistibly attracted by the very anxieties we find most terrifying; we are drawn to them by a primitive excitement that arises from flirtation with danger. Moths and flames, mankind and death – there is little difference."

NOTE

1   This is not to ignore the existence of audio and video versions of opera. It is simply to put these secondary manifestations in perspective: operas are almost always composed to be performed live.

REFERENCES AND FURTHER READING

Abbate, C. (1991). *Unsung Voices: Opera and Musical Narrative in the Nineteenth Century*. Princeton, NJ: Princeton University Press.

Bronfen, E. (1998). "Death and Aesthetics." In M. Kelly (ed.), *Encyclopedia of Aesthetics*, vol. 1 (pp. 507–10). New York: Oxford University Press.

Brooks, P. (1984). *Reading for the Plot: Design and Intention in Narrative*. New York: Knopf.

Conrad, P. (1987). *A Song of Love and Death: The Meaning of Opera*. New York: Poseidon Press.

Dollimore, J. (1998). *Death, Desire and Loss in Western Culture*. London: Routledge.

Elam, K. (1980). *The Semiotics of Theatre and Drama*. London and New York: Routledge.

Flachmann, M. (1992). "Fitted for Death: *Measure for Measure* and the *Contemplatio Mortis*." *English Literary Renaissance* 22, 222–41.

Freud, S. ([1905] 1953). "Psychopathic Characters on the Stage." In J. Strachey (ed.), *The Standard Edition of the Complete Psychological Works of Sigmund Freud*, vol. 7 (pp. 305–10). London: Hogarth Press and the Institute of Psycho-Analysis.

Goodman, N. (1968). *Languages of Art*. New York: Bobbs-Merril.

Jahn, M. (2003). "A Guide to the Theory of Drama. Part II of Poems, Plays, and Prose: Guide to the Theory of Literary Genres." <www.uni-koeln.de/~ame02/pppd.htm>.

Kermode, F. (1967). *The Sense of an Ending: Studies in the Theory of Fiction*. New York: Oxford University Press.

Kramer, L. (1990). *Music as Cultural Practice, 1800–1900*. Berkeley : University of California Press.

Lindenberger, H. (1984). *Opera: The Extravagant Art*. Ithaca, NY: Cornell University Press.

Mattingly, C. (1998). *Healing Dramas and Clinical Plots: The Narrative Structure of Experience*. Cambridge, UK: Cambridge University Press.

Miller, J. H. (1990). "Narrative." In F. Lentricchia and T. McLaughlin (eds.), *Critical Terms for Literary Study* (pp. 66–79). Chicago: University of Chicago Press.

Montagu, H. ([1631] 1971). *Contemplatio Mortis et Immortalitatis*. Amsterdam and New York: DaCapo Press.

Nattiez, J.-J. (1990). *Music and Discourse: Toward a Semiology of Music*, trans. C. Abbate. Princeton, NJ: Princeton University Press.

Nietzsche, F. ([1895] 1967). *The Birth of Tragedy* and *The Case of Wagner*, trans. W. Kaufmann. New York: Vintage.

Nuland, S. B. (1994). *How We Die: Reflections on Life's Final Chapter*. New York: Knopf.

Nuttall, A. D. (1996). *Why Does Tragedy Give Us Pleasure?* Oxford: Clarendon Press.

Phelan, J. (1996). *Narrative as Rhetoric: Technique, Audiences, Ethics, Ideology*. Columbus: Ohio State University Press.

Schechner, R. (1994). "Ritual and Performance." In T. Ingold (ed.), *Companion Encyclopedia of Anthropology: Humanity, Culture and Social Life* (pp. 613–47). London and New York: Routledge.

Schmidt, H. J. (1992). *How Dramas End: Essays on the German* Sturm und Drang, *Büchner, Hauptmann, and Fleisser*. Ann Arbor: University of Michigan Press.

Steiner, G. (1961). *The Death of Tragedy*. London: Faber and Faber.

Taruskin, R. (1992). "She Do the Ring in Different Voices." *Cambridge Opera Journal* 4, 187–97.

Turner, V. (1986). "Dewey, Dilthey, and Drama: An Essay in the Anthropology of Experience." In V. Turner and E. M. Bruner (eds.), *The Anthropology of Experience* (pp. 33–44). Urbana: University of Illinois Press.

Zopelli, L. (1994). *L'opera come racconto: modi narrativi nel teatro musicale dell'Ottocento*. Venice: Marsilio Editori.

30

Music and/as Cine-Narrative
or: *Ceci n'est pas un leitmotif*

Royal S. Brown

Although film music has become, over the last decade or so, the object of increasingly serious study, the movie score continues in most cases to be both used and perceived in only the most superficial of ways. Either film music is seen as a support, something to beef up the narrative at key dramatic moments and then make its way to recordings. Or – and to my mind this is becoming more and more the case – it is becoming a kind of blaring, close-to-nonstop wallpaper for a culture that seems increasingly incapable of doing anything, from running to having a cup of expensive coffee at Starbucks to buying groceries, without some kind of musical accompaniment that seems to grow louder with each passing year of the new millennium. How else to explain James Horner's crushingly overbearing, harmonically and melodically void, and, dare I say, derivative symphonic strains that accompany the eponymous disaster of *The Perfect Storm* (2000)? One might have naïvely supposed that the overwhelming sounds, even manipulated, of the wind and the waves would provide sufficient aural drama. Or how to explain the misguided need felt by the makers of the otherwise magnificent documentary, *Le Peuple migrateur* (Winged Migration, 2001), to weight down its spectacular images of birds and the planet Earth with frequent expanses of overly loud New-Agey music by Bruno Coulais when one would have thought, here even more so than in *The Perfect Storm*, that natural sounds would be just as much the point as the breathtaking and occasionally tragic images? Of course, were this a different essay, and were I in an even more cynical mood, I could suggest the seeds of a quasi *Brave New World* master narrative in the politics of a civilization that needs to keep its populace constantly numbed out on a drug euphemistically known as ambient music. But that, as the man says in *Irma La Douce*, is another story.

The examination of film music and its relation to cine-narrative has generally been an almost purely descriptive catalog of all of the various themes and motifs in a given score and their tie-ins to various characters, situations, and places that turn up in the film, with little or no thought given as to why, just for starters, the filmic text needs these nonvisual doublings. Of course, there's no question that, early on in particular, film scores were often put together in such a literal-minded fashion that they encouraged this type of reading. In many of the scores penned by Max Steiner, for example, leitmotifs and other types of doubling amount to what Claudia Gorbman (1987), in her pioneering book *Unheard Melodies*, has dubbed "hyper-explication," a process typical of Hollywood's eternal need to dumb down both its product and its consumers. But even the heavily leitmotivic score often extends miles beyond the implications of hyperexplication, whether by the critics or the composers. In its best manifestations, such as in most of the small number of scores (relatively speaking) composed by Erich Wolfgang Korngold, a rich assortment of themes and motifs often provides the building blocks for long cues in which the music is structured in such a way as to produce a quasi-contrapuntal paralleling of the written and visual texts. An excellent example of this is Korngold's score for the 1940 film *The Sea Hawk* (see Brown 1994: 97–120).

What I propose to examine here, then, is not the ways in which music supports and/or hyperexplicates the diverse elements of cine-narrative, but rather some of the quasi-narrative properties generated out of the many codes, particularly harmonic, built into the structure of Western music, and how these codes interact with, and actually comment on, the various visual and narrative codes of commercial cinema. Typically, we think of narrative as a representation of something that takes place in which characters and events are elaborated over a certain period of chronological time. Typically, music is considered, in its "absolute" manifestations at least, as a wholly nonrepresentational art form which, like narrative film and literature, needs chronological time to present its text, but whose ties to any possible world remain abstract at best. Within this perspective it would seem impossible to develop anything resembling a musical narratology. Put another way, those who theorize music as a privileged art form foreclose the rich potential of at least certain musical texts as a form of narrative in and of themselves. On one end of the scale, we have Canadian musicologist/sociologist John Shepherd, who, early on in his book *Music as Social Text*, notes the following:

> If human language is important to facilitating a clear distinction between thought and the world on which thought operates, then other modes of communication, in making their materiality felt, remind us of our connectedness to the materiality of the world as signified. Music … is most notable among these other modes of communication.
>
> … [P]ost-Renaissance, "educated" men became so aware of the potential for separating the meaning of a word from its referent, and so seduced by the intellectual power this represented in terms of manipulating and controlling the world, that they had difficulty seeing beyond the immediate implications of their own cleverness. In acting as an antidote to this tendency, the very fact of music as a social medium *in sound* reminds us, not so much of what has been lost, but of that of which we have ceased to be publicly enough aware.
>
> (Shepherd 1991: 6)

Shepherd's perspective, an interesting one to be sure, actually invites an application of the Lacanian topography of the orders of the Real and the Symbolic: It is in the very nature of the various modes of discourse that are the *raison d'être* of the Symbolic order to alienate the subject from the Real by separating the sign from the referent; but music, by stressing the *materiality* – which includes sound, although we generally don't tend to think of sound in such terms – of its own particular mode of discourse, at least offers the potential of avoiding that alienation through a more or less direct presentation of or from the Real. At the other end of the scale we have a post-Platonist such as Schopenhauer, who suggests that "music is by no means like the other arts, namely a copy of the Ideas, but the *copy of the will itself*, the objectivity of which are the Ideas" (Schopenhauer 1969: 257). Similarly, the antimateriality Symbolist poet Stéphane Mallarmé wrote that poets need to reclaim from music what rightfully belongs to them, and that "Music, in all fullness and evidence, and as the whole of the relationships existing in everything, results not from the elementary sonorities of the brass, the strings, the winds . . . but from intellectual enunciation at its peak" (Mallarmé 1896: 367–8; my translation). Within the neo- or post-Platonist perspective as well as from the more nihilistic viewpoint of Mallarméan Symbolism, then, music appears to be the ideal hypersymbolic mode of discourse for bringing about a highly desirable alienation from the material world. This perception can take place – paradoxically, if we consider Shepherd's remarks – precisely because music *is* a medium in sound, since sound, particularly within the worldview of modernity dominated by what one writer has referred to as the hegemony of vision (Levin 1993), does not appear to represent anything at all. And so, in order to represent – and therefore to be able to generate – narrative, music must be tied in to some specific kind of "program," whether overt, such as in the Berlioz "Symphonie Fantastique" (1830) or hidden, as in the dialogue between Orpheus and Eurydice in the second movement of Beethoven's Fourth Piano Concerto from 1808, for which one musicologist makes an extremely convincing case (see Jander 1985), or the passionate love affair encoded by Alban Berg into his 1925–6 *Lyric Suite* (see Perle 1995), or even the sexual violence that feminist musicologist Susan McClary find in the recapitulation in the first movement of Beethoven's Ninth Symphony. McClary describes the movement as "one of the most horrifying moments in music, as the carefully prepared cadence is frustrated, damming up energy which finally explodes in the throttling, murderous rage of a rapist incapable of attaining release."[1]

But music does not have to be specifically programmatic in order to generate narrative. Susanne K. Langer has noted, for instance, that music reflects "the morphology of feeling" (Langer 1957: 238). This morphology, with its patterns of tension, release, active expectation (see Meyer 1956), and what might be termed "active memory" – generated in particular by the harmonic and structural codes of Western music – has much in common with narrative. If one can invoke the Lacanian Real here, it is not so much through the materiality of sound but rather via a particularly direct access to affect. "The *symbolic*," on the other hand, "comforts by covering over the real of *affect*. One could even consider naming it as the realm that negotiates *affect* precisely because it offers the safety and comfort of distance from the *real*" (Ragland 1997: 1094). If, then, music in its normal course can be said to offer a more or less unnegotiated, unmediated path at least to the morphology of feeling, it is a well-known characteristic of film music that in many instances it accesses the domain of affect with an immediacy generally unfound in more traditionally developed works, from songs to symphonies. This immediacy may be said to represent one of film music's greatest assets, but it has also been the object of vituperative criticism from film-music detractors.

But one can go further still. Much later in *Music as Social Text* Shepherd, in writing about the "functional tonality" that dominates Western music, including most of that heard on the music tracks of narrative films, perceptively suggests a perspective diametrically opposed to his early proposition of music as a "medium in sound," quoted above:

> Functional tonal music is about sequential cause and effect – a cause and effect which depends, in the fashion of materialism, upon the reduction of a phenomenon into "indivisible" and discrete, but contiguous constituents that are viewed as affecting one another in a causal and linear manner. The analysis of functional tonal music often concerns itself with "showing" how the final satisfying effect of stating the tonic chord is "due" to previously created harmonic tension. It is no accident that completed and satisfying harmonic passages are frequently referred to as "harmonic progressions."
>
> (Shepherd 1991: 124)

What Shepherd is suggesting is that the harmonic, rhythmic, and formal structures, among other things, of Western music tie this art, along with all of the others, in with the worldview of modernity, which demands what it considers to be realism from its art forms in their representation of both materiality and of time. In Western music the moments of sonorous materiality are linked together in quasi-causal chains leading to a resolution that implies mastery and control of materiality, which is wholly consistent with the ethos of modernity and the countless narratives via which it manifests itself. From this perspective, one could modify Langer's axiom to suggest that music reflects the morphology of the modernist worldview. In other words, the sense of satisfaction, even of relief, produced, for instance, by the eventual return of the home key – or, as another example, of the principal theme – in a work of music reflects the need for closure in a culture that depends upon cause and effect to explain away just about any occurrence, whether "real" or narrative.

It is hardly surprising, then, that one major scholar, structural anthropologist Claude Lévi-Strauss, finds much in common between music and one of the richest manifestations of narrative, myth:

> [M]yth and music share [the characteristic] of both being languages which, in their different ways, transcend articulate expression, while at the same time – like articulate speech, but unlike painting – requiring a temporal dimension in which to unfold. But

this relation to time is of a rather special nature: it is as if music and mythology needed time only in order to deny it. Both, indeed, are instruments for the obliteration of time. Below the level of sounds and rhythms, music acts upon a primitive terrain, which is the physiological time of the listener; this time is irreversible and therefore irredeemably diachronic, yet music transmutes the segment devoted to listening to it into a synchronic totality, enclosed within itself. Because of the internal organization of the musical work, the act of listening to it immobilizes passing time.... It follows that by listening to music, and while we are listening to it, we enter into a kind of immortality.

(Lévi-Strauss 1969: 15–16)

Lévi-Strauss's myth/music parallel depends first and foremost on the unfolding of the text over diachronic time. This dependence puts his theoretical perspective at odds with that of his earlier text, "The Structural Study of Myth" from 1955.[2] There he stresses paradigmatic structure and synchronic time to such an extent that he ends up boiling the entire Oedipal mythology down to a paradigmatic opposition between the autochthonously created being versus the sexually reproduced being, while also downplaying the role of mythic narratology. Major arguments against Lévi-Strauss's almost purely paradigmatic approach to myth have been posed by such scholars as John Peradotto (Peradotto 1984), who stresses both paradigmatic and syntagmatic order in the creation of the mythic text. Similarly, Terence S. Turner notes that "The sequential pattern of the narrative, although it is an irreversible form of temporal organization [i.e., quasi-historical], is not 'diachronic' in the sense of historical time (i.e., a relatively disorderly or randomized process whose organization is expressed in 'statistical' rather than 'mechanical' terms: (Lévi-Strauss 1953: 528))"; rather, "Myths ... provide synchronic models of diachronic processes..., directly at the level of their organization as temporal sequences, through the correspondence between their sequential patterns and aspects of the diachronic processes they 'model'" (Turner 1969: 43).[3]

These theoretical perspectives immediately give rise to the problem of the distinction between myth and narrative, a distinction that certainly seems blurred in Terence Turner's presentation. The late Russian semiotician Jurij Lotman, for instance, presents solid criteria for distinguishing between the mythic text and what he refers to as "plot narration" (Lotman 1979). On the other hand, the synchronic component, posited by Turner, of even the most "realistic" of narratives at least begins to move that text in the direction of myth. While it is well beyond the scope of the present study to examine this problem in any detail, I would propose that, as is so often the case, it is impossible to draw a clear line distinguishing the one from the other: any narrative, at least in structure if not in content, offers elements of myth, and myth must be elaborated in some type of narrative form in order to be communicated. It may certainly be that all mythic narratives are generated from Lévi-Straussian oppositional pairings, but these remain an abstraction until they are elaborated in some form, which is inevitably narrative. Even paintings such as "Oedipus and the Sphinx" by Ingres (c. 1826) and Moreau (1864) present the viewer not just with a key element of the well-known classical Oedipal story but of an encounter – almost erotic in the Moreau – between a (naked) man and a (female) monster that implies an entire narrative even for those not acquainted with the Greek versions of the myth. I would suggest that the more a given narrative stresses, in form and/or content, the synchronic over the diachronic, the paradigmatic over the syntagmatic, the more it is *perceived* as mythic. I would further suggest that the cine-narrative, with its ability, in an art form that appears to mimic the reality we live in, to manipulate images of time and space with montage and music, offers a particularly fertile ground for the mythic or quasi-mythic narrative.[4]

Verbal narrative can and does, of course, generate synchrony through, for example, the reprise of certain motifs. But the reprise of a visual image, such as the point-of-view shot of Scottie looking down accompanied by the famous zoom-in/track-out–track-in/zoom-out camera work in Hitchcock's *Vertigo* (1958), has a quality of instantaneity generally lacking in verbally elaborated motifs. This quality at least partially liberates it from the diachronically elaborated narrative structure, and therefore allows it to generate a more purely structural synchrony. The motif in film music, by dint of being liberated from the developmental patterns characteristic of nonfilm music, particularly concert music, likewise has something of that same quality of instantaneity while also benefiting from music's status as a nonrepresentational art, which allows it, like the visual image, to stand at least partially apart from the diachronically elaborated narrative structure. If, indeed, the novels of Alain Robbe-Grillet often behave like films (the author's pronouncements to the contrary notwithstanding) or works of music, it is because of the same kind of immediacy in the motifs, whose reprises often appear to be independent of diachrony altogether, either because of their apparent arbitrariness, or because of the novelist/filmmaker's conscious or unconscious serialization of the various motifs.[5] Turner's narratological arguments also reveal the weakness of the attacks on novelistic narrative led by André Breton and the Surrealists[6] and on both novelistic and cine-narrative proposed by Robbe-Grillet as *nouveau roman* theorist,[7] who sees the narrative time of traditional novels and films as nothing more than an imitation of historical time.

Going beyond the manifestations of synchrony in narrative discussed above, I propose at this point the application of an additional dimension by introducing the narratological concept of the "temporal categories" (Tarasti 1994: 8) implied by a series of linguistic terms – inchoativity, durativity, and terminativity – particularly durativity – put forth by Tarasti via Greimas (1983: 119) but strangely not pursued by either. Used in linguistics to label aspects, that is, semantic representations of event structure, particularly in verbs, these terms have an obvious application to narrative structure, in which there is generally presumed to be a beginning (inchoative), middle (durative), and end (terminative), although not necessarily in that order, as New Wave filmmaker Jean-Luc Godard is reported to have said. Any particular narrative element, within whatever medium, can be said to be encoded in ways that imply all three of these categories in varying degrees, with the heaviest weighting determining the temporal function played by a given element at a given point within the overall narrative structure.

One is reminded of the sentence that, according to André Breton, French poet Paul Valéry refused to write – *La marquise sortit à cinq heures* (The marquise went out at five o'clock) – precisely because, once written, that sentence implies so much narrative movement forward that Valéry would have been obliged to write a novel (see Breton 1966: 15). Thus the sentence itself, as potentially the first one of the narrative in a book one has opened, has, by dint of its physical position, a strong inchoative function, with a strong durativity also implied by the pages and pages of sentences that follow, and terminativity supposed by the solid probability that there will be a final, complete sentence, *Finnegans Wake* notwithstanding. More importantly, the presence of a marquise as a character is all but guaranteed to suggest interesting aristocratic adventures to come (durativity), a constant, particularly in the early history of the French novel, on which the reader will want to follow through. The French verb *sortir* suggests not so much the completed act of going out (terminativity) as, by dint of its literary past tense (the so-called *passé simple*), the very *pastness* that is essential to almost every novel ever written (Robbe-Grillet notwithstanding) and, for that reason, the guarantor of the storytelling mode that will keep the narrative moving forward (durativity). It also suggests the beginning (inchoativity) of an adventure yet to be told (durativity). The time of going out (five o'clock) is the classic, early-evening hour at which the aristocracy just begins to come to life. Alfred Hitchcock, in suggesting that "the secret of suspense in a film" is "never to begin a scene at the beginning and never let it go on to the end" (McGilligan 2003: 422), provides an almost perfect definition of narrative durativity. Tarasti, who also frequently invokes the Greimasian term "isotopy" ("a set of semantic categories whose redundancy guarantees the coherence of a sign-complex . . . " [Tarasti 1994: 304]), makes convincing arguments for the existence of exactly this kind of narrative structure, in which inchoativity, durativity, and terminativity work off each other in a fairly balanced relationship, in works of "absolute" concert music that have no obvious program. What I am going to suggest throughout much of the remainder of this essay, on the other hand, is that music as it is generally applied to film tends (1) to carry the transparency of motivic reprise to something of an extreme, and (2) to be weighted much more strongly toward durativity than its counterparts in concert music. The film score, then, by subverting diachrony through the cyclicity of its motivic structure and through unbalancing the chronological implications of beginning, middle, and end contributes mightily to the impression we have of much cine-narrative as a mythic or quasi-mythic text.

As an extremely simple illustration of musical narratology as it relates to film, I have chosen the title sequences of two very different films, *The Best Years of Our Lives* (1946), based on a novel by MacKinlay Kantor, directed by William Wyler with music by Hugo Friedhofer, and *North by Northwest* (1959), directed by Alfred Hitchcock after an original screenplay by Ernest Lehman, with a score by Bernard Herrmann. The Main Title cue for *The Best Years of Our Lives*, a mere 23 measures running

71 seconds that run behind very simple title cards, offers an almost aggressive example of "functional tonality": after a two-bar introduction that presents what will become the bridge theme, the opening theme, played in four unison horns and the cellos, stays solidly around the key of C major with only a single accidental until its seventh measure. At that point a dramatic chordal figure takes over, moving from an E♭-major chord to a D♭-major chord to a B♭-major chord to a G-major chord before finally – and very predictably – resolving on a C-major chord. The bridge theme, which features dramatic octave-leaps upward that borrow their rhythmic configuration from the opening theme, starts to modulate, only to quickly give way to a reprise of the main theme and its C-major tonality. Further tying the music in to the norms of cultural modernity (as opposed to artistic modernism, which opposes those norms) is, in my opinion, the theme's very regular 4/4 meter (the norm of countless works of Western music), which I would propose suggests not the diachronic movement of the music, which would be the time over which it elapses, but rather stands as an image of diachrony, of quasi-historical time. In other words, the rhythmic structure characteristic of much Western music makes explicit something – the passage of time in regular intervals – that would basically remain implicit in the time given to the listening to a particular work. Some composers, such as Franz Joseph Haydn in the second movement of his Symphony No. 101 ("Clock," 1794), actually go so far as to use the evenly measured rhythmic structure to imitate the ticking of a clock. Of course, within this regularly beaten meter the number of configurations working both with and against the beat is all but infinite, with the regular beat serving as a point of reference against which what might be called "psychological" or "creative" time is experienced. Composer Elliott Carter has gone so far as to literalize this concept in certain works, such as his 1948 Cello Sonata, about which he has written that one of the first movement's basic ideas lies in "the contrast between psychological time (in the cello) and chronometric time (in the piano), their combination producing musical or 'virtual' time" (Carter 1977: 272). I would modify Carter's statement to read "metronomic" rather than "chronometric" time, the metronomic time being that element that provides an *image* of chronometric time but that, strictly speaking, is not the same as chronometric time.

Also reassuring to listeners of *The Best Years of Our Lives* is the initially very predictable structure of the theme as a whole, which acts as if it is going to follow one of the patterns, built on the so-called "four-bar phrase," of the traditional ABA song form, with the initial "A" in eight bars, the bridge (B) in four, and the reprise acting as if it is going to return to eight. On at least three different levels, then, the music's basic language and structure suggest a kind of down-to-earth normality, wholly consistent with the film's home-town Americana setting. The music suggests this normality to such an extent that deviation from the expected, one of the principal generators of aesthetic effect and affect, not to mention dramatic narrative, in temporally elaborated works of art (see, once again, Meyer 1956), does not seem to figure into the equation other than in the intangible beauty and warmth present in the music from the outset, in the slightly more obvious isotopic characteristic that the entire Main Title grows out of a single very simple musical idea, and in the unexpected appearance of the mildly chromatic chord motif.

But just at the point where the Main Title seems well on the way to completing its ABA song form, with two bars reprising a variant of the A section, and resolving solidly into C major, everything breaks down. After a brief crescendo, the next two bars, the first marked *subito*, suddenly hush down into two varied reprises of the chord motif, by far the most chromatic and unstable segment of the Main Title whole. That motif returns a third time in its original form (with a slight rhythmic variation), leading the "Main Title" back to C major, except that, here, the resolution remains unstable, with two shifts back and forth between an unstable changing chord and C major providing a musical segue into the opening shot at an airport where a soldier returning from World War II (Dana Andrews) is trying to get a plane back to his home town. Significantly, the music, which has come to a rest on a sustained C-major chord, stops short, cutting off most of the final two measures in the score manuscript in which muted trumpets quietly play a fragment – the opening three notes – of the A section in a manner that suggests the "taps" bugle call. What starts out, then, appearing to be a musical entity unto itself, dictated by its own laws of closure and spiced up with the characteristic cine-affect, suddenly loses that stability and, on a purely structural level, implies nonclosure and narrative continuation, that is, durativity. It needs to be stressed that what the music evokes is not intranarrative instability, although one finds plenty of that as the film progresses, but rather the lack of closure inherent in narrative openings, although it is expressed and created according to the codes of cine-musical narrative rather than the visual/verbal ones.

It is obvious that composer Friedhofer had something of a quasi-narrative segue in mind by the way he composed the final two measures of the Main Title for *The Best Years of Our Lives*, and more particularly in the way he toggles back and forth between the unstable chord progression and the C-major chord that resolves, but is also momentarily unresolved by, those chords. But Friedhofer's version still offers a sense of musical – cine-musical, if you will – closure, whereas the way in which the Main Title ends several seconds into the opening action sounds like a rather hasty piece of scissor-work by the music editor. Whereas this sort of practice is the bane of existence for those who make a distinction between film and "serious" music, it is not only justifiable, it is even, in many instances, desirable in the creation of cine-narrative nonclosure. What I am suggesting here is that, in narrative films such as *The Best Years of Our Lives* and countless others, the Main Title serves not just as a musical prelude to get the emotional juices flowing but also as the first sentence, if you will, of the narrative itself. Since this first sentence takes shape in the nonreferential language of instrumental music, I would be tempted to extend Langer's formula to suggest that, in instances such as this, film music has the paradigmatic function of reflecting the morphology of narrative – in this case of narrative openings. Interestingly, in the posttitle sequence, paradigms of movement forward continue not just in the initial obstacle-to-be-overcome narreme (returning soldier Dana Andrews cannot get a flight home, while the rich businessman behind him in line gets a seat right away) but also in visual terms, in this case the airplane itself, as we will see below.

The opening of *North by Northwest* works in remarkably similar ways. Of course, the title sequence, designed by Saul Bass working on his second Hitchcock film, is twice as long and hundreds of times more visually interesting than that of *The Best Years of Our Lives*. In addition, Herrmann's hyperkinetic fandango Overture, while taking off and theoretically landing in the key of A minor, ventures into much more dissonant and chromatic harmonic territory and substantially more flamboyant instrumental territory than Friedhofer's mellow prelude of everyday heroism. Further, Herrmann, who methodically avoided the four-bar-phrase precisely because he knew that musical structure would work against cine-narrative structure (see Brown 1994: 289–93), builds the Overture to *North by Northwest* almost entirely out of motivic fragments defined in the brief one-bar phrases of the Overture's 3/8 meter. These fragments, more often than not, literally repeat in a second bar, with broader melodic development replaced, as the Overture moves forward, by the harmonic sequence, wherein the same phrase gets repeated, often several times, at different pitch levels. But as in *The Best Years of Our Lives*, the *North by Northwest* title sequence, which visually "modulates" from abstract diagonal lines against a green background to a Manhattan office building with the same patterns to the hustle and bustle of New York City crowds in various locations, including Grand Central Station, the musical score continues into the film's opening shots, here suspending abruptly on an unstable seventh chord that suggests the beginning of narrative movement rather than the end of purely musical movement. Those acquainted with concert versions of the Overture, which includes all of those on recording save the original music tracks released on a Rhino Movie Music CD in 1995, will have noticed that these versions, unlike what is heard in the film, all end on a whopping V7-I cadence in A major, which casts the experience into quite a different shade. One might have supposed that here, as in the Main Title for *The Best Years of Our Lives*, the cadence was written into the original score, and that the excision of these final two chords was, again, the work of the music editor. But this does not turn out to be the case. In correspondence I had with Christopher Husted, Manager of Bernard Herrmann Music (www.bernardherrmann.com) and curator of diverse materials related to the composer, Husted noted that the Overture as heard in the film is a somewhat shortened version of the cue, composed before the Overture, entitled "The Wild Ride," which accompanies Cary Grant's drunken careenings in a car in which he has been forcibly placed by the bad guys in hopes of bringing about his "accidental" demise. The sequence, both visually and musically, comes to an end as Grant slams on the brakes to avoid an accident at an intersection and is rear-ended by two cars, the second of which belongs to the local police. Rather than providing musical closure, the cue comes to an ambiguous halt on that suspended chord in the midrange brass.

Statements, via chordal or melodic structures, among other things, of and in the home key (C major for the *Best Years of Our Lives* Main Title, A minor for the *North by Northwest* Overture) in a work of tonal music can be described as both strongly inchoative and strongly terminative in their temporal implications, since the key theoretically determines both the starting and the ending points. Sections that depart from the home key, on the other hand, are more strongly durative in nature, since, among other reasons, the work theoretically could not start or end within the parameters defined by these departures. The Main Title for *The Best Years* both starts and ends in C major, with an additional element of terminativity provided by the return to the "A" theme. At the end of the *North by Northwest* Overture a fast downward run in the high winds (with prominent piccolo) followed by a loud chord repeated several times seems to promise a return, via a cadence leading to a whopping final chord, to the home key (A major in the concert versions, which represents a change of mode but not of key). But although the Main Title for *The Best Years* does in fact end on a C-major chord, the two measures in which the chord toggles twice back and forth between more unstable harmonic material, and the cutting of the quasi-taps coda in the score's final two measures (which also creates a rhythmic imbalance, since the final chord gets chopped off after less than a beat) mitigate the impact of the terminativity here. *North by Northwest*'s Overture, on the other hand, crushingly cuts into the innate terminativity of a tonal conclusion by sustaining on a seventh chord that the demands of tonality should cause to resolve (into the home key) but that simply stops. In both cases, particularly *North by Northwest*, purely musical terminativity has given way to a kind of durativity that promises the entire narrative to come. Or, to be more precise, since the end of both cues coincides with the ending of the title sequence, one might refer here, if you'll pardon the oxymoron, to a "terminative durativity" of the type that leads audiences into countless cine-narratives in sound films at least into the 1960s.

I would in fact suggest that, while there is no question that film music often creates leitmotifs that "identify" such things as characters, situations, and places, and while one of the principal justifications of film music has always been to reinforce the affective impact of dramatic situations in a medium whose apparent realism can seem excessively cold (see Brown 1994: 12–37), one of the most overlooked functions of film music is to provide, often through violations of strictly musical codes, what might be referred to as metanarrative paradigms of durativity. By this I mean that, in one of its most important tasks, film music often rises above the types of action-specific reinforcement that bring criticism upon the heads of its composers to reinforce spectator expectations not just of events internal to the narrative but in fact of the ongoing durativity of the narrative itself. Countless are the film-music cues that undercut the inchoativity and terminativity innate to tonality by subverting the purely musical types of movement generated by the tonal system. Paradoxically, in fact, the more harmonically static a cue is musically, the more durative its impact tends to be cine-narratively. A particularly outrageous example of this can be found in the "Laser Beam" cue in John Barry's score for the James Bond thriller *Gold-finger* (1964), which accompanies a major threat to 007's career as a laser beam heads straight for his crotch. As I have noted elsewhere (Brown 1994: 46–7) the entire cue, which runs nearly three minutes, plays over the same sustained F-minor added-second chord, wholly typical of Barry's Bond sound, as the same eight-note motif gets repeated identically some 12 times, followed by another 12 repetitions of two notes from that motif in a seemingly interminable crescendo. As the villain shuts off the laser beam just in time, the ongoing F-minor added-second chord simply continues for a few more seconds without resolving. Interestingly, the visual action at this point – one of the villain's henchmen walks over to Bond, points a gun at him, and fires, with Bond then slumping back onto the table to which he has been tied – has massive terminative implications, thus creating a quasi-contrapuntal interaction between apparent terminativity in the visuals and durativity in the music, which lets us know that Bond's career as a lover has not yet come to a blazing end.

If the visual/musical "counterpoint" in the *Goldfinger* sequence depends on contrast, one could say that, in both *The Best Years of Our Lives* and *North by Northwest*, a visual motif of durativity – airplanes in *The Best Years* and all manner of vehicles in *North by Northwest* – complements the musical durativity. In other words, vehicles in these two films serve not simply as important elements of the diegesis but, perhaps more importantly, their visual presence generates narrative durativity right through to the end of the films. In *The Best Years* it is a plane that, at the film's opening, carries the three returning World War II veterans back to their native city (this to the tune of the repeated bridge motif from the Main Title), while, at the end, it is a whole passel of junked airplanes that will, by providing raw material for prefab houses, lead the most down-and-out of the three veterans (Dana Andrews) into a new job and a new marriage – durative terminativity, if, one more time, you'll pardon the oxymoron: the classic aspect of the happy ending (in which case tragedy would be terminative terminativity). In *North by Northwest* no sooner do the titles end than we see a New York City bus close its door in the face of director Alfred Hitchcock, who will remove himself to the director's chair as his surrogate, Cary Grant, gets (1) in and out of numerous taxis; (2) kidnapped and transported in a car to Glen Cove, Long Island; (3) forcibly intoxicated and then loaded drunk into a stolen car; (4) into a train from Grand Central Station to Chicago; (5) attacked in the middle of nowhere by gun-bearing thugs in a crop-dusting airplane; (6) back to Chicago in a stolen pick-up truck; (7) loaded into an airplane to Rapid City, South Dakota, by a government official (Leo G. Carroll); (8) taken by an ambulance into woods near Mount Rushmore where he is reunited with his ladylove (Eva Marie Saint); (9) free just in time to save his lady-love from boarding an airplane from which she was to be thrown to her death; (10) into the upper berth, with his ladylove/new (third) wife, in the sleeping car of another train last seen entering a tunnel, finally providing quasi-coital terminativity to this complex labyrinth of vehicular durativity. Hitchcock has said of *North by Northwest* that, "When I start on the idea of a film like that, I see the whole film, not merely a particular place or scene, but its direction from beginning to end. I do not have the vaguest idea of what the picture will be about" (Truffaut 1984: 319). Vehicles in the film function almost as abstract carriers of that beginning-to-end durativity.

Interestingly, however, the Overture music, whose frenetic pace would also seem to link it to the vehicle motif, does not reveal a one-for-one relationship to that motif, nor are any of the *Best Years* motifs (the opening four notes, the five-note chordal theme, and the opening four notes of the bridge) specifically associated with vehicles – or anything else. In *North by Northwest*, the Overture, while providing motivic fragments that show up throughout, also appears more or less *in toto* at three different points: the title sequence, the "Wild Ride" sequence, and, with many variations, during the final chase sequence over Mount Rushmore. One might have expected it to also provide what the cue sheets refer to as "backing" during the crop-duster attack, but this sequence remains unscored until the end, after the plane crashes into a gas truck. Beyond its function as a signifier of narrative durativity, then, the Overture music and its various motifs, rather than having action- or character-specific implications, also function as musiconarrative isotopies that give, in an abstract way, an overall coherence to the filmic text. Even more importantly, the nonleitmotif character of this music also allows it to signal, with the kind of transparency suggested above by Lévi-Strauss, what Turner refers to as the synchronic function of narrative patterns. This effect may be even more obvious in *The Best Years of Our Lives*. Although one writer refers to Friedhofer's score as "perhaps the best example" of the use of the Wagnerian leitmotif in films (Prendergast 1977: 73), and although the music does in fact offer several place- and character-specific motifs (the theme for Wilma being the most notable example), by and large its music functions in a broader and very nonleitmotivic way. The three basic motifs defined above of the Main Title simply float freely throughout the movie, sometimes isolated, at other times presented in alternate orders from their appearance in the Main Title, but never attaching themselves to anything more specific than the feeling for the entire movie as generated by the Main Title music. While imparting, with a transparency that music's nonreferentiality makes possible, isotopic coherency to the narrative, these recurring motifs also function as quasi-mythic paradigms that help the viewer "read" and feel the filmic time as narrative, in spite of its very specific historical references.

What I am suggesting, then, is that while film music has in fact been guilty throughout its history of a reasonable, perhaps even unreasonable, amount of leitmotivic literal-mindedness, it has also, even in most of its worst examples, provided movies with a kind of ongoing commentary on and parallel creation of both the syntagmatic/durative and the synchronic/paradigmatic structures essential to narrative. I am also suggesting that this commentary and creation are made possible through, among other things, the frequent violation of concert-hall syntax as well as through the nonaction-specific isotopic mobilization of both entire themes and fragments from them throughout the film. Carried forward on musically generated durativity, these motifs and fragments "immobilize passing time." Or, as T. S. Eliot puts it in the first of his *Four Quartets*, "Only through time time is conquered." In its best examples, such as *The Best Years of Our Lives* and *North by Northwest*, the rich interaction of musically, visually, and verbally generated structures creates a kind of meta-text whose "story" is the very substance of narrative. Lest we forget, the ultimate revelation in *North by Northwest* turns out to be a piece of 35 millimeter film.

NOTES

1 See "Getting Down off the Beanstalk: The Presence of a Woman's Voice in Janika Vandervelde's *Genesis II*," in *Minnesota Composers Forum Newsletter* (January 1987), n. p. In the revised version of this article that appears in McClary (1991: 112–31), the author has considerably mitigated the language of the original.

2 A slightly modified version of the article appears in Lévi-Strauss (1963: 206–31).

3 The Lévi-Strauss reference is to an article entitled "Social Structure," in A. L. Kroeber (ed.), *Anthropology Today: An Encyclopedic Inventory*. Chicago: University of Chicago Press, 1953, pp. 524–53.

4 This is one of the principal points of a book on which I am currently working, provisionally entitled *Images of Images: Myth, Lacan, and Narrative Cinema*.

5 See Brown (1990).

6 See in particular the first *Manifeste du surréalisme* (1924), which can be found in André Breton (1966: 15–18).

7 See in particular Robbe-Grillet ([1961] 1989).

REFERENCES AND FURTHER READING

Breton, A. (1966). *Manifestes du surréalisme*. Paris: Gallimard.

Brown, R. S. (1990). "Serialism in Robbe-Grillet's *l'Eden et après*: The Narrative and Doubles." *Literature/Film Quarterly* 18(4), 210–20.

Brown, R. S. (1994). *Overtones and Undertones: Reading Film Music*. Berkeley: University of California Press.

Carter, E. (1977). *The Writings of Elliott Carter: An American Composer Looks at Modern Music*, ed. Else and Kurt Stone. Bloomington: Indiana University Press.

Gorbman, C. (1987). *Unheard Melodies: Narrative Film Music*. Bloomington and Indianapolis: Indiana University Press.

Greimas, A. J. (1983). *Du sens II*. Paris: Seuil.

Jander, O. (1985). "Beethoven's Orpheus in Hades: The *Andante con moto* of the Fourth Piano Concerto." *19th Century Music* 8(3), 195–212.

Langer, S. K. ([1942] 1957). *Philosophy in a New Key: A Study in the Symbolism of Reason, Rite, and Art*, 3rd edn. Cambridge, MA: Harvard University Press.

Lévi-Strauss, C. (1963). *Structural Anthropology*, trans. C. Jacobson and B. Grundfest Schoepf. New York: Basic Books.

Lévi-Strauss, C. (1969). *The Raw and the Cooked: Introduction to a Science of Mythology, I*, trans. J. and D. Weightman. New York: Harper/Colophon.

Levin, D. M. (ed.) (1993). *Modernity and the Hegemony of Vision*. Berkeley: University of California Press.

Lotman, J. (1979). "The Origin of Plot in the Light of Typology," trans. J. Graffy. *Poetics Today* 1(1–2), 161–84.

Mallarmé, S. ([1886] 1996). "Crise de vers." In *Oeuvres complètes* (pp. 360–68). Paris: Gallimard/ Bibliothèque de la Pléiade.

McClary, S. (1991). *Feminine Endings: Music, Gender, and Sexuality*. Minneapolis: University of Minnesota Press.

McGilligan, P. (2003). *Alfred Hitchcock: A Life in Darkness and Light*. New York: Regan Books.

Meyer, L. B. (1956): *Emotion and Meaning in Music*. Chicago: University of Chicago Press.

Peradotto, J. (1984). "Oedipus and Erichthonius: Some Observations of Paradigmatic and Syntagmatic Order," ed. L. Edmunds and A. Dundes. *Oedipus: A Folklore Casebook* (pp. 179–96). New York and London: Garland.

Perle, G. (1995). *Style and Idea in the* Lyric Suite *of Alban Berg*. Hillsdale, NY: Pendragon Press.

Prendergast, R. (1977). *Film Music: A Neglected Art*. New York: W. W. Norton.

Ragland, E. (1997). "Lacan and the Subject of Law: Sexuation and Discourse in the Mapping of Subject Positions that Give the Ur-form of Law." *Washington and Lee Law Review* 54(3), 1091–118.

Robbe-Grillet, A. ([1961] 1989). *For a New Novel: Essays on Fiction*, trans. R. Howard. Evanston, IL: Northwestern University Press.

Schopenhauer, A. (1969). *The World as Will and Idea*, vol. 1, trans. E. F. J. Payne. New York: Dover.

Shepherd, J. (1991). *Music as Social Text*. Cambridge, UK: Polity Press.

Tarasti, E. (1994). *A Theory of Musical Semiotics*. Bloomington: Indiana University Press.

Truffaut, F. (1984). *Hitchcock*. New York: Simon and Schuster.

Turner, T. S. (1969). "Oedipus: Time and Structure in Narrative Form." In R. F. Spencer (ed.), *Forms of Symbolic Action: Proceedings of the 1969 Annual Spring Meeting of the American Ethnological Society* (pp. 26–68). Seattle and London: American Ethnological Society/University of Washington Press.

31

Classical Instrumental Music and Narrative

Fred Everett Maus

From the 1970s onward, a number of musicologists have explored relationships between classical instrumental music and narrative. Such relationships have long been familiar in cases of program music, for instance Hector Berlioz's *Fantastic Symphony*, a composite work in which a verbal text by the composer spells out a narrative that the musical sounds can be heard to illustrate (see Kivy 1984: 159–96). But the late twentieth-century musicological developments that I discuss here concerned "purely instrumental" music that lacks an explicit literary program originating with the composer.

At their strongest, some treatments suggested that nonprogrammatic instrumental music can be a form of narrative representation. Other treatments explored analogies between instrumental music and discourses normally understood as narrative. I prefer the latter approach: questions about whether some kind of music is an instance of narrative can run aground on issues about essential properties of narrative, not a fruitful preoccupation for musicology.

Some musicologists have understood exploration of nonprogrammatic instrumental music and narrative as a new research paradigm, an approach to recalcitrant theoretical issues of meaning and practical issues of criticism. The association of instrumental music with narrative was an attractive alternative to purist accounts (like Hanslick's 1986) in which instrumental music is nothing other than engagingly patterned sound, and to narrowly emotion-based accounts that have often dominated philosophical discussions of music.

In these developments, one can identify a first stage, perhaps taking Edward T. Cone's book *The Composer's Voice* (1974) as a starting point, extending into the early 1990s. In this stage, discussions of music that drew on analogies to narrative took an optimistic tone, as though new conceptualizations could resolve long-standing critical and philosophical problems. Still, despite persistent optimism, the texts from this period were, by and large, curiously noncumulative: different authors, and even different texts by the same authors, seemed to start over repeatedly rather than building on earlier accomplishments.[1]

A second stage, during the late 1980s and early 1990s, may have been predictable. Several musicologists and other writers disparaged recent reliance on narrative conceptions for understanding music, instead exploring failures of analogy between instrumental music and narrative. Some writers suggested that ideas of narrative would not be valuable for music criticism and sought to discourage further work in the area.

Problems with Analogies Between Music and Narrative

Some of the new essays focused, perhaps overemphatically, on particular claims. For instance: musical form typically involves extensive repetition of events (Kivy 1993); music has no past tense (Abbate 1991); music has no subject and predicate (Nattiez 1990). These observations (slightly weird in themselves – who needs to be told such things?) figured in arguments against the critical and theoretical assimilation of instrumental music and narrative. On a plausible reading, these arguments share a simple structure. Identify a necessary condition of narrative representation. Then argue that music cannot satisfy that necessary condition. It follows that music is not a form of narrative representation.[2] So, for instance, if narrative representation requires something like a past tense, but music always or normally lacks such a feature, then any general account of "music as narrative" is in trouble.

Arguments like these suggested the need for care in articulating claims about music and narrative. But they did not prove that analogies between music and narrative are useless. For one thing, such arguments are most telling as objections to the claim that some music really is a kind of narrative. Someone interested in analogies to narrative can refine an account in response to these arguments, rather than abandoning the line of inquiry.

Grant that music lacks a device with the function of a past tense, allowing present discourse to depict past events. Perhaps, then, listeners typically imagine the events in a musical plot not as recounted in a narrative voice, but rather as occurring in the present time of the listener's perception, like the events of an ordinary stage play.

Musical form often involves extensive literal or near-literal repetition. But the sequence of musical events in a composition nonetheless invites comparison to the unfolding of a narrative plot. So the contribution of concrete material musical sound to "musical plot" must differ from the role of concrete material words and sentences in literary narrative. To many people, patterns like sonata form resemble a story, in which the concluding section resolves tension and imbalance. The final section largely repeats material from earlier in the piece, and this resembles, in its effect, a denouement in a literary work. However, one would not expect the denouement of a stage play or novel to comprise extensive literal repetition of earlier events or language.

Nonetheless, rather than abandoning the intuition of commonality between literary denouement and musical recapitulation, one can suggest that musical denouement uses special means, among them extensive repetition.

And if musical syntax lacks any distinction resembling that of subjects and predicates in language, then music cannot use a subject–predicate structure to tell a story by naming objects (including, of course, characters) and attributing actions and qualities to them. If music sometimes seems, nonetheless, to evoke actions and/or characters, questions arise about how this can happen. Why can listeners sometimes hear a series of musical sounds as a sequence of actions or other events in a dramatic story? If a listener hears actions, who are the agents? To what extent can the musical sounds of a particular composition, along with some established normative practice of interpretation, determine specific answers to these questions? To what extent is the determination of specific actions, agents, and so forth a matter for imaginative creativity by individual listeners? Around 1990, I suggested that listeners can hear actions in music by understanding musical events in relation to imagined intentions; that musical actions have general qualities in common with other actions, as well as having specifically musical descriptions; and that musical agency is typically indeterminate.[3] Other accounts of musical action and agency are possible.

It is interesting to consider general objections to comparisons between instrumental music and narrative, along with possible responses to the objections. But the more rewarding issues concern the undeniable appeal that many listeners and critics find in narrative-like conceptions of instrumental music. A good way to explore the nature and appeal of narrative analogies is to leave the level of abstract general argument and consider scholarly and critical texts that have used such analogies in specific interpretations. I turn now to three essays that make a more constructive or optimistic use of ideas about narrative.[4] Two of these are classic essays from the years before controversies about narrative approaches became prominent; the third, Marion A. Guck's essay published in 1994, proceeds as though those controversies have not taken place (and was first drafted in 1989, again before negative discussions of music and narrative became common). When I ponder the strong appeal of analogies between music and narrative, I still find myself turning to exploratory essays like these, rather than to polemical essays against such work.

An Immigrant Pitch

I begin with Guck's essay, "Rehabilitating the Incorrigible," in part because of its methodological clarity (Guck 1994c). Guck responds to several methodological essays by the composer and music theorist Milton Babbitt. Through his writings in the 1950s and 1960s and many years of teaching at Princeton University, Babbitt was one of the strongest influences on the new professional field of music theory. This technically oriented field became particularly coherent and sophisticated in North

America in the second half of the twentieth century. Typically, music theorists offer intricate analyses and generalizations about music, drawing primarily on the information that is verifiable in the scores of musical works. Music theory has normally addressed patterning of sound, without raising questions of meaning or historical and cultural context. The austerity of the field owes much to Babbitt's methodological writings; thus, in questioning those texts, Guck engages a crucial point of origin of contemporary music theory.

Dismayed by the chaos he perceived in description and evaluation, Babbitt (2003) urged music theorists to adopt scientific goals and procedures. Emulating the intolerance of logical positivist philosophers, Babbitt expressed alarm at the prevalence and power of meaningless, logically ill-formed, and incorrigible language in music criticism. Though Babbitt's position seems integrated, Guck identifies various strands of it that can be evaluated separately. For instance, Babbitt sometimes stated pragmatic goals for descriptions of music: when successful, descriptions may "extend and enrich" one's "perceptive powers," "granting additional significance to all degrees of musical phenomena" (Guck 1994c: 62, 64, 73, quoting from Babbitt [1952] 2000: 24). Such goals do not entail the scientific approach that Babbitt also endorses and are at odds with the objectifying language that theorists favor, which often lacks clear relevance to listeners' experiences.

Much of Guck's presentation responds to a particular moment in one of Babbitt's essays. Astutely, Guck identifies a subtle incoherence in Babbitt's response to an analytical description by musicologist Hans David. David identifies a certain note in a Mozart composition as "unexpected." Babbitt's rebuttal seems, initially, to dismiss any such claim as having a "dubious status," by which Babbitt would probably mean that it has no content; but then Babbitt seems to *argue against* the claim, offering evidence against it, as though it is meaningful but false. From this inconsistency, Guck infers that Babbitt does in fact have a sense of how one might support the musical descriptions that, nonetheless, he seems to dismiss: "Babbitt indicates how personal statements might be rehabilitated when he refutes David's statement by producing evidence" (Guck 1994c: 61).

Guck elaborates an alternative description of the same note in the slow movement of Mozart's Symphony No. 40, since she agrees with Babbitt that "unexpected" is not a helpful term. Her description resembles David's in being a report of her own experience, rather than an impersonal description of data in the score. But unlike David, she supports her account with careful description of musical detail, drawing on technical analysis and other resources; thus she hopes to bring her account of personal experience closer to Babbitt's standards of communication.

From her initial sense of the particular note, C-flat, as "portentous" when it occurs in m. 53, Guck moves to an extended account of the roles of other C-flats across the whole movement. Her account combines technical description, the kind that Babbitt encourages as giving determinate content to musical descriptions, with a sustained figurative description. The pitch C-flat, now understood as an enduring individual, unified across the various momentary occurrences of C-flats, is an "immigrant" to the key of E-flat major.[5] To call a pitch an "immigrant" is to personify it; to trace the different roles that the immigrant pitch adopts in an alien tonality is to create a narrative about that character. The narrative traces different attitudes and roles of the pitch, for instance, distinguishing occasions when it "quietly took up its place" from others when it "evidenced a tendency to draw attention to itself" (Guck 1994c: 69). The "portentous" moment is one in which the pitch begins to act on its "impulse to transform its environment" (p. 70). But the narrative ends with a stable relation between the pitch and its context, one in which C-flat has become the tonic pitch of its own key and that key has been shown in a clear relation, distinct but subordinate, to the main tonality. The pitch "has been, so to speak, naturalized, though its foreign accent remains" (p. 70).

While Guck's essay does not begin from the topic of "music and narrative," it reaches that topic promptly as Guck elaborates an alternative to Babbitt's scientific norms for music theory and analysis. Guck notes that the language of her story about an immigrant resembles metaphor, and could be considered figurative. She also suggests that it could be understood as fictional (following Kendall Walton [1990], she interprets such fictional discourse as stating the content of a listener's imaginative activity).

A summary will facilitate comparison of Guck's essay and other approaches to music and narrative. Guck creates a determinate protagonist for her narrative by personifying a recurring pitch. She traces its successive interactions with its surroundings. Doing so, she tells a story about an immigrant, in which moments of self-assertion lead to a naturalization that permits the immigrant's local power and preserves identity. Guck does not claim that her narrative reveals the meaning of the composition. On the contrary, she explicitly presents the narrative as something concocted by an individual listener, in an effort to communicate how she hears particular moments. In communication about music, as expounded in Guck's essay, individual listeners explain their experiences to others, and construction of a narrative can be an *ad hoc* device to help with this communication.

A Rebellious Piano

Solo concertos provide, in the solo instrumental part, an obvious candidate for a "protagonist" in a dramatic encounter with the orchestra; many descriptions of concertos rely on this possibility. According to a classic essay by Donald F. Tovey, from 1903:

> Nothing in human life and history is much more thrilling or of more ancient and universal experience than the antithesis of the individual and the crowd; an antithesis which is familiar in every degree, from flat opposition to harmonious reconciliation, and which has been of no less universal prominence in works of art than in life. Now the concerto forms express this antithesis with all possible force and delicacy.
>
> (Tovey 1903: 7)

Among recent musicologists Joseph Kerman (1992, 1999) has particularly emphasized the dramatic potential of the concerto texture. An essay by Susan McClary, published a few years before the groundbreaking feminist essays in *Feminine Endings* (1991), makes an impressive contribution to this area of criticism, by taking seriously political aspects of the interaction of individual and group. McClary wants to show, in opposition to received ideas about Mozart, that his music deals with social issues in a tense complex way.

McClary identifies a general plot succession for the eighteenth-century concerto, the kind of recurring succession that Anthony Newcomb labels a "plot archetype" (see below): "the stable community [withstands] the adventures and conflicts of the soloist, and they [are] reconciled to coexist in mutually beneficial bliss" (McClary 1986: 138). Against this background, she notes three peculiarities of a Mozart movement, the slow movement of the Concerto in G, K. 453. One is its use of a recurring motto theme, strangely distinct from the other material of the piece. The other two peculiarities concern the piano part: its complex affect differs strikingly from that of the orchestra, and it tends to move rapidly through many different keys.

McClary's detailed description of the movement identifies three elements. The first, the orchestral motto, which has religious connotations, gives way to the second, conspicuously conventional secular music, also in the orchestra (McClary 1986: 142–5). A third element, the solo part, enters in a way that seems to reject the motto, and it also "strikes out against the placidity offered by the group" (p. 146). This conflict develops to form a drama, unfolding in "a world that contains transcendental ideals, social order, and subjective alienation" (p. 155).

By the end of the first large section of the movement (the exposition), the solo part has been "re-assimilated," reaching a "tentative détente" with the orchestra. But the development reopens the conflict. The piano eventually "throws the orchestra's would-be influence off altogether and lays bare its despair" (McClary 1986: 145); in doing so, it arrives at the dominant of a very remote key (C-sharp minor, in a C major movement).

But, in an extraordinary passage, the orchestra returns the piece to C major in a few brief measures of chromatic motion, a transition that McClary calls "irrational." McClary suggests that this procedure "shows the authoritarian force that social conventions will draw upon if confronted by recalcitrant non-conformity" (McClary 1986: 151). The return is to the opening motto, now in the piano part. McClary, recalling its religious quality, suggests that the movement has dramatized "the initial resistance to but eventual acceptance of some principle that *transcends* both the social order and individual subjectivity" (pp. 152–3). The rest of the recapitulation sustains the resolution of these three elements. However, McClary argues that unresolved tension remains in the movement as a whole: "the piano was an unlikely participant in the celebration of its own submission. The happy ending, the requisite closure, was attained at too high a cost" (p. 158).

Guck's and McClary's narratives are thematically similar, taking shape as dramas of separation and reconciliation, despite the fact that one writer takes as protagonist a pitch, the other an instrumental part. Epistemologically the essays are at opposite poles. McClary does not ask her readers to take an interest in her personal musical experiences as such, nor does she draw attention to her own act of fabricating a narrative description. Instead, she offers a confident account of the meaning of the Mozart composition. However, support for her interpretation rests on the appeal of her description of the music; thus, somewhat like Guck, she "invites you to match your hearing with mine or to imagine a new hearing that could be described by you in the same terms" (Guck 1994c: 63).

Disavowal and Acknowledgment

Anthony Newcomb's long essay on Schumann's Second Symphony begins by noting a puzzle about the Symphony's reception: admired in the nineteenth century, the work fell from favor in the twentieth century. "This suggests that our problems with the piece may be rooted in current analytical tools for absolute music" (Newcomb 1983–4: 233). Thus Newcomb writes in order to revive historically appropriate interpretive tools. The essay draws on many different resources to offer an account of the composition "as composed novel, as a psychologically true course of ideas" (p. 234). These include thematic transformation (along with a suggestion that "we do well to think of the thematic units partly as characters in a narrative" [p. 237]); biographical information about Schumann; semiotic or expressive aspects of musical style; and thematic allusions to music by Bach and Beethoven. Newcomb also proposes that the Symphony as a whole instantiates a multimovement "plot archetype." A plot archetype, according to Newcomb (p. 234), is "a standard series of mental states." Beethoven's Fifth and Ninth Symphonies, for example, share the plot archetype of "a psychological evolution, such as suffering followed by healing or redemption."[6] According to Newcomb, nineteenth-century critics understood Schumann's Second Symphony as another instance of that archetype (p. 234).

Newcomb's interpretation, then, shows how the Second Symphony instantiates this general progression. I shall summarize a crucial portion of the interpretation, Newcomb's attractive view of the third and fourth movements. Newcomb describes these movements in terms of a series of emotions, along with subjective stances toward those emotions.

The sadness of the third movement, ending in "resignation and near stasis," gives way suddenly to apparent happiness at the beginning of the last movement: "Schumann begins the last movement with an abrupt disjunction, juxtaposing passive resignation and active triumph" (Newcomb 1983–4: 243). But the contrast is too harsh; the sense of relief seems forced, amounting to a denial of the reality of the previous sadness. As the fourth movement unfolds, there is an attempt to establish a connection to the past, through a restatement of the opening melody of the third movement, revised to sound cheerful in accord with the current mood. But this jolly revision also seems forced, inappropriate as a response to the third movement. Finally, the fourth movement returns frankly to the painful affect, along with thematic material, of the third movement, acknowledging the previous sadness before moving to a sober and satisfactory resolution. The "psychological truth" of this "course of ideas" is that suffering must be acknowledged and integrated. Understood this way, the whole musical texture seems to depict the successive states of a single protagonist.[7]

The fourth movement has puzzled twentieth-century commentators in its failure to exemplify any standard formal pattern for last movements (such as rondo or sonata). Newcomb explains its unfamiliar pattern as a result of its problematic opening. The movement becomes a satisfactory conclusion to the whole Symphony by replacing its initial material, "a rough shout of affirmation" (Newcomb 1983–4: 243), with more emotionally appropriate thematic material. It fails to make sense in standard formal terms, but this failure can be explained by more basic needs of emotional and dramatic appropriateness.[8]

If Guck and McClary distinguish separate agencies within the music, Newcomb instead identifies an internal conflict within an encompassing protagonist, whose shifting response to past sadness creates a fourth movement with an unusual sequence of events, incoherent when regarded in nondramatic formal terms. Like Guck, Newcomb praises a narrative style of description, contrasting it with the limited resources of modern technical analysis. Like McClary, he identifies a general plot pattern, common to a number of compositions, and narrates an individual, somewhat complex, instance of the pattern. Like McClary, and unlike Guck, he regards his essay as an inquiry into the meaning of the composition; he explicitly engages documents of reception history to justify his account, as McClary does not. Nonetheless, crucial aspects of his interpretation depend, finally, on the plausibility of his personal responses to the music. He offers no historical documents in support of the narrative of denial and acknowledgment that is basic to his interpretation, instead expecting that readers will test the account in their own experiences.

Poetics of Musical Description

Various general issues arise from these essays. One that seems fundamental is the tension between two approaches: one that uses narrative to communicate a personal experience of music, and one that offers hermeneutic and historical claims about the meanings of musical works. Excellent recent work continues to show this difference in emphasis; I think of Charles Fisk's (2001) individualized synthesis of years of intense reflection on Schubert's piano music, and Richard Will's (2002) historical account of the "characteristic" symphony, which culminates in richly informed readings of two Beethoven symphonies.

But, while noting this difference, one should be careful not to stage a simplified melodramatic opposition between sheer autobiography and sternly impersonal history. For one thing, I already noted that McClary and Newcomb rely, at crucial points, on personal insight that does not have specific support from historical documentation; the same is true of Will's book and probably any interesting critical description. On the other hand, if one understands Guck's description as *ad hoc* interpersonal communication of experience, one should not miss the ways, unthematized in her essay, that her narrative conforms to shared habits. In its personification of an obtrusive pitch, its tale of contestation among pitches and key areas, its plot of individuation and reconciliation, even its basic form as narration, her account recognizes and reinforces transpersonal norms of musical narration.[9]

I want to consider, though, another issue about these texts. Returning first to McClary's essay, I note an intriguing feature. The elements – transcendental ideals, social order, and subjective alienation – that shape McClary's account of the Mozart movement also structure her depiction of herself and her present surroundings. McClary writes in order to dissent from the conventional contemporary understanding of Mozart, striking out against the placidity with which contemporary audiences receive Mozart's works. And she identifies Mozart's role in contemporary culture with the transcendental – as she puts it, "we still seem reluctant to let go of the classical music through which we yet have (the illusion of) access to transcendental truth" (McClary 1986: 131). Contemporary audiences, the contemporary image of Mozart, and McClary, form the same configuration as the orchestra, religious motto theme, and soloist, in Mozart's concerto.

McClary is aware of this isomorphism: it forms the basis of an attractive ironic turn in her argument. On her account, music that dramatizes the tensions among the transcendental, the social group, and the individual, has come to serve a conventional social group as an emblem of the transcendental. And so "what began life as a critique becomes a flat affirmation of precisely that which it tried to rupture" (McClary 1986: 162). Further, McClary observes that different listeners will respond differently to the unfolding of the narrative. She formulates these differences in terms of identification, suggesting that "a listener who tends to identify with flamboyance or noise in the face of order will probably hear the soloist as a sympathetic protagonist" (p. 147). Still, she does not direct attention to the precision of the match between her implicit self-depiction and the rebellious protagonist in the concerto. McClary's essay creates matched images of herself and the piano protagonist in the Mozart movement, and locates them in similar worlds.[10]

Newcomb's essay also shows an entanglement of his musical example and his musicological thematics. He claims that musical scholars have forgotten a humanizing mode of interpretation, commonplace in the nineteenth century, replacing it with a more mechanistic analysis of structure. To illustrate, he tells of a finale that initially disavows certain emotional states and then abandons conventional structural patterns in order to reconnect with them. Schumann's Symphony joins Newcomb in warning of the dangers of denying one's emotional life.

Guck's tale of an immigrant relates to her musicological goals in various ways. As commonly understood, figurative language, which Guck recommends to literal-minded music theorists, is language that migrates from its home, where it functions literally, to new contexts, where it becomes newly meaningful while retaining its strangeness. Guck herself, elaborating her narrative, becomes something of an immigrant: "In telling my tale, I will be on dangerous ground, because I conceive of the immigrant C-flat as animate and motivated – but I intend to stay here" (Guck 1994c: 68). More broadly, Guck's desire to move into the public realm of professional discourse, while retaining explicit reference to her subjective responses, resembles the immigrant's effort to fit in while retaining identity.

In another essay, Guck reflects on her professional work in similar terms. She discusses her projects, undertaken as a female theorist in a predominantly male and masculine field, and summarizes:

> I've talked about my work as different from traditional or conventional music theory and about being an outsider. I may sound bitter about it, but I don't think I am. I would like to see inroads made from the margin to the center, not to replace the old center but to create a more integrated and balanced music theory for the sake of refining and enriching what we can notice and take pleasure in.
>
> (Guck 1994a: 40)

Like the C-flat in the Mozart piece, Guck has "survived, in some ways even succeeded," in a difficult environment; she sometimes finds herself "speaking as though my work stands in opposition to traditional analysis," when her more basic goal is to "enlarge its scope" by adding a distinctive, personal voice (Guck 1994a: 37).

What should one make of these matches between musicologists and musical protagonists? It would be possible to respond negatively, finding the essays to be, in some damning way, self-involved, as though the alleged musicological content is some sort of personal projection. This would be reductive. The interpretive content in these essays, as well as the authorial self-depictions, are plausible by standards held within their scholarly audience; otherwise the essays would never have been taken seriously.

Less punitively, one could say that these essays reveal the individualized personal involvement that is central to musical meaning and provides content to musical narratives. Understood that way, they would begin to resemble some writing on music that has emphasized the personal nature of musical understanding, sometimes through the creation of idiosyncratic narratives. Guck has written usefully about the subtle depictions of personal investment in analytical writing (Guck 1994b). Feminist and queer scholars sometimes write from individual subjectivities, shaped in part by socially constructed identities, and sometimes such writing offers idiosyncratic narrative interpretations (Caputo and Pegley 1994, Maus 1996, Brett 1997). But the mirroring patterns I have described are different from explicit assertions of personal involvement; it is not clear how to understand this difference.

Perhaps one could begin to develop a poetics of a certain kind of musicological essay, the humanistic critical essay that takes a stand against dehumanizing norms and draws upon a privileged musical example for support. What effects are possible when a text conjures up a bold individualistic scholar and an eloquent musical composition, the two complementing and echoing each other?[11] Surely such patterns, suggesting mutual insight between the musicologist and the music, contribute to an effect of musicality in an essay. No doubt this intimacy of musicologist and composition also helps explain why many readers, like me, are moved by such writing.

Related broader questions come to mind. One could ask, for instance, about the professional habit in which a musicological essay conjoins an innovative theoretical claim, often in a sketchy programmatic form, and a single privileged musical example. Given the difficulty of proving general claims from a single example, one might not expect this pattern to be common in musicological writing. But it is, not least in the literature on music and narrative. How do such conjunctions of example and generality function? Do they, in some way, inhibit sustained theoretical thought and the accumulation of insights from one essay to another? Why, nonetheless, do intelligent, careful attempts at general theory about music and narrative seem comparatively bland and unmusical?[12]

In any case, it seems that a consideration of issues about music and narrative leads readily to a consideration of the poetics of texts about music and narrative. This is a welcome reduction in idealization: a representational conception of discourse about music gives way to a more concrete attention to texts about music in their literary and pragmatic aspects.

Narrative and Performance

I shall close by indicating another kind of idealization that is pervasive in discussions of music and narrative. My questions in the preceding section will not keep me from developing the present argument with reference to a specific example, displaying my own "narrative" thinking about music.

As Newcomb noted, Beethoven's Fifth Symphony exemplifies a certain kind of musical narrative. Many listeners have felt that it somehow tells a story, extending across all four movements, through musical means, without requiring the assistance of a verbal text. This common idea comes, in part, from the obvious contrast between the outer movements, suggesting a plot in which conflict leads to triumph (conforming to Newcomb's plot archetype). The unusual return of the scherzo in the last movement also suggests a dramatic motivation. Apart from these large-scale issues, the first movement, with its vehemence and contrasts, suggests some kind of conflict, again implying some kind of story.

Hector Berlioz wrote vividly about the piece, understanding the symphony as a depiction of Beethoven's "intimate thoughts," and in the first movement he heard "the chaotic feelings that overwhelm a great soul when prey to despair," comparable to "Othello's terrible rage on hearing of Desdemona's guilt from Iago's poisonous lies." More specifically, Berlioz pointed to the movement's contrasts, interpreting them psychologically: "at times it is a frenzy that explodes in a terrifying outcry, at times an extreme dejection that expresses itself only in regrets and takes pity on itself." According to Berlioz, the movement represents the extremes of emotion that are possible within a general mood of despair, ranging between violent anger and hopeless passivity.

To exemplify his generalizations, Berlioz describes one particular passage, evidently the passage leading to the recapitulation:

> Listen to the gasps in the orchestra, to the chords in the dialogue between winds and strings that come and go, sounding ever weaker, like the painful breaths of a dying man. Then their place is taken by a phrase full of violence, as if the orchestra were revived by a flash of anger. Note this trembling mass as it hesitates for a moment, then dashes headlong, splitting into two fiery unisons like two streams of lava; and then say whether this impassioned style is not beyond and above any instrumental music ever written.
> (Berlioz 1994: 19–20)

Berlioz's description identifies four distinct stages in the passage, as though the protagonist's experience passes through four phases: increasing weakness, a sudden revival of energy through anger, momentary hesitation, and then headlong motion, as though a volcano has built up enough pressure to explode, or as though the protagonist's fiery anger decisively overcomes fatigue and hesitation.

The development in Beethoven's first movement has two parts, each beginning with a sequence. Each sequence contains two similar members followed by something that could have been a third member, but the third passage diverges and becomes much longer than the model. The second part of the development works with the horn theme that opened the second group, taking it sequentially through G major and C major. The music moves to F minor, and begins the horn theme again, but proceeds to work motivically with the first two notes of the horn theme, subsequently reducing the motive to only one note. Berlioz describes the events from this F minor passage to the beginning of the recapitulation. It is easy to hear, first, the exchanges between winds and strings; second, an abrupt loud interjection; third, a momentary hesitation as the exchanges between winds and strings return; and finally, the loud canon that leads to the recapitulation.

Now, what happens if one listens to a performance, with Berlioz's description in mind? It depends on the performance. That will be my point.[13] (And from here on, a reader who wants to evaluate my descriptions will need, sooner or later, to turn to the recordings I mention. However, someone who simply reads through the remainder of this chapter can get a sense of the issues that interest me.)

In general, Toscanini's 1933 performance seems to match Berlioz's description nicely. It becomes remarkably quiet in the passages of wind and string chords, as well as remarkably slow, "sounding ever weaker" as though undergoing a terminal loss of energy. In one way, however, there is a subtle failure of match between Berlioz's description and Toscanini's performance. In Berlioz's description, the decisive revival of energy seems to come when loud music first interrupts the quiet chords; the subsequent brief return to the quiet chords is a momentary hesitation before the loud music continues. But Toscanini's performance softens the first interruption, as though the protagonist cannot completely shed the mood of the quiet chords. Toscanini saves a more decisive contrast for the loud canon that leads to the recapitulation. He differentiates the passages partly by his treatment of the ambiguous low chords that both end the chordal passages and begin the interruptions, minimizing the first of these and emphasizing the second.

Despite differences, it is possible to enjoy Toscanini's performance while retaining Berlioz's general sense of this passage – that it concerns a dangerous drop in energy, through "extreme dejection," and an abrupt recovery through something like anger. But one has to change the details of the story. A different performance could match Berlioz's story more precisely, by increasing the aggression of the first orchestral interruption.

Though Toscanini's drop in tempo is quite beautiful, creating a vivid effect, it does not derive from any explicit indication in Beethoven's score. It is interesting to compare the effect of a more "literal" reading, such as the 1944 performance by Artur Rodzinski. I find that Rodzinski's steadiness changes the effect of this passage. The chordal antiphony remains mysterious, and some effect of decreasing motion is inevitable, because of the slowing harmonic rhythm. But the relentless pulsation contradicts the slowing harmonic rhythm, creating a peculiar tension. Berlioz's description is less helpful in thinking about this performance, since the description fails to capture this combination of stasis and relentlessness. Rather than trying to imagine the passage, as Rodzinski performs it, in Berlioz's terms of fatigue or decline, I prefer Scott Burnham's narration, in which the passage "constitute[s] something like the eye of a hurricane, or the uneasy respite of a battle . . . These chords are like the suddenly audible respirations of a nervous soldier" (Burnham 1995: 48). Burnham's military reference suggests that even this quiet passage can be heard as manly and vigorous, though momentarily constrained.

Rodzinski's performance has another important effect: the lack of rhythmic fluctuation isolates the oboe solo in the recapitulation, so that the solo stands alone as a startling departure from the tempo. Rodzinski heightens this effect by moving promptly to the half-cadence that precedes the solo. The Toscanini performance, already very quiet after the motto statements, slows down to approach the oboe solo. Not only does this integrate the solo with the immediately preceding passage, it also recalls the slackening in the development. Thinking again in Berlioz's style, one can hear the burst of energy that begins Toscanini's recapitulation as short-lived, falling back almost immediately to lassitude.

Toscanini's 1952 performance is continuously tense and agitated. Though always fast, it shows a nervous uncertainty about the exact tempo, manifested in part through imperfections of ensemble. These qualities are exciting, if nerve-wracking. The end of the development bears little relation to the passage as played in 1933. At the beginning of the F minor section, Toscanini actually broadens a bit for the first loud chords, and then picks up the tempo as the chords become quieter. As the first loud interruption approaches, the wind chords begin to anticipate the beat slightly, and the last wind chord even has a crescendo. It is as though the chords are reaching forward toward the loud passage, almost as though it is a goal.

At this point, further analytical comments will be helpful for readers who can follow them. I mentioned that the second part of the development begins with a sequence, moving from G major to C major and on to F minor. While the third section, with its antiphonal chords, breaks from the motivic sequence, nonetheless it moves on to B-flat minor, thus continuing the descending fifths. This could be alarming; take the pattern further and the music will be remote from the home key. But the fifth motion ends as the winds lead the passage instead to G-flat minor. While this may seem exceedingly remote from C minor, Beethoven treats it as F-sharp minor, raises the upper voice from C-sharp to D, and thus reaches V / V. That is when the first interruption occurs.

The enharmonic pun creates an intriguing ambiguity. Heard simply as moving to G-flat minor, the passage seems to drift; heard as escaping from the sequential pattern and moving toward a possibility of large-scale return, it seems ingeniously purposeful. Toscanini's 1933 performance does not treat the chordal passage as goal-directed, but in his 1952 performance, it is as though the music consciously approaches a point of resolution.

Roger Norrington's 1989 performance is as regular as Rodzinski's but quite fast, with startling blurts from the winds and brass. Among various interesting features, there is an extraordinary emphasis on the G-flat major chord, just as the music moves away from F minor. In some ways it is a wonderfully engaging performance. Its energy and fierce tempo live up to this movement's reputation for aggression, and the noisy unpredictable winds and brass make the music unusually frightening. However, the soft chords that approach the recapitulation seem almost ordinary in comparison to the other performances. Their gentle seesawing motion is rather pretty. What strikes me most about them is their relative calm, and especially the brief respite from sudden loud noises.

As I hear it, the loud G-flat chord that I mentioned has two main effects. Somewhere in this passage, there is a reorientation of large-scale meter. At the beginning of the F minor passage, the measures group in twos, and after the B-flat minor chord arrives, the position of weak and strong measures has reversed. Norrington's loud chord invites listeners to reorient at the earliest possible opportunity; the other performances leave an ambiguous group of five measures. (Norrington reinforces the new large-scale meter with quite a heavy arrival on the B-flat chord.) The other effect of the loud chord, especially at this brisk tempo, is to associate the first G-flat chord with the subsequent arrival at G-flat minor, making the intervening chords sound like motion within a sustained harmony. This creates a remarkably simple structure of three long spans – nine measures of F minor, sixteen measures of G-flat major changing to G-flat minor (reinterpreted as F-sharp minor), and eight measures of D major. The forced metric reorientation, which might seem undesirable in itself, makes sense as a way of shaping this long span of G-flat, beginning it cleanly on a downbeat.

While the performance imposes a rhythmic and harmonic lucidity that is missing from the others, it does so with a pleasingly paradoxical result. Norrington's performance creates an especially strong emphasis on the harmony that is furthest from the tonic. His crash landing on the first G-flat chord leaves it sounding arbitrary, as does its lack of a clear harmonic role. At first, it sounds like a pointless Neapolitan, then like a more appropriate VI of B-flat minor, and finally like the prevailing harmony of its own long span, appearing and eventually disappearing mysteriously. Perhaps, in this performance, the passage offers a brief image of gentleness and calm, shown to be unsustainable by its outrageously remote harmony.

I have been trying to exemplify a certain kind of thinking, one that is central to my conception of the relation between music and narrative. Sometimes, as the musicologists I discussed before all agree, when music is said to have a narrative quality, or to tell a story, it is because the music seems to have strong anthropomorphic effects, unfolding in a way that suggests a psychological or dramatic succession of events. This could be a starting point for the critical interpretation of compositions: perhaps one could try to recount the stories dramatized by various works. But what, for example, would be the story of the Beethoven passage that I have been discussing? Rather than hoping to associate a determinate story with a particular work, it may be more accurate, and ultimately more pleasurable, to recognize the diversity of the dramatic successions that different performers may create, even when starting from the same score. Thus the idealization that I mentioned, hardly confined to discussions of music and narrative, comes when critics attempt to specify the meanings or, more modestly, their personal experiences, of individual compositions, without taking into account the variety introduced by the creativity of performers.

A Third "Stage"

I have recommended that we ponder diverse performances, rather than interpreting a stable consistent work of Beethoven. The basic attitude, favoring attention to "performance" broadly understood, shapes other parts of this chapter. I recommended that we try out analogies between music and narrative, rather than affirming literal theoretical identities; and that we study the poetics of texts about music, noticing the tricks of literary construction that create images of music and subjectivity, rather than evaluating such texts as purely representational devices.

I mentioned a first, optimistic, stage of musicological work on narrative, in which the concept of narrative seemed to promise the resolution of traditional puzzles about musical meaning and interpretation; and a second, skeptical, stage, in which several prominent writers chastised musicologists for overidentifying music and narrative. I suppose we are now in a third stage, or nonstage, in which exaggerated claims, positive or negative, are no longer exciting. In my view, analogies to narrative can show their value for music criticism by the insights and experiences they produce, the relationships with music that they help to create. The notion of narrative, brought into interpretive relation with instrumental music, is neither heroic nor scandalously naïve. It is something to try, one way and another. I find this nonstage comfortable, inviting an experimental exploratory approach to the performances of music-critical thought.[14]

NOTES

1 Newcomb's essays (1983–4, 1987, 1992, 1997) are striking in that each takes on new theoretical concerns.

2 The structure resembles that of a famous formalist argument, Hanslick's (1986) attempt to prove that music cannot depict definite emotions. All definite emotions are identified by their involvement with a thought about an object; to depict a definite emotion, one must also depict the identifying thought about an object. But music cannot depict a thought about an object. Therefore music cannot depict definite emotions.

3 That is, events in music, when understood imaginatively as actions, have both specifically musical descriptions and more general descriptions using vocabulary shared with nonmusical behavior. For instance, a certain event might be a *cadence* (a certain type of musical action), and a *closing* or *articulation* (acts that also occur outside music). Regarding agency: various aspects of music can be anthropomorphized as agents in a story, but not decisively in relation to other alternatives. And listeners can enjoy following musical actions without needing determinate identification of agents. These claims have the effect of maintaining close contact between dramatic aspects of music and traditional musical analysis, and minimizing the intrusion of arbitrary or incorrigible individual fantasy (Maus 1988, 1991). In binding my account closely to relatively uncontroversial technical descriptions, I failed to address important ways that music becomes meaningful to individual listeners. I corrected for this, to put it mildly, in an autobiographical paper (Maus 1996).

4 In doing so I illustrate some issues, through examples, rather than generalizing. I have given a brief general account, with bibliography, elsewhere (Maus 2001).

5 Music theorists often distinguish between "pitches" and "pitch classes." A particular pitch, for instance middle C, belongs to a pitch class that includes Cs in all octaves. Strictly, the C-flat in Guck's story is a pitch class, not a pitch; but I will stay with the more informal and familiar term "pitch" to minimize unfamiliar technical language.

6 There is a discrepancy between the two formulations I have just quoted, since it is not clear that "healing" and "redemption" are mental states.

7 The relation between themes, as characters, and the unified subjectivity of the entire texture is not fully clear in Newcomb's account.

8 Newcomb notes that a "cheerful, rather frothy" finale has often been an option for ending a multimovement piece; thus he suggests that this movement shifts from an emotionally inappropriate, but stylistically feasible, option to an alternative, the "serious, weighty, reflective, summarizing finale." The shift is necessary because the previous movements have already evoked the plot archetype that will require the second sort of finale (Newcomb 1983–4: 243).

9 Maus (1991) goes into such matters.

10 Harold Powers, criticizing McClary's account from several perspectives, ends by emphasizing its personal qualities. He states that one should not be satisfied with work that describes "the individual personal responses, however vivid or perceptive, of twentieth-century critics motivated by social ideologies," and claims that "readings like McClary's collapse music from the past into

a present-day sensibility" (Powers 1995: 43). While I disagree with his evaluation, I agree that McClary's apparently objectifying account involves substantial self-representation and personal investment; that is part of what I like.

11 The present chapter illustrates this pattern with "humanistic" examples. Maus (2004) gives a related account of a technical essay by Allen Forte.

12 Fine attempts at general work in this area include Tarasti (1994) and Berger (1999).

13 In emphasizing the contribution of performance, I follow up on the ideas in Maus (1999).

Attention to performance has been a welcome development in recent musicology. The path-breaking polemical contributions, in my view, are the essays in Taruskin (1995). For a range of approaches, see Rink (1995). Nicholas Cook holds views similar to mine; see, for instance Cook (2002).

14 I am grateful to James Phelan and Peter Rabinowitz for excellent comments on the first version of this chapter. My ideas show the ongoing effect of years of conversation with Marion Guck and Joseph Dubiel.

References and Further Reading

Abbate, C. (1991). *Unsung Voices: Opera and Musical Narrative in the Nineteenth Century*. Princeton, NJ: Princeton University Press.

Babbitt, M. ([1952] 2000). "Review of Felix Salzer, Structural Hearing: Tonal Coherence in Music." In *The Collected Essays of Milton Babbitt* (pp. 22–30). Princeton, NJ: Princeton University Press.

Babbitt, M. (2003). *The Collected Essays of Milton Babbitt*. Princeton, NJ: Princeton University Press.

Berger, K. (1999). *A Theory of Art*. Oxford: Oxford University Press.

Berlioz, H. (1994). *The Art of Music and Other Essays*, trans. E. Csicsery-Rónay. Bloomington: Indiana University Press.

Brett, P. (1997). "Piano Four-Hands: Schubert and the Performance of Gay Male Desire." *19th-Century Music* 21(2), 149–76.

Burnham, S. (1995). *Beethoven Hero*. Princeton, NJ: Princeton University Press.

Caputo, V. and K. Pegley (1994). "Growing Up Female(s): Retrospective Thoughts on Musical Preferences and Meanings." In P. Brett, G. C. Thomas, E. Wood (eds.), *Queering the Pitch: The New Gay and Lesbian Musicology* (pp. 297–313). New York: Routledge.

Cone, E. T. (1974). *The Composer's Voice*. Berkeley: University of California Press.

Cook, N. (2002). "Music as Performance." In M. Clayton, T. Herbert, R. Middleton (eds.), *The Cultural Study of Music: A Critical Introduction* (pp. 204–14). New York: Routledge.

Fisk, C. (2001). *Returning Cycles: Contexts for the Interpretation of Schubert's Impromptus and Last Sonatas*. Berkeley: University of California Press.

Guck, M. A. (1994a). "A Woman's (Theoretical) Work." *Perspectives of New Music* 32(1), 28–43.

Guck, M. A. (1994b). "Analytical Fictions." *Music Theory Spectrum* 16(2), 217–30.

Guck, M. A. (1994c). "Rehabilitating the Incorrigible." In A. Pople (ed.), *Theory, Analysis and Meaning in Music* (pp. 57–73). Cambridge, UK: Cambridge University Press.

Hanslick, E. (1986). *On the Musically Beautiful: A Contribution Towards the Revision of the Aesthetics of Music*, trans. G. Payzant. Indianapolis: Hackett.

Kerman, J. (1992). "Representing a Relationship: Notes on a Beethoven Concerto." *Representations* 39, 80–101.

Kerman, J. (1999). *Concerto Conversations*. Cambridge, MA: Harvard University Press.

Kivy, P. (1984). *Sound and Semblance: Reflections on Musical Representation*. Princeton, NJ: Princeton University Press.

Kivy, P. (1993). "A New Music Criticism?" In *The Fine Art of Repetition: Essays in the Philosophy of Music* (pp. 296–323). Cambridge, UK: Cambridge University Press.

Maus, F. E. (1988). "Music as Drama." *Music Theory Spectrum* 10, 56–73. Also in J. Robinson (ed.) (1997). *Music and Meaning* (pp. 105–30). Ithaca, NY: Cornell University Press.

Maus, F. E. (1991). "Music as Narrative." *Indiana Theory Review* 12, 1–34.

Maus, F. E. (1996). "Love Stories." *Repercussions* 4(2), 86–96.

Maus, F. E. (1999). "Musical Performance as Analytical Communication." In I. Gaskell and S. Kemal (eds.), *Performance and Authenticity in the Arts* (pp. 129–153). Cambridge, UK: Cambridge University Press.

Maus, F. E. (2001). "Narratology, Narrativity." Grove Music Online, ed. L. Macy, www.grovemusic.com.

Maus, F. E. (2004). "The Disciplined Subject of Musical Analysis." In A. Dell'Antonio (ed.), *Beyond Structural Listening: Postmodern Modes of Hearing* (pp. 13–43). Berkeley: University of California Press.

McClary, S. (1986). "A Musical Dialectic from the Enlightenment: Mozart's Piano Concerto in G Major, K. 453, Movement 2." *Cultural Critique* 4, 129–69.

McClary, S. (1991) *Feminine Endings: Music, Gender, and Sexuality*. Minneapolis: University of Minnesota Press.

Nattiez, J-J. (1990). "Can One Speak of Narrativity in Music?" *Journal of the Royal Musical Association* 115, 240–57.

Newcomb, A. (1983–4). "Once More 'Between Absolute and Program Music': Schumann's Second Symphony." *19th-Century Music* 7, 233–50.

Newcomb, A. (1987). "Schumann and Late Eighteenth-Century Narrative Strategies." *19th-Century Music* 11, 164–74.

Newcomb, A. (1992). "Narrative Archetypes and Mahler's Ninth Symphony." In S. Scher (ed.), *Music and Text: Critical Inquiries* (pp. 118–36). Cambridge, UK: Cambridge University Press.

Newcomb, A. (1997). "Action and Agency in Mahler's Ninth Symphony, Second Movement." In J. Robinson (ed.), *Music & Meaning* (pp. 131–53). Ithaca, NY: Cornell University Press.

Powers, H. (1995). "Reading Mozart's Music: Text and Topic, Syntax and Sense." *Current Musicology* 57, 5–44.

Rink, J. (ed.) (1995). *The Practice of Performance: Studies in Musical Interpretation*. Cambridge, UK: Cambridge University Press.

Tarasti, E. (1994). *A Theory of Musical Semiotics*. Bloomington: Indiana University Press.

Taruskin, R. (1995). *Text and Act: Essays on Music and Performance*. Oxford: Oxford University Press.

Tovey, D. F. ([1903] 1935). "The Classical Concerto." In *Essays in Musical Analysis, 3: Concertos* (pp. 3–27). Oxford: Oxford University Press.

Walton. K. (1990). *Mimesis as Make-Believe: On the Foundations of Representational Arts*. Cambridge, MA: Harvard University Press.

Will, R. (2002). *The Characteristic Symphony in the Age of Haydn and Beethoven*. Cambridge, UK: Cambridge University Press.

RECORDINGS OF BEETHOVEN, SYMPHONY NO. 5, OP. 67

Roger Norrington, London Classical Players (1989). *Ludwig van Beethoven, 9 Symphonies*. EMI CDS 7 49852 2.

Artur Rodzinski, New York Philharmonic Orchestra (1944). *The Beethoven Recordings Vol. 2*. Fono Enterprise AB 78 923.

Arturo Toscanini, New York Philharmonic Orchestra (1933). *Toscanini Concert Edition*. Naxos 8.110801.

Arturo Toscanini, NBC Symphony Orchestra (1952). *Ludwig van Beethoven, 9 Symphonies*, Vol. 2. BMG 74321 55836 2.

32

"I'm Spartacus!"

Catherine Gunther Kodat

Of course, when two people do the same thing (and even more when two people say the same thing), the result is not the same.

> (György Lukács 1971: 291)

Geschichte zerfällt in Bilder, nicht in Geschichten. (History disintegrates into pictures, not stories)

> (Walter Benjamin 1982: 596, my translation)

I was disappointed in the film. It had everything but a good story.

> (Stanley Kubrick, on the release of *Spartacus*, in Nelson 192: 250)

As history, legend, and figure, Spartacus presents a special case for the narrative theorist. Given the formidable dimensions (one is tempted to say, the beefy proportions) of Spartacus, the frames crafted to contain or explain his figure have been many and various, ranging across a good chunk of recorded time – from Sallust's *Historiae* (Shaw 2001: 145–9) to the *Spartacus International Gay Guide* (Bedford 2001) – and through nearly every literary, visual, and performing art medium. Sifting through this material is the sort of job that uses up every free moment and then goes on to colonize other work, and thus I found myself, one schoolday afternoon not long ago, asking my sick-at-home son if he would like to join me in watching a videotape of the Bolshoi Ballet's 1968 production of *Spartak*. "Sure, mom," he said, settling in next to me as I fired up the VCR. "Is this the one where Spartacus wins?"

Good question. For why should Spartacus be of such interest to so many and for so long, given the fact that we know *exactly* what's going to happen to him? Indeed, the fate of Spartacus has been known longer than that of Jesus Christ and has provoked considerably less disagreement; how could anything so predictable remain so compelling? In a 1990 essay, J. Hillis Miller posed the generic version of this question – "Why do we need the 'same' story over and over?" – and concluded that "the answers . . . [to this question] are more related to the affirmative, culture-making function of narrative than to its critical or subversive function." Narrative repetition, he observed,

> may therefore have as its function . . . the affirmation and reinforcement, even the creation, of the most basic assumptions of a culture about human existence, about time, destiny, selfhood, where we come from, what we ought to do while we are here, where we go – the whole course of human life. We need the "same" stories over and over, then, as one of the most powerful, perhaps the most powerful, of ways to assert the basic ideology of our culture.
>
> (Miller 1995: 71–2)

Miller's diction is careful here – what narrative iteration "affirms" is "ideology," not "truth" – and in fact a crucial subplot in any history of contemporary narrative theory would trace the realignment of our critical project from defining universal human truths to describing mechanisms of cultural construction and surveillance (viz., the passage from F. R. Leavis, Cleanth Brooks, and Northrop Frye to Hayden White, D. A. Miller, and Judith Butler). Apt as Miller's observation undoubtedly is, it does not quite answer the challenge posed by Spartacus. As gleefully prescriptive as narratives of Spartacus's defeat undoubtedly were in the days of the Roman Empire, modern Spartacus narratives cannot be said to do the same cultural work: even Arthur Koestler's dystopic anticommunist fable *The Gladiators* ([1939] 1965) accepts the merit of the slaves' desire for freedom. We no longer have proslavery Spartacus narratives, but we should not assume that modern versions of Spartacus present a unified vision of freedom. For though the fate and figure of Spartacus are very old indeed, his narrative course through history (and his course through narrative history) has been such as to subject him to near-constant retro-fitting – an endless tinkering that cuts his narrative to fit the currently prevailing definition of freedom, a definition that is itself subject to change. The figure of Spartacus has found itself clothed in the freedom-forward fashions not only of Arthur Koestler, but of Voltaire, Karl Marx, Robert Montgomery Bird, Rosa Luxemburg, Josef Stalin, Howard Fast, Aram Khachaturian, Dalton Trumbo, Stanley Kubrick, and Briand Bedford (editor of the *Spartacus International Gay Guide*), to give a list by no means exhaustive but certainly representative in revealing an ideological heterogeneity profoundly irreducible to any single narrative of freedom.

It has never been doubted that, in 73 BCE, a gladiator named Spartacus led a breakout from a training center in Capua, an escape that grew to a slave rebellion lasting almost two years and ranging over the whole of the Italian peninsula before being crushed by the Roman Legion. But the earliest extant Spartacus narrative was written by Sallust many years after the rebellion; for centuries now that history itself has existed as a disintegrated collocation of narrative fragments, and the Spartacus narratives published after it (among the most famous those of Plutarch and Appian) are as notable for their many areas of disagreement as for their unique narrative properties. Attempts by various classicists and historians to cobble together some sort of imagined Spartacus *urtext* that would explain the motivation, aim, and effects of the rebellion are thought-provoking and of considerable speculative interest (see, for example, Bradley 1994 and 1998, and Shaw 2001), but, given the levels of disagreement among the classical source texts, they remain speculative.

This is not to say, however, that the many efforts to "tell" Spartacus are so peculiar to their moments of production that *no* common points emerge across narratives. It is, rather, to say that those common points invite a reading of the multiple Spartacus texts as examples of eidetic variation, a process J. M. Bernstein has characterized as "the imaginative act of producing deformations of some phenomenon" so that "one discovers what is invariant or essential to it" (Adorno 1991: 7). Bernstein's definition appears in the context of his discussion of the cultural criticism of Theodor Adorno, and though he borrows the phrase Edmund Husserl coined to describe his preferred method of phenomenological analysis, Bernstein makes clear that he does not mean to indicate that Adorno accepts Husserl's notion of "essential seeing" ("of course, Adorno is seeking after historical truth, not the ahistorical, rational essence of phenomena" [p. 7]). Nor do I wish to establish some sort of "essence of Spartacus" that might then work to distinguish the more "truthful" Spartacus narratives from those more clearly "ideological," for they are all ideologically motivated and do ideological work. Rather, casting Spartacus as a figure subject to eidetic variation through narrative allows us to view the multiple Spartacus iterations as a connected series of gestures in which what first appears as the strength of a single figure to hold together a crumbling narrative (the fragmentary, incomplete, and contradictory early histories of a slave rebellion in which Spartacus is the common thread) slowly becomes an exploration (really, a test) of the capacities of narrative to contain a single protean figure. As he moves from hero in the ancient chronicles to post-Enlightenment political symbol to Marxist martyr to Cold War spectacle to emblem of contemporary gay sexual liberation, Spartacus roils the always fluid relationship between figure and ground, image and narrative. Each reappearance of Spartacus is coincident with a change in the terms of the meaning of his significance; re-establishing his footing with each shift in the terrain, Spartacus battles on.

Why think of the multiple Spartacus texts as examples of eidetic variation, rather than narrative revision? Though I've indicated the source of my interest in Bernstein's appeal to Husserl in describing Adorno's work on the culture industry, a quick check in the *Oxford English Dictionary* makes clearer the advantages afforded by such an interpretive framework. There, "eidetics" itself is rather plainly defined as "the theory of perceptual images"; the phrase "eidetic image" arose in psychology during the mid-1920s as a description of a common visual phenomenon: the retention of an image in the field of vision after the image itself had been removed. The retained image is often experienced as something of a complementary "negative" of the original image, in that there are common properties shared by both the original and its ghost (usually shape), but also clear differences (usually color). However, "eidetics" as a term rapidly grew beyond this single meaning and came to encompass a whole class of visual phenomena, ranging from so-called "photographic memory" to the capacity for visual hallucination. What all these meanings have in common, though – what binds these phenomena together as a class – is their temporality: an eidetic image is an after-image, a kind of mental reviewing of an image that has passed. Thus the notion of eidetic variation keeps in suspension both the temporal property of narrative and the spatial dimension of the figure.

I mean to indicate two related but distinct ideas in employing the term "figure" rather than one more conventionally associated with narrative theory (such as "character"). In dance, the term figure has several interlocking meanings, one being the particular dancer's body, another being the gestures performed by that body. Thus I mean to acknowledge the special challenges posed by my attention to Yuri Grigorovich's ballet *Spartak*, where a term like "character" cannot account for the full range of activity within the narrative frame. *Spartak* is full of moving figures, and even though all contribute to the ballet's narrative, it would be a misrepresentation of the particular formal properties of dance – to the expressive spatiotemporal powers of *gesture*, which can only be manifested in figures (that is, bodies) and which works to create figures (that is, gestural phrases) – to conflate those moving figures with literary characters. This double sense of the figure as both material and form leads to my second aim, which is to honor the knottedness of the figure/ground dialectic, to highlight the oscillation informing what is conventionally taken to be hierarchical relationship. In dance, after all, moving figures (the corps) comprise the background as well as the foreground.

So: viewing the serial iterations of Spartacus as products of just such a process of eidetic variation, one that helps uncover what might, genealogically speaking, be called the "family resemblance" among them, has led me to make several observations. First, it is clear that the many versions of Spartacus both reflect and critique constructions of freedom particular to their given moments of production, and that those constructions are themselves genealogically connected. Second, this approach to the Spartacus narratives shows how difference emerges out of sameness; specifically, it reveals a growing link between homosexuality and the struggle for freedom. This link is most obvious in the Cold War "superpower" productions (Kubrick's film and Grigorovich's ballet), where a strong emphasis on a melancholic masculine identification with the hero ("I'm Spartacus!") marks the turn from Spartacus as narrative to Spartacus as figure – the attempted escape, as it were, of Spartacus (both character and story) from a particular kind of narrative demand. This struggle to escape from the imperatives of narrative becomes, over time, metonymically expressed as the struggle for sexual freedom – freedom from the reproductive mandate, freedom from a heterosexual narrative of sacrifice and perpetual deferral toward some invisible future – and it comes to stand, with Spartacus, as symbol of the struggle for freedom itself. Among other things, this careful attention to these variations on the theme of Spartacus gives us insight into the careful attention given to narrative in recent queer theory.

My third observation has to do with the relationship between narrative and figure as such. Spartacus begins as a fragment (in Sallust) and ends as a figure (in the *Spartacus International Gay Guide*), and the trajectory taking us from one to the other is, in many ways, a tour through narrative, a series of repeated experiments in the various properties of the relationship between figure and narrative ground. By figure here I mean those fraught constellations of incongruous and antagonistic forces whose meaning in large part derives from their power both to articulate and to contain irreconcilable tensions (so figures are both tropes and individuals); by ground I mean to indicate clearly teleological narratives. Various aspects of this relationship have captured the attention of literary scholars for some time now, though under the guise of other names and framed in subtly distinct fields of reference (Jakobson's metaphor and metonymy, for example, or de Man's semiology and rhetoric). This relationship more recently has been the subject of analyses by contemporary theorists, many (though not all) working under the rubric of queer theory – for example, Judith Butler, Gilles Deleuze, Lee Edelman, Paul Morrison, Gary Saul Morson, and Judith Roof – who share a view of the issue not as a set of formalist concerns derived from Gotthold Lessing's *Laocoön* (1984) but rather as an ethical and philosophical problem: narrative's capacity (or incapacity) to represent freedom. The gladiator slave who looks out at us today from the pages of the *Spartacus International Gay Guide* (and who in fact appears nowhere in the guide as either narrative or figure, but who rather presides over the text as a kind of controlling metaphor or beneficent eidetic ghost) perhaps may be thought of as a kind of Foucauldian countermemory, but, if so, his is a countermemory that seeks less a revision of the original narrative than a release from narrative *tout court*. To put it another way: over the course of this eidetic variation Spartacus becomes more queer, and in doing so his figure forces us to confront the degree to which narrative both produces a field of battle and determines the victor.

Thus we come back to the question with which I began: how is it that a figure seemingly chained to loss and defeat continues to incite interest? One could take the (very) long approach to this question, beginning with the Spartacus narratives of antiquity and proceeding through the sentimental nineteenth-century works of Robert Montgomery Bird, Elijah Kellogg, and C. Osborne Ward, but our purposes are equally well served by attending to some select uses of Spartacus in the twentieth century, starting with the example of Rosa Luxemburg's *Spartakusbund* and concluding with the spectacular Cold War productions of Kubrick and Grigorovich.

The importance of Luxemburg to our inquiry lies in her effort to make certain signal features of the sentimental nineteenth-century representations of Spartacus do duty in a modern political context. More than the nineteenth century representations, the twentieth-century Spartacus is strongly shaped by Marx's view of the gladiator as the "real representative of the ancient proletariat" (Marx 1942: 126), a view made flesh by Luxemburg's decision to don the mask of Spartacus and so take her place in a still-unfolding struggle for freedom. This appeal to Spartacus thus granted her movement a certain narrative structure and historical *gravitas*, but given the brutal repression of the *Spartakusbund*, this choice of model may seem horribly prophetic;

Luxemburg shared the same fate as her ancient forebear. In taking the mantle of Spartacus for her own, Luxemburg turned a political question of strategy into a rhetorical question of the capacity of the figure to generate a narrative departing from that which saw its first emergence. Thus, though Luxemburg succeeded in giving life to Marx's off-hand characterization of Spartacus as an early avatar of the proletariat, embodying a vision of Spartacus that would link him worldwide, and for generations, to revolutionary Marxism, the particularities of their shared fate impart the mordant after-taste of a sentimental politics. Luxemburg never articulated a notion of freedom that tied it to the bourgeois family (which had been the case with the nineteenth-century Spartacus), but her rhetoric of revolutionary nostalgia was shaped less by the belief in a restoration of a lost Edenic past than by the conviction that a history of defeats surely meant ultimate victory was at hand. The present's deadly struggle would redeem itself and that of the past, giving both coherent shape and meaning by giving birth to the perfected future.

Luxemburg's revolutionary Spartacus thus appears as the after-image of a nineteenth-century discourse yoking abolition with (bourgeois) family feeling, an afterimage Howard Fast's *Spartacus* sought to carry forward by reviving Popular Front appeals for unity and brotherliness in an early Cold War dominated by the forces of Stalin and McCarthy. In his 1990 memoir *Being Red*, and again in a preface to the 1996 edition of the novel, Fast describes how he was forced to bring *Spartacus* out himself in 1951 after seven publishers turned down the novel from fear of contact with a "known Red." In these retrospective accounts of the writing and publishing of *Spartacus*, Fast claims that "in the small-circulation publications of the left, the book was praised to the skies, but the mass-circulation, important papers of America brushed it off, saying that no publisher could be blamed for refusing a book by a red like Howard Fast" (Fast 1990: 293). Like Luxemburg, Fast wants to be Spartacus – though his is the Spartacus whose campaign, initially dismissed by Rome as barely worth notice, goes on to become a major Hollywood epic. The calculation informing Fast's rhetoric becomes clear when his description of *Spartacus*'s reviews is compared with the reviews themselves. Only Melville's notice for the *New York Times* comes close to fitting Fast's description (*Spartacus* is "a dreary proof that polemics and fiction cannot mix" [Heath 1953]); the majority of the reviews are respectful, if less than glowing. In fact the most critical reviews come from the left, among them Harvey Swados's notice in *The Nation*. Swados makes a point of sympathetically informing readers of the difficulties Fast overcame in getting *Spartacus* published, but goes on to say that the novel is "diffused and scattered," that "Mr. Fast's conception of history is not really much different from that of Cecil B. De Mille," and singles out for particular scorn the book's sexual politics: Fast "has provided Spartacus with a lovely and loyal wife named Varinia, and as if to make sure that we will not miss the point, he has contrasted their splendid fidelity with the homosexual carryings on of the degenerate members of the master class" (Swados 1952).

In fact, and as Swados's review helps us see, Fast takes pains in his 1990 memoir and 1996 preface to align the mainstream reception of his *Spartacus* with the contemptuous reception that greeted the original rebellion primarily in order to block recognition of the fact that the novel itself is something less than revolutionary: far from being a blistering critique of the US Cold War/McCarthyist cultural imaginary, *Spartacus* actually is coterminous with it. Fast's novel opens in the spring of 71 BCE, after the uprising has been put down, and concludes with a brief description of the postrebellion life of Spartacus's widow Varinia in a village in Gaul, where she remarries, raises eight children (including Spartacus's son), and dies, leaving her firstborn to carry on the work of revolution. Through this narrative structure, Varinia becomes the trace of Spartacus, the legible remainder of his figure and, thus, the screen on which (and through which) the meaning of his struggle is made comprehensible. Spartacus *does*; Varinia *is*, and her being ensures that his doing will not have been in vain. This is, of course, recognizably the Cold War gender ideology that helped dismantle such economic and social women's progress as was made during World War II; *Spartacus* differs from this gendered worldview only to the extent that, through Varinia, Fast fuses the redemptive Christian impulses of the nineteenth-century Spartacus figurations with Luxemburg's drive toward utopia in an effort to radicalize the "family values" implicit in a politics that sees freedom always (but also only) in the future: it's all for the sake of the children. Far from offering a radical dismantling of the near-hysterical valorization of the heterosexual and patriarchal family structure so crucial to the Red Scare, *Spartacus* embraces that structure as its own.

It is not surprising, then, that Fast's *Spartacus* is nearly frantically homophobic, despite the fact (or maybe because of the fact) that the figure of the homosexual turns out to be crucial to the novel: Spartacus's rebellion would not be told were it not for an erotic encounter between two men, for the narrative of the uprising enters the novel analeptically through the pillow talk of Marcus Licinius Crassus and the young patrician Caius Crassus. Thus the task of telling Spartacus – of giving narrative shape to his figure – thoroughly depends upon (rather than, as Fast seems to intend, departs from) a homoerotic relay of narrative transmission and reproduction. This open tension between the novel's twin obsessions – social revolution and sexual transgression – might be said to arise from Fast's shrewd sense of the relationship between titillation and sales, but this tension seems largely unintended; certainly, it is beyond the novel's efforts to contain and direct it by rearticulating the patriarchal family in a "radical" context. Rather, the tension may partly be seen as an effect of the novel's moment of production: it is precisely the sense of the future – the assurance that there *will be* a future – that had vanished with World War II's nuclear conclusion and the ensuing MAD (mutual assured destruction) diplomatic policies, a disappearance signaled by Faulkner's famous assertion that "there are no longer problems of the spirit. There is only the question: When will I be blown up?" (Faulkner 1967: 119). *Spartacus*'s appeal to futurity, so heavily dependent on heterosexual reproduction in service to "family values," rings hollow in such a climate, and Swados was correct to detect in the novel a texture of prefabrication that aligns it most closely not with a proletarian literary tradition but with a culture industry: Fast's "technicolor characters are determinedly banal, stubbornly refusing to speak in any other accents than those we have come to expect from the heroes and heroines of the movie epics" (Swados 1952). Through Kubrick, the translation of Fast's *Spartacus* from page to screen will exploit those accents, with revisionary consequences for Spartacus's figure that Swados probably could not foresee.

Before the US film, though, there was the Soviet ballet. As Fast was putting the finishing touches to his manuscript, Aram Khachaturian began work on a ballet score whose commission he had accepted years earlier. The Kirov Ballet's Nikolai Volkov had written the book for *Spartak* in 1938, at a time when the Spartacus rebellion was enjoying a vogue as a subject of study among Soviet scholars charged with proving Stalin's version of the "stage" theory of human progress. Among others, the historian A.V. Mišulin produced a series of works between 1934 and 1937 that explained the failed Spartacus rebellion in terms making clear its importance to the ultimate Soviet victory almost 2,000 years later. Mišulin termed the Spartacus uprising an actual revolution, and, in employing the state-approved typological method of historical analysis, made Spartacus "the herald of the first liberation movement in history" (quoted in Rubinsohn 1987: 8). In this way, Mišulin translated a narrative from antiquity into a proleptic allegory of contemporary political exigencies.

Khachaturian's decision to finally begin work on this heavily politicized narrative in 1950, over 10 years after accepting the commission, may itself have been politically motivated: in 1948, at the end of a three-day conference of Soviet composers assembled in Moscow at the behest of the Central Committee of the Communist Party, Khachaturian had been attacked by Andrei Zhdanov, Stalin's cultural watchdog, for producing work marked by the "atonalism, dissonance, and disharmony" of the "formalist and anti-people school" (Werth 1974: 29). Zhdanov's charges were codified in the Central Committee's Decree on Music, released one month after the conference, and there the "anti-democratic tendencies" of twentieth-century Western art music (as typified in the work of composers like Igor Stravinsky and the members of the second Viennese school) were denounced, and those Soviet composers deemed most guilty of indulging in "formalist perversions" were named – among them Dmitri Shostakovich and Sergei Prokofiev, as well as Khachaturian (Werth 1974: 29). At a reception held shortly after the decree, Khachaturian assured a Western journalist that the censure "shouldn't be taken too seriously," though he added ("a little wistfully," according to the journalist) that "there is going to be a reassessment of a lot of things; some of the works that I considered least important – such as some of my ballet music – will now be treated as important" (Werth 1974: 91–2). Thus Khachaturian began composing *Spartak* two years after his public chastisement at the hands of Zhdanov had made him realize that his ballet music had become an interest of the state. He completed it in 1954, one year after the death of Stalin, and the ballet was given its world première 10 months after Khrushchev's "secret speech" to the party condemned the "cult of personality" that had led to the brutal excesses of Stalinism. If one were looking for a signal example of the importance (and dangers) of attending to the relationship between art and its moment of political and economic production, one could hardly find a work more fraught by circumstance than Khachaturian's *Spartak*.

Spartak received its world première at the Kirov Theater on December 27, 1956, with choreography by Leonid Jacobson. This first production of the ballet unquestionably was an effort to produce a genuine socialist realist work, an "historically concrete depiction of reality in its revolutionary development" targeted toward "the task of educating workers in the spirit of Communism" (Brown 1991: 90). In this sense the work took its cue from the Mišulin histories of Spartacus: suffering the humiliations of the slave market, forced to kill in the arena, Spartacus is radicalized and leads his fellow gladiators in rebellion; his defeat and death are depicted as regrettable but necessary sacrifices endured on the road to the eventual (implicitly Soviet) liberation. But *Spartak* differs from Mišulin's histories in one respect: Spartacus is destroyed not by the combined forces of the extreme left and the petty bourgeoisie, but rather by sexual intrigue when Harmodius, a "comrade-at-arms" of Spartacus, is seduced by Aegina, the consort of Crassus, and consequently betrays his fellow rebels to the Roman army (Schneerson 1959: 88). Thus this first production of Khachaturian's ballet registers Spartacus's capacity to bring sex and politics into volatile relation such that lines of ideological allegiance, even within the strongly narrative tradition of socialist realism, become troublingly blurred. In other words, *Spartak* illustrates how the individual figure, even as it is subordinated to the sweep of a spectacular collectivist narrative, retains its capacity to interfere in that narrative.

However, no one would claim that the earliest productions of *Spartak* represented a clear and recognizable break with *zhdanovshchina*, which even after the deaths of Zhdanov and Stalin continued to influence Soviet artists and critics. Most likely because of its subject, *Spartak* wins the approbation of two state-sanctioned biographies of Khachaturian, which together assert that the ballet met strong public and critical approval at its première. But both studies allow that this first production was not without its flaws – flaws attributable precisely to its articulation of freedom, most particularly choreographic freedom. Yuzefovich asserts that Jacobson's unusual choreography – which abjured the specialized vocabulary of classical ballet in an effort to duplicate figures drawn from "ancient Roman vases and the friezes of the famous Pergamon Altar" (Yuzefovich 1985: 218) – was simply too innovative; Grigory Schneerson only notes that, after "the Soviet public acclaimed with enthusiasm the Kirov Theatre production" (Schneerson 1959: 89), the ballet immediately received quite different choreographic treatments in Prague and Moscow; those productions were no less (but no more) successful than the first. Not until Grigorovich's 1968 version for the Bolshoi would the Soviets have a triumphant *Spartak*; though, as we shall see, this production drew much of its power from its ability to emphasize the figural ambiguity of this once-Stalinized narrative.

With Kubrick's *Spartacus*, the eidetic series begins its turn away from a Spartacus subject to a utopic narrative of future freedom and towards a view of him as a figure *freed from* the narrative of the future. On the face of it, there seems little in the film to merit this claim: produced by Kirk Douglas's Bryna Productions and released by

Universal Studios in 1960, *Spartacus* is in many ways a completely conventional Hollywood toga movie. Yet it was precisely through an emergent gay sexual politics that Spartacus continued to signify for the late-Cold War US cultural imaginary, as the question of how to build a better future dissolved into the demand for freedom *now* – and that politics, while not explicit, is clearly detectable in the film.

The now-famous "snails and oysters" scene, in which Crassus (Laurence Olivier) attempts to seduce the slave Antoninus (Tony Curtis), would seem to be a logical place to begin a discussion of a queer *Spartacus*. The scene, which caused considerable discomfort for Production Code Administration censor Geoffrey M. Shurlock and which outraged the Legion of Decency, was cut from the film before its release (it was restored in the 1991 rerelease of the film), and it has been analyzed in several recent studies of Hollywood depictions of homosexuality (see Russo [1981] 1987 and Barrios 2003). But homosexuality in *Spartacus* does not begin (or end) with "snails and oysters": with his first appearance, in the first five minutes of the film, Peter Ustinov's Batiatus introduces to *Spartacus* what gay film critic Richard Barrios has called the "pansy note," playing his opening scene as interested inspector of masculine musculature for every double entendre under the location's Death Valley sun.

Ustinov and Kubrick's decision to render Batiatus sexually "suspect" is hardly surprising, given the long narrative tradition linking Roman slavery and sexual "decadence" that precedes the film and that made itself felt not only in Fast's novel but also in much of Dalton Trumbo's original screenplay (preserved in the Douglas and Trumbo papers in the Wisconsin Historical Society archives). What is perhaps surprising is that, as presented by Kubrick and Ustinov, Batiatus winds up a sympathetic, even heroic, character: Batiatus weasels out of Crassus's demand that he identify Spartacus, and it is he who drives the cart bearing Varinia and her infant to freedom. Batiatus's appeal depends upon a performance that emphasizes the roguish geniality typical of camp; placed next to his Nero of *Quo Vadis* (1951), Ustinov's turn in *Spartacus* is perhaps best described as a kind of camp redemption. And Ustinov's performance is only the most obvious queer aspect of the film; the Legion of Decency may have hoped that cutting "snails and oysters" would root out "inferences of homosexuality in a film which, at the same time, [Universal is] actively promoting as a valuable historical document for all school levels" (Barrios 2003: 273), but the gay ethos of *Spartacus* runs deep, ranging from the stylized sketch of a bare-bottomed gladiator that served as the film's promotional logo to Crassus's unexplained but obvious passion for the hero.

Even the first meeting of Spartacus and Varinia has its queer moment: "We recommend that you reconsider the line, 'I've never had a woman,'" censor Shurlock wrote to Universal officials after reviewing the script, understanding quite well that the line did not mean that Spartacus had never had sex (*Spartacus* 2001, Disc II of the 2001 Criterion Collection DVD of the 1991 restored print). As blocked and shot, in fact, the famous "snails and oysters" scene serves less to introduce homosexuality into *Spartacus* as something new than to finally reveal what had always been there: Kubrick parks the camera in front of a gauzy curtain stretched in front of Crassus's sunken tub, and the entire two minute scene unfolds behind the curtain without cut or camera movement. On the line, "my taste includes both snails and oysters," Antoninus draws the curtain aside as Crassus, wrapped in his robe, steps into the foreground. The literalized drawing aside of the curtain makes it plain: homosexual passion has always been part of Spartacus (and so, of *Spartacus*), just heretofore veiled and behind the scene.

Ustinov's contribution to *Spartacus*, then – a contribution that Kubrick approved – skews the film away from the heterosexual profamily earnestness of Fast's novel (and Trumbo's script) and towards a rather different reading of the relationship Spartacus's figure has to the narrative of freedom. It is this persistent queer undertone of *Spartacus* that Kubrick may have had in mind when he claimed (in an astonishing statement that makes no literal sense, given the antiquity of the Spartacus narrative) that "for once, the audience doesn't know what's going to happen next" (Nelson 1982: 250). Batiatus picks up and makes visible the latent liberatory homoerotics of a Spartacus considered as figure *and* narrative, an erotics articulated in what is the film's most famous scene: asked to reveal the subversive within their ranks, the men who have followed Spartacus through rebellion and defeat proclaim, over and over again, "I'm Spartacus!" In declaring their identification at a moment when such identification can mean only death, Spartacus's men refuse the narrative formula that would grant them life on the condition that they abandon their inappropriate and ungovernable attachment. Given the film's overdetermined cultural, political, and historical narrative frame, the men who proclaim this attachment openly are given the death they appear to demand in place of liberty. But Batiatus escapes that narrative frame, thus putting to question the capacity of that frame to completely contain the figures within it.

Eight years after Kubrick's film the Soviets, refusing to give up on Khachaturian's *Spartak*, handed the assignment of reviving the production to Bolshoi Ballet artistic director Yuri Grigorovich. Grigorovich recrafted the ballet as "a performance for four soloists and a corps de ballet" (Yuzefovich 1985: 227), placing Spartacus and his faithful Phrygia (the Soviet Varinia) in direct opposition to Crassus and the scheming Aegina. Such a move required a total transformation in the role of Crassus. In past productions the part was "hardly danceable" or "played by an extra" (Yuzefovich 1985: 227), a characterization no doubt meant to sharpen the work's didactic point by placing the freedom-loving, freely moving Spartacus in opposition to a stolid, tyrannical Crassus. Grigorovich, however, saw the relationship of Spartacus and Crassus not as a foregone conclusion but rather as the emotional center of the work, and the ballet's restructuring was undertaken chiefly with the aim of focusing attention on the relationship between these two men.

Grigorovich's production met with tremendous international acclaim precisely thanks to his decision to exploit the vexing figure/ground wobble that had seemed to mar past versions of the ballet. Rather than being about the power and beauty of the Spartacus rebellion as precursor of the Bolshevik revolution, *Spartak* was now about the power and beauty of the male figure (and I should be clear here: the beauty of the male figure does not translate straightforwardly into the power of an individual character, even though something of that power certainly makes itself felt). Grigor-ovich's *Spartak* offers "some of the most explosive choreography ever written for the male dancer" (Craine and Mackrell 2000: 216), and the explosiveness stems not only from the steps themselves but also from Grigorovich's decision to effect a kind of divorce from (and within) the narrative convention of the single leading couple, such that the erotic tension driving the traditional nineteenth-century story ballet (Prince Siegfried and Odette/Odile in *Swan Lake*, Prince Désiré and Princess Aurora in *Sleeping Beauty*, James and the Sylph in *La Sylphide*, Prince Albrecht and Giselle in *Giselle*) is reinvested in two men. Grigorovich's *Spartak* thus queered the Stalinist narrative of Spartacus in irrevocable ways, offering a new "stage theory" (so to speak) of human progress that seemed simultaneously to underwrite and subvert the author-ity and power of the Soviet state. Roman tyranny is matched by Roman glamour; in the climactic confrontation between Spartacus and Crassus, Spartacus chooses, almost inexplicably, to spare the Roman's life. Most striking of all are the bleak final moments of the work (Spartacus's death tableau mixes imagery of crucifixion and the martyrdom of St Sebastian, and is followed by a socialist realist pietà), which, in emphasizing the death of Spartacus and the grief of Phrygia (who has no children nor prospect of any), refuse any consolatory gesture towards future freedom – a remark-ably daring move given the standard Soviet practice of uplifting conclusions. In abjuring strict Zhdanovian notions of proper Communist art, Grigorovich produced a work that both accedes to and critiques the narrative demands of the state. *Spartak*

> expressed the qualities that Grigorovich had made his own: darkness, fatalism, and weight. Even as they soar, Grigorovich's protagonists are in chains, heavy with corrup-tion or the foreknowledge of death. Audiences, particularly in the West, reacted to this extreme application of ballet with stunned amazement. Although impeccably Soviet on the surface, the allegory worked both ways: was it the brave Thracians or the fascistic Roman legions who represented the Soviet state?
>
> (Jennings 1995: 76)

Grigorovich's elevation of the male figure emerged against a Soviet legal and cultural background of criminalized homosexuality and a near-institutionalized sexual prig-gishness: in 1934 Maxim Gorky had heralded the new Soviet criminal code – in particular Article 121, which made sodomy an offense punishable by up to five years' internment – as "a triumph of proletarian humanism"; two years later Nikolai Krylenko, the People's Commissar for Justice, "announced that homosexuality was a product of the decadence of the exploiting classes; in a socialist society based on healthy principles, such people ... would have no place" (Kon 1993: 92). Soviet homosexual repression is thus part of the narrative background to *Spartak*'s figure; knowing this background of sexual and cultural censorship heightens the sense of Grigorovich's *Spartak* as a kind of queer critique, coded, like Ustinov's camp Batiatus, to work both within and against the figure's political and social background. *Spartak* had its première on April 9, 1968; four months later Warsaw Pact tanks rolled into

Prague, and the post-Stalin Soviet cultural "thaw" was officially over. *Spartak*, however, went on to win extravagant critical praise both at home and abroad, and precisely because its elevation of figure over ground anticipated what might be called the politics of the figure that rose to replace the grand totalized narratives of freedom that came to a head and collapsed in the year of its première. What has been alternately praised and derided as "identity politics" – black power, feminism, gay liberation – can in part be seen as a move from a politics bent toward universal (yet uniform) freedom for all in some as-yet-unrealized utopian future to a strategic and idiosyncratic politics of freedom in and for the individual body, a freedom in which the ability of the figure to move both within and against the social narrative appears more attainable, but also more precious, than any totalized unity of figure and narrative.

As spectacle, both *Spartacus* and *Spartak* articulate a longing for freedom that uses the future perfect – it shall be so – to express a grief for an imagined past: it should have been thus. Such nostalgia for the future emerges chiefly in figural flashes, as history disintegrates into longing's projected *Bilder*. And so we arrive, in 1970, at the first edition of the *Spartacus International Gay Guide*, a vacation travel manual that, in its matter-of-fact, (im)modest way, articulates the generative paradox of Spartacus as one who urges both flight from Italy (the wish to escape from the dominant order in pursuit of private satisfaction) and a stand against Rome (the drive to destroy the dominant order in a battle for freedom). *The Spartacus International Gay Guide* thus executes a double figural movement that corresponds to the "affection image" in Deleuze's schematics of cinema: it is the "affection image" (paradigmatically, the face in close-up) that intercedes between and binds together the "perception image" (what we might simplify as the establishing shot) and the "action image" (the activity within the frame). Deleuze detects within this structure the "perpetual destiny" of cinema – "to make us move from one of its poles to the other, that is, from an objective perception to a subjective perception, and vice versa" (Deleuze 1996: 73) – and this destiny is also a narrative, a narrative of figure as narrative, of *Bilder* as history:

> [T]here is no subject which acts without another which watches it act, and which grasps it as acted, itself assuming the freedom of which it deprives the former. "Thus two different egos [*moi*] one of which, conscious of its freedom, sets itself up as independent spectator of a scene which the other would play in a mechanical fashion. But this dividing-in-two never goes to the limit. It is rather an oscillation of the person between two points of view on himself, a hither-and-thither of the spirit . . ." a being-within.
> (Deleuze 1996: 73–4; the internal quote is from Bergson 1975)

It is this oscillation, this being-within, that accounts for the process of eidetic variation and that drives our continued fascination with Spartacus. For if, as Judith Butler has pointed out, the process of becoming an independent subject is bound up with the process of subjection ("the subject loses itself to tell the story of itself, but in telling the story of itself seeks to give an account of what the narrative function has already made plain" [Butler 1997: 11]), then the story of a struggle for freedom that never arrives is *our* story. This oscillation informs our queer recognition that the figure (me, you) both *is* and is *a part* of (and so apart from) the narrative that bears it. We're Spartacus – or at least, we think we are. And whether truth or ideology, it seems that is one story we can never figure out, or hear often enough.

References and Further Reading

Adorno, T. (1991). *The Culture Industry: Selected Essays on Mass Culture*, ed. J. M. Bernstein. London: Routledge.

Adorno, T. and Horkheimer, M. ([1944] 1989). *Dialectic of Enlightenment*, trans. J. Cumming. New York: Continuum Publishing Company.

Appian. ([1913] 1995). *The Civil Wars*, trans. H. White. Cambridge, MA: Harvard University Press.

Barrios, R. (2003). *Screened Out: Playing Gay in Hollywood from Edison to Stonewall*. New York: Routledge.

Bedford, B. (ed.) (2001). *The Spartacus International Gay Guide, 2001–2002*. Berlin: Bruno Gmünder Verlag.

Benjamin, W. (1982). *Gesammelte Schriften*, vol. 5, part I (*Das Passagen-Werk*), ed. R. Tiedemann. Frankfurt am Main: Suhrkamp Verlag.

Bergson, H. (1975). *Mind-Energy: Lectures and Essays*, trans. H. W. Carr. Westport, CT: Greenwood Press.

Bird, R. M. (1935). *The Gladiator*. In A. G. Halline (ed.), *American Plays: Selected and Edited with Critical Introductions and Bibliographies* (pp. 155–98). New York: American Book Company.

Bradly, K. R. (1994). *Slavery and Society at Rome*. Cambridge, UK: Cambridge University Press.

Bradly, K. R. ([1989] 1998). *Slavery and Rebellion in the Roman World, 140 B.C.-70 B.C.* Bloomington: Indiana University Press.

Brown, M. C. (1991). *Art under Stalin*. New York: Holmes & Meier.

Butler, J. (1997). *The Psychic Life of Power: Theories in Subjection*. Palo Alto, CA: Stanford University Press.

Craine, D. and Mackrell, J. (eds). (2000). *The Oxford Dictionary of Dance*. Oxford: Oxford University Press.

Deleuze, G. ([1983] 1996). *Cinema 1: The Movement-Image*, trans. H. Tomlinson and B. Habberjam. Minneapolis: University of Minnesota Press.

de Man, P. (1979). "Semiology and Rhetoric." In *Allegories of Reading: Figural Language in Rousseau, Nietzsche, Rilke, and Proust* (pp. 3–19). New Haven, CT: Yale University Press.

Edelman, L. (1998). "The Future is Kid Stuff: Queer Theory, Disidentification, and the Death Drive." *Narrative* 6 (1): 18–30.

Fast, H. (1990). *Being Red*. Armonk, NY: M. E. Sharpe.

Fast, H. ([1951] 1996). *Spartacus*. Armonk, NY: North Castle Books/M. E. Sharpe.

Faulkner, W. (1967). "Upon Receiving the Nobel Prize for Literature, 1950." In J. B. Meriwether (ed.), *William Faulkner: Essays, Speeches, and Public Letters* (pp. 119–21). London: Chatto & Windus.

Foucault, M. (1977). *Language, Counter-Memory, Practice: Selected Essays and Interviews*, ed. Donald F. Bouchard. Ithaca, NY: Cornell University Press.

Heath, M. (1953). "War of the Gladiators." *The New York Times*, 3 February: 22.

Husserl, E. (1999). "Eidetic Variation and the Acquisition of Pure Universals." In D. Welton (ed.), *The Essential Husserl: Basic Writings in Transcendental Phenomenology* (pp. 292–9). Bloomington: Indiana University Press.

Jakobson, R. ([1956] 1987). "Two Aspects of Language and Two Types of Aphasic Disturbances." In K. Pomorska and S. Rudy (eds.), *Language in Literature* (pp. 95–114). Cambridge, MA: The Belknap Press.

Jennings, L. (1995). "Night at the Ballet: The Czar's Last Dance." *The New Yorker*, 27 March.

Kellogg, E. (1864). "Spartacus to the Gladiators." In G. S. Hillard (ed.), *The Sixth Reader*. Boston: Brener.

Koestler, A. ([1939] 1965). *The Gladiators*, trans. E. Simon, postscript by the author. New York: The Macmillan Company.

Kon, I. (1993). "Sexual Minorities." In I. Kon and J. Riordan (eds.), *Sex and Russian Society* (pp. 89–115). Bloomington: Indiana University Press, 1993.

Lessing, G. E. (1984). *Laocoön: An Essay on the Limits of Painting and Poetry*, trans. E. A. McCormick. Baltimore: Johns Hopkins University Press.

Lukács, G. (1971). "Critical Observations on Rosa Luxemburg's 'Critique of the Russian Revolution.'" In *History and Class Consciousness: Studies in Marxist Dialectics*, trans. Rodney Livingstone. Cambridge, MA: The MIT Press

Marx, K. (1942). Letter to Frederick Engels of February 27, 1861. In *Selected Correspondence of Karl Marx and Frederick Engels (1846–1895)* (pp. 126–7), trans. Dona Torr. New York: International Publishers.

Miller, D. A. (1981). *Narrative and its Discontents: Problems of Closure in the Traditional Novel*. Princeton, NJ: Princeton University Press.

Miller, D. A. (1988). *The Novel and the Police*. Berkeley: University of California Press.

Miller, D. A. (1992). *Bringing out Roland Barthes*. Berkeley: University of California Press.

Miller, J. H. ([1990] 1995). "Narrative." In F. Lentricchia and Thomas McLaughlin (eds.), *Critical Terms for Literary Study*, 2nd edn. (pp. 66–79). Chicago: The University of Chicago Press.

Morrison. P. (2001). *The Explanation for Everything: Essays on Sexual Subjectivity*. New York: New York University Press.

Morson, G. S. (1994). *Narrative and Freedom: The Shadows of Time*. New Haven, CT: Yale University Press.

Nelson, T. A. (1982). *Kubrick: Inside a Film Artist's Maze*. Bloomington: Indiana University Press.

Pelz, W. A. (1988). *The Spartakusbund and the German Working Class Movement, 1914–1919*. Lewiston, ME and Queenston, ONT: The Edwin Mellen Press.

Plutarch. ([1958] 1972). *Fall of the Roman Republic*, trans. R. Warner, introductions and notes by Robin Seager. London: Penguin Books.

Roof, J. (1996). *Come as You Are: Sexuality and Narrative*. New York: Columbia University Press.

Rubinsohn, W. Z. (1987). *Spartacus' Uprising and Soviet Historical Writing*, trans. J. G. Griffith. Oxford: Oxbow Books.

Russo, V. ([1981] 1987). *The Celluloid Closet*, revised edn. New York: Harper & Row.

Shaw, B. D. (2001). *Spartacus and the Slave Wars: A Brief History with Documents*. Boston: Bedford/St. Martin's Press.

Schneerson, G. (1959). *Aram Khachaturian*, trans. X. Denko. Moscow: Foreign Languages Publishing House.

Swados, H. (1952). "Epic in Technicolor." *The Nation*, 5 April, 174: 331.

Waldman, R. (1958). *The Spartacist Uprising of 1919*. Milwaukee, WI: The Marquette University Press.

Ward, C. O. (1907). *The Ancient Lowly: A History of the Ancient Working People from the Earliest Known Period to the Adoption of Christianity by Constantine*, vol. I. Chicago: Charles H. Kerr & Company.

Werth, A. (1974). *Musical Uproar in Moscow*. Westport, CT: Greenwood Press (1949).

Yuzefovich. V. (1985). *Aram Khachaturyan*, trans. N. Kournokoff and V. Bobrov. New York: Sphinx Press.

33

Shards of a History of Performance Art: Pollock and Namuth Through a Glass, Darkly

Peggy Phelan

As the work of Michel Foucault has demonstrated, certain forms of human thought and action are "invented" via the encounter between discourse and event (Foucault 1978). In this sense, we can say that performance was invented in the twentieth century. While people, animals, and machines performed before this period, the specific framework for understanding these sets of activities *as* performances emerged only in the twentieth century. Beginning with avant-garde experiments in Europe and Russia at the turn of the century, and flowering fully in the years after World War II, especially in Japan and Austria, performance histories are deeply entwined with the larger history of the twentieth century. In the early days of this new century, perform-ance emerges as a term whose meaning and import extend well beyond the realms of aesthetics or technology, and include politics, philosophy, economics, and assessments of all kinds (McKenzie 2000). While performance as concept and practice increasingly expands, attempts to recount its history risk becoming ever more fractured. Even if we confine our focus only to the realm of aesthetics, we find three competing narratives of the history of performance art, each claiming different points of origin, different signal events, and different prospects for the future. These narratives are:

1 Performance art emerges from the history of theater and begins as a counterpoint to realism.
2 Performance art emerges from the history of painting and gains its force and focus in "action painting."
3 Performance art represents a return to investigations of the body most fully explored by shamans and alternative practitioners of the healing arts (McEvilley 1998: 23–5).

All three of these narratives of the history of performance art are helpful. But since they tend to interpret performance as a kind of "add-on" to their primary interest (theater, painting, or anthropology/healing/spiritual practice), they give short shrift to the larger intellectual and aesthetic achievements (and failures) of performance on its own terms. Moreover, since these three explanations take the form of narratives, they frequently gloss over the deep resistance to narrative common to some of the most significant performances ever made. Thus a comprehensive history of performance would have to account for this widespread antinarrative attitude without defeating its point by virtue of its own narrative form.

Assuredly, many performances tell stories and/or are derived from sacred and mythological narratives. Nonetheless, the art of performance takes place exclusively in the present tense. Performance exists in the arc of its enactment; while sometimes this arc is structured as a narrative, the ontological quality of performance rests on its ephemeral nature (P. Phelan 1993). If we apply Dorrit Cohn's helpful axiom about temporality in typical narrative structure, "live now, tell later" (Cohn 1999: 96) we see that performance lives in the now, while narrative histories describe it later. Enacted in the present tense, performance lives, rather than tells, its meaning.[1]

In his account of the linguistic performative, J. L. Austin (1962) emphasizes the present tense form of the performative speech act. Arguing that performative speech acts make something happen in the act of utterance – "I promise," "I worry," "I bet" – Austin notes that when a performative speech act takes the future or past tense, it becomes a constative act and loses its force as action. Austin's argument helps illuminate the paradoxical nature of the ambition to create a narrative history of performance art. Precisely by taking a narrative form, this history risks missing the performative force of the art it seeks to comprehend. What would a history that tried to capture this force in its telling look like? Or to put it slightly differently, what would it take to create a performative account of a history of performance art? Jackson Pollock's action paintings and the narratives they have inspired allow us to see all three versions of the history of performance art at play in the same space. They mark the point of departure for the claim that performance emerges from painting (see Schimmel 1998 and Jones 1998). Pollock's paintings also function as dramatic visual theater in the photographs recorded by Hans Namuth in 1950, photographs that repudiate the psychological realism central to portrait photography in favor of the portrait of a man of action. Additionally, Pollock's painting, as recorded by Namuth, can be seen as ritualistic, shamanic performance, replete with references to Native American sand painting (Soussloff 2004). Pollock's paintings and Namuth's photographs conspire to create a significant, albeit dense, condensation of the three competing narratives of the history of performance art.

Action painting, such as Yves Klein's "living paint brushes" and Pollock's poured paintings, are central moments in the history of performance art. In these works, the final product, the painting as object, is less important than the act that brought that art into being. The arc of Pollock's hand as it flies across the canvas dripping paint, like the paint-splashed torsos of Klein's models pressing hard against the prepared surface of the canvas, move the emphasis in visual art away from the quality of the completed art object toward the complex drama of the act of composition. As a result, interest in the artwork shifts from the object to its maker, and more specifically, since the maker's action is ephemeral, to frozen images of its maker. At the heart of this performance-centered view of painters and painting, therefore, photography plays a complicated role.

When photography was first made popular in the nineteenth century, it seemed to represent the triumph of mimetic aspiration that had fueled painting for centuries. Photography's ability to document subtle detail accurately seemed to portend the death of painting.[2] But rather than destroying painting, as some nineteenth-century commentators predicted, photography served to advance it. Freed from the task of resemblance, painting went on to experiment with other possibilities in its form. From analytic cubism to abstract expressionism, painting became increasingly robust as photography became more ubiquitous.

Walter Benjamin was the first to note that photography renders all visual arts photographic: "Anyone will be able to observe how much more easily a painting and above all, a sculpture or architecture, can be grasped in photographs than in reality" (Benjamin [1931] 1980: 212). But often this "ease" fundamentally distorts the painting, sculpture, or architecture. Art that resists photography's flat square frame risks, in a literal sense, not being seen. Discussing the early history of photography, Benjamin dwells on the long exposure times needed for portraiture: "The procedure itself caused the models to live, not *out* of the instant, but *into* it: during the long exposure they grew, as it were, into the image" (Benjamin [1931] 1980: 204, original emphasis). This act of growing into the image, a condensation of live movement into the arresting square of photographic light, introduces a new mode of performance into the history of visual art. Photography exposes an aspect of performance designed to enhance the art of photography itself. This exposure in turn transformed painting's relationship to performance. In the mingling of painting and photography at the heart of the encounter between Pollock and Namuth a blur developed. This blur, at once optical and ontological, has obscured some of the most radical possibilities inherent in the concept and practice of action painting. Working under the cover of the pure documentary, Namuth's photographs are themselves artfully designed performances. The point of view of most of the shots emphasizes the figure in the midst of an all-over field: both walls and floor teem with paint. Moreover, the space of the photograph flattens the field in which Pollock worked and almost absorbs his figure (see Clay 1977 and Krauss 1980 for fuller discussion of Namuth's photographs). Both artists worked in deference to the art and action of the other. This deference may well have been motivated by ambition, reverence, and/or commercial and historical aspirations. But whatever the motivation, the story of their encounter has become the main kernel in the narrative of action painting, some 50 years on.

I

In his introduction to the valuable catalog, *Out of Actions: Between Performance and the Object 1949–79*, Paul Schimmel (1998) claims Jackson Pollock as one of the four fathers of performance art (it's always ironic that in real life paternity is often denied, while in history writing not a mother can be found and fathers are everywhere). Schimmel invites his reader to revisit the primal scene in which Pollock was christened as a performer: Harold Rosenberg's 1952 essay, "The American Action Painters." In his famous argument, Rosenberg claimed, "at a certain moment the canvas began to appear to one [North] American painter after another as an arena in which to act — rather than as a space to reproduce, re-design, analyze or 'express' an object, actual or imagined. What was to go into the canvas was not a picture but an event" (Rosenberg 1952: 22). Schimmel admits that Rosenberg's essay "encouraged a myth" about Pollock, but he happily exploits it as a founding text in the history of performance art.

Rosenberg never names Pollock directly in his essay. Nor does he analyze any specific painting. Nor does he mention Namuth's work. Yet the essay is widely understood in the way Schimmel employs it: "In overstating the case for the performative qualities of Pollock's painting, action painting, and the New York School in general, Rosenberg encouraged a myth that has been more protean for subsequent generations of artists than the canvases themselves. His words, coupled with Namuth's famous photographs, mightily enforced a monocular view of Pollock's contribution" (Schimmel 1998: 19). A series of narratives, both verbal and visual, that "tell the story" of Pollock's paintings constitute the framework of this monocular view. Taken together, however, these narratives work to repress the antinarrative stance of the poured paintings. In focusing on Pollock's method of painting – did he drip, pour, or splatter the paint? – and indeed on his difficult life, art criticism and theory have failed to confront the force of the antinarrative stance of the paintings themselves. More than being simply nonfigurative as most abstractionists were, Pollock took especial delight in rupturing the assumption that his work could be "translated" by critical descriptions. "There was a reviewer a while back who wrote that my pictures didn't have a beginning or any end. He didn't mean it as a compliment, but it was. It was a fine compliment. Only he didn't know it" (quoted in Roueché 1950: 16).

The poured paintings, Pollock's singular achievement in the work he did between 1947 and 1950, abandoned figuration and the traditional task of "copying" an object (real or imagined) more generally. The poured paintings are densely layered, colorful surfaces;[3] each line seems overtaken by another; the best of them resist chaos and confusion by an appeal to rhythm and movement; the visual is rendered musical; color, symphonic. Pollock's best paintings come to us as fully present objects. "My paintings do not have a center," Pollock explained, "but depend on the same amount of interest throughout" (quoted in Goodnough 1951: 60). Pollock's paintings are radically open, and indeed, the best seem not so much "finished" as "filled out" (or perhaps filled in and filled up). This wide-open quality has much in common with the epistemological horizon of the present tense. Pollock's paintings come to us in a state of almost ecstatic suspension; they resist both the pleasures and the traumas of the completed story.

In so doing, they also reject the primary mode of art criticism up until World War II (P. Phelan 2004). In the prewar period, those who wrote about painting devoted themselves to the narrative exposition of the journey of color and line across canvas. But with the advent of Pollock's poured paintings and Namuth's documentation of them in 1950, this exposition was at once impossible and also decidedly beside the point. Pollock's paintings and his collaborative work with Namuth initiated a specific challenge for both painting and the discourse about it. In other words, while Pollock pursued "all-over painting" on his canvases, he implicitly asked his viewer to find a way to enter the painting that did not rely on the rules of perspective or narrative coherence. He was asking for something that was, and is still, extremely radical – but before his invitation could be absorbed it got displaced by his encounter with Namuth, and the photographs and film became the point of entry.

The reasons for this are manifold, but they include the affinity between photography and writing and the disharmony between abstract painting and criticism. Pollock's best paintings resist narrative's past and future tense by occupying a vivid present. Thus it is worthwhile to examine a further displacement: from the photographic record of Pollock painting to the written record. I want to look closely at what writing about action painting enacts, because it is here that the scholarly field operates most decisively to re-create the history of the form. As Rosenberg put it: "To form a School in modern times not only is a new painting consciousness needed but a consciousness of that consciousness – and even an insistence on certain formulas. A School is the result of the linkage of practice with terminology – different paintings are affected by the same words" (Rosenberg 1952: 22). Part of what a school requires, then, is a set of words and a style of address. Just as action painting created a new "event," it also created the need for a performance-minded criticism. Rosenberg understood that Pollock's painting demanded a new language and critical entry point but he himself was unable to provide it. A generous reader could conclude that Rosenberg's failure to name a single artist or to analyze any specific painting was an attempt to honor the actionists' abandonment of figuration and narrative. A skeptical reader might suggest that Rosenberg's essay is more interesting as a meditation on writing than it is on painting, and indeed that his essay, as Barbara Rose has claimed, does not concern "painting at all; he was describing Namuth's photographs of Pollock" (Rose 1980, n.p.). The elision between Pollock's paintings, Namuth's photographs, and the writing about them opens up a place where a different kind of history of performance art might be written.

No less than Rosenberg, I want to form a School. Having attempted to teach the history of performance art for 19 years now, I see the value of a comprehensive narrative of the form. But performance art has been extremely unruly in its relationship to chronology, documentation, media, and politics. Performance art works to unsettle the distinction between subject and object, between doing and telling. Rather than writing a nonfiction narrative of the history of performance art in the past tense, I want to allow the transformative aspects of performance to inspire a new writing, a performative writing that remains alive to action, whose telling force resides in each breath of the renewing present tense.

II

How then to find a mode of address that is closer to the language and aspiration of the art one wants to discuss? Narrative is a necessary but not sufficient mode for a performative history of performance art. For if the poured paintings are belated traces of ephemeral acts like dancing with a wet brush and an open can of commercial paint, then how much more belated is critical commentary on it? Since photography, and now, as Pepe Karmel (1998) has meticulously demonstrated, digital computer composites derived from Namuth's negatives and contact sheets can document how the paintings came to be, why do we need criticism at all? Donald Judd's assessment of the problem raised by Pollock's work in 1967 is still largely true: "art criticism [of Pollock] is very inferior to the work it discusses . . . It would take a big effort for me or for anyone else to think about Pollock's work in a way that would be intelligible" (quoted in Rose 1980: n.p.). This "big effort" has been replaced by a lot of intriguing, often brilliant, sidesteps of the central problem, which is a problem of narrative. Pollock's poured paintings refuse to tell a story, and more, they resist the stories we would like to tell about them. They do this by fully inhabiting the present tense. In making the poured paintings, Pollock did not do any predrawing or sketching. The painting came to be in the act of pouring, dancing, and establishing "contact" with the emerging landscape. In his encounter with Namuth, however, Pollock's energetic embrace of the present tense was framed by Namuth's lens. The photographs give us a before and after, a past and future tense, that the paintings themselves, and, in a sense, the painter himself, refused. They have allowed art historians and critics to overlook the antinarrative achievement of action painting at its best.[4]

So thoroughly has photography informed our sense of visual history, we have forgotten what was at stake in the collaboration between Pollock and Namuth. The best of the still photographs were made in 1950, when Pollock was deeply engaged in the poured paintings. In "Photographing Pollock," Namuth's 1980 recollection of his encounters with the painter, he describes meeting Pollock at an exhibition in East Hampton and suggesting that "it might be a good idea if you let me come and photograph you while you are painting." Pollock was initially reluctant but then he "promised he would start a new painting for me, and perhaps, finish it while I was still around." Namuth's "for me" is telling: with that phrase the photographer takes his first explicit steps toward imagining himself as the progenitor and inspiration for Pollock's painting. In the oral history interview Namuth did with Paul Cummings in 1971, nine years before his published memoir, Namuth says nothing of this promise. He simply says that they arranged a time to meet. In the published version, when Namuth arrives at the appointed time, Pollock reports flatly that he had finished the painting and there was nothing for Namuth to photograph. Defeated, Namuth asks if he can at least see the studio. Pollock, accompanied by the painter Lee Krasner, his wife, agrees to take Namuth to the small shed where he painted. Namuth continues:

I looked aimlessly through the ground glass of my Rolleiflex and began to take a few pictures. Pollock looked at the painting. Then, unexpectedly, he picked up can and paintbrush and started to move around the canvas. It was as if he suddenly realized the painting was not finished. His movements, slow at first, gradually became faster and more dance-like as he flung black, white, and rust-colored paint onto the canvas. My photography session lasted as long as he kept painting, perhaps half an hour. In all that time, Pollock did not stop. How long could one keep up that level of physical activity?[5] Finally he said, "This is it."

(Namuth 1980, n.p.).

There are many questions worth asking about this recollection, but for now I will concentrate only on the central one: why did Pollock decide that the painting he had just declared finished was actually unfinished? The intervening action between the statement of its completion and Pollock's decision to keep painting, or perhaps more accurately to repaint and paint over the painting, was Namuth's "aimless" shooting. Just before he began shooting, Namuth remembers, "Blinding shafts of sunlight hit the wet canvas making its surface hard to see. There was complete silence. I looked aimlessly through the ground glass of my Rolleiflex and began to take a few pictures. Pollock looked at the painting..." Might it be that these "blinding" light rays caused Pollock himself to "lose contact" with his painting? Pollock was famous for insisting that he liked to have "contact" with the texture of his painting, and when they later created the voiceover for the movie in which he paints on glass, Pollock remarks that he lost contact with the painting and had to begin again.

Although Pollock worked on the floor, he intended his work to hang on the wall: thus his sense of how his work looked often underwent many permutations. None of these involved a predetermined idea of beginning or end. Krasner recalls: "Working around the canvas – in the 'arena' as he called it – there really was no absolute top or bottom. And leaving space between paintings, there was no absolute 'frame' the way there is working on a pre-stretched canvas. [...] He hated signing. There's something so final about a signature" (Krasner, n.p.). The signature edits and cuts into a field larger than the object cut from it. In Pollock's first encounter with Namuth, the difficulty of securing an ending is manifest. Pollock seems both to lose and to renew contact with his painting in the "blinding shafts of sunlight," refracting off the finely ground glass of Namuth's lens.

Pollock sees Namuth as a witness who cannot see and this failure prompts Pollock to repaint and/or to continue painting. Such a continuation/repetition within the field of the canvas transforms the completed painting into a "new" painting. This trans-formation has the advantage of restoring Namuth to his position as progenitor of Pollock's new painting. But it also works to obscure the more startling fact that the painting's status as finished is so provisional. Pollock's decision to paint anew the painting he had previously declared complete is made possible by a break in the traditional understandings of what a painting is and what a painting does. While the usual understanding of "action painting" successfully makes the case that a painting is an action, what has been overlooked is the fact that, at least in Pollock's case, that action has no discernible beginning, middle, or end. It as if Pollock wanted to enliven painting as a noun by expanding the possibilities of painting as a verb. Taking action right to the edge of what is still recognizably painting, Pollock himself sometimes seemed unable to discern if his efforts still counted *as* painting. Krasner recalls: "Jackson experienced extremes of insecurity and confidence.[. . .] In front of a very good painting [. . .] he asked me, 'Is this a painting?' Not is this a good painting or a bad one, but a *painting!*" (Krasner 1980, n.p., original emphasis).

For Pollock, there really is no such thing as a "finished" painting – there are instead "full" canvases. The radical concept of perpetually "open" paintings inaugurated by action painting remains a repressed topic in art history.[6] This repression stems partially from discrepancies in the archival record. For example, in his essay for the 1998 catalog, Karmel includes Reuben Kadish's photograph of Pollock sitting in front of his painting, *Guardians of the Secret* (1943), in his 8th Street apartment in New York (Karmel 1998: 127–9). But that painting is remarkably different from the one that art historians think of when they see that title. Two versions of the same painting, both hung on walls in seemingly complete form, and two photographic documents of each give the lie to the concept of the "original" at the heart of both the modernist and capitalist economy (Krauss 1985). Here, the photographic record seems almost too full, contaminating the purity of the archive by introducing numerous versions of paintings all seemingly complete. What Pollock's work opens up is the possibility of an archive of ever-changing versions of the same paintings, versions which "pause" at different moments in the ongoing act of completion. A good many of these pauses have been recorded photographically (Pollock complicated the possibility of a stable archive even further by changing the titles of many of his paintings). Pollock's long preoccupation with numbers, both on the surfaces of his early paintings and as titles for the poured paintings, might well be a way of registering his sense of painting's resistance to singularity. When Clement Greenberg, often said to be the most influential of all of Pollock's commentators, remarked that the all-over paintings are "knit together of a multiplicity of identical or similar elements" that are repeated throughout the canvas, without "beginning, middle or end" (Greenberg 1948: 482), he came close to aligning painting with an aspect of performance that has little to do with action painting as it is commonly understood. This is where we can begin to glimpse Pollock's painting in its most radical aspect. Multiple versions of the same painting are akin to different performances of the same act, the same play. The repetitious and recursive quality of Pollock's painting, as both verb and noun, allowed Pollock to create paintings that risk their own disappearance and invisibility within the lens of a narrative art history deeply invested (in all senses) in a teleological master plot replete with action heroes and one-of-a-kind great works.

The present tense quality of Pollock's understanding of painting has been forgotten by art historians eager for the consolations of a secure ending. This has put enormous pressure on the end point of Pollock's poured paintings and on the end point of his life as well. That ending began to be written and absorbed in the elevation of Namuth's photographs and memoir into a kind of "pure" documentary record. In this record,

Namuth is all powerful: he inspires the painter to work anew on a painting already declared complete, and more crucially, his efforts to capture Pollock's methods by filming the painter working on glass, pushed Pollock off the wagon.[7] The same night they finished filming, Pollock resumed drinking, after two years of sobriety. Art historians, biographers, and the Hollywood film community are all in agreement: Pollock's performances for Namuth's camera ended his greatest works, and perhaps ended the man himself.

Perhaps. But perhaps after all this time we might yet get out from the enormous weight of this surety. The poured paintings, for Rosenberg, are dramatic dialogues. "Each stroke had to be a decision and was answered by a new question. By its very nature, action painting is painting in the medium of difficulties" (Rosenberg 1952: 48–9). The difficulties come, I believe, not so much from the canvases, but rather from the questions they raise about how to discuss them. The almost ecstatic suspensions of Pollock's paintings that I alluded to earlier can certainly be seen as "difficulties." But the paintings can also be seen as lyrical celebrations of flow. The movement across Pollock's surfaces is dense, but it is also majestic, engaging, fully present. The anguish and emotional turmoil that many see in the paintings might be the result of reading them through the lens of Pollock's end, his death, a death that is itself suspended between narratives of suicide, murder, and tragic accident. But before turning to that event, let's pause for a moment on the overdetermined encounter between painter and photographer, as narrated by Namuth.

Namuth's narrative tells us much more about what happened for him out in the barn than it sheds light on Pollock. The painter is a moving figure illuminated only as light filters through the lens of Namuth's prose. In the space between these three sentences of Namuth's record, "the action" of the actionist painting is born: "I looked aimlessly through the ground glass of my Rolleiflex and began to take a few pictures. Pollock looked at the painting. Then, unexpectedly, he picked up can and paintbrush and started to move around the canvas." These gestures across the immense field of *One: Number 31, 1950* (about 10 ft by 16 ft) recorded by Namuth produce the vocabulary and discourse of action painting. Namuth's first published comment about the session, "It was a great drama," underlined and gave language to the photographs he produced. "The flame of explosion when the paint hit the canvas; the dance-like movement; the eyes tormented before knowing where to strike next; the tension, then the explosion again" (Namuth 1951). These "tormented eyes" were what kept the two men at their dance, both trying to see and to be seen as great artists. It was not long before they found a conflict. One looks "through" a glass lens but one looks "at" a painting. Suppose the canvas could itself function as a glass? Pollock had been experimenting with making cutouts within the surface of his painting for some time, intent on revising the traditional figure/ground relation. In *Out of the Web: Number 7* (1949), for example, the cutout shapes reveal the brown fiberboard beneath the canvas. Splattered with small daubs of paint, these cutouts help unify the swirling pattern on the surface, even while they upset the boundary between figure and ground central to narrative painting.

Namuth, afire with his quest to see Pollock's creativity ever more fully, soon wants a more mobile camera to record the actions of the painter. Karmel carefully analyzes the black and white film (Karmel 1998: 106–11) that resulted from Namuth's first efforts with the movie camera.[8] I will concentrate here on his second effort, the color film that concludes with the extraordinary glass painting. Namuth was not satisfied with the black and white film.

> I soon found that a film, like a short story, needs a beginning, middle, and an end. It wasn't enough to show a painter painting. I wanted more [...] I wanted to show the artist at work with his full face in view, becoming part of the canvas, inside the canvas so to speak – coming at the viewer – through the painting itself.
>
> (Namuth 1980, n.p.)

Discontent with documenting from the outside, Namuth wants to enter the painting with Pollock. (In the winter of 1947–48, Pollock had commented: "When I am *in* my painting, I'm not aware of what I am doing.") They decided that the best way to do this would be for Pollock to paint on glass.

Perhaps if we focus on the allure of the glass for Pollock and Namuth we can gain access to the drama of the encounter between the painter and the photographer in the transformative film they made together. Whereas in the still photographs Pollock seems to be the object of a seemingly neutral documentary impulse, the strange point-of-view shots of the movie make such illusionary neutrality impossible to sustain.[9] Shooting from beneath the mounted glass on which Pollock paints, Namuth seems to embrace the traditional shot/counter-shot structure of narrative cinema. In this tradition, the point-of-view shot of the protagonist is expected. But Namuth withholds this shot because of the actual architectural arrangements of the filming. He lies on the ground and positions himself where the canvas might be if Pollock were working on the ground. Shooting up into the glass suspended halfway between them, Namuth captures Pollock looking at the painting but cannot show us what he sees. By filming only his own gaze at Pollock, Namuth's film unwittingly suggests that there is something besides paint caught within the glass that screens him from Pollock. The camera's focus passes beyond the glass of the painting and encompasses the blue sky above Pollock's head. This shimmering blue of the sky fades as the film continues, coloring the glass painting itself. Pollock becomes the figure in the field of Namuth's lens even as the painter tried to avoid the pull of narrative carried by the figurative in his own work.

What transpires as each man performs on different sides of the glass canvas, the glass lens? If Pollock "dances," Namuth surely partners him. Two mediums. Two men. Too much?

III

"The Story of Jackson Pollock and the Allure of Glass," that's what I'd like to read, to write, to know. It's gotta be the glass. Shattered. Refracted. And still beckoning.

It's gotta be the glass. Object relations: I wish Pollock had gone to a Winicottian rather than a Jungian when he explored his unconscious. Glass contains light. It's heavy. It can ground you in a sea of alcohol. It can hold the paint when the paint won't dry. It can layer the colors so you can make weight literal – emphasis added, like a writer with italics. Glass is necessary to a (good) mirror, but if you grind up the former, no one minds, unless you put it in your skin. If you put it to sleep in the sea's paint, if you dance in front of its ground lens, you'll be fine. Right?

One good glass deserves another. Painting on glass and watching Namuth's glass lens capture him, Pollock seems to have rekindled a desire for another glass. "I saw him there with two larges glasses filled to the brim with bourbon. I protested, but he had already emptied his glass, his first drink in two years. It was not long before he had a second" (Namuth 1980, n.p.). The painting was finished, so, perhaps, why not the painter? Why not be done with the infernal dancing, filming, starting and stopping, reshooting the same acts over and over? It was not the camera that was mechanical during this shooting; it was the artist who was asked to repeat his entrance into the frame, into the glass canvas, again and again. "Can you do it again, one more time, but this time, can we do it on glass?"

It's gotta be glass. End it by finally going into the glass, going through the glass painting. "I am the painting" and the painting cuts. Shards of light open the skin, while shafts of light blind. The glass calls and cuts, screens and reflects. Finally Namuth says the film is finished. They go inside and Pollock pours two glasses of bourbon. Lee Krasner has arranged a dinner party. Ten guests. Pollock is already in the can: Namuth's film preserves his gestures with pigment in light. His actions, like his paintings, are no longer ephemeral. Indeed, his actions become a way to open the discourse about his painting.

Pollock is the figure in the painting now, his actions are the events that make the painting, but it's no longer his painting. The glass cuts both ways. Ten guests at the table. He is being served up. Different memories recorded about the food, the date (Potter 1985: 129–30). Some guests agree that Namuth and Pollock were each accusing one another of being a "phony." A bad performer. A fake. There is a difference between creating and recording. Belatedly Pollock discovers this, after he is in the can, after the tumblers of bourbon cut through his throat, after two years dry. Pollock does not like losing. He turns the table. All the glassware breaks. Inner wars breaking out. Lee Krasner says the party will continue in the other room. Even now, the party still unfinished.

Later, the art historians said he made a Faustian bargain with the devil of Namuth's camera. Namuth's contact sheets, some five hundred images in all, caused him to lose contact with his painting. I don't think it's so simple; most bargains aren't. The canvas was glass. He left it outside. A kind of window in a field in Long Island. But where were the inner rooms? The island surrounded everywhere by water. Pollock had already painted Moby Dick *(1943): a field of blue with scratches of tic-tac-toe, a topsy-turvy ship. What holds the whiteness of the whale? Who is the captain in the game of being blue?*

Pollock, they said, was never the same after Namuth finished filming. After the first glass, he kept drinking. He lost his way. Driving home one night after too many glasses of too much alcohol, Pollock took a curve too quickly. He was with Ruth Kligman, a young painter with whom he was having an affair, and Ruth's friend, Edith Metzger. The women were screaming for Pollock to slow down, but he was listening to the tires screeching, to the wind, and then he went off the road, flew above the glass windshield, and into a tree. Pollock and Metzger died instantly; after a long recuperation, Kligman recovered. Greenberg, the critic who did the most to establish Pollock's reputation while the artist was alive, refused to speak at his funeral, because he viewed the accident as a murder-suicide.

On his last night, Pollock broke the glass, shattered narrative and entered myth. He became a celebrity, founded a School. Dead at 44, he was turned into a father of performance art, an American hero, a mythic, laconic cowboy. Edith Metzger is largely forgotten. Kligman is remembered for her memoir, Love Affair, *that tells the story of their relationship and Pollock's death, and for her friendship with Andy Warhol, who called her "the car wreck girl."*

Through a glass, darkly. Flying through the narrative that embedded him in a "medium of difficulties," Pollock entered myth. Edith Metzger played the role of his sacrificial victim. Right from the beginning, when Pliny describes the origin of the first painting and remarks that the artist was a sailor about to go on a long sea voyage and wanted to leave his image with his beloved, art-making has been unduly burdened with attention to the narrative situation of the artist. Thus we know more about Pollock's drinking habits than about the order of his interest in Melville. (How the man wanted to drown! The Deep *(1953) is just an ice cube floating on the surface of his thirst.)*

"Criticism," Andy Warhol told Bob Colacello, "is so old-fashioned. Why don't you just put in a lot of gossip?" (Colacello 1990: 62). But that's what we already do. Pollock, they say, went to seed after Namuth turned off his camera. But the actions of artists are not contained only in the objects that remain after the events they brought into being come to an end. These actions are like the light held in glass: they ripple and enlighten, obscure and flatter. Through a glass, lightly. Through a glass, darkly. Pollock's paintings refuse narrative because they are about motion that never finds its destination; they repeat lines because the line is broken. The trauma of that brokenness makes linearity inadequate after the war, after photography displaces painting's ethical and aesthetic force in a world in which everything must be mediated and seen through glass. Everything screened, nothing direct. Pollock's paintings are unphotographable, although Pollock in the act of painting, performing for the lens, is the image that launched a history of a living art form called performance art. Pollock's paintings refuse to succumb to photography's more general conquering of all visual art.. They remain forever in motion, suspended there in the pulsating blur between shattering glass and endless ground.

Notes

1 Thanks to Jim Phelan for helpful advice about this section of my argument. Suzanne Fleischman (1990) argues that the proper tense of narrative is the past; the use of the present tense, she claims, renders discourse as either lyric or drama. Pollock's paintings combine elements of both; indeed, it would not be far off to claim that Pollock creates "lyrical dramas." See J. Phelan (1994).

2 The literature about this topic is vast. But Trachtenberg (1980) has assembled a superb collection of the most important debates in the nineteenth and early twentieth centuries.

3 Toward the end of 1950, Pollock created *Number 32, 1950*, a large (8 ft by 15 ft), black painting on an off-white canvas. In 1951 and 1952, Pollock continued to work with black and white almost exclusively. One of the best

of these is *Echo: Number 25, 1951*. Black and white are, of course, colors, but since photography and its vocabulary are so dominant, sometimes the black and white paintings are mistakenly assumed to be without color.

4 In describing Pollock's paintings as antinarrative I do not mean to imply there are absolutely no stories at work in the paintings. Nor do I mean to overlook the connections between the "trace" of the ephemeral act of action painting that remains on the canvas and the "trace" of the past that photography captures. But I am saying that the narratives inspired by photography are far more congenial to critical writing than are the traces of the past that constitute the surface of Pollock's paintings.

5 Namuth, perhaps unwittingly, responds to the forceful present tense of Pollock's painting here as he switches from his past tense narration to the eternal now of this question.

6 It should be noted that my sense of what is radical about action painting differs markedly from what Rosenberg thought it was. The best discussion of Rosenberg's work I've read is Orton (2000).

7 The completed glass painting, *Number 29, 1950*, is now owned by The National Gallery of Canada, Ottawa.

8 Soussloff (2004) has an excellent discussion of Namuth's black and white film that differs markedly from Karmel's.

9 Krauss (1980: n.p) deconstructs this apparent neutrality.

References and Further Reading

Austin, J. L. (1962). *How To Do Things With Words*. Oxford: Oxford University Press.

Benjamin, W. ([1931] 1980). "A Short History of Photography." In Alan Trachtenberg (ed.), *Classic Essays on Photography* (pp. 199–216). New Haven, CT: Leete's Island Books.

Clay, J. (1977). "Hans Namuth: Art Critic." *Macula* 2: 24–5.

Cohn, D. (1999). *The Distinction of Fiction*. Baltimore, MD: Johns Hopkins Press.

Colacello, R. (1990). *Holy Terror: Andy Warhol Close Up*. New York: HarperCollins.

Fleischman, S. (1990). *Tense and Narrativity: From Medieval Performance to Modern Fiction*. Austin: University of Texas Press.

Goodnough, R. (1951). "Pollock Paints a Picture." *Artnews* 50 (3): 38–41, 60–1.

Greenberg, C. (1948). "The Crisis of the Easel Picture." *Partisan Review*, 15 (April): 481–4. (Also reprinted in *Clement Greenberg: The Collected Essays and Criticism, Volume. 2: Arrogant Purpose, 1945–49* (pp. 222–4), ed. J. O'Brian. Chicago: University of Chicago Press, 1986.)

Foucault, M. (1978) *The History of Sexuality, Volume 1: An Introduction*. New York: Random House.

Jones, A. (1998). *Body Art: Performing the Subject*. Minneapolis: University of Minnesota Press.

Karmel, P. (1998). "Pollock at Work: The Films and Photographs of Hans Namuth." In K. Varnedoe with P. Karmel, *Jackson Pollock* (pp. 87–137). New York: The Museum of Modern Art/Harry N. Abrams.

Krasner, L. (1980). "An Interview with Lee Krasner Pollock by B. H. Friedman." In B. Rose (ed.) *Pollock Painting* (n.p.). New York: Agrinde Publications.

Krauss, R. (1980). "Reading Photographs as Texts." In B. Rose (ed.), *Pollock Painting* (n.p.). New York: Agrinde Publications.

Krauss, R. (1985). *The Originality of the Avant-Garde and Other Modernist Myths*. Cambridge, MA and London: The MIT Press.

McEvilley, T. (1998). "Stages of Energy: Performance Art Ground Zero?" In M. Abramović, *Artist Body, Performances 1969–1998* (pp. 14–25). Milan, Italy: Charta.

McKenzie, J. (2000). *Perform – Or Else!* New York and London: Routledge.

Namuth, H. (1951). "Jackson Pollock." *Portfolio: The Annual of the Graphic Arts* 3, n.p.

Namuth, H. (1971). "Hans Namuth Oral History Interview Conducted by Paul Cummings." Smithsonian Archives of American Art, <artarchives.si.edu/oralhist/namuth71.htm>.

Namuth, H. (1980). "Photographing Pollock – A Memoir." In B. Rose (ed.), *Pollock Painting* (n.p.): New York: Agrinde Publications.

Orton, F. (2000). "Action, Revolution and Painting." In F. Frascina (ed.), *Pollock and After: The Critical Debate* (pp. 261–87). New York: Routledge, 2nd edn.

Phelan, J. (1994). "Present Tense Narration: Mimesis, the Narrative Norm, and Positioning the Reader in *Waiting for the Barbarians*." In J. Phelan and P. Rabinowitz (eds.), *Understanding Narrative* (pp. 222–45). Columbus: Ohio State University Press.

Phelan, P. (1993). *Unmarked: The Politics of Performance*. New York and London: Routledge.

Phelan, P. (2004). "Lessons in Blindness from Samuel Beckett." *PMLA* 119.5 :1279–88.

Potter, J. (1985). *To a Violent Grave: An Oral Biography of Jackson Pollock*. New York: G. P. Putnam's Sons.

Roueché, B. (1950). "Unframed Space." *The New Yorker* 26 (24), 5 August: 16.

Rose, B. (1980). "Namuth's Photographs and the Pollock Myth." In B. Rose (ed.) *Pollock Painting* (n.p.). New York: Agrinde Publications.

Rosenberg, H. (1952). "The American Action Painters." *Artnews* 51 (8): 22–3, 48–50.

Trachtenberg, A. (ed.) (1980). *Classic Essays on Photography*. New Haven, CT: Leete's Island Books.

Schimmel, P. (1998) *Out of Actions: Between Performance and the Object 1949–1979*. Los Angeles: Museum of Contemporary Art.

Soussloff, C. M. (2004). "Jackson Pollock's Post-Ritual Performance: Memories Arrested in Space." *TDR: A Journal of Performance Studies* 48 (1, T181): 60–78.

Epilogue

34

Narrative and Digitality: Learning to Think With the Medium

Marie-Laure Ryan

We all know that computers are programmable machines. This means, technically, that they execute commands, one after the other, in a tempo regulated by the pulses of an internal clock. This also means, in the domain of artistic expression, that the behavior of digital objects is regulated by the invisible code of a program. This program often plays a double role: it presides over the creation of the text, and it displays it on the screen. If we regard dependency on the hardware of the computer as the distinctive feature of the medium family known as "digital" (or more commonly as "new media"), then the various types of text-creating and text-displaying software (also known as "authoring systems") should be regarded as the submedia of digitality. It is evident that developments on the level of hardware had a crucial impact on the features of digital texts: for instance, faster processors and expanded storage capabilities allowed the integration of text, image, and sound, while the creation of large computer networks allowed communications between multiple users and the collaborative construction of the text. But the form and content of digital texts, as well as the reader's experience, are also affected by the underlying code.

In this essay I propose to revisit the evolution of digital narrative over the past 25 years, presenting it as the story of the relations between software support and textual products and asking of each authoring system: what are its special affordances, and how do these affordances affect the construction of narrative meaning? Though my study will cover multimedia narratives, I will limit my investigation to texts that rely on language as their principal mode of presentation. This means that I will ignore video games, one of the most productive domains of narrative activity in digital media.

Before embarking on this investigation, let me enumerate the properties of digital systems that I regard as the most relevant for narrative and textuality:

1 *Interactive and reactive nature*: the computer's ability to take in voluntary or involuntary user input and to adjust its behavior accordingly.
2 *Volatile signs and variable display*: what enables bits in memory to change value, causing pixels on the screen to change color. This property explains the unparalleled fluidity of digital images.
3 *Multiple sensory and semiotic channels*: what makes the computer pass as the synthesis of all "old" media.
4 *Networking capabilities*: the possibility of connecting computers across space, bringing their users together in virtual environments.

A text that takes advantage in a narratively significant way of one or more of these properties is a text that thinks with its medium. This is not the case of all digitally encoded narratives. When Stephen King posted one of his novels on the Internet in order to bypass the publisher (an experiment that eventually failed), he was using the networking capabilities of the computer as a channel of transmission, not as a means of expression. He may have been thinking with the medium in economic terms, but he was certainly not doing so in narrative terms. Thinking with the medium is no easy task for authors of narratives (or, should one say, for designers of narrative experiences), because only the third of the above properties is inherently supportive of narrative meaning. Interactivity breaks the linear flow of narrative and removes control from the designer; volatility impedes the thorough scrutiny of the text that is often necessary to appreciate the subtleties of narrative meaning; and networking – by this I mean connecting a large number of users for a live exchange – is more likely to produce undisciplined chat than the collaborative production of a sustained narrative action.

Whether or not a text thinks with its medium is a value judgment rather than an objective observation. This judgment acknowledges the text's ability to create an original experience which cannot be duplicated in any other medium, an experience which makes the medium seem truly necessary. Thinking with the medium is not the overzealous exploitation of all the features offered by the authoring system, but an art of compromise between the affordances of the system and the demands of narrative meaning. Nor is thinking *with* the medium synonymous with thinking *about* the medium, a formula which describes the currently fashionable habit of sprinkling digital texts with theoretical comments on the nature of digital textuality. A work that truly thinks with its medium does not have to think about it, because it inspires readers to do the thinking themselves.

I

The first narrative genre that grew up and ran exclusively in a digital environment was a purely textual hybrid of game and literature known as Interactive Fiction (henceforth abbreviated as IF). The classics of the genre are the games produced by the now defunct company Infocom, especially the 1980 Zork adventures, but the literary minded will mostly remember *Mindwheel*, a so-called "electronic novel" written by the poet Robert Pinsky (1984). Born in the early 1980s, when personal computers first made their appearance, IF is a dialogue system in which the user, manipulating a character (henceforth referred to as the avatar), interacts with the machine not through the selection of an item from a fixed menu, but through a relatively free production of text: the user can type whatever he or she wants, though the parser associated with the system will understand only a limited number of verbs and nouns. "In this genre of fiction," says the website of Inform, the authoring system most commonly used nowadays for the production of IF, "the computer describes a world and the player types instructions like **touch the mirror** for the protagonist character to follow; the computer responds by describing the result, and so on until a story is told."[1]

All narratives can be said to describe a world, but the engine that operates IF goes one step further, in that it not only evokes a world through visible text, but also constructs a *productive* model of this world through computer-language statements that the player never gets to see. These statements specify the general laws that define the user's range of options, and determine the results of the avatar's actions. For instance, if Coca-Cola is described as both liquid and toxic in the computer's world-model, and if the user makes the avatar drink a can of Coke, the action will result in the avatar's death. When the player takes an action, the system updates its model of the current state of the fictional world, for instance, by canceling the attribute "alive" of the avatar after he ingests poison. When the attributes of an object change, so do the various actions to which the object lends itself. This type of productive engine is known as a simulation, a concept that contrasts with standard narrative representation: whereas narrative representation usually recreates past events (real or fictional), simulation produces events looking forward, as we do when we live our lives, and it generates different courses of events with every run of the program, depending on the player's input.

The coherence of the stories generated by the system is guaranteed by the world-rules, and by the fact that every episode involves the player's character. When the world-rules are inconsistent with each other, or with common world knowledge, the narrative becomes illogical or unpredictable. For instance, if Coca-Cola is not defined as liquid, the system will block the avatar's attempt to imbibe the substance with the message "you cannot do that." In a standard narrative there is no need to mention that Coke is liquid, because the reader will make the inference on the basis of real-world experience; but in IF, every relevant property must be specified in the invisible code, since the proper development of the narrative depends as much on the knowledge-base of the computer as on the reader's inferential capabilities – and unlike the reader, the computer cannot make inferences on the basis of life experience!

The design of the world-model that underlies IF begins with the creation of a geography made up of distinct sites (or "rooms," in the jargon) connected by a network of passageways. The underlying map of the fictional world specifies what sites are adjacent to every location, and what objects are contained in the various areas. From the cave of the robbers, for instance, it may be possible to go east to the forest, or to crawl west through a narrow shaft to the secret room that holds the treasure, but the player cannot go through the wall to the north or to the south unless he or she picks up a magic pebble on the floor of the cave. To move efficiently around the fictional world, the player needs to construct a mental or graphic map of its spatial organization.

The prominence of the geographical layout, and the fact that texts of IF are games, predisposes these texts to an epic structure or to a mystery-story framework that foregrounds the theme of the quest. In this archetypal pattern, the player-hero receives a task, and to accomplish this mission, sets out on a journey through the fictional world. During this journey the player visits various places and solves various problems with the help of objects or information gathered along the way.

Though the world-model allows different narratives to unfold – in principle a new one for each game-session – these narratives are not all equally satisfying to the player: some end with the fulfillment of the mission, others lead to the death of the avatar. To parody Tolstoy, we can say that the unhappy narratives are unhappy in many different ways, while the happy narratives all follow the same route. It is, however, important to distinguish the variable stories created by the player's actions from the predetermined "master narrative" (or narratives) written into the system as the solution(s) of the game. Whereas one player will make 10 unsuccessful attempts to open the door that leads to the treasure, another will use the right tool straight-away. The adventures of these two players (or rather, of their avatars) in the game-world will produce different sequences of events, and bring different text to the screen, but both players will eventually perform the same actions to complete the master plot.

Reading (and playing) for the masterplot is not the only way to approach IF, or computer games in general. For the true connoisseur, one of the special pleasures of the genre lies in trying to evade the control of the game-designer, in the best tradition of deconstructive reading. A world-model in which every law, as well as every property of every object, must be specified is bound to present inconsistencies and fatal omissions – "bugs," in the programming jargon. The subversive reader will engage in an active search for these bugs, in the hope of coaxing unplanned stories or delightful nonsense out of the system. Espen Aarseth (1997: 123–4) describes a particularly amusing bug in Marc Blank's *Deadline* (1982), a mystery story in which the player must find the murderer of a wealthy businessman, Mr Robner. If the player maliciously decides to interview Mr Robner himself, the system will forget that he is dead, and the player will be able to strike up a conversation with him. The system will not allow the player to arrest Mr Robner for his own murder, invoking insufficient evidence, but if the player shoots Mr Robner, the system will declare the mystery solved, and will send the player to jail.

For the narratologist, IF is a goldmine of illocutionary situations, discourse modes and interplay of diegetic levels that expands significantly the technical repertory of language-based narrative. Usually told in the second person and in the present tense, IF is one of the rare narrative forms where the use of "you" enters into a truly dialogical rather than merely rhetorical relation with an Other, and where "present" denotes narrow coincidence between the time of the narrated events and the time of the narration. Rather than imaginatively pre-existing to the act of narration, the events of the fictional world are made to happen at the very moment of their description through the performative force of the discourse that appears on the screen. Or to be more precise, they happen as soon as the user presses the return key, for narrative time is suspended when the user types a response.

The most distinctive narratological feature of IF, when compared to either print narrative or to the other digital forms discussed in this essay, is the construction of the story through a movement that leads in and out of the diegesis – in and out of the fictional world. Standard narrative fiction adopts a unified, world-internal point of view. But in IF, some utterances can be attributed to a narrator situated within the fictional world, for instance:

> Player: Kill Mr. Robner.
> System [as narrator]: With a lethal blow of your hand, Mr. Robner falls dead. Your mind becomes confused amidst strange screaming, yelling, and the pangs of your conscience. "How could I have done it?" you ask yourself, as you hear the distant sound of police sirens. Sergeant Duffy and two other officers enter and grab you rather unceremoniously.
> (Blank 1982, quoted in Aarseth 1997: 123–4)

while others (marked in italics in the example below) represent an external voice, the voice of the system that produces the story in collaboration with the player:

> System [as narrator]: A plain metal door faces you to the east, near the alley's end. It's firmly shut.
> Player: Open door.
> System: *You don't see how.*
> Player: Scream in despair.
> System: *That's not a verb I recognize.*
> (Plotkin, *Spider and Web*)

This game of in-and-out of the fictional world opens the possibility of metaleptic transgressions of ontological boundaries. For instance, the members of the fictional world are not supposed to be aware of the existence of the system that operates them – no more than the characters of a novel are supposed to be aware of their fictionality. But conventions exist to be broken: as Nick Montfort (2003) observes, a character in Steve Meretzky's *Planetfall* comments, within the IF world, on the use of the SAVE directive, which, as part of the system, is external to the fictional world. When the player types SAVE, the character exclaims: "Oh boy, are we going to try something dangerous now?"

The player's input displays the same variety of positions with respect to the diegesis as the system's responses. When dialoguing with a character, the player speaks in the name of his or her avatar, within the fictional world, and the player's input is an integral part of the narrative. For instance:

> System [as character]: You're going to start by telling me how you got through that door. Do you understand me?
> Player [as avatar]: Yes.
> System [as narrator]: The man nods briefly – a man satisfied with the least important detail.
>
> (Plotkin, *Spider and Web*)

On the other hand, when players make their avatar perform an action, usually through a two-word sentence, their input is not treated by the system as part of the narration, but as a command external to the text. The system fulfills the command by expanding the player's input into a more vivid description of the event, and by detailing its consequences:

> Player: Kiss Gil.
> System [as narrator]: You purse your sensuous lips and give one of the bums a medium-long, fairly wet kiss.
>
> (From Robert Pinsky, *Mindwheel*, quoted from Campbell 1987: 78).

Much – arguably too much – has been made of the creative role of the reader in digital environments. The fact that the system of IF rewrites most of the player's input puts a serious damper on the claim that interactivity turns the reader into a coauthor. Even though players interact through language, most of their contributions are treated as paratext, and they are not allowed to participate directly in the writing process.

Still, by inviting the reader to become in imagination not merely an anonymous recipient of a report of past events, as does standard fiction, but a personalized member of a fictional world and an active participant in a pseudo-live action, IF pioneered a type of narrative experience that takes full advantage of the interactivity of digital media, and that represents consequently the purest form of thinking with the medium. Video games added sensory channels to IF, and they allowed users to interact in real time rather than in suspended time through keyboard input that simulates physical action, but they owe much of their popularity to the same idea of impersonating an active character in a fictional world.[2]

II

In the late 1980s two factors contributed to the temporary demise of purely text-based interactive fiction.[3] For lovers of games, the fatal blow was dealt by the improvement of graphic interfaces. The text screen of the earlier Zork episodes looked rather bleak, compared to the visually rendered game-world, the film clips, and the talking characters of the later installments. Meanwhile, for lovers of literature, IF was outstaged by hypertext, a new digital genre that burst onto the scene with a blaze of theoretical publicity. How could a mere game compete in intellectual sophistication with a genre that was heralded as the verification of the ideas of Barthes, Foucault, Derrida, Deleuze, Guattari, and Kristeva on the nature of textuality? [4]

Most of us associate hypertext with texts composed from the late 1980s to mid-1990s with the authoring program Storyspace: works such as Michael Joyce's (1987) *afternoon: a story*, Stuart Moulthrop's (1991) *Victory Garden*, and Shelley Jackson's (1995) *Patchwork Girl*, all sold by Eastgate Systems. Storyspace was designed with a certain type of literary text in mind,[5] namely large projects representing the digital equivalent of the novel, and for many readers this model has come to pass as the canonical form of hypertext narrative: *afternoon*, and to a lesser extent *Victory Garden* and *Patchwork Girl*, are indeed regarded as the classics of the genre.

Compared to the Infocom engine Storyspace is a very simple program. There is no need to write code, and the composition process is only slightly more complicated than writing with a word processor. While Infocom fictions enable the reader to communicate with the machine through language, Storyspace responds exclusively to the clicking of the mouse.[6] And while Infocom constructs a world on the basis of rules which can be regarded as a rudimentary artificial intelligence component, Storyspace limits its operation to the mechanical combination of textual fragments, without any knowledge of their content. This means that instead of keeping an internal representation of the evolving state of the fictional world, and of sifting a database of logical rules to decide which episodes can follow one another, Storyspace only needs to perform jumps to certain memory addresses and to display their data when the user clicks on a word designated as link. Storyspace hypertexts are much more deterministic in their mode of operation than interactive fiction.

A Storyspace hypertext is a network of links and nodes, also called lexia. The lexia correspond to units of text – the digital equivalent of the page. When the user clicks on a link, the system displays a new page on the screen. Since there are usually several links on a page, the reader can activate several different lexia, which means that the order of presentation of the lexia is variable. This property of hypertexts is generally known as nonlinearity, though multilinearity would be a better term, since the reader's choices inevitably result in a sequential order. In most texts the words that serve as anchors to the links are marked with special fonts, to make them visible to the reader; but this feature is optional. In *afternoon*, for instance, the links remain hidden. This turns the reader's exploration of the text into a blind navigation, or into a search for Easter eggs – the Easter eggs of what Joyce calls "the words that yield."

To help authors keep the complexity of the database under control, Storyspace generates a map that shows the current state of the developing network of links and nodes. Some of the finished products, for instance *Patchwork Girl*, make these maps available to the reader as part of the interface while others, such as *afternoon*, keep the map hidden. The possibility of consulting the map makes it possible to bypass the system of links designed by the author. In *Patchwork Girl*, the reader can indeed reach any node visible on the map by clicking on its image. But because the networks of Storyspace hypertexts are much larger that what can be shown on a screen, maps cannot be displayed in their totality, and they never allow free movement through the text.

Reinforcing the name of the program, the feature of the map accounts for what has become the most lasting legacy of Storyspace: the conceptualization of hypertext narrative in terms of spatial metaphors, such as the labyrinth or the Garden of Forking Paths. The Storyspace toolbox facilitates the creation of dense networks of links, but the complexity of these networks usually give the reader the sense of being lost in a maze, because the proliferation of choices turns navigation into a series of blind decisions, and because heavily connected networks create the possibility of running in circles.[7] But if Storyspace frames the act of reading as an exploration of textual space, this space has nothing to do with the imaginary geography of a fictional world, as it did in IF. Textual space is determined by the two dimensions of the text map, which itself is the graphic representation of the network of links and nodes that underlies the text. This space is purely virtual, because the text itself is stored in computer memory as a unidimensional string of zeroes and ones. As Alan Turing has indeed demonstrated, all computable tasks can be performed by a machine that reads an infinitely long tape.

To open a new type of space, Storyspace hypertexts sacrifice another dimension of literary narrative, namely the reader's immersion in the stream of narrative time. The fragmentation of the hypertext format stands in the way of the feverish anticipation that we call "reading for the plot." There are no thrillers, no suspense stories, no dramatic curves of rising and falling tension in hypertext fiction. Suspense effects are highly dependent on the management of what the reader knows and does not know at every moment of the reading experience; but when the linearization of the text is left to the reader – which means generally that it is left to chance – the author cannot control the disclosure of information. In a Storyspace hypertext, the plot is not something that reveals itself in response to the reader's desire to know what happens next; it is rather an image that the reader constructs by traveling through the virtual space of the text, collecting narrative fragments at every stop, and trying to assemble these fragments into a meaningful pattern. This mode of reading can be compared to the activity of putting a jigsaw puzzle together by picking up individual pieces and connecting them into a picture that makes visual sense. The main difference between puzzles and hypertext lies in the fact that hypertext, in keeping with postmodern aesthetics, may prevent the formation of a complete picture, or that it may lead to the construction of many conflicting partial images.

Some theorists (e.g., Landow 1997) have argued that every itinerary through hypertext fiction produces a different story, but this claim is unrealistic, because it would mean that the events represented in the lexia can be endlessly permuted, and still yield a coherent narrative sequence. This is to forget that narrative meaning is fundamentally linear. Since it is regulated by the one-directional relations of causality, psychological motivation, and temporal sequence, narrative meaning cannot be freely created by the reader, and it cannot emerge from a partly random combination of textual fragments. In IF the narrative coherence of the various traversals was insured by the logical rules, by the fact that all episodes involved the player's character, and by the general assumption that their order of presentation corresponds to their chrono-logical order in the storyworld. But in Storyspace hypertext the reader is external to the text, and the system cannot control his or her itinerary beyond the current node.[8] This make it impossible to insure that the succession of lexia will respect narrative logic. What differs with every reading is not story but discourse, not the narrated events themselves, but the dynamics of their disclosure.

But the reconstruction of a reasonably consistent story from a scrambled discourse would quickly become a tiresome activity if the reader's role were exhausted by the metaphor of the jigsaw puzzle. Any picture can be cut up, boxed, and sold as a puzzle. A rigid mapping of hypertext onto puzzles would therefore mean that the significance of the reader's involvement is independent of the narrative content of the text. From a literary point of view, the best hypertexts are those that manage to present the reader's activity of moving through the network and reassembling the narrative as a symbolic gesture endowed with a meaning specific to the text, a meaning which cannot be predicted by reading the medium as a built-in message, as Marshall McLuhan's famous formula advocates. This ability to adapt the narrative subject matter and the role of the reader to the hypertextual mechanism is what I call thinking with the medium. Here are two examples of this type of thinking.

The short story *Twelve Blue* by Michael Joyce contains several narrative subworlds, each inhabited by different characters, but connected by common themes. (Foremost among them is the theme of drowning.) An interface of colorful threads, which suggests destiny lines, dangles the promise of stories. By clicking on a thread of a given color the reader is able to follow the life of a certain character for a limited time, but the thread eventually decays, and the reader is switched to a different plot line, as if memory had failed, or as if the synapses of the brain had suddenly fired in another direction. The whole process resembles stream of consciousness, except that the stream runs through the minds and private worlds of many characters. The random activity of clicking and bringing text to the screen thus mimics the mysterious functioning of memory, the fluidity of dream, and the operation of a collective consciousness. But it is only because the colored threads can keep us for a while in the world of the same individual that we become familiar with the inner and outer lives of characters and learn to care for them. Joyce has successfully streamlined navigational choices to enhance narrative interest.

In Shelley Jackson's *Patchwork Girl*, the reader's clicking symbolizes the activity of sewing a crazy quilt from different pieces of material cut out from old garments. The quilting theme allegorizes the postmodern practice of constructing a text out of disparate, often recycled, elements. *Patchwork Girl* abounds indeed in intertextual allusions, and includes both narrative fragments and theoretical considerations on the nature of its medium. But the reader's symbolic stitching also simulates the activity of two female figures: the heroine Mary Shelley (a fictional counterpart of the author of *Frankenstein*), who assembles a female monster by sewing together body parts collected from different women; and the author, Shelley Jackson, who constructs a narrative identity for the monster from the stories of these women.

III

The next milestone in the evolution of digital narrative is the development of two features of digital systems: the ability to encode and transmit visual and audio data efficiently; and the ability to connect personal computers into a world-spanning network. In the mid-1990s, digital narratives developed into multimedia texts, and the Internet became their primary mode of distribution. Since downloading is still slow, and space is limited on websites, this encouraged the creation of short texts. The major influence on the form of today's digital works is the widespread adoption of a program named Flash produced by Macromedia which allows what is called the "streaming" of information: when the user downloads a Flash movie – as the products are called – from the Web, the movie can start playing on the user's screen before all the data has been downloaded.

A program of superior multimedia capabilities, Flash can handle a wide variety of objects: text, bitmaps, vector graphics, and sound files. Unlike Storyspace it comes with a programming language that enables the user to specify the behaviors of these objects, such as undergoing transformations when the mouse cursor traverses certain areas of the screen. The label of "movie" that designates Flash products underscores another major difference from Storyspace: a shift in emphasis from spatial navigation to temporal dynamics. The forward movement of the movies allows animation effects, but the designer can control the flow of time, for instance, by making the movie stop on certain frames until the user activates a button or by looping back to a previous frame. Sometimes the Flash movie imposes its tempo on the user; sometimes users are able to determine how much time they want to spend on a certain frame. This temporal game of give and take, which makes it possible to alternate between the leisurely reading experience of books and the relentless forward movement of cinematic movies, is what makes interactive digital texts truly unique among media.

The emphasis of the program on temporal dynamics does not mean that Flash products neglect spatiality: the author works with a spatial display, called the stage, as well as with a temporal one, the timeline. But space in Flash means primarily the *visual space* of the stage, rather than the *topographical space* of a fictional world, as it does in IF games, or the *structural space* of the text, as it does in Storyspace hypertexts. This visual space is structured as a series of layers that give some depth to the image: an object located on a top layer will be in the foreground, and will partially hide the objects of a lower layer. One of the most productive effects of this lamination is the possibility of making objects emerge from the depth of the digital palimpsest when the user mouses over certain "hot spots."

It is difficult to predict where narrative is headed in the age of Flash. Most applications so far have been minigames, visual works, random combinations of sound, text, or picture fragments known as "remixes," "theoretical fictions" that privilege metatextual comments at the expense of narration,[9] concrete poetry, or visual adaptations of print poems. All we can say at the present time is that Flash narratives, because of the length restriction, will be neither the complex labyrinths of Storyspace nor the time-consuming quests of IF. It is impossible to give in the restricted space of this essay an idea of the variety of the current production. I will therefore limit my discussion to two texts that put Flash or Flash-like effects in the service of radically different aesthetic agendas: the first a postmodern exercise in antinarration; the second an attempt to facilitate the construction of narrative meaning through graphic design.

My first example accomplishes the paradoxical feat of rejecting both the linearity of narrative meaning and the nonlinearity of hypertext. Judd Morrissey's *The Jew's Daughter* (2000) presents itself at first sight as a standard Storyspace hypertext, but there is only one link per screen, and the reading sequence is strictly determinate. When the user mouses over a link, part of the screen replaces itself, but the new text is inserted without visible mark somewhere in the middle of the screen, leaving the rest of the page unchanged. Only those gifted with perfect recall will be able to tell what is new and what is old. The only clue to the location of the new text is a nervous twitching of the affected area when the substitution takes place. Since it is impossible to return to the previous screen, the reader cannot compare the two lexias. This formula is designed to frustrate memory, and without memory, of course, the reader cannot construct a stable narrative world nor a consistent narrative action. The replacement of only part of the text does not move the plot forward; it merely suggests other directions the plot could take, other situations from which it could develop, other stories that could be explored. The textual algorithm is truly a machine for generating unfulfilled possibilities. To salvage some intelligibility, readers will interpret the replacement mechanism as a symbolic gesture; but the meaning of this mechanism is itself an open field: does the text allegorize the radical instability of meaning, does it signify the absence of an external reference world and of real events to narrate, does it imitate the random meandering of thought (the text presents itself as an interior monologue reminiscent of a Beckett novel), or does it simulate the dynamics of the writing process – the replacement standing for false starts and for the technique of "cut-and-paste"? Whatever the reader decides, once he or she forms an interpretation there is little incentive to explore any further. What is the point of reading if you cannot remember anything? The text is readable on the metanarrative, but not on the narrative level.

For the reader who likes to explore a text systematically, one of the most frustrating aspects of classical hypertext is the impossibility of following several routes simultaneously, or to move back and forth between these routes.[10] In her mini-hypertext *My Boyfriend Came Home from the War* (1996), the Russian author Olia Lialina proposes a clever solution to this problem – or rather a clever alternative to what is usually a deliberate design philosophy. Though the text was not written in Flash, but in HTML code (which means that the programmer did it the hard way, by writing code, what a Flash user can do by clicking and dragging the mouse), it has become a classic of its generation. The narrative begins with a unified screen displaying the phrase "My boyfriend came home from the war; after dinner they left us alone." The first click divides the screen into two separate windows showing, respectively, two dejected people looking in opposite directions and the frame of a window, which suggests that the lovers, far from being left alone, are placed under surveillance by the reader and the family. The next click further splits one of these windows in two, and so on until the screen is partitioned into some 16 distinct spaces that contain either text or a picture. When the reader reaches this bottom level, text replaces itself in the various windows with each mouseclick, telling a linear story through a broken dialogue. The important feature, the one that distinguishes *My Boyfriend Came Home from the War* from Storyspace hypertext, is that when the reader explores a window, the others remain visible on the screen, offering alternative stories, and the reader can always switch from one window to another. Here the text truly functions as its own map, but this map is dynamic, altering itself as the reader progresses. At any given time, it shows which frames hold content to be explored, and which ones are no longer active: when a window has been exhausted, it turns black, telling the reader that its narrative thread has come to an end. Reading the text thus becomes a game of opening and emptying windows as if they were boxes.

From a thematic point of view, the splitting of windows suggest the multiple possibilities that arise when a soldier returns to his girlfriend after a long separation – renewed flame, estrangement, infidelity, disappointment – but the successive divisions of the screen also symbolize the divisiveness of war, the growing apart of the lovers, and the failure to communicate that takes place in most scenarios. Only two of the threads end on a positive note: "Together forever," or "Look it's beautiful"/"kiss me"; but they are the shortest, and they may represent no more than wishful thinking. Other scenarios show the stalling of the boyfriend when asked to set a date for the wedding ("Will you marry me"/ "tomorrow"/ "No better next month and the weather must be better. Yes, next month. I'm happy now"), the girlfriend being questioned by her lover about her faithfulness during his absence ("You don't trust me, I see"/ "But it was only one. Last summer . . . And if you think . . . Why should I explain? . . . Don't you see") or the boyfriend sheepishly breaking up with a lame excuse and a vacuous promise ("Guys change; don't worry; I'll help you").

Through its choice of a simple, yet poignant story tailored to the size of the screen, a story that leaves large gaps to be filled in by the reader, and through its efficient visual interface to the idea of multiple narrative possibilities, Lialina's text proposes a powerful demonstration of what it means to think with the medium. *My Boyfriend*

Came Home from the War achieves an all-too-rare reconciliation of narrative coherence, human interest, and digital presentation.

Depending on whether we think with the medium or think from the more familiar point of view of traditional literature, we will judge the current achievements of digital narrative in two contrasting ways. Some people will say: the electronic medium has produced nothing comparable to Shakespeare's tragedies, to Proust's *A la recherche du temps perdu*, or even to the great classics of the cinema. Digital textuality has failed to become a major force on the literary scene, the computer is no substitute for the book, and there is little hope that this situation will ever change. These people are both right and wrong: right because Proust's novels have nothing to gain by offering multiple choices, nor Shakespeare's tragedies by allowing the spectator to manipulate a character; and because print narrative is not threatened to go out of fashion. But they are also wrong, because you don't take something that works and try to fix it. Digital texts should not be expected to be enhanced versions of the novel, of drama, or of the cinema. Their achievements reside in other areas: freely explorable narrative archives; dynamic interplay between words and image; and above all active participation in fantasy worlds. Digital narrative is only a failure if we judge it by the criteria of the literary canon, this is to say, by the criteria of another medium.

NOTES

1 <www.inform-fiction.org/introduction/ index.html>.

2 I am aware that some scholars consider computer games, because of their simulative engine, incompatible with narrativity, which they associate with a retrospective representation of past events: for instance, H. Porter Abbott (2002) and Espen Aarseth (2004). For a counterposition, see Marie-Laure Ryan (2002).

3 IF survives in small Internet niches, practiced without commercial and theoretical pressures by enthusiastic writers and programmers who freely share their work with a devoted community.

4 See in particular Landow (1997).

5 Storyspace was not primarily designed for literary texts. The main use of the system – and of hypertext in general – is the construction of informational databases.

6 Storyspace allows the reader to write notes in special areas, the digital equivalent of scribbling in the margins of a text, but these notes are external to the text, and they do not move the plot forward.

7 This possibility explains the lack of closure of most Storyspace hypertexts. By titling her book on hypertext *The End of Books – or Books Without End*, J. Yellowlees Douglas (2000) suggests that endless circling is a deliberate artistic choice rather than a design flaw.

8 In Storyspace, a feature known as a "guard field" can prevent the reader from reaching a lexia before a certain other lexia has been visited, but this feature allows only partial control over the reader's itinerary.

9 For instance Talan Memmott, *Lexia to Perplexia* <www.altx.com/ebr/ebr11/11mem/>.

10 *afternoon* actually made it possible to follow several paths simultaneously by allowing the reader to split the screen into several windows; each window would contain a different path. But the complexity of the textual network quickly outgrew the graphic capability of the system: the screen had not enough room for all of the choices. The feature was dropped in later Storyspace hypertexts.

REFERENCES AND FURTHER READING

Aarseth, E. (1997). *Cybertext. Perspectives on Ergodic Literature*. Baltimore, MD: Johns Hopkins University Press.

Aarseth, E. (2004). "Quest Games as Post-Narrative Discourse." In M.-L. Ryan (ed.), *Narrative Across Media: The Languages of Storytelling* (pp. 371–6). Lincoln: University of Nebraska Press.

Abbott, H. P. (2002). *The Cambridge Introduction to Narrative*. Cambridge, UK: Cambridge University Press.

Blank, M. (1982). *Deadline*. Cambridge, MA: Infocom.

Bolter, J. (1991). *Writing Space: The Computer, Hypertext, and the History of Writing*. Hillsdale, NJ: Lawrence Erlbaum.

Campbell, P. M. (1987). "Interactive Fiction and Narrative Theory: Towards an Anti-Theory." *New England Review and Bread Loaf Quarterly* X (1): 76–84.

Douglas, J. Y. (2000). *The End of Books – or Books Without End? Reading Interactive Narratives*. Ann Arbor, MI: University of Michigan Press.

Hayles, N. K (2002). *Writing Machines*. Cambridge, MA: MIT Press.

Jackson, S. (1995). *Patchwork Girl*. Cambridge, MA: Eastgate Systems.

Joyce, M. (1987). *afternoon, a story*. Cambridge, MA: Eastgate Systems.

Joyce, M. (1996, 1997). *Twelve Blue: Story in Eight Bars*. World Wide Web hyperfiction. Postmodern Culture and Eastgate Systems, <www.eastgate.com/TwelveBlue>.

Landow, G. (1997). *Hypertext 2.0: The Convergence of Contemporary Critical Theory and Technology*. Baltimore, MD: Johns Hopkins University Press.

Lialina, O. (1996) *My Boyfriend Came Home From the War*, <www.teleportacia.org/war/>.

Manovich, L. (2001). *The Language of New Media*. Cambridge, MA: MIT Press.

Morrissey, J. (2000). *The Jew's Daughter*, <www.thejewsdaughter.com/>.

Montfort, N. (2003). "Toward a Theory of Interactive Fiction." <nickm.com/if/toward.html>.

Moulthrop, S. (1991) *Victory Garden*. Cambridge, MA: Eastgate Systems.

Murray, J. (1997). *Hamlet on the Holodeck: The Future of Narrative in Cyberspace*. New York: Free Press.

Plotkin, A. *Spider and Web*. <ftp://ftp.gmd.de/if-archive/games/infocom/Tangle.z5>.

Pinsky, R. (1984). *Mindwheel : An Electronic Novel*, S. Hale and W. Mataga (programmers). San Rafael, CA: Brøderbund Software Corporation.

Ryan, M-L. (2001). *Narrative as Virtual Reality: Immersion and Interactivity in Literature and Electronic Media*. Baltimore, MD: Johns Hopkins University Press.

Ryan, M-L. (2002). "Beyond Myth and Metaphor: Narrative in Digital Media." *Poetics Today* 23 (4): 581–610.

35

The Future of All Narrative Futures

H. Porter Abbott

The future will always trump prediction, whenever prediction involves complex phenomena like narrative. So this chapter does not aim to predict. Its subject instead is how we do and do not predict, that is, narrativize, the future. The focus is on both our narrative entertainments and the larger narrative arenas of life, and how they possibly relate. If this enterprise is predictive it is so only in suggesting how things have been, are, and ever shall be. But a good way into the subject is to look at what people are currently predicting for the future of narrative.

I

Predictably, what is being predicted on all hands is that the future of narrative is connected to the future of technology. Advances in digitization, connectivity, graphical manipulation, parallel processing, modal interfacing, virtual reality (VR), Flash, and much else have enabled striking transformations of the feel and texture of narrative, whether as hypertext fiction, interactive fiction (IF), text adventures, cybertexts, MUDs (multiuser domains), MOOs (object-oriented MUDs), MMORPGs (massively multiplayer online role-playing games), theme-based amusement park rides built around popular films, or any number of hybrids. There are two principal originating strains of this frenetic invention: in print narrative and in games.[1] Harbingers in print are reading-order optional texts like Marc Saporta's *Composition 1* ([1960] 1963), Julio Cortázar's *Hopscotch* ([1966] 1971), and B. S. Johnson's *The Unfortunates* (1969). In the field of games the commonly referenced antecedent is the intensely narrativized role-playing game that caught fire in the late 1970s, *Dungeons and Dragons*. If much has transpired over the last quarter century, enthusiasts agree that we are still only at the beginning – an "incunabular" phase that corresponds to the first 25 years of the printed book.

Taking a hard look at how e-innovations are transforming narrative, insofar as they can be considered narrative (I'll get back to this), one can isolate two closely interrelated shifts. The first is an expansion of the narrative domain and a corollary intensification of focus on the details of the discourse, often at the expense of story and even of closure. Visitors to the Aladdin ride in Walt Disney World are permitted physically to navigate within the domain of a narrative that was originally presented as a linear experience rendered in only one way, that is, as a film (Murray 1997: 49–50). This freedom, however limited, to move about within a physical amplification of a familiar narrative matches the experience of MUD/MOO/MMO (hereinafter MUD) gamers. Gamers explore and help create the inner world of games like *Asheron's Call*. The bones of the story emerge as the game progresses amid a welter of activity, much of which has nothing to do with the story.

Similarly, hypertext readers navigate back and forth among the "lexias" of fictions like Michael Joyce's *afternoon, a story*. Readers differ as to whether there is a coherent story in *afternoon* among its many story hooks, but unexhausted fans feature the way its 539 lexias gain energy through the strategic withholding of information and the (possibly) infinite postponement of closure. In hypertext fictions, the expansion of the narrative discourse often includes the generation of multiple story possibilities by stacking competing stories on the same or conflicting narrative detail. In this regard, the commonly referenced ancestor text is Borges's "Garden of Forking Paths." Borges's story actually closes emphatically, but the theory it conveys – that from one moment to the next any person inhabits an infinitude of potential stories, any one of which may or may not intersect with any one of the infinitude inhabited by anyone else – can be actualized in the complex lexial webs of hypertext fiction. Attention is redirected from a linear chain of suspense and surprise to the *frisson* of gathering indeterminacies.

The second narrative shift, inseparable from the first, is heightened "interactivity" or the engagement of reader/spectators in shaping the narrative discourse. Interactivity is a matter of degree, ranging from comparatively passive to comparatively active forms of reader engagement: what Marie-Laure Ryan (2001) refers to as "selective" and "productive" interactivity. At one end is the minimal freedom enjoyed by readers of hypertext fiction to create the order of the narrative discourse by selecting from a palette of hypertext lexias fabricated in advance by an author. At the other end is a reliance on readers or gamers actually to produce segments of the narrative discourse in an individual or collaborative enterprise, the outcome of which is not known in advance. Closer to this latter end of the spectrum are MUDs, in which players, through their "avatars" (characters they control within the action), commonly generate a great deal of supplementary action, fighting, marrying, and generally socializing. All of this unpredictable activity takes place within an at times many-venued domain, which in turn is the product of a team of fabricators who operate behind the scenes. These extradiegetic authors are also responsible for a variety of obstacles and means of escape (often magical), threatening and friendly entities, both monstrous and human, and an overarching skeletal story.

In much of the literature on the future of narrative, interactivity is a kind of gold standard. Janet Murray in *Hamlet on the Holodeck* (1997) deploys as a running motif the "holodeck" that appears in installments of *Star Trek*: a wrap-around, holographic production in which the default narrative accommodates the active presence of a spectator/performer by responding in words and actions to the things he or she says and does within the ongoing mimesis of events. More exclusively, Espen Aarseth in *Cybertext* draws a sharp distinction between "hypertext," a term he reserves for texts in which reader options are all fixed in advance, and "cybertext," which denotes "a work where the user can contribute discursive elements to the effect that the 'theme' of the 'discourse itself' is unknown in advance or subject to change" (Aarseth 1997: 49).[2]

The first general point I want to make, however, is that these diverse experiments in technologically assisted narrative, wonderful and promising as they are, do not represent a revolution or even a minor change in the enduring structures of narrative. Narrative will continue to be narrative, so in this sense the future of narrative is the past of narrative. This is not out of sync with the positions of Murray, Douglas, Ryan, and most other forecasters. "Hypermedia fiction and digital narratives . . . will morph and evolve during the years ahead," writes Douglas. "What will not change are the things that have always engaged us: the strings of cause and effect; generalizations about character and motivation we accrue from our study of outward dress, manner, tics; the dense weave of micro-and macroplots; and, always, underlying all of it, words, words, words" (Douglas 2000: 171).

II

But do the innovations nonetheless augur a general shift in cognition and behavior? After all, the technological revolution has made these innovations swiftly accessible to an enormously expanded consumer base. Are we not becoming, culturally, even globally, more participatory, less keenly focused on the end of the story, more prone to want to cruise around and even do things in the multiple inner spaces of narrative? Are we all perhaps undergoing some kind of universal cultural morphing, with the emergence of a new episteme – a postmodern sea-change marked by an abandonment of "master-narratives" (Lyotard) and an embrace of "rhizomatic" thinking (Deleuze)? In a rich importation of post-structuralist thought into the study of narrative, Andrew Gibson argues that not only is this happening but that the whole field of narratology is stuck in an outdated structuralist frame of mind wholly inadequate to this deep shift in our ways of knowing and communicating. Gibson argues that narratology is dominated by a retrogressive illusion of unitary wholeness, of fixed narrative space with fixed points of reference, of hierarchical thinking and a general privileging of the word over vision, and as such "produces a resistance to postmodernity" (Gibson 1996: 21). In this view, interactive fiction is a clear indicator of where the cultural action is: "Narrative space is now plastic and manipulable. It has become heterogeneous, ambiguous, pluralized. Its inhabitants no longer appear to have an irrefutable or essential relation to any particular space. Rather, space opens up as a variable and finally indeterminate feature of any given world" (p. 12).

But can the quality of these experiments, together with the analytic mode that Gibson argues is appropriate to them, be called *the future* of narrative? Gibson's rhetoric wavers between prediction and exhortation, but insofar as he is predicting, the odds are stacked against a deep shift of this sort. This is my second point – which is not at all to say that there won't continue to be significant shifts in the entertainment market with significant shifts in segments of the readership. I look forward to engaging with Hamlet on the holodeck ("Hamlet, wouldst thou please get a move on"). But though the holodeck may be *in* the future of narrative, it can't *be* the future of narrative. To begin with, the vast quantitative bulk of narrative will continue to thrive in the "natural-language narratives" of everyday life. This production of narrative in the course of any conversation is of a piece with the production of narrative for commercial consumption. Roughly 90 percent of narrative on CDs and the Web replicates the book and film industry, where linear stories of the pursuit of love or revenge thrive unabated. Again, the future of narrative would seem to be the past of narrative.

There's more to this point. A year after Lyotard first published his *Reflections on Time* ([1988] 1991), Francis Fukuyama first articulated his theory of "The End of History." Proposed in the immediate aftermath of the fall of the Berlin Wall, Fukuyama's theory was the exact antitype of Lyotard's theory of the abandonment of historical master-narratives. It promulgated a ringing endorsement of the idea that history is not only narratable but has followed the course of a universal master-narrative, now arriving at its end. "[T]here is a fundamental process at work that dictates a common evolutionary pattern for *all* human societies – in short, something like a Universal History of mankind in the direction of liberal democracy" (Fukuyama 1992: 48). Fukuyama wrote with a polemical weather-eye trained on the academy, and his capitalizing of "Universal History" is only one of many ways he invited the storm that broke over his head. The ensuing fight gave Fukuyama's work sustained attention and in certain quarters added luster. But the theory itself electrified not simply the political right but a significant segment of a reading public starved for some confirmation that history did have a story, one with closure, and, needless to say, a good place for themselves in its happy ending.

Is Fukuyama's idea a cultural anachronism? To call it an anachronism, of course, is to imply that there is another masterplot than his, unfolding in linear time. But in fact Fukuyama's kind of story, a story of extended conflict, crowned by triumph, thrives everywhere on the globe. On September 11, 2001 – we all know this story – planes were converted to bombs by pilots with deep convictions about the story of their lives, a story of conflict and eventual triumph, with sufficient exactness of detail to specify the number of virgins awaiting them in Paradise. These pilots inhabited stories that were already "written." And their stories in turn inhabited a larger story, a master-story of cosmic history. There is no doubt that the terrorists are a small aberrant fragment of what goes by the name of Islam. But in its skeletal shape, the larger story of Islam, with the emphatic closure of its already written conclusion, is a story that hundreds of millions of people worldwide live within throughout their daily lives.

Not uncommonly in the West one hears the argument that Islam is itself a kind of anachronism, that in global terms it is culturally backward, even medieval. This is why, it is argued, Islamic societies can't compete in the modern world. They lack the cultural flexibility, the necessary range of options available to liberal democracies. Yet within days of the attack on the twin towers, President Bush told us that we were now engaged in a war between Good and Evil, one in which "God is not neutral" (Bruni 2002: 257). As many have noted, in so characterizing the conflict the president not only acceded to bin Laden's narrative construction of the meaning of this story but adopted many of his terms. Yet "acceded" and "adopted" are not the right words, since the idea of such a universal story, though with Good and Evil differently assigned, had already been a part of the President's thinking. It was this that led him to talk publicly (and so damagingly) about a "Crusade," a term as positive for him as it was negative for the Islamic world. Some White House insiders have suggested that, like the terrorists, the president sees his own personal story as embedded in a larger story, that this crusade "must be God's intention for him" and that "his leadership at this time of crisis was part of God's plan" (Bruni 2002: 256).

Is Bush, then, an anachronism? Not, I would argue, in this regard. Nor is his idea necessarily a Republican construction. Shortly after 9/11, it was a Democrat, Senator Byrd, who told him "there's an army of people who believe in divine guidance and the Creator. . . . You stand there. Mighty forces will come to your aid" (Woodward 2002: 46). If Byrd is a southern gentleman of the old school, he nonetheless invoked an idea that regenerates insistently out of American soil. Nor do such masterplots, Islamic or Christian, lose their power by apparent failure in the world of action. Frank Kermode, in his enduring book *The Sense of an Ending* (1966), has shown how such stories retain their power despite endless postponements of their endings. An ancillary feature of my second point, then, is that in spheres of practical action, especially political action, the rhetorical power of historical and cosmic narrative is an indispensable resource. Most such narratives are not as institutionally orthodox or explicit as those I've produced above. But with whatever religious tincture, or lack of it, such predictive narratives rally the troops. This apparent fact of social psychology promises to continue into the indefinite future, despite incursions of the unclosed, the digressive, the meandering, the alinear, and the polysemous.

III

Is there, then, no correspondence between what is happening to e-entertainments and those rugged narrative structures through which we live our lives and nations conduct their business? If, for example, readers of conventional linear narrative entertainments correspond to those few for whom the future is written in its entirety (Wahabists,

Calvinists), to what in the larger sphere do MUD gamers and readers of hypertext fiction correspond? This question lies within another: to what extent are we dealing here with narrative at all? And this, within yet another: when does something stop being narrative and start being something else?

One answer to the last question is: when the linear gives way to the lyrical, that is, when attractions of the discourse – aesthetic and emotional – absorb attention at the expense of the story. Works like Michael Joyce's *afternoon* and, even more, Robert Kendall's *A Life Set for Two* (1996) are arguably more lyrical poem than narrative, insofar as the immersive process of continual lexial recombination sufficiently displaces the pull of the story line for an ever deepening immersion in a world of thought and feeling. Pursued far enough, such "twisting" of narrative discourse, to use Nelson Goodman's (1981) term, will eventually displace a text from the broad category of narrative into something else. This kind of genre-creep in hypertext fiction has frequently been noted. George Landow, for example, argued that hypertext linking is, by its nature, poetic: "the link, the element that hypertext adds to writing, bridges gaps between text – bits of text – and thereby produces effects similar to analogy, metaphor, and other forms of thought, other figures, that we take to define poetry and poetic thought" (Landow 1997: 215).

Another answer to the question of where narrative leaves off and something else begins is when the story is no longer felt to precede the telling. In some way, illusory or real, fictional or nonfictional, stories wait to be told. Narrative is a "recounting," to use the word Gerald Prince uses to define it (Prince 1987: 58). Narrative recounts even in cases of "anterior narration," that is, narration that precedes the events narrated (pp. 57–8), since the future, as in God's prophecies, is in some way already there, available to be narrated. This is why most science fiction can be related in the past tense entirely without puzzlement. But even future tense narrative conveys a sense of something already there to be recounted, if only in a place called the future. Michael Frayn underscores this paradox in the opening sentence of his future tense novel, *A Very Private Life*: "Once upon a time there will be a little girl called Uncumber" (Frayn 1967: 3). The future world of the novel is asserted as already occupying a place in time. Monika Fludernik (1996) rightly points out that Frayn's novel, though set in the future, is marked by a large preponderance of present-tense constructions: "And then, one day when she is up in the little outside world at the top of the secret stairs, her elbow bangs against something sticking out. She pulls at it, and a great section of wall comes swinging back, filling the darkness with light" (Frayn 1967: 12). This is the "future present," an exact analog of the "historical present" (the rendering of past action in the present tense) and most likely as common to novels set in the future as the historical present is to novels set in the past. Both use the present tense to "recount" action that in some way is already there to be recounted. Fludernik's other example of a future tense fiction in English is Pam Houston's short story "How to Talk to a Hunter," a story that Fludernik contrasts with Frayn's novel in that "*will* is almost consistently read as a hypothetical *will* rather than a future tense" (Fludernik 1996: 256). Not "once upon a time" but "once upon a possible time." Yet here again, in this most tenuous of fictions, a hypothetical world is invoked, a world with its own narratable events. Given such a world, in other words, these are the events you can expect, the events that already belong to it.

One strong objection to the view that narrative always recounts comes from Jonathan Culler, who argued in a landmark essay that narrative is also governed by an opposite and irreconcilable "logic by which event is a product of discursive forces rather than a given reported by discourse" (Culler 1981: 175). Readers acquire a whole complex of expectations with regard to the "necessity" of having events turn out in one way rather than another. Events come after the discourse in the sense that they are generated by "the demands of signification." But that Culler has to strive to awaken us to this other logic shows how deeply embedded is our way of thinking about the events of narrative. Even if you are making up a story for a child, doing it right on the spot, and she knows this, she still hears you "recounting" events. She may complain about the ending, and you may provide a different one, but she is nonetheless hearing you render events that in some way precede the rendering. In short, Culler's take on narrative does not contradict the argument that, however paradoxically coexistent with its opposite, the sense of the precedence of the event (true or false, fictional or nonfictional) is a *defining condition of narrative*. There are of course other defining conditions of narrative, but this one is also present wherever there is narrative.

So when do we traverse from narrative to the prenarratable, from recounting events to events as they happen? We would seem to get closest with what has been called "simultaneous narration": narration that cannot be "normalized" either as narration in the historical (or future or hypothetical future) present or as interior monologue. Literally understood, simultaneous narration involves no gap at all between the event or experience and the narration of it. Some modes come close to this, but fall short. In Richardson's *Pamela* or Poe's "MS. Found in a Bottle," for example, the employment of the device of "writing to the moment" assumes a large enough gap to permit the events to be recorded. Even in what Christian Paul Casparis (1975) calls "current report" – announcing sports events or news as it happens – there is an awareness, as we read or listen, of those split seconds of mediation that take place as the traces of events pass from the always vanishing instant of the absolute present into the medium that conveys them. But in works without such devices, like Coetzee's *Waiting for the Barbarians*, the narrative gap is much harder to perceive: "With a pole and a white linen shirt I make a banner and ride out towards the strangers. The wind has dropped, the air is clear, I count as I ride: twelve tiny figures on the side of a rise . . . " (Coetzee 1980: 69). Dorrit Cohn argues that such first-person novels, "*globally* narrated in the present tense," represent "the most serious challenge to the accepted truth that "narrative is past, always past," since "the temporal hiatus between the narrating and the experiencing self . . . is literally reduced to zero" (Cohn 1998: 97, 107).

This is one of those points where it is important to stress that the narrator's (or narration's) relation to what is narrated is not the same as the reader's relation to the narrative. As long as the question of the pastness of narrative is confined to the former, simultaneous narration is a unique violation of the "rule" and carries with it its own unique effects on the reader. But if we look to the way the reader apprehends the novel itself, we have to leave this limited circle of concerns. Therefore, though we assume that for the narrator of *Waiting for the Barbarians* the future, in James Phelan's words, "is wide open," we also "read with the assumption that Coetzee has shaped his novel, has given it some kind of teleology" (Phelan 1994: 223). In other words, the story is already there, packaged in a book. As readers, we know this. The story already stretches from event A to event Z, even though the discourse that gets us from the one event to the other is simultaneous narration. In the same way, certain devout religious believers are convinced that the story of the world is already accomplished, though it unfolds in a mode of simultaneous narration.

That narrative is a form of "recounting" has kept a significant number of narratologists from defining plays and movies as narrative. In these media, the argument goes, there is no re-counting. As Prince says of the events in drama, "rather than being recounted, [they] occur directly on stage" (Prince 1987: 58). I don't want to dispute this exclusion, but instead to propose that it is the same intuitive logic (and in line with the final point above) that adds its own weight when scholars include drama and film among the narrative forms. In this view, dramas and films are not presentations but re-presentations of a story that has pre-existed as a script or screenplay or novel or history or myth or an idea in someone's head and that has subsequently passed through transformative processes including rehearsals or editing. Dramatic productions and films (both of them forms that thrive on modes of simultaneous narration) are nonetheless fabricated objects that convey a story and that can convey it again and again. Such is the intuition on this side of the argument. But the strong point here is that the term "narrative" as it is generally used, even by those of quite opposed views about the limits of narrative, includes the idea that the story is already there to be rendered. In this sense, there is always a gap between narration and the prenarratable – that is, those events, past, present, future, hypothetical, conditional, known, unknown, scripted, unscripted, imaginary, or real, that are grist for the mill of narration.

IV

This brings us back to the holodeck, because what happens there is not an evolution or extension of narrative but local abandonments of narrative. When I get my chance to introduce my own words into *Hamlet*, and Hamlet responds with his appropriately adaptive words ("I'm thinking!"), we both will have stepped for the moment across narrative's defining gap into the prenarratable. Such a moment is prenarratable in the same sense that life is prenarratable. As yet, of course, there are no holodeck productions, but such moments have opened up in the traditional theater, most aggravatingly when a cell phone goes off. More like what happens on the holodeck is the (no doubt apocryphal) moment in the fifth act of *Richard III* when John Barrymore spoke those famous lines "A horse! A horse! My kingdom for a horse!"

(V: iv, 7) and a man in the audience laughed out loud. Without skipping a beat, Barrymore turned, pointed at the man, and cried: "Saddle yon braying ass!" For that moment, Barrymore had stepped over the gap. He was no longer engaged in a dramatic recounting of Shakespeare's *Richard III* but inventing the prenarratable (which I now can narrate).

What is most interesting about the evolution of MUDs is their porosity with regard to the prenarratable. What stops the action and makes the heart jump when the prenarratable intrudes into traditional dramatic productions is much of the draw for the players of MUDs, especially in their massively multiuser versions. MUDs, though often referred to as narratives, descend, as I've said, more directly from games (rule-bound contests). In their descent from games, they acquired equipment with a high degree of narrativity (quests, dungeons, monsters). In both loosening the tight constraints of traditional games and acquiring narrativity (but without the constraint of a tightly scripted and all-comprehensive narrative), MUDs opened up spaces in which the spectator/participants could freely develop much prenarratable action. The quest, the plot-points, the scenery, the host of hostile or friendly agential characters, and other narratable elements are provided by the game-masters. After the fashion of narrative, these elements are *already there*. What is not yet there is all the meandering business that will be invented by the players.[3]

I don't think it is a stretch to see in this infiltration of the prenarratable, as with the free, poetic recombinations of hypertext fiction, a restless dissatisfaction with the givenness of narrative. The kind of slowing down that these intrusions create is different from the time-honored modes of retardation that are an essential part of all successful narratives. Retardation accentuates our interest in the story by keeping us in suspense. Spontaneous eruptions of the prenarratable are willful abandonments of the story, continual wanderings away from the plot-points. Indeed, some of these sites have devolved toward the condition of chat-rooms. Whether or not they go that far, such entertainments match the evanescence of story and the movement toward the condition of poetry in passively interactive hypertext fictions like Joyce's *afternoon*. Both resist narrative's ultimate obedience to the containment of story.

However, it is not only in their willfully anarratological character that these interactive entertainments become interesting in the larger narrative context of practical behavior, but also in the containment of that interactivity. Their freedom of interactivity is restricted to quarantined eruptions of the prenarratable (MUDs) or limited recombinations of the preselected (hypertext fiction). To whatever extent these kinds of interactive freedom are extended (toward lyrical anarchy or chat room discourse), they are extended within the finite lexias of hypertext fiction or the skeletal narrative contests of MUDs. We noted above that the diverse and widely practiced entertainments of reading and viewing narrative correspond to the comparatively rare practice of reading all events past and future as already written. In contrast, the e-entertainments I have been discussing correspond at the larger level to contained abandonments of given structures: committee-meetings, battles, conferences, construction work, seminars *with* their coffee-breaks, R & R, and other forms of ateleological churning. At the extreme end are parties, wakes, talk shows. At the level of politics, these extreme forms are signally ineffective. If the happenings of the 1960s, the rave events of the 1980s and 1990s, and the flash mobs of the new millennium all take their identity against the containment of narrative teleology, they also, like MUDs, accept kinds of containment in both space and time that effectively quarantine their impact. Moreover, and by their nature, they rob themselves of narrative's immense rhetorical power, thus keeping them from making significant interventions at most levels of practical life. They would appear rather to operate in a kind of antithetical symbiosis with decision-making power – as ideas of anarchy that sustain the narrative dominants they oppose.

As a rough draft, then, of a taxonomy of the filiations between entertainments and the larger spheres of practical life, we can start with the following homology:

Living as reading/as game	**Contained anarchic social behavior**
Reading traditional narrative	Reading/arranging hypertext fictions
Playing traditional games	Playing within MUDs

V

At the level of entertainment, there is an additional distinction, one that seems to have eluded most predictors. In the chart above, I have distinguished four basic forms of event-based fictions that fall into the two categories: traditional narratives and traditional games on the left and, on the right, passively interactive hypertext fictions and those MUDs where prenarratable behavior takes place within narrative and gamelike constraints. But what if the constraints were so light that the prenarratable took over the business of generating not only intermediary stretches of the prenarratable but the *story* itself? Examples of this would be thoroughly collaborative MUDs and hypertext narratives in which the story itself is generated by the participant-writers.[4] It is important to stress that I am referring here to the experience of these writer/players at the time of composition and not to the experience of some reader reading the finished work. Were you to read through a fiction on a collaborative site, knowing full well that it had been improvised on the spot by numerous participant-writers, you would still read it in the same way as the child hears you when you make up a story, as re-counting. The reason for this is simple: it's narrative.

The key distinction, then, is between narrative and the prenarratable, that is, between the experience of the reader and the experience of the writer. In effect, while the writer is creating the story discourse, he or she crosses over to the other side of Culler's (1981) "double logic," experiencing events as coming after the discourse. This parallels the effect in those local creations of the prenarratable in MUDs that simply emerge, from moment to moment, with no feeling that they are somehow already there. Yet to the extent that such local role-playing performances take place within a story, however hidden – what Aarseth (1997) calls "intrigue" – to that extent the sense of being in Culler's other "logic" of narrative is limited. By contrast, in a collaborative fiction that writes itself as it proceeds, or a multiuser game as free of constraint as *A Tale in the Desert* (a 2003 game by eGenesis), where players not only engage in social engineering but create an entire history of a portion of Egypt, the story itself is not yet "written" and will only take shape as words are expressed or moves made.

I am putting some strain on Culler's conception of the second logic of narrative, since he sees it as still an aspect of narrative, while I am putting it outside narrative in the realm of the prenarratable. What I am talking about is the experience of emergent form, of the coming into being of events, regardless of expectations, indeed, against expectations. This state of not knowing, of inhabiting the prenarratable, is quite simply the experience of writing that writers often speak of when they are writing well. As John Fowles put it, speaking of novelists, "It is only when our characters and events begin to disobey us that they begin to live" (Fowles 1969: 81). Characters "mutiny," to use Forster's word (1927: 66), in the same way they do in Flann O'Brien's *At Swim-Two-Birds* when they plot to kill their author in his sleep. There is a great range of testimony on this point.[5] In such writing, characters and events appear to create themselves entirely beyond the control of the author who, in theory at least, is inventing them. There is also a body of evidence linking this condition of novelists with the childhood phenomenon of "imaginary companions" who similarly operate with complete autonomy relative to the children who imagine them (Watkins 1986: 91–103, Taylor 1999: 148–52). Writers, of course, can plan out their fictions and force their characters to follow preconceived courses, but such writing is, in effect, "readerly" to the extent that the narrative is known in advance of the narrating. What I am isolating here is the way the future, not just in the minor details of the discourse but in the story itself, germinates in the writing. In the process it creates what was heretofore unknown. This is Tolstoy discovering *as he writes* and with great surprise that Vronsky is going to attempt suicide in *Anna Karenina* (Gifford 1971: 48). The story is not there until the discourse makes it.

What does this correspond to in the larger narrative sphere? It corresponds, basically, to an abandonment of prediction. When we don't read life as narrative, the absence of the future is absolute. Nothing is there yet. Life is not "written." In this sense, if I may continue to appropriate (with some distortion) a distinction from Barthes ([1970] 1974), it is a "writerly," rather than a "readerly" attitude toward the business of living, though an important corollary of this effect is that, once written, the past becomes absolute. The complete taxonomy, then, looks like this:

Living as reading/game	Contained anarchic social behavior	Living as writing
Reading traditional narrative	Reading/arranging hypertext fictions	Writing narrative
Playing traditional games	Playing within contained MUDs	Playing open MUDs

For most of us, living our lives at the top level of this taxonomy, life is a blend of reading and writing. Simply to survive, we must all be equipped to read as well as to write our lives, perhaps in equal measure. On the one hand, though only a few of us may be possessed by the conviction of a detailed masterplot within which our lives unfold, we all send out mental scripts to guide us, and sometimes we follow them. On the other hand, not only do things constantly happen to us without warning, rather in the way Fowles's character Charles happened to him, but we often improvise responses without thinking. With greater or less conviction we project scripts in the form of plans, agendas, plots, regimens, recipes, schemata, trying to *read* them even as we *write* the details, improvising and revising, and, as needed, relocating the main events forward into the future.

At the level of entertainment, though, what is striking is how much more activity there is on the left-hand side of the paradigm than on the right-hand side. It may be that writing, as I am using the term, is simply too difficult or requires too great a gift to have wide appeal as an entertainment. But then making up stories and games comes quite naturally to children. So it is possible that the reason there is so little activity on the right-hand side of the taxonomy is that we simply get too much of the condition of writing in our lives. I think we must yearn for those entertainments that take place within the security of the written. If the middle category of entertainments expresses a rejection of narrative containment, it does so within the security of a narrativized and game-like domain. In the same way, anarchic social behavior is usually quarantined in some way and largely immune from anything but random political effect. In short, there is much containment in this diagram and little risk. After all, it is as hard to live with the absolute absence of the future as it is with the absolute finality of the past. This is yet another reason, if I may cautiously predict, why the often wonderful developments in the technology of entertainment will continue largely to take place within constraints, narrative or otherwise, that give us the illusion that time itself has a shape and that somehow we are equipped to read it.

NOTES

1 In this essay, I define "narrative" as the representation of an action and "game" as a rule-bound contest involving one or more players.

2 Many practitioners of interactive fiction jealously limit the definition of IF to "text adventures," that is, "works that simulate a virtual world and allow a single user to meaningfully interact with it by issuing natural-language commands." This definition would exclude "hypertext literature, multiplayer games, and collaboratively written novels" (Nick Montfort, personal communication).

3 To a lesser degree, "reality TV" has much the same hybrid character as multiuser RPGs: a containing, narrativized game structure, within which there is room for local incidents of prenarratable action. Much of the audience appeal of these contests must derive from the opportunity to observe actual lives taking shape under pressure, but the containment of the game structure is even more pronounced than that of most MMRPGs.

4 Frankly, I have yet to find a good example of collaborative fiction on the web. All the credible examples I know of are novels published in book form in which each chapter is written by a different author, *seriatim*, and with no overarching scheme: e.g., *The Floating Admiral*

(1931), *Naked Came the Stranger* (1969), *S* (1991).

5   Watkins cites a number of these, including this one from the popular children's writer Enid Blyton: "Sometimes a character makes a joke, a really funny one, that makes me laugh as I type it on my paper – and I think, 'Well, I couldn't have thought of that myself in a hundred years!' " (Watkins: 97).

References and Further Reading

Aarseth, E. J. (1997). *Cybertext: Perspectives on Ergodic Literature*. Baltimore, MD: Johns Hopkins University Press.

Barthes, R. ([1970] 1974). *S/Z*, trans. R. Miller. New York: Noonday Press.

Bruni, F. (2002). *Ambling Into History: The Unlikely Odyssey of George W. Bush*. New York: HarperCollins.

Casparis, C. P. (1975). *Tense Without Time: The Present Tense in Narration*. Bern: Francke Verlag.

Coetzee, J. M. (1980). *Waiting for the Barbarians*. Harmondsworth, UK: Penguin.

Cohn, D. (1998). *The Distinction of Fiction*. Baltimore, MD: Johns Hopkins University Press.

Cortázar, J. ([1966] 1971). *Hopscotch*, trans. G. Rabassa. New York: New American Library.

Culler, J. (1981). "Story and Discourse in the Analysis of Narrative." In *The Pursuit of Signs: Semiotics, Literature, Deconstruction* (pp. 169–87). Ithaca, NY: Cornell University Press.

Douglas, J. Y. (2000). *The End of Books – or Books without End? Reading Interactive Narratives*. Ann Arbor: University of Michigan Press.

Fludernik, M. (1996). *Towards a "Natural" Narratology*. London: Routledge.

Forster, E. M. (1927). *Aspects of the Novel*. New York: Harcourt, Brace & World.

Fowles, J. (1969). *The French Lieutenant's Woman*. New York: New American Library.

Frayn, M. (1967). *A Very Private Life*. New York: Viking.

Fukuyama, F. (1992). *The End of History and the Last Man*. New York: The Free Press.

Gibson, A. (1996). *Towards a Postmodern Theory of Narrative*. Edinburgh: Edinburgh University Press.

Gifford, H. (ed.) (1971). *Leo Tolstoy: A Critical Anthology*. Harmondsworth, UK: Penguin.

Goodman, N. (1981). "Twisted Tales: or Story, Study, and Symphony." In W. J. T. Mitchell (ed.), *On Narrative* (pp. 99–115). Chicago: University of Chicago Press.

Johnson, B. S. (1969). *The Unfortunates*. London: Panther Books/Secker & Warburg.

Kendall, R. (1996). *A Life Set for Two*. Cambridge, MA: Eastgate Systems.

Kermode, F. (1966). *The Sense of an Ending: Studies in the Theory of Fiction*. London: Oxford University Press.

Landow, G. P. (1997). *Hypertext 2.0*. Baltimore, MD: Johns Hopkins University Press.

Lyotard, J.-F. ([1988] 1991). *The Inhuman: Reflections on Time*, trans. G. Bennington and R. Bowlby. Stanford, CA: Stanford University Press.

Murray, J. H. (1997). *Hamlet on the Holodeck: the Future of Narrative in Cyberspace*. New York: The Free Press.

Phelan, J. (1994). "Present Tense Narration, Mimesis, the Narrative Norm, and the Positioning of the Reader in *Waiting for the Barbarians*." In J. Phelan and P. J. Rabinowitz (eds.), *Understanding Narrative* (pp. 222–45). Columbus: Ohio State University Press.

Prince, G. (1987). *A Dictionary of Narratology*. Lincoln: University of Nebraska Press.

Ryan, M.-L. (2001). *Narrative as Virtual Reality: Immersion and Interactivity in Literature and Electronic Media*. Baltimore, MD: Johns Hopkins University Press.

Saporta, M. ([1960] 1963). *Composition No. 1*, trans. Richard Howard. New York: Simon and Schuster.

Taylor, M. (1999). *Imaginary Companions and the Children who Create them*. New York: Oxford University Press.

Watkins, M. (1986). *Invisible Guests: The Development of Imaginal Dialogues*. Hillsdale, NJ: The Analytic Press.

Woodward, B. (2002). *Bush at War*. New York: Simon and Schuster.

Glossary

actant: in structuralist narratology, any of the basic roles in the action structure of a narrative. Greimas, who originated the term, described six actantial roles (subject, object, sender, receiver, helper, and opponent), but the term is often used more loosely to refer to a character considered in terms of his or her structural function in the action – a hero (subject) or villain (opponent), for instance. The same actantial role can be held by more than one character (there may be many opponents, for example) in a given narrative; similarly, the same character can perform more than one actantial role (for example, a character who is initially a helper may also be an opponent). See also **passant**.

analepsis, analeptic: flashback. Analeptic passages interrupt the forward movement of narrative time by narrating material (events, an image, a figure of speech) from an earlier time in the chronology.

antinarratable: that which, according to a given narrative, should not be told, due to social convention or taboo.

attached text, or contingent text: one in which the primary "I" is assumed to be the author of the work; one whose meaning depends on the equation of the textual **voice** with that of the author. Editorials and scholarly essays are attached texts.

auditory percept: the subjectively perceived auditory object resulting from the translation, by the hearing process, of the acoustic waveform into meaningful sound. Distinguished from "sensations" and "concepts," the percept is produced by a complex interaction of physiological and cognitive processes.

auditory restoration, or continuity effect: the perceptual filling in of missing sound when it has been masked or replaced by louder sound of similar frequency. When the gap is filled by such noise and not by silence, we perceive the obliterated or interrupted sound as steady or continuous, unless we have other cues to the contrary.

auditory streaming, auditory scene analysis, or perceptual/auditory grouping: the process of perceptually organizing the single continuous waveform produced by multiple sound sources into separate meaningful sounds. Streaming includes perceiving sounds (including harmonics and reverberations) as emanating from a single source (stream integration or fusion) and processing them into different streams (stream segregation or fission).

auscultation, auscultize, auscultator: terms referring to the perceptual representation of sound in literature (who hears?), paralleling the terms **focalization**, focalize, and focalizer. Auscultation may be regarded as a subspecies of the broader concept focalization (who perceives?) or distinguished from focalization if the latter is used specifically to refer to sight (who sees?).

authorial audience: the hypothetical ideal audience for whom the author constructs the text and who understands it perfectly. The authorial audience of fiction, unlike the **narrative audience** (defined below), operates with the tacit knowledge that the characters and events are synthetic constructs rather than real people and historical happenings.

catachresis: an anomalous trope in which a word with a known literal meaning is used as the name of something that has no literal name. The commonest examples tend to be parts of the human body projected on the natural world, as in "face of the mountain," or "tongues of flame."

chronotope: the temporal and spatial dimensions of narrative **discourse**. Bakhtin coined the term in "Forms of Time and of the Chronotope in the Novel" and defined it as "the intrinsic connectedness of temporal and spatial relationships that are artistically expressed."

coreference: see **reference**

countermemory: a term drawn from the work of Michel Foucault that indicates lost or hidden cultural practices (memories, narratives) brought to light by genealogical investigations of history.

culture industry: a phrase coined by Theodor Adorno and Max Horkheimer, deployed most famously in *Dialectic of Enlightenment*, to describe the application of Fordist principles of mass production and consumption to the creation and dissemination of cultural artifacts.

deixis: the function of certain words (demonstrative pronouns, definite articles, temporal adverbs) to locate referents in place and time relative to the speaker's location. In a narrative utterance such as "I realized that this apple was now better than that orange," "this" and "that" have the **deictic** function of indicating that the apple is closer to the "I" than the orange, while "now" has the deictic function of indicating both some change over time and the speaker's current realization. The juxtaposition of "now" with "was" – an adverb conveying the present with a verb conveying the past – is linked to the narrative convention of the past tense often functioning to signify the present time of the narrated events.

detached text: one in which the author's identity is understood as dissociated from the identity of the textual "I"; one in which the author cannot be equated with the textual "I" or in which the relation between the author and the primary "I" is not consequential for textual meaning. Advertisements and national anthems are detached texts.

dialogism: according to Bakhtin, a property of the language of novels whereby utterances or instances of **discourse** in a novel, whether associated with characters or the narrator, are oriented toward other utterances, either within the same novel or outside it in the wider social arena. That is, utterances anticipate other utterances, respond to them, polemicize against them openly or surreptitiously, mimic or parody them, and so forth. Some types of discourse (e.g., **free indirect discourse**) incorporate both parties to this dialogue within their own structure, and so are said to be "double-voiced."

diegesis: (1) the narrative world, whether fictional or nonfictional; and (2) telling, as in summarizing or commenting, as opposed to showing via dialogue or performance. The first sense of the term provides the root for a family of terms: **extradiegetic** refers to situations that are not properly part of the main narrative world; a narrator who is not part of the action he or she narrates is an extradiegetic narrator. **Intradiegetic** refers to situations within that main narrative world; an intradiegetic narrator is one whose narration is framed by another narrator as Marlow is in Conrad's *Heart of Darkness*; that frame narrator is extradiegetic. (Note, however, that an intradiegetic narrator can also be a heterodiegetic narrator, if he or she does not participate in the action narrated; Chaucer's pilgrim narrators on their way to Canterbury, for example, are both intradiegetic and heterodiegetic.) See also **heterodiegetic narration, homodiegetic narration**, and **metalepsis**.

discourse: the set of devices for telling a **story**, including vision or **focalization** (who perceives?), **voice** (who speaks?), duration (how long it takes something to be told), frequency (whether something is told in singulative or iterative manner), and speed (how much story time is covered by a stretch of discourse). In structuralist narratology, discourse is regarded as the "how" of narrative, distinct from the "what" – character, event, and setting.

disnarration: a technique in which a narrator recounts something that does not happen.

ekphonesis: the representation of a musical or sound composition in a literary work.

ekphrasis: the representation of a visual composition in a literary work.

equivocal text: one in which the primary voice of the text is assumed to be at once associated with and independent of the author's voice; one in which the relationship between the "I" of the text and the author's "I" is indeterminate or variable. Novels and poems are equivocal texts.

existential mechanism: a reading-hypothesis that links and resolves problematic elements of a fictional text in terms of some reality model, like the world of science fiction or of Kafka's "Metamorphosis."

extension: the process by which a new narrative imitates an original, but does not constitute a sequel to it (does not continue the life of the original characters); rather the new narrative places the new characters in situations parallel to those experienced by the original characters.

fabula: the sequence of a narrative's events in chronological order; more generally, the what of narrative before it is rendered in **discourse**.

fictive, fictional, fictitious: these terms are often used synonymously, but can be usefully distinguished as follows: **fictive** means "fiction producing, imaginative," and applies to (authorial) **discourse**; **fictional** means "characteristic of fiction, imagined," and applies primarily to **story** (note, however, that a *represented* discourse would normally be fictional, not fictive); and **fictitious** means "unreal, imaginary," and applies to the events and existents, or the particulars, of story.

focalization: the answer to the question "who is perceiving?" in narrative **discourse**. Gérard Genette noted that the term "point of view" conflated two distinct aspects of narrative discourse: voice (the answer to the question "who is speaking?") and vision or focalization. Since Genette's identification of the concept, narratologists have been debating how best to describe it and account for its effects.

free indirect discourse: a locution in a narrative in which the narrator represents a character's speech or thought by blending the character's expression with his or her own. In direct discourse, the narrator would quote the character's thought: "He thought, 'I am going home to sleep it off.'" In indirect discourse, the narrator would report the character's thought: "He thought that he would go home to sleep it off." In free indirect discourse, the narrator would drop the framing "he thought": "He would go home to sleep it off."

functional mechanism: a reading-hypothesis that imposes order on divergent and discontinuous textual elements in terms of the (e.g., thematic, rhetorical) ends that require that divergence.

genealogy: for Foucault, a practice of historical writing, indebted to Nietzschean critique. As Foucault explains in "Nietzsche, Genealogy, History," the practice attends to the "accidents, the minute deviations – or conversely, the complete reversals – the errors, the false appraisals, and the faulty calculations that gave birth to those things that continue to exist and have value for us" and so "discover[s] that truth or being do not lie at the root of what we know and what we are, but the exteriority of accidents."

generic mechanism: a reading-hypothesis that explains a work's simplifications of reality and other discordances by appeal to its kind, as when we say that comedy typically makes its older characters function primarily as obstacles to the lovers of the younger generation.

genetic mechanism: a reading-hypothesis that resolves fictive oddities and inconsistencies in terms of the causal factors that produced the text without coming to form part of it, for example, the creative process.

heterodiegetic narration: Gérard Genette's term for narration in which the narrator exists at different level of existence from the characters.

heterotopia: an external place that is simultaneously "real" (limited, concrete, not utopian) and also full of relational references to other places and disciplinary institutions. The term is Foucault's neologism in "Of Other Places" to refer to actual places that acquire intense meanings through their existence within a larger set of spatial and temporal social relations – for example, cemeteries, brothels, prisons, theaters, honeymoon hotels, museums, libraries.

historical present: in both ordinary speech and narrative art, the narration of past events and experiences in the present tense. As such, it is distinguishable from narration in the present tense of events as they occur (**simultaneous narration**).

homodiegetic narration, or character narration: Gérard Genette's term for narration in which the narrator exists at the same level of existence as the other characters. When the character narrator is also the protagonist, homodiegetic narration can be further specified as autodiegetic.

hypertext: a collection of texts or text fragments interconnected by links. The presence of a plurality of links out of a given fragment creates a choice of reading orders which gives hypertext what is generally called a nonlinear character, though multilinear is a more appropriate term, given the inevitable linearity of language. Primarily a mode of access to documents within a database, hypertext is the basic structure of Internet sites, but the format has also been used in literary narrative, both print and digital. Digital hypertext fiction allows the reader to click on highlighted links to move to new segments (words, graphics, sounds) of the narrative. See also **interactivity, lexias**.

implied author: the version of the real author responsible for the choices that create the narrative text as "these words in this order" and that imbues the text with his or her values.

informant: an unself-conscious transmitter, or quotee, whose originally private **discourse** mediates and serves another's higher-level, framing communication. The informant thus opposes the narrator as well as the author. Examples range from the secret diarist to the vocal soliloquist to the interior monologist.

integration mechanisms: the means by which readers transform apparent textual incongruities into coherent parts of the larger text. See the five particular mechanisms: the **existential**, the **functional**, the **generic**, the **genetic**, and the hypothesis of **unreliable narration**.

interactive fiction: a purely textual type of computer game in which the user solves problems by participating in a dialogue with the machine. The player of interactive fiction impersonates a character in a fictional world by typing sentences which count in the fictional world as the actions of the character. The system updates the state of the fictional world in response to these events, and the player gives new input, in a feedback loop that runs until a terminal state of winning or losing is reached.

interactivity: participation of reader/spectators in the actual production of the narrative text, especially participation that affects the information displayed to the reader/spectator. Interactivity is mainly a property of digital texts, thanks to the feedback loops through which computers accept input that determine their inner state and their output. Multipath texts realized in print are sometimes regarded as interactive, though these texts lack the dynamic behavior and agency of digital texts. Interactivity can be either strictly selective or productive: in the selective variety the user's participation is limited to clicking on hyperlinks, while in the productive form, the user's input consists of text or simulated actions that become events in a fictional world.

lexias: (1) a term introduced by Roland Barthes referring to the "contiguous fragments" that make up a narrative. Generally brief, though arbitrary in length, they are the "units of reading" as determined by the reader. (2) In **hypertext** fiction, a term borrowed from Barthes by George P. Landow and now generally used to refer to fragments of hypertext narrative, fashioned as such by the writer yet commonly arranged in an order devised by the reader.

mediation: **mimetic** motivation; that is, the process by which elements of a text are made to seem inevitable as a result of their conforming to (some model of) reality. Mimetic motivation thus has two main branches, the existential (appealing to whatever counts as objective reality) and the perspectival (a subject's distinctive, fallible view of reality).

medium: a channel of transmission or a type of material support for information. From the point of view of narrative theory, medium is a mode of encoding and transmitting narrative information that makes a difference as to what kind of stories can be told, how they are told, and how they are experienced. Print is one kind of medium; film is another. Medium is distinct from genre in that it consists of properties and limitations inherent to its material realization, while genre is defined by human-made conventions.

metalepsis: the breaking of the conventional barriers between diegetic levels, as, for example, when John Fowles has his extradiegetic narrator in *The French Lieutenant's*

Woman enter the diegesis (narrative world) of his protagonist Charles Smithson. See **diegesis**.

mimetic/mimesis: mimetic refers specifically to that component of character directed to its imitation of a possible person. It refers generally to that component of fictional narrative concerned with imitating the world beyond the fiction, what we typically call "reality." Mimesis refers to the process by which the mimetic effect is produced, the set of conventions, which change over time, by which imitations are judged to be more or less adequate.

mise en abyme: the device of having part of a text mirror in miniature the larger text; for example, Shakespeare's use of the play within the play in *Hamlet*.

motivation: According to Russian Formalist theory, the process by which elements of a text (especially but not exclusively elements of **discourse** or "devices") are made to seem inevitable rather than arbitrary, and integral rather than anomalous. Elements may be motivated, and their presence justified, either in terms of their contribution to aesthetic and rhetorical effects, or, in **mimetic** motivation, by appeal to some model of reality, that is, in terms of their "realism." Elements deliberately left unmotivated are "laid bare," exposed *as* formal elements rather than assimilated to larger compositional or mimetic patterns.

narratee: the audience directly addressed by the narrator; the degree to which this audience gets characterized varies widely.

narrative audience: the observer role within the world of the fiction, taken on by the flesh and blood reader in that part of his or her consciousness which treats the fictional action as real. The narrative audience position, like the narratee position, is subsumed within the **authorial audience** position.

narrativity: the formal and contextual qualities distinguishing narrative from non-narrative, or marking the degree of "narrativeness" in a **discourse**; the rhetorical principles underpinning the production or interpretation of narrative; the specific kinds of artifice inherent in the process of narrative representation.

neonarrative: strategies for stretching generic boundaries to include matter that would previously have been unnarratable in a given genre.

paralepsis: narration that reflects a greater knowledge than the narrator could presumably have; in other words, narration in which the narrator tells more than he or she knows.

paralipsis: narration that does not reflect the narrator's full relevant knowledge; in other words, narration in which the narrator tells less than he or she knows.

paranarratable: that which, according to a given narrative, would not be told, due to literary convention.

passant: a character viewed from the perspective of the impressions registered on him or her, rather than from the perspective of the actions he or she performs. A term introduced in Rabinowitz's chapter in this volume as a contrast to **actant**.

path: a character's order of experience, which may or may not coincide with the order of events in the **story** or in the **discourse**.

performative: a term from speech act theory, invented by J. L. Austin to name an enunciation which is not "constative," that is, not a putative statement of fact capable of being either true or false, but a speech act that makes something happen. A performative, in Austin's phrase, is a way of doing something with words. For example, when the minister or duly authorized civil official says at the end of a marriage ceremony, "I now pronounce you husband and wife," he or she performs the act of marrying the couple.

primacy effect: our tendency to accept as valid the information we are initially given, even when that information is contradicted later in the same message.

prolepsis, proleptic: flash-forward; the temporal counterpoint to **analepsis**. Proleptic passages interrupt the steady forward movement of narrative time by narrating material located in the narrative's future.

prosopography: literally the writing (*graphy*) of a mask or persona (*prosopon*), it incorporates the trope of prosopopoeia, in which a dead or absent entity is given a persona and a voice, and refers to the practice of representing the history of a nation or community as a set of representative persons, in collections of their names, portraits, and biographies. It has also referred to methods of historical analysis that compare data about the lives of groups of people in antiquity or the middle ages – when records are scarce – or modern times, when statistics about parentage, marriage, or life expectancy are ample. Less formally, it refers to collections of short biographies (collective biography) in general.

reference: the relation between an instance of a referring expression (a proper noun, definite noun phrase, pronoun, or demonstrative) and a referent (a specific person, object, place, event, etc.). Reference resolution is the interpretative act of assigning a referent (on a pragmatic and semantic basis) to an instance of a referring expression in a given context. **Coreference** is the relation between two instances of the same or different referring expressions that can be attributively (in discursive terms) or referentially (in terms of the referent) identified with each other.

second-degree text: any text that plays off an older, pre-existent text; parodies, **extensions**, and sequels are all examples of second-degree texts.

self-consciousness: a discourser's awareness of communicating with some audience. An authorial privilege by definition, it is delegated to narrators (or speakers/writers outside narrative) and denied to informants, with significant implications for how their respective performances as transmitters operate and make sense.

simultaneous narration: present tense narration in which there is no apparent gap between the time of the narration and the time of the event or experience narrated: in simultaneous narration living and telling occur simultaneously. See **historical present**.

sjuzhet: the **fabula** rendered in a specific narrative **discourse**; the synthesis of **story** and discourse.

soundscape: the sonic equivalent of landscape. An environment of sound, especially as it is perceived and understood by the listener or listeners. A term first employed by R. Murray Schafer, in the World Soundscape Project, along with other terms for discussing sound environments, such as soundmark (landmark), sound signal (figure), keynote sound (ground), and earwitness (eyewitness).

speech act: from the point of view of speech act theory, any utterance is not only constative (saying something) but also performative (doing something). A speech act is a purposeful, communicative use of language involving a locutionary act (producing a grammatical utterance); an illocutionary act (a purpose achieved in the process of performing the locutionary act, e.g., asserting, promising, warning, requesting, commanding); and potentially a perlocutionary act (a purpose achieved by means of performing the illocutionary act, e.g., informing, convincing, dissuading, etc.). Speech act theory resists the assumption that language use can be understood independently of its context, or purely in relation to its propositional truth value. See also **performative**.

story: the what of narrative: character, events, and setting are elements of story; the events in chronological order constitute the story abstracted from the **discourse**.

subnarratable: that which, according to a given narrative, need not be told, because it is so "normal" as to go without saying.

supranarratable: that which, according to a given narrative, cannot be told, because it is ineffable or inexpressible.

transposition: the process by which a new text changes an imitated text; the new text preserves a clear association with the original, but alters or even reverses its significance by modifying setting, tone, plot, and/or characters. Unlike parody and pastiche, the imitative text has serious purposes.

undecidable: a term used to describe a text that is open to two (or more) incompatible readings, each (or all) of which can be amply supported by textual evidence.

unnarration: a technique in which a narrator asserts that what happened cannot be retold in words, or explicitly indicates that what happened will not be narrated because to do so would be impossible.

unreliable narration: within the rhetorical theory of narrative, narration in which the narrator's reporting, reading (or interpreting), and/or regarding (or evaluating) are not in accord with the implied author's. There are six main types of unreliable narration: misreporting, misreading, misregarding; underreporting, underreading, and underregarding. The two main groups can be differentiated by the activity they require on the part of the authorial audience: with the first group – misreporting, misreading, and misregarding – the audience must reject the narrator's words and reconstruct an alternative; with the second group – underreporting, underreading, and underregarding – the audience must supplement the narrator's view. Within Yacobi's complementary approach, unreliability is a reading-hypothesis that is formed to resolve textual problems (from unaccountable detail to self-contradiction) at the expense of some mediating, perceiving or communicating agent – particularly the global narrator – at odds with the implied author. See also **integration mechanisms**.

voice: in traditional narratology the answer to the question "who is speaking?" in narrative **discourse**; more generally, the term refers to the way in which choices of diction and syntax convey values and thus a sense of a speaker. Studying the distribution (who gets to speak) and authority (how much weight does the speech have) of voice is one way to study the politics of narration.

Index

Aarseth, Espen 518, 519, 531, 538–9
Abbate, Carolyn 442, 443, 467
Abbott, H. Porter 15–16, 150–1, 193
Abish, Walter
    Alphabetical Africa 173
Ackerman, J. S. 294n
actants 184, 372, 375–6, 542
actual audience *see* audience, actual
Adams, Hazard 175
Adams, Timothy Dow 340
addresseelessness 244–5
Adorno, Theodor 486
Ahmad, Aijaz 204n, 363
Aird, Catherine 341
Alcott, Louisa May 223
Allende, Isabel 356, 358
Alter, Robert 296n
Althusser, Louis 45
Amis, Martin 103
anachrony 137, 138, 139, 378
    see also order
analepsis 39, 137, 542
Anderson, Benedict 338
Anderson, Paul Thomas: *Boogie Nights* 228
Andrews, William 420
Anthony, Susan B. 337, 339, 343, 344, 350, 353
antinarratable 7, 222, 224–5, 228, 231, 542
antinarrative in law 420
Antoni, Janine 367–8
apologue 169
Aristophanes: *Thesmophoriazusae* 178n
Aristotle 25–6, 33n, 240, 336n, 443–4, 448

Poetics 28
Armstrong, Nancy 37
Ashe, Penelope: *Naked Came the Stranger* 541n
ars moriendi 446
Arterburn, Jerry and Steve: *How Will I Tell My Mother?* 399
attached texts 6–7, 208–18, 542
Atwood, Margaret: "Happy Endings" 175
audience 4
    actual 9, 83–6, 243, 299, 307
    authorial 83–6, 94, 182, 323, 543
    implied 118–19, 243
    narrative 182, 548
auditory perception 382–3, 387, 390, 542
auditory restoration 542
auditory scene analysis 389, 542
auscultation 12, 385–96, 396n, 542
    in Woolf 386–96: *Between the Acts* 392–4; "Kew Gardens" 12, 386, 388, 391; *Mrs. Dalloway* 386, 387–8; "Time Passes" 389–92, 393; *The Years* 12, 390–5
Austen, Jane
    Emma 236
    Northanger Abbey 214
Austin, J. L. 30, 134
    performative speech 500
author
    collaborative 399–411
    flesh and blood 75–86, 92, 243, 299, 301, 307–8, 359, 361
    implied 3–4, 9, 42–3, 50, 75–86, 89–92, 94, 99–105, 109, 110, 114, 115, 209, 211, 243,

Index compiled by Aaron McKain

CPSIA information can be obtained at www.ICGtesting.com
Printed in the USA
BVOW100058170413

318374BV00011B/188/P